Produced in Toronto, Ontario, Canada. Distributed by the University of
Wisconsin Press, 114 N. Murray, Madison, WI 53715, USA

ISSN 0734-8665
ISBN 0-9682722-3-1

Cover: Josef Bierbichler as Galileo and Robert Gwisdeck as Andrea in the
1997 Berliner Ensemble production of *Leben des Galilei*, directed by B.K.
Tragelehn (photo by Ute Eichel).

Officers of the International Brecht Society:

Alexander Stephan, President, Department of German, 314 Cunz Hall, 1841 Millikin Road, Ohio State University, Columbus, OH 43210-1229, USA.
email: stephan.30@osu.edu

Erdmut Wizisla, Vice-President, Chausseestr. 125, 10115 Berlin, Germany
email: bba@adk.de

David W. Robinson, Secretary/Treasurer, Department of Literature and Philosophy, Georgia Southern University, Statesboro, GA 30640, USA.
email: DWROB@gasou.edu

Gudrun Tabbert-Jones, Editor, *Communications*, Department of Modern Languages, Santa Clara University, Santa Clara, CA 95053, USA
email: gtabbertjone@scuacc.scu.edu

* * *

Internet Website address: http://ployglot.lss.wisc.edu/german/brecht

* * *

Membership:

Members receive *The Brecht Yearbook* and the biannual journal *Communications of the International Brecht Society*. Dues should be sent in US$ to the Secretary/Treasurer or in DM to the Deutsche Bank Düsseldorf (BLZ 300 702 00, Konto-Nr. 76-74146):

Student Member (up to three years)	$20.00	DM 30,-
Regular Member,		
annual income under $30,000	$30.00	DM 45,-
annual income over $30,000	$40.00	DM 60,-
Sustaining Member	$50.00	DM 80,-
Institutional Member	$50.00	DM 80,-

* * *

Submissions:

Manuscripts should be submitted to *The Brecht Yearbook* on hard copy (double-spaced) and/or diskette. They may also be sent as email attachments. Endnote format should be internally consistent, preferably following *The Chicago Style Manual*. Address contributions to the editor:

Stephen Brockmann, Department of Modern Languages, Carnegie Mellon University, Baker Hall 160, Pittsburgh, PA 15213-3890, USA
email: smb@andrew.cmu.edu

Inquiries concerning book reviews and conference participation should be addressed to:

Marc Silberman, Department of German, 818 Van Hise Hall, University of Wisconsin, Madison, WI 53706, USA
email: mdsilber@facstaff.wisc.edu

The International Brecht Society

The International Brecht Society has been formed as a corresponding society on the model of Brecht's own unrealized plan for the Diderot Society. Through its publications and regular international symposia, the society encourages the discussion of any and all views on the relationship of the arts and the contemporary world. The society is open to new members in any field and in any country and welcomes suggestions and/or contributions in German, English, Spanish or French to future symposia and for the published volumes of its deliberations.

Die Internationale Brecht-Gesellschaft

Die Internationale Brecht-Gesellschaft ist nach dem Modell von Brechts nicht verwirklichtem Plan für die Diderot-Gesellschaft gegründet worden. Durch Veröffentlichungen und regelmäßige internationale Tagungen fördert die Gesellschaft freie und öffentliche Diskussionen über die Beziehungen aller Künste zur heutigen Welt. Die Gesellschaft steht neuen Mitgliedern in jedem Fachgebiet und Land offen und begrüßt Vorschläge für zukünftige Tagungen und Aufsätze in deutscher, englischer, spanischer oder französischer Sprache für *Das Brecht-Jahrbuch*.

La Société Internationale Brecht

La Société Internationale Brecht a été formée pour correspondre à la société rêvée par Brecht, "Diderot-Gesellschaft." Par ses publications et congrès internationaux à intervalles réguliers, la S.I.B. encourage la discussion libre des toutes les idées sur les rapports entre les arts et le monde contemporain. Bien entendu, les nouveaux membres dans toutes les disciplines et tous les pays sont accueillis avec plaisir, et la Société sera heureuse d'accepter des suggestions et des contributions en français, allemand, espagnol ou anglais pour les congrès futurs et les volumes des communications qui en résulteront.

La Sociedad Internacional Brecht

La Sociedad Internacional Brecht fué creada para servir como sociedad corresponsal. Dicha sociedad se basa en el modelo que el mismo autor nunca pudo realizar, el plan "Diderot-Gesellschaft." A través de sus publicaciones y los simposios internacionales que se llevan a cabo regularmente, la Sociedad estimula la discusión libre y abierta de cualquier punto de vista sobre la relación entre las artes y el mundo contemporáneo. La Sociedad desea, por supuesto, la participación de nuevos miembros de cualquier área, de cualquier país, y acepta sugerencias y colaboraciones en alemán, inglés, francés y español para los congresos futuros y para las publicaciones de sus discusiones.

Contents

EDITORIAL   ix

MEMOIR

Bertolt Brecht
    Postkarten an Max Hohenester 7. und 26. August 1915   1

Jürgen Hillesheim and Erdmut Wizisla, Berlin
    „Was macht Deine Dichteritis?"
    Bertolt Brecht im Bregenzer Land   3

Irma Commanday and Mordecai Bauman, New York
    In Praise of Learning: Encounters with Hanns Eisler   15

Stephan Suschke, Berlin
    Geniales Kind im Mörderhaus   35

PERFORMANCE

B.K. Tragelehn, Berlin
    Der Fall G/B   47

Alexander Stephan, Columbus
    Zurück in die Zukunft des politischen Theaters?
    Soeren Voima schreiben mit *Das Kontingent*
    Brechts *Maßnahme* weiter   61

Alexander Stephan and Soeren Voima
    Interview mit Soeren Voima zu *Das Kontingent*   73

Hector Maclean, Melbourne
    Gestus in Performance: Brecht and Heiner Müller   81

Ulrike Garde, Melbourne
    "Never in body and seldom in spirit":
    Australian Productions of Brecht's Plays
    and Their Reviews from 1945 to 1998   101

Denise Varney, Melbourne
    Performing Sexual Difference:
    a Feminist Appropriation of Brecht   127

Meg Mumford, Glasgow
    Gestic Masks in Brecht's Theater: A Testimony to
    the Contradictions and Parameters of a Realist Aesthetic 143

THEORY AND SOURCES

Daniel Müller Nielaba, Erfurt
Wie Dichten *Lesen* schreibt. Zur Poetologie
der Intertextualität beim jungen Brecht,
am Beispiel der Ballade „Das Schiff"   173

Robert Kaufman, Stanford
Brecht's Autonomous Art, or More Late Modernism!   191

Bettina Englmann, Augsburg
„Es gibt eine Überlieferung, die Katastrophe ist."
Erinnerungskultur versus „Kult der Erinnerung"
in Bertolt Brechts *Lukullus*-Texten (1939)   213

Dorothee Ostmeier, Eugene
Bertolt Brecht and the Internet   235

Astrid Oesmann, Iowa City
From Chaos to Transformation:
Brechtian Histories *Im Dickicht der Städte*   257

Max Statkiewicz, Madison
Brecht's (Non-)Philosophical Theater   277

James K. Lyon, Provo
Brecht's Sources for *Furcht und Elend des III. Reiches*:
Heinrich Mann, Personal Friends, Newspaper Accounts   295

FORUM

Hans-Albert Walter, Hofheim/Taunus
Hier wird Brecht gespuckt oder
„*Kim*: konnte nicht ermittelt werden."
Die skandalöse Kommentierung von Brechts Briefen   307

Barbara Brecht-Schall, Berlin
Letter   316

BOOK REVIEWS

Antony Tatlow, Simone Barck, Sara Freeman, Sabine Gross,
Herbert Knust, Karl-Heinz Schoeps, Petra Stuber, Thomas Engel,
Helen Fehervary, James K. Lyon, Jutta Phillips-Krug   319

BOOKS RECEIVED   363

Editorial

The essays in this volume divide (by chance) almost equally into practice and theory. As Mordecai Bauman points out in his Memoir, you can't have a practice without a theory. But whoever encounters Brecht must also conclude that you can't have the theory without the practice. The pudding has to be eaten to be put to the proof. How nutritious this interaction always is can be seen in the work of such distinguished practitioners with deep roots in the Brecht tradition as B.K. Tragelehn and Ekkehard Schall, as well as in Alexander Stephan's essay showing the fascinating re-emergence of *Die Massnahme* as a work of great contemporary relevance. We also see Brecht giving his uniquely practical and perceptive advice about masks — as useful today as ever. Hector Maclean demonstrates that the Gestus lives as a practical tool, and Denise Varney, that feminist appropriation is very much part of the continuing interaction. Brecht the poet is also seen as essentially performative, in his early poetry as well as in his interest in Shelley, and in his philosophical ideas.

That Brecht has minimal relevance is a hardy perennial, but one has only to consult the Yearbook essays of the past few years and the Book Reviews, to see that academics and theater practitioners all over the world are continually discovering new facts, new interpretations, and new use-values. The historical perspective in this volume is equally wide-ranging, from the young Brecht on vacation around Lake Constance, seemingly unaware of the Great War raging, to Mordecai Bauman unwittingly singing Hanns Eisler for an audience of 22,000 in Madison Square Garden, to the Brecht of the Weimar Republic making a posthumous connection with the Internet and corporate globalization. The extent to which he pops up productively in unexpected places became clear to me in a recent concert in Toronto given by the extraordinary baritone Matthias Goerne. Romantic Lieder of exile and alienation by Schubert formed the theme of the performance. They were punctuated by Eisler's and Brecht's *Hollywood Elegies*. Delightfully shocking in their astringency given the context, these songs suddenly hoisted the recital, both form and content, into contemporaneity.

With the next volume, editorial responsibility moves to Stephen Brockmann in Pittsburgh. Volume 27 will focus on Brecht and Beckett, but as usual all essays around and about Brecht are welcome. Since 1995 I have been supported in every way by Marc Silberman, who deserves special thanks, as does the editorial board. John Willett has been a source of help and inspiration. So have Erdmut Wizisla and the staff of the Brecht Archive. I am grateful also to Mordecai and Irma Bauman in New York for being there, now, to show an affirming flame.

Maarten van Dijk, Toronto, October 2001

"How is your Poetitis?" Bertolt Brecht in the Bregenz Region. Postcards to Max Hohenester, 7 and 26 August 1915

Two previously unknown postcards from Brecht, dating from the late summer of 1915, have been found among the papers of Max Hohenester, a friend of Brecht's during his days in Augsburg. They are among the earliest biographical documents of Brecht's life and relate an episode that closes a gap in the chronology of Brecht's life. In August of 1915 the young writer undertook a roughly three-week trip with Fritz Gehweyer to the area around Bregenz. The postcards provide insight into the intellectual life of Brecht the schoolboy, who was filled with the desire to be a great writer, who stylizes himself in the manner of Nietzsche's philosophy as a genius, and who, as early as 1915, demonstrates remarkable virtuosity in his use of language. Another thing becomes clear: the war, which had already gone on for almost a year, is evidently of no importance for Brecht: he enjoys his vacation untroubled. What is important is the development of his literary talent; day-to-day politics leaves him cold.

Postkarten an Max Hohenester
7. und 26. August 1915

Bertolt Brecht

Eugen Brecht   [Schröcken], 7.8.15
Bis Montag Reutte

Mein Lieber!
Tour über Bregenz nach Schröcken. Schön bei schönem Wetter, das
wir seit Bregenz haben.
Ich gedenke, einen Zyklus v. Gedichten zu schreiben, „Das Fest d.
Erde". Was macht Deine Dichteritis?
In 1 Woche werd ich bei Dir vorsprechen.
Leider sind die Nächte trüb, zu windig für ein Übernachten in einer
Heuhütte.
Hast Du übrigens schon Deine beiden Gedichte an eine Zeitung
geschickt? Hoffentlich, hm? Wenn wir vom Ertrag derselben nach
München gingen? Ich bringe doch auch welche nach Augsburg zurück!
Es ist hier sehr einsam. Gott sei Dank. Es gibt kein dummes Gewäsch.
Gehweyer und ich haben uns schon ganz schön angeschwiegen.
Jetzt gerade ziehen wieder Wolken übern Berg. Wo sollen wir hin? Wir
haben kein Ziel.
Gruß Dein
BEugen Brecht
Gruß an, na wie heißt er denn? An Deinen Freund halt.
[Viele Grüße Gehweyer]

                                                Lindau, 26.8.15
Mein Lieber!
Ich schreibe es an heißem Sommersonnentag im Boot. Die Nächte
wandre ich draußen am weißen Kai (auf sehr verbotenen Wegen) u. seh
den mondfunkelnden See glänzen.
Schwing auf, mein Herz, die Zeit ist Wunders voll!...etc!

New Essays on Brecht / Neue Versuche über Brecht
Maarten van Dijk et al., eds., *The Brecht Yearbook / Das Brecht-Jahrbuch*
Volume 26 (Toronto, Canada: The International Brecht Society, 2001)

Wenn ich an euer armes Augsburg denk! Freilich träume ich manchmal im Boot, in den hohen Himmel starrend — ich schwinge mich hinauf in den Himmel, über die winkeligen Gassen u. die Eselswiese u. die dummen Affengesichter glotzen staunend empört herauf und ich fliege über sie alle weg, in den Himmel auf der großen Karusellschaukel!....!? Also *doch* auf Wiedersehen mit Grüssen (auch an Fohrer und Schultz, der aber die Karte nicht lesen soll, gelt.)
Dich grüßt –
Dein treuer
Eugen Brecht

„Was macht Deine Dichteritis?"
Bertolt Brecht im Bregenzer Land

Jürgen Hillesheim und Erdmut Wizisla

Während der letzten fünfzehn Jahre wurden, im Vergleich mit anderen herausragenden Autoren des 20. Jahrhunderts, außergewöhnlich viele Texte aus Brechts Jugendzeit entdeckt und veröffentlicht, die seine literarischen Anfänge in einem helleren Licht erscheinen lassen. Man denke an den langen Brief an Therese Ostheimer (1988 publiziert),[1] an das „Tagebuch No. 10 (1989),[2] die Briefe an Paula Banholzer (1992)[3] und schließlich die Schülerzeitschrift „Die Ernte" (1997).[4] Manche These der Forschung musste aufgrund der neuen Textbasis korrigiert werden, andere wiederum wurde bestätigt, darüber hinaus entscheidende neue Erkenntnisse gewonnen. In diese Reihe der neu entdeckten Texte Brechts aus der Jugend fügen sich die beiden im Jahr 2000 aus Augsburger Privatbesitz zur Publikation zur Verfügung gestellten Postkarten Brechts an seinen Freund Max Hohenester vom 7. und 26. August 1915. Sie sind trotz ihrer Kürze im Aussagewert nicht nur den anderen in den letzten Jahren gefundenen und veröffentlichten Dokumenten durchaus vergleichbar, sondern gehören zu den frühesten Zeugnissen dieser Art überhaupt: Nur fünf ältere Briefe Brechts sind überliefert.[5] Darüber hinaus erzählen sie eine bisher völlig unbekannte Episode aus der Jugend des „Stückeschreibers" und füllen damit eine weitere Lücke in der Chronologie seines Lebens.

* * *

Man weiß seit langem, dass Brecht mit Fritz Gehweyer vom 10. bis 13. August 1918 einen Ausflug in den Bayerischen Wald machte,[6] der offenbar sehr harmonisch verlief.[7] Brecht hatte in dieser Zeit mit Gehweyer bereits weniger zu tun, als in den Jahren zuvor. Dieser hatte schon 1914 Augsburg verlassen, um in München die Kunstakademie zu besuchen. Die beiden Postkarten belegen nun, dass die gemeinsame Tour im August 1918, als Gehweyer längst nicht mehr zum engsten Kreis um den jungen Dichter gehörte, gewissermaßen an „alte Zeiten" anknüpfte. Denn genau drei Jahre zuvor machten beide schon einmal einen Ausflug, und zwar in das Bregenzer Land, und blieben, wie die Daten der Karten ergeben, mindestens 20 Tage, für siebzehnjährige Schüler damals eine erstaunlich lange Zeit. Dabei hatte man offenbar

New Essays on Brecht / Neue Versuche über Brecht
Maarten van Dijk et al., eds., *The Brecht Yearbook / Das Brecht-Jahrbuch*
Volume 26 (Toronto, Canada: The International Brecht Society, 2001)

zunächst geplant, früher zurückzukehren: Am 7. August schreibt Brecht, dass er in einer Woche bei Hohenester „vorsprechen" werde, was nicht anders zu deuten ist, als dass er ursprünglich dann wieder zurück in Augsburg sein wollte. Dafür spricht auch die Formulierung „Also *doch* auf Wiedersehen" („doch" von Brecht unterstrichen) in der Karte vom 26. August, was wohl so verstanden werden muss, dass das ursprünglich ins Auge gefasste Wiedersehen verschoben wurde, nun allerdings „doch" bevorsteht. In diesem Zusammenhang ist zu erwähnen, dass Hohenester offenbar schon wusste, dass Brecht nicht wie eigentlich geplant nach Augsburg zurückkehren wollte, da in der zweiten Karte der nun längere Aufenthalt mit keinem Wort erwähnt ist, Brecht also voraussetzt, dass sein Freund Kenntnis von der Änderung des Urlaubsplanes hat. Dies ist nur so zu erklären, dass Brecht ihm entweder noch eine dritte, nicht überlieferte Karte geschrieben hat, die wohl nicht allzu lange nach dem 7. August entstanden sein muss, oder dass Hohenester über jemand anderen, dem Brecht ebenfalls schrieb (Eltern oder andere Freunde), erfahren hat, dass er nun länger im Bregenzer Land bleibt.

Offenbar haben Gehweyer und Brecht ihren Urlaub spontan verlängert — Grund dafür könnte die gute Stimmung (trotz des gelegentlichen gegenseitigen „Anschweigens") und das Wohlbefinden sein, das sich in den Postkarten überdeutlich mitteilt. Der gemeinsame Ausflug 1918 kann von diesem Aspekt aus betrachtet durchaus als Versuch gesehen werden, diese Atmosphäre der ersten Reise in einer anderen Zeit und unter anderen Umständen nochmals „aufleben" zu lassen, was, wie Brechts Brief an Paula Banholzer zeigt, offenbar geglückt ist.

Weder der Aufbruch zur Tour in das Bregenzer Land noch die Rückkehr lassen sich genau bestimmen. Als „terminus ante quem" für die Rückkehr muss der 15. September gelten, denn einen Tag später begann das neue Schuljahr 1915/1916,[8] zu dem Brecht wieder rechtzeitig am Realgymnasium sein musste. Eine wesentlich frühere Heimreise ist jedoch wahrscheinlicher: Vorwegnehmend sei darauf hingewiesen, dass Brecht sich offenbar auf den „Plärrer," Augsburgs großes Volksfest, freut, das jeweils Anfang September beginnt.

Berücksichtigt man die konkreten Angaben Brechts und die Stempel auf den Postkarten, kann folgender Reiseverlauf als möglich in Betracht gezogen werden: Brecht und Gehweyer fuhren wahrscheinlich mit dem Zug bis nach Lindau, das als „Stützpunkt" gedient haben könnte, von dem aus die beiden Wanderausflüge unternahmen. Dass ein großer Teil des Weges tatsächlich zu Fuß und ohne feste Übernachtungsplanung zurückgelegt wurde, ergibt sich aus Brechts Bemerkungen, dass beide vor dem Regen fliehen müssen, nicht wissen, wohin sie sollen und dass es zu kalt für ein spontanes Übernachten in einer Heuhütte sei. Eine größere Tour führte die beiden, wie Brecht schreibt, „über Bregenz nach Schröcken," das über vierzig Kilometer Luftlinie vom Bodensee entfernt ist. Etwa auf halbem Weg liegt Reutte, wo mindestens zwei Tage Rast gemacht wurde und Brecht die erste Postkarte schrieb, die dann in Schröcken aufgegeben wurde. Der Grund, warum gerade Schröcken beider Ziel war, ist durchaus zu vermuten: Ganz in der Nähe des Ortes ist das Quellgebiet des Lechs, der durch Augsburg fließt und das Stadtbild entscheidend prägt. Seine Auen, nicht weit entfernt vom Wohnhaus der Familie Brecht, gehörten zu den bevorzugten Aufenthaltsorten des jungen Dichters und seines Freundeskreises, und nichts liegt näher, als dass beide den Fluss, der von Kindheit an zu ihrem Alltag gehörte, an seinen Ursprüngen erleben wollten. Spätestens am 26. August war man dann wieder zurück in Lindau, wo man das Fluidum des Bodensees genoss und Brecht die zweite Postkarte schrieb.

* * *

Fritz Gehweyer also begleitete Brecht, der Empfänger der Postkarten ist Max Hohenester, gegrüßt werden soll unter anderem Karl Schultz (der erwähnte Fohrer ist nicht zu ermitteln, auch nicht Hohenesters Freund, dessen Name Brecht nicht einfällt). Damit ist Brechts Beziehungsfeld der damaligen Zeit abgesteckt. Nicht die bekannten Namen wie Georg Pfanzelt (der allerdings einer Art literarischem „Interessenkreis" angehören sollte, den Brecht gemeinsam mit anderen im September 1915 gründen sollte),[9] Rudolf Hartmann, Otto Müllereisert oder Caspar Neher (an den bis zu dieser Zeit nur ein einziger Brief Brechts überliefert ist),[10] die später den so charakteristischen Freundeskreis um Brecht maßgeblich bestimmen sollten, spielen eine Rolle, sondern die Clique, mit der er 1913/1914 die „Ernte" herausgab. Neben dieser Zeitschrift und dem „Tagebuch No. 10" stellen die Karten damit außer Zweifel, dass es eine Vorstufe jenes späteren berühmten Freundeskreises gab. Er bestand aus anderen Personen, war durchaus von Dauer (mindestens zwei Jahre), und die Ziele und Ideale waren bereits denen der späteren Brecht-Clique sehr ähnlich. Man litt an „Dichteritis": Gleichgesinnte fanden sich zusammen, die sich enthusiastisch mit Literatur beschäftigten und schriftstellerisch produktiv sein wollten. Es herrschte eine „Atmosphäre gemeinsamer Euphorie."[11] Und was später charakteristisch für den Kreis sein sollte, ist erstaunlicherweise auch schon 1915 eine Tatsache: Im Mittelpunkt stand Brecht, von dem dieses Hochgefühl, die Begeisterungsfähigkeit für Literatur, die beinahe alles andere überdeckte und fester Bestandteil des Lebens war, ausging.

Karl Schultz, 1898 in Mannheim geboren und am Realgymnasium eine Klasse unter Brecht, ist eher eine Randfigur. Einige sehr kurze und wenig aussagende „Glossen und Witze" für die „Ernte"[12] sind von ihm überliefert. Fritz Gehweyer (1897–1918)[13] indessen gehörte zu den engsten Freunden, wurde jedoch in der Forschung zum jungen Brecht lange Zeit zu wenig gewürdigt. Er war der Sohn eines Kaufmanns, der in Augsburgs Innenstadt ein Textilgeschäft besaß. Gehweyer und Brecht waren in den ersten Jahren der Gymnasialzeit in einer Klasse. Im Schuljahr 1912/1913 wurde Gehweyer nicht versetzt, 1914 musste er die Schule verlassen und zog nach München um. Gemeinsam mit Gehweyer gab Brecht die „Ernte," sein erstes ernst zu nehmendes literarisches Projekt, heraus, wobei Gehweyer für die Illustrationen verantwortlich war. Nach dessen Schulabgang blieb der enge Kontakt noch über ein Jahr bestehen. Nach Ausbruch des Ersten Weltkriegs stellten beide eine Reihe von Postkarten für die Kriegsfürsorge des Roten Kreuzes her: Brecht schrieb jeweils ein Gedicht, das Gehweyer dann in Jugendstilmanier mit Zeichnungen versah. Brechts Verbindung mit Gehweyer ist die erste mit einem künstlerisch Begabten einer anderen Sparte, dessen Talent er für die eigene Kunst fruchtbar machen konnte und deutet auf viele andere Freundschaften Brechts voraus, etwa auf die mit Neher, Weill, Eisler und Dessau. Gehweyer meldete sich freiwillig zur Front. 1918, unmittelbar vor Ende des Kriegs und nur einige Wochen nach dem gemeinsamen Ausflug in den Bayerischen Wald, kam er ums Leben, wie zuvor auch seine beiden älteren Brüder Georg und Franz. Noch heute zeugt ein Gedenkstein auf dem Augsburger Westfriedhof von diesem Familienschicksal.

Ebenfalls zum engeren Kreis um Brecht gehörte in dieser Zeit Max Hohenester (1897–1956).[14] Zunächst am Realgymnasium eine Jahrgangsstufe höher als Brecht, kam er, als er im Schuljahr 1910/1911 eine Klasse wiederholen musste, in dessen Parallelklasse. Hohenesters Vater war Schneidermeister. Er betrieb in der Augsburger Innenstadt ein Geschäft. Die Familie wohnte in der Jakoberstraße, wohin auch die beiden Postkarten adressiert sind, keine fünf Gehminuten von Brechts Wohnung in der Bleichstraße entfernt. Hohenester war einer der wichtigsten Mitarbeiter der „Ernte," die meisten Beiträge, von denen Brechts abgesehen, stammen von ihm. Er verließ 1914 das Gymnasium mit dem „Einjährigen" und begann eine Banklehre, meldete sich jedoch schon bald freiwillig zum Kriegsdienst. Zunächst noch dem Kreis um Brecht zugehörig, verlief sich die Freundschaft etwa ab 1916; nur noch selten begegnete man sich. In einem Brief an Neher äußert Brecht sich überaus spöttisch über Hohenester als Soldat.[15] Nach der Rückkehr aus dem Krieg wurde Hohenester Journalist. Für verschiedene Augsburger Zeitungen arbeitete er zunächst als Lokalredakteur, dann als Schriftleiter. 1922 wurde er Schriftleiter und 1. Beisitzender der neu ins Leben gerufenen „Literarischen Gesellschaft Augsburg," die er mitbegründet hatte. 1923 verfasste er für den „Erzähler," der literarischen Beilage der „Augsburger Neuesten Nachrichten," einen äußerst positiven Beitrag über Brecht, in dem er ihn gegen Angriffe verschiedenster Seiten in Schutz nimmt.[16] Weiterhin erwähnenswert ist Hohenesters Engagement im Bereich des katholischen Journalismus. Während der Zeit des Dritten Reichs arbeitete er als Schriftleiter der „Nationalzeitung" und trat der NSDAP bei. Nach dem Zweiten Weltkrieg war Hohenester an der

Neugründung der „Augsburger Theatergemeinde" beteiligt. 1951 wurde er zum 1. Vorsitzenden des Bundes der Theatergemeinden Westdeutschlands ernannt, in dessen Eigenschaft er sich um das Werk Brechts, der ihn bei einem Entnazifizierungsverfahren entlastet haben soll,[17] verdient machte.

Die beiden Postkarten Brechts aus dem Jahr 1915 gelangten in den Besitz von Hohenesters in Augsburg lebender Tochter Irmingard Oelkrug, die sie aufbewahrte und im August 2000 freundlicherweise zur Veröffentlichung zur Verfügung stellte.

* * *

Ähnlich wie der Brief an Therese Ostheimer vom Juli 1916 sind Brechts Postkarten, trotz der völlig anderen Situation — Therese Ostheimer will er auf sich aufmerksam machen, weshalb er sich explizit mit seiner literarischen Bildung rühmt, Max Hohenester hingegen schreibt er aus dem Urlaub — nichts anderes als eine Selbstdarstellung und -stilisierung. Der Gymnasiast lebt für die Literatur; sein ganzes Denken und Streben ist darauf ausgerichtet, zu dichten und seinen Weg als Schriftsteller zu machen. Auch der Urlaub wird, trotz der sicherlich anstrengenden Wandertouren, dazu genutzt, literarisch zu arbeiten. Dabei scheint Brecht von seinem Talent tief überzeugt zu sein und davon, dass er einmal zu den ganz großen Dichtern zählen wird. Wie zu Zeiten der „Ernte" und später stetig, geriert er sich gleichzeitig auch als Förderer: Er animiert Hohenester dazu, eigene Gedichte zum Abdruck einzureichen, verkehrt mit ihm in der Art eines Dichter-Kollegen. Dies entspringt indessen keineswegs reiner Selbstlosigkeit. Zwar will er Hohenester und später andere durchaus zu literarischer Arbeit anregen, deren Talent fruchtbar machen. Darüber hinaus jedoch ergibt sich aus dieser Art des Förderns auch eine Hierarchie: Brecht ist derjenige, der, wie schon zuvor in seiner Eigenschaft als Redakteur und Herausgeber eines literarischen Blattes, bereit ist, für andere „etwas zu tun" und setzt damit voraus, dass er dies auch kann. Damit nimmt er eine Metaebene ein, gibt sich als Mäzen und als eine Art von „Literatur-Manager." Dass Brecht schon zuvor bei der „Ernte" und auch später immer wieder auch von den Inspirationen seiner Freunde profitierte, steht außer Zweifel und ist ein charakteristisches Merkmal dieser literarischen Clique[18] und auch in späten Schaffensphasen kennzeichnend für den Autor.

Ebenso markant ist, dass Brecht von Beginn seines literarischen Schaffens an stets auch vom materiellen Wert seiner Arbeiten überzeugt ist und mit ihnen immer Geld verdienen will, sie als Einkommensmöglichkeit betrachtet. Dichtung ist niemals nur Selbstzweck, sondern geht einher mit wirtschaftlichen Interessen — eine Sichtweise, die Brecht, in verschiedener Ausprägung, sein ganzes Leben lang beibehalten sollte. Bereits bei der „Ernte" ist das so: Bevor das Projekt konkret wird, lässt er sich die geschäftliche Seite durch den Kopf gehen: „Dann bei Gehweyer. Wir besprachen eine Zeitung –.[...] Er verlangte 1 M fürs Schreiben. Ich sollte dann die Zeitung redigieren, konzeptieren, hektographieren und verbreiten. U. dafür Gewinn — 25 Pfennig! Er hält mich scheint's für dumm."[19] Paula Banholzer schreibt er im Januar 1919 in durchaus ähnlichem Zusammenhang, bezugnehmend auf sein Drama „Trommeln in der Nacht": „Vormittags schreibe ich an dem Stück, das 10000 Mark einbringt."[20] So auch in der Karte an Hohenester vom 7. August: Er rechnet mit dem Honorar der Gedichte beider und überlegt, ob man davon nicht nach München fahren könne. Dies ist der erste überlieferte Hinweis darauf, dass Augsburg schon bald für Brechts literarische Ambitionen zu eng und provinziell sein und er sich nach München orientieren wird, um dort in Künstler- und Theaterkreisen Bekanntschaften zu machen und sich zu etablieren. Dass er zumindest daran denkt, gemeinsam mit Hohenester nach München zu fahren, belegt, dass er in dieser Zeit nicht nur ein Freund oder Bekannter Brechts ist, sondern zum engeren literarischen Kreis um den werdenden Schriftsteller gehört.

* * *

Die Texte sind gespickt mit literarischen Anspielungen: „Ich gedenke einen Zyklus von Gedichten zu schreiben, ‚Das Fest d. Erde,'" teilt er in Inhalt wie Wortwahl unbescheiden mit und nimmt nicht nur die Pose des souveränen literarischen Genius ein, der gleich eine komplette Gedichtsammlung plant, sondern er zeigt sich auch offenkundig inspiriert von Gustav Mahlers „Das Lied der Erde," ein Zyklus von Orchestergesängen, der erst 1911, nach Mahlers Tod, in München uraufgeführt wurde. Nach der Glosse „Wagner" aus der „Ernte",[21] in der Brecht sich mit Hans Pfitzner, Max Reger und Richard Strauss beschäftigt, ist dies ein weiterer Beleg dafür, dass er sich sehr früh nicht nur in der Literatur, sondern auch in der zeitgenössischen Musik erstaunlich gut auskennt. Zudem erweist er sich mit der Anspielung auf Mahler als „Kind seiner Zeit" und ist damit in durchaus „guter Gesellschaft": Denn kein anderer als der ihm später so verhasste Thomas Mann befasste sich intensiv mit Mahlers Werk, dem er mit der 1912 erschienenen Novelle „Der Tod in Venedig" ein literarisches Denkmal setzte.

Auch Johanna Spyris Jugendroman „Heidis Lehr- und Wanderjahre" (erschienen 1880) ist Brecht offensichtlich bekannt. Auf das hier propagierte „einfache," aber naive Leben nicht ohne Bösartigkeit und Spott anspielend, teilt er mit, „daß die Nächte zu kalt seien, um in „einer Heuhütte zu übernachten" — ein Fingerzeig auf ein Motiv aus Spyris Roman.

Die wichtigste literarische Anspielung liegt jedoch in Brechts Selbststilisierung: Der große Geist wandelt auf „sehr verbotenen Wegen," setzt sich von den „dummen Affengesichtern" ab und sucht die Einsamkeit von Nacht und Natur, um sich „wachend und schweigend" dem eigenen Genius zu überlassen. Dies ist der Gestus von Nietzsches Zarathustra, der gleichfalls die „Herde der Mittelmäßigen" hinter sich lässt, um in einem Zustand der „Immoralität," eines „Jenseits von Gut und Böse,"[22] aus sich selbst heraus Werte zu schaffen. Und wie Zarathustra macht Brecht diese Distanz zwischen dem Einen und den Vielen in seiner Vorstellungswelt auch sichtbar. Zarathustra verlässt die Seinen und begibt sich auf einen Berg, stellt damit die beiden Ebenen des Höheren und Tieferen real her. So auch bei Brecht: Er erhebt sich in den Himmel, fliegt, ist somit im Sinne des Wortes „über" den „Affengesichtern," denen nichts bleibt, als empört zu ihm heraufzuschauen. Dass Nietzsches *Also sprach Zarathustra* in dieser Zeit im Kreis um Brecht tatsächlich ein wichtiges Thema ist, dokumentiert sein Brief an Fritz Gehweyer, den er nur etwa drei Wochen später, am 20. September 1915, schreiben wird: „Wir lesen zusammen *Hamlet*, eine Szene. Über Zarathustra wird gesprochen."[23] Die Pose geht indessen weit über die anderen literarischen Anspielungen hinaus. Denn es deutet sich eine intensive Nietzsche-Rezeption an, die, obwohl in der Forschung lange in Frage gestellt,[24] in *Baal* und vielen Gedichten der *Hauspostille* ihren Höhepunkt erreichen und auch Brechts späteres Werk beeinflussen sollte.[25] Es ist der erste Hinweis auf eines der wirkungsvollsten und nachhaltigsten Leseerlebnisse aus Brechts Jugendzeit überhaupt. Es zeigt sich darüber hinaus, wie früh bei Brecht „Dichtung und Wahrheit," ineinander fließen: Dass er die Karte vom 26. August tatsächlich in einem Boot schreibt, darf wohl ebenso bezweifelt werden, wie beispielsweise später seine Behauptung, er habe das Gedicht „Erinnerung an die Marie A." während einer Zugfahrt von Augsburg nach München verfasst.[26] Vielmehr nutzt er abermals die Gelegenheit zur Selbststilisierung, künstlerische Individualität, Virtuosität und Schöpferkraft zu demonstrieren, wie später so oft in Briefen und biographischen Aufzeichnungen.

In einem weiteren Punkt deutet dieses Miteinander von Phantasie und Realität über sich hinaus. Auch wenn man von Brechts sprachlich und gedanklich virtuosem Traum vom Fliegen absieht, entsprechen die Texte vorwiegend nicht einer Alltagssprache, wie man sie in einer Postkarte erwarten könnte, sondern sie sind — die Karte vom 26. August beinahe vollständig — Dichtung. Formulierungen wie „Sommersonnentag," „mondfunkelnder See," „Wir haben kein Ziel" muten an wie Lyrik. Brecht artikuliert sein Weltgefühl unmittelbar in Dichtung. Es wird ein Kennzeichen seines ersten großen Dramas *Baal* sein, dass der Protagonist — der im übrigen teilweise ebenfalls als Selbststilisierung des jungen „Stückeschreibers" gilt — sich nicht nur dann poetisch ausdrückt, wenn er eigene Werke vorträgt, sondern auch die Dialoge des Dramas wirken wie Gedichte: „es gibt keine Differenz, nicht einmal einen sprachlichen Unterschied zwischen Poesie und Wirklichkeit."[27] Dass diese Art der Sprache nur innerhalb des engsten literarischen Kreises um Brecht als akzeptiertes und gar bevorzugtes Kommunikationsmittel dienen konnte, ist beinahe selbstverständlich. Deshalb verbietet Brecht Hohenester auch, die Karte vom 26. August Schultz lesen zu lassen, der beiden nicht so nahestand. Der lyrische Duktus war Brecht offenbar ein wenig peinlich, wenn es um jemanden ging, der nicht, wie Hohenester und er selbst, an „Dichteritis" litt.

* * *

Und noch etwas wird in der Karte vom 26. August erstmals indirekt erwähnt: Der Augsburger Plärrer, jenes bis heute zweimal im Jahr stattfindende Volksfest, das eines der bevorzugten Ziele des späteren Kreises um Brecht werden sollte und, ähnlich wie der Lech und seine Auen, in seinem Jugendwerk allenthalben präsent ist. Brechts Sprache ist, wie schon angedeutet, bereits geprägt von einem wirkungsvollen Miteinander aus Sentiment, Romantik und Witz. Naturerleben, das eigene literarische Potenzial und das Bewusstsein, etwas Besonderes zu sein, lassen ihn über alles hinwegschweben. Der Himmel, in den er sich erhebt, ist allerdings — der Augsburger Himmel, denn die „große Karusellschaukel," auf der er, als ein markantes Requisit seiner Jugendzeit, fliegt und die ihn auch wieder, um bei diesem Bild zu bleiben, auf den Boden zurückbringen wird, steht natürlich auf dem Plärrer, der unmittelbar nach Brechts Rückkehr beginnen wird oder zumindest noch nicht beendet ist und auf den er sich offensichtlich freut.

A propos Augsburg: In kalligraphischer Hinsicht ist auffällig, dass Brecht, neben den üblichen und bei ihm durchaus bekannten Unterstreichungen, mit denen er Worte akzentuiert, die Begriffe, die ihm offenbar besonders wichtig sind, mit einem zusätzlichen Linienschwung versieht: „Gedichte," „Augsburg" und vor allem den Namen, den sich der werdende Dichter gibt. Dabei präsentiert er eine bisher nicht überlieferte Variante. In der Zeit der ersten Veröffentlichungen in der „Ernte" und wenig später in Augsburger Tageszeitungen experimentierte er mit den Namensformen „Eugen Brecht," „Bertold Eugen" und „Berthold Eugen," um die geläufigsten zu nennen. Hier nun überrascht er mit der humoristischen Variante „BEugen Brecht," eine Kontraktion aus „Berthold" und „Eugen," die mit Sicherheit nicht für eine Publikation bestimmt war, vielleicht aber gelegentlich intern im Freundeskreis Verwendung fand.

* * *

Ein letzter Punkt ist bemerkenswert: Die Karten entstehen in einer Zeit, während der in der Heimatstadt mit der Novelle „Dankgottesdienst" einer aus der Reihe von nationalistischen Texten Brechts[28] in der Zeitung abgedruckt wird und — so die landläufige Meinung — er sich intensiv mit dem Krieg auseinandergesetzt und begonnen habe, sich zum Pazifisten zu entwickeln. Von existenziellen Konflikten dieser Art ist in den Karten schlechterdings nichts zu bemerken. Die Stimmung ist alles andere als nachdenklich oder gar betrübt. Völlig unbekümmert kann Brecht die Ferien genießen, intensiv die Natur erleben. Ihn interessiert das tagespolitische Geschehen nicht. Dieses ist sehr fern, nicht nur räumlich, sondern vor allem auch gedanklich. Was einzig zählt und ihn beschäftigt, ist die Entfaltung seines literarischen Talentes, sein Fortkommen als Autor. Sogar der bevorstehende Plärrer scheint ihm wichtiger als der Krieg, dessen Auswirkungen in Form erster Todesnachrichten und nach Augsburg heimkehrender Verwundeter in dieser Zeit schon mehr als deutlich wahrgenommen werden konnten. Bestätigen diese Karten somit nicht, was immer schon vermutet wurde:[29] Dass die deutsche Außenpolitik und das Kriegsgeschehen Brecht letztlich einen Dreck scheren und er seine patriotisch anmutenden Texte nur schreibt, damit er endlich eigene, wenn auch zunächst noch unter Pseudonym erscheinende Werke in gedruckter Form bewundern kann? Freilich nimmt er dafür zumindest vorübergehend in Kauf, Zugeständnisse an die Zeitungsredakteure und damit an den nationalistischen Zeitgeist zu machen. Ihm deshalb einen Vorwurf zu machen, würde nichts anderes bedeuten, als eine moralisierende Position einzunehmen, die Brecht nur wenig später in seinen Werken, die die Doppelbödigkeit des Bürger- bzw. Kleinbürgertums demaskieren, aufs Korn nehmen wird.

ANMERKUNGEN

[1] Bertolt Brecht: „Brief an Therese Ostheimer." In: *Sinn und Form. Beiträge zur Literatur.* 40–1988, S. 5–7. Vgl. dazu: Helmut Gier: „Der Gymnasiast und seine erste Liebe." In ebd., S. 8–15.

[2] Ders.: *Tagebuch No. 10, 1913.* Hrsg. Siegfried Unseld. Frankfurt/M. 1989.

[3] Ders.: *Liebste Bi. Briefe an Paula Banholzer.* Hrsg. Helmut Gier und Jürgen Hillesheim. Frankfurt/M. 1992.

[4] *Bertolt Brechts „Die Ernte." Die Schülerzeitschrift und ihr wichtigster Autor.* Hrsg. Jürgen Hillesheim und Uta Wolf. Augsburg 1997. Mit Ausnahme der Beiträge Brechts zur „Ernte," Heft 2, sind alle hier genannten Texte enthalten in: Bertolt Brecht, *Große kommentierte Berliner und Frankfurter Ausgabe.* Hrsg. Werner Hecht, Jan Knopf, Werner Mittenzwei und Klaus-Detlef Müller. Berlin, Weimar, Frankfurt/M. 1987–1998; im folgenden abgekürzt „GBA."

[5] Vgl. GBA, Bd. 28, S. 7–17.

[6] Vgl. Werner Frisch und Kurt Walter Obermeier: *Brecht in Augsburg. Erinnerungen, Dokumente, Texte, Fotos*. Berlin, Weimar 1986, S. 107f. Die Vermutung, dass Brecht diesen Ausflug gemeinsam mit seinem Vetter Fritz Reitter gemacht habe (Werner Hecht: *Brecht Chronik 1898–1956*. Frankfurt/M. 1997, S. 58), ist nicht zutreffend. Brechts Beziehung zu den beiden Vettern Fritz und Richard Reitter verschlechterte sich bereits 1913 (Vgl. Brecht [Anm. 2], S. 45, 90, 92), und man behielt auch in den folgenden Jahren diese Distanz. Nur noch bei Familienfeiern war man zusammen. Darüber hinaus bestätigte Fritz Reitter, der heute hochbetagt im Bergischen Land lebt, im August 2000, dass er 1918 nicht gemeinsam mit Brecht im Bayerischen Wald war.

[7] Vgl. GBA, Bd. 28, S. 63–65.

[8] Vgl. Jahres-Bericht über das Königliche Realgymnasium zu Augsburg im Schuljahre 1914/15. Augsburg 1914, S. 61.

[9] Vgl. GBA, Bd. 28, S. 6.

[10] Vgl. ebd., S. 15-17.

[11] Tom Kuhn: „,Ja, damals waren wir Dichter.' Hanns Otto Münsterer, Bertolt Brecht und die Dynamik literarischer Freundschaft." In: *Der junge Brecht. Aspekte seines Denkens und Schaffens*. Hrsg. Helmut Gier und Jürgen Hillesheim. Würzburg 1996, S. 50.

[12] Vgl. Brechts „Die Ernte" (Anm.4), S. 125.

[13] Zu Fritz Gehweyer vgl. ebd., S. 32–36.

[14] Zu Hohenester vgl. Jürgen Hillesheim. *Augsburger Brecht-Lexikon. Personen - Institutionen - Schauplätze*. Würzburg 2000, S. 99f.

[15] Vgl. GBA, Bd. 28, S. 40.

[16] Vgl. hierzu: Jürgen Hillesheim: „,Nichts für literarische Sonntagsjäger.' Wie Bert Brecht in seiner Geburtsstadt plötzlich zum Thema wurde und was die Lokalpresse dazu beitrug." In: *Augsburger Allgemeine Zeitung*, 20.12.1999.

[17] Vgl. Brief von Irmingard Oelkrug vom 31. Januar 2000 an Jürgen Hillesheim, Bertolt-Brecht-Archiv.

[18] Vgl. dazu Kuhn (Anm. 11), S. 58.

[19] GBA, Bd. 26, S. 69.

[20] GBA, Bd. 28, S. 71.

[21] Vgl. Brechts „Die Ernte" (Anm. 4), S. 83f.

[22] Vgl. Friedrich Nietzsche: *Kritische Studienausgabe der sämtlichen Werke in 15 Bänden*. München, Berlin, New York 1980, Bd. 5, S. 18.

[23] GBA, Bd. 28, S. 18.

[24] Vgl. hierzu: Hans-Thies Lehmann und Helmut Lethen: „Verworfenes Denken. Zu Reinhold Grimms Essay ‚Brecht und Nietzsche oder Geständnisse eines Dichters.'" In: *Brecht-Jahrbuch* 1980. Hrsg. Reinhold Grimm und Jost Hermand. Frankfurt/M. 1981, S. 149f.

[25] Vgl. Christoph Subik: *Einverständnis, Verfremdung, Produktivität. Versuche über die Philosophie Bertolt Brechts.* Klagenfurt 1982, S. 56.

[26] Vgl. GBA, Bd. 11, S. 318.

[27] Jörg-Wihlem Joost, Klaus-Detlef Müller, Michael Voges: *Bertolt Brecht. Epoche - Werk - Wirkung.* München 1985, S. 94.

[28] Vgl. hierzu: Helmut Gier: „Brecht im Ersten Weltkrieg." In: *1898–1998. Poesie e politica. Bertolt Brecht a 100 anni dalla nascita.* Hrsg. Virginia Cisotti und Paul Kroker. Mailand 1999, S. 39–51.

[29] Erstmals wohl bei Reinhold Grimm: „Brechts Anfänge." In: *Aspekte des Expressionismus. Periodisierung, Stil, Gedankenwelt.* Hrsg. Wolfgang Paulsen. Heidelberg 1968, S. 151.

Irma Commanday Bauman and Mordecai Bauman in July 1998, at Lake Constance, after attending Hanns Eisler's 100th birthday symposium in Berlin

In Praise of Learning:
Encounters with Hanns Eisler

Irma Commanday and Mordecai Bauman

The first time I heard Mordecai Bauman sing the Brecht/Eisler song "In Praise of Learning" from *Mother* was at a Town Hall symposium sponsored by the magazine *New Masses*. How could I have known that it would change my life? And what was I doing there? Maybe he invited me, maybe I was curious about his performance. Neither of us remembers. It's quite enough to say that I never forgot it and that the song still resonates in my head. Today, June 18th, 2001, as it coincidentally happens, is our fifty-seventh wedding anniversary, an appropriate date to think about Eisler's enormous impact on our lives, both politically and aesthetically.

We had first met in the cast of the Britten/Auden opera *Paul Bunyan* in May 1941. Mordecai (known to his intimates as Mordy), sang the part of the Narrator; I was a Frontier Woman, a member of the chorus. Soon we were taking walks together in the park during breaks in rehearsals, and it wasn't long before we knew we were committed to each other. The opening choral number speaks the theme of our life together:

> Once in a while the odd thing happens
> Once in a while, the dream comes true,
> And the whole pattern of life is altered
> Once in a while, the moon turns blue.

Eisler's arrival in America in 1935 put a new spin on the musical life of this country and on many American composers as well. Few people are still alive in the U.S. who knew and worked with Eisler. As his music is revived and made more easily available, musicians and scholars seek Mordy out to discuss Eisler's work, bringing new relationships and activity to our lives.

They met in 1935. Mordy had recently graduated from the Juilliard Graduate School and Columbia College. The composer Elie Siegmeister, Mordy's fellow student at the Juilliard, recommended him to accompany Eisler on a tour throughout the U.S. He traveled with Eisler to nine cities, (Boston, New York, Chicago, Detroit, Pittsburgh, St. Louis, Berkeley, San Francisco, Los Angeles), singing songs Eisler set to poems by Brecht. The tour was arranged by members of Lord Marley's Com-

New Essays on Brecht / Neue Versuche über Brecht
Maarten van Dijk et al., eds., *The Brecht Yearbook / Das Brecht-Jahrbuch*
Volume 26 (Toronto, Canada: The International Brecht Society, 2001)

mittee to raise funds for children who were victims of Nazi fascism. The first concert was in Boston. The next one, in New York, was at Mecca Temple on 2 March 1935, Mordy's twenty-third birthday. Eisler accompanied him at the piano. The hall was packed. They never again had such large audiences; Eisler never complained about the public; he said the people could not understand the music because they were unprepared.

Mordy and Eisler were together frequently after the tour while Eisler was in New York. On one occasion Eisler and Brecht were invited to a party at the Soviet Union Consulate; Eisler asked Mordy to go with them and sing some of his songs. Mordy often joined them at the historic rehearsals of the Theater Union production of Brecht's play *Mother*.

Eisler was short, paunchy, and quite bald, with poor teeth. Careless in dress, he worried about his health, often complaining that he didn't feel well. He had wonderful ideas about how to sing and was a fine musician. He insisted that a pearl-shaped tone was not acceptable, that one must aim at sense, not sensibility; that words came first. (This was very important to Mordy, of course — but pearl-shaped tones! That was how he was trained to sing at the Juilliard.) Eisler was also a stickler for detail. A sociable man, he loved good food, good wine, and good talk

Mordy remembers episodes and anecdotes from the 1935 tour. Each city had a different character. Detroit was in the middle of a severe depression, the weather was dreadful, the audience sparse. There was so little to do that Eisler began to work on his *Deutsche Sinfonie*. He thought of using the melody of "The Peat Bog Soldiers" as the theme of the symphony, but later changed his mind.

In contrast, the Pittsburgh concert was a great success. A local resident, Jessie Lloyd O'Connor, wife of the writer Harvey O'Connor, suggested they might find a similar reaction in McKeesport, a nearby steel town suffering drastic unemployment. A union organizer tried to set up a meeting. The union hall was closed; a room with a piano was found, a few members showed up. Mordy sang a couple of the Brecht/Eisler songs. The material was unfamiliar, and few of the men understood Brecht's poetry and point of view. "Over their heads," Mordy said.

Years later, in 1943, Mordy was program director at the United Service Organization (USO) in Washington. One of his tasks was to visit military men recovering from battle wounds or fatigue. In a hospital he met a young solder who told Mordy he was from McKeesport. "McKeesport!" Mordy exclaimed. "I've been in McKeesport." As they talked, Mordy asked the soldier what his plans were after he left the army. "Never to go back to McKeesport," he exclaimed. And that response might explain the disinterest of the audience when Mordy and Hanns performed there.

In St. Louis they stayed in separate rooms in a large private home. Eisler got up in the middle of the night and instead of finding the bathroom he opened the wrong door, fell down a flight of stairs and fractured his arm. They found an accompanist to join them. It was in that city that Eisler said to Mordy: "I want you to meet Bertolt Brecht. He's the most important poet of our time and he happens to be here visiting Elisabeth Hauptmann." In Hauptmann's house the friends talked animatedly. Hauptmann, Mordy remembers, was very attractive, comfortable with Brecht, enjoying Eisler's charm and wit. Mordy didn't understand much of the conversation but felt he was in the presence of genius.

In San Francisco they lived in great style, meeting local celebrities: among them were Haakon Chevalier, a victim of the attack on Robert Oppenheimer; the distinguished anthropologist Paul Radin; and Louise Branston, a prominent San Francisco cultural leader who had arranged the Berkeley concert. Eisler wanted to meet the labor agitator, Tom Mooney, whose imprisonment was protested internationally. Louise was a member of the committee trying to prove his innocence and was permitted occasional visits. She took Eisler and Mordy across the bay to San Quentin. Mooney told Eisler about prison life, how the temper of the times swayed the attitude of his treatment in prison. When the country was in a progressive period he found he was given privileges, when a reactionary government was in power those privileges were taken away and he became the victim of restrictions. He no longer spoke as an individual but as a cause. Eisler was most interested in the experience of a political prisoner in America, aware that his escape from Germany saved him from a fate much worse than Mooney's.*

A San Francisco paper said of Mordy's singing on 16 March 1935:

On the tour Eisler is accompanied by a soloist who is said to be an uncommonly fine baritone, Mordecai Bauman. In New York, Bauman made a sensation with songs and ballads by Eisler, sung to the composer's accompaniment. He was acclaimed, not merely because he could sing, but

* Thomas L. Mooney was born in Chicago in 1883. He was a labor agitator, a leader in several violent labor struggles in California. He was convicted as a participant in bomb killings at the San Francisco Preparedness Day Parade in 1916, and sentenced to death. His case aroused international interest because of belief in his innocence, and questionable testimony at his trial. In 1918 he was sentenced to life imprisonment. In 1939 Governor Olson of California pardoned him unconditionally. He died in 1942. He was the source of one of the well-known political jokes of the period. During a rent strike in a cooperative apartment owned by a large New York City union, tenants carried signs as they marched up and down the street, picketing the managers: "No Rent Raise." "Improve the Maintenance." "We need Better Security." And "Free Tom Mooney!" After long negotiations, the managers finally met with the strike leaders: "We'll keep the rents low, we'll work to improve maintenance. But *how* can we free Tom Mooney?"

also because he revealed himself as a great interpreter. In other words, unlike many singers, he doesn't take the vitality out of his songs by devoting himself merely to musical sound. He thinks about the words. Every word he pronounces distinctly. What the words say he lights up. He's evidently one of those rare singers who recognize that singing is exalted speaking, designed to express both feeling and ideas.

The Hollywood-style part of the tour began at the airport in Los Angeles. Arrivals in other cities were quiet; they were met by the chairman of whatever committee was sponsoring the local concert. The committee organizing the Hollywood concert was the League Against War and Fascism. At the airport in Los Angeles they were surprised to find a large delegation in thirty limousines. It felt like a parade. They were overwhelmed with enormous bunches of roses, an unexpected, breathtaking experience. Later they found out that the father of one of the committee members, Seema Matlin, was a rose grower! She drove them to the Biltmore Hotel where they were shown to a suite of rooms. They were treated like VIPI (Very Important Persons Indeed!). In other cities they had generally been taken to the home of one of the committee members; never before to a hotel. This, they felt, was truly movieland style.

It was suggested that they "freshen up," because a press conference was to take place in a few minutes. And in a little while reporters and photographers arrived to interview the famous German exile. Hanns was in his element.

In 1935 the American public didn't believe that concentration camps existed or that Germans would seriously carry out a program of genocide. Hitler was just another authoritarian personality who was trying to improve the German condition. The Hearst reporter used this opportunity to insinuate that the only purpose of Hanns's visit was "communist propaganda." Eisler knew how to parry the questions, and he brought off the interview with élan. Before they had a chance to relax after the press conference, however, they discovered the truly true Hollywood style. Hanns had taken off his tie and started to unpack. But a committee member announced: "We've rented the suite *only* for the interview; now we will take you to your real quarters." The committee made the most of their arrival at the least cost. The next day newspapers featured Eisler's picture and interview, emphasizing the points he made, announcing the forthcoming concert (see Appendix 2). Then they were given splendid hospitality by distinguished members of the film community where they each had a comfortable room in a movie star's house, plus swimming pool.

At Madison Square Garden on 23 January 1939, the New York Committee of the Communist Party honored the fifteenth anniversary of Lenin's death with a play by Hoffman Hays, with music by Herbert Haufrecht and "John Garden." It was a pageant that lasted for about an hour and played with enormous success to 22,000 spectators. Hays began his story with an episode from the Colonial period of American history and ended with the release of Tom Mooney from San Quentin Prison. The play was directed by Jules Dassin and made use of 250 actors, orchestra, and vocal music, as well as choreography. It was presented in pantomime on a platform raised in the center of the auditorium, with the audience banked around all four sides.

Music, voices and sound effects were synchronized with the action on stage from a booth a hundred feet away, using giant overhead amplifiers. This difficult method of production was necessary so that the audience of 22,000 could hear. Mordy sang "John Garden's" song "Sweet Liberty Land" and "Building North America" by Herbert Haufrecht. The enthusiastic *New York Times* reviewer of this great occasion reported that "Mordecai Bauman's excellent interpretation of Haufrecht's and Garden's music fortified and complemented the dramatic action of the play." It was only later that Mordy learned from Herb Haufrecht that "John Garden" (John for Johannes, and Garden for the location), was in fact Hanns Eisler, who was in New York secretly, without a visa. As he was more or less in hiding he worked through Hays, so Mordy naturally did not see him on that occasion.

In 1939 Mordy found Eisler again quite by chance at the Palacio de Bellas Artes in Mexico. Mordy was there as the baritone soloist accompanying Anna Sokolow's dances, including Elie Siegmeister's "Strange Funeral in Braddock, Pennsylvania." Sokolow had choreographed a dance to this dissonant and harrowing piece about a worker who fell into a vat of molten steel. It was the major work in the repertoire, always a success with audiences. One day in May Mordy was standing in the orchestra pit next to the piano waiting for the dance to start. He looked into the audience and saw Hanns Eisler and his wife Lou. They had a great reunion. Their presence in Mexico changed Mordy's plans. Eisler asked Mordy if he could help find a house in Mexico City to rent for some months.

Mordy's high school Spanish lessons would make the search easier, and thus he found the Turkish Ambassador's house in Chapultapec Heights. Eisler invited him to stay on as his guest. The tour was coming to an end and Mexico City appealed to Mordy, so he decided to stay on for a while. The Eislers were joined by their friends, Dr. Henrietta Begun, a gynecologist, and her husband Hans Schröter, a former Communist member of the Reichstag.* Exiles from Germany, the two cou-

---

* We lived in Cleveland from 1946 to 1952. One of our friends was the acoustic engineer Joseph Begun, called Semi. One Christmas Semi went to Mexico to visit his sister. Mordy suddenly remembered that he had lived with her and the Eislers. Semi called us the moment he came home: he had made the same connection with Reni.

ples had never lived so luxuriously. There were three servants to take care of them: a housekeeper, a cook, and a chauffeur. The Mexicans lived in a small house on the property. The living room was decorated in a colorful Turkish "harem" style: the furnishings were elaborate, the chairs large and comfortable. On the wooden backs of the enormous sofas carved snakes slithered around, their eyes green bulbs that lit up at night.

During the run of Anna Sokolov's dance company, Ted Allan, the Canadian co-author of *The Scalpel, the Sword: the Story of Dr. Norman Bethune*, came to a performance. He told Mordy that Clifford Odets was also in Mexico. Mordy had shared a cabin with Odets in 1930, during an unforgettable summer at Camp Scopus, an adult camp in the Adirondacks. Odets, a budding playwright, was in charge of the evening theatrical programs, Mordy was his assistant. In Margaret Brenman's biography of Odets she quoted Mordy:

> ...[He] recalled him as a "loner with a friendly — sometimes knowing — smile, but never a laugh. He seemed always to be watching and listening: A lot of his quality was in his eyes — unwavering, as though looking through you. It was as though he was searching for himself and hoping to find it in somebody else."
>
> The eighteen-year-old Bauman, seeing Romain Rolland's play, *Beethoven* [the reference should actually be the book *Jean Christoph*, based on Beethoven's personality] under his arm, decided that Odets saw himself as the great and suffering romantic composer. "He was protective of me as if I were a younger brother or even like Beethoven's nephew — I think he liked the idea I was a singer and had won a scholarship to Juilliard."

Eisler had been invited to teach at the Mexico City conservatory by Sylvestre Revueltas, but his real purpose in going to Mexico was to immigrate legally to the United States, to settle and find work. He was familiar with Odets's reputation and success and was excited by the opportunity of meeting him in this informal atmosphere. Odets was looking for material *and* excitement, and he was aware of Eisler's important contribution to the plays of Brecht and to the music of the time. A few years later, Odets invited Hanns to visit him in Hollywood where he wrote the music for several of Odets's movies. Eisler became involved in the film colony and was closely associated with Charlie Chaplin and Fritz Lang. He and Odets remained good friends and continued to correspond for many years. The letters are included in a book of Eisler's correspondence, edited by Jürgen Schebera.

From that moment on Mordy and Eisler only heard of each other through professional activities. During the war years Mordy performed in New York, worked for the USO in Washington, and was eventually drafted into the Army in 1943. Eisler, on the other hand, remained in Hollywood, close to his former teacher, Arnold Schönberg, and had enough work in the movie industry.

Mordy continued to sing Eisler's songs and they became part of his permanent repertoire. His name became identified with "In Praise of Learning", "Forward, We've not Forgotten," "Peat Bog Soldiers," "United Front." He sang for progressive causes everywhere. Whenever he sang those songs they elicited immediate response and rapport with the audience. They became so popular that Eisler/Brecht and American Labor Songs were finally recorded on a label called "Timely," with a chorus conducted by Lan Adomian. Eisler accompanies "Rise Up." Marc Blitzstein is at the piano for the other numbers.

The records reached a reasonably large audience, were favorably reviewed, and were the first workers' protest songs to be recorded in the U.S. Even today, we still meet people who identify Mordy with those records; many progressives still treasure them.

Eisler and Brecht read newspapers regularly, assiduously following the political machinations of the moment. They were never able to break through to the media to get their own point of view across. Eisler referred to those who misunderstood his position as "gangsters." On the other hand, both Brecht and Eisler were unhappy with the adulation of progressive supporters who had no concept of world politics and really didn't understand their work. Eisler said of them that they had "all heart and no head."

In the spring of 1978 Mordy read an item in the *New York Times* Travel Section about a memorial symposium in Berlin celebrating Eisler's work on his 80th birthday. Albrecht Betz arranged for us to be invited by Eisler's widow, Steffi. One of the most exciting moments for us at the Eisler *Tage* was when we met two Soviet musicologists, Gregori Schneerson and Israel Nestev. Schneerson took Mordy's hand and said: "Mordecai Bauman! I've had your name on my desk since 1935, and now we meet! We must go together and see Ernst Busch." Busch had just come out of the hospital and was recuperating at home. Schneerson arranged for the visit. Busch was in a bathrobe; his elegant wife served tea and we tried to say something in German. "Kinder-Deutsch" I called it. At one point Schneerson said: "We have to sing 'The Peat Bog Soldiers.'" No one remembered the words. Mrs. Busch rummaged through the library to find an old song book; it was 45 years since Eisler had written the arrangement for the concentration camp song. Mordy and Busch, elderly singers, and Schneerson, Albrecht Betz and Nestev, musicologists from different countries, sang together and wept.

During the week of the seminar we gave Eisler memorabilia to his archive. The musicologists at the symposium had never seen the recordings Mordy made with Eisler in 1935. We gave the three 78 rpm records to the archive. We still had copies of Eisler's songs, music that Hitler destroyed; they are now where they belong, in the historic Eisler archive.

Hoffman R. Hays, translator of Brecht poems, wrote a play *Daniel Drew* with music by Eisler It was a project that never got off the ground. Juliette Hays, Hoffman's widow, sent a copy of the play to the archive. We also brought a copy of Brecht's New York production script of *Mother* and Workers Song Books in which Eisler's songs were published. The music of greatest interest to the musicians and organizers of the conference was the manuscript that Eisler had composed for the pageant, *A Song About America*, written by Hays for a Madison Square Garden event under the auspices of the Communist Party. The work was not familiar to any of the assembled participants, for the apparent reason that Eisler could not risk identifying himself with such an event, and had chosen "John Garden" as a pseudonym.

The moment that had by far the greatest impact on our lives came when Mordy was delivering his brief comments at the 80th birthday symposium. He said that Eisler always told him that when the war was over he would invite Mordy to visit him in Berlin. Being in Berlin represented "closure" of his association with Eisler. That was a new "buzz word" for us in 1978. Now we don't use it any more; it has become ubiquitous and boring. The young American interpreter could not think of a proper translation for the word. From the back of the auditorium came a voice: "*Entschuldigen Sie*, perhaps I can help." Jürgen Schebera came up to the platform and made the reference clear. He was in the process of writing a book about Eisler. We promised to send him a picture of Mordy at twenty-three. "Please call me when you come to Leipzig," he said.

"We're not going to Leipzig," we said. Jürgen was astonished. "How can you be here and *not* go to Leipzig?" When we thought about it, we realized how foolish it would be to skip Leipzig. We went to Leipzig partly because Jürgen reminded us that it was Eisler's home town, but mainly because Bach spent twenty-seven years there as Kapellmeister for the city.

It may seem like a *non sequitur* but it's important to report here that Mordy spent the summer of his seventeenth year reading the plays of George Bernard Shaw; he was especially impressed by the Prefaces. One GBS comment from "Maxims for Revolutionists" influenced him for years: "He who can, does. He who cannot, teaches." He was determined to always "do," which meant he would never agree to teach. But in later reading he discovered Bach as pedagogue. That changed his attitude toward his own work, and eventually led him to establish the summer arts workshop, Indian Hill. He wanted to direct a school where teachers lived and worked intimately with artistic and talented students, as Bach lived with boys in the St. Thomas Choir. Twenty-five summers directing Indian Hill defined Mordecai Bauman as an educator who influenced hundreds of talented students who continue the teaching tradition identified with Bach. Experiencing the atmosphere of the St. Thomas Church was awesome. When we recovered our equilibrium Mordy said: "It will be Bach's 300th birthday in 1985; we have to do something to celebrate that. We'll make a documentary film about Bach. We have seven years to accomplish that." It took twelve.

What an adventure that became! Mordy was sixty-six years old and had never made a film. He would never have dreamed of such a project if we had not come to the Eisler Tage, if we had not met Jürgen, if we had not gone to Leipzig. When Mordy talks about his collaboration with Eisler he repeats what a significant influence it was in his artistic growth. And he led us back to Bach.

Some years later we visited Brecht's home, now a museum. It was a Saturday morning, a quiet time in East Berlin. The front entrance was closed; we wandered up and down the street and discovered the cemetery across the alley where Brecht, his wife, Helene Weigel, the philosopher Hegel, Eisler, and our friend Lin Jaldati are buried. Finally we saw a worker opening a side door to the house; he motioned us in. We met a charming young woman who offered to show us around. She assumed we were English. When we told her we were from New York she wondered what Americans were doing in East Berlin. She had never met anyone from the U. S. Mordy said he had known Brecht and wanted to see where and how he lived. She was certain that Werner Hecht, director of the museum, would want to meet us.

Hecht invited us to have tea in his rooms above the museum. Mordy talked about the Eisler tour; Hecht asked Mordy where he had met Brecht. "In St. Louis," said Mordy.

"Brecht was never in St. Louis," asserted Dr. Hecht.

"But I know that's where I first met him," Mordy claimed. "He was visiting Hauptmann."

"Oh, I guess you're right. I know *she* was in St. Louis, and of course Brecht might have visited her there!"

One day in 1984 we had a telephone call from Europe. A young man identified himself: "My name is John Highkin and I'm calling from Cambridge, England. I'm writing a play about Hanns Eisler, and I understand that you sang his songs. Can I use you in the play?" John was working toward his Master's degree at Cambridge; he asked John Willett, the British scholar and translator of Brecht's works, for names of Eisler colleagues in the U.S. Willett suggested that John call Mordy, who became a character in the play *More than a Fair Trial*. It was performed during that summer in Cambridge, at the Edinburgh Fringe Festival and at the Berliner Ensemble. (In Cambridge Mordy's role was played by a woman.)

In 1992 another unexpected call came from a professor at Indiana University, Ronald Cohen. He was collecting American Labor and Protest songs from 1926 to 1953 for a project to produce CDs of hundreds of old records. Included are labor songs, the Brecht/Eisler songs that Mordy introduced and recorded with Eisler in the U. S., and "Strange Funeral in Braddock" by Elie Siegmeister. A German firm, the Bear Family, released the set of ten CDs titled: "Songs for Political Action," in May 1996. A book of stories about the music and the performers, with lyrics of the songs and many photographs are included in the handsome edition. It is because of that project that the sixty-year-old pristine 78 rpm records we have kept so carefully were digitized. Mordy is heard singing nine songs.

In 1993 we were able to see a German documentary film about Eisler. There were several people in the film whom we know: Lou Eisler-Fischer, Hanns's second wife, the one Mordy knew best; Hilda Eisler, Gerhart Eisler's widow (recently deceased); Georg Eisler, Hanns's son by his first wife (also deceased). And some well-known artists: Wolf Biermann, Gisela May, Ernst Busch, Therese Giehse and Brecht. And we saw a brief view of Eisler's house in Berlin, familiar to us now, focusing on his piano. Sting opens and closes the documentary, singing his own excellent arrangements of two songs with words by Brecht. In English translation they are "To My Little Radio Set" and "Where the Wind Blows."

Almost sixty years after those years with Eisler, we read an announcement in *The Berkshire Eagle* (a Massachusetts newspaper) about a program of Brecht/Eisler and Rilke in an unlikely place, Housatonic, Massachusetts. Housatonic is a small village near Great Barrington; most of the buildings that housed large paper mills are now empty. Today its fame is based on Arlo Guthrie's rap song "Alice's Restaurant." Housatonic was not only an unusual place to bring the works of Brecht, Eisler and Rilke together, but the combination of the three is awkward. Albrecht Dümling, Director of the Eisler Society, wrote: "Brecht and Eisler only liked Rilke in their youth, but turned away from him later."

We had to attend this extraordinary event in a building we knew well. It was in a loft, up a long flight of narrow stairs, above a lumber supply store. The Swiss actress, Graziella Rossi, created the program. She was anxious to meet us and hear about Mordy's friendship with Eisler. The producer, Alexander Souri asked Mordy to say something about his association with Brecht and Eisler, at the performance.

"Who's Eisler?" the man behind us asked. Ess White — yes, that *is* his name — turned around and said: "Stuart, this man can and will tell you all about Eisler at the end of the program." The impressive performance was very well received, though it was in German. Graziella was terrific: dramatic, attractive, portraying the under and overtones of Brecht's poetry.* The German actor, Nikolaus Deutsch, partnered her

---

* In 1998, honoring the 100th anniversaries of both Brecht's and Eisler's births, Graziella produced and performed in *Die Massnahme* for an audience of over a thousand people in Zurich.

with strength and compassion.

Mordy gave a two-minute talk about his memories of Eisler and Brecht and their collaboration. He read Brecht's poem "In Praise of Learning" and played the 1935 recording. What's historically interesting about that poem is the translation. Mordy's friend Henry Mins changed the British translation into American vernacular, words that would be more easily understood when sung. Mordy himself changed "You must be ready to take *over*," to "*power*" which is a less accurate translation; but with a consonant making it easier to project the final, most important word. A truly accurate translation would be: "You must take over the leadership," impossible to sing. Because Henry Mins translated Brecht's poem and Mordy changed the final word, Brecht told the Un-American Activities Committee in 1947: "No, those are not my words."

From 1978 to 1988 we traveled to both East and West Germany to explore the places where Bach had lived. We filmed the program in May 1988. DEFA. the TV company in the GDR was our local producer. As we began the editing process, we realized that we could not afford to film in West German cities. Fortuitously, two Berlin film-makers came to the U.S. to finish their film *My Name is Bertolt Brecht; Exile in America*. Norbert Bunge and Christine Fischer-Defoy, two attractive and talented young Germans, came to our apartment to talk to Mordy. As he piqued their interest with his Eisler stories, Norbert asked him if he would be in the film. Mordy agreed, and appeared in the broadcast on PBS/TV. Parts of the interview were edited out; this is the unedited version.

The narrator, Alan Marks (the late American pianist), introduced the film in a voice-over:

> New York: focus of Bertolt Brecht's fascination with America in the twenties. 1933: Brecht's *Threepenny Opera* is staged in New York. 1935: Brecht's first visit to the states. The production of *Mother*, with music by Hanns Eisler ends in disaster. Brecht's theories of Epic Theatre are totally incomprehensible. Disillusioned, Brecht returns to Denmark. His songs remain.
>
> In 1935 Hanns Eisler tours the USA with the American singer Mordecai Bauman. Several records are produced.

Mordy is on screen, sitting in our living room

> Here's one of the three records that we made with Eisler's music and Brecht's words: the "United Front" song which is a real popular piece of music with a real lilt to it so that people can sing and march at the same time. It became very popular all over the world; everybody sang it.

While he speaks, the record is on the screen, the chorus and Mordy singing:

> At that time there was a big movement for a united front against fascism
> And it is what I became involved in: this progressive movement to stop
> fascism wherever it was.

On the screen now is an old portrait of Eisler and Brecht. Mordy continues:

> I think Eisler was trying through his whole life, his total life, to represent a
> new kind of man. I think Brecht was trying to represent a new kind of
> theatre. He was a new kind of writer. I think what he was saying was something
> that we still haven't really accepted in America: the idea that a
> theatre piece is also a learning piece. I felt that what Brecht had brought,
> not only to the theatre but also to the musical idiom, was the concept that
> became very popular -maybe ten or twenty years later — which was expressed
> in our terms as "cool." Everything was "cool." But what it meant
> was: you said something that had a really *hot* message, but you didn't say
> it with passion; you said it with "*Verstand*" (Intellect).

Mordy walks into the New School auditorium, across the street from
our apartment. As he walks toward the stage he is speaking in a voice-
over:

> It's over fifty years since Eisler was welcomed here at the New School in a
> welcoming concert. The concert was organized by the American Music
> League, which was a group of workers' musical organizations. Marc Blitz-
> stein played the piano for me, and I sang some of Brecht's songs that Eisler
> had written. For instance, his famous "In Praise of Learning," which came
> from the play *Mother*, that Brecht had done from the novel by Gorky. In a
> house of learning, "Praise of Learning" is not a bad song to remember.

And he sings the first verses without accompaniment.

During the summer of 1993 we heard of another Eisler connection:
his music was played for the first time, as far as we know, at Tangle-
wood. Oliver Knussen conducted the chamber music piece *Fourteen
Ways to Describe Rain*. Although Eisler is well-known and respected in
Europe, in the U. S. most music lovers don't know who he was. Now
because of the 100th anniversary of the births of both Eisler and Brecht
we were surrounded by Eisler connections. The Brecht/Eisler work,
Deutsche Sinfonie was played by the American Symphony Orchestra
in New York, Rhombus, a Canadian television production company,
with ZDF/TV in Berlin and Holland TV, produced *Solidarity Song*,
another video biography of Eisler. Mordy was interviewed for the film,
sitting on our apartment roof garden, in April 1995. Larry asked him to
sing "Forward, We've Not Forgotten." Mordy tried, hesitated, then
admitted: "well, I've forgotten" [the words]. Eberhard Rebling, former
director of the Hanns Eisler Conservatory in Berlin, told us that it was
an indication of how Eisler's name and music was not remembered.
"Even Mordy forgot!"

It is a poignant film, telling the story of Eisler's struggles. His teacher, Arnold Schönberg, disapproved of his political activities. Although he thought of Eisler as one of his most gifted students, Berg and Webern — politically more acceptable — became better known. The film describes the many tragedies in Eisler's life, but also many successes.

Günter Mayer, editor of Eisler's written works, sent us a twenty-seven page critique of many errors in directorial judgment he found in the film. He feels that Eisler's life was not as tragic as it was presented. Although he had many problems in Germany, both because of Hitler and from the East German bureaucracy, when he returned from exile it was to great acclaim. He wrote the national anthem of the GDR, and the music conservatory in East Berlin was named the Hanns Eisler Schule. Now there is a revived interest in Eisler's music, partly because of the TV documentaries. Sting's recording of "To My Little Radio Set," and especially Matthias Goerne and Fischer-Dieskau's recordings of Eisler songs. Reunification of Germany made it possible to re-issue Eisler's music originally recorded on IPS in the former German Democratic Republic; many CDs are available in U. S. record stores.

Not altogether unexpectedly we were invited to participate in the 100th birthday seminars about Hanns Eisler. June 24, 1998 found us in Berlin as guests of the Eisler Gesellschaft. Thirty-six enormous cranes hovered over Berlin, an incredible sight, making it difficult to get around the city. There was so much construction, so many road blocks and narrowed streets that many taxi drivers — in both east and west sections of the city — could not find our destinations.

Jürgen Schebera interviewed Mordy at the first meeting of the conference. First, I thanked all our friends for their help. Mordy was fluent, articulate, witty. We were surprised, however, to read the long news item about the conference: Headlined: "Mordecai Bauman, a shrewd story teller!" First Paragraph from *Der Tages Spiegel*: KULTUR, *June 30, 1998*:

> Mordecai Bauman remembers his 23rd birthday fondly. In the year 1935 the young graduate of the Juilliard School was the first American to perform Eisler, with the composer at the piano, in New York. The tour went on to 50 [sic] U.S. cities. Now, at the age of 86, a shrewd story-teller, "Mordy" sits here in the Berlin Institute for Music Research, as the honorary guest of the International Hanns Eisler Society for "The First International Hanns Eisler Colloquium." Bauman made the "Solidarity Song" well know in the U.S., and sang the "Ballad of the Peat Bog Soldiers" in German in various places, the only song he sang in the original language. He remembers Eisler as tremendously entertaining, but "very serious," bursting with energy, dressing carelessly, not a good pianist, but "a great performer." As an observer, he knows exactly why *Mother* was not a success in the U.S. Neither the excellent actors nor the director understood Brecht.

A last-minute foundation grant supported a concert of Eisler songs and piano pieces. Steffi Eisler asked us to sit with her. Next to her was Gisela May, the remarkable Eisler interpreter. She surprised the large audience by singing three Eisler songs after the scheduled perform- ances. Steffi complained throughout: "It's too long! Hanns always said that an hour and a quarter is enough for any concert! It's much too long!"

H.K. Gruber, called "Nali" by his friends, conducted the EOS or- chestra in New York in April 2001, in works of Eisler and Weill and his own orchestral pieces. Larry Weinstein, director of *Solidarity Song* introduced Mordy to him, saying that Mordy had known Eisler and Brecht and lived with Eisler in Mexico for a month. "I need two months with you!" Nali said. So we invited him to have lunch with us. A propos of Mexico he told us about a wonderful American flutist he conducted in the Mexico City Symphony Orchestra. "She was a student at our school, Indian Hill," I told him. He was astonished that we knew so many people in common, a common enough occurrence for us. Then he told us a story I enjoy repeating: a famous professor in Vienna had a coterie of admiring students around him. He had an enormous reputation as a great teacher; however students were surprised that he seemed to care so little about them that he never kept their names on file. A student complained unhappily, asking: "Don't you want to know how our careers develop?" The professor replied: "The world is round. We will certainly meet again."

Appendix 1

Excerpts from a letter from MB to R.G. Davis, concerning his article, "Music for the Left," about Charles Seeger, Pete's father, in *Rethinking Marxism*, 2.4 (Winter 1988): 9–25.

Seeger's rejection of Eisler as European is specious. His score for *Song About America*, written with Hoffman Hays for the Madison Square Communist Party meeting, is as popular and American as anything one might identify as American. "Sweet Liberty Land" from that score is a favorite of Pete's. Eisler's "United Front" song was a great success in the U.S., as was "Die Moorsoldaten." (Peat Bog Soldiers). The question is not one of European or American music, but good or bad music. Of course each (and every) country's music has a distinctive sound and rhythm. But much of Eisler's music had an international appeal. He was a hit wherever he went...and I don't need to argue about Brecht's universality.

Seeger was a populist and a musicologist — a wonderful human being. He is the perfect example of the intellectual in political life, which he could take or leave.

Eisler's part in the struggle of the left is quite different from Seeger's. Eisler was an ardent believer in socialism and chose to work openly in the workers' movement. He broke with his mentor, Schoenberg, conducted workers' choruses, wrote for the left-wing press and used his music as a political weapon. He worked to improve the condition of the workers. In "Music and Politics" he wrote: "A great culture begins with the creation of a high standard of living for all."

Eisler has not been eliminated. His music is still performed in Europe, and the left has not yet developed a history of its own cultural achievements. Historians are now writing about women, blacks, Indians and others who have been neglected — in time we will discover the achievements of the left.

Eisler influenced many musicians, but his stay in the U. S. was both short and isolated. It was almost entirely confined to the film industry. When he was hounded out of this country it didn't increase his popularity.

There must be more to workers' culture than picket line protests. "We are the World" may be great to raise money to fight famine, but it doesn't give the worker a clue as to *why* the famine. That's the difference between Seeger — and Eisler and Brecht. Eisler and Brecht wanted their works to educate the audiences; Seeger's approach is more romantic and emotional. (The picket lines haven't had a new song since Maurice Sugar wrote "Sit Down.") It would be wrong to think that European workers are much more sophisticated in their music than Americans. One of Eisler's aims was to replace the "beery" songs with more militant ones. It is necessary to have a theory in order to have a practice.

Appendix 2

Article from *The Los Angeles Examiner*, March 1935, by Roger D. Johnson:

MUSICIAN, NAZI BANNED, HERE FOR RECITALS

Record breaking systems have no allure for Hanns Eisler, refugee German composer. In his case, phonograph records bearing his music were ordered destroyed, his music burned and all singing societies were forced to stop singing his songs under penalty of imprisonment after Adolph Hitler came into power.

Driven out of his apartment by Storm Troopers who "confiscated everything but one shirt, one suitcase and a toothbrush," this musician has been living as a wanderer in London, Paris and other cities of

Europe. [Actually, Eisler was in Vienna, having been warned by Brecht to leave Europe.]

Here to give lecture recitals during the next 10 days, Mr. Eisler is stopping at the Biltmore Hotel, following his arrival by airplane yesterday from San Francisco.

MODERNISM BANNED

"Hitler is destroying the cultural life of his people," Mr. Eisler claims. "Jews are not the only ones persecuted. He subdues everyone who shows any signs of arousing the population, no matter what the field may be. Nothing modern is permitted in art, literature or music. Hitler wants slow romantic and sentimental music that will dull the population, serving as a narcotic and stunting their minds."

Of course his close associates hold the same views he has. "They must, or be wiped out. Everyone remembers that [Hitler] shot his close friend, Ernest Roehm, within six weeks after he had issued a public letter praising him. Americans returning from the Saar plebiscite [where they were the guests of Hitler]...naturally have a good report to give. They were shown only the things Hitler wanted them to see during their short stay. Give me eight days and plenty of money and even I could make every city in the United States look attractive to strangers. I could make Shanghai, one of the worst cities in the world, look beautiful through such methods."

HITLER DOOM SEEN

Short life for Hitler was predicted. "It is shown by history that such dictatorship cannot last," Mr. Eisler said. "He will never die in bed but through violence. When he does, there will be a terrific fight for power among his followers but I think the German people will eventually regain control of their own country."

NO ATTRACTION HERE

After appearances here, including a recital Sunday night at 1441 N. McCadden Pl., Mr. Eisler and his baritone soloist, Mordecai Bauman, will leave for Chicago. On April 12, his newest symphony will be performed in England under the baton of Ernest Ansermet, director of the London Symphony Orchestra. "American motion pictures hold no attraction for me," he admitted. "Only if a story of unusual possibilities were offered would I work here. I have a contract for more pictures in England."

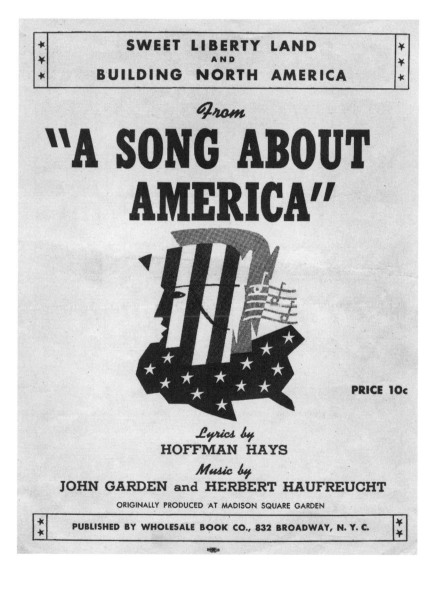

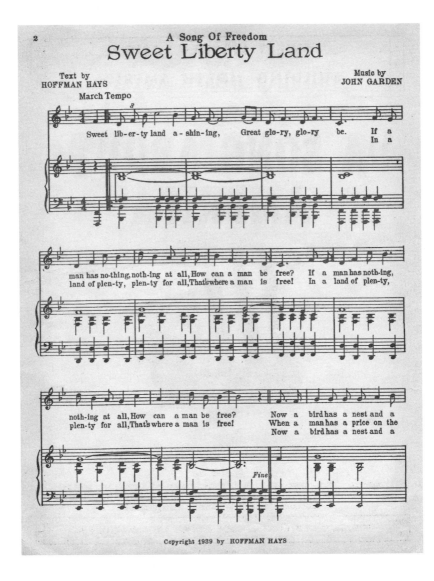

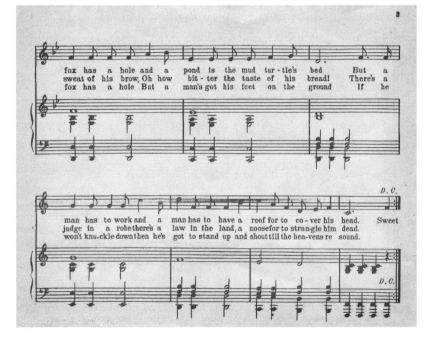

Brilliant Child in the Murder House

On the occasion of Ekkehard Schall's seventieth birthday, the author reflects on Schall's career as an actor, a man of the theater, and a member — through marriage — of the Brecht family. In particular Schall's relationship to Brecht himself is considered. Schall's famous performance as Arturo Ui is remembered, along with Heiner Müller's poetic reaction to that performance. Although the author views Schall's career as having been shaped by numerous political and personal constraining factors, he sees Schall's negotiation of these constraints as remarkably successful and considers Schall one of the greatest German actors of the twentieth century.

Geniales Kind im Mörderhaus

Stephan Suschke

Ein Schwert kann zerbrochen werden und ein Mann
Kann auch zerbrochen werden, aber die Worte
Fallen in das Getriebe der Welt uneinholbar
Kenntlich machend die Dinge oder unkenntlich.
Heiner Müller

Eigentlich dachte ich an einen road movie über Schall. Weil die Geschichte an einem Nachmittag auf dem Fahrrad beginnt. Ich fahre mit dem Fahrrad die Schönhauser Allee hinauf, am Polizeirevier 76 vorbei, lasse den Jüdischen Friedhof hinter mir und etwa auf Höhe Luitpold-Bierstuben, (da, wo früher der Franz-Klub war) hatte ich die Eingebung eines Titels. Ich schiebe dessen Verlockung sofort beiseite, weil er nach West-Feuilleton klingt, die Häme schwingt mit. Einzig der Ort macht mich unsicher, es ist ein literarischer Ort, der Ort einer Erzählung: "...nur die U-Bahn schoss flink wie immer zu ihrem hochgelegenen Bahnhof hinauf." Ich mag ihn wegen eines einsamen Moments in einem großen Zimmer mit weißem Flügel und wegen eines alten aufrecht sitzenden Mannes mit ebenso weißem Haar. Der alte Mann saugte an seiner Pfeife und ich sprach mit ihm über seine Biographie, kurz bevor Karl Corino versuchte, Hermlin von dessen Biographie zu enteignen. Aber es geht um Ekkehard Schalls Leben und das ist eine andere Abteilung, obwohl sie ohne Leute wie Hermlin nicht möglich gewesen wäre. Bei allem, was folgt, gilt es, eins festzuhalten, ob einem das gefällt oder nicht: Schall gehört zu den größten deutschen Schauspielern des vergangenen Jahrhunderts, das wäscht ihm kein Regen ab, das steht in tausenden von Kritiken, in Kritiken aus aller Welt. Gegen die untergehende Sonne fahre ich mit meinem Fahrrad in Richtung Danziger Straße, frühere Dimitroff, ein Flugzeug setzt in der scheinbaren Verlängerung der Schönhauser Allee zur Landung an: „An den bewährten Triebwerken der Firma Pratt & Whitney / die die Maschine über Oranienburg hinunterschrauben, / entgegen den Havelseen und den Waldgebieten im Norden; / entgegen dem dörflichem Flughafen Tegel" beschrieb Uwe Johnson dieses Einschweben in die „Selbständige politische Einheit Westberlin" irgendwann in den siebziger Jahren, an einem Tag an dem Ekkehard Schall vielleicht den Ui spielte oder Coriolan. Schall war berühmt, als ich geboren wurde.

New Essays on Brecht / Neue Versuche über Brecht
Maarten van Dijk et al., eds., *The Brecht Yearbook / Das Brecht-Jahrbuch*
Volume 26 (Toronto, Canada: The International Brecht Society, 2001)

Es ist auch eine Zeitreise, aus dem Frühling des Jahres 2000 in die 50er Jahre, als Autos in Berlin selten waren. „Wir haben mit der Vergangenheit abgeschlossen, aber die Vergangenheit nicht mit uns", sagt die off-Stimme ein paar Tage später im neuerbauten Cinemaxx an derselben Ecke, um Tom Cruise mit einem vergessenen und verdrängten Leben zu konfrontieren. Und sein Gesicht wird sehr leer sein. Aber ich radele auf die Danziger zu, gegen die untergehende Sonne. Das Flugzeug braucht endlos in meiner Erinnerung, etwa solange, bis ich den Titel verwerfe: „Baal im Kaschmirmantel," aber ich bin angekommen an der Ecke Danziger. Berlin — Ecke Schönhauser.

Ich habe Schall an einem 1. Mai kennengelernt, Anfang der 90er Jahre. Damals wurde der „Kampftag der internationalen Arbeiterklasse" Mai noch gefeiert, eine sich langsam in den Abend hineinfressende Sauferei. Von der Maifeier des Deutschen Theaters, draußen auf dem Platz, in das dunkle Herz des Berliner Ensembles — der Kantine. Axel Werner sass da, Castorf, ein paar andere und am Schauspielertisch saß Ekke, wir kannten uns flüchtig, setzten uns und kurze Zeit später beschimpfte Castorf Schall, alles lief auf eine Prügelei hinaus, bei der Castorf wahrscheinlich verloren hätte, aber der Streit wurde verlegt in Schalls Wohnung. Es gab Whisky und Dosenbier — Castorf schlief schnell auf der Ledergarnitur ein — der Abend endete friedlich im Morgen. In Peter Voigts Film *Dämmerung — Ostberliner Boheme der fünfziger Jahre* werden auch die verschwundenen Kneipen der fünfziger Jahre abgefahren, der Esterhazy-Keller, die Hajo-Bar, die Koralle und Schall sagt: „Wir nahmen natürlich in Anspruch, dass man mal saufen durfte, wenn man frühmorgens Probe hatte, allerdings nicht vor Vorstellungen." Der Film ist in das warme Licht von Erinnerung getaucht, die Sehnsucht nach einem zurückliegenden Aufbruch bestimmt den Film und eine Stelle bei Kafka: „Wir wurden aus dem Paradies vertrieben, aber zerstört wurde es nicht. Die Vertreibung aus dem Paradies war in einem Sinne ein Glück."

Berlin — Ecke Schönhauser also, Ortsbestimmung und Titel eines der schönsten Filme über die fünfziger Jahre. Es ist die Zeit der Spionage, die Zeit der Schieberei. Schall spielt einen Halbstarken, der durch eine unglückliche Verkettung von Zufällen an die Ränder des kriminellen Milieus gerät, ehe er von der DDR wieder an die Brust genommen wird: „Warum kann ich nicht leben, wie ich will. Warum habt ihr lauter fertige Vorschriften. Wenn ich an der Ecke stehe, bin ich ein Halbstarker, wenn ich boogie woogie tanze amerikanisch, wenn ich das Hemd über der Hose trage ist es politisch falsch. Mir braucht keiner zu helfen. Jeder macht seine Erfahrung selber." Ein Text, wie von Schall selber. Er brilliert mit bescheidener Genauigkeit, den Mund auch beim Sprechen kaum öffnend. Ein Gesicht voller Unschuld, in das sich nur manchmal Züge unvorstellbarer Härte einschreiben, dabei immer etwas Stures, Eigenes. Eine andere Figur — Typus bürgerlicher Gegner —

äußert sich: „Psychologisch ist der Westen im Vormarsch. Dieses ganze System wird zusammenbrechen. Deutschland ist schließlich nicht A-sien." 33 Jahre später stelle ich fest, dass der „Gegner" Recht behalten hat. Es ist ein warmer Frühlingstag: gleiche Stelle: Ecke Schönhauser; eine der letzten Ecken Berlins, wo die neue Mitte noch nicht die Geschichte wegsaniert hat. Das Kapital hat Besitz genommen, an der Ecke Kastanienallee die Sparkasse, Ecke Eberswalder die Berliner Bank wenige Meter entfernt die Dresdner. Wo im Film noch der Konsum stand, hat Rossmann eine Filiale. Die Untergrundbahn donnert über die grüngestrichene Brücke, an deren Geländer statt des *Neuen Deutschlands* die Springerpresse wirbt: ("Und wenn der Springer noch so hetzt, die DDR, die fetzt, die fetzt," hieß es in den siebziger Jahren im DDR-Radio). Aus der Eberswalder wälzt sich ein endloser Autostrom in die Danziger, bevor die Ampel die Schönhauser freigibt.

Tage später in der Straßenbahn auf dem Weg zu Schall, erinnere ich ein Gespräch mit Friedrich Dieckmann: „Die Ära Berghaus war ein Aufbruch, sowohl was neue Autoren anbelangte: Hacks, Mickel, Heiner Müller, also die zuvor auch am BE gewaltsam zurückgedrängte DDR-Dramatik, wie auch das Verhältnis zu den Brechtschen Modellen, die nicht mehr einfach übernommen wurden, sondern wirklich kritisch, manchmal auf eine verstörende Art befragt wurden. Das BE unterstand damals, wie später in der Wekwerth-Ära, einer Doppelherrschaft: Ruth Berghaus war die Intendantin, Barbara Brecht-Schall verfügte über die Brecht-Rechte, also über die Möglichkeit, ob das Ensemble seinen grundlegenden Autor spielen könne. Deren Verhältnis zueinander wurde auf verschiedene Weise beschrieben: Einigen erschien deren Verhältnis zu dem Ring des Brecht-Erbes wie das von Kriemhild und Brünhilde im Nibelungen-Ring, das Lindenblatt im Rücken des Theaters war dessen festgehaltene Rolle als Brecht-Monopol Bühne, während Schleef der Meinung war: Millionärinnen tun sich nichts. Er irrte, denn beim Theater hörte nicht nur die Freundschaft auf, sondern auch jegliche Rücksichtnahme. 1975 verweigerte Barbara Brecht-Schall die von der Berghaus schon vorbereitete Inszenierung der *Dreigroschenoper*. Der Öffnungsversuch der Berghaus-Ära scheiterte am Widerstand des politbürokratischen Apparats und der Erbeverwaltung, also ein Doppelnelson aus Ost- und Westzensur, denn der Eingriff aus Eigentumsbefugnissen ist ja ein Topos des Westens. 1977 gab die Intendantin auf, die Dynastie setzte auf Wekwerth."

Das Haus, in dem Schall und seine Frau Barbara in der Friedrichstraße wohnen, steht neben einem plattgewalzten Areal, wo einst das Hotel Adria stand, unweit der Weidendammer Brücke. An den Wänden des Hausflurs Graffitis, die Fliesen auf dem Boden haben eigenwillige, fast orientalische Muster. Die alten Stromleitungen liegen über Putz, das Holzgeländer ist kunstvoll verziert, vor den Wohnungstüren schmale Spiegel, in denen der Besucher Zeit hat, sein Äußeres zu kor-

rigieren. Schall, wie immer in unseren Begegnungen freundlich, sach-
lich, in einer Leinenhose, breite Hosenträger über dem T-Shirt: „Ich
habe keine Entzugserscheinungen vom Theater" sagt er, und ich versuche ihm zu glauben. Ich denke an Geschonnek, einen Satz zu Schall in
Duell Traktor Fatzer, „Wie man aufwächst, denkt man." und frage ihn
nach Magdeburg: "Ich stamme aus einer kleinbürgerlichen Familie,
Tabakwarenhändler en gros. Bücher gab es, im Herrenzimmer, Lexika,
die üblichen Romane und das Gesundheitsbuch mit der aufklappbaren
Frau. Ein bisschen so wie überall." Das Kriegsende war für ihn keine
Befreiung, eher „ein Vakuum, ein Abbruch — man erfuhr, das was
gestern war, durfte man nicht mehr vertreten. Begonnen mit dem Theater hat es im Krieg in der Bismarck-Schule. Der Deutsch- und Lateinleh-
rer Hinze organisierte Schüleraufführungen — „ich spielte die Bäuerin-
nen in den Volksstücken von Hans Sachs, und die Rüpelszenen aus
Shakespeares *Sommernachtstraum*. *Gyges und sein Ring* von Hebbel
im Stadttheater gab endlich den Anstoß: der Vorhang ging auf und
hinter einer Säule trat der Schauspieler Romano Merk hervor und sagte
als Kandaules: ‚Heut' sollst du sehn, was Lydien vermag.' Da wusste
ich, so imposant möchte ich auch auftreten." Er lernte die Ringerzäh-
lung, sprach vor, und lernte am Schauspielstudio Magdeburg neben
der Schule, er war 16. Sein Agent vermittelte ihn erst nach Frank-
furt/Oder: „Busch hat dort angefangen und meine Tochter Johanna."
Später nach einem Vorsprechen an die Neue Bühne, dem späteren
Maxim-Gorki-Theater.

Das erste Vorsprechen bei Brecht war schief gegangen, er durfte
weder Schiller noch Hauptmann vorsprechen, sondern Nico Dostals
Eva im Abendkleid. Anschließend das Rundgedicht „Ein Hund kam in
die Küche," als achtzigjähriger Greis, dreißigjährige Frau und als zwölf-
jähriges Kind. Trotz des Fehlschlags gab er nicht auf, bewarb sich noch
einmal, diesmal für die Rolle des José in *Die Gewehre der Frau Carrar*.
Gefordert war ein romanischer Typ, er ließ sich die Haare blauschwarz
färben, und bekam die Rolle, sicher nicht nur wegen der Haare. Die
entscheidenden Jahre, Jahre des Lernens bei einer Ausnahmefigur vom
Range Brechts begannen. Schall bezeichnet sich als ein bisschen ver-
rückt: „Ich ging auf die Bühne wie ein aufgepumpter Pneu, dann zog
ich das Ventil raus, pssssssss." Dagegen hat Brecht gearbeitet: „Er hat
mir den Eindruck vermittelt auch mit geringer Lautstärke ausdrucksstark
zu sein. Ich hatte immer wieder Rückfälle, wo ich das vergaß. Einmal
schrie mich Brecht, der ziemlich laut schreien konnte, an: ‚Jung-
Siegfried, Hofschauspieler.' Nach der Probe trat er im Dunkeln aus
dem Hauseingang der Kammerspiele auf mich zu: ‚Nachher war's besser.' Durch die Angriffe aus Ost und West wusste man nach kurzer
Zeit, dass es etwas Besonderes war, am Berliner Ensemble zu spielen.
Man kriegte ein Elitebewusstsein." Schall redet auch über *Winter-
schlacht*, die Inszenierung Brechts, die ihn krisengeschüttelt zurück-

ließ, obwohl es einen kleinen Zettel gibt: „„lieber Schall, wenn ich das sagen darf: ich finde den hörder jetzt von großer art, ihr b.' Am nächsten Tag wollte er ihn zurückhaben — und das war der Beginn meiner großen Krise, weil ich in der zweiten Vorstellung die Figur, wie er meinte, eigenmächtig verändert hätte." „Wir haben mit der Vergangenheit abgeschlossen, aber die Vergangenheit nicht mit uns," denke ich, während Schall weiterspricht: „Wir waren immer im Nachteil, dass wir zu den älteren Schauspielern kein Lehrer-Schüler-Verhältnis hatten, die waren Vorbild, auch in ihrer Biographie, in ihrer Lebenshaltung, man kam eigentlich nicht an sie ran, die wussten es immer besser."

Während des Gesprächs immer wieder sehr genaue Beschreibungen von Kollegen: „Busch war ein merkwürdiger Schauspieler, weil er nicht bereit war, sich der Rolle zu nähern, sondern die Rolle musste zu ihm kommen. Bei der Weigel war es so, dass sie sich fast demütig einer Rolle unterordnete. Ich war dazwischen. Ich bin wegen meines leidenschaftlichen Exhibitionismus zur Bühne gegangen und das wollte ich nie aufgeben." Irgendwann, ich frage Schall danach, was sie während der endlos anmutenden Probenzeit von 9 Monaten gearbeitet hatten, kommt Schalls Frau Barbara, sie wird sich in der Folgezeit immer wieder in das Gespräch einschalten: „Papa hat gesagt, ein Elefant trägt zwei Jahre, ein Karnickel drei Monate. Aber beim Elefant kommt auch ein Elefant heraus." (Durch meine Arbeit am Berliner Ensemble war ich mittelbar oder unmittelbar von ihren Entscheidungen betroffen. Deshalb hatte ich immer ein kompliziertes Verhältnis zu ihr. Aber bei aller Rigidität ihrer Entscheidung kommt man an ihrer Persönlichkeit nicht vorbei, egal, ob sie recht hat oder nicht, ob man sie mag, oder nicht. Ich denke an das Emigrantenkind — „enemy alien" — das erst in Amerika, dann in Deutschland Fremde war und sich durchsetzen musste. Es entschuldigt nichts, aber erklärt manches.)

Wir reden über Berlin-Ecke Schönhauser, warum Schall so wenige Filme gemacht hat. Er bekennt, dass es ein großes Glück für ihn war, mit Brecht zu arbeiten und zugleich ein Unglück: „Die anderen waren alle eine Stufe tiefer. Die Höhe war einfach nicht zu halten, und dadurch wurde es schwieriger mit anderen zu arbeiten. Das betraf nicht die großen Inszenierungen, die mit Palitzsch/Wekwerth und Wekwerth/Tenschert in den ersten Jahren nach Brechts Tod entstanden sind — Wekwerth konnte sehr scharf analytisch denken, und hatte eine wunderbare Art einen Gedanken, einen realen Punkt zu treffen. Diese intellektuelle Strenge wurde ästhetisch vom Palitzsch umgesetzt. Die Grobheit des Wekwerthschen Arrangements wurde durch Palitzschs Eleganz verfeinert." Beider *Ui*-Inszenierung hat Schall weltberühmt gemacht, sie lief 584 mal, Schall setzte sich dafür ein, sie abzusetzen, „weil ich eines Tages merkte: Ich konnte dem Burschen nicht mehr richtig böse sein." Wochen vorher hatte Heiner Müller eine Vorstellung gesehen und ein Gedicht geschrieben, das in keiner Ausgabe zu finden ist:

FÜR EKKEHARD SCHALL
Als zum 532.mal auf der Bühne stand
In der Rolle des Arturo Ui der Schauspieler
Ekkehard Schall, verließ der von ihm porträtierte
Adolf Hitler, mit Neugier auf die berühmte Darstellung
(Deren Ruhm sich herumgesprochen hatte
Unter den Toten sogar) heimlich sein Bunkergrab
Und reihte sich ein unter die Zuschauer im Berliner Ensemble
Und es geschah, daß er nicht erkannt wurde
Von dem genaueren Abbild, sondern unbemerkt
Kleiner und kleiner werdend zurückschwand in seine Versenkung
So daß er genannt wurde von nun an
Von den anderen Toten nicht mehr mit seinem
Vorübergehenden Namen
Adolf Hitler, sondern nur noch
Arturo Ui

In der politisch und für die Geschichte des Berliner Ensembles interessierende Zeit wird das Gespräch unschärfer, ohne dass Schall ausweicht, dazu ist seine Sicht auf die Dinge zu eindeutig. 1969 versuchte Wekwerth zusammen mit Kurt Hager Helene Weigel zu entmachten. Wekwerth hatte eine neue Strategie, und die Voraussetzung diese umzusetzen, war die Entmachtung der Matriarchin. Grundlage war Ulbrichts Aufsatz über neue Leitungstätigkeit, in der nur Genossen in leitenden Positionen sitzen durften. Der Putsch misslang, die Weigel war, außer, dass sie eine vorzügliche Theaterleiterin und erstklassige Schauspielerin war, auch die Inhaberin der Brecht - Rechte, die nach ihrem Tode auf die drei Kinder übergingen. Wir sind bei der Berghaus-Zeit angelangt. Er beschreibt den ästhetischen Punkt der Differenz präzise: „Die Schwierigkeit, die sich herausstellte, waren die immer mehr zunehmende Choreographien der Aufführung, die Vorgänge wurden zurückgedrängt, es war eine starre mechanische Wiedergabe." Es kam zum Bruch, Barbara Schall kann sich nicht an das Verbot einer Inszenierung der *Dreigroschenoper* erinnern, sie hätte später Wekwerth vorgeschlagen, dass die Berghaus die *Dreigroschenoper* inszeniert. Auf die Frage der Einflussnahme der Familie auf die Rechte antwortet sie: „Ekke hat sich prinzipiell nie eingemischt." Barbara Brecht-Schall erzählt, dass „Ekke" Gast am Berliner Ensemble und auf die schwarze Liste gesetzt wurde. Er durfte nicht nach „drüben." Es kam zur Allianz mit Wekwerth. Wekwerth wurde Intendant, Schall sein Stellvertreter: „Hager hat uns verdonnert: Versucht es zusammen!" Praktisch hätte er kaum Einflussmöglichkeiten gehabt, künstlerisch wäre die Zeit außer manchen Rollen wenig ertragreich gewesen.

Ich frage noch nach seinem Training und er führt mich in den Nebenraum, wo mehrere Maschinen stehen, die von Schall bearbeitet werden. An der Wand Plastiken seines Freundes Igael Tumarkin, mit dem Gesicht von Schall in unterschiedlichen Rollen. Als ich ihn bitte, ihn fotografieren zu dürfen, stellt er sich bereitwillig daneben. Zum Schluss trinken wir zusammen einen Grappa. Barbara entlässt mich mit der Bitte, die eine Aufforderung ist, zur Autorisierung und ich bin draußen auf der Friedrichstraße. Langsam gehe ich in Richtung Chausseestraße, um Dieckmanns *Coriolan*-Beschreibung aus dem Brecht-Archiv zu holen: „Ja, es ist in der Schallschen Darstellung, etwas kindlich Ungebärdiges, naiv Trotziges in seinem Betragen..." vorbei am Dorotheenstädtischen Friedhof. Über der ehemaligen Wohnung Brechts das Archiv. Auf dem Weg dorthin passiere ich einen Glaskasten mit einem Brecht-Gedicht, denke beim Lesen an Peymann. Mich ärgert die Billigkeit meiner Assoziation: „die neuen Antennen / verkünden die alten Dummheiten."

Vor der Brecht-Buchhandlung steht Werner Riemann, Assistent am BE seit 1959, blickt ins Schaufenster, wo ein gelber Reclam-Band von Kierkegaard „Über die Angst" liegt. Ich überlege, ob ich Riemann nach Ekke fragen soll, denke Ekke, nicht Schall, aber lasse es. Ich überleg, ob Ekke Angst gehabt hat in seinem Leben, denke über den Schmerz nach und mich erstaunt diese merkwürdig ungebrochene, total intakte Existenz. Ich hätte gern mit ihm über den Tod gesprochen, über Brüche — aber wo ist das Gesicht hinter dem Gesicht, wo ist der wirkliche Gedanke hinter der Sprache. Tage später werde ich diesen Punkt verfolgen, in einem Gespräch mit Hans-Joachim Frank. Aber ich bin auf dem Weg zu Ulrich Wüst.

Ich erzähle Ulrich Wüst, weshalb ich da bin: Wegen eines Satzes, den der alte Geschonnek in Heiner Müllers Inszenierung *Duell Traktor Fatzer* gesagt hat: „Wie man aufwächst, denkt man." Ulrich Wüst ist in der gleichen Stadt wie Schall geboren und als mir der Satz von Müller/ Geschonnek einfiel, fielen mir Wüsts Fotografien ein. Sie entstanden vor zwei Jahren in Magdeburg auf endlosen Wanderungen durch seine fremde, nahe Heimat — ich erinnerte mich an sie, weil ich den Nachkrieg spürte, die von diesen Photographien ausging. Überdehnter Nachkrieg wird Wüst im Gespräch sagen. Fotos ohne Menschen, das endlose Warten auf den Augenblick, wo die Erde unbewohnt ist wie der Mond. Die Häuser auf den Photographien sind zwei-, manchmal dreistöckig, der Putz bröckelt, man denkt, dass es einer der endlosen Vormittage am Sonntag ist oder der Sonnabendnachmittag — es ist heiß, alle warten auf den Regen oder die Fußballübertragung von *Sat 1*. Die Tristesse verstärkt durch die vergeblichen Versuche der Werbung — das Design bestimmt das Bewusstsein. Aus Magdeburg muss man wegwollen, wenn man Künstler werden will, wie aus Gelsenkirchen, Großenhain, Ambach, oder Weimar, Städte über die Therese Giehse sagte: in der Provinz kann man lernen, aber nicht bleiben — Photographien von einem untergegangen Stern. Fast zwanghaft wiederholt sich der denkmalgeschützte Schornstein von SKET, einziges Wahrzeichen einer Industriebrache, deren Wurzeln älter sind als die DDR - der Vorgänger des Schwermaschinen Kombinat Ernst Thälmann, waren die Krupp-Gruson-Werke — „Wie man aufwächst, denkt man" sagt Geschonnek vor sich hin/zu in *Duell Traktor Fatzer*. In Heiner Müllers theatralischem Krebsgang durch die deutsche Geschichte, seiner wichtigsten und zugleich erfolglosesten Inszenierung am Berliner Ensemble, war die Besetzung exemplarisch: Erwin Geschonnek kehrte nach fast vierzig Jahren an das Berliner Ensemble zurück und spielte sich selbst als alten Genossen, Gegenpol zu Bernhard Minetti als altem Schauspieler der zwei Jahre später Ui/Wuttke/Hitler die Schauspielkunst beibringen wird. Eine andere Besetzung war Schall. Er spielte zusammen mit Geschonnek und Hermann Beyer Müllers theatralische Auseinandersetzung mit dem 17. Juni 1953. Ich erinnere mich gut an beide. Wie Geschonnek mühsam nach seinem Stock angelt, sich auf den Tisch stemmend, aufsteht und „Madrid du Wunderbare" singt, und an Schall, wie er, nachdem klar ist, das die russischen Panzer kommen, abgewandten Gesichts nach dem Parteiabzeichen sucht. Er findet das kleine Blechschild und heftet es sich mit einer Mischung aus Renitenz und Unverfrorenheit, fast mechanisch, ans Revers. Und eine andere Stelle erinnere ich: Sein letzter großer Ausbruch in *Fatzer*. Schall spielte es als Kommentar auf die einsetzende strafrechtliche Verfolgung der DDR-Polit-Elite. Die alte Bundesrepublik wähnte sich damals noch in der Unschuld der unbefleckten Empfängnis. SED war Synonym für politische Kriminalität schlechthin, unvorstellbar, dass eine Partei der Bundesrepublik in einem solchen Kontext je erscheinen könne: Schall tobte, einen Stuhl als Krücke nutzend, gefesselt in einem Teermantel, einer Erfindung des Malers Mark Lammert, sich zu Tode schreiend, mit äußerster Beherrschung und äußerster Wut:

> Noch nicht dem letzten räudigen Hund
> Werden wir zumuten, Platz zu nehmen
> Auf euren dreckigen Gerichtsbänken
> Eures dreckigen Staates.
> Ein Klumpen Natur.

Tage später sitzt Hans-Joachim Frank mir gegenüber in einem kleinen Café in der Hannoverschen Straße. Frank leitet das Theater 89, ein Theater, das durch seine professionellen Schauspieler und Arbeiten zu den besten Berlins gehört, auch wenn sich das nicht in seiner lächerlichen Subvention widerspiegelt. Er kam 1973 als 19jähriger an das Berliner Ensemble und ist Schalls vorerst letzter Regisseur in Christoph Heins *Bruch*. Er hat in Schalls einziger Inszenierung *Eduard II.* gespielt und neben ihm in vielen Aufführungen. Noch einmal wird das fertige

Bild, das man von Schall hat, relativiert: „Er hat nie faktisch die Macht, trotz der körperlichen Nähe zu den Brecht-Erben. In der kleinen Theater-Politik konnte er nie Entscheidungen treffen. Es werden Berichte kolportiert, in denen Wekwerth Schall als Feind der Partei bezeichnet hat. (Auch diese Beziehung, wie so viele im Berliner Ensemble eine Hassliebe, auch weil sie eine Beziehung Abhängiger war). Schall hat das natürlich gemerkt, und als er Wekwerth kurzzeitig als Stellvertretenden Intendant vertrat, und eine Sitzung im Intendantenzimmer stattfand, hatte er große Scheu, sich auf den Stuhl der Weigel zu setzen. Er war in einer schwierigen Situation. Er brauchte einen Regisseur, darum wusste er, aber er hatte durch seinen Ruhm und durch die Verbindung zu Barbara eine fiktive Macht, vor der die Regisseure scheuten." (Ich erinnere mich an eine Äußerung Schalls in einer Auswertung zu *Turandot*: "Die Schauspieler sind nicht hergenommen worden, das merkt man ihnen an. Das muss jetzt grob geschehen. Ihr habt nicht mit ihnen Krieg geführt und ihnen das verboten und jenes erlaubt." (22.1.1973) — Ich ist immer der Andere.) „Aus dieser Hilflosigkeit begann er plötzlich, alles um sich herum zu organisieren. Da war er auch nicht unbedingt fein. Als er bei der *Mutter*-Inszenierung schon im Widerstreit mit der Berghaus lag, sagte er kurz bevor der Vorhang aufging: ‚Hast du dich schon eingekrüppelt für die Scheiße.' Sein Problem: er kam aus Magdeburg, war ein schwer begabter Kleinbürger, der immer zwischen die Fronten geriet. Das hängt natürlich auch mit seiner traumatischen Beziehung zu Brecht zusammen, der den berühmten ‚ihr hörder ist von großer art'-Zettel nach der zweiten Vorstellung zurück verlangte. Brecht, später die Berghaus, und auch Wekwerth, die haben Gott gespielt, mit unwahrscheinlicher Klasse, aber auch mit großer Brutalität. Die Ritsch sagte, ‚das ist ein Mörderhaus.' Aus dieser Verletzung von Brecht, die traumatisch war, und eine Karriere beenden kann, kam die Panzerung, dass solche Schocks nie wieder hochkommen. „Wie man aufwächst, denkt man," sagte Geschonnek. Diese Erlebnisse, die aus der Brecht-Zeit kamen, wurden weitergegeben, von der Berghaus, später natürlich auch von Wekwerth. — Am besten war er, wenn er Kleinbürger gespielt hat, Ui oder Iwagin in Müllers *Zement*. Die Heldenrollen waren immer problematisch, was jetzt sicher anders ist. Man unterschätzt auch den wahnsinnigen Druck, unter dem Schall gestanden hat. (Schalls Frauen- und Saufgeschichten, kurze Momente der Entspannung vor dem wieder und wieder ausgeführten Sprung in die Haifischbecken.) Letztendlich musste er die großen Vorstellungen immer auch tragen und das hat er fast immer geschafft. Dafür haben sie ihn geliebt und gehasst."

Wir sprechen über seine Inszenierung *Der Bruch*. „Er war nicht misstrauisch, sondern hat sich erstklassig vorbereitet und war wahnsinnig diszipliniert. In Niedergörsdorf (einer Spielstätte des Theaters 89, im Kulturhaus einer ehemaligen sowjetischen Kaserne) hatte er als

Garderobe ein Zimmerchen, ohne Wasser, mit herunterhängenden Tapeten. Er ist jeden Tag zwei Stunden hin und zwei zurück gefahren ohne mit der Wimper zu zucken. Wenn wir mal vor 50 oder 60 Leuten gespielt haben, hat er das niemals irgend jemand merken lassen. Er gehört zu den Leuten die nicht zynisch sind, als Schauspieler nicht verkommen, nicht abgewichst. Eigentlich ein großes Kind."

Ekkehard Schall wird siebzig. Selten habe ich Leute so verschieden über einen Menschen sprechen hören, selten hat eine Persönlichkeit Menschen so gespalten. Hass und Verachtung auf der einen Seite, Ehrfurcht und Verehrung auf der anderen. Diese Polarisierung ausgehalten zu haben, bescreibt Schalls Qualität.

Ekkehard Schall als Arturo Ui in *Der aufhaltsame Aufstieg des Arturo Ui,*
Berliner Ensemble 1959
Regie: Manfred Wekwerth / Peter Palitzsch
[Foto: Vera Tenschert, Bertolt-Brecht-Archiv]

The Case of G/B

The author reflects on his experiences directing Brecht's *Galileo* at the Berliner Ensemble in the late 1990s. For Tragelehn, Brecht saw himself reflected in the figure of Galileo, and hence the play's criticism of its protagonist is also Brecht's own self-critique. Tragelehn explains his attempt to emphasize the conversational, open nature of *Galileo*, which he distinguishes from parable plays like *The Good Person of Szechwan*.

Der Fall G/B

B.K. Tragelehn

Vorbemerkung   Unter dem kleinen Aufsatz, einer Art Arbeitsresümee, steht das Datum der letzten Vorstellung, drei Tage vor dem Beginn der Umbauarbeiten im Theater am Schiffbauerdamm. Zu der Zeit gab es bei der neuen Direktion Überlegungen, die Aufführung weiterzuspielen, mit Umbesetzungen, und mit der Möglichkeit dies und jenes zu ändern. Die Vorstellungen waren immer gut besucht, die Überlegung lag nahe. Die Feuilletons jedoch hatten keinen Brechtreiz verspürt, sondern Brechreiz. (Thomas Wieck hat in *TdZ* 1998/2 dazu etwas gesagt.) Dass aber auch Rezensenten die Intention der Aufführung wahrzunehmen vermochten, zeigte ein kleines südwestdeutsches Blatt: *Am Anfang tritt Karl-Heinz Tittelbach auf, ein in Zirkus, Film und Theater erfahrener kleinwüchsiger Schauspieler, der diverse Schrecken des Klein-Seins schildert. Was solls? Das Fragezeichen bleibt bohrend im Raum. Galileo...tritt als nächster auf, nackend, wäscht sich. Wieder ein Fragezeichen. Wieder keine Antwort. Dunkel Genossen ist der Weltraum sehr dunkel: dieser Satz, weiß auf schwarz, zieht sich als Band über die drei Wände der Guckkastenbühne...Die ist ziemlich leer ansonsten. Stühle stehen verloren im kahlen Mauerwerk auf dem durch ein blendend weißes Klebeband zweigeteilten Boden. Auch das provoziert Fragen, die unbeantwortet bleiben. Zu einem Abend vieler offener Fragen hat Regisseur B. K. Tragelehn Galilei arrangiert. Das macht durchaus Sinn. Handelt es sich doch um ein Stück des Fragens...* (Die Rezension von Peter Claus, überschrieben *Genosse Galileis Fragen*, stand am 17. 12. 1997 in der Zeitung *Die Rheinpfalz*.) Die Bühne war von Schliecker, die Musik von Goldmann, den Galilei spielte Bierbichler, seine Tochter Virginia Mira Partecke, Premiere war am 12. Dezember 1997.

1   Der Triebtäter mit dem schlechten Gewissen, dem es trotzdem wieder passiert: das war es, was Brecht von Busch verlangt hat, in den Proben der Schlussszene. Busch wollte lieber jemanden spielen, der oben schwimmt. Er war lange genug unter Wasser gewesen. Da war dann auf der Probe einer zu sehen, den es zerreisst — hinaus über die Zerrissenheit des alten Gefangenen über der Frage, ob er sein Manuskript herausrücken will oder nicht. Das war einer der nachhaltigen Eindrücke von den Proben im Winter 1955/56. Der andere, unvermittelt daneben: Brecht als Galilei. Die Art, wie Brecht vorsprach (sehr

New Essays on Brecht / Neue Versuche über Brecht
Maarten van Dijk et al., eds., *The Brecht Yearbook / Das Brecht-Jahrbuch*
Volume 26 (Toronto, Canada: The International Brecht Society, 2001)

viel) und vorspielte (sehr wenig) — nein, sein ganzer Habitus: G steht und geht und redet und blickt wie B. G ist B.

Die überlieferte Formulierung aus einem Gespräch nach der ersten Niederschrift: *die Darstellung der großen Prozesse sei mit dem Stück technisch gelöst* (was immer das heißt), war von trügerischer Objektivität. Sie verschleiert, dass das *Portrait of the Artist as Galileo Galilei* mehr noch als ein Selbst-Porträt eine Selbst-Denunziation war. Brecht hat sich die Hexenmaske Bucharins aufgesetzt. (So wie er sich, zu besichtigen auf dem Schnappschuss von einer Weihnachtsfeier in Kalifornien, hinter einem Sessel stehend, die Arme eingestemmt, den Schnauzbart des neuen Papstes vorgehängt hat.)

Als 19-jähriger habe ich die Proben in Berlin staunend verfolgt, ohne die Bedeutung zu erfassen. Dazu war die Erfahrung von Jahren nötig. Für Brecht war sie alt. Und war wiedergekehrt am 17. Juni 1953. *Der 17. Juni verfremdet die ganze Existenz*, schrieb er ins Tagebuch. Es blieben ihm drei Jahre und zwei Monate, um die Erfahrung zu bearbeiten. Er dachte erst an Coriolan, und entschloss sich dann, als Busch den nicht spielen wollte, zu Galilei. Er konnte die Proben nicht mehr beenden. Die Variante einer Episode in der 13. Szene, ein Paralipomenon der ersten Niederschrift, wurde sein Testament. Die Ausgrabung, aus einer seiner vielen Mappen, fällt in sein letztes Vierteljahr.

2   Heiner Müller, im Gespräch mit Heise, noch in der DDR, in den achtziger Jahren, stellt die Frage erst einmal so wie Brecht sie gestellt hat: *Preis oder Verdammung* Galileis. Aber Brecht ist es passiert (das ist das Resüme meiner Eindrücke aus seinen Proben), dass er, mit der Absicht die Verdammung zu zeigen, Galileis Tragödie zeigt. Und die ist seine eigene. Und deshalb weiß er nichts davon. Und auch das Stück weiß nicht. Es fragt. Die Tragödie, jenseits von Dafür und Dagegen, kommt am Ende zu keiner Formel, keinem Urteil im gewöhnlichen Sinn des Wortes. Mit der sogenannten Selbstverurteilung formuliert Galilei den Riss: eben seine Tragödie.

Das Urbild der Zerreißung des Intellektuellen ist die Auslegung der Aktäongeschichte in Giordano Brunos 18. Sonett in den *Eroici furori*.

DAS URBILD NACH BRUNO
für Josef Bierbichler/Galilei

Die Meute los gelassen hetzt zur Jagd
Auf ungewisser Fährte. Aktäon wagt
Ihr folgend sich ins finstere Dickicht heute
Dringt bis zum Ufer vor und sieht im Fluss
Göttlich im Sonnenlicht den Wellen Kuss
Die Schönheit. Und der Jäger wird zur Beute:
In einen Hirsch verwandelt wird er jetzt
Von seinen eigenen Hunden tot gehetzt.

Leben des Galilei, Probenfoto: B.K. Tragelehn (Regie), Mira Partecke
(Virginia)
Berliner Ensemble 1997
[Foto: Ute Eichel]

Er sieht die Schönheit. Und zahlt mit dem Leben.
Diese Geschichte will ein Gleichnis geben:
Ich wars der meine eigenen Gedanken
Zur Jagd hetzt. Ihre Meute meuternd Schranken
Durchbrechend hat mit unbarmherzigen Bissen
Sich auf mein Herz gestürzt. Und es zerrissen.

Zur Vorgeschichte der aktäischen Hunde, wie Bruno von ihnen spricht, gehören die griechischen Erinyen, die römischen Furiae; in der deutschen Sprache ist (nach Christianisierung und Reformation) der Begriff *Gewissensbisse* übriggeblieben. Müller bringt es, Jahrzehnte nach Brecht, auf den Punkt, sprachlos: *Zerreißung der Photographie des Autors.* Eine Bühnenanweisung ist das Herzteil der *Hamletmaschine.*

Die Schöne, die Aktäon sieht, ist die Wahrheit. Dass im Gedicht die Schönheit die Wahrheit vertritt (repräsentiert), ist nichts Vages, keine Ungenauigkeit, sondern bohrt in der Wunde. Die Schönheit beruht auf dem strahlenden Schein einer Ordnung. Und die großen Entdeckungen, was entdecken sie? Eine neue Ordnung. Immer löst eine Ordnung die andre ab. Für Galilei obenauf die Frage: rücke ich mit meiner Arbeit heraus, der Entdeckung einer neuen Ordnung. Und darunter die Frage: bin ich verblendet. Er ist am Ende fast blind. Heute noch sagt man den Kindern, dass sie blind werden, wenn sie direkt in die Sonne sehn.

In dem Gespräch mit Heise zitiert Müller dann Bernard Dort mit dem Satz, dass das Stück *eine Tragödienstruktur hat.* Er kommt sozusagen von der anderen Seite her zur Tragödie, von der Lesart der Rechtfertigung. Die lag in der DDR nahe, weil es da immerzu darum ging, wie man das, was man macht, durchbringt, mit (fast) allen Mitteln. Das war schon eine Intention von Brechts erster, der dänischen Fassung gewesen, geschrieben in den Jahren des doppelten Schreckens, den Dreißigern. Das Stück sollte die Illusionen über die *neue Zeit* zerstören. Zugleich wird *die neue Zeit* als solche behauptet. *Die neue Zeit* ist die nach 1917. In dieser Konstellation war G gleich B.

3   Die in L.A. ausgenommen, hatten alle Aufführungen einen reichen und repräsentativen Rahmen, auch und gerade die berühmt gewordenen. Sie zeigten immer das Bild eines berühmten Schauspielers mit einem edlen Rahmen darum herum. Dagegen die schwarze Höhle, zweigeteilt durch einen weißen Strich, mit den hellen Stühlen in der Runde und mit der Schrift an der Brandmauer rundum (dem Satz von Gagarin *Dunkel Genossen ist der Weltraum sehr dunkel*), als Fernrohr ein Lichtstrahl: das war ein Raum, in dem die Verhandlung, die unabschließbare Debatte, Platz hatte sich zu entfalten.

Leben des Galilei: Josef Bierbichler (Galilei), Robert Gwisdek (Andrea),
Berliner Ensemble 1997
Regie: B.K. Tragelehn
[Foto: Ute Eichel]

Der Eindruck der Grabeshöhle (aus der Schwärze) hat nichts Niederdrückendes (auch weil die Bühne die Bühne bleibt und die Schwärze nicht Stimmung erzeugt). An das, was diese Höhle beherbergt, kann sich Hoffnung knüpfen, denn die Toten sind nicht tot, wenn wir sie nicht verdrängen. Eine Zukunft der Gattung gibt es nicht ohne ihre Geschichte. Es wird nicht Vergangenheit durch Sichhineinfühlen vergegenwärtigt (denn, mit Klaus Heinrich zu reden, *die Farben der Vergangenheit auftragen, heißt die Fragen der Vergangenheit abschneiden*) — sondern es wird herausgeschnitten das, was uns betrifft. Galilei meets Brecht, Brecht meets us. Und jeder nimmt, was er braucht.

Drei Monate nach Abschluss der ersten Fassung hatte Brecht ins Tagebuch geschrieben, das Stück sei *technisch ein großer Rückschritt*. Es müsse neu geschrieben werden: *alles mehr direkt, ohne die Interieurs, die „Atmosphäre," die Einfühlung*. Die Aufführung in L.A. und ihr kondensierter Text bewegten sich in die Richtung. Wir gingen aus von dieser Aufführung (die gut überliefert ist: ich hatte im Herbst 1955 aus einem Schuhkarton voll Fotos das Modellbuch gemacht für Brechts Proben, und es gibt auch einen Schmalfilm von Ruth Berlau, den das Regieteam vor Probenbeginn ansah und an dem ich das Modell kontrollieren konnte. Tatsächlich war es möglich gewesen, ohne Kenntnis der Aufführung, die Fotos in die richtige Reihenfolge zu bringen, die Bilderzählung war also einleuchtend). Das war als Ausgangspunkt schön und gut, aber wir haben uns nicht schnell genug weiterbewegt. Bierbichler drängte, und viel zu spät habe ich das Podest und die Hänger, die wir auf die Bühne gestellt hatten, Theatertheater, abgeräumt. Schliecker reagierte, indem er den weißen Strich zog, der durch die Höhle schneidet.

Die Schwächen der Aufführung sind meiner Säumnis geschuldet. (Grund war, denke ich, eine Art Instinkt-Unsicherheit, Folge der Ratifizierung der geschichtlichen Niederlage.) Die Zeit war jetzt knapp, und wir konnten nicht alle Überlegungen weiter verfolgen. Aber wir hatten, eine Woche vor der Premiere, endlich den Raum, den wir brauchten. Und kamen zurück auf eine Ausgangsüberlegung: *das talking*. Bei Brecht, gerade in Texten aus dieser Zeit, wird nämlich getalkt: im *Messingkauf*, in den *Geschäften des Herrn Cäsar*, in den *Gewehren der Frau Carrar*. Die Debatte, die Diskussion ist etwas Brecht Eigentümliches, und das war festzuhalten. Ganz zuletzt kam noch der Entschluss dazu, im Zuschauerraum das Licht anzulassen. Diese Massnahme gilt im Theater als der Konzentration abträglich. Aber die Leute im Parkett sollten die eigenen Reaktionen auch sehen können. Die Debatte bleibt so nicht auf die Bühne eingeschränkt.

Die Lebensstationen Galileis, Szene für Szene, gerieten in der Debatte in Bewegung, d. h. die Trennung zwischen den Szenen wurde übergangen, die Szenen gingen über ineinander, das Licht nicht aus.

Das Besondere jeder Situation (das war der Gedanke) wird in dem bewegten und bewegenden, in dem verwickelten und verwickelnden Streit deutlicher als in der äußeren Abteilung. Erst im zweiten Teil der Tragödie sind Stationen, eine nach der andern, die Schritte ins Ende, Agon. Ist es das Ende? Ja und nein. Unsinnig zu leugnen oder zu verdrängen, dass es sich um einen Prozess handelt. Brecht will dem Prozess des Schicksals den Prozess machen. Der Prozess G endet. Der Prozess B endet. Aber der Prozess der Gattung geht weiter im Parkett. Und so bleiben auch der Prozess G und der Prozess B offen.

Die Lebenszeit des Einzelnen (seine Geschichte) und die Zeit der Geschichte (der Gattung) treten auseinander. Die Vergänglichkeit macht aus der Tragödie das Trauerspiel.

4 Wenn man einen Riesen zeigt, muss man auch einen Zwerg zeigen. Für den großen Mann muss irgendwer bezahlen, viele müssen das, Frau und Kind und Schüler. Und das Männlein? *Dies Männlein ist der Insasse des entstellten Lebens.* Das was vergessen wird, und das was vergisst.

Der Zwerg führt das Publikum an — im doppelten Sinn des Wortes. Zweifellos ist der Zukurzgekommene boshaft. Und seine improvisierte Conference, in der er aus seinem Zwergenleben erzählt ehe er die folgende Szene ankündigt, kann nicht ohne Pein sein für den Zuschauer. Es ist eine Unverschämtheit, dass dieses Männlein nicht unter den Tisch gekehrt und dem Blick entzogen ist. Aber nein, seine Rolle ist einsehbar, und der Zuschauer soll über die Peinlichkeit hinweg steigen. *Liebes Kindlein ach ich bitt / Bet fürs bucklicht Männlein mit.*

Kann man sich noch einfühlen in einen Helden, wenn ein Zwerg ihn vorführt? Das Stück ist zwar noch eines mit Protagonist. Aber das Theater muss das nicht sehenden Auges nachvollziehen (z. B. durch reiche Rahmung). Denn der Protagonist ist ein Problem, im Theater wie im Leben. (Das Problem wurde ehemals mit dem Begriff *Personenkult* euphemistisch umschrieben.) Die Verblendung ist beides zugleich: abstoßend und mitreißend, und beides ist gefährlich. Und nicht nur für den Verblendeten. Das steht im Text: *Unglücklich das Land, das keine Helden hat. / Unglücklich das Land, das Helden nötig hat.* (Schon in Müllers erstem Stück, *Lohndrücker*, ist Balke kein P mehr. Es hat so etwas wie eine *sozialistische Dramatik* tatsächlich gegeben.)

5 Was bei uns ausfiel, ist die Karnevalsszene. Das ist ein Mangel, der das Ganze betrifft. Was fehlt, ist der Bruch mit dem Verfahren, der es erst einsehbar macht als Verfahren. Einmal hätte die Debatte unterbrochen werden müssen, einmal hätte ein Bild zu sehen sein müssen. Ja, mach nur einen Plan: Wir hatten einen schönen, der falsch war, eine Einlage von einer oberbayerischen Rockgruppe — und konnten uns nicht überzeugen, dass er falsch war, weil es aus ganz äußerlichen (organisatorischen) Gründen nicht dazu kam, ihn auszuprobieren. Dabei war es ganz einfach: ein Lied war da, wir brauchten ein Bild. Die wimmelnden Massen und Masken Ensors zeigen das, was man sieht, wenn einmal der lastende Stein aufgehoben wird. Wir hätten eins der Ensorschen Bilder einer Menschenmenge in Masken nehmen können als eine Art Zwischenvorhang. Und vor dem hätte dann Goldmanns schönes Lied mit dem Gewicht gestanden, das ihm zukommt. (Goldmann hat eine von der als Theater-im-Theater geschriebenen Kabarettnummer sehr abweichende Textfassung komponiert, zusammengesetzt aus Brechtschen Entwürfen. Kern bleibt aber, oder wird, als ein Refrain, nur deutlicher, die verräterische Zeile mit den drei Binnenreimen: *Macht man den Strick uns ums Genick nicht dick, dann reißt er!*)

Eine Korrektur an Brechts Auffassung (kaum am Text) ist das Zurücknehmen der Behauptung von so etwas wie einer revolutionären Situation. Die ist für 1630 unzutreffend. Und ebenso 1938, 1945, 1953 und 1956, 1997. Die Szene ist eine *Traumszene*, hat Dieckmann gesagt. Eine Wunschtraumszene. Ein Wunsch Galileis — also ein Wunsch Brechts. Damit das herauskommt, ist entscheidend, dass das Lied Galilei singt. Bierbichler hat es sehr schön gesungen, aber innerhalb der Handlung (am Ende des Festes in Rom, auf dem er die Verwarnung der *Hauptverwaltung für ewige Wahrheiten* entgegennimmt), eine Notlösung. Der nächste (wirklich nötige) Schritt wäre gewesen, es aus der Handlung herauszulösen und ihr entgegenzustellen, an der richtigen Stelle, wo Brecht es hingesetzt hat: vor die Verhaftung.

6 In Berlin war für Brecht der 17. Juni 1953 ein Anstoß, wie es in L.A. der 6. August 1945 war. (Im Kalten Krieg blieb aber die Drohung der einen Seite für die andere Seite gut verwendbar als *dicker Strick*. Die Berliner Fassung, 17. Juni hin 17. Juni her, ist angstvoll dominiert von der Damoklesbombe.)

Wir hatten es versucht, und den Maler in sein Bild gesetzt. Auf einer unserer Proben saßen G und B (B mit ins Gesicht gezogener Mütze) in Front zum Publikum in der Mitte der Bühne auf dem Boden nebeneinander, getrennt nur durch den weißen Strich quer durchs Schwarz, und sangen gemeinsam den Refrain *Macht man den Strick...* Vor dem Lied (war unsere Überlegung) sollten Filmbilder vom 17. Juni 1953 gezeigt werden. Wir haben uns einen Stapel Fernseh-Dokumentationen angesehen. Schön waren die Bilder vom ersten Tag: die Demonstrierenden, mit strahlenden Gesichtern, in breiten Reihen, die ganze Straße in Besitz nehmend. Aber davon gab es nur Fotos, Filmkameras waren noch nicht zur Stelle gewesen. (Die Dokumentationen behalfen sich und fuhren die Fotos mit der Filmkamera ab.) Dann, am zweiten Tag, vor laufenden Kameras die Wende zu dem, was in Müllers *Germania Tod in Berlin* heißt: *Wortsalat aus Freiheit Deutsch Totschlagen Aufhängen*. Und wir wollten doch den Karneval.zeigen und nicht den Aschermittwoch! Wenigstens das Phantom der Freiheit! Der Wunsch Gs, der Wunsch Bs ist auch mein Wunsch — und (wenigstens) Bierbichler einschließend kann ich sagen, unser Wunsch. (Die gleiche Wende *sechsunddreißig Jahre später vom Ruf Wir sind das Volk zum Ruf Wir* sind ein Volk.)

7 Die zweite Korrektur ist die Verwendung der Variante der dänischen Fassung als Epilog. Brecht hatte sie 1956 noch selber in das 1957 posthum erschienene Heft 15 der *Versuche* aufgenommen. *Der alte Galilei liest Montaigne*, d.h. er lässt sich, fast blind, von der Tochter die Deckeninschriften der Bibliothek Montaignes vorlesen, und kommentiert sie. Die Szene funktioniert dramaturgisch als wirkliches Ende, letzte Station. Aber als eine letzte Station ohne Urteil. Wenn man will: als Übergang (Übergabe) des Ganzen an die Zuschauer. Die Wirkungsweise ist wesentlich musikalisch. Virginia liest die angestrichnen Stellen vor: *lento continuo regulare*, Galilei kommentiert: *vivace* (aber ohne Bewegung des Körpers). Einmal schweigt er, *Generalpause*. Die Tochter sieht ihn an, und als er nichts sagt, kehrt sie zum Buch zurück und zum nächsten Satz. (*Musikalisch*: d .h. nur, dass hier das Verhältnis des Sprechenden zum Text so ist, wie es immer sein sollte. Er soll sozusagen die Noten treffen. Es muss der Satz gesagt, und nicht versucht werden, Bedeutung auszudrücken. Versucht man das, wird der Satz unverständlich, d. h. der Zuhörer kann sich keinen Reim drauf machen, keinen Sinn drin finden. Der Sinn wird ihm vorweggenommen.)

Galileis letzte Replik: *Lauter* (auf die Inschrift: *Bewundernswert ist das Gute*) ist *der Ruf nach der Vereinbarung des Unvereinbaren*, sagt Klaus Heinrich.

8 Sonst orientiert sich unsere Fassung grundsätzlich an der Knappheit der zweiten, der amerikanischen. Die Knappheit führt im Deutschen in die Richtung der Diktion in den ersten Stücken Müllers.

Zuerst ist das eine Tempofrage. Das Tempo des Transportes ist im englischen Text höher als im deutschen, ein Auto gegen ein Pferdefuhrwerk. (Das erinnerte mich an meine erste Lektüre von Müllers *Lohndrücker* im Frühjahr 1957. Gewohnt an das Tempo Brechts habe ich gleich in der ersten Szene, die keine Buchseite lang war, weg gelesen über eine Regiebemerkung: *Der Geheimrat kichert*. Die Sprüche der Arbeiter über das Arbeiterbier bringen den heruntergekommenen Geheimrat zum Kichern. Das verändert die Situation. Die Handlung war einen Schritt weitergegangen, und ich hatte den Schritt nicht bemerkt.)

Der Tempounterschied der Fassungen liegt nicht nur an der unterschiedlichen Geschwindigkeit der beiden Sprachen. Der englische Text (Laughton hat da wie ein Filter gewirkt) scheidet alle Malerei aus, und er verweigert fast ganz die Wertung von Figuren oder einzelner Haltungen von Figuren. Dahinter steht eine englische Tradition, literarisch und theatralisch. (Das *talking play* ist etwas anderes als das *Konversationsstück*). Die Aufführung hätte so zu so etwas wie einer Talkshow werden können (zugegeben einer idealen, die des deutschen Fernsehens muss man vergessen) — mit Durcheinanderreden, Aufeinanderprallen und einbrechenden Pausen. Erzeugt wird dann der Impuls, sich einzumischen, mitdiskutieren zu wollen. Bierbichler führt das beispielhaft vor, und seine Unmittelbarkeit (Unmittelbarkeit in der Diskussion, damit die Diskussion als Mittel erscheint) hat einige Schauspieler auch mitgenommen. Aber im Ganzen ist das nur ansatzweise realisiert. (Die Voraussetzungen waren von der Fassung des Textes gegeben. Vorabwertungen der Gegenkräfte im Text waren gestrichen.)

9 Überhaupt Bierbichler. Nachdenken ist der Grundgestus dieses Schauspielers, dem er alle Gesten, das Material, Elemente gegenwärtiger Realität, aussetzt: sie sind so einer Versuchsanordnung unterworfen. Schon dadurch, dass er sein Herkommen nicht verleugnet und seine bayrische Diktion nicht unterdrückt, unterwirft er die Worte, die er dem Dichter nachspricht, einem *Test*. (Tatsächlich besteht eine gute Aufführung aus einer Abfolge von vielen *Tests*.)

Der Schauspieler muss eine Sache zeigen, und er muss sich zeigen. Er zeigt die Sache natürlich, indem er sich zeigt, und er zeigt sich, indem er die Sache zeigt. Obwohl dies zusammenfällt, darf es doch nicht so zusammenfallen, dass der Unterschied zwischen diesen beiden Aufgaben verschwindet: das sagt Brecht. Und Benjamin schließt an: *mit andern Worten, der Schauspieler soll sich die Möglichkeit vorbehalten, mit Kunst aus der Rolle zu fallen. Er soll es sich, im gegebenen Moment, nicht nehmen lassen, den (über seinen Part) Nachdenkenden vorzumachen.* Bierbichler spielt in der Vorstellung nicht anders als auf der Probe, kein Unterschied, ob er das Nachdenken dem Regisseur oder dem Zuschauer vormacht. Er probiert etwas so und er probiert es so. Er kann sich selber unterbrechen. Er korrigiert sich, auch mitten in der Aufführung, nicht immer zur Freude der anderen Darsteller. Immer probieren, das heißt alles was einem begegnet auf die Probe stellen, einen Text, eine Figur, ein Stück (und die andern Beteiligten, das Theater, das Publikum, die Gesellschaft. Nicht zuletzt sich selber).

10 An der Vorstellung vom *epischen Theater* ist ihr Untergrund wichtig, den Brecht nicht mitformuliert hat. *Sagen lassen sich die Leute nichts, erzählen lassen sie sich alles.* Der Satz ist von Benjamin. Als Beispiel nimmt er Herodots Erzählung von dem Ägypterkönig Psamenit, der besiegt ist von Kambysis, und zusehen muss, wie seine Tochter zum Brunnen geht, Wasser zu holen als Magd, und wie sein Sohn vorbeigeführt wird zur Hinrichtung. Er senkt den Blick und zeigt keine

Jörg Michael Koerbl (Sagredo), Josef Bierbichler (Galilei)
Leben des Galilei, Berliner Ensemble 1997
[Foto: Ute Eichel]

Regung. Als aber ein alter Diener vorbeigeführt wird unter den Gefangenen schlägt er sich an Kopf und Brust und bricht in Tränen aus. Wir fragen uns: Warum klagt er erst beim Anblick des Dieners? Benjamin vergleicht die Erzählung mit den Samenkörnern, die jahrtausendelang in den Grabkammern der Pyramiden verschlossen waren und bis heute ihre Keimkraft bewahrt haben.

Erzählen heißt eine Geschichte frei halten von Erklärungen. Die Moral ist eine Antwort der Leute. Der Schauspieler des epischen Theaters hat nichts zu sagen, er hat nur zu zeigen. (Den Pfarrer kann der Komödiant dann nichts mehr lehren.) Und die Formel *Gesten zitierbar machen*, zu der Benjamin Brechts Beschreibungen kondensiert hat, lässt einen sofort an Kafka denken, an die Isolierung der Gesten, das Weglassen des Bezugssystems. (Bei Brecht exemplarisch in *Dickicht*.) Zitieren ist ja ein Ausschneiden aus einem Zusammenhang. Gesten auszusieben und anzuordnen auf ein Ergebnis hin, das vorher feststeht, eine Lösung, eine Moral, ein Urteil: das baut Parabelstücke wie z. B. *Sezuan*, von dem Brecht im Tagebuch selbstkritisch sagt: *Dem Ausgerechneten entspricht das Niedliche*. Das ist das, was das Berliner Ensemble nach Brechts Tod kanonisiert hat, und damit den Schwenk vollzogen zum Staatstheater, zur Affirmation. Die Aufführung von Baierls *Frau Flinz* hat, vier Jahre nach Brechts Tod, den Punkt gesetzt. Mutter Courage will am Krieg ihren Schnitt machen und verliert durch den Krieg ihre Kinder. Frau Flinz verliert ihre Kinder an den Sozialismus — und gewinnt sie natürlich dadurch. Hans Mayer nannte das Stück *Mutter Courages Himmelfahrt*. Brechts Marxismus-Begriff, der von Korsch kam: Kritik (das Programm der Rückkehr nach Deutschland hieß: *zwanzig Jahre Ideologiezertrümmerung*), wurde preisgegeben. So haben die Hüter des Hauses einen lastenden Alb im Haus hinterlassen. Von Haus aus (als gewöhnliche Redewendung gesagt) ist aber *Galilei* ein solches Stück gerade nicht. Erst die dritte, die Berliner Fassung kann so gelesen werden: eine Moralität, die ihr Exempel statuiert, indem sie die Gesten bewertet, eine erschrockene Hilflosigkeit.

Benjamin schreibt über Brecht in der Form des Kommentars, der von der Klassizität seines Gegenstandes ausgeht. Aber die Kommentare enthalten unausdrücklich Kritik. Die Kritik setzt den Hebel an den gleichen Punkten an wie dann die Fortschreibungen Brechts durch Müller. Der Drehpunkt ist dort, wo der Maler in sein Bild hinein geht. Und so war es kein Zufall, dass ich von Brecht gerade *Baal* und *Galilei* inszeniert habe, Quasiautobiographie.

Der Dialog mit den Toten darf nicht abreißen, bis sie herausgeben, was an Zukunft mit ihnen begraben worden ist.

27 .04. 99

Josef Bierbichler (Galilei), Robert Gwisdeck (Andrea)
Leben des Galilei, Berliner Ensemble 1997
Regie: B.K. Tragelehn
[Foto: Ute Eichel]

Back to the Future of Political Theater?
With their Production of *Das Kontingent*, Soeren Voima go on writing Brecht's *Die Maßnahme*

In 2000 the TAT in Frankfurt and the Schaubühne in Berlin staged Soeren Voima's *Das Kontingent*, a new play which in content and form closely resembles Brecht's *Die Maßnahme*. The Communist International has now become the UN; oppression and war unfold in a fictitious Chechnya/Bosnia instead of China; the idealistic comrade who must be liquidated because he undermines the mission of the collective is a young American from Dayton, Ohio. Modern music, choric speech and a uniformly gray stage set are used to prevent emotional identification with the characters and the story they tell about ethnic violence, murder, rape and a World Bank which pretends to help the victims.

It has been argued that *Das Kontingent*, which was recently shown at the UN headquarters in New York, could mark the beginning of a new political theatre. In an interview the collective author Soeren Voima prefers to talk about a "theatre of affirmation" which presents the conflicts of our time without taking sides and does so in an entertaining, futuristic laboratory setting.

Zurück in die Zukunft des politischen Theaters? Soeren Voima schreiben mit *Das Kontingent* Brechts *Maßnahme* weiter

Alexander Stephan

Als am 3. Februar 2000 bei der Premiere von Soeren Voimas *Das Kontingent* in der Berliner Schaubühne ein Chor von UNO-Soldaten sein letztes Lob auf die „glücklichen Völker" unseres „glücklichen Jahrtausends"[1] ins Publikum gesungen hatte und das Licht ausging, war möglicherweise etwas besonderes auf dem deutschen Theater geschehen. In seltener Einheit lobten die Feuilletons von *FAZ*[2] und *Neuem Deutschland*,[3] *Süddeutscher*[4] und *Berliner Zeitung*,[5] *Zeit*[6] und *tip*,[7] dass den Regisseuren Robert Schuster und Tom Kühnel mit *Das Kontingent* eine Erneuerung des politischen Theaters gelungen sein könnte.[8] In der Pause und auf dem Nachhauseweg seien, so die Berichte weiter, diskutierende und nachdenkende Zuschauer gesichtet worden, die den Prosecco in ihren Kühlschränken erst einmal warten ließen. Ohne Murren nahmen Kritiker verschiedenster politischer Couleur die Erschießung eines jungen, idealistischen Amerikaners durch eine ebenfalls junge Frau hin, die wie einst Ulrike Meinhof mit einer Maschinenpistole auf der Bühne herumfuchtelt. Willig, ja mit einer gewissen Begeisterung, ließen sich Publikum und Kritik auf eine Diskussion um humanistische Grundwerte aus der Mottenkiste der Aufklärung ein — Freiheit, Menschenwürde, eine Neuordnung der Welt—, denen das Feuilleton seit zwanzig Jahren keine Zeile mehr gewidmet hatte, außer wenn es darum ging, die sogenannten 68er lächerlich zu machen oder die DDR-Ikone Christa Wolf zu demontieren. Lang vergessene Kunstgriffe des Theaters werden in den Besprechungen wiederentdeckt, Verfremdungseffekt, Dialektik, Parabelform. Und wie um das Skandalon auf die Spitze zu treiben, konstatiert der Chor der Kritiker unisono, dass dem Frankfurter TAT, das *Das Kontingent* nach Berlin gebracht hatte, die Neubearbeitung und Aktualisierung eines Stükkes gelungen sei, das seit Jahrzehnten zu den politischen Kotzbrocken des deutschen Theaters zählt und noch vor kurzem, anlässlich einer Neuinszenierung nach weit über einem halben Jahrhundert Verbot durch den Autor, mit Eifer als „Agitprop-Oratorium und ‚RAF-Schlüsseltext'"[9] verdammt worden war: Bertolt Brechts Lehrstück *Die Maßnahme*.

In der Tat ist die Handlung von Soeren Voimas Überraschungser-

New Essays on Brecht / Neue Versuche über Brecht
Maarten van Dijk et al., eds., *The Brecht Yearbook / Das Brecht-Jahrbuch*
Volume 26 (Toronto, Canada: The International Brecht Society, 2001)

folg *Das Kontingent* — über den „Autor" ist später noch mehr zu sagen — jedem, der Brechts *Maßnahme* kennt, (fast) vertraut: Eine Gruppe von jungen Soldaten soll im Namen der UNO in einem Bürgerkrieg im Kaukasus Frieden stiften. Der strikte Auftrag des Kontingents lautet, absolute Neutralität zu wahren und sich unter keinen Umständen in die regionalen Konflikte einzumischen. Ein junger Amerikaner, nicht zufällig gebürtig aus Dayton, Ohio, vermag sich angesichts der Ungerechtigkeiten und Greuel, die er hilflos mit ansehen muss, nicht an diese Vorgaben zu halten. Fünfmal verletzt er die kalten, bürokratischen Regeln der UNO, als er emotional auf das Elend um ihn reagiert und als Mensch dem geknechteten Menschen zum Helfer wird („DER JUNGE AMERIKANER Hier gilt es nicht mehr nachzudenken! Wer fühlt, was er sieht, muß handeln!"[10]). Die neuen, womöglich noch größeren Leiden, die er dadurch provoziert, verlangen nach einer radikalen Lösung. Bevor der Soldat aus Dayton den Auftrag der Blauhelme total kompromittiert, wird er von einem weiblichen Mitglied des Kontingents erschossen. Ein Gerichtsspiel, in dem alle Beteiligten ihre Positionen noch einmal erklären und die entscheidenden Situationen nachspielen dürfen, überlässt es einem Chor (und den Zuschauern) zu urteilen, ob der Amerikaner zu recht oder zu unrecht von seinen Kameraden getötet wurde.

Keine Frage also — Soeren Voimas *Das Kontingent* und die vom TAT nach Berlin gebrachte Inszenierung sind über weite Strecken Brecht pur. Wurde damals, 1930, der Konflikt zwischen KP und Kuomintang in China als Material für das Theaterexperiment der *Maßnahme* benutzt, steht jetzt ein futuristischer Kaukasus im Zentrum, der sehr real an die heutige Situation in Tschetschenien, in Bosnien und im Kosovo erinnert. Überraschend unvermittelt und problemlos geraten KP und UNO in dieselbe Ecke: Der Anspruch der Avantgarde der Weltrevolution, alle Völker und Menschen mit Hilfe einer grauen Theorie zu nivellieren, unterscheidet sich kaum von der aseptisch-rigiden Charta des Völkerbunds und den Methoden der Weltbank, arme Länder durch Sparmaßnahmen für wohlhabende Investoren attraktiv zu machen. Hier wie dort bleiben die, denen die Welt nicht gehört, ohne Hoffnung auf der Strecke, chinesische Kulis ebenso wie arme kaukasische Bergbewohner, Reisbauern und streikende Fabrikarbeiter nicht anders als protestierende Studenten und eine inguschetische Bibliothekarin. Individualität ist bei der einen wie der anderen Organisation nicht gefragt, was dazu führt, dass Brechts Kommunisten ihre Gesichter hinter Masken verstecken bzw., wenn nötig, in einer Kalkgrube auslöschen, und Voimas internationaler Kontingenttruppe in einem boot camp bei Philadelphia die nationalen Eigenarten, Sprachen und Biographien aus dem Gedächtnis getrieben werden. Und wer für die Armen dieser Welt Mitleid zeigt und sich wie der junge Genosse durch das Zerreißen der marxistischen Klassiker gegen die totale Macht der

Menschheitsbeglücker stellt bzw. wie der junge Amerikaner die UNO-Charta bespuckt, wird hier wie da kurzweg liquidiert:

> DER KONTROLLCHOR
> ...fandet ihr keinen Ausweg, zu erhalten den jungen Kämpfer dem Kampf?

> DIE VIER AGITATOREN
> Bei der Kürze der Zeit fanden wir keinen Ausweg...
> Auch ihr jetzt denkt nach über
> Eine bessere Möglichkeit.[11]

> DER JUNGE AMERIKANER
> Wußtet ihr keinen anderen Weg?

> DIE SOLDATIN
> Hilflos
> Ohne Haß
> Und ohne Reue,
> Voll Sympathie für sein Gefühl
> Doch wissend um die Forderung des Rechts
> Antworteten wir:

> DIE SOLDATEN
> Nein.[12]

Doch nicht genug der Parallelen zwischen *Kontingent* und *Maßnahme*. Denn nicht nur der Inhalt der im Januar 2000 fertiggestellten Arbeitsfassung von Voimas Schauspiel entspricht über weite Strecken dem Lehrstückklassiker von Brecht, auch die Form der beiden Parabelspiele weist eine Vielzahl von Gemeinsamkeiten auf. Gemäß den klassischen Regeln des Verfremdungseffekts verweigert *Das Kontingent* durch Rollentausch, chorische Einlagen und eine moderne, antiemotionale Musik die Möglichkeit, sich mit der Handlung und den Handelnden zu identifizieren. Die Reihenfolge der Prüfungen, durch die der junge Amerikaner fällt — die Überwachung eines Wahlkampfes in Dagestan am Kaspischen Meer, der Besuch einer Delegation der Weltbank in einem vom Bürgerkrieg zerstörten Land, die Verteilung von Essensrationen in Tschetschenien und die Bewachung einer Brücke in einer von ethnischen Konflikten geteilten Stadt—, ist wie bei Brechts Theaterexperiment austauschbar. Durch die Struktur der Gerichtsverhandlung wird das Ergebnis des Spiels im Spiel zu Beginn vorweggenommen und damit das Interesse vom Ausgang auf den Gang der Ereignisse gelenkt. Und selbst jene an den Zuschauer gerichtete Pause, die Klaus Emmerich 1997 für die *Maßnahme*-Inszenierung am Berliner Ensemble schmerzhaft in die Länge gezogen hatte, findet sich in *Das Kontingent* wieder:

DIE SOLDATIN
Und auf uns gerichtet die Augen der Welt
Trafen wir unsre Entscheidung:
Die Gewalt der Waffe
Anzuwenden im Sinne des Ganzen
Zum Schutz und im Dienste des Rechts,
Und nicht zu dulden
Den Unduldsamen.

Pause

CHOR
Welche Welt wiegt auch nur ein
Menschenleben auf?

DIE SOLDATIN
Keine.
Ohne Hoffnung
Auf eine bessere Welt,
Einzig mit dem Willen
Leben zu retten
Töteten wir.[13]

Wie ein Zitat, um nicht zu sagen Plagiat — denn Brecht und sein Lehrstück werden an keiner Stelle in *Das Kontingent* erwähnt — wirkt, wen kann es noch wundern bei so vielen inhaltlichen und formalen Übernahmen, auch die Inszenierung des TAT-Teams um Tom Kühnel und Robert Schuster. Geschickt installiert Jan Pappelbaum die abweisende Mechanik der UNO-Welt in die kalte Betonkonstruktion der Berliner Schaubühne, deren monotones Grau kaum durch das blasse Blau der schlapp von ihren Masten hängenden Fahnen der UNO aufgelockert wird. Wie bei Brecht bleibt die offene, auf drei Seiten von Zuschauern umzingelte Bühne frei von unnötigen Utensilien und Dekorationen. Kühl und futuristisch wirken die von Elina Schnizler entworfenen Anzüge der Kontingentmitglieder und lenken so, wie die schwarzen Outfits von Brechts Genossen in Emmerichs *Maßnahme*-Inszenierung, nie vom Text ab. Nach dem Prolog, wo bei der Vorstellung der Soldaten des Kontingents noch ein wenig Komik aufkommt („FÜNFTER SPIELER Hallo, ich bin Christoph. Ich bin neunzehn fünfundneunzig geboren... Beim Kontingent gefällt es mir richtig gut. Ich bin hier der Koch."[14]), imitiert der Vortrag der Schauspieler mit seiner vor allem in den chorischen Passagen fast unerträglich abweisend-stilisierten Rhythmik die Brecht-Vorlage derart deutlich, dass der leise Verdacht aufkommt, das Regieteam könnte sich über den Meister lustig machen. Und auch die über weite Strecken das Spiel dominierende Musik — komponiert von dem Italiener Matteo Fargion und vorgetragen unter der Leitung von Philipp Vandré durch das Kammerensemble Neue Musik Berlin, das bereits bei der Wiederaufnahme der *Maßnah-*

me am BE erfolgreich mitgewirkt hatte und mit seinem Namen auf die Kontroverse um die Uraufführung des Brecht/Eisler-Spiels zurückgreift — erinnert in ihrer trockenen, unpathetischen Art ohne weiteres an den avantgardistischen Beitrag des klassenkämpferischen Neutöners Eisler zur Arbeitermusikbewegung der zwanziger und dreißiger Jahre, freilich ohne die Qualität der Vorlage zu erreichen.

Soweit die Parallelen zwischen Brechts *Maßnahme* und Voimas *Kontingent*. Spannender als die nicht zu übersehenden Gemeinsamkeiten zwischen beiden Stücken sind freilich die Unterschiede, auch wenn deren Aufspüren entschieden schwieriger und nicht immer befriedigend ist.

Zunächst und vor allem muss es hier um die Figur des jungen Amerikaners gehen, der, logisch kurz nach Ablauf jenes 20. Jahrhunderts, das man das „amerikanische" genannt hat, den jungen Kommunisten ersetzt, ähnlich wie die UNO an die Stelle der kommunistischen Weltrevolution gerückt ist. Glücklich, überglücklich, ist dieser junge Mann in einem hoch kultivierten, kaum mehr realistisch wirkenden Amerika aufgewachsen, in dem allenthalben Demokratie, Freiheit und Wohlstand herrschen. „Sorglos"[15] durfte er dort zwischen Cappuccino und „Bach, gespielt von Gould," leben, mit Tennisschlägern und Weingläsern hantieren („Für jeden Wein gab es ein Glas") und in „„Die Kunst der Gegenwart'"[16] lesen, bis er eines Tages, wann und warum genau wird nicht klar, "die täglichen Bilder des Schreckens und der Willkür in den Nachrichten... nicht mehr länger mit ansehen" kann: „Deshalb komme ich zu euch.... Mein Privileg schmerzt mich: Ein Recht muß allen Menschen gelten!"[17]

So weit so gut als freie Weiterdichtung der *Maßnahme* — würden Soeren Voima ihren Amerikaner nicht von Anfang an aus jener Rolle fallen lassen, die der junge Genosse vorgespielt hatte. Nur mit großem Widerwillen akzeptiert der Mann aus Dayton nämlich die für den Ablauf des Stücks entscheidende Vorgabe der UNO, dass die Mitglieder des Kontingents, die u. a. aus Deutschland, Finnland, Mexiko und dem Sudan kommen, ihre Identität und Herkunft auslöschen müssen, um in den Krisengebieten neutral zu bleiben:

> DER JUNGE AMERIKANER
> Ich glaube an die Demokratie, in der ich aufwuchs.
> Ich glaube an die Freiheit, die ich genoß...
> Und ich verstand, daß das Recht der Menschen auch der Durchsetzung bedarf, daß die Verletzung dieses Rechts verfolgt werden muß. Und daß die Verfolgung nicht an den Grenzen der Länder Halt machen darf.[18]

Ohne jene bedingungslose Entindividualisierung freilich, die in *Die Maßnahme* von Anfang an vorgegeben ist, weil die drei Agitatoren und der junge Genosse ohne Biographien auf die Bühne kommen, besteht kaum eine Hoffnung, dass der Amerikaner sich bei den verschiedenen

Prüfungen richtig, d. h. frei von Emotion, Mitgefühl und einem regionaltypischen Demokratieverständnis verhalten wird. Der kleine Rest von „Spannung" auf den Ausgang der einzelnen Episoden, den das Original trotz der Vorwegnahme des Endes am Anfang zu erzeugen vermochte („DIE VIER AGITATOREN Wir melden den Tod eines Genossen."[19]), ist der Neuauflage damit weitgehend abhanden gekommen. Entsprechend undramatisch und voraussehbar wirkt die Liquidierung des Störenfrieds aus Ohio, auf die sich Voimas Spiel langsam hinarbeitet. Das bei Brecht ebenso entscheidende wie umstrittene Einverständnis des jungen Genossen in seinen Opfertod wird dem Amerikaner nie abverlangt. Keiner der UNO-Soldaten bietet dem Verurteilten Trost. Und da das Gesicht des Mannes aus Dayton von Anfang des Stückes an immer offen, arglos und nackt bleibt (und das Kontingent nie von Verfolgung durch die Mächtigen bedroht ist, weil es sich selber im Besitz der Macht befindet), gibt es auch keinen Grund, dieses Antlitz nach der Erschießung in einer Kalkgrube auszulöschen.

Ähnlich aktuell, doch womöglich noch interessanter als der junge Amerikaner, ist die Figur eines Journalisten, die Voima dem Stück hinzufügen. Elend, Mord und Vergewaltigungen nämlich finden in unserer zeitgenössischen Welt der totalen Nachrichten, glaubt man diesem unangenehm selbstsicher daherkommenden Vertreter der Medien und seinem Vordenker Michel Foucault, nur statt, wenn sie auf Bildern und in Filmen festgehalten oder auf der Bühne thematisiert werden („JOURNALIST Unfaßbares, namenloses Leid braucht ein Gesicht."[20]). Ein individueller Autor, der wie Brecht die Verantwortung für das Gezeigte und Gesagte übernimmt (sieht man einmal von den jüngsten Angriffen auf Brechts Urheberschaft ab), ist — immer noch nach Foucault — obsolet geworden. Namen- und gesichtslose Kollektive haben längst seine Rolle und die seiner Figuren übernommen als passive Opfergruppen, in Gestalt von moralischen Instanzen wie dem multinationalen Kontingent, als Massenmedien, Fernsehen und Internet, als undurchschaubare Megaorganisationen wie UNO und Weltbank, in Form von Ensembles wie — jetzt sei es gesagt — dem anonymen Autorenkollektiv Soeren Voima,[21] als Theatergruppen wie die von TAT und Schaubühne, deren Mitglieder offen auf der Bühne ihre Rollen tauschen, als Masse von Zuschauern, als Leser dieses Aufsatzes usw.

Lösbar ist die Aufgabe, die dem Kontingent und den im Richterstuhl sitzenden Zuschauern gestellt wird, deshalb wohl, dies der letzte wichtige Unterschied zu Brechts *Maßnahme*, nicht mehr. Dazu fehlt es den Handelnden in der Zukunft der Zeit um 2040 und den Urteilenden von heute an der nötigen Überzeugung, sprich: an einer handfesten Ideologie, deren Fahne kräftiger leuchtet als die blassblaue der UNO. Könnte es also sein, dass das Autorenteam die immer gleichen, leeren Phrasen der Menschheitsbeglücker nur noch mit müder Ironie aufs Papier zu bringen vermag und den didaktischen Habitus des Weltver-

besserers Brecht längst ad acta gelegt hat? „Glückliches Jahrtausend,"
„Gleichheit aller Geschlechter und Rassen," „Würde und Wert jedes
einzelnen Menschen," „Freiheit," „Frieden"[22] steht da zu Anfang des
Prologs. „Glückliche Menschheit," „schönste aller Welten," „Recht,"
„Moral"[23] echot der Chor nach 50 Seiten voller Mord, Totschlag und
Vergewaltigung mit ungebrochenem Pathos am Schluss des Stücks.
Passé wären dann, wenn hier in der Tat Ironie mit im Spiel ist, selbst
jene Alternativen, die Brecht mit dem *Jasager* und *Neinsager* probte;
aufgegeben die hellwache Resignation am Ende von Max Frischs *Biedermann und die Brandstifter*, das im Untertitel „Lehrstück ohne Lehre"
genannt wird; indiskutabel geworden die selbstgerechten, flammenden
Aufrufe, mit denen das politische Theater der sechziger Jahre auf die
Missstände unserer Welt hingewiesen hatte, die, keine Frage, 1930
ebenso wie heute und in der Zukunft Veränderung bitter nötig hat.

Bernd Stegemann, Dramaturg am TAT und Teil von Soeren Voima,
kennt solche Zweifel nicht, wenn er mit der Chuzpe des Dreißigjähri-
gen *Das Kontingent* per Manifest kurzweg zum „ersten politischen
Theaterstück des neuen Jahrhunderts"[24] erklärt. Andere Mitglieder der
jungen Theaterkollektive aus Frankfurt und Berlin tragen neben jener
Portion Mut, die nötig ist, um Brechts mit Hohn und Hass überschütte-
te *Maßnahme* aus der Mottenkiste des Theaterfundus zu zerren und auf
den letzten Stand der Dinge zu bringen, einen ähnlich wachen politischen Instinkt mit auf die Bühne. Sorglos proklamierten so vor kurzem
die neuen Hausherren der Schaubühne, Thomas Ostermeier und Sasha
Waltz, zu Anfang ihrer Intendantur, dass das Theater in einer Zeit „der
völligen Unterwerfung unter die Gesetze des Marktes... (wieder) der
Ort einer Bewusstwerdung und damit einer Repolitisierung"[25] werden
muss — und setzten gleich danach Inszenierungen von Alfred Jarrys
Anarcho-Klassiker *Ubu!*, Lars Noréns Assozialenstück *Personenkreis
3.1* und Falk Richters Kosovo-Langeweiler *Peace* in den Sand. Und
Soeren Voima, die neben ihrem „Modellstück" *Das Kontingent* für das
weniger erfolgreiche Spiel *Deutsch für Ausländer* zeichnen, haben in
einem anderen Manifest, das ebenfalls Brechts Theorien nahe steht,
ohne sich von ihnen gängeln zu lassen, kurz und bündig ihr Theater in
Frankfurt, das TAT, zu einer „Forschungseinrichtung" umdeklariert:

> Der Wille zur Veränderung steht für uns nicht am Anfang. Dazu ist uns
> der ideologische Boden entzogen... Die Debatte um eine einheitliche
> Theaterästhetik interessiert uns deshalb nicht. Jeder Bereich der Wirklich-
> keit braucht einen anderen Umgang. Erst auf dieser neu zu schaffenden
> Grundlage ist zu entscheiden, was verhandel- und veränderbar ist. Die Er-
> forschung der Wirklichkeit ist affirmativ. Sie kritisiert nicht, sie dokumen-
> tiert. Sie begibt sich in die Phänomene und versucht, ihr Eigenleben und
> ihre Gesetzmäßigkeiten darzustellen. Nur durch die affirmative Beobach-
> tung bekommt die Wirklichkeit bestimmbare Konturen.[26]

Nimmt man dazu die laut vorgetragene Drohung des aus Wien

zugereisten Altmeisters Claus Peymann, der Berliner Republik von Brechts Theater aus das Fürchten zu lehren, dann könnte sich — ungeachtet der Flops von George Taboris Stück über Brecht und das FBI (*Die Akte Brecht*) und Franz Xaver Kroetz' Petra Kelly/Gert Bastian-Spiel *Das Ende der Paarung*, Richters *Peace* und Christoph Schlingensiefs viel gescholtenen Flüchtlingslagerinstallationen — der Verdacht erhärten, dass Deutschland zu Anfang des 21. Jahrhunderts so etwas wie eine kleine Renaissance des politischen Theaters erlebt.

Um so überraschender ist es, dass Soeren Voima mit *Das Kontingent* Ende 2000 von der UNO eingeladen wurden, nicht auf den Balkan, um Blauhelmsoldaten auf ihren nächsten Einsatz vorzubereiten, sondern in die Zentrale nach New York, wo Bürokraten der Weltorganisation im Zuschauerraum saßen, die am nächsten Tag in irgendeinem Krisengebiet Frieden stiften sollten.[27] Und auch ein Oberleutnant der Bundeswehr ließ — anders als einst Brechts kritische Genossen aus der KPD — seine Mitmenschen per Leserbrief wissen, dass er sich und seinen Einsatz in Mostar in dem Spiel wiedererkenne. Nur die Erschießung des jungen Amerikaners wolle er, wer kann es ihm verübeln, lieber als „theatralische Überspitzung"[28] verstanden wissen.

ANMERKUNGEN

[1] Soeren Voima: *Das Kontingent.* Berlin: Henschel Schauspiel, Arbeitsfassung, 31. 1. 2000, 49.

[2] Matthias Ehlert: „Die Verfremdung der Verfremdung. Lehrstück: Die Uraufführung von Sören Voimas ‚Kontingent' an der Berliner Schaubühne." In: *Frankfurter Allgemeine Zeitung* v. 5. 2. 2000.

[3] Gerhard Ebert: „Glückliche Menschheit?" In: *Neues Deutschland* v. 7. 2. 2000.

[4] Georg Diez: „Erschießt die Idealisten! Tom Kühnel und Robert Schuster inszenieren ‚Das Kontingent' an der Berliner Schaubühne." In: *Süddeutsche Zeitung* v. 5./6. 2. 2000.

[5] Roland Koberg: „Weitere Maßnahmen. Das Frankfurter TAT von Tom Kühnel und Robert Schuster zeigt an der Schaubühne 'Das Kontingent'." In: *Berliner Zeitung* v. 5./6. 2. 2000.

[6] Gerhard Jörder: „Im Ernstfall." In: *Die Zeit* v. 10. 2. 2000.

[7] Peter Laudenbach: „Blauhelm-Maßnahmen. Uraufführung: Die Schaubühne zeigt ‚Das Kontingent' von Sören Voima." In: *tip* 4/2000.

[8] Vgl. dagegen weiter unten das Gespräch mit Soeren Voima sowie einen Bericht im *Spiegel* Nr. 39/2000 („Pseudo-Genies"), in dem davon die Rede ist, dass das Theater am Turm, das eben erst „mit Tamtam" aufgebrochen war, „um ‚neue Formen' zu finden," mit einer Tschechow-Inszenierung jüngst „vom modischen Posieren zur Kunst der Verkörperung" vorgedrungen sei.

[9] „Mit Gewalt die Welt ändern." In: *Spiegel* 39/1997, 231.

[10] Voima, *Kontingent*, 45.

[11] Bertolt Brecht: *Die Maßnahme. Kritische Ausgabe mit einer Spielanleitung von Reiner Steinweg.* Frankfurt: Suhrkamp 1972, 32. (=edition suhrkamp, 415.)

[12] Voima, *Kontingent*, 48.

[13] A. a. O., 47–8.

[14] A. a. O., 2.

[15] A. a. O., 6.

[16] A. a. O., 11.

[17] A. a. O., 6.

[18] A. a. O.

[19] Brecht, *Maßnahme*, 7.

[20] Voima, *Kontingent*, 32.

[21] Peter Laudenbach: „Der Geheime. X Personen erfinden einen Autor: Sören Voima." In: *tip* 4/2000. Hier heißt es u. a.: „Den wenigen biografischen Angaben, die über Voima in Umlauf sind, ist zu entnehmen, dass er 'im Durchschnitt 30 Jahre alt' ist und 'zum größten Teil in Frankfurt am Main' lebt... Er hat aus Foucaults These vom Tod des Autors die radikalstmögliche Konsequenz gezogen. Er ist ausschließlich in seinen Texten vorhanden."

[22] Voima, *Kontingent*, 4.

[23] A. a. O., 49.

[24] Michael Hierholzer: „Menschenrecht statt Menschlichkeit. Eingreiftruppe im Kaukasus: Tom Kühnel und Robert Schuster inszenieren Soeren Voimas Thesenstück über die Paradoxien einer universell geltenden Moral." In: *Frankfurter Allgemeine Zeitung*, Sonntagszeitung Bühne 2/2000.

[25] „Vorrede" (www.schaubuehne.de)

[26] Sören Voima, „Die Gesellschaft des Theaters" (www.dastat.de)

[27] Edmund L. Andrews: „U.N. Peacekeepers in the World According to Brecht." In: *New York Times* v. 21. 11. 2000 (Nachdruck in *International Herald Tribune* v. 22. 11. 2000).

[28] Daniel Henke: „Soldaten sind denkende Wesen." In: *Frankfurter Allgemeine Zeitung*, Sonntagszeitung Bühne v. 20. 2. 2000.

Interview mit Soeren Voima zu *Das Kontingent*

Alexander Stephan und Soeren Voima

Frage: Herr *Voima*, neben *Das Kontingent* sind in diesem Jahr Stücke herausgekommen wie das Kosovo-Spiel *Peace* von Falk Richter und Christoph Schlingensiefs Flüchtlingsinstallation an der Volksbühne in Berlin. Andere sollen im ehemaligen Jugoslawien recherchieren. Ist die Zeit wieder reif für ein politisches Theater?

Voima:[1] Na ja, die Versuche, die es da gibt, zeigen ja schon die Schwierigkeiten mit dem politischen Theater. Unter politischem Theater versteht man in der Regel eine Art Tendenztheater. Und das ist bei all den genannten Versuchen nicht der Fall. Es wird keine Tendenz verfolgt, sondern es wird eine politische Ratlosigkeit aufgezeigt. Eher handelt es sich um Theater mit einem politischen Inhalt, einem politischen Sujet. Es ist eine Definitionsfrage, ob wir das jetzt politisches Theater nennen würden, was wir hier machen.

Frage: Aber Sie haben doch gesagt *Das Kontingent* wäre das erste politische Theaterstück des neuen Jahrhunderts.

Voima: Das habe nicht ich gesagt, das stand in einer Kritik. Aber vielleicht ist es das ja tatsächlich. Es zeigt eben was politisches Theater noch sein kann, wenn man diesen Begriff überhaupt noch gebrauchen will. So wie er am Anfang des vergangenen Jahrhunderts gebraucht wurde, ist der Begriff sicherlich nicht mehr verwendbar.

Frage: Aber warum dann die Anknüpfung an die *Maßnahme*, die zweifellos ein sehr politisches Stück ist?

Voima: Eben aus diesem Grund. *Kontingent* spielt mit diesem Stück, das fast hundert Jahre alt ist und aus einer Zeit kommt, als solche Richtungsangaben noch möglich waren. Es spielt damit, das ich eine Struktur übernehme, auch behaupte es gibt eine Ideologie, die man ähnlich behandeln kann. Nur die Lösungsmöglichkeiten sind nicht mehr so einfach zu formulieren. *Kontingent* bleibt eher eine Falluntersuchung. *Die Maßnahme* ist auch mehr als ein politisches Zeitstück gewesen, sonst hätte sie nicht so lange überlebt. Viele andere Agitpropstücke dieser Zeit kennt heute niemand mehr. Was Brecht versucht hat, ist eine aktuelle Thematik zu nehmen und trotzdem eine große Tragödie zu schreiben.

Frage: Sind *Maßnahme* und *Kontingent* eher formale Experimente oder inhaltliche?

---

[1] Die drei Mitarbeiter des Theater am Turm in Frankfurt, mit denen dieses Gespräch im November 2000 geführt wurde, wollen als Soeren Voima und nicht als Einzelpersonen sprechen.

Voima: Das lässt sich nicht trennen. Der eigentliche Kern ist, eine Ästhetik, die man eher mit einem kommunistischen Inhalt in Verbindung bringt, mit einem anderen Stoff zu verknüpfen. Um dieses Spiel mit Form und Inhalt geht es in *Das Kontingent*. Trennen lässt sich das nicht, denn die Ästhetik ist Bestandteil der Aussage. Das Stück war immer auf eine bestimmte Ästhetik hingeschrieben — das Oratorienhafte, das Betonen des schönen Bildes, das Weglassen von Blut und extremen Grobheiten. Was man vielleicht mit dem Stichwort affirmativ beschreiben könnte.

Frage: Sind Sie deshalb so gut bei der Kritik weggekommen, weil *Das Kontingent* kein altmodisches politisches Stück ist? Es sind ja an sehr gegensätzlichen Orten sehr positive Kritiken erschienen, etwa in der FAZ und im *Neuen Deutschland*, der *Süddeutschen Zeitung* und der *Berliner Zeitung*.

Voima: Ich glaube es war eher die Überraschung, dass man überhaupt so einen Versuch wagt. *Das Kontingent* schwimmt im dramaturgischen Fahrwasser von Brecht und bezieht sich auf ein funktionierendes Modell. Es gibt eine ganze Reihe von Leuten, bei denen das auf der nostalgischen Ebene läuft, die sich wünschen, wieder mehr ein solches Theater zu sehen. Auf der anderen Seite gibt es viele, die eher das ironische Spiel mit einer Theaterform genießen.

Frage: Dass die Welt eine andere geworden ist seit 1930 sorgt Sie da nicht?

Voima: Das eigentlich Interessante an *Das Kontingent* ist ja, dass die Welt nicht so anders geworden ist. Die Grundthese ist, dass sich die herrschende Ideologie des Kapitalismus im wesentlichen nicht unterscheidet von einer kommunistischen Ideologie, weil man bei beiden Ideologien in letzter Konsequenz beim Glauben ankommt. Auf der anderen Seite unterscheiden sich diese Ideologien fundamental, weil der Kapitalismus auf einen hochgezüchteten Individualismus abzielt. In diesem Sinn ist *Kontingent* nicht die Tragödie des Kapitalismus. Wenn in dieser totalitären Theaterform ein Chor auftritt, dessen Mitglieder alle gleich angezogen sind und chorisch singen „zehnmilliardenfacher Mensch" und in einem völligen Zurückgetretensein in das Kollektiv das Individuum feiern, liegt darin die eigentliche Spannung des Stücks. Aber man kann das hin und herwenden wie man will, weil das Kollektiv auch im Marxismus nicht Selbstzweck ist. Es geht dort auch immer um die Verbesserung der Lebensbedingungen des Einzelnen. Deswegen funktioniert *Die Maßnahme*. Man muss aber auch sagen, dass es sich in beiden Fällen um Kollektive in Ausnahmesituationen handelt. Das ist im einen Fall eine Gruppe von illegalen Kämpfern und im anderen eine Militäreinheit. Es sind also beides Spezialgruppen, die zur Durchsetzung einer Idee spezielle Formen des Kampfes einsetzen.

Frage: Heißt das dann, dass man die Kommunistische Internationale mit der UNO gleichsetzen kann?

Voima: Strukturell ja. Zumindest arbeitet die UNO mit ähnlichen Emblemen und ideologischen Signalen wie die KI. Sie hat aber ein völlig anderes Menschenbild. Das Menschenrecht geht für die UNO auf einen bestimmten Humanismus zurück und auf eine Eigenwertigkeit des Individuums, während sich bei der Kommunistischen Internationale ein Weltgeist blutig oder unblutig durchsetzen soll. Gleichzeitig wird aber in der *Maßnahme*, wie in allen Stücken von Brecht, auch an das Elend und die Lebenssituation des Einzelnen appelliert.

Frage: Könnte man sagen, dass die von Brecht eingesetzten formalen Mittel wie der Verfremdungseffekt heute abgenutzt wirken, weil sie längst von Werbung, Medien und Politik in Beschlag genommen worden sind?

Voima: Ich glaube, wenn man diesen Maßstab anlegt, dann gibt es nur ganz wenig, was man überhaupt noch benutzen kann. Es wird vom Betrachter ohnehin alles als verfremdet angesehen. Es gibt gar kein nicht verfremdendes, illusionistischen Theaterspiel mehr.

Frage: Warum haben Sie *Das Kontingent* in die Zukunft verlegt?

Voima: Weil *Das Kontingent* ebenso wie *Die Maßnahme* nur funktioniert, wenn man anerkennt, dass die Methoden, die gelehrt werden, die richtigen sind. Und die richtigen können sie nur sein, wenn sie erfolgreich waren. Im Kosovo zum Beispiel ist es so, dass man heute noch gar nicht weiß, ob es sinnvoll war, dass die NATO dort eingeschritten ist. Das Stück braucht diese Setzung, wenn es rückwirkend untersucht, welche Fehler gemacht worden sind. Das ist die inhaltliche Affirmation.

Frage: Gibt es da einen Bezug zur World Trade Organization und zu den Protesten gegen die WTO etwa in Seattle? Immerhin kommt die Weltbank in *Kontingent* auf die Bühne.

Voima: Das Prinzip der Affirmation zieht sich ja eigentlich durch das ganze Stück. Es gibt die Setzung, dass der Globalisierungsprozess und das wofür die UNO steht ganz ernst und positiv zu betrachten sind. Da ist wieder der Anknüpfungspunkt zum Marxismus. Die Weltbankleute bei uns versuchen wirklich, die Probleme zu lösen.

Frage: Ironisch oder echt?

Voima: Für das Stück ist es erst einmal absolut notwendig, das positiv aufzufassen, z. B. die Argumentation der Weltbank nachzuvollziehen. Außerdem steht unter allem unausgesprochen: „Der Siegeszug der westlichen Demokratie." Da ist natürlich auch Ironie dabei, wenn man das so absolut setzt.

Frage: Warum wird denn in *Das Kontingent* aus dem jungen Genossen ein junger Amerikaner?

Voima: Amerika ist heute die einzige Supermacht und damit der Vorreiter der westlichen Welt. Der *Frage*, ob man die Menschenrechte, an die man glaubt, weltweit durchsetzen soll auch wenn dabei Leben geopfert werden, wird in den USA anders, offener, unverschämter ausgetragen.

Frage: Sie verändern noch etwas anderes in *Das Kontingent*: Der Amerikaner wird von einer Frau erschossen. Ist das eine Quotenlösung oder erinnert es an die RAF?

Voima: Das ist eher eine dramaturgische Lösung, denn die Aktion des Amerikaners wird von einer Vergewaltigung ausgelöst. Dadurch, dass eine Frau das Eingreifen verhindert, wird die Spannung im Stück größer.

Frage: Noch mal zurück zur UNO. *Das Kontingent* ist gerade in diesem Monat in New York im UNO-Hauptquartier aufgeführt worden. Wie ist es dazu gekommen?

Voima: Einmal im Jahr geht eine Wirtschaftdelegation aus Frankfurt in die USA, und da bringt die Stadt Frankfurt immer ein kulturelles Geschenk mit. Weil das UNO-Gebäude staatenloses Gebiet ist, ging das mit dem Stück ziemlich problemlos, obwohl es noch nie Theater in der UNO gegeben hat. Abgesehen von einer Zuschauerin, die meinte, dass die UNO angegriffen wird, haben vor allem die Amerikaner das Spiel ziemlich naiv aufgenommen, weil man *Die Maßnahme* dort ja nicht kennt.

Frage: Brechts Vorlage ist doch aber auch hierzulande kaum noch jemandem bekannt, weil *Die Maßnahme* bis vor kurzem für Aufführungen gesperrt war.

Voima: Aber unter Linken in der Bundesrepublik hat *Die Maßnahme* doch eine große Rolle gespielt, weil das quasi das Handout der RAF war. „Töten im Auftrag der Partei" — so kann man das Stück natürlich lesen. Außerdem bestand ja schon vor 1933 im deutsch-nationalen Lager die Meinung, dass hier endlich einmal eine Ideologie vorgetragen wird, die man selbst schon lange vertreten hatte. Etwas ähnliches ist auch dem *Kontingent* passiert. Es gab Vorwürfe aus dem linken Lager, das sei faschistisches Theater, weil wir für die Staatsräson und gegen den Einzelnen eintreten. Einigen Mitgliedern der PDS Bundestagsfraktion hat das Stück dagegen gut gefallen, weil sie auf das richtige Abstraktionsniveau gekommen sind. Sie haben verstanden, dass das Problem „objektiv" unlösbar ist, und folglich nur politisch gelöst werden kann. Damit begreift man Politik wieder ganz im Sinne der platonischen Unterscheidung von Meinung, die die Politik bestimmt, und Wissen, das die natürliche Wahrheit beschreibt. Bei Abstimmungen nach den Aufführungen war immer die Hälfte der Zuschauer für den Amerikaner und die andere Hälfte der Zuschauer für das Kontingent. Außerdem gab es im Publikum Diskussionen, ob das Stück eine Art Nullaussage macht oder ob wir Partei ergriffen haben. Es war immer völlig widersprüchlich. Und das ist für mich eigentlich politisch.

Frage: Das würden Sie bei Brecht nicht so sehen, weil der seine Ideologie hatte?

Voima: Brecht war theatralisch einfach intelligenter als er als Politiker war. Das ist das Gute an der *Maßnahme*. Außerdem ist da was von Brecht selber drin, von einem bürgerliche Individuum, das den letzten Schritt nicht mitgeht.

Frage: Gab es noch andere Vorbilder für sie, etwa Max Frischs *Biedermann und die Brandstifter* oder das Oratorium *Die Ermittlung* von Peter Weiss?

Voima: Nein, eigentlich nicht. Wir haben als Raster eigentlich nur *Die Maßnahme* benutzt.

Frage: Wie ist es denn mit der Musik? Es gibt Leute, die meinen, dass die Musik, die Hanns Eisler für *Die Maßnahme* geschrieben hat, revolutionärer war als Brechts Text.

Voima: Die Musik war bei Probenbeginn noch gar nicht fertig. Das lag daran, dass Matteo Fargion gesagt hat, er könne die Musik erst zuende bringen, wenn er den Text vor sich hat.

Frage: Das hört sich an als habe Fargion die Begleitmusik für ein Stück geschrieben und nicht wie Eisler eine Musik, die in sich selber formal oder inhaltlich revolutionär sein sollte.

Voima: *Die Maßnahme* war nur möglich, weil es damals diese Arbeitersingebewegung gab. Solche Andockungspunkte haben wir heute nicht mehr. Dazu ist die Musik mittlerweile auf einem ganz anderen Entwicklungsstand. Das Ziel war, eine Musik zu haben, die gefällt und den Inhalt positiv transportiert, aber nicht zum Musical wird.

Frage: Soeren *Voima* hat vor einiger Zeit in einem Manifest gesagt: „Die Erforschung der Wirklichkeit ist affirmativ. Sie kritisiert nicht, sie dokumentiert." Setzt sich *Voima* damit von Brecht ab, der die Welt nicht nur erforschen, sondern verändert wollte?

Voima: Die *Frage* ist, ob ich Wirklichkeit mehr verändere, indem ich sie kritisiere oder dokumentiere.

Frage: Lernen soll bei *Voima* also der Zuschauer und nicht, wie bei Brecht, in erster Linie der Theaterschaffende?

Voima: Bei Brecht hat auch nicht der Spieler gelernt. Da ist er in seiner Praxis anders als in seiner Theorie. Wir lernen natürlich auch bei *Das Kontingent*. Aber letztendlich geht es um einen Theaterabend, den man produziert, um ästhetisches Vergnügen und Unterhaltung. Wir sind Künstler, die in einem subventionierten Staatstheater Kunst machen, in das Leute, die es sich leisten können, gehen und sich einen schönen Abend machen. Ich glaube, da darf man sich keine Illusionen machen.

Frage: Wenn Sie schon die Welt nicht verändern wollen, wird das Theater für Sie dann vielleicht wieder zu einer moralischen Anstalt?

Voima: Also, moralisch, das ist schwer. Was gibt's zu lernen? Wir bringen ja nicht neue Tatsachen, die man lernen könnte. Im besten Fall hat der Zuschauer eine Möglichkeit, über das Stück zu reflektieren. Der Witz ist, einen Abend lang die Grundlagen der westlichen Demokratien abzuarbeiten, das Poetische im Bekannten zu finden. Das Exotische — Drogentote, Minderheiten und Asoziale — kommt uns dagegen abgeschmackt vor und hat mit unserem Leben wahrscheinlich weniger zu tun als im Theater behauptet wird. Das Markierte erzeugt eine Art Pseudobewegung, ohne gedanklich etwas auszulösen.

Frage: Nun hätten Sie sich bei Brecht auch eine andere Vorlage aussuchen können als *Die Maßnahme*. Etwa *Der guten Menschen von Sezuan*, der auf die new economy unserer Zeit passt. Warum ausgerechnet *Die Maßnahme*?

Voima: Wir hatten 1993, also kurz nach der Wende, schon einmal *Die Maßnahme* inszeniert, absolut unironisch, und damals gesagt, man müsste das eigentlich noch einmal aktualisieren. Die Gelegenheit kam dann, als holländische UNO-Soldaten bei Srebrenica nicht eingriffen als serbische Soldaten vor ihren Augen anfingen, Frauen zu vergewaltigen und die holländischen Soldaten daraufhin in Holland vor ein Gericht kamen wegen unterlassener Hilfe.

Frage: Herr *Voima*, gibt es zur Zeit einen Trend im deutschen Theater?

Voima: In der TAZ wurde gerade geschrieben, dass das TAT mit dem Theater der Affirmation vielleicht gescheitert ist, aber das einzige deutschsprachige Theater sei, das überhaupt über ein Konzept verfügt.

Frage: Was meinen Sie mit affirmativem Theater?

Voima: Die Gegenstände so darstellen, dass der Zuschauer in ein widersprüchliches Verhältnis zu ihnen gerät. Der Zuschauer erhält also nicht die Tendenz, sondern den Widerspruch einer Wahrnehmung geliefert. Dabei muss der Darstellungsvorgang dem Gegenstand gegenüber ein liebevoller sein, weil sich der Zuschauer sonst mit dem Besserwissen derjenigen synchronisiert, die ihm die Situation zeigen. Der

Witz der Affirmation ist, dass sie die Widersprüche sichtbar macht, ohne sich auf die eine oder andere Seite zu stellen. Das ist keine Erfindung von uns, aber eine Neuentdeckung für das Theater, das seit '68 diesem mittlerweile leerlaufenden kritischen Impuls, diesem Rumgeschreie verhaftet war. Paradoxe finde ich im Theater spannender als Lösungen, die ohnehin immer zu kurz greifen.

Frage: Würden Sie denn behaupten, dass Wirklichkeit erst geschaffen wird auf dem Theater? Sie haben einen Journalisten im Stück, der sagt, dass durch seine Bilder erst Realität entsteht.

Voima: Nicht die Wirklichkeit wird geschaffen, sondern ein bestimmter Zugriff auf die Wirklichkeit wird vermittelt durch die Medien und das Theater. Auch die Medien sind eine Realität. *Das Kontingent* ist also so etwas wie Brecht mit Niklas Luhmann. Es ist der Versuch, den Eigenwert der Systeme sichtbar zu machen. Das geht nur von innen heraus, auch auf die Gefahr hin, dass einem strategische Dummheit vorgeworfen wird.

Herr *Voima*, ich danke Ihnen für dieses Gespräch.

Gestus in der Aufführungspraxis

Dieser Aufsatz will nicht nur den Begriff Gestus als Teil der Theorie Brechts sondern auch seine Rolle in der Theaterpraxis des Berliner Ensembles untersuchen. Zunächst wird festgestellt, dass Gestus im Zusammenhang mit anderen wichtigen Elementen wie z.B. Fabel, Charakter, Diskontinuität diskutiert werden muss. Dass Gestus beim Autor entsteht, kann man ohne weiteres annehmen, aber es ist wichtig anzuerkennen, dass auch andere daran beteiligt sind, vor allem die Schauspieler. Brechts Zusammenarbeit mit Charles Laughton ist vielleicht das bekannteste Beispiel dafür, denn die Sprache (und deshalb der Text) war nicht der bestimmende Faktor. Laughton konnte nämlich kein Deutsch und Brecht beherrschte nicht völlig Englisch. Die Haltung des Schauspielers und vor allem der Körper bestimmen in dieser Situation den Ausdruck des Gestus. Der Gestus erscheint bekannterweise nicht nur bei Brecht, sondern taucht auch bei vielen anderen Autoren auf. Heiner Müller ist ein gutes Beispiel dafür, denn er hat den Begriff wie auch den Gebrauch davon übernommen.

Gestus in Performance
Brecht and Heiner Müller

Hector Maclean

(For Patrice Pavis)

The Brecht fashion is past. Let us begin to work with Brecht. (Manfred Wekwerth. 1976)[1]

What then is a social gest (how much irony has reactionary criticism poured on this Brechtian concept, one of the clearest and most intelligent that dramatic theory has ever produced!)? (Roland Barthes, 1977)[2]

The old lady squatting in front of the mound of mangos picked him instantly. As soon as the young man in the worn T-shirt, old shorts and cheap thongs approached, she ceased bargaining and snapped at his mother: "Why are you haggling with me? Your son is rich." Hung was astounded — he'd carefully removed his watch and dressed in old clothes before going to the local market. What gave him away, he asked the woman. "Two things," she replied. "Clean heels and the way you walk. It's obvious — you're not afraid of the authorities."

This incident, narrated in the *Melbourne Age* newspaper of 11.1.1992 (p.21) by a reporter who was certainly not thinking of Brecht, fulfils the requirements of Gestus, for which it is hard to find a better concise definition than that of John Willett in 1959: "It is at once gesture and gist, attitude and point: one aspect of the relation between two people, studied singly, cut to essentials and physically or verbally expressed. It excludes the psychological, the subconscious, the metaphysical unless they can be conveyed in concrete terms."[3] One may add the complicated and contradictory nature of Gestus, to which Willett also refers. In a useful addition to this definition, D'cruz[4] and Mehigan[5] add change of status or "loss of face," an external revelation of concealed ideological relationships and a "change or transformation in the presented performance text." It is really only the last to which

New Essays on Brecht / Neue Versuche über Brecht
Maarten van Dijk et al., eds., *The Brecht Yearbook / Das Brecht-Jahrbuch*
Volume 26 (Toronto, Canada: The International Brecht Society, 2001)

my example does not refer. It is certainly a performance text, but not in the ordinary sense.

What is lacking in the narrative I have quoted is the context and the larger story which provides that context. As we shall see, both enrich the little moment of street theatre, but it should be noted that they are not absolutely necessary for the incident to have its effect. To a certain degree the incident is autonomous. I shall return to that point later.

The background to the story can be quickly sketched in: Hung, the young man in the story, is a Vietnamese who had left Vietnam at the age of sixteen, settled in Australia for thirteen years where he acquired a good education and eventually returned to Vietnam as an employee of an Australian company. The point I wish to make at this stage is that, while the incident above is fully "gestic" in terms of Brechtian theatre (despite certain ideological ironies at the time), the larger story is not yet theatre, does not constitute what Brecht would call Fabel.

I have started in this way because it has seemed to me for some time that at least some of the confusion which surrounds Gestus derives from the vagueness with which it is used in association with textual, and, much more, with performance structures in the theatre. It might be useful therefore to begin by isolating as far as possible some of the main problems which the term throws up:

(a) Brecht himself admitted that Gestus is a vague concept, though it should be noted that he was talking about the "total Gestus of a play," (der Gesamtgestus eines Stückes) and that "the questions which have to be put in order to define it cannot be specified." (man kann nicht die Fragen angeben, die gestellt werden müssen, ihn zu bestimmen) [6]

(b) The link between Gestus and Fabel and the translation of both terms create confusion with related terms such as "plot," "story," "narrative" and the structuralist "fabula."

(c) Though Gestus tends to originate in the word, that is not always the case, as I shall show. Whatever the case, its destination is certainly the performance or the workshop floor. Despite this the term is mostly discussed in relation to a printed text, often with minimal reference to performance (e.g. Jameson's recent *Brecht and Method*).

(d) The probability that this dominance of text, however much it is questioned, privileges intentionality (of playwright, director and actor) and tends to leave out of account the actual generation of Gestus on the workshop floor and in the rehearsal space. It tends to ignore also the potential contribution of the audience.

(e) Because Brecht says very little about the body in his theoretical writing, there is an assumption that he pays little attention to the body both in theory and practice. Thus the question of a link between body and Gestus is seldom discussed.

(f)   The tendency to assume that Gestus is a purely Brechtian phenomenon, despite the fact that he quotes examples from other playwrights.
(g)   The fact that Brecht made little use of his theory in workshops.

The main thrust of my argument will relate chiefly to (d), (e) and (f). Let
us take the lines from the poem, "Brief an den Schauspieler Charles
Laughton, die Arbeit an dem Stück ,Leben des Galilei' betreffend":

> Immerfort wandelte ich mich zum Schauspieler, zeigend
> Gestus und Tonfall einer Figur und du
> Wandeltest dich zum Schreiber. Weder ich noch du
> Sprangen aus unserm Beruf doch.[7]

It may be argued that this is an exceptional case, insofar as there was a
language barrier. The English of the one was limited, the German of the
other as good as non-existent. Yet my point is not negated by that but
rather reinforced (Brecht the "actor, showing Gestus and intonation" —
Neither you nor I discarded our profession"). The communication between the two is as great as, possibly even greater than, that between a
German actor and the German author/director. Brecht commented on
his work with Laughton in great detail and with enormous enthusiasm.
     Before developing this theme, however, it should be placed in
context and related to other important concepts.

FABEL

One of the basic components in the construction of performance involves close links between Gestus and Fabel, as Brecht himself has
pointed out: "Das große Unternehmen des Theaters ist die *Fabel*, die
Gesamtkomposition aller gestischen Vorgänge..."[8] There are two common misunderstandings associated with Fabel. It is often confused with
"plot," but plot (or "sjuzet"), as Elam points out, is "the organization in
practice of the narration itself," as distinct from "fabula," the "basic
story-line of the narrative,[9] i.e. the bare bones of the story. However,
Elam makes only a perfunctory distinction between narrative and
drama — the latter is "acted rather than narrated"[10] — and appears to
accept that the concept of the structuralist fabula can be applied
equally as well to drama as to narrative. There are considerable problems involved in equating *fabula* with theatre, definitions which apply
also to Elizabeth Wright's definition of Fabel as "the moral of the story
not in a merely ethical sense, but also in a socio-political one."[11] While
both Elam and Wright acknowledge the performance element, neither
takes sufficient account of the very great differences which it makes in
the construction of such forms as Fabel.

A more balanced approach is given by Manfred Wekwerth, himself a director and one of Brecht's most trusted colleagues in his last years: "The Fabel of a play is often understood to be a self-contained plot, rather like the sort contained in an opera guide.... Brecht understood Fabel as the totality of all incidents (Vorgänge), which emancipate themselves on stage into gestic attitudes (Gestus)."[12] Notice the use of the word "emancipate" which I have purposely translated literally and of "attitudes" (Haltungen) which are so often restricted to the abstract social concept. There are several interesting features in this statement, but the operative words are "on stage." The Fabel ceases to be text-bound and is translated to the performance space.

It is Wekwerth's comment on the gestic attitudes which I want to stress. Peter Brooker, in a chapter on Gestus, makes the point that it is "designed to make the 'story' [=*Fabel*] element of epic theatre more immediately accessible and intelligible."[13] I would go further than that and assert that Fabel in the performance space is to a considerable extent created by Gestus, in Brecht's words "the complete fitting to-gether of all the gestic incidents" (die Gesamtkomposition aller Vorgänge),[14] not the other way round. One can put a narrative onto the stage, but it will not be Fabel or, for that matter, theatre in any sense of the word until all the elements which create the Gestus of each incident or sequence have been worked out.

The basic structural unit of Brecht's plays is not the scene, as is still quite often assumed, but the sequence or even the micro-sequence, one sentence or one action such as a laugh or the opening of a door. Even the so-called basic Gestus ("Grundgestus") which Brecht claimed to sum up a whole play or a whole scene is a single, and apparently simple, incident: Woyzeck buying the knife, Mephisto's bet with God, Grusche's tug of war with the governor's wife in the chalk circle. We can see that Wright's notion of a "moral" is neither Fabel nor Gestus, for it not only ignores the *accumulation* of events but it is far too imprecise. A moral is the judgment after the performance rather than an element in the performance itself. The emphasis must be on the concrete and discrete part as opposed to some kind of overriding totality; the discrete incidents which are "knotted" together in the creation of epic theatre are gestic incidents, and the incidents become Fabel (and theatre) only when their particular Gestus been worked out.

I do not know whether Brecht wrote his plays according to these principles, and it is not very important whether he did or not. What is important is that he expected his actors to proceed along these lines:

> Von Satz zu Satz vorgehend, gleichsam sich über seine Figur vergewis-sernd, an den Sätzen, die sie sprechen und die sie hören oder empfangen soll, von Szene zu Szene Bestätigungen und Widersprüchlichkeiten sam-melnd, baut der Schauspieler die Figur auf. Diesen Prozeß des *Nachund-nach* prägt er seinem Gedächtnis tief ein, damit er am Schluß seines Stu-

diums imstande ist, die Figur auch für den Zuschauer in dem Nachundnach ihrer Entwicklung vorzuführen. Dieses Nachundnach muß bleiben.

(Progressing from sentence to sentence, as it were assuring himself of his character, the actor builds up his role on the sentences he is to speak and which he is to hear and perceive, collecting from scene to scene confirmation and paradox. He engraves this step by step process deeply into his memory, so that at the end of his study he is in a position to present the role to the audience also in the gradations of its development. This gradation has to be retained...)[15]

And he emphasizes that the actor must not proceed from a total view of the play, for that will result in a stereotyped or derivative approach to both play and character:

Ein solches schrittweises Vorgehen ist besser als ein deduktives, ableitendes, das, von einer möglichst schnell, nach womöglich flüchtiger Durchsicht der Rolle gefaßten Gesamtvorstellung des darzustellenden Typus ausgehend...

(Such a gradual procedure is better than a deductive or derivative one. The latter bases itself on a total concept of the type to be presented which is arrived at as quickly as possible after a cursory glance through the role...)[16]

It is here that we can see the basic difference between Brecht's use of the Fabel and the *fabula*, introduced by the Russian formalists and adapted by theatre semioticians in the seventies. Discussing the use of *fabula* in relation to drama, (though not, it should be emphasized, referring to Brechtian theatre as such), Keir Elam observes: "It is only at the level of the *fabula* or story that the series of distinct actions and interactions of the plot are understood to form coherent *sequences* governed by the overall purposes of their agents. Macbeth's plan to seize the throne provides the chief interpretative frame for the play...."[17] It is precisely the coherence of the sequences, the notion that one central action or motivation can shape the interpretation of a whole play, which Brecht so vehemently denied. For him the play should not be dominated by the concept of Macbeth as the man saying: "I'm destined for higher things."[18] And it is for this reason that he insisted that the succession of incidents be seen not as a continuous flow but as discontinuous, and that each incident is enabled to contradict the previous one even as it carried the action a stage further. Again it is the operation of Gestus which is decisive.

THE INTERVAL

Discontinuity is a constant theme in Brecht's theory and practice: "...the progress of the Fabel is discontinuous, the unified whole consists of autonomous parts which can, indeed must, be confronted immediately with the corresponding part events in reality" (Die Fortfüh-rung der Fabel ist hier diskontinuierlich, das einheitliche Ganze besteht aus selbständigen Teilen, die jeweils sofort mit den korrespondieren-den Teilvorgängen in der Wirklichkeit konfrontiert werden können, ja müssen.)[19] Since Brecht, both the focus on the gestic incident and its separation from the surrounding action have been admirably described by Roland Barthes. He describes epic theatre as "successive tableaux"[20] and goes on to say that "Brecht's theatre, Eisenstein's cinema are series of pregnant moments."[21] I have some difficulty with the fact that "tab-leau" is referred to as an "action picture" and that "pregnant moment" derives from Lessing's *Laokoon*, referring to the moment in the story chosen by the *sculptor* as the most significant in a series of incidents. Certainly that moment proceeds directly out of the previous one and directly precedes the next, but the choice of sculpture somehow seems to negate the reality, the dynamism and above all the changing nature of the performance space. That aside, I know of no other approach which so well points to the significance, the autonomy and the sepa-rateness of the gestic incident. Interestingly Walter Benjamin very early recognized the structural nature of Gestus when he said that "unlike people's actions and endeavours, it [Gestus] has a definable beginning and a definable end. Indeed, this strict, frame-like, enclosed nature of each moment of an attitude which, after all, is as a whole in a state of living flux, is one of the basic dialectical characteristics of the ges-ture."[22] And Herbert Blau refers again to both attributes in his book, *The Audience*, when he speaks of: "the arresting interval of the Brechtian Gestus" combined with "the pregnancy of the question sus-pended in the Gestus."[23]

If the gestic incident and the discontinuity of the action are crucial for the creation of Fabel and hence for theatre, and if the interval or the pause is necessary for the signaling and greater effectiveness of the Gestus which is to be shown, then we have to consider what actually happens on stage. Here the pause tends to indicate change of direction or of register. The most obvious signals are mechanical ones, those which are best known involve the actor's body, the actor's pause. I have seen Ekkehard Schall, a finger showing the moustache, act a Hit-ler, then in a flash and a total change of body's expressiveness becom-ing a humble figure squatting on the ground. It is worth noting that one can observe a similar phenomenon in the Noh theatre, especially in comic situations where an actor "changes gear," entering a sequence which contradicts in style or tone the previous one. Indeed the interval often announces this fundamental change, not only in body but also in space: "A woman sits, and around her walls with windows move into place" ("Die Welt des Bühnenbauers ist einigermaßen verkehrt. In ihr laufen die Personen herum mit Zimmern um sich oder eine Maschine hinter sich oder Treppen unter den Füßen....Eine Frau sitzt, und um sie schieben sich Wände mit Fenstern."[24] I remember vividly this bodily gear shift when it was used by Ernst Busch with the Berliner Ensemble in 1957. Between the fourth and the fifth scene in *Der kaukasische Kreidekreis,* as he left the singer's position outside the proscenium arch, he announced with a wry/sly grin over his shoulder to the audience: "now I'm going to play Azdak," and his body abandoned the singer's bearing as he disappeared through the curtain onto the stage. It is always interesting to observe the interaction of body and frame — the one creates the other.

CHARACTER

In his discussion of Gestus, Patrice Pavis emphasizes not only the link with Fabel but also the way in which Fabel influences and is influenced by character.[25] It is well known that, for Brecht, character is not a fixed concept, that it is not a "grease stain in a pair of pants" ("ein Fettfleck in der Hose. Da kann man reiben und wischen, wie man will, er drückt sich immer durch."), which keeps coming through, no matter how hard one rubs at it.[26] It changes as circumstances change. Hence the links with Fabel and the role it plays in helping to shape the social energies which create and re-create the conditions in which Gestus can operate.

In traditional Brechtian terms "it is what happens *between* people that provides them with all the material that they can discuss, criticize, alter." (Denn von dem, was *zwischen* den Menschen vorgeht, bekommen sie ja alles, was diskutierbar, kritisierbar, änderbar sein kann.)[27] So it is in the space between the characters that the focus of Gestus resides, it is here that the spring of the action is to be found. There is no transfer of (the actor's) inner reality to the outer world; rather it is the other way round. Jan Knopf points out: "Thus the Gestus notion frees itself from the subjective and transfers its emphasis to the intersubjective..."(Damit löst sich der Gestus-Begriff vom Subjektiven und verschiebt seine Bedeutung zum Intersubjektiven...)[28] He then goes on to remind us that the expression of subjectivity is not excluded but is drawn from and made accessible through outer reality.

It is a not unimportant distinction, but let us rather look at an example from Brecht's own practice, bearing in mind that it is practice and not merely theory. I refer to a report by Hans Joachim Bunge concerning a rehearsal sequence in *Der Kaukasische Kreidekreis* from November 1953, that sequence in Scene 3, where Grusche buys milk for her baby from an old peasant who overcharges her. Bunge emphasizes that the actions do not stem from inherent characteristics (the "motherly" nature of Grusche or the "evil" nature of the peasant) but from the fact that there is a situation of warfare, that marauding troops infest the countryside, that the peasant has lost his goats to them and has little milk left. This is the reason the peasant opens his door cautiously, since it will be necessary to push it shut again quickly if Grusche is not alone. All this seems to be in accordance with the way real people act. But it's fairly dull and predictable; it simply makes the peasant into a suspicious type. So the need is felt to perform several layers of behavior. After considerable discussion and experimentation the actors arrive at a tentative solution: the peasant sells Grusche the jug of milk (still at a high price of course), but he does not simply stay guarding the doorway. He follows her — after first barring the door behind him — to where she is giving the child the milk. Partly he has developed sympathy for her plight, partly he wants to keep an eye on the jug.

This an inadequate précis of a rehearsal process which takes fourteen pages to describe. What lies behind those processes is summed up as follows:

> Der Regisseur könnte jetzt vorspielen, wie er sich das Auftreten des Alten denkt. Aber das tut er nicht, ihm liegt offenbar daran, daß der Schauspieler selber den Gestus der Figur findet. "man muß sehen können," sagt er, "daß der Bauer auch anders sein kann. Wenn der Krieg sich so entscheidend auf sein Verhalten auswirkt, wie könnte man sich den Bauern vor dem Krieg vorstellen? Wahrscheinlich kam selten ein Mensch vorbei, und der Bauer war bei der Ankunft eines Fremden eher erfreut statt mißtrauisch...."Wir müssen suchen, wo wir solche Mehrschichtigkeit zeigen können," sagt der Regisseur.[29] (..."We have to try and show this kind of multi-layering," says the director.)

The use of the word "multi-layering" or "Mehrschichtigkeit" is particularly valuable in this context; the infusion of Gestus, the potentially contradictory motivations governing the peasant's conduct, into each speech and action results in rich theatre, a series of moments in which the internal contradictions and multi-layering of emotions demand one's interest, whereas the bland stereotyping that one is familiar with in too many theatres would leave us cold.

THE BODY

In reading much of what Brecht has to say in his theoretical writing about the building of a role — and that includes most of the passages I have quoted above — one could be forgiven for thinking that the development of character is largely text-based and that the actor develops the character *only* by examining the text "sentence by sentence." There is a wide-spread assumption that Brecht may talk about the actor but never about the body. Thus Elin Diamond appears to be justified in saying: "Although he [Brecht] talks a lot about pleasure, it is the pleasure of cognition, of capturing meaning; Brecht does not apparently release the body, either on stage or in the audience. The actor's body is subsumed in the dialectical narrative of social relations..."[30] In using the words "on stage" and "in the audience" Diamond is clearly working on the assumption that the production of a Brecht play derives entirely from text and written commentary, implicitly making the statement that the theory dominates the stage. Unfortunately this is all too often the case, especially in the mainstream theatres of any country. It is not Brecht who is unwilling to release the body; it is the directors who shape his plays as "classics," according to a tradition which they mistakenly believe to come from Brecht himself and the Berliner Ensemble. To work in two dimensions simply should not be considered when dealing with theatre, and certainly the practice of unquestioningly imitating what appears in the photographs of the "Modellbuch" should be avoided, for it tends to produce disastrous results.

One must agree then that Brecht, in his theoretical writing, pays little attention to the body. Which makes it all the more important to consider what he has to say about the body in the context of commenting on various productions of his own plays, in his discussion, for example, of the very physical statements of bathing and eating in *Das Leben des Galilei*. In the commentary on Laughton's Galileo he says:

> So kommt es, daß wir, unseren ‚Faust' aufführend, ...ihn jeder Sinnlichkeit entkleiden und das Publikum dadurch in eine vage Stimmung versetzen, in der es fühlt, es habe etwas mit allerhand Gedanken zu tun, ohne einen einzigen zu fassen. L. benötigte nicht einmal irgend welche theoretische Information über den Stil....So vermochte er die widerspruchsvolle Person des großen Physikers in voller Leiblichkeit zu entwickeln, ohne seine eigenen Gedanken darüber zu unterdrücken oder aufzudrängen.

> ([W]hen we [i.e. the Germans] stage a performance of our *Faust*...we strip it of all sensuality and thus transport the spectators into an indefinite atmosphere where they feel themselves confronted with all sorts of thoughts, no single one of which they can grasp clearly. L[aughton]...was able to unfold the great physicist's contradictory personality in a wholly corporeal form, without either suppressing his own thoughts about the subject of forcing them upon us.)[31]

To take one example Brecht gives of Laughton's approach: „Sein Spiel mit den Händen in den Hosentaschen beim Planen der neuen Forschungen reichte an die Grenze des Anstößigen."[32] ("His [Laughton's] sensual walking, the play of his hands in his pockets while he is planning new researches, came close to being offensive.")

That is probably a form of "pleasure" not many would choose, but it is not as if the generation of meaning from physical interaction is limited to *Galileo*. Quite apart from the enormously sensual earlier plays such as *Baal*, there are the bodies in the tobacco shop of Shen Te, in *Der Gute Mensch von Sezuan*, or the delight in tumbling bodies, in a confined space climbing over and under each other, during such scenes as the wedding of Grusche and the peasant in *Der Kaukasische Kreidekreis*. The latter was superbly and hilariously "overdone" in the Berliner Ensemble production of 1957.

However, it is mainly in relation to Gestus that I wish to show the involvement of the body. In his admirable essay on Gestus Patrice Pavis points out: "Brechtian gestus, with its sole ambition to represent certain social relationships mimetically, is not a sex-specific notion," and goes on to say that, when Mother Courage bites the coin there is nothing typically feminine or masculine about it.[33] This is unarguably correct, if there is no performance context. Indeed, Diamond is also technically correct in complaining that Brecht "exhibits the blindness typical of all Marxist theorists regarding sex-gender configurations."[34] What worries me is that such criticisms in effect may be seen to extend the statement to performance as well. It is certainly in order to separate Brecht's theory of Gestus from the practical application whilst one is discussing theory. But I would maintain that in the context of perform-ance there is more often than not a whole range of physical characteris-tics which include sex-specific behavior. What is described as Laugh-ton's "Arbeitsgestus" in "Aufbau einer Rolle" — too involved in his work to take notice of his daughter — tends more towards the male. A clearer example, the transformation scene in *Der Gute Mensch von Sezuan* — Shen Te assuming the bearing, the clothing and the behavior of Shui Ta, the woman playing the man — notoriously involves "sex-gender configurations."

There is one area in particular in which the body performs an es-sential role, and that is the Gestus of showing, probably the most basic form of Gestus. That is apparent in Brecht's *Die Straßenszene* and in-deed in our example of the returned Vietnamese at the beginning of this essay. Jameson makes considerable mention of this but mainly in the context of teaching. Certainly that is correct but is too narrow. A text can only indicate the possibilities, the body is essential for its completion. There is an interesting example in Scene 7 of *Der Gute Mensch von Sezuan*. A child goes to a dustbin, looks around timidly, scrabbles in the bin and begins to eat what it has found. When Shen Te "lifts up the child and expresses her horror at the fate of poor children in a speech, showing the audience his dirty mouth" and tells the audi-ence to "observe the greyness around his mouth."[35] The sequence throws up fascinating problems involving the body, as we discovered in a workshop for drama teachers at the then Institute of Education at the University of Melbourne. How do actors show a dirty mouth (apart from the use of make-up)? Can one show it perhaps by hiding it?

One statement which Brecht makes, in that part of the Laughton commentary I quoted earlier, strikes me of particular importance, namely his belief that a lack of sensuality encourages an "indefinite atmosphere" in the audience and that, without the contribution of the body, thoughts cannot be grasped clearly. One of the most important attributes of Gestus is precisely the clarification, even more the sharpening of the point being made. And one can hardly imagine a more graphic way of showing the link between body/intellect and desire than by showing a Galileo indulging in thought while playing with his testicles.

What does concern me nevertheless is the assumption which seems to be implicit in Brecht's more theoretical writing that there is a hierarchy within the actor and that the body is always subservient to the brain. What I am thinking of here is the near universal agreement that the Brechtian actor is a creature of the intellect. I submit that Brecht does not always say that and certainly not in his Laughton commentary. Is it not more likely that it was not the intellect but the *body* of Laughton which discovered the means of expressing the sensuality of the character?

HOW IS GESTUS ARRIVED AT?

This leads into the question of what controls/creates Gestus, a question which is almost as broad as the one which asks how theatre is made. And yet it is worth asking at least, even if we arrive at no definite conclusion, because it should provide a pointer to the use of Gestus in situations outside the context of Brechtian theatre. In the case of Brecht there is, as we have seen, a strong tendency for critics to derive Gestus solely from the text. In a typical approach Horst Turk discusses *Leben des Galilei* in great detail from the point of view of Gestus. Nevertheless his greatest concession to the actual stage is still text-bound: "Ob ein dramatischer Text gestisch ist oder nicht, läßt sich zunächst an den Regiebemerkungen ablesen."[36] (Whether a dramatic text is gestic or not can be read first of all from the stage directions." Turk does, it is true, list the Laughton commentaries and the accounts of the Berlin rehearsals in his footnotes, but makes no use of the abundant evidence they contain. Most commentators who discuss Gestus acknowledge that it is the actor who is responsible for the final shape of Gestus, but the implication is almost always that he/she, in the first and indeed the last instance, works from the text.

I should like to take up two periods — separated by ten years — of the *Galileo* rehearsals of Scene 14, effectively the last scene in most productions: the Laughton period of Hollywood in 1945 and the Busch period of Berlin in 1955. When Galileo hears from Andrea that Federzoni has given up research and has returned to lens-grinding, he laughs and remarks that Federzoni should have learnt Latin. It is the laugh which constitutes the Gestus. In Käthe Rülicke's account of the rehearsal of 28.12.1955, with Ernst Busch as Galileo, the moment is described as follows:

> Wenn Galilei hört, daß Federzoni wieder Linsen schleift, muß nach der Regieanweisung im Buch Lachen kommen. Busch lachte mit dem Gestus: „Das geschieht ihm recht. Wer kein Latein kann, kann eben nicht studieren." Aber er brachte auch heraus, daß er nicht über Federzoni lachte, sondern über die Ungeheuerlichkeit des Vorgangs: über eine Gesellschaft, in der solche merkwürdige Dinge passieren. Nicht bitter, sondern belustigt lachend, zeigte er das Bildungsprivileg einer Klassengesellschaft bereits als merkwürdig; er brachte sogar heraus, daß vom Standpunkt einer klassenlosen Gesellschaft gesehen Komik in dem Vorgang war.[37]

At the time (1947) that stage direction was not in the text, a fact which needs to be emphasized. Thus there is a certain irony in the fact that the stage direction in the final version of the text, in direct contrast to what is believed by Turk and others, owes its existence to the actor. For it was the direct result of Laughton's work with Brecht in the creation of an English text:

> Das Lachen auf dem Bild war durch den Text nicht provoziert, und es war schrecklich. Sarti, der einstige Lieblingsschüler, kommt zu Besuch, und Virginia bespitzelt die mühselige Unterredung. Galilei erkundigt sich nach seinen ehemaligen Mitarbeitern, Sarti gibt rücksichtslose Auskünfte, berechnet, den Lehrer zu verletzen. Sie kommen auf Federzoni, einen Linsenschleifer, den Galilei zum wissenschaftlichen Mitarbeiter gemacht hat, obgleich er nicht Latein verstand. Als Sarti berichtet, er sei wieder zurück in seiner Werkstätte, Linsen schleifen, antwortet Galilei: "Er kann die Bücher nicht lesen," und dann läßt L. ihn lachen.[38]

There are two fascinating things about these accounts. Rülicke writes as if she is unaware of Brecht's account of Laughton's contribution, and yet her interpretation of the Gestus is the exact reverse of the earlier interpretation. Furthermore Busch's Galileo is represented as kindlier than Laughton's, although Brecht is believed to have sharpened the condemnation of Galileo in the later version in order to show the scientist as criminal. Of course it has been reported that Busch worked against Brecht's wishes, as his personal sympathy for Galileo grew.

Even more interesting for my purposes is Rülicke's statement that the laughter derived from the text, whereas the author/director, as we have seen, states specifically that it originated with Laughton. Thus it is a case of the actor not following the intention of the author but working, it seems, against the grain of the text. The author/director is surprised by the laugh and even finds it shocking. And then the laugh later becomes enshrined in the text.

What I have been trying to show in discussing the link between Gestus and performance is the fact that the author's intentions, whose importance need not thereby be diminished, should certainly not automatically be imposed on the performance text. I have argued that it is not merely the author's intentionality which should be examined critically but also that of the director and indeed of the actor. Equally, more detailed records might well have shown that stage and lighting design may well have contributed. And finally, of course, the spectators would clearly have constructed their own interpretation.

There is inevitably no reliable documentation of spectator contribution as such, although some indication may be found in the fact that audiences "demonstrated for and against Galileo" when the production was taken to Paris after Brecht's death.[39] For Brecht, spectator contribution has always tended to be a definite affirmation or rejection. It is that which points most clearly perhaps to the difference between him and an author such as Heiner Müller.

BEYOND BRECHT: HEINER MÜLLER

In considering the possibilities of constructively using Gestus in a contemporary situation, Heiner Müller is perhaps the most useful choice to take as an example, since he both rejects and continues Brechtian tradition; in addition he shows, as we shall see, that he is aware of Gestus as a term and a concept. However, one of the points of difference between Brecht and Müller lies in their attitude to Fabel. Brecht was emphatic that there is an autonomy of the individual parts, that the presentation of Fabel need not result in an absolute whole, as would be appropriate for Aristotelian drama, but he clearly did not go as far as Müller with his bold juxtapositions across the centuries and the genres. What Müller substitutes in place of a linear sequence is history, not history as story, but history as intertextuality or as quotation, what Müller calls "Zitatgestus" or "Gestus of quotation," a very postmodern form of Gestus. Müller feels that the presentation of history (presumably also myth) by itself is of no interest unless it is commenting on the present. Thus, in a statement about his play *Philoktet,* he remarks:

> Jeder Vorgang zitiert andere, gleiche, ähnliche Vorgänge in der Geschichte soweit sie nach dem Philoktet-Modell gemacht wurde und wird. Der Kessel von Stalingrad zitiert Etzels Saal.... Die Reflektion der Vorgänge durch die Figuren, gedanklich und emotionell, hat ebenfalls Zitatcharakter. Der Zitatgestus darf Intensität und Spontaneität der Reaktionen nicht schmälern. Einfühlung im Detail bei Verfremdung des Ganzen. Die deutschen Soldaten haben im Kessel von Stalingrad die Lektion der Nibelungen nicht gelernt. Die wiederholte Einmaligkeit muß mit zitiert werden.
>
> (The cauldron of Stalingrad quotes the hall of Attila....The German soldiers in the cauldron of Stalingrad did not learn the lesson of the Nibelungs.)[40]

Clearly such quotations by themselves do not yet constitute Gestus for they are far too general (in fact are similar to the social and political "moral" contained in the notion of Fabel put forward by Elizabeth Wright), but they point the way to a link with history of the kind to which Roland Barthes is referring when he says: "...the gesture bears the weight of history: its pregnancy brings together the past...the present.... The pregnant moment is just this presence of the absences..."[41]

It is in this way, a radical and startling juxtaposition of history and the present, that Müller achieves Gestus. In the context of performance the best example may be found in a video, taken from German TV and made in the Schauspielhaus in Bochum, which shows a scene, "Brandenburg Concerto 2," from his play *Germania Tod in Berlin*. It takes place in the reception room of a castle in what was East Germany, shows a pompous, more than life-size Empire chair and a diminutive Frederick the Great scuttling between the legs of the chair, then driving away a workman (a modern subject of the DDR). The workman goes up to Frederick, now perched on the chair, legs dangling, seizes Frederick's cane and breaks it. Whereupon Frederick leaps onto the workman's back, a veritable Old Man of the Sea, the weight of imperial bureaucracy borne by the subject workman. This is a series of gestic moments, though the last is the sharpest and most telling. It is worth adding that Müller himself chose the scene to illustrate that juxtaposition of past and present, and, in answer to the question, "Wie soll denn dieser Anachronismus eigentlich funktionieren?," he tells the story as follows:

> Da ist 1949 oder 50 eine Feier in einem Schloß oder einem ehemaligen Schloß, einem Regierungsempfang. Und da wird unter anderem auch ein Maurer, der Held der Arbeit ist, eingeladen. Es fällt ihm schwer, sich am kalten Buffet zurechtzufinden. Er hat noch nie vor einem Kalten Buffet gestanden, wo es zwei Sorten von Kaviar gibt und das alles. Und dann kommt ein Funktionär und fragt ihn, warum er so finster blickt. Der Maurer sagt, er finde sich nicht zurecht mit derlei Sachen. Der Funktionär fragt ihn, was er möchte. Und der Maurer sagt ihm, er möchte ein Kotelett und ein Bier. Das kriegt er schließlich auch und setzt sich damit auf einem Empirestuhl und fühlt sich da ganz wohl. Doch dann kommt Friedrich der Große als Vampir und versucht, ihn aus diesem Stuhl zu vertreiben. Das klingt zwar jetzt etwas komisch, ist aber ein Beispiel für das, was ich meine. Weil natürlich das preußische auch etwas ist, was die DDR zu tragen hat, in vieler Beziehung. Da war ein Beamtenstaat und ein Staat, wo die Leute zu Untertanen erzogen wurden. Und das bot sich an in der Situation nach 45.[42]

Frederick the Great is here the "presence of the absences"; he is metonymic for the Prussian state and bureaucracy which he fostered so sedulously and, it is implied, for the DDR as well. Certainly the play does not offer an absolute Fabel, but in other respects the scene admirably fulfils the requirements of Gestus. When Frederick the Great is quoted we have quotation as Gestus, "Zitatgestus."

Of course the scene is in several ways non-Brechtian: the entirely unrealistic, non-rational and grotesque appearance of Frederick the Great which creates ambivalence and a considerable uncertainty as to the interpretation of several of the "gestic" moments, (the play ran into trouble in the DDR, and the video I mentioned came from Bochum in West Germany), often leaving the spectators to construct their own meanings. Where Brecht knew how he expected the audience to react, and was often enough disappointed when it reacted the "wrong" way, Müller is apt to respond to accusations that he leaves his audience in a state of confusion with something like: "That's their problem."

Earlier I mentioned Benjamin's description of a "strict, frame-like, enclosed nature of each moment of an attitude." Müller is of course capable of creating a frame, but he is just as likely to break it. The play in which this kind of Gestus may most readily be observed is *Hamletmaschine*. In the video of a rehearsal of the play by students of the Department of Angewandte Theaterwissenschaft at the University of Gießen and directed by Müller himself, the second scene opens with the Gestus of Ophelia standing in a coffin[43] and wearing a bridal veil. Whilst Ophelia's death occurs at the end of the fourth act of *Hamlet*, in the Müller version it appears much earlier, except of course that here she reverses the story, she rejects the fate she suffers in Shakespeare's play and becomes the other Ophelia, the one the river did not keep: "yesterday I stopped killing myself." She has stopped being victim, has become active, violent and aggressive, smashing "the tools of my captivity."

Thus the body of Ophelia and the coffin in which she stands receive a double significance, the known death of the intertextual reference and the shock of the "resurrection." The sharpness of the transformation which takes place is also increased through an intertextuality with the submissive and resigned Shakespeare figure, a passivity present in her very absence; but equally the violence of the new Ophelia conjures up both the figure of Electra and, so Müller informs us elsewhere, that of the modern German terrorist, Ulrike Meinhof — the play was written after all in 1977.

In another frame-breaking moment of *Hamletmaschine*, the actor who plays Hamlet steps out of his role, takes off make-up and costume and becomes the Actor Who Plays Hamlet. He tears up a photograph of the author, Heiner Müller. Here the subjective dominates and dictates action or rather non-action. Having translated himself out of the Danish monarchy into a time of revolution more suited, it is claimed, to the character he represents, Hamlet then rejects history altogether and withdraws total passivity and self-disgust. He plays also a self-critique of the author, who divided himself for so many years between the two Germanies, between communism and capitalism, and could not make up his mind to choose one over the other. It is not merely the strong subjective element operating here, the desire of mind *and* body to be free of all feeling, to become a machine ("ich bin eine Schreibmaschine" is a form of linguistic and physical Gestus), but there is a radical fragmentation of the subject, shown in a variety of ways but most sharply in the tearing-up of the photograph.

Gestus then, I would maintain, functions just as well in the postmodern theatre as it does in the modernist Brecht. The rejection of linear Fabel and history, the breaking as well as the construction of the frame, the subjectivity as distinct from the "expression of subjectivity" (Müller's Hamlet is multiplied sometimes by three, even becomes a "chorus") all create a pattern of postmodernism which permits and encourages the creation of Gestus.

In this essay I have had three main aims: to re-examine the concept of Gestus in such a way as to relieve some of my own confusion and perhaps to encourage others also to think further about it; to explore its operation as far as possible, given the difficulty in obtaining documentation, in the performance space and through the body; finally to investigate the possibilities of using the concept outside the traditional Brechtian theory and practice.

NOTES

[1] Manfred Wekwerth, *Brecht? Berichte Erfahrungen Polemik* (München: Hanser, 1976); "Die Brecht-Mode ist vorbei. Beginnen wir mit Brecht zu arbeiten." 89.

[2] Roland Barthes, "Diderot, Brecht, Eisenstein: in *Image-Music-Text* (Glasgow, Fontana, 1982), 73.

[3] John Willett, *The Theatre of Bertolt Brecht* (London: Methuen, 1959), 175.

[4] Glenn D'cruz, "Illuminating Gestus towards a Political Theatre" in *Antithesis*, 4.2 (Melbourne, 1991): 64–65. Also valuable is the list of markers (71).

[5] Tim Mehigan, "Brecht and Gestus. The Place of the Subject" in *Faultline*, 2 (1993): 73–94.

[6] Brecht, "Über den Gestus," *Gesammelte Werke*, 16 (Frankfurt/M: Suhrkamp, 1967): 753.

[7] Brecht, "Brief an den Schauspieler Charles Laughton," *Gesammelte Werke*, 10:938.

[8] Brecht, "Kleines Organon für das Theater"65, *Gesammelte Werke*, 16:693.

[9] Keir Elam, *The Semiotics of Theatre and Drama* (London & New York: Methuen, 1980), 119.

[10] Ibid.

[11] Elizabeth Wright, *Postmodern Brecht. A Representation* (London & New York: Routledge, 1989), 28.

[12] Manfred Wekwerth, *Notate über die Arbeit des Berliner Ensembles 1956 bis 1966* (Frankfurt/M.: Suhrkamp, 1967), 34.

[13] Peter Brooker, *Bertolt Brecht: Dialectics, Poetry, Politics* (London & New York: Croom Helm, 1988), 51.

[14] Brecht, "Kleines Organon für das Theater" 65, 693.

[15] Brecht, "Aufbau einer Figur" (Construction of a Character) in *Gesammelte Werke*, 15:398.

[16] Ibid., 399.

[17] Elam, *The Semiotics of Theatre and Drama*, 123–24.

[18] Brecht, "The Film, the Novel and Epic Theatre," in *Brecht on Theatre*, 49.

[19] Brecht, "Der Messingkauf," in *Gesammelte Werke*, 16:655.

[20] Barthes, "Diderot, Eisenstein, Brecht," 72.

[21] Barthes, 73.

[22] Walter Benjamin, "Studies for a Theory of Epic Theatre," in *Understanding Brecht*, trans. Anna Bostock (London: Verso, 1984), 24.

[23] Herbert Blau, *The Audience* (Baltimore & London: The Johns Hopkins University Press, 1990), 336.

[24] Brecht, "Fixierung des Raums bei induktiver Methode" in *Gesammelte Werke*, 15:450.

[25] Patrice Pavis, "On Brecht's Notion of *Gestus*" in *Languages of the Stage* (New York: Performing Arts Journal Publications, 1982), 40.

[26] Hans Joachim Bunge, "Brecht probiert" in *Sinn und Form, 2. Sonderheft Bertolt Brecht* (Berlin: Rütten & Loening, 1957), 324.

[27] Brecht, "Kleines Organon für das Theater" 65, 693.

[28] Jan Knopf, *Brecht-Handbuch Theater* (Stuttgart: Metzler, 1980), 392.

[29] Bunge, "Brecht probiert," 325.

[30] Elin Diamond, "Brechtian Theory/Feminist Theory. Towards a Gestic Feminist Criticism," in *The Drama Review*, 32.1:88.

[31] Brecht, "Nachträge zu: Aufbau einer Rolle" in *Materialien zu Brechts "Leben des Galilei,"* zusammengestellt von Werner Hecht, ed. Suhrkamp (Suhrkamp Verlag, Frankfurt/M., 1963), 76

[32] Ibid., 51

[33] Patrice Pavis, "Brechtian Gestus and Its Avatars in Contemporary Theatre," *Brecht 100 ⇔ 2000, The Brecht Yearbook 24* (University of Wisconsin Press, 1999): 183. I am most grateful to Patrice Pavis for an ongoing exchange of views on *Gestus* and other points of common interest.

[34] Diamond, 89.

[35] Brecht, *Der Gute Mensch von Sezuan* (London: Eyre Methuen, 1977), 77.

[36] Horst Turk, "Das gestische Theater B. Brechts" in *Études Germaniques* (Jan–March, 1989), 42

[37] Käthe Rülicke, "Leben des Galilei. Bemerkungen zur Schlußszene" in *Sinn und Form*, 299

[38] Brecht, "Aufbau einer Rolle/Laughtons Galilei," in *Materialien zu Brechts 'Leben des Galilei,'* zusammengestellt von Werner Hecht, edition suhrkamp, (Frankfurt /M., 1963), 69; or: *Modellbücher des Berliner Ensembles* (Henschelverlag, Berlin 1956), 60

[39] John Fuegi, *The Essential Brecht* (Los Angeles: Hennessy & Ingalls, 1972), 175.

[40] Heiner Müller, "Drei Punkte. Zu Philoktet," in *Material, Texte und Kommentare*, ed. Frank Hörnigk (Göttingen: Steigl, 1989), 61.

[41] Barthes, "Diderot, Eisenstein, Brecht," 73

[42] Müller, *Gesammelte Irrtümer — Interviews und Gespräche* (Frankfurt/M.: Verlag der Autoren 1986), 37–38.

"Never in body and seldom in spirit" ("Nie im Fleische und selten im Geiste"): Australische Inszenierungen Brechtscher Dramen und Besprechungen zwischen 1945 und 1998

Die oben zitierte Bemerkung eines australischen Regisseurs, der eine bedeutende Rolle in der australischen Rezeption Brechts gespielt hat, dient als Ausgangspunkt für den vorliegenden Artikel zur Rezeptionsgeschichte von Brechts Dramen in Australien. Anhand von Inszenierungen und Pressespiegeln wird untersucht, wann und wie Brechts Dramen aufgeführt wurden, welche intellektuellen und dramaturgischen Funktion diese Inszenierungen erfüllten und ob sie im Sinne Brechts waren. Ergänzt wird das Gesamtbild der australischen Rezeption Brechts durch die Analyse von Edith Andersons englischer Übersetzung von "Vergnügungstheater oder Lehrtheater?", die das australische Verständnis der Brechtschen Theorien zum Theater entscheidend geprägt hat. Aufgrund der australischen Inszenierungsgeschichte und insbesondere aufgrund neuerer erfolgreicher Aufführungen schließt sich der Artikel der Forderung zahlreicher Forscher und Regisseure an, das Konzept einer Inszenierung im "Geiste" Brechts nicht länger als an orthodoxe Modelle gebundene "Werktreue" zu interpretieren, sondern freiere, dynamische Interpretationen zu fördern, die sich Brechts Dramen zueigen machen und auf diese Weise in Australien und weltweit einen neuen Zugang zu seinem Werk und einen transkulturellen Mehrwert ermöglichen.

"Never in body and seldom in spirit"
Australian Productions of Brecht's Plays
and Their Reviews from 1945 to 1998

Ulrike Garde

I n 1979, at the height of Australian interest in Brecht and his plays, Australian director Wal Cherry, one of the key figures in the local reception of Brecht, summarized the Australian reception of Brecht as follows: "Brecht was never in Australia in body and seldom in spirit."[1] This article examines the validity of Cherry's remark by turning the spotlight on the Australian reception of Brecht's plays from 1945 to 1998 and asks what could be understood by "in spirit" in this context.

If Brecht's physical presence was an issue in Australia, Cherry was right; unlike the United States, Australia was never a place of exile for Brecht and, unlike Britain, it was not a country for which Brecht prepared a production of one of his plays directly. Australians were only exposed to an "authoritative" production, which followed Brecht's *Modellbuch* closely, in 1973, when Joachim Tenschert directed *Mother Courage* for the Melbourne Theatre Company (MTC). Although Tenschert had originally intended to adapt the *Mother Courage Model* for the performance in Melbourne and considered the play's parable "übertragbar, übersetzbar"[2] for local audiences, he did not realize his plans because of a range of contingent circumstances.[3] As a result, Australian theater critics considered Tenschert's production as reflecting Brecht's "spirit" to the extent that it represented "the authentic version"[4] of the play; it was thought to show "how a definitive production should be done."[5] In this respect the production represented an eye-opener for many. Yet the majority of critics and spectators did not consider this version as setting down any sort of standard for future productions. This "authentic" mounting had come too late in the Australian reception history to have any practical consequences for the performance of Brecht's plays either in the established Australian mainstream theaters or in newer alternative theater circles. Critics thought Tenschert's version mainly of interest as a "museum piece," "undeniably out of its epoch."[6] Apparently it broke "no new ground" and failed "to really grip Melbourne audiences as fully as it might."[7] These responses reflect the fact that Australian directors did not generally feel the need to honor Brecht's "spirit" in the sense of attempting to copy his original produc-

New Essays on Brecht / Neue Versuche über Brecht
Maarten van Dijk et al., eds., *The Brecht Yearbook / Das Brecht-Jahrbuch*
Volume 26 (Toronto, Canada: The International Brecht Society, 2001)

tions; and audiences and critics did not expect them to do so.

Neither did the majority of Australian productions convey the impression that Brecht was considered a political ally. At the beginning of the period of reception under consideration, in the 1950s and early 1960s, the New Theatre groups, who had been the first to stage plays by Brecht in Australia,[8] were the only ones to declare political motives for staging one of his plays. This is also reflected in *The Exception and the Rule* as their favorite choice of play. Yet as the groups were closely associated with the Communist Party they did not represent a mainstream movement.[9] An Australian political theater with a broad audience simply did not exist at the time.[10]

Directors and critics in mainstream theaters tended to treat the aesthetic elements of Brecht's theories in isolation, neglecting the strong link between his political and aesthetic ideas. As in other English-speaking countries, Brecht became popular as a "tamed" classic with a particular focus on the production of the so-called "humanist" plays of his middle period like *Galileo, Mother Courage, The Good Person of Szechwan* and the slightly later *Caucasian Chalk Circle*.[11] The latter became his most frequently performed play in Australia.

It was only from the second half of the 1960s that a broader use of theater as a means of political expression evolved with the emergence of more dynamic alternative theaters. The formation of companies such as La Mama and the Australian Performing Group (APG) in Melbourne accompanied a general change of political climate.[12] Brecht's plays fitted quite naturally into this climate which welcomed social and political commentary and this led to the only period when Australians considered Brecht's plays relevant to their own society without changes to the original texts.

While these alternative theater groups remained faithful to the dramatic texts they felt free to alter Brechtian performance traditions without giving much thought to potential misrepresentations of Brecht's "spirit." In 1975, for instance, the APG, under the direction of Lindzee Smith, staged *The Mother* in an "environmental" style, using the possibilities of "bivouac theatre." The actors performed each scene of the play in a different part of the performance space situated in an old Pram Factory, making use of the entire space available in the building; the audience was equipped with folding chairs with which they followed the play around.[13] Vlassova's role was distributed among four actors.[14]

The production is an illustration of how, in line with the *Zeitgeist*, this group applied a questioning attitude towards authorities and traditions — to Brechtian performance traditions too. Lindzee Smith commented that "Some people, who were doing Brecht's work after Brecht's period of influence — like the Berliner Ensemble at a certain stage — were paying some sort of lip-service to his ideas; I think once the ideas had been assimilated they then were useful for adaptation for a new generation of theater artists to use."[15]

This open declaration of confidence becomes all the more significant when viewed in the context of the Australian cultural phenomenon known as "cultural cringe," a term that had been coined by Arthur A. Phillips in 1950,[16] which described Australians' intimidation by, and subservience to, British culture, and, in the theatrical sphere, to Anglo-Celtic,[17] and later, American culture. By challenging the predominance of any kind of tradition, the alternative theaters of the "New Wave" were the first to openly challenge the models which had been blindly accepted for as long as Australian theater was under the spell of "cultural cringe" and in doing so they displayed an attitude which would be labeled "irreverent" or "bold" in years to come.

Admittedly Australian directors had been modifying Brecht's plays to suit local theatrical norms before the shift in attitude and expectations brought about by the "New Wave" Theatre and with the approval of many critics. However, the approach taken by such directors differed from the "bold" approach in that it was generally done without reflection and thus cannot be interpreted as a sign either of confidence or of indifference to the plays' textual bases and performance traditions. Until the mid-1960s, and in many cases after that time, the majority of Australian directors took their primary aim to be the reproduction of Brecht's plays according to a "spirit" they believed to be faithful. At the time, explicit defiance of the "untouchable" status of a dramatic text or a performance tradition in programme notes or reviews was inconceivable.[18]

On stage, though, directors did adapt their productions to the predominant theatrical norms of what is often referred to as "Australian naturalism," a production style, including acting style and stage design, which attempted to create the illusion of real life on stage. It tended to eschew any form of theater associated with "artiness" because it could disturb the direct contact between the subject matter and the spectator and led to what might be called "invisible form."[19] While individual critics' expectations varied as to specifics[20] there was general agreement that this style should enable audiences to feel "compassion" for a play's characters.[21] As a result Brecht's plays were commonly reduced to bare storyline, in turn becoming predominantly displays of emotion; their critical components, and in particular their political implications, together with Brechtian staging techniques, were often entirely neglected.

Although this practice was clearly incompatible with Brecht's concept of theater and its function, no clash of expectations was openly discussed at the time. In some cases, it was not even recognized and this is partly due to the state of information about Brecht's theories on theater which, for Australians, largely depended on English translations. Despite the merit of introducing readers to Brecht's theoretical considerations, many early translations were in parts misleading as, for example, is the case of Edith Anderson's translation of "Vergnügungstheater oder Lehrtheater?" under the title "Theatre for Learning" for a 1958 issue of the Australian literary magazine *Meanjin*.[22] This publication was crucial for the local reception of Brecht's theories as it provided Australians with the well-known table contrasting "Dramatic Form" with "Epic Form" that was frequently referred to by reviewers. Moreover, its publication preceded the first professional English performance of a play by Brecht in Australia: Wal Cherry's 1959 production of *The Threepenny Opera* for the Union Theatre Repertory Company (UTCR), the precursor of the MTC.[23]

While rendering *Verfremdung*, or rather *Entfremdung*, carefully as "de-familiarization," the quality of the remainder of Anderson's translation is affected by the differences in her world views to Brecht's. Unlike Brecht, Anderson seems to consider the individual as essentially free from social pressures and instead caught up in moral dilemmas. When Brecht states "Der *Mensch* wird als bekannt vorausgesetzt" ("Dramatische Form") and that "Der *Mensch* ist Gegenstand der Untersuchung" ("Epische Form"), Anderson applies the idea to the stage only and renders the two claims respectively as "The *character* is a known quantity" and "The *character* is subjected to investigation."[24] The translation in other words disguises the fact that Brecht ultimately wanted the changes presented on stage to be connected to a transformation of man as a member of society outside the theater. This translation also makes it difficult to see Brecht's subsequent distinction between "Man unchangeable" ("Dramatic Form") and "Man who can change and make changes" ("Epic Form").

Anderson's table concludes by contrasting "The world as it is" ("Dramatic Form") with "The world as it is becoming" ("Epic Form"). But it omits Brecht's logical conclusion from this: "Was der Mensch tun soll / Seine Triebe" ("Dramatische Form") and "Was der Mensch tun kann / Seine Beweggründe" ("Epische Form").[25] The latter distinction is surely of great importance for it makes a strong point about the "old" theater where the character is the site of conflict between nature and idea, between the shortcomings of human existence and a moral imperative and it opposes this view of theater and the world to the "new" theater where man reacts to socially determined situations, but where critical insight into this situation allows him a measure of control and responsibility.

The moral conflict of the "old" theater also comes to the fore in Anderson's rendering of audience reactions which Brecht had added to the table. The original has the audience of the "epic theater" respond with "So darf man es nicht machen." Anderson's version reads "People shouldn't do things like that." Implicit in the original is the idea of *how* something is done in a social context, consequently a questioning of the circumstances and the social context under presentation. Anderson's translation on the other hand transforms this into a question of *what* is being done framed in terms of a failure of morally adequate behavior. Willett's translation of the same from 1964 as "That's not the way" confirms this analysis.[26]

There can be little doubt that Anderson's translation resulted in a misinterpretation of Brecht's ideas, this in turn contributing to the false impression that adapting Brecht's plays to the naturalistic repertoire did not conflict with Brecht's "spirit" — in other words with his original intentions. (In this context, it is all the more disturbing that Anderson's translation has been reprinted without modifications in the recently published *Brecht Sourcebook*.)[27]

This misreading is reflected in the way in which critics retrospectively assessed the MTC's standard practice of turning Brecht's plays into naturalistic productions after Tenschert's production of *Mother Courage*. Thus Ian Robinson made the comment: "The Melbourne Theatre Company finally discovered Brecht's plays about three years ago. Now they have discovered Brecht."[28] Unlike Robinson, Geoffrey Hutton endorsed the adaptations of Brecht's plays to the conventions of Australian naturalism and the theater of illusion. He wrote in hindsight about John Sumner's 1971 production of *The Caucasian Chalk Circle* for the MTC:

> It was engrossing theatre, never relaxing the pressure or the sense of surprise through its six long scenes. (...) Perhaps it should have been drier and more didactic, but I would not have changed it."[29]

The legacy of Australian naturalism has exerted and continues to exert an influence on Australian theater.[30] On stage the effects were most clearly visible until the height of the reception of Brecht in the late 1970s. However, it bears repeating that, parallel to the ongoing practice of adapting Brecht's plays to these predominant Australian theatrical norms, a first shift in expectations took place in the late 1960s and early 1970s, together with the emergence of alternative theater companies.

One director illustrating this shift was Wal Cherry who claimed in 1979 that Brecht had been "seldom in spirit" in Australia. After a study tour of theater in Europe, including a visit to the Berliner Ensemble, he introduced Australian audiences to Brecht through *The Threepenny Opera* in 1959. At the time, Cherry, like his audiences and critics, was still preoccupied with familiarizing himself with Brecht's ideas. His approach was specific in so far as he hoped that Brechtian theater would act as a catalyst for improving contemporary Australian theater, which he described as "a naturalistic orchestration of the wit and the word" dominated by an acting style he characterized as "make-believe-I'm-a-fairy."[31]

As far as the political dimension of *The Threepenny Opera* was concerned, Cherry made it clear he did not entirely reject Brecht's political commitment, though he did not seem ready to adopt it fully either. In an article written shortly after he had seen performances by the Berliner Ensemble, entitled "Brecht's Theatre in East Berlin," he noted that the plays were principally "concerned with man's political awareness" adding however that "man is more than politically aware."[32]

A certain ambivalence also characterizes his programme notes for *The Threepenny Opera* and they serve as the illustration *par excellence* of how Brecht's political message was toned down by Australian interpreters of all descriptions. Cherry began his interpretation of the play as follows:

> Brecht took Gay's plot, and many of his characters, and by placing them in the world of contemporary business methods, proceeded to infer that there were many similarities between the laws which govern the activities of beggars and criminals and the laws which govern the world of morality and commerce.[33]

However, the power of this interpretation was attenuated because Cherry did not apply it to contemporary conditions in Australia. Instead of reinforcing the underlying political intention, he undercut it in the anticlimactic sentence which follows: "It [*The Threepenny Opera*] is a bitter stabbing work, a true play of the underdog, an opera for the poor."[34]

Although the expression "underdog" originates in the America of the 1900s,[35] it is a term close to Australians because of what might be described as its "Australianist legend,"[36] which can be traced back to the support system of convicts transported to Australia. Dennis Carroll, in his book *Australian Contemporary Drama*, refers to "the 'mateship' or brotherhood of working men" as "an especially hallowed relationship"[37] and many people would still regard this as valid today.[38]

Although the concept of the underdog is closely associated with "his fight against society,"[39] the subversive content of this is toned down to mere "fighting against the odds."[40] More importantly, the underdog is usually an individual — although sometimes helped by his "mates" — who "has little status in society"[41] and who struggles against the hardship of life with the intention of surviving but without striving to change social conditions. Thus Australians related to Brecht's plays presenting working-class characters on stage[42] without taking up the political message which Brecht attached to them.

By referring to the familiar figure of "the underdog," Cherry not only cast Brecht's political message in terms of the "Australianist legend," but he also toned down the message considerably, thus avoiding being dismissed as a "Communist" himself. As explained earlier, political theater was not yet generally acceptable at the time.

Cherry's mode of interpretation was taken up and reinforced by the theater critic of the leading Melbourne newspaper, *The Age*. The critic elaborated Cherry's opening remark as follows: "John Gay's 18th century *Beggar's Opera* is turned into a modern opera for the poor, a bitter lecture on loving the destitute."[43]

This tendency to turn Brecht into a humanist bears direct comparison with the reception of Brecht in other English-speaking countries. American director Peter Sellars' remark that "Brecht has been domesticated like a lap-dog. At the best, the productions show the storyline and not much more"[44] can be easily applied to the greater parts of the playwright's reception in Australia.

In Cherry's 1959 production, this tendency seemed to be endorsed indirectly by means of the table contrasting "Dramatic Form" with "Epic Form" which the director had included in the programme notes. Anderson's translation, including the key phrases which she had misinterpreted, provided the theoretical background which seemed to justify the adaptation of Brecht's work to a "humanist" agenda. By 1975, though, Cherry's attitude towards Brecht's work had changed in line with the times. In that year, he directed *The Threepenny Opera* again, this time for New Opera South Australia with John Willett as dramaturge. Willett has documented his contribution to this performance in *Theatre Quarterly*.[45]

The production differed substantially from Cherry's first because he was now prepared to adapt Brecht's play to contemporary Australian circumstances. Apart from Willett's influence, Cherry's concern reflected the recent priority given to social relevance in Australian productions in general.

Cherry and Willett intended to update the social and political references of *The Threepenny Opera* in order to make it topical for Australian spectators in 1975. As Jim Sharman had done in a 1973 production,[46] they set the play in Australia. They created a framework for the original text, which used the Australian Anzac myth.[47] As part of the framework, a group of returning soldiers, gathering in a quarantine shed, introduced the play they were going to perform while waiting. Cherry and Willett also decided on minor changes to *The Threepenny Opera* itself in order to stress the play's topical significance for the audience.

The most important contribution to the play's topicality however was supplied by Australian political events of the time, that is Prime Minister Whitlam's dismissal by the Governor-General in 1975. Willett and Cherry drew parallels between the Governor-General's intervention, which effectively rescued the opposition of the time by putting it into power,[48] and Macheath's salvation via a *deus ex machina* in *The Threepenny Opera's* finale. Brecht's original was modified to read as follows:

And so to save our unsuccessful crook / The Crown itself will let him off the hook.
Chorus: Hark, who comes? / The Crown itself to the rescue comes, rescue comes (etc.). (...)
(Then Mrs. Peachum, *allegro moderato*)
So it all turned out nicely in the end. How nice and peaceful everything would be if the Governor General would always see things our way...[49]

Reactions towards this updated finale were positive. Kenneth Hince described the alterations as "a little cosmetic surgery" when reviewing the production for *The Australian* noting that

We now have a coloring of troops and Australian uniforms, and odd spots of the text have taken a new twist, notably in the happy ending with its bland reference to the Kerr–Whitlam confrontation.[50]

Willett himself concluded that it was "the only production of this work I've ever seen which seemed to make sense." Yet despite the successful adaptation, he remarked that the production's effect was not exactly what he had hoped for. According to his account, *The Threepenny Opera* played to full houses, but failed to "*hit* the modern public."[51]

Willett gave two possible reasons for this. In the first instance, he considered it problematic that the text was performed by opera singers who had been trained, as Willett put it, to "speak with a higher level of poshness on stage, and sing posher still."[52] In a wider context, this points once again to the influence of "cultural cringe" which had resulted previously in the Australian accent having been banned from the stage.

A second reason for the production's reduced impact lay according to Willett in the very nature of *The Threepenny Opera* and its performance history. In Willett's own words,

The Threepenny Opera remains an almost impossibly difficult work to put over. You can vulgarize it, you can appeal to nostalgia, you can make a *Cabaret* of it, you can make it seem topical by changing its message and its meaning. But you cannot ever recapture the shock effect of its original production in 1928 which came less from any real political relevance than from the form adopted, the language used, and the unexpectedness of the level at which this new mixture of words, music and theatre was pitched.[53]

Despite Cherry's and Willett's efforts to reinvigorate the social and political relevance of the play and to use Brecht's aesthetic devices in a fresh context, this play with music still appeared like a classic. Not only in Australia but world-wide, such an assessment represents a death sentence for Brecht's work unless a way can be found in which the original impact of his plays and, in particular, of *The Threepenny Opera* can be restored.

It is possible that Willett and Cherry's approach itself might contain the key to the problem. The two had modernized Brecht's original aesthetic including many of his devices, for example by replacing the half-curtain by tarpaulins; but they did not change the way in which these devices worked. And yet could Brecht's original aesthetic devices still be utilized effectively in 1975 in the same way they had functioned when Brecht first put them into practice?

In his review, Hince ruled out this possibility, assessing the accomplishment of Cherry's (and Willett's) production as a paradoxical one: "Because it is so true to Brecht's own notions of the theater, Wal Cherry's new production is an ambiguous thing. The more it succeeds, the greater its failure" because "Brecht's gambits in theater have been well played out in 50 years."[54]

Thus Cherry's and Willett's production and its reception raise some significant wider questions: How could Brecht's plays and his theatrical devices be reinvigorated? Is a new approach to Brecht's work necessary and helpful in this respect? Does the notion of a performance in Brecht's "spirit" need to be re-assessed in the context of a new approach?

Although the number of Australian performances of Brecht's plays peaked in the last years of the 1970s, the majority failed to address these questions; most productions were conservative in their choice of play and in production style. The exceptions were James McCaughey's production of *Baal* in 1977 and Wal Cherry's production of *Private Life of the Master Race* in 1978.[55] McCaughey's choice of play corresponded to preferences in West Germany where the focus of attention had moved to Brecht's so-called "open" plays like *Baal*, *In the Jungle of the Cities* and *Mahagonny*.[56] Thus, by choosing parts of his dramatic œuvre that Australians had yet to become acquainted with, these few productions gave an indirect answer to the question as to how to refresh the interest of contemporary audiences in Brecht's dramatic work.

At the same time, the dilemma was aired at the theoretical level. The great interest in Brecht in the late 1970s not only led to an increase in the number of productions, which made easy access to the more familiar plays possible but also enabled theoretical discussions to take place; visits by John Willett and Martin Esslin and a series of articles related to Brecht, published in *Theatre Australia*,[57] nourished a climate of discussion about Brecht's work.

Apart from Cherry's remark that begins this article, *Theatre Australia's* section on Brecht contained an article by Esslin called "Grass vs. Brecht: *The Plebeians Rehearse the Uprising*"[58] and an article by playwright and director Roger Pulvers entitled "What is Brechtian in 1979?" which centers on Pulvers' latest play *Bertolt Brecht Leaves Los Angeles*.[59]

In a passage reminiscent of Willett's views of 1975, Pulvers argued:

> The set "Brechtian" ways may not work any more. (...) In a particular de-
> vice [sic] which Brecht himself used has been so successfully integrated
> into what is now considered the conventionally dramatic, it may have lost
> its effectiveness.

On the one hand, Brecht's legacy, including both his dramatic theory and methodology, pervades "everything we see on the stage" to such an extent that his impact on Australian theater might be seen as an ongoing one, as Robyn Archer has pointed out.[60] Thus his influence exceeds the mere number of productions. On the other hand, this very aspect of the reception has reinforced the tendency to view Brecht's plays as classics. Pulvers drew the conclusion that "The worst thing we can do — the most essentially un-Brechtian — is to treat him as any orthodoxy. "Brechtian," for me at least, is above all *irreverence*."[61]

In short, Pulvers' definition of "in spirit" took up the approach which the APG had used in their production of *The Mother* in 1975, particularly as regards the production style, and anticipated the "bold" approach which Barrie Kosky was to suggest two decades later. For Pulvers, as for Kosky, this "irreverent" attitude was strongly connected to the notion of "owning" the resulting production; hence the subtitle of Pulvers' article was "My Brecht."

Yet in practice the 1980s did not prove to be conducive to an "irreverent" approach towards Brecht's plays. It seemed as though Australians had had their fill of Brecht and the number of plays performed fell sharply to less than half of the performances staged in the 1970s.[62]

At the time, conditions for the reception of Brecht's plays were unfavorable from both the socio-political and theatrical point of view. In cultural affairs, the new political leaders ceased to see themselves as patrons of the arts as their predecessor Whitlam had done. An economic climate marked by financial deregulation, economic rationalism and big-borrowing entrepreneurs together with the prevailing attitude of "greed is good"[63] created a climate that was not auspicious for the reception of Brecht or his sense of political idealism.

Nimrod and the APG, the two major theater companies that constituted the "New Wave" Theatre, had lost momentum, making way for a great number of small theater companies which competed for funding. Because Brecht's plays are generally thought to require big casts and hence big budgets, the mood of financial constraint discouraged productions of his plays, especially by small alternative companies. As a result many productions were of the conventional Brecht repertoire and took place within the theatrical mainstream at the MTC in Melbourne,[64] the STC in Adelaide, the QTC in Brisbane and the Canberra Opera. One notable development though, was that Brecht's plays started to spread beyond the major cities in the late 1980s,[65] with some productions linked to community theater which might be said to have represented the new momentum in an Australian theater that was otherwise characterized by a "post-boom feeling."[66]

In the 1990s, the Australian Brecht-fatigue lingered on. Although, on the whole, the decade was a politically stable one without major upheaval, a recession was one factor seen as preventing a return to the level of funding the arts had seen in the 1970s. Funding cuts and an obsession with marketing and administration led some to declare that "Australian theatre is over."[67] According to Julian Meyrick, the fragile market in the theater industry, with its high labor costs, had caused alternative and mainstream theaters alike to resist adventurous programming.[68] Once again, productions of plays by Brecht were hampered by a reputation for high production costs. Unlike in the United States, where Carl Weber noted that the interest in Brecht appeared "to have been revived," precisely because of economic reasons and "the recession and a growing awareness of social crisis at the beginning of the 1990s,"[69] similar economic and social factors in Australia failed to create a renewed interest in Brecht.

Apart from such generally unfavorable conditions, the low interest in Brecht can be attributed to his image having been tainted in two ways. First, attitudes towards Brecht were affected by doubts cast by John Fuegi on Brecht's personal and political integrity and his accusations and their immediate aftermath had a negative influence on the Australian perception of Brecht.

In the second instance, Brecht's popularity decreased because of crucial social and political changes taking place in Europe at the end of the decade. As in the case of Fuegi's accusations, it is difficult to specify how much the change in the world's political configuration and the resulting skepticism towards left-wing political thinking have influenced decisions not to stage plays by Brecht. However, programme notes and reviews show clearly that directors and critics were mindful of these changes affecting the political aspects of Brecht's work.

As far as style and form are concerned, Brecht's plays suffered from the ongoing problematic status of a classic in need of reinvigoration for the contemporary Australian stage. Directors attempted to solve these problems in various ways. In the context of an intensified search for meaningful ways of producing Brecht's plays in the 1990s, both directors and critics showed awareness that quality translations were the basis for any successful text-based production. Thus Richard Wherrett based his 1996 production of *Galileo* for the Sydney Theatre Company (STC) on a new version by David Hare. Three years earlier, Jean-Pierre Mignon had asked Australian playwright Humphrey Bower to provide a new translation for the production of *Mother Courage* at Anthill Theatre (Australian Nouveau Theatre) in Melbourne. Bower's efforts resulted in a translation which rendered the spirit of Brecht's original with an Australian flavor and it was well received. In her review, Ellen Fidavila expressed the notion of "ownership" of the text when she noted:

"Bower's Brecht sings of Fitzroy Street corners."[70] Despite the fresh translation, the production style was surprisingly conventional for an alternative company well known for courageous stagings of contemporary European plays. Ultimately, both Wherrett's and Mignon's productions failed to grip audiences.

A different approach was taken by Simon Phillips in staging The Threepenny Opera for the STC in 1994. His production can be interpreted as an attempt to come to terms with both the challenges represented by Brecht's ideology and his theatrical devices. Aware that the collapse of left-wing regimes had detracted from Brecht's image as a politically engaged playwright, Phillips recommended a "reassessment of the polemical playwright"[71] and interpreted The Threepenny Opera as a "plea for compassion."[72] Phillips' interpretation was based on the final hymn which, according to the programme notes, was taken as an appeal to the spectators' conscience, effectively ignoring Brecht's stated intentions and the genesis of the text, the Ludenoper, which indicates that the play's happy end was designed as a highly ironic manipulation of audience expectations and theatrical norms. Critic John McCallum subsequently criticized Phillips for converting "the play into a bourgeois lament for the individual failure of compassion" and for some changes to the script preventing the production from revealing "the criminal base of bourgeois capitalism."[73]

As far as formal aspects of The Threepenny Opera are concerned, like Willett and Pulvers before him, Phillips acknowledged the fact that Brecht's aesthetic devices had lost their original effect. In his own words he felt the urge to "rekindle the aspects which made Brechtian theater so revolutionary in its day, many of which have now been so absorbed into our theatrical culture as to be taken for granted."[74] Like Willett and Cherry, he saw reinvigorating Brechtian devices rather than replacing them by new ones as the key to the problem of waning effect.

While critics could neither agree on the effectiveness of this strategy nor on the production's overall achievements they all sought to engage with the question of how a play by Brecht could be staged for contemporary Australian audiences. Ultimately this means that Phillips' approach was at least partly successful because it stimulated an intense debate about this crucial issue and thus reanimated and enlarged discussion of Brecht's work. Thus John McCallum asked in The Australian what "Brechtian" could mean and David Gyger, in Theatre Australasia, reflected on the "creative core of this work."[75]

The centenary of Brecht's birth, although not officially marked in Australia, saw a number of notable productions of Brecht's work. Robyn Archer performed a collection of songs, mainly by Kurt Weill and Hanns Eisler, which had been originally devised to accompany an exhibition of George Grosz's drawings from between the wars (Weimar Republic 1919-1932).[76] In Kabarett, Archer was accompanied by Michael Morley who also contributed to the programme notes an assessment of cabaret from a contemporary point of view. He noted:

> Above all, the cabaret offers an opportunity for what perhaps might now be termed post-modernist performance possibilities. Philosophy can rub shoulders with vulgar jokes, lowbrow art can clash with highbrow musical craft; the naïve can jolt the sharply intellectual; jazz and blues can jostle for attention with the folk-song and parodies of the classical *Lied.*[77]

In practice Archer and Morley chose to build on the cabaret's ability to work as an umbrella for a great variety of performance material. Due to its inherent flexibility, its form needed neither to be adapted nor reinvigorated. The relevance of the lyrics remained the sole concern. Introductions and comments served to place the various texts within a contemporary framework; for instance, the "Song of Sexual Obsession" was dedicated to Bill Clinton. The updating process was completed by slightly modifying some texts and as a result, audiences and critics took away an impression of urgency and relevance.[78] Archer and Morley had made effective use of a form of presentation which was not bound to a clearly laid out text sequence that was expected to be faithfully reproduced on stage. Both the possibility of mixing different styles and of topical commentary made it much easier to make material relevant to contemporary audiences than was the case with Brecht's plays.

Michael Kantor's production of *The Caucasian Chalk Circle* for Belvoir Street Theatre, Sydney, nevertheless illustrates how this can be done effectively. Kantor took an approach which could be labeled "bold," to use a term coined by Australian director Barrie Kosky, who, from the outset of his career as a director, had suggested taking a fresh confident look at classical plays from foreign countries, in effect advocating what Pulvers had described in 1979 as "irreverence" towards traditional approaches and authorities. Promoting a less text-based approach, free from the limitations set by performance traditions or the "institutionalization of style," Kosky demanded: "We have to be bold."[79] The suggestion was that audiences should be able to "assume ownership" of the performances presented to them, the overreaching aim being to turn historically and culturally distant texts into relevant cultural experiences for local contemporary audiences. Within an academic context, a "bold" approach towards Brecht's work had already been employed effectively in Australia[80] and Kantor's contribution was to apply such an approach successfully to a production outside the academic context in a way that Australian audiences could engage with.

Kantor's mounting[81] differed significantly from the majority of productions of Brecht's plays that have been under consideration thus far in the sense that he did not attempt to stage a faithful imitation of model productions, nor try to revive isolated elements of Brecht's work.

Instead, he and his company treated the original features of Brecht's play as a basis from which they built a production of their own. In an interview, Kantor described the mixture of Brechtian elements and his company's contribution by noting: "We developed a text that was contemporary for us, but still strongly Brecht."[82] In this context, a "bold" approach resulted in Kantor making Brecht's text, method and ideology, stand the tests of time and validity. In more specific terms this meant personalizing the play's ideology and using only those Brechtian devices that were considered appropriate for their reading of the text.

Choosing *The Caucasian Chalk Circle* meant taking a fresh look at the most frequently staged play by Brecht in Australia. Working on the script, Kantor consulted a range of translations and adapted the original in several ways, basing his production on the "core narrative." He transposed the story into a "modern Eastern European environment" and "established references to contemporary Georgian political history."[83] The action of the original was reconstructed to take place over a 24-hour period.

One of Kantor's wider aims was to relate the play's central themes to contemporary socio-political conditions. Kantor proposed to re-critique Brecht's ideological positions, but maintain a "broadly socialistic, humane type of personal politics." The production was designed to "bring to life a whole lot of (...) pertinent issues," such as "what it is to be a parent [and] what it is to be in charge of another person" nowadays. [84] The narrative was placed in a broader context, with the aim of showing "a clash between political activity and personal politics and how you as a person relate to politics and the machinations of power."[85]

The effects of personalizing Brecht's ideology were clearly illustrated by the singer's role in the production. Kantor chose to "double up" the child representing the infant by use of a rectangular light box for most of the performance as well as having a real child accompany the singer and witness his own story. This in turn allowed actor-singer Paul Capsis to alternate between commentary for the audience for the purposes of *Verfremdung* and delivering a personal comment directed at the child who was at his side. This interpretation was characteristic of Kantor's approach to Brecht in so far as it shows that he considered some of Brecht's ideas as valid but only if modified and adapted to contemporary conditions.

Similarly, under Kantor's direction, Grusha's escape became a nightmarish and chaotic flight, structured around the leitmotif of her acceptance and rejection of the responsibility of being in charge of the child. Centering on themes such as personal responsibility and personal encounters with political forces, Kantor's production reflects a contemporary tendency to spurn world views which make claims to universal validity, such as those represented by radical left-wing ideologies.

However, the major difference between Kantor's *Caucasian Chalk Circle* and other productions which suppressed the ideological position underlying Brecht's play is that Kantor seemed strongly committed to a truly Brechtian questioning of social and political reality and to an overt display of the Brechtian spirit of doubt. By not providing the answers to the questions raised in the production he took a position similar to Brecht's skeptical attitude towards the world, thus relating to Brecht's "spirit."

The skeptical attitude inherent in the production points to the loss of any secure system of beliefs and in accordance with this the trial that is part of the play allowed only for a glimmer of hope. Where earlier Australian interpreters had read the trial and its outcome as a happy end, Kantor interpreted it as follows:

> [In our version] the trial takes place in the heat of the day, in a shimmering kind of stillness. (...) The hypocritical, but fascinating figure of the judge creates in this moment of stillness the slightest reminiscence of justice — and then it is gone.[86]

Brecht had sought to counterbalance the accidental nature of the trial's outcome by demanding a changed concept of ownership in the play's frame, thus proposing a utopian solution to the conditions the play itself describes. The hope which fuelled Brecht's belief in utopia has been lost. From the bleaker point of view of Kantor, the proposition at the end of the play to allocate everything to "those who are good for it" is not so much a promise as a challenge; in the performance of Paul Capsis the idea even comes across as vaguely threatening.

Kantor's world view translated into a new approach to the formal aspects of the play and production style. Thus Kantor added grotesque elements, such as excessive repetitions. A simple action, such as arriving in a room and sitting down on a chair, became distorted to the degree of becoming grotesque. Unnatural increases in the speed of certain actions worked in the same way and a grotesque figure reminiscent of Stalin was introduced.

Nightmarish images were made to predominate and for this purpose Kantor and designer Dorotka Sapinska stylized the set, creating a series of spaces "which were architectural rather than realistic, that continually evolved." [87] These spaces were made from steel, wood and paper. The atmosphere created by the stage design was reinforced by a disturbingly loud sound design, based on the sounds of a record player jumping as well as those of the rumbling of tanks and a child's heartbeat. These "were all fused together to create an evocative space,"[88] a dream-like atmosphere which did not correspond to Brecht's analytical presentation of socio-political processes. Against such a background, the story's fairytale elements which Australian directors had repeatedly relied upon to turn *The Caucasian Chalk Circle* into escapist theater, became downright sinister. Yet, as John McCallum observed, Kantor managed to counterpoise the bleak atmosphere with "emotionally moving and hugely entertaining" moments so as to do away with "any lingering suspicion that Brecht is somehow earnest, austere and polemical."[89]

In summary, Kantor's production introduced Australians to new avenues from which to approach Brecht and the production of his plays, showing that looking at Brecht through Australian eyes no longer necessarily implied an Australian setting.[90] Along the way he proved that a production of a play by Brecht does not necessitate a large budget or a big cast when actors are versatile enough to play several roles and the stage design is simple but inventive.[91] More importantly still, Kantor applied a "bold" approach successfully and stylishly to one of Brecht's plays that had become a classic of the Australian theater and was as in danger of becoming "museum theatre"[92] as it was in the rest of the world.

It was an undertaking that was well received by critics.[93] Both John McCallum, in *The Australian*, and Diana Simmonds, in the *Bulletin*, praised the production for having "remade" and "reconfigured" *The Caucasian Chalk Circle* "for a new generation."[94] The sense in which Kantor had enabled audiences to "assume ownership" of the production was captured by Bryce Hallett who summarized Kantor's achievement in a review for the *Sydney Morning Herald* by saying that "Kantor and his collaborators plug into tradition to arrive at a vocabulary in accord with Brecht's [modernist] approaches yet free-spirited and committed enough to make the parable decisively their own."[95]

It is possible to see in this production in particular a shift in attitude towards Brecht's work both on an international and local level. In Australia, Kosky has applied his notion of a "bold" approach to Brecht and has proposed to "de-Brecht" him, referring to recent changes at the Berliner Ensemble.[96] Internationally, Brecht's work is currently seen by many as offering an opportunity to explore critically new territory in terms of both content and style.[97] Scholars and theater practitioners are keen to stress that a dynamic approach towards Brecht's texts corresponds to Brecht's own method, as described by Heiner Müller: "Wenn der Brecht probiert hat, hat er auch den Text vergessen, hat er das Stück vergessen, ihn interessierten dann die Schauspieler mehr als der Text."[98]

Brecht was not only flexible in adapting his texts to the needs and constraints imposed by actors and circumstances; it is well known that he even wrote numerous revised versions of his plays and adopted an aggressive attitude towards classic texts.[99] In short, his own conduct invites a creative handling of his texts, including the "bold" approach.

It might indeed be high time to fill out the concept of what is Brechtian "in spirit" and to move away from "faithfulness" as the crucial criterion for assessing whether a production is in accordance with Brecht's "spirit." Just as Brecht adapted *Mother Courage* for London audiences, theater companies should feel encouraged to adapt their productions to the requirements of contemporary local audiences. On this view of the matter, a "bold" approach and a production in the "spirit" of Brecht do not necessarily exclude each other.

In Australia, in particular, this would appear a promising way to reinvigorate the dormant classic of the theater; the rediscovery of Brecht in Australia must be a corollary of seeing Brecht from an Australian point of view, through a wide and multi-faceted one. If it is true that the Australian "cultural cringe" is giving way to a generalized feeling of cultural confidence and assertiveness then an Australian look at classical plays could potentially by very rewarding. As Australian writer David Malouf points out: "There is a peculiar freshness and originality in the way we take what is classic and remake it as our own."[100]

In the spirit of building on this suggestion of Malouf's the following could stand as a motto for future productions of Brecht's plays: "Er hat Vorschläge gemacht. Wir haben sie weiter entwickelt."[101]

NOTES

[1] Wal Cherry, "Bertolt Brecht. Production in Australia," *Theatre Australia* 3.11 (1979): 14.

[2] "Transposable, translatable." See "Als Parabel ist diese Bildwelt [aus *Mutter Courage*] übertragbar, übersetzbar: sie kann Wahrzeichen sein für eine heile Welt, die den Krieg nicht oder nicht unmittelbar kennengelernt hat." Letter to Richard Prins and Hugh Colnan, 6.4.73. Regarding the information on *Mother Courage* enclosed in his letter, Tenschert intended it to provide "stimulations and suggestions [as to] what can be used, what can be developed and modified, what must be changed."

[3] Ian Robinson's review for the *National Times* (2.7.73) shows that the MTC favored spending money on an expensive set rather than on additional rehearsal time which would have allowed Tenschert and the actors to adapt the play to the contemporary Australian political context.

[4] G. Hutton, *The Age*, 22.6.73.

[5] John Sumner, *Recollections at Play. A Life in Australian Theatre* (Melbourne: Melbourne University Press, 1993), 249.

[6] Barrie Watts, *The Australian*, 29.6.73.

[7] Ian Robinson, *National Times*, 2.7.73. To many spectators, Tenschert's *Mother Courage* compared unfavorably to John Ellis' and Elijah Moshinsky's very successful 1967 production for the Melbourne Youth Theatre.

⁸ In 1939, New Theatre performed *Señora Carrar's Rifles* in New South Wales. This was followed in 1941 by *The Informer,* a segment from *Fear and Misery of the Third Reich.*

⁹ The isolation of New Theatre in the 1950s is revealed by the fact that in some places, newspapers refused to publish their advertising and to review their productions; see Philip Parsons et al., eds., *Companion to Theatre in Australia* (Sydney: Currency Press, 1995), 200.

¹⁰ Similarly, West Germans were reluctant to embrace the political message of Brecht's plays during the Cold War. See Michael Schneider, "Bertolt Brecht — Ein abgebrochener Riese. Zur ästhetischen Emanzipation von einem Klassiker," 26, in *Vorbilder,* ed. Jürgen Manthey et al., (Reinbek bei Hamburg: Rowohlt, 1979), 25–66, Klaus Völker, "Productions of Brecht's Plays on the West German Stage, 1945–1986," 63, in *Re-interpreting Brecht: His Influence on Contemporary Drama and Film,* ed. Pia Kleber and Colin Visser, (Cambridge: Cambridge University Press, 1990), 63–75.

¹¹ Cf. Peter Brooker, *Bertolt Brecht : Dialectics, Poetry, Politics* (London: Croom Helm, 1988), 182; and Maro Germanou, "Brecht and the English Theatre," 213, in *Brecht in Perspective,* ed. G. Bartram et al., (London: Longman, 1982), 208–24.

¹² In Sydney, Nimrod was founded. However, according to Melbourne theater critic Leonard Radic Nimrod was less radical in political terms: "The Nimrod was more businesslike and practical, with none of the APG's radicalism." In Leonard Radic, "Theatres come and Theatres go," 474 *Pearls before Swine: Australian Theatre Criticism. Meanjin* 53.3 (Spring 1994): 473–78. My performance records show that Nimrod only became interested in Brecht's plays in the late 1970s.

¹³ Brian Davies' production of *The Exception and the Rule* for La Mama in 1969 was characterized by a similar approach.

¹⁴ This device aimed to show that "the play is about all mothers in general, so it does not really matter who is portraying the part; (...) this is not the story of one person but the story of mothers all over the world in every country," Personal interview with L. Smith, 26.10.98. It was also thought to add a feminist aspect to the play in the International Women's Year; see *The Australian,* 20.8.75, *National Times,* 1.9.75. Critics' reactions towards the production were divided. Robin Prentice called the performance "a kind of adult 'kindy'" (*Nation Review,* 22.8.75); John Smythe thought it "not without contemporary significance to the inquiring mind," (*The Melbourne Times,* 22.8.75) and Garrie Hutchinson concluded: "If you are at all interested in anything theatrical or political, you cannot afford to miss it." (*The Australian,* 20.8.75).

¹⁵ Personal interview, 26.10.98. A similar, non-reverential, attitude is apparent in the APG's agenda from 1972, entitled "Why are we here?": "Political reasons. The state of the nation is about as rotten as proverbial Denmark's... Theatrical reasons. Australian theater in this century has been morally bankrupt, formally obsolete, politically irrelevant and not Australian in any recognisable way." *National Times,* 6.9.81.

[16] Cf. Arthur A. Phillips, "The Cultural Cringe," *Meanjin* 9.4 (Melbourne: University of Melbourne, 1950): 299–302.

[17] Irish playwrights exerted an influence on Australian playwrights.

[18] Exceptions were John Ellis' productions of *The Caucasian Chalk Circle* and *Mother Courage* in collaboration with Elijah Moshinsky in 1966 and 1967. Ellis remembers that one result of Moshinsky's unorthodox approach was that "within the theatre world, Moshinsky's work was seen by many as precocious" at a time when "any classic, including modern classics, were seen in reverential terms," Personal Interview, 27.3.00.

[19] John McCallum, *Some Preoccupations in Australian Theatre Criticism from 1955 to 1978* (M.A. Thesis, University of NSW, 1981), 141.

[20] Some reviewers stressed the formal aspect; they associated "naturalism" with the "well made play" and they saw the play as a character study with a psychologically motivated dramatic development. Others emphasized the content; in this case, "naturalism" meant the aim to represent "authentic" Australian life on stage. Frequently, the qualities of "truth" and "humanness" were also associated with naturalism. Of general importance was that the Australian vernacular and accent could be heard on stage.

[21] John McCallum explains that it was often implied in reviews "that it is compassion which is the mechanism by which fully-rounded characters are made interesting on stage." John McCallum (1981), 158, 161.

[22] In *Meanjin* (Melbourne: University of Melbourne, 1958), 300–307. For the German original see Bertolt Brecht, *Schriften 2 (1933–1942)*, ed. Werner Hecht et al. *Werke. Große kommentierte Berliner und Frankfurter Ausgabe*, vol. 22.2 (Berlin / Frankfurt/M., Aufbau / Suhrkamp, 1993), 106–16, hereafter GBA.

[23] In 1958, two amateur productions could be seen at the University of Melbourne: *Mother Courage* was performed in German at the Department of Germanic Languages and *The Caucasian Chalk Circle* was played in English by the Marlowe Society.

[24] "Theatre for Learning," 302; underlined by me.

[25] "What man should do / His drives," "What man can do / his motives." My translation. Another important omission is that of "Theatre for Pleasure" in the title. As the essay is quoted by reviewers under this title right from the start and even Willett does not restore it to its full length, the shortened title probably contributed to the prejudice that Brecht's theater is didactic and boring without trying to entertain the audience.

[26] "Theatre for Pleasure or Theatre for Instruction," 71, in John Willett, ed., *Brecht on Theatre. The Development of an Aesthetics* (London: Methuen, 1964), 69–77.

[27] Carol Martin and Henry Bial, eds., *Brecht Sourcebook* (London: Routledge, 2000), 23–30. This publication does not refer to the article's publication in *Meanjin* but to its reprint in *TDR* in 1961, 6, no.1.

[28] *National Times*, 2.7.73.

[29] Geoffrey Hutton, *It Won't Last a Week! The First Twenty Years of the Melbourne Theatre Company* (Melbourne: Sun Books, 1975), 75.

[30] This is illustrated by the continuing success of plays by Australian playwright David Williamson on the mainstream stage.

[31] *The Age*, 5.7.58. In the article, Cherry pointed out the merits of "Brecht's Theatre in East Berlin."

[32] *The Age*, 5.7.58.

[33] Programme notes.

[34] Programme notes.

[35] Cf. Robert K. Barnhart, ed., *The Barnhart Dictionary of Etymology* (New York: H.W.Wilson, 1988), 1184.

[36] Cf. H.G. Kippax (about Douglas Stewart's *Ned Kelly*): "Here all the birds in the bush of the 'Australianist' legend come home to roost — the underdog and his fight against society (...)" 15, in Harry G. Kippax, "Introduction," in *Three Australian Plays* (Melbourne: Penguin, 1963), 7–21.

[37] Dennis Carroll, *Australian Contemporary Drama* (Sydney: Currency, 1995), 4.

[38] Australian comedian Rod Quantock noted: "I get very nostalgic and angry and depressed. (...) We are losing a lot of things: mateship, egalitarianism, then there's the fact that 30 per cent of Australians live on or below the poverty line." *The Age*, 10.6.98.

[39] Harry G. Kippax, "Introduction."

[40] Margaret Lee, in *The Age*, 27.6.98; see also J.R.L. Bernard et al., eds., *The Macquarie Dictionary*, 3rd ed. (Macquarie University: The Macquarie Library, 1997), 2299: "the loser or expected loser in a competitive situation, fight etc." and Judy Pearsall, ed., *The New Oxford Dictionary of English* (Oxford: Clarendon, 1998), 2014: "a competitor thought to have little chance of winning a fight or combat."

[41] Judy Pearsall, (1998), 2014.

[42] Australian playwright Daniel Keene considers Australia "basically a blue-collar country, no matter how much people like to think we aren't" and writes his plays about "poor people," *The Melbourne Review*, 15.11.95.

[43] *The Age* Theatre Critic (no name given), *The Age*, 10.1.59.

[44] Carl Weber, "'Wie ein Schoßhund domestiziert.' Bertolt Brecht im amerikanischen Theater," *drive b. Theater der Zeit / Brecht Yearbook* (1997), 60–62: "Der Regisseur Peter Sellars spottet, daß 'Brecht wie ein Schoßhund domes-

tiziert worden sei,' und daß 'die Aufführungen bestenfalls die Fabel zeigen und kaum mehr.'"

[45] John Willett, "Brecht's *Threepenny Opera* at the Adelaide Festival Centre," *Theatre Quarterly* 7.26 (1977): 101–110. This article is one of the rare resources documenting in writing the challenges which theater practitioners faced when producing Brecht rather than the critics' reactions. The introduction to the article, however, records the year of Cherry's first production wrongly as 1956. For Willett's influence on the Australian reception of Brecht, cf. my doctoral thesis on *The Australian Reception Of Austrian, German And Swiss Drama: Productions And Reviews Between 1945 And 1996* (Monash University 2000).

[46] For his production at the Old Tote, the precursor of the STC, Sharman adapted *The Threepenny Opera* to the Australian depression.

[47] The Anzac myth, whose name derived from the initials of the Australian and New Zealand Army Corps, "rests upon the assumption that Australia 'came of age' as a nations when the Anzacs landed on Gallipoli on 25 April 1915," in Jan Bassett, *The Concise Oxford Dictionary of Australian History* (Melbourne: Oxford University, 1994), 8.

[48] About a fortnight before rehearsals began, the Liberal and Country Parties decided to block the budget of Whitlam's government. Willett described in his casebook how Malcolm Fraser, the leader of the opposition, tried to blackmail Whitlam into holding a general election, which Fraser would win according to the polls. Willett commented: "But by the time the budget had been referred back to the Senate for the third time (...) public opinion had swung against him [Fraser] and the polls started to favour Labor. Who let Fraser off this hook? Who else but the Governor General (...)." John Willett (1977), 108.

[49] Cf. the original: [Peachum] "Und darum wird, weil wir's gut mit euch meinen / Jetzt der reitende Bote des Königs erscheinen." (...) [Chor] "Horch, wer kommt! / Des Königs reitender Bote kommt!" (...) [Frau Peachum] "So wendet alles sich am End zum Glück. So leicht und fröhlich wäre unser Leben, wenn die reitenden Boten des Königs immer kämen." in Bertolt Brecht, *Stücke 2*, GBA 2 (1988): 307–8.

[50] *The Australian*, 11.12.75.

[51] John Willett (1977), 110; italics by Willett.

[52] John Willett (1977), 104. If this resulted in a distinguished British accent prevailing in the performance, Brecht's intentional use of social and regional variations of language must have lost its effect, indeed. Yet, the Australian accent would have been very suitable for rendering subtle meanings because it is characterized by "a colourful sense of language and a splendid accent which can be used either to point up class barriers or to cross them" as Cherry noted later on, in Wal Cherry (1979), 14.

[53] John Willett (1977), 110.

[54] *The Australian*, 11.12.75.

[55] McCaughey staged *Baal* in 1977 in the Back Theatre of the Pram Factory, its only Australian performance so far. Cherry had already directed *The Seven Deadly Sins* for New Opera in South Australia before directing this version of *Fear and Misery of the Third Reich*. Innovative impulses also came from the APG. In 1978, the group arranged readings of *The Days of the Commune* and in the same year they presented texts and songs from *Man is Man* and from *The Threepenny Opera*.

[56] Cf. Klaus Völker, (1990), 66.

[57] Robert Page and Lucy Wagner, "List of Brecht Productions," *Theatre Australia* 3, no. 11 (1979): 15.

[58] Esslin was in Sydney to direct a staged reading of Günter Grass' play. It is noteworthy that this reading had been organized by the Goethe-Institute in Sydney and that the first doubt on Brecht's integrity was cast by Germans. The Goethe-Institute also organized a lecture by Esslin and a discussion between him and Willett.

[59] Roger Pulvers, "What is Brechtian in 1979?," *Theatre Australia* 3.11 (1979): 20. Born in America, Pulvers was living in Australia at the time.

[60] Cf. Robyn Archer, "Brecht Today: An Australian Perspective," 144, in *Brecht Then and Now, The Brecht Yearbook* 20, ed. John Willett (Waterloo: University of Wisconsin, 1995), 144–47.

[61] Roger Pulvers (1979), 20.

[62] Cf. Appendix I and II of my doctoral thesis.

[63] Roger McDonald, "Mr Humphries Short History of Australia," *The Weekend Australian*, 13.2.1999, 4–6.

[64] A production of *The Good Person of Szechwan* at the MTC in 1981 represented an exception. Its director, Bruce Myles, surprised his audiences, including critic Suzanne Spunner, because "MTC are not known for their innovative Brecht productions," *Theatre Australia*, Sept. 1981, 34.

[65] In 1989, Des Davis directed *Mother Courage* in Wollongong, a co-production with the School of Creative Arts of the local university. In 1990, Des James directed *The Threepenny Opera* in Wagga Wagga, a town of about 50, 000 people. Amongst the performances which took place outside the major theater capitals Geoff Hooke directed *The Threepenny Opera* with the Darwin Theatre Company in 1989. In the same year, *The Threepenny Opera* was also performed at the West Australian Academy of Performing Arts, directed by John Milson.

[66] Peter Fitzpatrick, *After "The Doll." Australian Drama since 1955* (Melbourne: Edward Arnold, 1979), 157; see also Leonard Radic, *The State of Play* (Ringwood: Penguin, 1991), 170. Financially, community theater was encouraged through the funding provided by the specially created Community Arts Board as part of the Australia Council; see Leonard Radic (1991), 180.

[67] Julian Meyrick, "Cutting the Fringe," 20, *The Australian's Review of Books* 4, no. 5 (June 1999): 19–27.

[68] Julian Meyrick (1999), 20.

[69] Carl Weber, "Brecht and the American Theatre," 348, in *A Bertolt Brecht Reference Companion*, ed. Siegfried Mews (Westport, Connecticut: Greenwood, 1997), 339–55.

[70] *In Press*, 16.6.93; cf. also Helen Thomson's comment: "Humphrey Bower's new translation is excellent, idiomatic without anachronistic slang, its rhythms and emphasis are just right." *The Australian*, 7.6.93.

[71] Cf. "A reassessment of the polemical playwright is overdue, says Phillips, as Brecht seems to have fallen into disrepute of late." Interview with Joyce Morgan, *The Australian*, 26.8.94.

[72] Director's note, Programme notes.

[73] *The Australian*, 9.9.94.

[74] Director's Note, Programme notes.

[75] *The Australian*, 9.9.94, *Theatre Australasia*, Oct. 94.

[76] See programme notes. The lyrics were predominantly by Brecht, but *Kabarett* also included some texts by Felix Gasbarra, Friedrich Hollaender, Erich Kästner, Joachim Ringelnatz and Kurt Tucholsky.

[77] Programme notes.

[78] See Deborah Stone, *The Age*, 20.11.98; Helen Thomson, *The Age*, 23.11.98. The performance's relevance is of even greater importance when compared to those cabaret evenings which still have a strong tendency to "romanticize" the repertoire for audiences who prefer to focus on the music with the lyrics being sung in German; see Robyn Archer (1995), 147.

[79] Barrie Kosky, *Speech at the Shakespeare Youth Festival 1999 (Sydney Seymour Centre)* (Radio National, ABC, 2000, Jan.7).

[80] For instance, Denise Varney deconstructed *The Good Person of Szechwan (Sichuan)* from a feminist postmodern point of view when staging the play in 1993 with theater students from the University of Melbourne. See Denise Varney, *Feminism and Performance: Theorising New Performance Modes for Feminist Theatre* (Doctoral Thesis, University of Melbourne, 1998).

[81] For simplicity, I shall refer to the production as "Kantor's production" while keeping in mind that it emphasized a collaborative process; see Ruby Boukabou's description in *Revolver*, 21.9.98.

[82] Personal interview, 26.10.99.

[83] Personal interview, 26.10.99.

[84] Stephen Dunne, *SMH*, 11.9.99.

[85] Personal interview, 26.10.99.

[86] Personal interview, 26.10.99.

[87] Personal interview, 26.10.99.

[88] Personal interview, 26.10.99.

[89] *The Australian*, 18.9.98.

[90] See "It is not the Australian setting which makes a play work [for Australian audiences], it is a good theatrical idea; ideas, image and sound have to resonate and mean something for an audience." Personal interview, 26.10.99. A similar approach has been used in university productions such as Rachel Fensham's and Louise Taube's *Pretty Bourgeois*, based on *The Seven Deadly Sins*. This production with students from Monash University's Department of Drama and Theatre Studies presented "a journey from 1933 (...) to the present (...), travelling to seven Meccas of the twentieth century — Paris, New York, Melbourne, London, San Francisco, Tokyo, Berlin." Course outline, semester II, 2000.

[91] In Kantor's production, eight actors played fifty eight roles. Weber quotes a similar approach advocated by Schechner. The latter notes: "Brecht is a storyteller, his plays can be done in a storytelling technique with six actors and some musicians... The plays don't need lavish production, we did *Mother Courage* with a few ropes." In Carl Weber, "Brecht and the American Theatre," (1997), 352.

[92] Kosky used the expression in Kosky (2000). See also "The Deadly Theatre," in Peter Brook, *The Empty Space* (London: Penguin, 1968), 11–46.

[93] See *Daily Telegraph*, 18.9.98, *Revolver*, 21.9.98, *Sunday Telegraph*, 20.9.98.

[94] *The Australian*, 18.9.98, *Bulletin*, 29.9.98.

[95] *SMH*, 18.9.1998.

[96] Kosky (2000).

[97] Thus Simon McBurney concludes: "When the copyright laws are over, Brecht will return to the theater more strongly than he has done since his death." in Simon McBurney, "Waiting for the End of the Copyright Laws," *drive b. Theater der Zeit / Brecht Yearbook* (1997), 30–32.

[98] Heiner Müller, "Die Form entsteht aus dem Maskieren. Ein Gespräch mit dem diesjährigen Büchner-Preisträger Heiner Müller," 88, *Theater Heute. Jahrbuch* (1985): 88–93. "When Brecht rehearsed [a play] he forgot about the text, he forgot about the play, he was then rather interested in the actors than in the text." Some scholars support their argument by quoting Heiner Müller's following comment: "Brecht gebrauchen, ohne ihn zu kritisieren, ist Verrat." Heiner Müller, "Keuner $\pm$ Fatzer," 21, in *Brecht-Jahrbuch 1980*, (Frankfurt/M.: Suhrkamp, 1981), 14–21. However, they generally ignore the context of Müller's words, and that he was referring to the betrayal of history rather than of Brecht.

See for example Elizabeth Wright, *Postmodern Brecht. A Re-Presentation* (London: Routledge, 1989), 74–76. The fact that Müller invites creative work with his texts has led to considerable interest in his plays in Australia, especially at universities.

[99] See "Einschüchterung durch die Klassizität," in Bertolt Brecht, *Schriften 3 (1942–1956)*, GBA 23 (1993): 316–18 and Brecht's response to the survey "Wie sollte man heute Klassiker spielen?" in Bertolt Brecht, *Schriften 1 (1914–1933)*, GBA 21 (1992): 182.

[100] David Malouf, "Foreword," in Helen Marion Nugent, *Securing the Future. Major Performing Arts Inquiry. Final Report* (Canberra: Department of Communications, Information Technology and the Arts, 1999), 20–21.

[101] Bertolt Brecht, *Gedichte*, GBA 14 (1993): 191.

Die Aufführung sexueller Differenz: Eine feministische Aneignung von Brecht

Dieser Aufsatz untersucht eine Aufführung der Melbourne University in 1993 von Brechts Santa Monica Fassung von *Der Gute Mensch von Sezuan*, unter dem neuen Titel, *The Good Person of Sichuan*. In der Doppelrolle als Regisseurin und Forscherin war die Schriftstellerin an der Möglichkeit im Stück interessiert, Sex und Gender ungewohnt darzustellen. Indem die weibliche Shen Te und der männliche Shui Ta zusammen als äußere Zeichen an dem Körper des Schauspielers dargestellt wurden, bot die Aufführung verschiedene Lesarten eines fließenden und formbaren Genders dar. In dieser Analyse liegt die Faszination in der Art und Weise, wie die Figur in der Aufführung die Fragestellungen über Sex, Gender und sexuelle Differenz so fließend und zweideutig personifizieren kann und dabei feministische Theorie auflädt. Für die feministischen Zusehauerinnen schlägt die Shen Te/Shui Ta Figur eher den multiplen als den fixierten Standort des Subjekts vor.

Performing Sexual Difference:
a Feminist Appropriation of Brecht

Denise Varney

Contemporary theory has a tendency to needle away at perform-ance and the critical relation between theory and practice is never more troubled than in Brechtian theatre. Brecht's play texts are inscribed with both theory and practice but they also tell of bygone times, of a belief in an intact Marxism and social progress. What are the possibilities for a Brechtian theatre to speak to current obsessions with sex and gender, postmodern pluralism and the apparent collapse of the fable as a form that speaks its times.

This article examines a Melbourne University production of Brecht's Santa Monica version of *Der Gute Mensch von Szechwan*, translated by Michael Hofmann. Given the new title, *The Good Person of Sichuan*, the translation was commissioned and staged by Deborah Warner and the National Theatre, London, in 1989. The Santa Monica version, written for the American stage during Brecht's exile, features a pared-down narrative and reduced list of characters, a feature that per-suaded Warner and Hoffmann that it was better suited to a contempo-rary audience than the longer original. While long plays are no longer fashionable, the National Theatre decision also attests to a further wan-ing of interest in the full working-out of the original texts.

The Melbourne University performance was similarly drawn to the shorter version, but it intended to use the savings in time to investigate a set of questions concerning Brecht and feminism. The piece was pre-sented as a full-scale student production in the University's theatre, The Open Stage (there had been an earlier performance of *The Good Per-son of Szechwan* in The Open Stage in 1980, directed by Sue Nevile). In the combined role of director and researcher, I was concerned with the way in which feminist theory has needled away at Brecht and how this might be played out in performance. The tension between past practice and present concerns is best understood within the broader context of the historicization, to heed Herbert Blau, of the Brechtian project for the contemporary period. One of the driving forces of the performance was the interrogation of recent feminist writings on Brecht with a view towards the revisioning of Brecht for feminism, a move I acknowledge as an appropriation, for better or worse, in the title of this essay.

New Essays on Brecht / Neue Versuche über Brecht
Maarten van Dijk et al., eds., *The Brecht Yearbook / Das Brecht-Jahrbuch*
Volume 26 (Toronto, Canada: The International Brecht Society, 2001)

The production concentrated its revisioning of Brecht for feminism on the creation of *mise en scène*. This was because any revision of the play text (even if rewriting were allowed by copyright law) runs into the problem of the tightly woven and theoretically inscribed composition that resists change. Brecht's dramaturgy continues to weigh heavily on the creative development of the plays in performance. Notwithstanding these constraints, my production was interested in how far we could stray from and derail the original text, to reposition the play within a contemporary context.

But before moving on to analyze the production, I want to take some time to set out the main lines of feminist critiques of Brecht and of the *The Good Person of Szechwan* specifically. My survey is highly selective and limited to English language essays and books. The production of *The Good Person of Sichuan* will then be positioned as a response to these critiques.

SHEN TE/SHUI TA: SEXUAL STEREOTYPING AND GENDER FLUIDITY

Brecht fell from grace in feminist circles during the 1980s when he was associated with a form of misogynist sexual stereotyping that, it was said, absented real historical women, including his female collaborators, from the master fables of history and class consciousness (Lennox 1978, Herrmann 1990, Wright 1994, 121). A consensus of sorts was reached that Brecht exhibited a typical "Marxian blind spot" towards the role of sex and gender in the social constitution of the female subject. Anne Herrmann criticized the construction of Shen Te, the prostitute with the heart of gold and soon-to-be new mother, as an instance of the persistence of the "eternal feminine" in writing that on other counts represented a new way of thinking about representation in performance. While there is no doubt about the historical facticity of a "Marxian blind spot" towards gender, this is not to say that the plays remain bound to the period and its thinking.

Following a more productive critical line, Alisa Solomon looked beyond stereotypical images of women to consider the possibilities of the Shen Te/Shui Ta figure as a critique rather than a reinforcement of conventional gendered subject-positions (1994). Soloman was not the first feminist critic to argue that the lack of critical attention on the formal elements of the plays had contributed to a misreading. I have long thought that within these kinds of critiques, there was a feminist blind spot to the productive possibilities of *Verfremdungseffekt* and *Gestus*. Solomon rightly pointed to the use of the male/female character as a representation of social contradiction as a very useful way to estrange the contradictions of the male/female binary. The critical possibilities of staging sexual difference as a representation of the wider problem of the binary opposition of male and female, man and woman, masculine and feminine challenge feminists to find the openings in the plays to stage the problematics of sexual difference. Exposing the "structurality of the structure" of these binaries, to apply Derrida's phrase, is quite different from the consideration of the male and female types represented within that frame (Derrida 1981, 278). When Herrmann wrote that Shen Te is "conceivable only in relation to the masculine," she was closer to the issue of sexual difference than she owned. (Herrmann 1990, 302). As Elin Diamond has explained,

> When the performer "plunges into visibility" (in Peggy Phelan's fine phrase), s/he enters a space that, since the 1970s, feminist theory has described as socially, culturally, and psychically predicated on sexual difference. (Diamond 1997, 151)

As the masculine is constructed on the feminine character, the possibility exists for a feminist performance to critique conventional representations of sexual difference through the demonstration of gender as a fluid and strategic theatrical performance. Rather than performing the plays as misogynist constructions, it is now possible to stage the Shen Te/Shui Ta figure as a progressive and malleable figure and to play with the theatrical possibilities this suggests. Despite the political and historical formation of the plays, the example of *The Good Person of Sichuan* will demonstrate that the plays are open to a range of feminist possibilities.

THE GOOD PERSON OF SICHUAN AND THE ESTRANGEMENT OF GENDER

One of the possibilities involved historicizing Brecht, turning his own techniques of estrangement and distantiation against the assumptions that underpinned the original theory and practice.

To this end, we claimed "the good woman" as a feminist subject and turned much of the *mise en scène* into a feminine space. Appropriating masculine dialogue for the feminine subject, female actors played the three gods and Wang the Waterseller as well as other minor characters. Our fictional Sichuan was a postmodern space that was severed from its orientalist past and released from the onus of representing Brecht's critique of capitalism and Christianity. The ideological unity of Brecht's fable was ruptured by a visual text composed of objects from different historical periods, modes of production and social control. Neon signs and moody dark lighting attempted to re-inscribe the text with the techniques of postmodern theatre and mark the distance between tradition and the contemporary.

In terms of the unspoken dialogue, that which Patrice Pavis refers to as the "discourse of the *mise en scène*" (Pavis 1992, 34), the re-inscription of the play text began by revising the situation of enunciation for the verbal text. Whereas in the text Shen Te makes her first appearance halfway through the Prologue, in my production her first appearance is brought forward to the opening moments of the play.

DESCRIPTION OF THE OPENING MOMENTS OF THE PERFORMANCE

As Wang begins to speak, a female performer enters wearing a pair of black loose cotton trousers and a loose-fitting red satin blouse. The performer's long hair is tied back in a ponytail and make-up is minimal. She is barefoot and carries a pair of grubby white high-heeled shoes. A plastic feminine facemask hangs around her neck. The performer stops slightly upstage of Wang and places the shoes at her feet. She then puts on the mask and becomes the dramatic character Shen Te. Once she puts on the mask, she makes her presence known to Wang whose recognition of her as Shen Te assists in the establishment of the character's identity. As if to confirm the moment, Wang offers Shen Te some water from a cup. Shen Te accepts the cup but rather than drinking from it, tips the water over her dirty feet and washes them with her hands. Wang tells her about the gods and how they are expected any minute. Her feet clean after a fashion, Shen Te puts on her high-heeled shoes. The putting on of the shoes, and a *gestic* change in demeanor, marks the beginning of another character layer — the performer plays Shen Te who now plays the part of the prostitute. As other characters such as the Carpenter and the Gentleman enter, Shen Te, not wanting to be seen out on the street, slips away. She conceals herself from view with her hand as she crosses and exits behind the plastic that lines the stage left and right performance space walls.

When a female actor plays a female character, the estrangement of gender (here femininity) is problematic given the iconicity between actor and character. Whereas in the text, the difference or distance between the performer's female body and the male character she plays is clear, the text does not imagine the showing of the distance. Instead, the Brechtian text turns a blind eye to the iconicity between the performer's body and the female character, with the effect that embedded in a work of epic theatre is the kind of mimetic representation more often found in the dramatic theatre that Brecht criticized. If this is followed, as in conventional performances of the play, the feminine remains an unexamined body.

In my production, the female performer is distanced from the character through a number of devices. First, there is the much-quoted Brechtian estrangement device of the half-face mask. But here the mask draws attention to the performance of the feminine rather than, as in the more traditional performances, the estrangement between actor and character. Furthermore, traditional performances of *The Good Person of Szechwan* use the mask to show the masculine character. In this production, the distancing effect of the mask is aimed at the iconicity between the female performer and the female character she plays. In addi-

Figure 1. Shen Te with Wang the Waterseller. Open Stage, Melbourne, 1993.

tion to interrupting the seamless continuity between performer and character, the mask represents a heightened femininity, a deliberate adoption of the role. The high cheek-bones, the high-arched and fine eyebrows, the smooth plastic surface, neat nose and red lips of the mask parody and enlarge idealized femininity, the femininity most often associated with masculine desire (*fig. 1*).

The mask is a concretization of the Irigarayan notion of playing the feminine as a "playful repetition" (Irigaray 1985, 76). Making the signs of femininity visible is another aspect of *Verfremdung* in so far as the latter foregrounds aspects of language, gesture and tone which normally blend into the background. Shen Te's mask makes the signs of femininity visible. It shows femininity as a plastic "man-made" surface to be put on and taken off by the performer. The performer plays with the mask, touches it, adjusts it and wears it for the spectator. Her playfulness gives her control of the image, taking away her historical subordination as female dramatic character. The mask also shows femininity as a surface without a correlating interior. It draws attention to the signs of gender inscribed on its surface and to the distance between it and the body that manipulates it.

The performer demonstrates self-inscription — she stands, as a subject herself, in the space marked by performance and demonstrates the putting on of the mask of gender, the adoption of a sexual identity. She writes her own body into the performance and erases it under the mask. The representational system at work in the performance space absents natural subjects and replaces them with theatricalized signs.

The distancing of the performer from her own gender employs the mask in a way that was not originally intended by Brecht, but neither is it precluded by the dramatic theory or the play texts. The more traditional Brechtian performances use mask to mark the distance or difference between the performer's and the character's social attitudes. My production argues that if Shui Ta is an impersonation, a male character placed on a female body, then so is Shen Te an impersonation, a female character placed on a female actor. This was not to suggest that underneath the mask is Judith Butler's shibboleth, the pregendered "person," but to show that gender, like class, is not outside "the political and cultural intersections in which it is invariably produced and maintained" (Butler 1990, 3).

In the text, the female body is represented as unruly and unreliable. Shen Te throws herself into Yang Sun's arms in a *storm of emotion*, gets pregnant, feels dizzy and cries out in despair. Shen Te's female body gets wet in the park and succumbs to her biological destiny. From the dramatic text it is possible that in the case of Shen Te:

> Female sexuality and women's powers of reproduction are the defining (cultural) characteristics of women, and, at the same time, these very functions render women vulnerable, in need of protection or special treatment,

as variously prescribed by patriarchy. (Grosz 1994, 14)

Yet it is at the moment of Shen Te's self-definition through the discovery of her powers of reproduction, that the female character subverts the cultural inscriptions of frailty. The female actor's body, meanwhile, does not get wet in the park and does not get pregnant, feel dizzy or grow fat. The consciously-controlled female body of the actor shows that unruliness and frailty is not the defining characteristic of femaleness. Rather, it is a casting decision as to how frail or robust the Shen Te character will appear on stage.

PERFORMING SEXUAL DIFFERENCE: SHEN TE/SHUI TA

The second change to the dramatic text involved the Shen Te/Shui Ta transition. In the text, Shen Te exits at the end of Scene 1 and returns after an Interlude to begin Scene 2 dressed as Shui Ta, who is described in the text as a young gentleman dressed in a mask and suit. It is not necessarily apparent to the audience that Shui Ta is Shen Te; this is not revealed until The Song of the Defenselessness of the Gods and the Good. By Scene 7, the prosperous Shui Ta is expensively dressed and fat/pregnant (*fig. 2*).

In a move against the tradition of a complete costume change for Shui Ta, the suit was discarded in favor of an overcoat. The coat was made visible in the space from the beginning of the performance hanging on a coat-hanger in the downstage left area of the space. A pair of men's shoes was placed on the floor underneath an old man's herringbone coat that had seen better days on a much larger man and that hung loosely around the female performer's body. Hanging on the suspended coat-hanger, and visible to the spectators from the moment they entered the space, the coat carried a load of signification that was less easily definable than a businessman's suit, the sign *par excellence* of the modern masculine subject. The overcoat belongs to the streets, it conceals what is underneath; the suit belongs to bourgeois social and economic spaces and is associated with respectability, power and authority. In opting for the more ambiguous signifier of the overcoat, the performance emphasized male power as something that moves in public space but remains concealed (*fig. 3*). At the same time, however, placed on the double sign, the only partially concealed body of the female performer and the character of Shen Te, the masculine is defamiliarized and disempowered. On her body, male power is a surface, the performance of an attitude backed by hastily adopted representational systems, which give it credibility.

The pockets of the coat held a mask and a microphone (*fig. 4*). The mask was not the conventional theatrical half-face with moustache, but a surgical pressure-mask worn by burn patients (*fig. 5*). The pressure-mask bore no immediate relation to the coat, with the effect that the

Figure 2: Conventional
figuration of Shui Ta.
Open Stage, Melbourne.
1980.

Figure 3: Shui Ta and overcoat. 1993.

Shui Ta figure was a montage of unrelated signs whose only unity was their placement on the one body. The performer's body visually linked unrelated objects, disturbing the expectation that dramatic costume is a coherent signifier of socially stable dramatic character. The pressure-mask evoked the burnt body: the body whose surface is made up of grafts, a surface made of fragments and held on by a tight material-surface. The effect also suggested the balaclava of the terrorist or criminal, the comically "terrifying" mask of the wrestler, the executioner's hood and the head of the cyber body. It had a criminal, comic, sinister and monstrous look. In performance, the mask exceeded these connotations and initiated its own dramatic trajectory. As a sign it was characterized by its lack of closure.

At the end of Scene 1, during the Interlude and in preparation for the entry of Shui Ta in Scene 2, the performer puts on the coat, the shoes, the mask and the microphone in full view of the spectator. The cross-dressed figure of Shen Te/Shui Ta is an incomplete transition. It is a shabby and decrepit version of Shui Ta. There is no transformation of one character into another, only imperfect and shabby theatricality. Diamond suggests that the cross-dressed figure that is "not quite perfect" heightens the critique of gender norms (Diamond 1997, 46).

The incomplete cross-dressing of Shui Ta foregrounds gender, shifts the focus away from the drama of the class-struggle. It continues through to the representation of a number of characters. The bourgeois Man and Woman, who cross the stage in the Prelude, blur the boundaries of the masculine and feminine through their costumes and accessories. The man wears a pin-stripe suit, but neither a shirt nor a tie. Instead, he wears a woman's pearl necklace. The Woman wears a man's dark suit and a pink woman's hat. The incomplete cross-dressing plays with gender codes drawing attention away from the representation of social types based on class (*fig. 6*). The effect is to show that masculine and feminine identities are alterable, and not fastened onto a sexed body. Elin Diamond theorizes that the estrangement of sex and gender in cross-dressing theatricalizses gender. Demonstrating gender through a citation of stylized acts, cross-dressing critiques the way in which the "dominant culture understands [gestures, appearances etc.] as indices of feminine and masculine identity" (Diamond 1997, 46). Within *The Good Person of Sichuan*, the other characters perform a "mode of belief" (Butler 1990, 271) in the incomplete cross-dressing, and the spectator views that belief for what it is — a performance, an agreement and a kind of contract between stage and auditorium.

The performance of gender is foregrounded with astonishing clarity in the "Song of the Defenselessness of the Gods and the Good." Solomon argues that the song is the "theatrical crux" of the play in which the dialectic of "things as they are and, at the same time, as other than they are" is most forcefully presented. She asks:

Figure 4: Shui Ta with mask and microphone with Yang Sun. 1993.

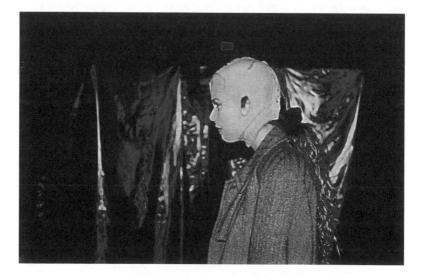

Figure 5: Shui Ta. 1993

> Who sings this song? That is, what stage persona commits the action of —
> in Brecht's words — zeigen gestus ("handing over") "The Song of Defense-
> lessness"? (Solomon 1994, 44)

Solomon's answer draws attention to the actor's demonstration of how she performs both Shui Ta and Shen Te in the performance. The song calls for the actor to show "Shen Te *playing* Shui Ta," invoking the "Not-But" element of the *Verfremdungseffekt*, as the performer not only plays Shen Te, but also Shui Ta. In this sense, the *Verfremdungseffekt* is inscribed in the play, as a product of the writing process, an inescapable element of performing the part.

In the performance, Shen Te begins the song in her own voice and, as she sings, puts on Shui Ta's coat and the shoes. She takes a few steps, puts on his mask and the microphone and carries on singing in a voice that is marked as "his" by the amplification. The spectator sees the cross-dressing take place and is simultaneously made aware of its social context. Crucial to the demonstration is that it is not accompanied by a change in subjectivity. The words of the song betray no shift from a female to a male perspective. Nor does the music alter its rhythm or tempo to mark the transition from female to male. It is only in the following scene in the Tobacco Shop that Shui Ta's language and point of view differ from Shen Te's.

Solomon had shifted the focus of feminist debates about the play from the dramatic text, on which much early criticism is based, onto the performance. The metatheatrical element in the Song is crucial to the creation of *Verfremdungseffekt* through the *Gestus* of showing. And it is through this showing, as Solomon points out, that we see Shui Ta as an invention or "impersonation" performed by Shen Te, and Shen Te, in turn, as an impersonation performed by the actor. Through this tripartite model, neither Shen Te nor Shui Ta has a relation to the real.

This reveals, ironically, that Brecht (himself/themselves) had already set up the possibility for the estrangement of gender. The text provides the impossible situation that induces Shen Te to take a desperate measure. The solution is *gestic*: Shen Te disguises herself as her male cousin Shui Ta and disappears. As the fable unfolds, invisibility protects Shen Te and improves her prospects, but it also complicates matters, particularly as the male body begins to display ambiguous markings — is it fat or pregnant? In addition, the invisible subject is always in danger of being heard and audible female sobs finally point to her concealed presence. Shen Te is a female character who attempts to "unmark" herself as feminine in order to improve her prospects in the world. Her performance as feminine is marked with goodness and kindness, that are exposed as "sucker values" within the inverted moral climate of Brecht's capitalist society. These are the imperatives from which she seeks escape. Peggy Phelan has written of the relative value of bodies marked as feminine and masculine:

> The male is marked with value; the female is unmarked, lacking measured value and meaning....He is the norm and therefore unremarkable; as the Other, it is she whom he marks. (Phelan 1993, 5)

Phelan goes on to argue that there is, nevertheless, power in being unmarked, that visibility can be a trap. Shen Te learnt this lesson well. Phelan cautions against the assumption that visibility is the starting-point for political action. There are times, she says, when it is better for the disenfranchised to remain invisible, although this should not be a long-term strategy. Visibility attracts unwanted attention: "it summons surveillance and the law; it provokes voyeurism, fetishism, the colonial/imperial appetite for possession" (1993, 6). As a prostitute, Shen Te's visibility invoked all these incursions. In the performance, as soon as the citizens of Sichuan enter, Shen Te averts her gaze, covers her face and goes indoors because her visibility is not free but for sale. Invisibility becomes, for her, a form of resistance. The binary of "the power of visibility and the impotency of invisibility" is shown to be false because it rests on the assumption that visual representation has truth value. *The Good Person of Sichuan* allows, through the contradictory operations of the Shen Te/Shui Ta double, for a disturbance of the notion that visual representation has truth-value.

These examples point to the way the Shen Te/Shui Ta character offers multiple reading possibilities. One of these is that as a female playing a male, gender is shown to be a social and cultural inscription. Using gender as the position from which the performer distances herself from the dramatic character subverts the Brechtian imperative that the class war provides the grounds for distantiation. But no sooner has this subversion been affected, than the ground shifts again. Shen Te/Shui Ta's gender, like gender itself, is a far less stable point than the old class-based binary of ruler and ruled. The Shen Te/Shui Ta character is gendered as a binary, but she is also differentiated within, producing, in the process, another reading of sexual difference. Theoretically, Shui Ta is the concretization of the view that gender is a cultural and social construction grafted onto the body, and on that view a *Gestus* revealing the social formation of gender. It is also a concretization of sexual difference within the subject itself, an actualization as Diamond argues, of the "Not-But" aspect of *Verfremdungseffekt* applied to sexual difference. Shen Te/Shui Ta embodies sexual difference, not as the difference between the two characters, but as sexual difference within the one performing body. In performance, the body of the performer — its sexual identity, its gender, its subject position — shifts before the spectator's eyes, suggesting a fluidity within the sexual identity of the subject itself.

This is what makes the Shen Te/Shui Ta character suitable for feminist performance. On this analysis, it is of no consequence whether, as separate characters, Shen Te and Shui Ta represent sexual stereotypes.

The fascination is with the way in which the character in performance can be seen to embody, so ambiguously and fluidly, the questions of sex, gender and sexual difference that energize feminist theory. For the feminist spectator, the Shen Te/Shui Ta figure suggests the multiple rather than the fixed subject-position.

Elin Diamond writes of the political potential of theories of difference and recuperates Brecht, through the "Not-But," for a politics of sexual difference:

> Keeping differences in view instead of conforming to stable representations of identity, and *linking those differences to a possible politics* are key to Brecht's theory of the "not...but," a feature of alienated acting that I read intertextually with the heterotopia of difference. (Diamond 1997, 48)

The notion of the "Not-But" ensures that the meaning of each action contains difference that always undermines the authority of the visible or present on stage. Shen Te as Shui Ta points to and conceals the feminine as a site of difference from the masculine, but also shows the shifting point between visibility and invisibility of the feminine and the masculine and the spaces between those two poles. It is a shifting point within Brecht's theory that has the potential to deconstruct its phallogo-centric basis from within and open it up to a more fluid politics.

My production was enlivened by the fact that performance is always in a position to mark the historical distance between the time of its writing and its staging. Brecht was historically positioned in a masculine world, but he was also positioned in a world that was different on a number of political, aesthetic and theoretical fronts. Brecht himself expected dramaturgy to change with history so that critique could keep up with changing circumstances:

> The epic theatre is chiefly interested in the attitudes which people adopt towards one another, wherever they are socio-historically significant (typical). (Brecht 1984, 86)

The attitude that Brecht as a social subject adopted to other subjects (women) becomes eminently suitable material for epic theatre today. Brecht's notion of "the historicizing theatre" allows for the interrogation of every piece of action, including his own, for its historical significance. The discursive and material construction of the categories of sex and gender was not made visible in his play texts. These categories were not, in Brecht's time, widely understood as discursive systems with a different history and set of practices from the class war. Despite that, the treatment and use of sexual difference in the play is ambiguous, open and both within and outside the economic frame. *The Good Person of Sichuan* is significant today because it represents capitalism's contradictions in terms of sexual difference.

Figure 6: The Gentleman and Woman. Prologue. 1993.

Play Texts

Brecht, Bertolt. 1987. *The Good Person of Szechwan*. Trans. John Willett. London: Methuen.

————. 1989. *The Good Person of Sichuan*. Trans. Michael Hofmann. London: Methuen.

Articles and Books

Brecht, Bertolt. 1984. *Brecht on Theatre*. Ed. & trans. John Willett. London: Methuen.

Butler, Judith. 1990a. *Gender Trouble: Feminism and the Subversion of Identity*. London & New York: Routledge.

Case, Sue-Ellen. 1983. "Brecht and Women: Homosexuality and the Mother." In *The Brecht Yearbook,* vol.12.

Derrida, Jacques. 1981. *Writing and Difference.* London and Hanley: Routlege & Keegan Paul.

Diamond, Elin. 1997. *Unmaking Mimesis: Essays on Feminism and Theatre.* London & New York: Routledge.

Fuegi, John, Gisela Bahr and John Willett. 1987. *The Brecht Yearbook,* vol. 13. Detroit: Wayne State University Press.

Grosz, Elizabeth. 1990. "Inscriptions and body-maps: representations and the corporeal." In *Feminine/Masculine/Representation.* Ed. Terry Threadgold and Anne Cranny-Francis. Sydney: Allen & Unwin.

———. 1994. *Volatile Bodies: Toward a Corporeal Feminism.* London: Routledge.

Herrmann, Anne. 1990. "Travesty and Transgression." In *Performing Feminisms: Feminist Critical Theory and Theatre.* Ed. Sue-Ellen Case. Baltimore, Md.: John Hopkins University Press.

Irigaray, Luce. 1985. *This Sex Which Is Not One.* Trans. Porter, C. Ithaca & New York: Cornell University Press.

Kebir, Sabine.1989. *Ein akzeptabler Mann? Brecht und die Frauen.* Köln: Pahl-Rugenstein.

Lennox, Sara. 1978. "Women in Brecht's Works." *New German Critique.* No.14. Spring.

Lug, Sieglinde. 1984. "The 'Good' Woman Demystified." *Communications from the International Brecht Society.* Vol.14 (1), Nov.

Pavis, Patrice. 1992. *Theatre at the Crossroads of Culture.* Trans. Loren Kruger. London & New York: Routledge.

Phelan, Peggy. 1993. *Unmarked: the Politics of Performance.* London & New York: Routledge.

Solomon, Alisa. 1994. "Materialist Girl: *The Good Person of Szechwan* and Making Gender Strange" *Theater.* Vol.25. No. 2.

———. 1997. *Re-Dressing the Canon: Essays on Theatre and Gender.* London and New York: Routledge.

Tabbert-Jones, Gudrun. 1995. "The Construction of the Sexist and Exploiter Bertolt Brecht." In *Brecht Then and Now. The Brecht Yearbook,* vol. 20. University of Wisconsin Press.

Willett, John. 1967. *The Theatre of Bertolt Brecht .* London: Methuen.

Wright, Elizabeth. 1994. "The Good Person of Szechwan: Discourse of a Masquerade." In *The Cambridge Companion to Brecht.* Ed. Peter Thomson & Glendyr Sachs. Cambridge: Cambridge University Press.

Performances cited

The Good Person of Sichuan. 1989. National Theatre, London. Trans. M. Hofmann. Dir. Deborah Warner. Des. Sue Blane. Fiona Shaw as Shen Te.

———. 1993. The Open Stage, University of Melbourne. Dir. Denise Varney. Des. Norman Price.

The Good Person of Szechwan. 1980. The Open Stage, University of Melbourne. Dir. Sue Nevile.

„Gestische Masken in Brechts Theater: Ein Zeugnis der Widersprüche und Parameter einer Realismusästhetik"

Brechts Haltung zum Realismus förderte eine reiche Verbindung gegensätzlicher Stile und Annäherungen, die ein Austausch zwischen Konkretheit und Abstraktion, Natürlichkeit und Stilisierung, Buchstäblichkeit und nicht buchstäblicher Mimesis ermöglichten. Ergänzend zu der Untersuchung jener Verbindung, verfolgt dieser Aufsatz den oft übersehenen Punkt, wie Brechts Realismus die gestischen Experimente der TheaterpraktikerInnen, insbesondere der SchauspielerInnen, umschrieb. Neben der Folgeleistung in der Unterdrückung der Formen, die, so glaubte Brecht, *nicht* zu der intelligiblen Erklärung der Realität dienen konnte, wird seine populistische Bevorzugung spielerischer deiktischer, lakonischer und lesbarer Stile analysiert. Die Untersuchung der stilistischen Umgrenzungen wird anhand einer Konzentrierung auf Gestus unternommen, ein Hauptvehikel seiner realistischen Haltung. Gestus in ihrer historischen Ausübung wird dann mit einer Studie über Brechts Gebrauch von Masken, die insbesondere auf die Archivforschung des vom in 1953 Berliner Ensemble aufgeführte Stück *Der Kaukasische Kreidekreis* beruht, beispielhaft erläutert.

Gestic Masks in Brecht's Theater:
A Testimony to the Contradictions
and Parameters of a Realist Aesthetic

Meg Mumford

Time and again Brecht's socialist theater has been celebrated as a balance of contradictory artistic tendencies, of avant-garde and realist or of experimental and popularist art forms.[1] One of the reasons for this emphasis is that within his historical context Brecht seemed to offer an exemplary and rare union of politically "popular" and avant-garde artistic trends.[2] A campaigner against the stultifying aspects of the Soviet socialist realist aesthetic, he has been acclaimed for having inspired experimentation amongst his literary successors in the former GDR.[3] Brecht's vigorous defense of artistic experimentation and the transformative use of even styles and forms belonging to conservative traditions was closely allied with his realist interventionist attitude. However, I would argue that insufficient attention has been given to the way that same attitude circumscribed the performer's experimental gesture in both Brecht's theorizing and his practice. My contention is that the circumscription of experimentation was brought about by a conflicting popularist insistence on the concrete and *intelligible* explication of reality and the "non-transformability" of some forms for that purpose. Without detracting from the celebration of Brecht's theater as a unique and rich unity of diverse forms, the following discussion also considers the way his popular realist union of oppositions — concreteness and abstraction, naturalness and stylization, literal and non-literal mimesis[4] — was a synthesis which rested on the suppression of some experimental styles and approaches.

John Fuegi has already pointed out that Brecht's theater practice involved a contradictory play between the two ends of the mimesis continuum, a mode he characterizes as the mixed mimetic style.[5] However, Fuegi dissociates this mode from Brecht's realism, describing it instead as an idiosyncratic trademark of a theater genius, a constant feature of all Brecht's work, even that of the pre-Marxist period.[6] By contrast, I would suggest that Brecht's realist attitude is a major determinant of style in Brecht's theater and that there is a continuity between Brecht's pre-Marxist and Marxist-inspired realism. This connection is manifest in the recurring phenomenon of the artistic defamiliarization of social reality through the juxtaposition of literal mimesis and non-

New Essays on Brecht / Neue Versuche über Brecht
Maarten van Dijk et al., eds., *The Brecht Yearbook / Das Brecht-Jahrbuch*
Volume 26 (Toronto, Canada: The International Brecht Society, 2001)

literal distortion. To point to a continuity in Brecht's attitude towards art and reality is not to blur the distinctions between his early and later realism, not least of which is the shift in Brecht's understanding of social actuality as it began to embrace the analytical research of the "new sciences," Marxism in particular. Rather, to recognize the continuity of not only style but *attitude* between Brecht's pre-Marxist and post-1926 work is to affirm a connection between his realist approach to art and his stylistic preferences.

A further limitation of Fuegi's analysis is the way it confines itself to eulogizing the contradictory style as "a "self-reflexive" mimetic mode well suited to twentieth-century experimentation both in the arts and in the sciences."[7] Of the few critics who have considered the stylistic nature of performance in Brecht's theater, most have lauded its experimental nature, stressing the fact that Brecht "encouraged the use of a wide variety of performance techniques," both on paper and in practice.[8] Ernst Schumacher's comparisons of Brechtian acting with Asian forms of performance, by contrast, constitute one of the few investigations of the stylistic parameters of Brecht's realism. Schumacher claims that gestures "aimed at making a social gesture conspicuous" and which serve a "mainly socially critical "enlightening'" function have to remain "closely related to *mimesis*, the imitation of "real life," the direction towards naturalness."[9] While Schumacher somewhat neglects the play between literal and non-literal mimesis in Brecht's work, his suggestion that even the stylized gesture in Brecht's theater must relate analogically and legibly back to familiar social behavior was a source of inspiration for this paper's investigation of the boundaries of gestural experimentation.

The nature and parameters of Brecht's realist aesthetic is here approached via a focus on "gestus," a key performance concept and technique which, as I will argue, is a major vehicle of Brecht's realist agenda. Gestus entails the aesthetic gestural presentation of the socioeconomic and ideological construction of human identity and interaction. Here "gesture" denotes the corporeal movements, positions and vocal activities of the performer/character's body and quasi-gestural extensions such as costumes, make-up, props and masks out of which the gestus is constituted. In accordance with Brecht's frequent usage, the term "gestic" (the adjectival version of "gestus") henceforth will be employed to denote performance oriented around the externalization of socially significant attitudes and comportments rather than simply "gestural" performance. By "significant" Brecht meant those humans and events which are most decisive for the developmental processes of society, for socialism and the progress of humankind rather than simply the most frequently occurring or strikingly visible and obvious.[10] In order to exemplify gestic practice, I have chosen to focus on Brecht's use of masks, particularly in the Berliner Ensemble's 1953 version of

The Caucasian Chalk Circle which employed masks in a fashion unprecedented in Brecht's career. Not only does the historical reconstruction of Brecht's practical work with masks, based on original archive research, provide a necessary supplement to Schumacher's analysis of mainly theories and play texts, but it memorably demonstrates Brecht's interest in the externalization of the socially significant, that is, in the creation of gestus. In addition, mask work constitutes one of the most overtly stylized aspects of Brecht's approach to performance and, as such, lends itself to an examination of the nature of formal experimentation in his theater.

REALISM AND GESTUS: CONCRETE AND ENABLING ABSTRACTION

A *Haltung* and its Artistic Realization

B recht was keen to assert that realism was a Marxist revolutionary *Haltung* not a particular style.[11] The term *Haltung*, which Darko Suvin has described as a "fruitful polysemy or pun meaning bearing, stance, attitude, posture, behavior, and also poise or self-control"[12] was used by Brecht to signify both attitude (mental and emotional responses) and comportment (full bodily expression of social bearing and position-taking). *Haltung* is intimately related to Brecht's concept of gestus in that it frequently appears in discussions of what a gestus is intended to demonstrate. In "A Short Organum for the Theatre," gestus is described as the fusion of *Haltung* and social relations:

> The realm of *Haltungen* adopted by the characters toward one another is what we call the gestic realm. Bodily disposition/attitudes [*Körperhaltung*], tone of voice, and facial expression are all determined by a social "Gestus': the characters curse, compliment, instruct one another, and so on.[13]

Elsewhere gestus is more clearly distinguished from *Haltung* as a term which is not only sociological in orientation but an aesthetic reference to an *artistic display* of social behavior. For example, in "Short Description of a New Technique of Acting which Produces a *Verfremdungseffekt*," Brecht described gestus as "the facial [*mimische*] and gestural expression of the social relationships prevailing between people of a given period" and the working out of scenes "in which people behave in such a way that the social laws under which they are acting are made visible."[14] In his comments on the New York performance of *The Mother*, Brecht stressed that the gestus, "purely aesthetically speaking," had to be carefully selected so that it was "significant and typical."[15] "On Gestic Music," one of Brecht's fullest explications of the concept, illustrates the creative nature of this selection process when it gives the example of how a gestic artist is one who turns a simple reflex action, like a defensive attitude towards a dog, into an episode which reveals the battle an ill-clad person has to wage against watch dogs.[16] Thus gestus refers not only to human behavior in general but to the artistic practice of selecting, defamiliarizing and showing significant *Haltungen* in order to create a vivid embodiment of social causality.

Brecht's pronouncements on gestus demonstrate how that concept was underpinned by his realist *Haltung*, by his political and philosophical attitude towards both the world and the function of art. That attitude was a socially critical interventionist one which by the late 1930s was in accordance with the theories of historical and dialectical materialism. As an historical materialist, the realist was involved in the class struggle on behalf of the proletariat:

> Realistic means: revealing the causal complex of society/ unmasking the ruling view points as the views of the rulers/ writing from the standpoint of the class which has the most wide-ranging solutions ready for the most pressing difficulties in which human society is caught/ emphasizing the element of development/ concrete and enabling abstraction.[17]

The realist's strategic task was to further the proletarian cause by defying the false pictures manufactured by the ruling class.[18] With the aid of the new sciences — sociology, Marxist economics and behaviorist psychology — the causal nexus underpinning capitalist society was to be exposed and revealed as controllable.[19] As a dialectical materialist, the realist was also to present reality in its contradictory complexity.[20] Brecht argued that a realist practitioner should be able to employ whatever forms are useful for the illumination of social contradictions.[21] He campaigned vigorously against any attempts to define realism in terms of a single form, criticizing Georg Lukács's exclusive promotion of organicist nineteenth-century bourgeois realism and his parallel disdain for avant-garde art. Brecht condemned Lukács's exaltation of bourgeois realism as "formalist" and presented the counter-notion of a realism "wide and political, sovereign over all conventions."[22]

Although Brecht was keen to point out that realism was a matter of *Haltung* rather than style, the components of this attitude obviously have stylistic implications. For example, in his definition of "realistic," quoted above, Brecht mentions that realist art must be *concrete and enable abstraction*. In his discussion of Brecht's realism, Ritter suggests that this combination of the concrete and abstraction are related to and can be illuminated through a Brechtian pairing which has a more direct connection with aesthetics, that of "naturalness" and "stylization."[23] Brecht described the activity of stylization as the turning of an actor's work into art and the "bringing out" and intensification of the "natural." The purpose of stylization was to demonstrate to the public what is socially important in the depicted fable.[24] Realistic stylization, then, is an artistic version of scientific abstraction and a type of V-effect which involves the defamiliarizing demonstration of significant episodes and segments. The structural implications of abstraction are interruptive theater, one characterized by a series of frame-like gestures and gestural complexes (tableaux and episodes) which interrupt and retard the action, giving the spectators an opportunity to intervene mentally in the stage events by allowing time and space to reflect between each gestural segment. The framed segments also point to their own constructedness, standing for the artistic choice of sections of reality, and thereby draw the spectator's attention to the production of meaning and constructed/re-constructable nature of the social world.[25] The sensual implication of abstraction is theater which preserves and artistically intensifies the "natural."

In a discussion of the type of stylization which preserves the "naturalness of gestures and intonations," Brecht gives as an example Weigel's performance of the protagonist's bread-baking activity in his Spanish Civil War play *Señora Carrar's Rifles*, interestingly one of the least avant-garde and most naturalistic of his works. Brecht explains that when Weigel shows the bread-baking she presents it as something particular and absolutely "untransportable," the bread-baking of Señora Carrar on the evening her son is shot (by fascists as he is fishing in the village harbor). Brecht goes on to describe the bread-baking as bringing much together, including: the baking of the last loaf, protest against another activity — like fighting, and its function as the clock for the course of events — Carrar's transformation from a pacifist to an armed republican revolutionary takes as long as it does for a loaf of bread to be baked sufficiently.[26] The type of stylization approved here involves the selection and isolation of one mundane gestural complex which is socially significant insofar as Carrar's bread-baking highlights her domestic role as contributor to the material needs of her family, forced to live at subsistence level as members of a fishing community torn apart by war. The domestic bread-baking also exposes her neutral pacifist attitude, helping to embody the way she turns her back on the violent revolutionary activity in which her husband was fatally involved, focusing solely on home and hearth instead. In the context of a fascist onslaught, her pacifist *Haltung* jeopardizes her ability to fulfill both her domestic role and the historical struggle of all impoverished workers for a better world. Through its combination of socially significant gestural complexes and artistic condensation (for example, Carrar's transformation is contained within the short period it takes to bake the loaf) the realist stylization process produces a historical gestus.

Although Brecht does not directly explain in what sense Weigel's showing of the bread-baking preserves "naturalness" it is apparent that such a performance entails a degree of imitation if not "literal mimesis," i.e. a tendency towards verisimilitude. In the opening of the article paragraph on "Style and Naturalness" which immediately precedes the bread-baking example, Brecht appears to equate "naturalness" with the socio-historically specific particular and "earth-bound."[27] By "earth-bound" I mean identifiably or recognizably connected to carefully observed phenomenal reality. Naturalness is also closely connected with both the contradictory flux of life and the concrete:

> The naturalness of the gestures and intonations must not be lost during the process of selection. It is not a matter of stylization. In the case of stylization gesture and intonation "mean something" (Fear, Pride, Pity, etc.). A gestus that is brought about through such stylization reduces the flux of reactions and actions of the characters to a series of rigid symbols. What results is a type of script with script characters of a very abstract nature and the portrayal of human behavior becomes schematic and lacks concreteness.[28]

To exclude naturalness (through a *non-realistic* form of stylization) is to reduce both "the flux of reactions and actions" and the concreteness of the portrayal. Through the examination of the artistic vehicle of concreteness — naturalness — it becomes evident that Brecht regarded the concrete not only as an actual substance or thing, any material expression, but as pertaining to realities or actual instances which are not only socio-historically specific but maintain the contradictory flux of the real.[29] Here he appears to add to the common usage of the term "concrete" ideas drawn from Hegel's conceptualization of the concrete as a "unity of differences" and Marx's definition of the concrete as "the concentration of many determinations, hence unity of the diverse."[30] Rather than supplying a one-sided abstract image, withdrawn from its context of inter-connection and inter-dependence with other things,[31] the process of abstraction was to highlight the concrete, the socio-historical specificity and contradictoriness of the natural.

The bread-baking maintains concreteness in that it preserves the carefully observed actions of a particular historical figure while also generating a unity of contradictions, such as that between Carrar's desire to provide for her family and the pacifist neutral stance which nullifies her very ability to do so. Brecht argued that it was important to make depictions as concrete as possible, for this made it easier for the spectator to adopt the attitude of one who makes analytical comparisons: "Lear behaves in such and such a way, do I?"[32] Although the "Style and Naturalness" paragraph with its bread-baking example illustrates the role of naturalness and its connection to the concrete more so than the process of stylization and its link with abstraction, some aspects of the latter — the process of selection, isolation, condensation — are suggested. One formal implication of the naturalness/stylization interplay is the resultant combination of literal and non-literal mimetic gestures. Non-literal mimesis, the opposite extreme of the mimetic continuum, involves the playful re-presentation of the original, its defamiliarizing distortion.

From Brecht's description of the realist's *Haltung* it is obvious that the purpose of providing art which is concrete and enables abstraction is to benefit the cause of the people, the oppressed proletariat in particular. In other words, the realist's art should also be "popular." As he had done in the case of realism, Brecht defined "popular" art as distinguished by its allegiance to a political *Haltung* rather than a particular set of styles.[33] Popular art not only represented the view point of the revolutionary proletariat but strengthened and corrected its stance. In order to do so it adopted and transformed the traditional art forms of the oppressed. However, this did not mean that the popular artist was restricted to popular traditions. Theoretically any forms, new or old, popular or avant-garde, could be utilized for the revolutionary purpose.[34] However, only those forms which fulfilled both the celebratory *and* the pedagogical ends could be considered. This limited the range of possibilities to the types which would both appeal to the proletariat's *Verstand* ("reason," "intellect") and be *Verständlich* ("comprehensible, intelligible").[35] Preferred models included the playfully deictic and laconic styles of the street ballad-singers and fair performer, the legible miming of circus and silent-cinema clowns and the externalizing style of Asian theaters. By "intelligible" Brecht did not mean "simplistic" but "as simple as possible, as intelligible as possible" given the complexity of contemporary subjects.[36] His version of realism prioritized not only *concrete* but lucid and deictic or *intelligible* expressions.

GESTUS AND THE REALIST *HALTUNG*

Before exploring further the stylistic implications of Brecht's realism, it is necessary to explore in greater detail how gestus relates to the realist framework. Gestus embodies both the realist *Haltung* and its formal implications. The gestic performer is a realist in that s/he exposes underlying structures and ideologies of social reality and their changeability. A gestus is at once concrete and the product of abstraction. Concreteness is ensured in that closely observed, contradictory and historically specific comportments are imitated. The process of abstraction is the isolation and gestic magnification, through retardation, exaggeration, and so on, of the comportment's socially significant features. In one of his short philosophical Meti works on human behavior, one which describes the development of a new gestic language, Brecht writes that it is precisely the illumination of *Haltungen* which leads to the desirable simultaneity of naturalness and stylization.[37] Art oriented around the gestus gives rise simultaneously to literal mimesis and gestural experimentation. As Terry Eagleton cogently observes, this is because the defamiliarization of social reality depends on the simultaneous positing and subverting of the solid anterior existence of that reality.[38] In addition, the gestus of showing — the performer's clear demonstration that s/he is a performer and one who critically re-presents the behavior of an historical character and/or who critically narrates historical events — which Brecht regarded as the most fundamental *Haltung* of the actor,[39] is the playful moment of making *intelligible*.

The relation between Brecht's realist notion of art and the gestic practice can be clarified through a concrete example (pun intended). As Ritter points out, Brecht's essay "Expanse and Variety of the Realistic Style of Writing" from 1938 contains an analysis of a poem which usefully demonstrates the relation between realism and gestic practice. The poem under analysis is Percy Bysshe Shelley's "The Mask of Anarchy." Although the poem was written more than a century before Brecht constructed his realist aesthetic, he praises it as a realist piece of writing for the following reasons:

> So we follow the procession of anarchy towards London and see great symbolic images and know at every line that here reality is given its chance to speak. Here not only was Murder called by its proper name but also that which called itself Law and Order was unmasked as Anarchy and Crime. *And this "symbolic" style of writing did not at all hinder Shelley from being very concrete. His flight did not lift itself too high above the earth.* [italics added][40]

At the level of *Haltung* the poem is both realistic and gestic in that it unveils the oppressive mechanisms of the status quo. Written after the Peterloo Massacre in Manchester in August 1819, a brutality instigated by drunken militiamen in the service of the conservative Tory government, the separate verses portray Murder, Fraud, Hypocrisy and Anarchy as costumed in the masks of statesmen of the day. The depiction of Murder is as follows:

> II
> I met Murder on the way -
> He had a mask like Castlereagh -
> Very smooth he looked, yet grim;
> Seven blood-hounds followed him:
>
> III
> All were fat; and well they might
> Be in admirable plight,
> For one by one, and two by two,
> He tossed them human hearts to chew
> Which from his wide cloak he drew.[41]

In terms of style the poem exemplifies the relation between the concrete particular and the moment of abstraction. Concreteness is ensured in several ways: the use of actual statesmen's names and distinctive features and acts associated with them; the inclusion of social practices such as the bloodsport involving hunters and hounds; and, in verses not given above, references to historical facts such as high infant mortality in the early nineteenth century. The illumination of social contradictions, through the showing of a conflict between the leaders' actions and their leadership roles, also ensures the concreteness of the poem.[42] The concrete particulars are then estranged, via the abstraction and stylization process, in this case through metaphorical devices which forge disturbing connections. For example, the face of the British Foreign Secretary and leader of the Tories, Robert Stewart Castlereagh, is likened to the deceptive mask worn by Murder. Statesman, misguiding appearances and the grim reaper find themselves inextricably linked. The metaphorical *Haltungen* and gestures selected for the Murder figure, such as the tossing of human hearts to a retinue of fat bloodhounds, link the power gestures of the ruling class with the oppression of the faceless multitude.[43] One of the poem's central abstraction techniques is the subversion of the structural device central to religious allegories and morality plays: instead of finding suitable embodiments for teaching spiritual or moral concepts, Shelley removes concepts such as Murder and Fraud from the pedestal of the abstract and reveals them as the material attitudes and actions of historical leaders.

The abstraction of historically significant comportments is a gestic technique. Two other notable abstraction devices in the poem are equally typical of Brecht's gestic practice. Firstly, there is the element of framing and isolating, structural features which arise from the frame-like quality of gesture, the discrete entity Walter Benjamin has posited as central to Brecht's interruptive theater.[44] The overall structure of Shelley's poem consists of the linking together of small scenes, each a framed picture or separate gesture of social attitudes and relations, which together constitute a fable about the procession of power from Manchester to London. And secondly, the poem is oriented around the exposure of *Grundhaltungen*, basic or fundamental attitudes/comportments. The *Grundhaltung* of the society described is captured through the metaphor of mask-wearing: the gestus of deception and ignorance. The poem's narrator figure combats this *Haltung* through critical and interventionist commentary: the gestus of unmasking. In reflection the poem, hailed by Brecht as realist synthesis of the concrete and symbolic, is in effect gestic. Significantly, what Brecht emphasizes as praiseworthy about Shelley's combination of symbolism and the concrete is not only the interplay between the two but the way the artistic flight does not "lift itself too high above the earth." Ritter interprets the latter comment as an approval of Shelley's realist *Haltung*. While the poem may seem to distance itself from reality through the artifice of mask metaphors and other such symbols, it is actually directly concerned with reality.[45] But Brecht's comment also illuminates the parameters of the realist gestic *style*: the artistically stylized must be drawn from and visibly refer back to the concrete events and *Haltungen* which constitute reality.

THE CONTRADICTORY REALIST AESTHETIC

Multiple Forms of Artistic Experimentation

B recht's insistence on artistic freedom stems from his perception of the political function of art: the revelation of social reality and its changeability through the enlightening and pleasurable manipulation of form. For a realist it was important to highlight and adapt to changes which had taken place in society by responding with new techniques: "Petroleum resists the five-act form."[46] The stylistic means were thus variable according to the dictates of time and place.[47] The "realistic" nature of a form was also historically relative. A realistic form of the nineteenth century, one which influenced and was influenced by that context, would probably not prove realistic in the twentieth century.[48] By employing new techniques the realist not only reflected historical change but provided a model for revolutionary experimental praxis by showing how reality could be altered through artistic shaping.[49] The artistic shaping, however, had to be oriented around practical ends:

> Art does not become unrealistic when it alters proportions but when it changes these in such a way that the audience, if they were to make practical use of the portrayals for insights and impulses, would founder in reality.[50]

In other words, the introduction of aesthetic experimentation into the theater was one prerequisite for the audience's transformation into social experimenters and activists.[51]

In his criteria for experimental theater Brecht stressed not only uniqueness and historical relevance but variety. He believed it was imperative that socialist realism should employ many types of acting, for if it remained one style it would become monotonous, satisfy too few needs and, consequently, die out.[52] Not only the revolutionary introduction of unique and varied forms but the sensually pleasing nature of artistic mastery was crucial to the interventionist:

> The theatre has delicate colors, pleasant and significant grouping, original gesticulation, in short, it has *style* at it disposal, it has humor, fantasy and wisdom in order to master the ugly.[53]

Gestic experimentation had revolutionary power in that it testified to humankind's transformative powers while simultaneously engaging the spectator in a pleasurable experimental process.

As a practitioner Brecht was an eclectic who revelled in stylistic multiplicity. His own work combined a great variety of formal influences which he made his own — ranging from Chinese acting techniques to the Bible, from the poetry of Villon to that of Kipling.[54] He once characterized his play output during the exile period as "abnormally disunified in every way," encompassing ceaselessly changing genres: biography, "gestarium," parable, character comedy in the folk vein and historical farce.[55] Brecht defended avant-garde techniques, such as the inner monologue and montage, and his own magpie collection of varied genres and styles by claiming that it was not the technique itself which was crucial so much as the way it was utilized:[56]

> In the theatre reality can be portrayed in factual and in fantastical forms. The actors may not use make-up — or hardly any — and claim to be "absolutely natural," and yet everything can be a swindle; or they can wear masks of a grotesque kind and present the truth.[57]

What Brecht seems to be arguing is the autonomy of artistic forms from ideology. That is, the form or technique — the "natural" or the grotesque masks — should not be regarded as the direct expression of an ideology nor as permanently tied to their current uses. Old forms could be transformed for progressive purposes.

Suppressed and Prioritized Forms

It is the issue of autonomy of form which provides the key to the tension within Brecht's realist aesthetic. For alongside upholding autonomy and experimentation, Brecht maintained that form and ideological content were closely interconnected. In some cases he tended to regard form and content as inseparable and to classify certain modes of representation, or the technical devices which constituted them, as narrowly partisan distortions of reality. That is, as irretrievably bound to undesirable conservative and mystifying uses. Such forms could never serve the realist task of revealing social causality.[58]

The desire to harmonize content and form is reiterated throughout Brecht's writings.[59] In the case of the bourgeois realists upheld by Lukács, Brecht maintained that it would be difficult for socialist authors to appropriate any techniques from nineteenth-century realism as these techniques were bound to an ideological tendency. He insisted that new content, such as the proletarian standpoint, simply could not be squeezed into a bourgeois method of representation.[60] In a similar vein he claimed that the V-effects in Chinese theater were not "transportable" as they were tied to a theater whose conception of society was false.[61] Nevertheless, he did manage to appropriate techniques, such as empathy and presentational styles of acting, from both bourgeois and Chinese theater. Some critics have attempted to explain this contradiction, between indivisible unity of form and content and transportability of technique, by interpreting Brecht as meaning that the contextual features of a technique which form part of its content, the aims of the artist and the historical situation which comes to bear on it, remain connected to the technique only when the unity between form and content is preserved.[62] The upshot of this argument is, presumably, that once a technique or form is separated out from its original context it can receive new contextual features better suited to contemporary socialist needs. However, this explanation does not account for the fact that Brecht rejected some forms because, regardless of aims or situations, they could never meet the criteria of concreteness and intelligibility.

A theoretical statement on signs and symbols from 1936 sheds further light on the nature of such forms. Here certain types of symbolism are described as "empty" and "dangerous" because they do not provide any "levers for reorganization," by which Brecht seems to mean that they do not present the world as re-constructable. One clarifying example he provides is the symbolic use, in Ernst Krenek's "scenic cantata" The Fortress (1924), of a fortress to represent a factory. What Brecht disliked about this symbolism was the way the fortress was supposed to symbolize all factories, irrespective of historical place or situation, and that the fortress should remain the same throughout the different scenes. This type of symbolism was empty and dangerous because it presented mankind as "governed by a few ideas or by basic drives of an eternal nature."[63] The "few ideas" reduce the factory to a non-contradictory entity, unaffected by historical context and therefore, unchangeable. As a dialectical materialist the realist would have to avoid such schematic non-dialectical stylizations at all costs.[64] They simply did not accommodate the concrete.

In the example Brecht provides of a realist scenographer's vision of a factory, he describes socially significant iconic and indexical signs.[65] Brecht is keen to emphasize that the signs used by the realist scenographer are not "mathematical symbols" or "abstractions" but authentic second-hand objects which display the traces of history and social functions.[66] If a factory were to be depicted by a realist, relevant iconic signs might include a gateway and a trolley which the workers can use during their breakfast break. The gateway and trolley are also indexical signs and metonyms in that they signify the factory through contiguity.[67] These signs must also be a "realistic reference to the environment of the people of the drama" and one which "gives information about the social processes which are in operation and those which should be initiated."[68] In the case of the factory, Brecht points out that the social process which can be revealed and changed is the contradiction between production and exploitation. Gestic signs which might serve this purpose include: wage lists, a photo of the factory owner, a page from a product catalogue, and one of those magazine-type propaganda photos where workers dressed in their Sunday best are shown posing in a spanking new canteen, an image underlined by the caption "Our Workers In The Breakfast Break." The interaction of the signs, such as the juxtaposing of workers forced to use the trolley as a place to rest and the propaganda canteen photo, makes the display of the contradiction between production and exploitation even more concrete.

Brecht's reticence about some Futurist art forms also shows that concreteness involved not only preserving the socio-historical and dialectical features of social reality but the maintenance of a recognizable connection to that reality. In a brief discussion of a Futurist art piece titled "Portrait of Lenin," the artistic distortion is criticized precisely because this connection is not maintained. The sculptural portrait Brecht describes consisted of a large cucumber placed on top of a large cube. Both objects were painted red. Brecht interprets the portrait in a somewhat po-faced manner, possibly unaware of or irritated by its humorous playfulness, as an attempt to depict Lenin as unlike anything which had ever yet been seen and to erase everything from the "bad old days." What he pinpoints as the shortcoming of the portrait is that it simply did not remind the spectator of Lenin at all. The result was an abstract symbol which totally removed any similarity or physical connection between sign and object. Brecht qualifies his statement by explaining that an image bearing greater resemblance to Lenin would prove equally unsuitable if it were unable to remind the viewer of Lenin's style of fighting.[69] To criticize the cucumber-cube portrait is not to affirm naturalist literal mimesis. Nevertheless, some identifiable similarity between the gesture and the object it refers to must be maintained.

Brecht's utilitarian approach to art forms also excluded abstract and formalist art. In the article "On Non-Representational Art" written in the late 1930s, Brecht characterized such art as a ruling class attempt to veil social truth. He regarded the abstract mixing of lines and colors, as making "things" unrecognizable and as generating vague, imprecise feelings. A painting of an obscure red object might make someone cry because they think of a rose, and others will respond to it with tears because they think of a child lacerated by air bombs and streaming with blood, he observed. In Brecht's eyes the abstract red object serves no social purpose as it neither reveals specific social problems nor arouses specific emotions, such as anger at injustice, which would precipitate solutions. He characterized abstract art, which emphasized the material quality of its signs rather than making its social meaning intelligible, as formalist.[70] While the aesthetics espoused by Marx recognized in art an element of self-purpose, a celebration of the productive human capacity for playful material activity,[71] Brecht presented art which revels in form as a ruling class tool for diverting attention away from the social function of art.[72] The over-emphasis on the pleasures of form in the theater also signalled an underlying vacuous content and was to be viewed as symptomatic of decadent ruling class.[73] A gestic theater which emphasized the clarifying presentation of the social gist could not embrace formalist and abstract forms.

Parallels can be drawn between Brecht's hostility to purely formal experimentation and Lukács's anti-formalist rejection of avant-garde art as decadent. The points of overlap between their distinct models of realism can be explained in terms of a shared historical setting and mutual Marxist concerns. Both developed their theories of realist art during the thirties in the context of the rise of fascism in Europe and of the cultural policies of the Comintern's Popular Front period. Brecht's anti-formalism can be related to the anti-fascist and Popular Front arguments that modernist trends in literature reflected an irrationalism which in turn could be identified with fascism. Although Brecht campaigned against the indiscriminate and stifling repression of modernist art, suggesting instead that some could be transformatively utilized, he shared Lukács's uneasiness about any forms which might obfuscate the connections between ideology, economics and social history.[74] Fredric Jameson attempts to explain Brecht's response to art as "a historical or generational accident" which simply spells out "the limits of Brecht's personal tastes."[75] However, while the response is indeed socio-historically specific it illuminates not simply Brecht's personal tastes but the boundaries of his realist political agenda.

In summary, it is the realist insistence on the concrete and intelligible concretization of social actuality which provides the parameters of the revolutionary experimentation. Brecht's version of realism does offer a politically valuable alternative to the model promoted by Lukács. It is an alternative which encourages innovation in the shape of multiple genres and styles, deliberate self-reflexive theatricality instead of photographic superficiality, transformative utilizations of old styles, the mixing of avant-garde and popular forms, beauty in groupings and framed gestures and suggestive metonymic images. However, the realist agenda which encourages the experimental impulse is also the source of its circumscription. In Brecht's realist art the process of abstraction must not only stem from but refer back to the concrete. What characterizes some of the forms which Brecht rejects is the way the process of abstraction is emphasized at the expense of the concrete. Hence the fortress-factory, cucumber and cube "Portrait of Lenin," and the abstract painting of an obscure red object are regarded with wariness. The preferred forms and signs are those which maintain an homologous relation to the object or event they depict, such as Shelley's fantastical presentation of the masked figures, the factory trolley and propaganda photograph, and Weigel's display of Señora Carrar's bread-baking gestures. The political underpinnings of Brecht's realism are also embodied in the emphasis on the legible. The complexly simple, laconic and deictic forms of popular art, from ballad-singers to clowns, are suitable means for a revolutionary pedagogy which does not fly too high above the earth.

GESTIC MASKS: STYLIZED NATURALNESS

Masks and the Display of *Haltung*

B recht's theorizing about realism promotes a form of art characterized by an interplay between an interconnected series of binary
opposites: concreteness and abstraction, naturalness and stylization,
imitative literal mimesis and experimental non-literal mimesis. According to Brecht's description of gestic art as the illumination of *Haltungen*
leading to the simultaneity of naturalness and stylization, gestus is a
concept and technique which vividly embodies the interplay of such
opposites. It has been my contention that the illumination of *Haltungen*, in accordance with Brecht's popular realist criteria of concreteness
and intelligibility, circumscribes the play of non-literal mimesis. In the
following section I argue that the same interplay and circumscription of
that interplay is apparent not only in Brecht's theory but also in his
mask-work, especially at the Berliner Ensemble. One of the most vivid
manifestations of the extent to which Brecht's theater practice was oriented around the realist presentation of *Haltungen* is the prevalence of
the mask. Potentially an ideal vehicle for gestus, the mask is capable of
a vivid stylization of social inscription and comportment. The nature of
Brecht's masks and the way he encouraged the actors to use them
clearly demonstrate the extent to which gestic performance *practice*
was governed by the realist principle of a stylized naturalness, both
concrete and intelligible.

Here the term "masks" is used to denote either coverings worn over
the face or an alteration to the face and head by means of make-up and
special effects. Masks are frequently used to conceal the identity of the
wearer and replace it with a disguise. Brecht employs them in this fashion insofar as he conceals, partially or fully, the actor's own face, turning it into a *tabula rasa* ready to be inscribed upon. The masks form
part of Brecht's shift from what he called the *"mimische* principle" to
the "gestic principle," a shift he regarded as crucial to the realization of
gestus.[76] As Ritter notes, the shift involves the rejection of a "cultivation
of psychological conflicts" and their direct expression through facial
expression.[77] Here the term *"mimische"* does not mean simply "mimetic" so much as an entire tradition of psychological realist theater.
Brecht's criticism of that tradition is most fully expressed in a fragment
from *Der Messingkauf* dialogues:

> The art of *Mimik* [facial expressions] was given a tremendous boost when
> playwrights constructed long, tranquil, soulful acts and you could get good
> opera-glasses from the manufacturers. Faces had a lot going on in them in
> those days; they became the mirror of the soul, which meant that they had
> to be held very still, so that *Gestik* [gesticulation] dried up. It was all a mat-
> ter of feelings; the body was just a container for the soul.[78]

That Brecht associated the emphasis on facial expression with psychologizing is suggested by the way later in the fragment he attributes the emphasis to "the Russian school," meaning the Stanislavskian proponents of psychological realism. What the passage quoted also highlights is Brecht's rejection of a hierarchical *Mimik/Gestik* dichotomy in which facial expression of the soul occurs at the expense of gesticulation. Brecht's theater tended instead to reinstate and intensify *Gestik*.

This reversal can be related to Brecht's interest in the communicative model of gesture as a socially encoded expression, an interest manifest in his description of gestures as "the habits and customs of the body."[79] The latter are the embodiment of routinized behavior derived from a particular social background. As such they are much more visible traces of socio-economic inscription than facial expressions of the soul. The *Mimik/Gestik* reversal is also attributable to the close relation between *Gestik* and gestus in Brecht's theorizing. In accordance with conventional usage in the German language, Brecht often used gestus and *Gestik* interchangeably.[80] When Brecht sought to differentiate the two, he described gestus as an artistic and ideological selection and combination of gestures.[81] One rehearsal technique for developing the gestus (or gestural complexes) was the wearing of a facial mask in order better to concentrate on the selection and execution of non-facial gestures.[82]

Perhaps the central function of masks in Brecht's realist theater can be described as an inversion of the more common usage: demonstrative "unmasking" rather than concealment. They are the perfect tools for the deictic gestus of showing as they constantly draw attention to the fact that the actor is involved in a theatrical re-presentation. However, the realm of the re-presentable is circumscribed by the dictates of criticizing social reality. Animal, mythical or fantastical masks rarely appeared on Brecht's stage, which focused instead on amplifying social roles and class-determined behavior.

It is when Brecht began to establish his Marxist approach to theater that the mask becomes particularly prevalent on his stage. Prior to 1926, on the rare occasion that the mask appears, it has functions easily transferable to gestic theater. In *Edward II*, for example, the white-face mask of the soldiers who hang Gaveston serves the purpose of social commentary, insofar as it shows that the soldiers are the exploited henchmen of the status quo who submit out of habit, fear and exhaustion to the powers that be.[83] In *Man is Man*, premiered in 1926, four different masks are used to display Galy Gay's progression through different social identity phases according to the pressures of his environment.[84] When Brecht directed the play in 1931, in order to indicate that the other soldiers in the fable had been reduced to fighting machines, he gave them a type of mask based on grotesque distortions of certain facial features. The gestus of monstrous inhumanity was further

enhanced by equipping them with outsized hands, stilts concealed by
long trousers for increasing their height and restricting mobility, and
costumes extensively draped with weaponry and caked in substances
like lime, blood and excrement.[85] This extension of mask work into
imaginatively significant costuming is testimony to the way gestic characterization encouraged formal experimentation. Yet the image also
contains evidence of a deference to the concreteness of social reality.
The soldiers' faces and language are recognizably human, and their
costumes bear a striking resemblance to the soiled uniforms of "real"
war.

The task most frequently fulfilled by masks in Brecht's theater is the
presentation of socio-economic determination and the class struggle.
For example, in the Berlin production of *Puntila and his Servant Matti*,
masks clearly differentiated the ruling from the working classes. The
feudal land-owner Puntila, senior officials and professionals like the
Provost, Attaché, Judge and Lawyer, were allocated grotesque masks
and comically regal movements. Puntila's daughter Eva remained unmasked, perhaps to suggest that the process of molding this young volatile person into a proper landowner's daughter and mistress of the
house had not been completed. The chauffeur, the working women of
Kurgela, servants on Puntila's estate and the farm laborers were unmasked and moved "normally."[86]

In *The Caucasian Chalk Circle* production in 1954 the masks also
functioned gestically to illustrate the class struggle, although Brecht
attempted to make the differentiations less schematic and more subtle.
Not only the rulers and professionals but some of the servants and soldiers linked directly to the corrupt feudal apparatus wore masks:

> I don't know whether you have noticed that even amongst the oppressed
> such rigid mask pieces are used. Some of the servants in Act I have par-
> tially rigid faces. It is important to take care that you don't suddenly arrive
> at symbols, that you don't first pursue a scheme. The entire press have
> fallen into this trap in that they have constructed a fixed scheme: rich peo-
> ple — masks, poor — none.... We don't characterize the ruling class ac-
> cording to certain types of stiffness. Although it is true — as you can ob-
> serve from films — that the ruling class does display such rigidities; but the
> oppressed also display them. The servants in particular. It is well known
> that they can look to some extent even more master-like than their masters.
> Even in their case there are these distortions, arising not from their control
> over themselves but from the strong tendency to let themselves be con-
> trolled.... There are not only two opposites, but sometimes five. The live-
> lier things are the more oppositions there are too, the more differentiated
> the less schematic.[87]

It is arguable that Brecht is merely creating a slightly more complex
schema: all those who perpetuate the manipulative exploitation of the
ruling class — masks; all those who do not directly support this per-

petuation — none. However, the attempt to re-present the complexity of the concrete is evident. To match the multiplicity of differentiations masks of all varieties were designed. The Governor, Fat Prince Kazbeki and the armored soldiers who behaved like mercenary opportunists wore almost full-size masks.[88] The Governor's wife was given only a half-mask in order to ensure that her mouth be kept free for smiling at the Adjutant, a gesture which clearly demonstrated a flirtatious relationship. However, the lower area of her face was so heavily made-up and in a complementary style that she might just as well have been wearing a full mask.[89] Brecht was keen to distinguish the professionals, such as the Advocates and Doctors from the rulers to whom they had sold themselves, by lessening the size and rigidity of their masks.[90] The servants of the feudal aristocracy received small masks, each particularized according to the behavior of its wearer.[91] The major protagonists, the servant Grusha and Azdak, the poacher turned poor people's judge, remained unmasked in order to reinforce a sense of the humaneness of these anti-ruling class rebels.[92] Though Grusha's loyal and generous fiancé Simon was also a soldier, he bore no mask, but it has been suggested that his masculine beard conveyed some of the fear-inspiring aspects of his vocational identity.[93]

The Caucasian Chalk Circle: Opulent Realistic Masks

The gestic masks in *The Caucasian Chalk Circle* greatly enhanced the theatricality of the performance in that they often encouraged presentational body language in keeping with their own stylized nature. One result was the tendency to exaggerate gestures or to eliminate small detailed and seamlessly flowing movements. At a rehearsal of the panic scene in Act One where the palace household is forced to flee when the Governor is threatened with being overthrown, Brecht incited the actors to convert their (literal) mimetic skills into those of a mime artist:

> Barbara, you get very little out of the mask. The movements must be more idiosyncratic. In order to strengthen the slave-like, the look up and the fear must be exaggerated. Everything at the moment is unfortunately rather thin. You are obviously still preoccupied with the expression that you had before. However, everything must now be more mime-like. When you are frightened it doesn't show in your eyes but rather in your outstretched hands, for example, when you are frightened about being hit.[94]

The theatrical gestures of mime appropriate for mask-work also proved an ideal tool for making *intelligible* the socio-economically determined nature of a character's behavior. The simplification and reduction of movements dictated by the masks produced similar results:

> At the rehearsals with the masks designated for a number of characters (Governor, Prince Kazbeki, the Governor's wife, the Child Bearer) it turned out that the acting style demanded very economical and appropriately

mask-like movements.... Therefore Prince Kazbeki must relinquish the continual fanning movement; he fans only at the moment when he actually really gets hot, when the Rider from the capital city arrives. Only decidedly significant gestures can be retained.[95]

The fanning signals the Prince's anxiety that his plot to murder the Governor might be revealed if the Rider brings news of the uprising led by all the princes against the Grand Duke and his Governors. The gestic mask helped make the transition from more naturalistic detail to a single telegraphic piece of business which theatrically underlined the operation of the power politics illuminated by the play.

Although Brecht regarded mechanized-style acting with skepticism,[96] the rigidity of the masks encouraged stiff jerky movements and these types of gestures proved particularly suitable for illustrating the petrifaction of the parasitic class:

To the actor playing the Fat Prince Brecht said: "Care has to be taken, because all smooth movements don't have an effect. When you pull your head across and look at the heroic Rider, you must pull it as if it is fastened to an elastic band and when you pull against the elastic band you put it out of place. Do you understand?"
"Not completely."
"It's like this: when you make a movement with the head — in the mask — it is effective not when you perform it in a relaxed fashion, but when it is carried out in a jerky, conspicuous way, against the resistance of a rubber band, so to speak."[97]

When Brecht wanted to break up the flow of events in order to defamiliarize a situation, the jerky rhythms inspired and aided by the masks were also extended to working class characters. The following instructions to an actress playing a servant in the panic scene illustrate this aspect of interruptive theater:

"The folding together of things," Brecht directed at another actress, "is now also too small a gesture. We need jerky movements and not flowing ones — and when something flows, then a lot must flow very quickly until the movements suddenly cease. And the stopping must be very sudden and abrupt. Syncopations have to be introduced. You all must now use the masks."[98]

The rehearsal with the masks illuminates how the realist agenda was aesthetically realized through the gestic principle, the isolating and intensifying of significant *Haltungen*, and the extent to which that agenda encouraged gestural experimentation.

The masks are also testimony to the realist insistence on the concrete. In productions directed by Brecht the masks presented immediately recognizable concrete human faces. Often the actor's face provides the base of the mask to which extensions are added by means of materials which recreate the texture of the human body. According to production photos of *Roundheads and Pointed Heads* performed in 1936, the masks were facial extensions. Brecht described them as 20cm in height and as depicting disfigurements of features such as the nose, ears, hair and chin.[99] In the case of the Hua figures they were accompanied by overly large hands and feet. Grotesque exaggerations rather than, say, abstract geometrical shapes prevail.[100]

The masks for the 1949 *Puntila* production came not from the world of the Surrealists but were inspired by the caricatures of social and political life drawn by Honoré Daumier and George Grosz. They were the creations of make-up rather than a fitted cover. Puntila's featured a large bald head with a few strands of hair and during rehearsal Brecht described him as resembling Genghis Khan.[101] Brecht's insistence on the concrete is captured in a *Theaterarbeit* production note which attempts to explain why the masks are not examples of symbolism:

> The theatre merely adopts a position and intensifies significant characteristics from reality, such as physiognomical deformations that occur in the case of parasites.[102]

While the masks reflect the process of stylization they retain their naturalness, their recognizable connection with the concrete.

The *Chalk Circle* masks were comparatively formalistic in that they were fitted covers, modeled in some cases on the grotesque and hyperbolic types from *Commedia dell'Arte* or Asian theater. However, the function of the masks, and the actor's attitude towards them, remained consistent with Brecht's realism in a number of ways. For a start, the masks were justified "realistically" by the play-within-the-play device. The characters of the parable do not simply appear before the audience in masks. Instead, their entrance is preceded by a prologue in which members of two kolchos villages, in the wake of World War Two, enter into a debate about the ownership of a Caucasian valley. When a decision has been reached, the delegates from the Rosa Luxembourg kolchos entertain their guests by performing an old legend, "The Chalk Circle," which they claim contains a lesson relevant to the dispute at hand. The masks together with the costumes become a practical way for the villagers to present their clarifying folklore. They are shown as both utilitarian and pleasurable products of human creativity rather than formalist emblems representing mythical forces. The prevalence of the realist emphasis on "earth-bound" imitation of *Haltungen* is to some extent reflected in the fact that the masks were considered a novelty by the Ensemble company. Brecht had never worked with actors wearing such masks. Their designer, Karl von Appen, described the actors' initial reaction when they discovered that the masks demanded different comportments and speech techniques as being one of apprehension. According to Brecht the performers, some of whom had been in the

Ensemble for more than four years when rehearsals began, had not yet developed expertise in mime-work or other necessary skills.[103] This would suggest that the company had offered practically no training in highly stylized presentational forms of acting, which may be attributable not only to the nature of actor training in the GDR but to the Ensemble's orientation around the concrete illumination of *Haltungen*.

While the masks and new acting style can be regarded as artistic extensions beyond the parameters of previous training and performances, the boundaries set by the realist agenda were still firmly in place. They surfaced in incidents such as when the actors playing the Fat Prince and his Nephew rehearsed with temporary masks found amongst a store of fairytale equipment. Brecht was greatly amused by their appearance but, despite his strong desire to satirize all parasites, he made the comment "What a pity that we can't do such a thing."[104] The fantastically absurd was out of gestic bounds. Brecht also tried to ensure that each mask was individualized and that there would be no abstractions of faces.[105] The aim was to recreate and draw attention to a type of human, as Brecht explained to the costume designer Kurt Palm:

> Most actors have been wearing make-up temporarily only on the face. Now, however, it is necessary that they apply make-up totally — to the neck and presumably also to the ears. I'm not yet quite sure about the latter, but definitely the neck. And in keeping with the complexion of the mask. Otherwise everything will be terribly artificial, that is artistic and will come close to that famous Formalism so that an impression is created that you want particularly to show that a mask has been put on, instead of the fact that you just want to show another human — with the help of a mask.... However, the difference between the man himself and the mask that he has in front of his face must not be emphasized. There was a principle whereby this [difference] was emphasized. We don't want that here; here it should be total, that is mask, face and head must be one.[106]

During the rehearsals Brecht rejected not only "art for art's sake" but the total separation of actor and character. Moreover, during his discussion with the costume designer, Brecht agreed that the masks should be manufactured in accordance with "the naturalistic principle."[107]

Some of the actors' experiments with an acting style which would complement the masks were discarded for similar reasons. In an anonymous rehearsal commentary Ekkehard Schall's attempt to find a suitable comportment for the Adjutant is criticized for its lack of realism:

> Schall obviously searches for means of expression that provide a counterweight to the portrayal with masks....He tries to stylize the gestus of the scene, which is indeed a legitimate method, but ends up in the realm of the marionette. In the same way he prunes his language. He shortens an already formed text and shows only the formula. The vivid treatment of the word is lost; instead a process of rigidification is set in motion. However,

> this leads to the death of any speech that is intended to be a lively method for getting the flow of human interaction going. At best this treatment of speech might serve as an idea for the expressionists.... In a realistically formed artwork it is in the long run simply impossible to negate life. Schall's stylization demonstrates a hostile attitude towards the realistic continuation of the scene.... In terms of effect, he has the same problem as Herr Keuner's gardener: "Good, you have the sphere, but where is the laurel?"[108]

The actor-gardener had lost sight of the concrete tree in his pursuit of an artistic form and naturalness had been sacrificed to stylization.

The interplay between naturalness and stylization in Brecht's gestic mask-work carries the traces of his realist insistence on the concrete and the process of abstraction. The defamiliarizing hyberbolic distortions of form and movement which the masks present must nonetheless retain their connection to a particular human being and its historically significant behavior. In Brecht's practice, the balance between nature and style encourages the prioritization of forms which, in accordance with his theory, are invariably concrete and deictic in nature, serving to magnify and isolate typical *Haltungen* and social relations: iconic and metonymic signs bearing some resemblance or connection to the social object, grotesque caricatures, the exaggerations of comedic and communicative (as opposed to symbolic) mime, and the segmentations and syncopated rhythms of interruptive theater. The resulting experimentation, in accordance with the gestic principle, resurrects forms suppressed in the theater of naturalism and psychological realism. However, this gestural experimentation generates its own series of suppressions, particularly of "non-transportable" styles, those seemingly bound to conservative and mystifying uses and thus incapable of ever illuminating social causality: formalist symbolism, abstract and even absurdist fairytale forms and types of mechanization which fail to accommodate the contradictory flux of the real. Gestic performers, in both theory and practice, share something in common with Shelley's masked figures — their artistic flight is a series of deictic gestures bound for earth.

NOTES

[1] See Peter Brooker, "Introduction," in *Modernism/Postmodernism*, ed. Peter Brooker (London: Longman, 1992), 28, 39; Alan Lovell, "Brecht in Britain — Lindsay Anderson," *Screen*, 16.4 (1975/76): 62–63; Stanley Mitchell, "From Shklovsky to Brecht: Some preliminary remarks towards a history of the politicisation of Russian Formalism," *Screen*, 15.2 (1974): 78. Brooker speaks of a "popular, flexible and experimental realism," one that is pluralist, democratic and open to revision then as now. Anderson describes Brecht as never refusing the pull of either side of the conflict between firstly, wanting to work for the

benefit of the mass audience, and secondly, an interest in avant-garde art and its techniques. And Mitchell upholds Brecht as combining and transcending the two main streams of revolutionary art, Russian avant-gardism of the 1920s and the realist tradition. Critics who have referred to the boundaries of experimentation, but only fleetingly include: Ronald Taylor, "Presentation II" and Fredric Jameson, "Reflections in Conclusion," in *Aesthetics and Politics,* ed. Ronald Taylor (London: NLB, 1977), 65, 198, 206.

² Taylor, "Presentation II," 66–67.

³ Brecht, 11 December 1948, *Arbeitsjournal 2*, ed. Werner Hecht (Frankfurt/M: Suhrkamp, 1973): 870; Dennis Tate, "Breadth and Diversity: Socialist Realism in the GDR," in *European Socialist Realism,* ed. Michael Scriven and Dennis Tate (Oxford: Berg, 1988), 60–73.

⁴ "Mimesis" denotes the re-presentation of nature or human behavior. While art forms at both extremes have a common base — they both involve the act of re-presenting — literal mimetic art is often referred to as "representational" and non-literal mimetic art is commonly termed "non (or even anti)-representational."

⁵ John Fuegi, *Bertolt Brecht: Chaos, According to Plan* (Cambridge: Cambridge University Press, 1987), 36.

⁶ Fuegi, 2, 36.

⁷ Fuegi, 36.

⁸ See for example, John Rouse, "Brecht and the Contradictory Actor," *Theatre Journal*, 36.1 (1984): 37.

⁹ Ernst Schumacher, "Gestic Acting in Kabuki and Gestic Acting According to Brecht," *Maske und Kothurn*, 35.2–3 (1989): 70.

¹⁰ Brecht, "Das Typische," c. 1951, in *Grosse kommentierte Berliner und Frankfurter Ausgabe* (Berlin: Aufbau and Frankfurt/M.: Suhrkamp), cited as GBA 23:141; "[Notiz zum Typischen]," January 1956, GBA 23:381.

¹¹ Brecht, 26 November 1948, in Brecht, *Arbeitsjournal* 2:863; "Die Expressionismusdebatte," summer 1938, GBA, 22.1:419; "Praktisches zur Expressionismusdebatte," 423; "Zur Formalismusdebatte," March/April 1951, GBA 23:135.

¹² Darko Suvin, "Brecht: Bearing, Pedagogy, Productivity," *Gestos* 5.10 (1990): 12.

¹³ Brecht, "Kleines Organon für das Theater," summer 1948, GBA 23:89. See Brecht, *Brecht on Theatre*, 2nd ed., trans. and ed. John Willett (London: Eyre Methuen, 1974), 198, henceforth cited as BT.

¹⁴ Brecht, "Kurze Beschreibung einer neuen Technik der Schauspielkunst, die einen Verfremdungseffekt hervorbringt," c. early 1940, GBA 22.2:646; "Über die Verwendung von Musik für ein episches Theater," 1935, GBA 22.1:157–58. See also BT, 139, 86. The translation of *mimisch(e)* varies in accordance with the linguistic context. In his version of the "Kurze Beschreibung ..." text, Willett translates *mimische* as "mimetic." This is presumably because *mimisch*

means "with reference to *Mimik*," and while *Mimik* commonly denotes facial expressions, it can also signify corporeal expressions in general. However, if Brecht had wanted specifically to mean "mimetic" he could have used the German word *mimetisch*. Elsewhere Brecht uses the phrase "*mimische* principle" to mean the principle of psychologizing and naturalizing imitation, a meaning close to "mimetic." See "Über die Verwendung von Musik für ein episches Theater," 158 and BT, 86. However, in "Kurze Beschreibung..." Brecht is describing the component parts of a gestus and therefore I would suggest that the word *mimische* simply refers to facial expression just as *gestische* here simply refers to gestural expression.

[15] Brecht, "Anmerkungen zur ‚Mutter,' 1938, GBA 24:172.

[16] Brecht, "Über gestische Musik," July/August 1937, GBA 22.1:330.

[17] Brecht, "Volkstümlichkeit und Realismus [1]," June 1938, GBA 22.1:409. Here I have drawn upon Stuart Hood's translation of Brecht's article in Taylor, 82.

[18] Brecht, "Thesen über die Organisation der Parole "Kämpferischer Realismus"," 1935, GBA 22.1:137; "Einige Gedanken zur Stanislawski-Konferenz," April 1953, GBA 23:238.

[19] Brecht, "B124" from "Der Messingkauf," c. 1942–43, GBA 22.2:792.

[20] Brecht, "Sozialistischer Realismus auf dem Theater," September 1954, GBA 23:286.

[21] Brecht, "Volkstümlichkeit und Realismus [1]," 408; "Praktisches zur Expressionismusdebatte," 422.

[22] Brecht, "Volkstümlichkeit und Realismus [1]," 408–9; see also the commentary on this article, GBA 22.2:1032.

[23] See Hans Martin Ritter for a discussion of the parallels between the two pairings in *Das gestische Prinzip* (Cologne: Prometh, 1986), 116, 120.

[24] Brecht, "Kleines Organon für das Theater," summer 1948, GBA 23:96; "Antigonemodell 1948: Vorwort," February-April 1948, GBA 25:79.

[25] See Walter Benjamin, *Versuche über Brecht*, ed. Rolf Tiedemann (Frankfurt/M.: Suhrkamp, 1966), 9–10 on Brecht's interruptive gesture-based theater and Roswitha Mueller, "Montage in Brecht," *Theatre Journal*, 39.4 (1987): 474, 483 on the constructedness of Brecht's tableaux.

[26] Brecht, "Hervorbringen des V-Effekts," c. 1938, GBA 22.1:356.

[27] Brecht, "[Über sozialistischen Realismus]," September 1954, GBA 23:287.

[28] Brecht, "Hervorbringung des V-Effekts," c. 1938, GBA 22.1:356.

[29] Brecht, "Praktisches zur Expressionismusdebatte," 422.

[30] G. W. F. Hegel, *Lectures on the History of Philosophy*, vol. 1, trans. Elisabeth S. Haldane (London: Kegan Paul, 1892): 24; Karl Marx, *Grundrisse: Founda-*

tions of the Critique of a Political Economy, trans. Martin Nicolaus (London: Penguin, 1973), 101.

[31] See Wallace's guide to Hegel's use of the terms "abstract" and "concrete" in his "Prolegomena," in G. W. F. Hegel, *The Logic of Hegel,* trans. and ed. William Wallace (Oxford: Clarendon Press, 1874), lxxiii–lxxx.

[32] Brecht, "B69" from "Der Messingkauf," c. 1939–41, GBA 22.2:743.

[33] Brecht, "Volkstümliche Literatur," summer 1938, GBA 22.1:415.

[34] Brecht, "Volkstümlichkeit und Realismus [1]," 408, 412.

[35] "Volkstümlichkeit und Realismus [1],"406; "Volkstümliche Literatur," 416; "An Walter Ulbricht," 19 March 1951, in Brecht, *Briefe* 1, ed. Günter Glaeser (Frankfurt/M.: Suhrkamp, 1981): 650.

[36] BBA 49/5-6 as quoted in BT, 270; Brecht, "Volkstümliche Literatur," 415.

[37] Brecht, "Über die gestische Sprache in der Literatur," c. 1934, GBA 18:78–79.

[38] Terry Eagleton, *Against the Grain. Essays 1975–1985* (London: Verso, 1986), 168.

[39] Brecht, "Das Zeigen muß gezeigt werden," c. 1945, GBA 15:166.

[40] Brecht, "Weite und Vielfalt der Realistischen Schreibweise," July 1938, GBA 22.1:430; Ritter, 117–19.

[41] Percy Bysshe Shelley, "The Mask of Anarchy," in Shelley, *The Poetical Works of Percy Bysshe Shelley,* ed. Harry Buxton Forman (London, 1877), 156-57; Brecht, "Weite und Vielfalt der Realistischen Schreibweise," 425–26.

[42] Ritter, 118.

[43] Castlereagh was infamous for his bloody suppression of unrest in Ireland. Here Shelley blames him for his support of Austria and the reactionary Holy Alliance in Europe. The seven bloodhounds might be a reference to the fact that in 1815 Britain joined seven other nations in agreeing to postpone final abolition of the slave trade. The pro-war advocates in Pitt's administration had also been known as the "bloodhounds." See the commentary in Percy Bysshe Shelley, *Shelley's Poetry and Prose,* eds. Donald H. Reiman and Sharon B. Powers (New York and London: Norton, 1977), 301.

[44] Benjamin, 9–10.

[45] Ritter, 119–20.

[46] Brecht, "Über Stoffe und Form," March 1929, GBA 21:303.

[47] Brecht, "Über sozialistischen Realismus," c. 1938, GBA 22.1:463; "Volkstümlichkeit und Realismus [1]," 410.

[48] Brecht, "[Über Georg Lukács]," November 1938, GBA 22.1:485–87.

[49] Brecht, "Couragemodell 1949: Realistisches Theater und Illusion," 1949, GBA 25:176.

[50] Brecht, "Kleines Organon für das Theater," 96; see also BT, 204.

[51] Brecht, "An Eric Bentley," August 1946, in Brecht, *Briefe*:532.

[52] Brecht, "Der Neubauer, Der Mittelbauer, Der Grossbauer," 1953, GBA 25: 442.

[53] Brecht, "Anmerkungen zum Volksstück," September 1940, GBA 24:296–97.

[54] Eugene Lunn, *Marxism and Modernism: An Historical Study of Lukács, Brecht, Benjamin and Adorno* (London: Verso, 1985), 121.

[55] Brecht, 24 April 1941, in Brecht, *Arbeitsjournal 1*, ed. Werner Hecht (Frankfurt/M.: Suhrkamp, 1973): 274.

[56] Brecht, "Glossen zu einer Formalistischen Realismustheorie," 1938, GBA 22.1:465.

[57] Brecht, "Volkstümlichkeit und Realismus [1]," 410; see also BT, 110.

[58] See Brecht, "Die Expressionismusdebatte," 419; "Falsche Darstellungen neuer Stücke," 1931, GBA 22.1:166–67.

[59] See, for example, Brecht, "Formalismus-Realismus," c. 1951, GBA 23:148.

[60] Brecht, "Übergang vom bürgerlichen zum sozialistischen Realismus," 1938, GBA 22.1:460.

[61] Brecht, "Verfremdungseffekte in der chinesischen Schauspielkunst," 206.

[62] Lutz Danneberg and Hans-Harald Müller, "Wissenschaftliche Philosophie und literarischer Realismus," in *Exil*, Sonderband 1 (1987): 54–55. Lunn suggests that Brecht regarded artistic forms as relatively autonomous because he categorized them as "forces of production" and hence as separate from their class or ideological uses within the "current relations of production." See Lunn, 88. Why then, did Brecht treat some forces as if they were inseparable?

[63] Brecht, "[Kennzeichen und Symbole]," autumn 1936, GBA 22.1:263; "[Die Auswahl der einzelnen Elemente]," autumn 1936/early 1937, GBA 22.1:253. In a short piece from 1951 on Caspar Neher's set design for *Puntila and his Servant Matti*, Brecht noted that the symbolist stage of the expressionists and existentialists was not useful for realistic theater because it was oriented around the expression of general ideas. See Brecht, "Caspar Nehers ,Puntila'-Bühne," 1951, GBA 24:313.

[64] Brecht, "Ist "Die heilige Johanna der Schlachthöfe" ein realistisches Werk?," May/June 1935, GBA 24:105–6. In a letter to the artist Hans Tombrock in 1940 Brecht criticized symbolism along similar lines, and stated his preference for gestic art: "You see, I don't make much of symbols, schematic rubbish that "is supposed to mean something," like the wine in the Mass. How you position your people, in what attitudes towards one another, that's what matters." Brecht, "An Hans Tombrock," c. mid-1940, in Brecht, *Briefe*, 420; see also

Brecht, *Letters 1913–1956*, trans. Ralph Manheim, ed. John Willett (New York and London: Routledge and Methuen, 1990), 328.

[65] Here I am drawing upon C. S. Peirce's sign typology as described by Keir Elam in *The Semiotics of Theatre and Drama* (London: Routledge, 1980), 21–29.

[66] Brecht, "[Die Auswahl der einzelnen Elemente]," 252–53; "Aufbau einer Rolle: Laughtons Galilei. Vorwort," 1947–8, GBA 25:19.

[67] Drawing on the work of the linguist Roman Jakobson, Elam presents the argument that "realist" modes of artistic representation are largely *metonymic* in mode while "symbolism" is primarily *metaphoric*. See Jakobson as paraphrased in Elam, 28. Brecht tends to reject those types of symbols in which the connection between signifier and object is based on flights of fancy, fixed conservative traditions and mystical visions. This is not to suggest that his theater is bereft of all symbolic signs. A theater which presents social habits and practices will necessarily incorporate symbols from everyday life, from the religious cross to the emblematic advertisement signs hung up outside shop fronts in a street. Brecht's theater also utilizes the prime example of a symbol based on an arbitrary sign-object connection: the linguistic sign. Moreover, there can be overlap between certain types of indexical and symbolic signs. Nevertheless, Brecht does tend to prefer signs which preserve either a similarity or a connection with objects of reality they refer to. See Brecht, "Die Merkmale," autumn 1936/early 1937, GBA 22.1:248–49.

[68] Brecht, "[Kennzeichen und Symbole]," 263.

[69] Brecht, "Die Expressionismusdebatte," 419.

[70] Brecht, "Über gegenstandslose Malerei," c. 1939, GBA 22.1:584–86.

[71] Lunn, 11, 21.

[72] Brecht, "Über gegenstandslose Malerei," 585.

[73] Brecht, "Formalismus-Realismus," 148.

[74] Ronald Taylor, "Presentation I," in Taylor, 10–11.

[75] Jameson, 206.

[76] Brecht, "Über die Verwendung von Musik für ein episches Theater," 158.

[77] Ritter, 18.

[78] Brecht, "B160," from *Der Messingkauf*, c. 1945, GBA 22.2:821. See also Brecht, *The Messingkauf Dialogues*, trans. and ed. John Willett (London: Methuen, 1965), 28.

[79] Brecht, "Anmerkungen zur ,Dreigroschenoper,'" 1930, GBA 24:65; "Anmerkungen zu Oper ,Aufstieg und Fall der Stadt Mahagonny,'" autumn 1930, GBA 24:77.

[80] See, for example, Brecht, "Schminke," c. 1937, GBA 14:376; „,Noch zerfleischten sich unsere Völker," from "Brief an den Schauspieler Charles Laugh-

ton, die Arbeit an dem Stück 'Leben des Galilei' betreffend," c. 1946, GBA 15:180.

[81] Brecht, „Über die Verwendung von Musik für ein episches Theater," 158; „Gestik," c. 1951, GBA 23:188.

[82] Brecht, „Hervorbringen des V-Effekts," 355.

[83] According to Walter Benjamin, Brecht had claimed that the idea of epic theater first came into his head during the Munich production of *Edward II*. During the rehearsals Brecht was having difficulties staging the battle scene. He turned to Karl Valentin for advice, asking what was the matter with the soldiers. Valentin replied "they're pale, they're scared, that's what!" Brecht added "They're tired," whereupon the soldiers' faces were thickly made up with chalk, and the style of the production was decided. See Walter Benjamin, "Conversations with Brecht," trans. Anya Bostock in Taylor, 94; Brecht mentions the incident in the incomplete fragment "B30 Der Augsburger [1]," from "Der Messingkauf," c. 1939–41, GBA 22.2:722.

[84] Brecht, „Anmerkungen zum Lustspiel ‚Mann ist Mann,'" 1931, GBA 24:45.

[85] GBA 24:45; John Fuegi, 72–73.

[86] Brecht, "Die Masken," GBA (1951), 24:313. Another instance of gestic mask work in Brecht's theater is that of Shui Ta in *The Good Person of Szechwan*. The central character Shen Te intermittently disguises herself with the aid of a mask as Shui Ta, the fictitious cousin and successful businessman she is forced to invent in order to survive in the "free" market world. The mask adds a lifeless and rigid quality to Shui Ta. It works together with the depiction of "his" ever-widening girth (actually caused by the gradual advancement of Shen Te's pregnancy) to create the gestus of parasitism, of one who feasts on the lives of others.

[87] Brecht as quoted in Joachim Tenschert, "Über die Verwendung von Masken" in *Materialien zu Brechts "Der kaukasische Kreidekreis,"* ed. Werner Hecht (Frankfurt/M.: Suhrkamp, 1966), 107–8.

[88] Hans Bunge, *Der kaukasische Kreidekreis*, diary of a production, 5 May 1954, BBA 944/105.

[89] Tenschert, 108–10.

[90] Tenschert, 107; Bunge, 20 January 1954, BBA 944/60.

[91] Tenschert, 110.

[92] Hans Bunge, *Der kaukasische Kreidekreis*, diary of a production, 31 May 1954, BBA 945/62.

[93] Alfred D. White, *Bertolt Brecht's Great Plays* (London: Macmillan, 1978), 170.

[94] Brecht as quoted in Hans Bunge, 22 May 1954, BBA 945/31.

[95] *Der kaukasische Kreidekreis*, notes, 20 May 1954, BBA 943/68-69

[96] Brecht, "Aus einem Brief an einem Schauspieler," c. 1951, GBA 23:172.

[97] Brecht as quoted in Hans Bunge, 22 May 1954, BBA 945/31–32.

[98] Bunge, 31.

[99] Brecht, „Anmerkung zu ‚Die Spitzköpfe und die Rundköpfe,'" 1936, GBA 24:218.

[100] The closest a mask in Brecht's theater came to a geometrical design appears to have been in the 1948 production of his *Antigone* adaptation. The chorus of elders carried and rhythmically banged Bacchus staves topped by identical anonymous masks that resembled the naïve brown paper-bag efforts of children with painted facial features and straw-like hair. Nevertheless, the minimum image was retained. In addition to carrying masks on staves, the actors playing the elders wore heavy make-up which was supposed to portray the devastation inflicted on the face by the custom of rulership. These facial masks were clearly intended to magnify through realist exaggeration the corporeal inscription of hierarchical power relations. See Brecht, "Antigonemodell 1948: Vorwort," 80, and "Antigonemodell 1948," GBA 25:121–23, 160.

[101] Egon Monk, *Herr Puntila und sein Knecht Matti* rehearsal notes, 19 September 1949, BBA 1598/11.

[102] Brecht, "Caspar Nehers ‚Puntila'-Bühne," 313.

[103] Brecht as quoted in Tenschert, "Über die Verwendung von Masken," 111; Friedrich Dieckmann, 86. The lack of expertise in mask-work can in part be attributed to the anti-formalist and pro-Stanislavskian aesthetics of the GDR at that time. For example, in the early 1950s mime had been classified as "formalist" and was not included in the repertoire of acting schools, a classification which Brecht covertly questioned when he suggested in 1951 that mime should be introduced into the acting syllabus. See Brecht, "[Vorschläge für Schauspielerausbildung]," c. 1951, GBA 23:180, and the commentary on this fragment on 506.

[104] „Schade, daß wir so etwas nicht machen können." Brecht as quoted in Hans Bunge, 27 November 1953, BBA 944/18.

[105] Hans Bunge, 31 May 1954, BBA 945/62.

[106] Brecht as quoted in Hans Bunge, 28 May 1954, BBA 945/52–53.

[107] Bunge, 53.

[108] "Bemerkungen zur Darstellung des Adjutanten durch Schall," 4 December 1953, BBA 239/11.

How Writing Poetry Inscribes *Reading*. The Poetology of Intertextuality in the Young Brecht, Exemplified by the Ballad "Das Schiff"

According to received opinion, obscurity is characteristic of modernist poetry. Illisibility, resistance to clear understanding or, according to Adorno's dictum, "Mimesis ans Verhärtete," are considered the main tendencies of modern lyric writing. An analysis of Brecht's poem "Das Schiff," however, shows that *reading* as a form of non-hermeneutic, incessant understanding of the process of composition, is constitutive of the *writing* of modern lyrics. The poem metaphorizes Brecht's own readings of Baudelaire, Rimbaud and others in the poetological trope of *navigation* — a "static" rhetorical topos that is set into irresistible movement simply by its use in the poem. This dynamization of a fixed trope is demonstrated in the analysis of the poem to be itself an essential metaphor for the representation of the mediation between reading and writing in the context of modernity.

Wie Dichten *Lesen* schreibt.
Zur Poetologie der Intertextualität beim jungen Brecht, am Beispiel der Ballade „Das Schiff"

Daniel Müller Nielaba

Aus Bertolt Brechts Tagebuch, zum 15. September 1920: „Was ist ein Gedicht wert: Vier Hemden, einen Laib Brot, eine halbe Milchkuh? Wir machen keine Ware, wir machen nur Geschenke."[1] Die Notiz des zweiundzwanzigjährigen Dichters, die ich hier an den Anfang meiner Ausführungen stelle, ist eine literarische Bemerkung, in zweifacher Hinsicht: Sie bezieht sich auf Literatur, und sie *ist* Literatur. Die Semantik des Wortes „Machen," das in Verbindung mit „Waren" etwas anderes bedeutet als in Verbindung mit „Geschenken," verleiht der Bemerkung eine Doppeldeutigkeit, die es zu bedenken gilt. Gewiss: Der junge Brecht gibt sich hier selbstbewusst und überzeugt davon, für seine Kunst gebe es jenen Preis erst gar nicht, der ihrem Wert angemessen wäre. Andererseits aber gibt sich seine Frage nach dem Tausch-„Wert" eines Gedichtes überhaupt als eine rhetorische Frage zu erkennen: Zu einem sprachlichen Kunstwerk gibt es für ihn offenbar kein Gegenstück in der Form klingender Münze. Ein Gedicht lässt sich nicht übersetzen auf jene Ebene von Heller und Pfennig, der gegenüber Brecht als Autor und Geschäftsmann ansonsten ja durchaus keine Berührungsängste bekundet hat. Ein Gedicht zwar „hat" keinen Preis, keinen Gegen*wert*; zugleich aber scheint ihm ein Gegen*über*, ein ihm Anderes von Anfang an unentbehrlich zu sein: Im Gegensatz nämlich zu der „Ware," die, gleichgültig gegenüber ihren Abnehmern, dasjenige bleibt, als was sie „gemacht" wurde, wird das „gemachte Geschenk" genau dann erst zu dem, was es sein soll, wenn es an jemanden gelangt, der sich beschenken zu lassen bereit ist. An jemanden also, der jenen Dialog, der unabdingliches Element jeden Schenkens ist, aufzunehmen und weiterzuführen gewillt ist. Brechts Feststellung, wonach das Gedicht „nur" — und das heißt: ausschließlich — ein „Geschenk," ein zu vergebender Gegenstand aus sprachlichen Zeichen und eine Transfer—, eine Vergabebewegung durch Zeichen zugleich und immer schon sei, hat Konsequenzen für die Beurteilung des Entstehens von Lyrik, des „Machens": Ein Gedicht machen, dies folgt aus Brechts Bemerkung, heiße, ein „Geschenk" zu „machen," umfasse also in ei-

New Essays on Brecht / Neue Versuche über Brecht
Maarten van Dijk et al., eds., *The Brecht Yearbook / Das Brecht-Jahrbuch*
Volume 26 (Toronto, Canada: The International Brecht Society, 2001)

nem und untrennbar voneinander den Vorgang des Herstellens wie jenen des Weiterreichens von Gedichtetem. Ein „Geschenk machen" heißt, ein Angebot angenommen wissen. Es scheint also, dass dem Gedicht sein eigenes Gelesenwerden — ohne welches es seine Bestimmung als „Geschenk" hoffnungslos verfehlen müsste — schon im Stadium des „Machens," schon im Schreibprozess notwendig inhärent sei, es scheint, als ob das Schreiben von Lyrik unumgänglicherweise stets auch ein Schreiben von Lesen wäre.

Nun sagt Brecht allerdings nicht, das Gedicht habe schlechterdings *keinen* Wert. Das Buch sei „für den Gebrauch der Leser bestimmt" (11/39), so beginnt die Einleitung der *Hauspostille*, in der sich auch das „Schiffs"-Gedicht von 1919 findet. Und weiter heißt es über das Buch, mit dessen Titel Brecht an jenen religiösen Alltagsgebrauch anknüpft, wie er die spezielle Tradition christlicher Erbauungsliteratur seit Luthers *Kirchen- und Hauspostille* von 1527 prägte: Es solle „nicht sinnlos hineingefressen werden." Gut lesen statt schlecht fressen, sinnvoll verwenden statt „sinnlos" verschlingen, lautet hier die Lektüreanweisung. Der wirkliche Wert also eines Gedichts läge — wörtlich — in seinem „Gebrauch," wäre ein Gebrauchswert.[2] Und dieser wiederum bestimmt sich notwendig in Relation zu denjenigen, die ihn nutzen, den Gebrauchenden, den Lesenden also. Mit dem Lesen aber ist dieser Gebrauchswert des Gedichts eine Funktion genau desjenigen Prozesses, der seinen Status als „Geschenk" überhaupt erst hervorbringt: Der Wert des Gedichtes mithin erzeugt sich *selbst*, und zwar fortlaufend dort, wo es als jenes „Geschenk" gebraucht wird, das es Brechts Diktum gemäß „nur" ist. Konsequenterweise wäre dann Lyrik auch als das Medium einer Lese-Geschichte zu lesen, indem sowohl das Gelesenwerden wie das Gelesenhaben Konstituenten dessen wären, was das Gedicht von und durch sich „erzählt."

Selbstbezüglichkeit: Ein Begriff, den die Literaturwissenschaft, und zwar weitgehend unabhängig von einer nationalphilologischen Zugehörigkeit, üblicherweise dann benutzt, wenn es darum geht, die westliche moderne Lyrik zu charakterisieren. Moderne, so wie ich den Terminus mit Blick auf Lyrik und in Übereinstimmung mit einem relativ breit gefächerten Forschungskonsens hier brauchen will, bezeichnet eine spezifische — oft und geradezu einhellig als „dunkel" beschriebene — Weise des Dichtens, die sich von Baudelaire bis Celan durch diverse Sprachen und über manche geschichtliche Zäsur hinweg als Konstante beobachten lässt. Erhellend kann in diesem Zusammenhang die gebräuchliche französische Bezeichnung der *obscurité* moderner Dichtung wirken. *Obscurité* nämlich vertritt gleichwertig die Bedeutungen der Unverständlichkeit wie jene der Dunkelheit und zeigt damit deutlich an, dass das spezielle Nicht-Verstehbare hier in der Tatsache seiner metaphorischen Umschreibbarkeit immer schon einen möglichen Verstehensweg als Nachweis einer Übersetzbarkeit seines Bedeutens vorzeichnet: Was übersetzbar ist ins Bild eines „Dunkeln," kann kein Unverständliches schlechthin sein. Das in diesem Sinne moderne Gedicht — auch hierin herrscht in der Forschung weitgehend Überein-stimmung — bezieht seine Hermetik, seine relative Unzugänglichkeit aus der Tatsache, dass es nicht Welt abbildet, ja dass es die Referenz einer angeblich gesicherten Realität, auf die es verstehend zu beziehen wäre, geradezu aufkündigt. Stattdessen bildet es eigene Welten, Sprachwelten gleichsam, die zu entziffern sich der Leser auf wenig oder nichts anderes stützen kann als auf eins: Das *Gedichtete* selbst, die *verba dicta*, die Worte, die allerdings eben — und das macht die Schwierigkeit solcher Texte aus — sowohl der Gegenstand wie das Darstellungsmedium dieses Dichtens sind. „Mimesis ans Verhärtete"[3] lautete hiefür die bekannte Formel Adornos, eine ebenso düstere wie folgenschwere Festschreibung moderner Lyrik, zu der die Gedichte des jungen Brecht — von einigen Ausnahmen abgesehen[4] — durch die Forschung nicht unbedingt gerechnet werden. Das verbreitete Missver-ständnis, wonach Adorno hier einen traditionellen „Mimesis"-Begriff verwendet habe und dementsprechend von einer Abbildung als einer mimetischen Reproduktion des „Verhärteten" durch Kunst ausgegangen sei, soll hier selbstverständlich nicht wiederholt werden. Eine ganz wesentliche theoretische Anstrengung der *Ästhetik* Adornos ging un-zweifelhaft darauf hinaus, (moderne) Kunst als jene Darstellungsweise schlechthin zu erschließen, die das Verhältnis zwischen der Tendenz zu archaischem Abbilden einerseits und dem Diktat einer verdingli-chenden Ratio andererseits eben als ein (negativ) dialektisches ersicht-lich werden ließe. Das ändert allerdings nichts daran, dass Adorno mit seinem an Baudelaires Lyrik gewonnenen Befund, „Weltschmerz" laufe da „über zum Feind, der Welt," und der anschließenden Konstatierung, es sei hievon etwas „als Ferment aller Moderne beigemischt geblie-ben,"[5] diese in ihrem Verhältnis zu „Welt" festlegt auf eine Negativrefe-rentialität, die als Zuordnungskriterium nicht zuletzt darum problema-tisch bleibt, weil sie genau jene Möglichkeit einer grundlegenden Dia-logizität der Texte, die hier im folgenden an einem Beispiel erörtert werden soll, faktisch ausschließt.

Dass die „Male der Zerrüttung,"[6] die nach Adornos Überlegung als deren „Echtheitssiegel"[7] die Wahrnehmungs- und Darstellungsverfahren des modernen Dichters semiotisch beglaubigen, dass Bruch und Inkon-gruenz wie sie zu seinem Umgang mit Bildlichkeit gehören, nicht im hermetischen Zuschluss enden, dass vielmehr gerade aus der vermeint-lich rein auf sich bezogenen Beschäftigung des Dichters mit dem Ich und dessen Sprache eine radikal aufs Offene zielende Sprachkunst entstehen kann, ist eine Beobachtung, die an vielen Texten zu machen ist, eine Beobachtung, die das Diktum der mimetischen Relation zum Erstarrten — und sei es einer negativ-dialektischen des „goût du néant"[8] — in ein kritisches Licht stellt. Noch und gerade in ihrer vermeintlich *eindeutigen* Suspendierung eines vormals zumindest als Relation gesichert scheinenden Bezugs von Ich und Welt nämlich kann moderne Dichtung mehrdeutig sein. Was Arthur Rimbaud, auf den im folgenden zurückzukommen sein wird, schon 1871 aufs epochale Fazit brachte: „Je est un autre," das lässt sich gewiss dahingehend verstehen, dass das moderne poetische Ich sich selber unwiederbringlich entfremdet sei, dass dichtendes und gedichtetes Ich sich zueinander als Nonrelata, als ganz und gar Fremde verhalten. Manches in Rimbauds Texten spricht für diese Lesart, die aber, wo sie ausschließlich wird, zu unterschlagen droht, dass sich in dem Satz auch eine poetologische Emanzipierung verbirgt: Die Wendung, wonach jedes gesprochene, geschriebene Ich zu dem, der „Ich" sagt, in einer ergänzenden Alterität steht, die diesem die Freiheit eröffnet, ein wandlungsfähiges, metamorphotisches, ein immer neues und anderes „Je" in Text zu inkorporieren, es auf Sprachreisen zu schicken: Es abzusenden in Papier, gerade ohne sich selbst dabei mit aufgeben — im Doppelsinn gemeint — zu müssen.

„Wir machen nur Geschenke": Wie freizügig Brecht selber generell mit fremden Texten als angeblichen „Geschenken" umgegangen ist, wie unverfroren er von Anderen Verfasstes sich schreibend angeeignet hat — zum Gebrauche entwendet gleichsam —, gehört zu den Eigenheiten seines Schaffens, über die sich die Gemüter nicht weniger Kritikerinnen und Kritiker bis heute zu erhitzen vermögen. „Ich wälze" — notiert er im Oktober 1921 während der Arbeit an seinem Stück *Im Dickicht der Städte* — „den Rimbaud-Band und mache einige Anleihen. Wie glühend dies alles ist! Leuchtendes Papier!" (26/248). Nun: Das Prinzip, seine „Geschenke" auf Kosten zuvor getätigter „Anleihen" zu „machen" — und darauf schließlich läuft diese Rechnung hinaus — mag weder mit höheren moralischen Ansprüchen noch mit den Grundsätzen ökonomischer Vernunft in Einklang stehen: Als literarisches Produktionsprinzip bleibt es trotzdem genauer zu bedenken. Was Brecht an „leuchtendem Papier" lesend sich borgt bei Arthur Rimbaud, gibt er, so bleibt nunmehr am „Schiff" zeigen, den Lesenden weiter als ein Geschriebenes, das sich auch als eine Lektüre-„Anleihe" zu verstehen gibt. Als ein Sprachkunstwerk also, das — lesbar — Angelesenes umsetzt, Angeliehenes verarbeitet, und dabei die Lesenden an einem geschriebenen Lektüredialog teilnehmen lässt.

Es seien an dieser Stelle zwei knappe Thesen formuliert, die in einem das bislang Gesagte bündeln, wie die Richtung für meine weiteren Überlegungen anzeigen sollen:

Erste These: Es gibt nicht ungelesene Lyrik. Die Moderne hat diese Tatsache keineswegs erfunden, höchstens vielleicht bewusster sie zum Referenzpunkt ihres Schreibens gemacht, machen müssen, nicht zuletzt aus historischen Gründen: Die Geschichte der Lyrik ist, unter diskursgeschichtlichem Aspekt betrachtet, eben zugleich diejenige eines Übergehens von einem vielohrigen Hörpublikum zu einem privaten Lesepublikum. Dass Lyrik nicht mehr mit den *Ohren* gehört wird, sondern mit dem Sehorgan, ist Effekt eines geschichtlichen Wandels, der bereits den Prozess des Gedichte-Schreibens wesentlich mitbestimmt. Der lyrische Text — das Brechtsche Bild des „Geschenke-Machens" verweist darauf — antizipiert in seiner Struktur den Prozess seines Gelesen-Werdens. Lesen ist daher dem Gedicht nichts Fremdes in dem Sinne, dass es von außen an es appliziert würde. Ein Gedicht mithin kann, ohne explizit von sich selbst als einem poetischen Gegenstand zu sprechen, stets auch ein Gedicht übers „Geschenke-Machen" sein. Solche Selbstimplikation des Lesens ins Dichten, dies als Randbeleg für meine Behauptung, zeigt sich dem genaueren Blick schon im Titel von Brechts erster großer Gedichtsammlung: Die „Postille" nämlich, als welche der Autor sein Buch ja ausdrücklich betitelte, ist in der Geschichte der Erbauungsliteratur nichts anderes als das gebräuchliche Kürzel für die Bezeichnung „post illa verba texta," für Geschriebenes mithin *nach* vorgegebenen Worten, für einen Lesestoff, der sich selbst als ein geschriebenes Lesen zu erkennen gibt, als „lectio" oder „Lektion" eben, wie Brecht die verschiedenen Abteilungen der Sammlung tatsächlich betitelt. [9]

Zweite These: Als allgemeines Charakteristikum moderner Lyrik darf gelten, dass das Gedicht seine Referenz nicht mehr in Welt, Natur oder einer gesicherten Ich-Instanz hat, sondern in Sprache, in dem also, was zugleich Material wie Medium des Dichtens ist. Daraus jedoch folgt, dass solche Dichtung weniger „Mimesis ans Verhärtete" vollzieht, als vielmehr eine Umstülpung jenes historischen Mimesis-Konzepts praktiziert, das den Text gleichsam auf die Funktion des Nachäffens, des Nachbildens ex post festlegt. Was sich im modernen Gedicht darstellt, ist die Praefigurierung seines stets anderen, stets neuen Gelesenwerdens: Was sich durch das Gedicht vermittelt, ist also eine Metamorphose seiner selbst. Dies letztere wiederum impliziert eine Auflösung herkömmlicher Zeitstruktur: Metamorphotischer Text ist gedichtete Bewegung, ist also gleichsam ein Text ohne Ende, ist — nach Maßgabe seiner Grundstruktur des *hysteron proteron* — als ein rekkurrentes Zeichengebilde zu umschreiben.

Ein geschriebenes Lesen also und eine Metamorphotik ohne Ende sind die beiden Aspekte, denen nunmehr an Bord von Brechts Gedicht „Das Schiff" (11/46f.) besondere Aufmerksamkeit zu schenken bleibt. Literaturwissenschaftlich motiviert und legitimiert ist dieses Vorgehen durch die grundsätzliche Frage nach einer möglichen Transparenz jener vielzitierten Dunkelheit und Hermetik des modernen Gedichts.

> 1
> Durch die klaren Wasser schwimmend vieler Meere
> Löst ich schaukelnd mich von Ziel und Schwere
> Mit den Haien ziehend unter rotem Mond.
> Seit mein Holz fault und die Segel schlissen

Seit die Seile modern, die am Strand mich rissen
Ist entfernter mir und bleicher auch mein Horizont.

2

Und seit jener hinblich und mich diesen
Wassern die entfernten Himmel ließen
Fühl ich tief, daß ich vergehen soll.
Seit ich wußte, ohne mich zu wehren
Daß ich untergehen soll in diesen Meeren
Ließ ich mich den Wassern ohne Groll.

3

Und die Wasser kamen, und sie schwemmten
Viele Tiere in mich, und in fremden
Wänden freundeten sich Tier und Tier.
Einst fiel Himmel durch die morsche Decke
Und sie kannten sich in jeder Ecke
Und die Haie blieben gut in mir.

4

Und im vierten Monde schwammen Algen
In mein Holz und grünten in den Balken:
Mein Gesicht ward anders noch einmal.
Grün und wehend in den Eingeweiden
Fuhr ich langsam, ohne viel zu leiden
Schwer mit Mond und Pflanze, Hai und Wal.

5

Möw und Algen war ich Ruhestätte
Schuldlos immer, daß ich sie nicht rette,
Wenn ich sinke, bin ich schwer und voll.
Jetzt, im achten Monde, rinnen Wasser
Häufiger in mich. Mein Gesicht wird blasser.
Und ich bitte, daß es enden soll.

6

Fremde Fischer sagten aus: sie sahen
Etwas nahen, das verschwamm beim Nahen.
Eine Insel? Ein verkommnes Floß?
Etwas fuhr, schimmernd von Möwenkoten
Voll von Alge, Wasser, Mond und Totem
Stumm und dick auf den erbleichten Himmel los.

Vom *Lesen*, um hier an meine beiden Fragen anzuknüpfen, ist die Rede nicht in diesem Gedicht. Nur: Gibt es überhaupt eine Rede *von* hier, ist da ein Sprechen, das sauber zu scheiden wäre von dem, was es erzählt? Brecht lässt das lyrische Ich seines Textes, das „Schiff," sein allmähliches Untergehen erzählen, über fünf Strophen bzw. „acht Monde," gefolgt von einem epilogartigen Botenbericht „fremder Fischer," die einem unbestimmten Adressaten Mitteilung machen, bzw. „Aussage" über etwas von ihnen anscheinend Gesehenes. Ein Schiffbruch also, einer mit Zuschauern zwar, mit Augenzeugen allerdings, denen das Gesehene beim „Nahen" verschwimmt: Wie ließe sich dieses Versinken, dieses In-die-Tiefe-Gehen des Erzählsubjekts trennen von einem Erzählen, das einem Lesenden, je mehr er sich darin vertieft, bedeutungsmäßig zunehmend zerrinnt und zerfließt? Wie soll ein Erzählendes geschieden werden von einem Erzählten, wenn vom Ersteren nur gewiss ist, dass es ein „tiefes" Fühlen hat gerade um sein unterschiedsloses „Vergehen" im Gedicht, in dem also, *was* es erzählt, in dem *Wie* seines Erzählens zugleich? Zudem: Wo ein lyrisches Subjekt sein Untergehen beschreibt, wo die Tatsache der Beschreibbarkeit durch eine Ich-Instanz mithin gerade vom paradoxen Überdauern dieses eigenen Untergangs zeugt, da liegt implizit jenes hysteron proteron vor, von dem oben als dem Kennzeichen eines metamorphotischen Textes, eines Textes in Bewegung und Wandel bereits die Rede war. Die üblichen Leitkoordinaten, denen sonst das Geschäft der Auslegung, der Texterklärung sich anvertraut, führen bei diesem Gedicht allemal auf Sandbänke, lassen den Lesenden enden im Schlick vermeintlicher Realien, auf die sich das Gedicht gerade *nicht* bezieht:[10] Nichts, was sich festhalten ließe, an solch fischigem Stück Sprachkunst.

Das hybride Bild, als welches das Schiff im Botenbericht dem Text entgleitet, muss — im Gefolge dessen, was der Leser in den fünf vorangehenden Strophen an Durchlässigkeit und Metamorphotik wahrnimmt, an Umstülpung auch von Zeitstrukturen — keineswegs gegen das Sehvermögen dieser „Fischer" sprechen oder gegen deren Zuverlässigkeit als Augenzeugen: Denn in der Tat „verschwimmt" dieses „Schiff" auch den Lesenden beim „Nahen" im Lesen, in der Tat mutet das Gedicht selber als ein „Verschwommenes" an. Gänzlich ort- und herkunftslos scheint das Schiff zu driften durch den Text hindurch, und doch erzählt es mit seinem Präteritum, mit seiner Fülle deiktischer Temporalangaben — das Wort „seit," viermal allein in den ersten beiden Strophen, aber auch „einst," „jetzt" — von einer Vergangenheit, so als hätten die Lesenden diese zu kennen, als wäre das Wissen darüber vorauszusetzen, woher es kommt, dieses merkwürdige Wassergefährt.

Undurchschaubar und unvernehmlich, „stumm," entgleitet den Seeleuten das Schiff aus dem Gedicht. Bestätigt sich an dem Gedicht damit jenes Paradigma der Nichtverstehbarkeit, das spätestens seit dem folgenschweren Dictum Adornos der Lyrik der Moderne als Etikett anhaftet? Nicht trotzig erzwungene Unlesbarkeit, als Aufbegehren des Dichters gegen das Faktum seines Nichtmehr-Verstandenwerdens in einer kunstfeindlichen Welt, ist dasjenige, so bleibt hier zu zeigen, was Brechts Gedicht dem Leser als Schwierigkeit zumutet. Das führerlose Schiff, das sich vermischt mit dem, worin es schwimmt, bis es, wie der zweitletzte Vers feststellt, „voll" ist „von Alge, Wasser, Mond und Totem," formuliert seine Lesbarkeit selber in einer poetologischen Figur, über Kreuz nämlich, in einem Chiasmus also: Als Aufforderung, zugleich mit den Ohren zu lesen, mit den Augen zu hören. Mit den Ohren jenen Dialog zu lesen, den das Gedicht aufnimmt und weiterführt, jenes „Geschenk" mitklingen zu hören, als das Brecht hier offenbar die zahllosen anderen gedichteten „Schiffe" angenommen hat; an erster Stelle natürlich, es ist dies alles andere als ein neuer Forschungsbefund, „Le Bâteau Ivre" (1871) von Arthur Rimbaud.[11] Mit den Augen gleichzeitig gilt es hörend ein „Wie" des Textes wahrzunehmen, das jenen Klang in Schrift übersetzt, von dem das Schiff gleich in den ersten zwei Versen als von seiner Eigenbewegung spricht: Jenes ziel- und schwerelose Schaukeln und Schlingern, das sich in den fünf- bis siebenhebigen Trochäen als Rhythmus vernehmbar macht, den das Lesen auf- und übernimmt, wo es ihm folgt.

Dass Brecht mit diesem Gedicht einen Dialog, ein Gespräch anvisierte, hat er selber in lyrischer Form explizit gemacht, in einem fragmentarisch gebliebenen Gedichtentwurf von 1927 mit dem überaus vieldeutigen Titel „Liquidation vom trunkenen Schiff" (13/391). Die Überschrift lässt völlig offen, ob da ein Gedicht liquidiert werden soll, im Sinne eines Loswerdens, eines Notverkaufs, oder ob es bei dieser „Liquidation" um eine Verflüssigung geht, um ein neues Zu-Wasser-Lassen gar des „Schiffes": „Ich aber habe mit dem gesprochen / Was der Rausch von ihnen übrigließ / Immerfort von neuem nach Neuem aufgebrochen." Bei seinem Umgang mit dem „trunkenen Schiff" habe er „*gesprochen,*" Unterredung gehalten mit dem, was der „Rausch" — jener der Dichter, der Schiffe? — „übrigließ," heißt es, und dann folgt ein Vers, der ganz offenbar genau dieses „Übriggelassene," dieses dauerhaft Ansprechbare der Gedichte bezeichnet: Die Permanenz des Weggehens, des „Aufbrechens" sei es, eine Permanenz der Bewegung, die zugleich eine Unbeendbarkeit des Lesens impliziert, des stets „neuen" Sehens auf „Neues" hin. Seine Nicht-Fixierbarkeit also, ausgerechnet, sei dasjenige am Gedicht, was alleine fix und auf Dauer gesichert sei, als das, was fortgehend „übrig"-bleibe, „immerfort": immer-fort.

Allein, es bleibt die Frage offen, ob diese Dialogizität des Textes — mit Blick auf das „Schiffs"-Gedicht — ob sein Lesen nun nicht einfach *hinein*gelesen ist durch das jeweils hierzu verführte Lektüresubjekt. Das abschließende Gedicht der *Fleurs du mal* von Charles Baudelaire, einem Werk, dem Brechts *Hauspostille* — von der Forschung nach meinen Kenntnissen bislang unbemerkt — auch in der numerischen Übereinstimmung des Aufbaus mit ihren fünf „Lektionen" und dem Schlusskapitel einen unüberlesbaren Tribut entrichtet, heißt „Le Voyage." Dieses Gedicht, mit dem seinerseits das Rimbaudsche „Bâteau Ivre" in intimstem Dialog steht, endet mit der Anrufung des Todes als des „vieux capitaine," als des — (Rausch)Gifte, „poisons" verteilenden — Steuermanns eines Schiffes, dem nicht Himmel noch Hölle etwas bedeute, das nur hinuntergeleitet sein wolle, hinunter zu *Neuem*: „Ô

Mort, vieux capitaine, il est temps! levons l'ancre !"[12], und weiter, Vers 142f.: „Nous voulons, tant ce feu nous brûle le cerveau, / Plonger au fond du gouffre, Enfer ou Ciel, qu'importe? / Au fond de l'Inconnu pour trouver du *nouveau* !" — Genau mit diesem „Abtauchen nach Neuem," die Korrespondenz der Texte liegt offen, will Brecht „gesprochen" haben, ihm also gilt es als Lesebewegung in seinem Schiffs-Gedicht weiter nachzufragen.

Brecht greift bei seiner „Liquidation vom trunkenen Schiff" den Schluss der Baudelairschen „Fleurs du Mal" auf und gestaltet diesen als eine lyrische Neulektüre des zu seiner Zeit und in seinem Freundeskreis überaus populären Rimbaud-Gedichts „Le Bâteau Ivre." „Au fond du *bien*connu pour trouver du nouveau," ließe sich dieses Vorgehen in Abwandlung von Baudelaires Schlussvers umschreiben. Jenes „neue Von-Neuem," das, was sich in Brechts „Schiffs"-Gedicht, Vers 21 wörtlich als ein „anders noch einmal" ausgedrückt findet, das also, was sich als das Oxymoron einer „anderen Repetition des Selben" formulieren lässt, wird in Brechts Bearbeitung sichtbar auch als eine Lesegeschichte des „betrunkenen Schiffs": Und zwar als die Geschichte eines zunehmenden Zielloswerdens der Schiffsbewegung. Um diese Überlegung an den Texten zu konkretisieren, genügt es schon, sich die ganz unterschiedliche Richtung dessen vor Augen zu führen, was jeweils das lyrische Subjekt bei Baudelaire, bei Rimbaud und bei Brecht als sein Bewegt-Sein formuliert: In „Le Voyage" handelt es sich um ein „nous," das sich selber zum metaphorischen Schiff macht dadurch, dass es den Tod zu seinem „capitaine" ernennt. „In den Abgrund zu Neuem" lautet die vergleichsweise klare und lineare Zielsetzung *dieses* finalen Untergehens.[13]

Erheblich undeutlicher schon erscheint die Zielrichtung des „trunkenen" Textsubjekts in Rimbauds „Bâteau Ivre." In dem Gedicht ist nämlich genau jene semantische Differenz von „ancre" und „encre," von Anker und Tinte, aufgehoben, die Baudelaire in den Versen 137 und 139 seiner „Voyage" so ungemein prägnant zu Bedeutung gelangen lässt: Der einzige mögliche „Anker" von Rimbauds „Schiff"-Text *ist* nurmehr die Tinte, ist die „encre" der Fortschrift, der einzige Halt ist die Bewegung.[14] Gleich in den zwei ersten Verse schon wird evident, dass dieses „Schiff" die Entscheidung über seine Richtungnahme an keinen „capitaine" mehr delegiert.

> Comme je descendais des Fleuves impassibles
> Je ne me sentis plus guidé par les haleurs:
> Des Peaux-Rouges criards les avaient pris pour cibles
> Les ayant cloués nus aux poteaux de couleurs
>
> J'étais insoucieux de tous les équipages,
> Porteur de blés flamands ou de cotons anglais.
> Quand avec mes haleurs ont fini ces tapages

Les Fleuves m'ont laissé descendre où je voulais.[15]

Indem das Schiff unbeteiligte Ströme hinunterschwimmt oder gerade *weil* es sie durchschwimmt, als wären sie unbeteiligt an seiner Bewegung — es bleibt offen im Wort „comme" — fühlt es sich „unbesorgt" (V.5) gegenüber jedwelcher Besatzung, gegenüber jeder Ladung (V.6). Es ist nicht mehr gehalten, nicht mehr geleitet durch seine Treidler, mit deren Verstummen (V.7) das Schiff, das Gedicht die Bestimmung seines Nieder- oder Hinuntergehens selber übernimmt: „Les Fleuves m'ont laissé descendre où je voulais." Jedoch: Noch und gerade das vermeintlich ganz autonome und souveräne Wollen dieses Schiffes — sein „Vouloir" — gibt sich dem genaueren Blick zu erkennen als eine Funktion der Strömungen, als grundsätzlich abhängig von einem „laisser" nämlich (V.8), einem „Freilassen" oder „Nicht-Freilassen" durch diese „Fleuves."[16]

Das Brechtsche „Schiff" erklärt sich „gelöst," los*geworden*, von Anbeginn: Gelöst vom „Ziel" (V.2), von jenem Ziel eines „Neuen" im „Abgrund," wie es die Baudelairsche „Voyage" aufrechterhält, gelöst selbst von jener „Schwere" (V.2), jenem Eigengewicht, das das Rimbaudsche „Bâteau" noch zu einem Objekt von Wellen und Strömungen macht. Brechts „Schiff" wiegt selber nichts mehr, es ist kein Gegenstand mehr für die Wellen, weil es überhaupt kein „*Gegen-*" mehr ist oder hat. Es zeigt sich als ein loses, ein erlöstes Schiff, verwandelt durch das Medium, in dem es treibt, verwandelt durch all dasjenige, was sich in ihm — auf seiner Reise durch die unterschiedlichsten Lektüren — an Heterogenem angelagert hat: „Schwer," so lautet unmissverständlich Vers 24, ist das Schiff „*mit* Mond und Pflanze, Hai und Wal," nicht ohne sie. Damit ist Brechts Gedicht zugleich eine lyrische Interpretation von Lyrik, von „Le Voyage," „Le Bâteau Ivre" und anderen, es ist also, um hier an meine zwei Leitfragen anzuknüpfen, zugleich ein Gedicht über das Entstehen eines Gedichtes im Prozess seines Gelesenwerdens, ein Gedicht eben, das eine Poetologie der Lektüre formuliert. Ein Gedicht, das darstellt, wie ihre Lesegeschichte sich in Gedichten selber mitverlagert, sie fortlaufend verändernd, das aber auch den Lesenden zeigt, dass noch deren jeweilige Tätigkeit Teil ist dieser unabschließbaren Lektüregeschichte. Das Gedicht legt damit offen, rückweisend, dass und wie es aus Lese-„Anleihen" besteht, vorausweisend, dass es als „Geschenk gemacht" ist, dass es gelesen werden will.

Bereits in Rimbauds Gedicht — es mag dies meine Interpretation poetologischer Metaphorik bei Brecht vom allfälligen Vorwurf der Willkürlichkeit entlasten helfen — findet sich eine entsprechende Selbstreflexion des Dichtens, hier als die Frage nach der Relation zwischen einem sprechenden Ich im Text und dessen sprachlichen Ausdrucksmitteln, den Zeichen: „[...] je me suis baigné," heißt es da in Vers 21/22, „dans le Poème/De la Mer."[17] Das Enjambement dieser beiden ersten Verse der sechsten Strophe verschränkt nicht bloß zwei Gedichtzeilen, sondern auch — in gänzlicher Unentscheidbarkeit — verschiedene gleichermaßen plausible Lesarten: *Ist* dem „Bâteau" mit dem Meer sein ureigenes Element metaphorisch ein „Gedicht," oder aber *schafft* sich das lyrische Ich mit seinem „Poème de la Mer" erst dieses Meer, als sein Medium, das es zum Schwimmen benötigt? Das „Gedicht vom Meer," in dem das Schiff gebadet haben will: Ist es ein Gedicht, geschrieben *vom* Meer? Ist es ein Meeresgedicht im Schiffsgedicht, ein Gedicht *übers* Meer, als Binnengedicht des „Schiffes"? Oder *ist* das Gedicht selber, ist „Le Bâteau ivre" jenes Meer, in dem sein durch es geschriebenes Schiff sich „badet"? Ganz offensichtlich stülpen sich hier die Mittel des lyrischen Sprechens und das Subjekt dieses Sprechens in sich selbst dergestalt um, dass daraus fast unversehens die sprachliche Darstellung einer Ununterscheidbarkeit von sprechendem Ich, als dem lyrischen Subjekt, und von dessen Sprechen, als dem Medium des lyrischen Erzählens, resultiert.

Brechts Ballade, als Umschrift seiner Lektüren, lässt das Schiff von genau diesen so unterschiedlichen „Meeren" als den Medien seiner eigenen Herkunft erzählen, lässt es zugleich sich an- und auffüllen mit vergänglichem Leben, bis es in der vierten Strophe zu etwas kommt, das sich durch die erst- und einmalige Verwendung des Doppelpunkts im Gedicht sehr deutlich als Zäsur bezeichnet: Es beginnt im „Schiff" und aus ihm heraus, wie es heißt, zu „grünen" (V.20). Hört und liest falsch, wer in diesem „Grün" eine der „Vokalfarben" Rimbauds aufschimmern sieht? „U vert," das grüne U, heißt es in Rimbauds Gedicht „Voyelles"[18] ebenso wie in der lyrischen Prosa seiner „saison en enfer."[19] „U vert," mit dem feinen Unterschied allerdings, dass Rimbaud in dem einen Text das „U" an den Schluss der Vokalreihe stellt — AEIOU — in dem andern aber — dem griechischen Alphabet folgend — das „O." Die Position von „O" und „U" also ist ihm austauschbar, ist ihm *offen*. Brecht, fasziniert von Rimbaud und dessen „Wortalchimie," scheint hier genaustens hingehört zu haben: Sein Schiff „grünt" dort genau, wo es, wie Vers 23 sagt, nur noch „langsam[e]" Bewegung ist, nur noch „fuhr," und nichts als dies, wo es gänzlich durchlässig, gänzlich o/u-vert ist. „Grün und wehend" (V. 22), sagt das Ich, sei es nun „gefahren," dank dieser Offenheit seiner „Eingeweide," wie es im selben Vers über das Schiffs-Innere heißt: Es „grünt" etwas in ihm und wächst, ein Neuanfang bahnt sich an im Blick auf jenes Ende, von dem in Vers 30 dann explizit die Rede ist. Das „Grünen" erweist sich hier als die poetologische Metapher, in der sich vom Gedicht aus der Effekt seines Gelesenwerdens vorweg darstellt: Als Sprachbild für ein Weiterleben im Lesen, das das Schiff allein seinem eigenen Offensein und seinem Untergehen dankt, seinem „sich lassen" „ohne Groll," wie es in Vers 12 heißt. Lesen als Werden des Geschriebenen, aufgeschrieben im Gedicht: Auch das Befremdende jener Ich-Instanz in diesem Text, einem Ich, das mit dem eigenen Versinken etwas erzählt, was — in Übereinstimmung mit zeitlicher Logik — seinem Erzählzugriff entzogen sein müsste, klärt sich auf, im „klaren Wasser" *dieser* „Meere." Klärt sich auf als eine erste Lesestimme schon im Text selbst, als eine Stimme, die etwas liest, vorliest, das sie selbst nicht ist, etwas jedoch, an dessen Entstehung sie ursächlich beteiligt ist: Das Gedicht, in dem sie geschrieben steht.[20] Es „grünt," und das Schiff wird „wehend" (V. 22) in jenem Untergehen, das sich mittlerweile als ein Unter*reden* erwiesen hat. „Wehend": Der junge Brecht kannte sich mit Schwangerschaften und mit Wehen besser aus als ihm irgend lieb sein konnte. Hier allerdings bahnt sich eine Geburt anderer Art an, eine Neugeburt des Gedichtes aus sich selber, aus dem eigenen Rumpf heraus, ein Neubeginn des lyrischen Sprechens, der sich einzig aus dem eigenen Enden alimentiert.[21]

Die ungemein enge Bindung des jungen Brecht an die Figur und den Mythos „Rimbaud" ist im übrigen bekannt und braucht hier nicht durch eine lange Beispielreihe dokumentiert zu werden. Ein bedeutsames Detail in einem Text zu Rimbaud allerdings ist erstaunlicherweise bislang völlig unbemerkt geblieben. In einem der für diese Frage oft zitierten Gedichte Brechts, einem Fragment von 1921 stehen die Verse: „Wir sind in Pergament verdorben / Der ganze Tümpel ist vertiert / Nachdem Artur Rimbaud gestorben / Dem man ein Bein noch amputiert" (13/239). Brecht setzt hier mit dem Wort „nachdem" eine Deixis, die mit dem Tode Rimbauds den historischen Ausgangspunkt eines künstlerischen „Verderbens"-Prozesses markiert, der zugleich ein Vorgang des „Vertierens" und des allgemeinen Aufgehens in einem „Tümpel" sei. Genau diese Vertierung und Vertümpelung aber vollzieht sich offensichtlicherweise auch am lyrischen Ich der Schiffs-Ballade, so dass sich sagen lässt, es sei selbst in dieser Hinsicht ein Untergehen — das „Verderben" nach Rimbauds Tod — das sich in einem als die Voraussetzung und als der zu entrichtende Preis zu erkennen gebe für die Möglichkeit des Entstehens eines neuen Sprachkunstwerks, für ein neues produktives „Verderben" des Subjekts „in Pergament." Für diese grundsätzlich *positive* Konnotation des „Vertierens" und für seine organische Verbindung mit dem Prozess des Schreibens spricht im übrigen unüberlesbar der Schluss des *Hauspostillen*-Gedichts „Lied am schwarzen Samstag [...]," wo es heißt: „Leicht, *vertiert* und feierlich / *Wie ein Gedicht von mir*, flog ich durch Himmel [Hv. D.M.]" (11/76). Über die Gleichwertigkeit ihres „vertiert"-Seins stellt sich die Einheit von „Gedicht" und „Schiff" dar, und es zeigt sich zudem, dass das letztere für sein produktives Ein- und Untergehen im „Pergament," als jenem Papier, auf dem es geschrieben ist, des „Verderbens" von früherem Schreibmaterial, von früheren „Schiffs"-Texten bedarf.

„Jetzt, im achten Monde" markiert das lyrische Ich in Vers 28 des „Schiffs" eine späte Deixis, einen vermeintlich sicheren „Zeit-Punkt," der sich aber als reine Gedicht-Zeit erweist: Der „achte Mond" lässt seiner Bedeutung nach das *Untergehen* übergangslos in ein bevorstehendes *Niederkommen* mutieren, was den durch das Ich ausgesprochenen Wunsch nach einem „Enden" unversehens zur Hoffnung macht auf ein Neubeginnen. Ein Schiffbruch, ausgerechnet, als utopisches Bild? In Brechts Tagebucheintrag vom 24. September 1920 heißt es zum „Untergang" des deutschen Theaters:

> Jetzt verlassen die Ratten das Schiff [...] — Aber wir wollen uns in ihm einquartieren und die Beine gegen die Planken spreizen und sehen, wie wir das Schiff vorwärtsbringen. Vielleicht saufen wir das Wasser auf, das durchs Leck quillt, vielleicht hängen wir unsere letzten Hemden an den Mast als Segel und blasen dagegen, das ist der Wind, und furzen dagegen, das ist der Sturm. Und fahren singend hinunter, daß das Schiff einen Inhalt hat, wenn es auf den Grund kommt. (26/169f.)

Auch dies ein verschlungenes, ein rekurrentes Bild: Das „Schiff," ein Theater-Schiff, bewegt sich im Scheinwind seiner schreibenden Passagiere und wird schwer, inhaltsschwer von ihrem bloßen „Singen." Es sind also nichts als Gedichte — Brecht hat die Texte der *Hauspostille* bekanntlich zum Singen geplant, einzelne sogar selber vertont — die das Schiff hier „auf den Grund kommen" lassen, wie die genaue Formulierung lautet.[22]

Es darf dabei nicht vergessen werden, dass Brecht hier ein Bild zitiert, das seit der Antike eine Leitmetapher ist für ein bestimmtes Selbstverständnis von Poesie. Dichten hieß bei Vergil bereits „die Segel setzen," und wurde seither immer wieder umschrieben als ein „Ablegen vom sicheren Hafen," ein „Auslaufen zu Unbekanntem," Dichten hieß stets, „zu Schiffe fahren," durch die „klaren Wasser vieler Meere":[23] Das „Schiffs"-Gedicht kennzeichnet sich so auch von seiner Tropik her als ein Dichtungs-Gedicht, als ein Schiff, auf und mit dem sich Dichtung lyrisch *über*setzt. Es ist im übrigen, als gäbe das „Schiff" noch dem späten, dem nachdenklichen Brecht — dem zerrissenen auch — das Sprachbild schlechthin ab, wenn es um das Schreiben des „Machens" von Gedichten geht. Als ein Zitat seiner eigenen Tagebuchnotiz von 1920 zum „Theaterschiff" klingt, was er — mit einer feinen aber entscheidenden Nuance — 1953 seinen *Buckower Elegien* als Motto voranstellt: „Ginge da ein Wind / Könnte ich ein Segel stellen / Wäre da kein Segel / Machte ich eines aus Stecken und Plane" (12/310). Noch einmal reflektiert hier Brecht sein eigenes Dichten in der Schiffsmetaphorik: Was die „nautischen" Mittel des Schreibenden, was seine „Segel" betrifft, so ist die Haltung nicht anders als dreißig Jahre zuvor. Es taugt das „letzte Hemd" dazu, wie es in der oben zitierten Passage von 1920 heißt, es reicht ein Fetzen oder eine „Plane" auch nur: Auf seine Papiersegel also schiene der Dichter hier weiterhin zu vertrauen. Bloß: „*Ginge* da ein Wind," heißt es jetzt über die Antriebskraft der Poesie, eine Kraft, die der junge Brecht sich einst noch selber schaffen wollte, sie erdichten bzw. „ersingen" für seine Text-„Schiffe." Es *geht* — der

Irreales „ginge da" drückt es klar als ein Manko aus, als ein Defizit — es *geht* „da" kein Wind mehr für eine freie, schwimmende Lyrik, eine Schiffs-Lyrik. Es weht, im Vergleich zum Kunstwind der *Hauspostillen*-Gedichte, ein gänzlich anderer „Wind" durch das Brechtsche Arbeitszimmer von 1953, der rauhe Wind der Geschichte. Ein Wind, der fürs Machen wie fürs Verbreiten gedichteter „Geschenke" wenig günstig ist, ein Faktum, das Brecht im Motto zu den *Buckower Elegien* unüberlesbar zum Ausdruck bringt.

Brechts „Schiff," darauf hatte die erste meiner zwei Leitfragen gezielt, gibt sich als eine Fortschrift von Gelesenem zu lesen. Es zeigt sich damit als ein Lesen, das es — so die Richtung meiner zweiten Frage — gerade in seiner überaus „endlichen," weil so kompakten, so klar vom Anfang bis zum Ende überblickbaren Form eines Gedichts als unbeendbaren Prozess zur Darstellung bringt. Diese beiden Aspekte zusammengeführt, folgte daraus, dass das Gedicht selber die Signale beinhaltet, die den Lesenden zeigen, dass es kein „Ende" hat oder haben kann, dass sich vielmehr sein eigenes Enden als ein Neubeginnen gestaltet findet.

Auf die Bitte, es möge „enden," wandelt sich das Gedicht in einer Weise, die präzise dasjenige umsetzt, was in Vers 21 als *der* Effekt des „Grünens" am und im Schiff von diesem selbst beschrieben war: Sein „Gesicht" — sein Sehen und sein Aussehen also — wird, wie es heißt, „anders noch einmal." Das „Gesicht" des Gedichtes wird ein Gesehenes „fremder Fischer," das im „Nahen" diesen „verschwimmt," ein „Etwas," wie es zweimal genannt wird, das mit abnehmender Distanz dem festlegenden Blick sich entzieht. Dem *festlegenden* Sehen, gilt es zu betonen, jenem der Fischer nämlich, die den Erfolg ihrer Fahrt nach dem bewerten müssen, was am Grund des Netzes als ihr Fang hängen bleibt, nach dem, was sie als eine „Ware" dem Heimathafen zuführen können. Ihnen bleibt das „Schiff" sprachlos, „stumm," wie es im letzten Vers heißt. Anders ist es für jenen Leseblick, für jene Lektüre, von deren Effekt das Gedicht selber — mit dem „Grünen" und „Wehen" — genau besehen spricht. In Bewegung mit dem Gedicht, immerfort mit dem Text — um noch einmal den so genauen Ausdruck aus Brechts „Liquidations"-Fragment aufzunehmen — hat das Lesen hier keine „Ware" zum Ertrag, sondern einen Erkenntnisgewinn: Die Einsicht in die Beziehung von Text und Lektüre. Immerfort: Die Leserinnen und Leser, dies die ungemein frohe Botschaft von Brechts Gedicht, sie gehen nicht unter, sie bleiben oben und sie bleiben liquide, solange sie unterwegs sind auf Papierschiffen, auf geschenkten Anleihen.

ANMERKUNGEN

[1] Bertolt Brecht, *Werke*, Große kommentierte Berliner und Frankfurter Ausgabe, hrsg. Werner Hecht, Jan Knopf, Werner Mittenzwei, Klaus-Detlev Müller, Berlin/Weimar/Frankfurt/M. 1989ff., Bd. 26, S. 167. Ich zitiere im folgenden nach dieser Ausgabe, wobei die Zitate direkt im Haupttext belegt werden, und zwar jeweils in Klammern, unter Angabe der Bandnummer und der Seitenzahl.

[2] Brecht selber braucht den Ausdruck „Gebrauchswert" explizit in einem Entwurf, wo er feststellt, er halte die Form der Hauspostille „für eine ausgezeichnete, da sie den Inhalt seinem Gebrauchswert nach, den verschiedenen Bedürfnissen der Leser entsprechend, anordnet und bestimmt (23/202).

[3] Theodor W. Adorno, *Ästhetische Theorie*, hg. v. Gretel Adorno und Rolf Tiedemann, Frankfurt a.M. 1992, S. 39.

[4] Es sind m. W. in der Forschung erstmals Helmut Lethen und Hans-Thies Lehmann gewesen, die Ende der Siebziger Jahre auf einen möglichen Zusammenhang von „moderner Lyrik" und „Brechts Lyrik" überhaupt aufmerksam gemacht haben (Lehmann/Lethen [Hg.], *Bertolt Brechts „Hauspostille." Text und kollektives Lesen*, Stuttgart 1978, S. 11). Ansonsten bleiben die Gedichte der *Hauspostille* in Studien zur Moderne üblicherweise unerwähnt.

[5] Adorno, *Ästhetische Theorie*, [Anm. 3], S. 39.

[6] Ebd. S. 41.

[7] Ebd.

[8] Ebd. S. 40.

[9] Darauf, dass die „Lektionen" natürlich auch den Begriff der *lectio* beinhalten, dass sich also die *Hauspostille* schon von daher als eine Abfolge von geschriebenen *Lektüren* zu erkennen gibt, wird bereits hingewiesen bei Hans-Thies Lehmann, *Subjekt und Sprachprozesse in Bertolt Brechts „Hauspostille" (1927). Texttheoretische Lektüren*, Berlin 1978, S. 36.

[10] Wenn daher Helmut Lethen mit Bezug auf die Schlussstrophe sagt, „‚Fremde Fischer' geben auf einer Station der Küstenwache zu Protokoll, daß sie etwas sahen" (Helmut Lethen, *„Das Schiff*. Selbstkritik der Poesie," in: Lehmann/Lethen, *Bertolt Brechts Hauspostille* [Anm. 4], S. 99–121, hier: S. 103), dann ist dies nicht einfach deswegen falsch, weil die Analyse hier Elemente erfindet — „Protokoll," „Küstenwache" — für deren Gegebensein das Gedicht nicht den geringsten Anhaltspunkt liefert: Falsch ist es in einem viel grundsätzlicheren Sinn, dadurch nämlich, dass das Gedicht gerade ausschließlich Anhaltspunkte dafür gibt, dass es auf *keinerlei* extratextuelle, auf keine dem Leseprozess enthobene „Realien" referentialisierbar ist. Für das gesamte „Schiff" als den „Körper" des Gedichtes gilt dasjenige, was Brecht an anderer Stelle in der *Hauspostille* explizit als die Begehbarkeit der Papierstruktur durchs Lesen allein thematisiert: „Sie schlugen Löcher wohl in meine Wände / Und krochen fluchend wieder aus von mir: / Es war nichts drinnen als viel Platz und Stille / Sie

schrien fluchend: ich sei nur Papier" („Lied am schwarzen Samstag in der elften Stunde der Nacht vor Ostern," 11/76).

[11] Der Verweis auf Rimbauds Gedicht als Referenztext für die Schiffsballade von Brecht ist nahezu ein Gemeinplatz der einschlägigen Forschung zu Brechts Lyrik, von Schumann über Pietzker bis zu Jan Knopf. Auf die diversen impliziten und expliziten Rimbaud-Zitate speziell im Stück *Im Dickicht der Städte* hingewiesen hat Gerhard Seidel, „Frankreich im Werk Brechts. Bericht über eine Spurensuche," in: *Études germaniques*, 44 (1989), S. 4–16, hier: S. 7f. Auch Franz Norbert Mennemeier hat einige konkretere Bezüge zwischen dem Gedicht Brechts und dem „Bâteau Ivre" deutlich gemacht, ohne allerdings dem Aspekt des *Lesens* bei Brecht nähere Beachtung zu schenken (vgl. Franz Norbert Mennemeier, *Bertolt Brechts Lyrik. Aspekte, Tendenzen*, Berlin 1998, bes. S. 27ff.). Mennemeiers Befund, die Gemeinsamkeit von Brechts und Rimbauds Gedicht liege in der Tatsache, dass beidenorts „das Schiff als ‚absolute' Metapher eines universellen und intellektuellen Vorgangs" (ebd., S. 32) fungiere, halte ich für unzutreffend: Das Brechtsche „Schiff," ich unternehme es hier zu zeigen, ist nicht eine der sogenannten „absoluten Metaphern" moderner Lyrik, sondern ein Lese- und Schreibbild, das geradezu im Gegenteil die Verflüssigung und das In-Bewegung-Versetzen jedwelcher sprachlichen Absolutheitsmetaphorik selber mimetisch umsetzt. In diesem Punkt unterscheidet sich das Schiffsgedicht Brechts von seinen Bezugstexten, namentlich vom „Bâteau Ivre," für das schon Hugo Friedrich, in nach wie vor gültiger Weise, an mehreren Stellen „absolute Metaphern" lokalisiert und analysiert hat (vgl. Hugo Friedrich, *Die Struktur der modernen Lyrik*, Hamburg 1956, bes. S. 70ff.).

[12] Charles Baudelaire, *Oeuvres complètes*, Bd. I., Paris 1975, S. 134.

[13] Es ist dies jene Tendenz, die bereits Walter Benjamin in seinen Baudelaire-Aufzeichnungen als die Bewegung von Baudelaires Schreiben schlechthin ausgemacht und in einer gegenläufigen Verschlingung mit dem Charakteristikum von Nietzsches Schreibprozess zusammengebracht hat: „Bei Nietzsche liegt der Akzent auf der ewigen Wiederkunft, der der Mensch mit heroischer Fassung entgegensieht. Baudelaire geht es vielmehr um ‚das Neue,' das mit heroischer Anstrengung dem Immerwiedergleichen abzuringen ist" (Walter Benjamin, *Das Passagen-Werk*, hg. v. Rolf Tiedemann, Erster Band, Frankfurt a.M. 1983, S. 425).

[14] Insofern also, als es dabei um die Eigendarstellung einer selbsttätigen Schreibbewegung geht, bliebe zu fragen, ob man hier Hugo Friedrich tatsächlich folgen soll mit seinem Befund, „ungesagt, aber unmißverständlich" bedeuteten „die Vorgänge zugleich solche des dichterischen Subjekts" (*Die Struktur der modernen Lyrik*, [Anm. 11], S. 73).

[15] Artur Rimbaud, *Oeuvres complètes*, Paris 1972, S. 66.

[16] Dieser Befund steht im Gegensatz zur communis opinio der Rimbaud-Forschung, wie sie sich ausdrückt in Hermann Wetzels Formulierung, es sei zu „unterstreichen, daß Rimbauds chaotische Ausfahrt auf einen freien Willensentschluß zurückgeht" (Hermann H. Wetzel, *Rimbauds Dichtung. Ein Versuch, „die rauhe Wirklichkeit zu umarmen,"* Stuttgart 1985, S. 111). Von einer Affirmation der Fiktion eines „freien" Subjekts kann m.E. weder für Rimbauds

Gedicht noch für Baudelaires „Voyage" gesprochen werden, eine Erkenntnis, die das Brechtsche Gedicht als Erfahrung der eigenen Lesegenealogie umsetzt: Die Freiheit, von der das „Schiff" kündet, ist die Selbstbefreiung von der Fiktion des autonomen Subjekts im Text und das explizite Sich-Überlassen an die Schreib-/Lesebewegung, „ohne Groll."

[17] Rimbaud, *Oeuvres* [Anm. 15], S. 67.

[18] Rimbaud, „Voyelles," in: *Oeuvres* [Anm. 15], S. 53.

[19] Artur Rimbaud, *Une Saison en Enfer*, in: *Oeuvres* [Anm. 15], S. 106.

[20] In diesem Punkt scheint mir eines der avancierteren Lektüremodelle, wie es in der jüngeren Brecht-Forschung diskutiert wurde, revisionsbedürftig. Philip Thomson, *The Poetry of Brecht. Seven Studies*, Chapel Hill/London 1989, S. 29f., unterscheidet im Zusammenhang der *Hauspostillen*-Lyrik drei textrelevante Leser-Instanzen: "The *actual* reader [...], the *fictive* reader, a character created by the text [...] the *ideal* reader, created likewise by the text in the sense that the text implicitly envisages a reader whose role as addressee the text creates." Das Schiffsgedicht, so meine ich hier zu zeigen, fingiert gerade nicht ein Lesesubjekt, keinen impliziten Leser im Iserschen Sinne, sondern praefiguriert ein *Lesen* als die jeweilige Präsenz des Textes, in dessen stets neuem und anderem Vollzug ein möglicher „reader" überhaupt erst entsteht. Brecht akzentuiert entschieden die Transitorik und Vergänglichkeit allen Lesens, die keine *Festlegung* einer außertextuell abgesicherten und fixen Position eines Lektüresubjekts mehr erlaubt.

[21] Auch Mennemeier, *Bertolt Brechts Lyrik*, [Anm. 11] S. 29, erwähnt in diesem Zusammenhang die „Metaphorik der Schwangerschaft," ohne allerdings den weiteren Konsequenzen dieses „Wehens" als einer Selbstprokreation der Bildlichkeit, *im* Gedicht und dargestellt *durch* das Gedicht, nachzugehen.

[22] Brecht lässt hier selbstverständlich auch ganz deutlich die stehende Wendung des „Auf den Hund-Kommens" anklingen: Die Kunst ist auf den Hund gekommen und muss deswegen erst einmal „auf den Grund kommen," muss — im Bild des Gedichtes — „grün und wehend" untergehen, um überhaupt weiterbestehen zu können.

[23] Im Schiffsbild berührt sich demgemäss die traditionelle Selbstdarstellung des Dichtens mit einem der ebenso traditionellen, namentlich für die Barocklyrik als Topos zu bezeichnenden, Gegenstände lyrischer Dichtung: Dem Bild des individuellen Lebens als der *navigatio vitae*. Brecht gestaltet diese Metapher ganz offensichtlich als ein „Bild im Bild," indem sein „Schiff," als der herkömmliche sprachliche Bildträger hier selber untergeht, mithin dem vorgegebenen Lauf der *navigatio vitae* folgt, den es der Tradition folgend bloß zu repräsentieren hätte.

„Brechts autonome Kunst oder Mehr Spätmodernismus!"

Dieser Aufsatz rekonstruiert eine oft vergessene Geschichte: Brechts und Benjamins bedeutende Wiederbegegnung, angefangen im Sommer 1938, mit der Frage der romantischen, lyrischen Aura. Beide beginnen das Werk des englischen Dichters der Romantik, Percy Shelley, erneut zu lesen, zu übersetzen und zu überdenken; dies führt zu ihrer Neuerwägung des kritisch-progressiven Wertes der in der Romantik zuerst projizierten lyrischen Aura. Diese Begegnungen führen zu Benjamins brillanter Kompliziertheit einiger seiner früheren ästhetisch-politischen Ansichten über Allegorie und lyrischer Aura in der Moderne, andererseits zu Brechts Wiederaufnahme einer kritischen, negativ-auratischen Dichtung während der vierziger und fünfziger Jahre; und sie tragen zu Adornos späteren Überlegungen bei, wie die *via-negativa* Aura der lyrischen Poesie eine potentiell kritische moderne Ästhetik in Anspruch nimmt. In Hinblick auf die Zuversicht vieler linken Postmodernisten, wie sie die Brecht-Benjaminische Ansichten verstehen, die die modernistische ästhetische Aura hinter sich lassen oder abschaffen wollen, könnte die Neuerwägung dieser Materialien gegenwärtige Periodisierungen und Stilcharakterisierungen der Postmoderne und ihre oft verworfene Vorgeschichte umgestalten. Die Erkenntnis, wie eingehend Brecht und Benjamin (während und nach ihrem erneuten Lesen von Shelley) lyrische Aura und ästhetische Autonomie weiterhin aufgespürt haben, sollte tatsächlich gängige Standarddarstellungen wie sie wechselweise ein linker Tauschwertzynismus und ein mechanisch-reproduzierbarer Ausstellungswertavantgardismus bilden, erschüttern.

Brecht's Autonomous Art,
or More Late Modernism!

Robert Kaufman

Among the real pleasures of Fredric Jameson's *Brecht and Method* (1998) must be counted Jameson's characteristically penetrating attention to issues of form. Jameson's illuminating treatment of Brecht's formal engagements in art and theory support a powerful argument for the Brechtian aesthetic as nothing less than modern Marxism's dialectical relay switch between form and theory itself. In short — although Jameson doesn't put it quite this way — Brechtian form, with its crucial enactments of formal estrangement, teaches us via form to work *through* form towards theory (towards a theory, to be sure, of and informed by history). In a strong rewriting that in effect drafts into Brecht's construction brigade everyone from Descartes to Marx, Sartre, and Barthes, Jameson's name for this dynamically holistic formal process becomes *method*, or, better, *Brecht and Method*. Not the least fascinating maneuver here is the proximity Jameson implicitly establishes between Brechtian form and formal vocation in its classically Kantian and modernist senses. Like the latter two, Brechtian form, in Jameson's persuasive account, generates out of its at least provisional autonomy a critical purchase on the sociohistorical and on the potential for progressive or radical engagement with it.

Now Jameson — like Brecht himself — takes pains to distinguish the Brechtian case from bourgeois formalism (meaning Kant and romanticism) or even from Marxian formalism (meaning especially Adorno and high hermetic modernism). Yet to his credit, Jameson, rather than avoiding the evident and glaringly problematic overlap, goes so far as to court its recognition when he foregrounds Brecht's interest in that ostensibly high formalist phenomenon of both romantic and modern literature, *autonomization*. Certainly it is central to Brecht's art and Jameson's analysis of it that an otherwise merely formalist notion of literary autonomy, from the level of image or sentence right up to the institution of aesthetic autonomy itself, is to be "refunctioned" rather than simply ratified. But you may already have guessed that, if space permitted, I would be trying to show at length how in Brecht's art if not his theory such refunctioning finally reveals its identity with aesthetic form and aesthetic experience as such: which is to say that Brecht ultimately echoes the ways Marx *and* Adorno reimagine and radically

New Essays on Brecht / Neue Versuche über Brecht
Maarten van Dijk et al., eds., *The Brecht Yearbook / Das Brecht-Jahrbuch*
Volume 26 (Toronto, Canada: The International Brecht Society, 2001)

bless, with varying degrees of explicitness but hardly any important revisions, that good old-time Kantian aesthetic. I would also want to contend that far from this involving only a few privileged moments in Brecht's *oeuvre*, it is to be found virtually everywhere therein, hence also everywhere in Jameson's wonderful meditation on the Brecht *Werke*.

The present essay will focus on one generative instance, a terrifically charged intersection of literary, aesthetic, and sociopolitical history. This intersection has the added benefit of highlighting the fact that the undersong of formal aesthetic autonomy appears not only during Brecht's later years, amid his palpable concerns about post-humous influence and canonicity, but already within heated, earlier debates about artistic *engagement* and intervention.[1] Precisely here Brecht turns to a figure of special significance for radical and Marxian traditions, someone whose stand for "commitment" is paradoxically inseparable from formalist dedication to high lyric aesthetic autonomy: the English poet Percy Shelley. Elsewhere I've tried in a more sustained manner to trace this nineteenth-to-twentieth-century trajectory, with an eye towards unsettling recent "critique of aesthetic ideology" narratives about British romanticism and its modern aftermaths; those narratives, of course, often or usually invoke Marx and the Frankfurt School. But here, with the trepidation appropriate to an *Ausländer* who has wandered from his accustomed English-department territory, I'd like to stress the modern chapters of the story, and begin to think about how the Brechtian nexus at issue will finally set in motion key developments in poetics and critical theory for the post-1945 period, from Europe to Latin America to the U.S.

A few Anglo-American critics have briefly discussed Brecht's interest in Shelley. Steven Jones's *Shelley's Satire* significantly expands this body of commentary, not only by offering nuanced interpretation of Brecht's recourse to Shelley's *Mask of Anarchy* for his 1947 satiric poem "Der anachronistische Zug oder Freiheit und Democracy," but also by remarking the importance of Brecht's 1938 translation of, and essay on, Shelley's *Mask*.[2] (*The Mask of Anarchy* [1819] was one of Shelley's most celebrated responses to what was popularly known as Peterloo or the Manchester Massacre, an event in which armed cavalry attacked a huge but peaceful demonstration for parliamentary reform and workers' rights. The Manchester Massacre immediately achieved the iconic public, rallying cry status that something like the 1960 Sharpeville Massacre in South Africa, or the Edmund Pettus Bridge attack on African-American civil rights marchers, would come to have for a later period. At all events, the modern British labor and parliamentary-reform movements both treat the Manchester Massacre as a foundational moment.[3]) In a footnote, Jones gestures towards the

Robert Kaufman

importance of a crux somewhat beyond the limits of his own study, though happily consonant with it.[4] This crux has otherwise been virtually ignored by historians of literature, poetics, and critical theory. Jones notices that one of Walter Benjamin's posthumously published, extremely influential Baudelaire essays (written in 1938) presents a one-stanza quotation and two-sentence analysis of — along with a gnomic reference to — a then-unpublished Brecht translation of lines from Shelley's rollicking, "Satanic," anti-Wordsworthian satire *Peter Bell the Third*.[5] Jones also observes that *Peter Bell the Third*'s famous line about Hell being "a city much like London" reappears in Brecht's 1941 poem "Nachdenkend über die Hölle."[6] In fact, these materials are part of a larger cache, which plays a fascinating role in both modernist art and Critical Theory.

In 1936, Brecht, Lion Feuchtwanger, and Wili Bredel become the editors of the new, Moscow-based journal *Das Wort*. *Das Wort*, of course, is established by leftist exiles from the Third Reich as a Popular Front, Communist-led "anti-fascist literary journal"; it publishes texts by everyone from Thomas, Heinrich, and Klaus Mann, to Langston Hughes, Hemingway, Anna Seghers, Lukács, Benjamin, César Vallejo, and others. In June 1937, *Das Wort* publishes *The Mask of Anarchy*'s final fifty-five stanzas as translated by the expressionist poet, playwright, novelist and critic, Alfred Wolfenstein, who had fled Germany for Prague in 1934, and who would soon, upon the Wehrmacht's entry into Czechoslovakia, flee to France until it too would be occupied by Hitler.[7] Back in 1922, the publisher Paul Cassirer — Ernst Cassirer's cousin — had published a slim, gorgeous edition of Wolfenstein's Shelley translations, simply titled *Shelley Dichtungen*. (Wolfenstein had also written a translation-treatment of Shelley's play *The Cenci* for a 1924 Berlin theatrical production.) The *Shelley Dichtungen* had featured excerpts from Shelley's *Adonais*, *Hellas*, and *Prometheus Unbound*; from the entirety of various shorter works (such as "Alastor," "Ode to the West Wind," and "Hymn to Intellectual Beauty"); and a number of still shorter lyrics, including the explicitly political sonnet "England in 1819." Though the *Shelley Dichtungen* had not included *The Mask of Anarchy*, Wolfenstein, in the *Dichtungen*'s Nachwort [Afterword], quoted liberally from it.

Indeed, Wolfenstein's Nachwort to the *Shelley Dichtungen* is quite an undertaking, with great importance for the history of debate about the relationships between high, formalist aesthetic autonomy and more apparently interventionist poetics: Wolfenstein insists on the radical unity of Shelley's work, the ways that the seemingly abstract idealist and ostensibly concrete activist modes inhere within each other. Wolfenstein specifically transvalues — or bounces off Swinburne's transvaluation — of Matthew Arnold's notorious tagging of Shelley as

193

"the ineffectual angel"; Wolfenstein concedes that Shelley *was* angelic, provided one remembers the terrifying nature of angelic presence. Bringing together Shelley's *Prometheus Unbound* and the *Defence of Poetry*, the *Mask*, various Hölderlin poems, and a string of allusions highly resonant for a Left German tradition that tended to think in terms of Promethean assaults on the heavens (from Goethe's work, to Marx's and Engels's lines about the Parisian communards having "stormed heaven itself"), Wolfenstein maintains that Shelley's "idealism" is best understood as an expression of poetry's fierce judgment of a world built on oppression and suffering.[8]

In January 1938, six months after publishing Wolfenstein's *Mask* translations, *Das Wort* publishes a lengthy essay on Shelley by Walter Haenisch.[9] Haenisch had left Berlin for Moscow in 1931, to work on the *Marx-Engels Gesamtausgabe*. Haenisch's article on Shelley, less literary and more overtly focused on particulars of sociohistorical context than Wolfenstein's 1922 Nachwort, nonetheless shares affinities with it, above all, concerning the unity of Shelley's work. Haenisch treats many of the same poems as Wolfenstein, and, like him, stresses the significance of Shelley's having been primarily a high *lyric* poet — a crucial factor, Haenisch indicates, in Marx's and Engels's championing of Shelley. After discussing various poems in relation to their sociopolitical contexts, Haenisch suggests that an *oeuvre* encompassing both *Prometheus Unbound* and the *Mask of Anarchy* is at one with the project undertaken in *Das Kapital*. (Such an idealist-materialist coalition, incidentally, develops a parallel history on the Western side of the Atlantic in the same era, and one of its guiding lights is the Shelleyan [and, as Russell A. Berman has recently shown, the very steeped-in-German-philosophy] radical scholar-activist W.E.B. Du Bois. Du Bois's Shelleyanism is consciously taken up or shared by a range of figures across Left and African-American culture, extending all the way to Popular Front veterans like Ossie Davis, Ruby Dee, and the labor organizer Ella Reeve "Mother" Bloor, committed Shelleyans all.)[10]

So in 1937 and early '38, Brecht and Benjamin are reading all this Shelley-discourse in a journal they're both associated with and for which Brecht, in fact, serves, at times very ambivalently, as a principal editor. In June 1938, Benjamin joins Brecht in Svendborg, Denmark, where the two work together for several months, sharing ideas and manuscripts. In July, Brecht writes and hands to Benjamin a group of essays intended for *Das Wort*; there is evidence that Brecht may even have talked through the essays with Benjamin as he drafted them.[11] Some of these essays, which take issue with Lukácsian realism and defend the critical value of experimental art, have been familiar to Anglo-American readers since 1977, when they appeared in *Aesthetics and Politics*, and to German-reading audiences at least since the 1973 publication of *Die Expressionismusdebatte*.[12] Brecht went ahead and submitted the essays to *Das Wort*, which never printed them.[13] But in addition to fears about rocking the orthodox boat, the other editors of *Das Wort* may also have declined to publish these Brecht essays in order to protect Brecht himself. If so, they had good reason; which is to say, the materials of our story get grimmer: a few months after *Das Wort* had published Walter Haenisch's January 1938 Shelley essay, Haenisch became one among legions falsely accused, amid the general insanity in Moscow, of "Trotskyite" and/or "Social-Fascist" espionage. Haenisch was denounced and executed as a "people's enemy."[14]

One of these unpublished Brecht essays of July 1938 — which unfortunately is not included in either *Aesthetics and Politics* or in *Die Expressionismusdebatte*, and which has never appeared in translation — is "Weite und Vielfalt der realistischen Schreibweise [Range and Diversity of the Realist Literary Mode]."[15] The essay's central exhibit is Brecht's quotation, translation, and analysis of 25 stanzas from Shelley's *Mask*. (Brecht's crackling translation features, by the way, an almost absolute literalness that departs intriguingly from Wolfenstein's *Das Wort* translation of the *Mask* a year earlier.)[16] Brecht claims that "the great revolutionary English poet *Shelley*" demonstrates how a vital fusion of aesthetic experiment, speculative imagination, and song may lead to, rather than away from, critical mimesis of the real (the latter being virtually synonymous, throughout "Weite und Vielfalt," with commitment).[17]

At the same time that he translates and analyzes the *Mask*, Brecht also translates nine stanzas from Shelley's *Peter Bell the Third*, which apparently remain unpublished throughout Brecht's lifetime.[18] Brecht immediately gives his *Mask* essay-translation and the *Peter Bell* translation to Benjamin; Benjamin copies out the *Peter Bell* stanzas, preserving them in the pages we know as the *Passagen-Werk* or *Arcades Project*.[19] As already mentioned, Benjamin also quotes, and briefly comments on, *Peter Bell*'s "Hell is a city much like London" stanza in Benjamin's "The Paris of the Second Empire in Baudelaire" — an essay whose manuscript Benjamin gives to Brecht; Brecht in turn reads "The Paris of the Second Empire in Baudelaire" and copies out portions of it for the fragments *he's* writing on Baudelaire.[20] The Brecht-Benjamin interchange, amounting almost to collaboration, is so intertwined that it's hard to tell the order of influence among these July and August 1938 writings. At any rate, a common set of subsequently canonized images and ideas appears in Brecht's Shelley essay, Benjamin's Baudelaire essay, and then Brecht's Baudelaire meditations and later poetry.

Equall remarkable is an extended interpretive passage on Shelley and Baudelaire in the *Passagen-Werk*; based on Brecht's translation of the nine *Peter Bell* stanzas, it is clearly the fuller version of the supercompressed but better-known comparison of Shelley and the French poet that Benjamin offers in "The Paris of the Second Empire in Baudelaire." In the *Passagen-Werk* entry titled "Zur Bilderflucht in der Allegorie [On Image-Flight in Allegory]," Benjamin more extensively develops the comparison of Shelley and Baudelaire. The remarks gesture toward a sense of how the two poets' divergent approaches to allegory chart the mode's modern fate in general:

> The incisive effect [of Shelley's *Peter Bell*] depends...on the fact that Shelley's *grasp* [*Griff*] of allegory makes itself felt. It is this grasp that is missing in Baudelaire. This grasp, which makes palpable the distance of the modern poet from allegory, is precisely what enables allegory to incorporate into itself the most immediate realities... — Shelley rules over the allegory, Baudelaire is ruled by it.[21]

Benjamin says a good deal more, but his point isn't to proclaim Shelley the greater poet. He implies instead that a turn in modernity and the history of aesthetic "aura" has made Shelley's critical allegoresis unavailable to Baudelaire. Baudelaire's intermittently critical triumph will then be to make lyric poetry sing — severely and intensely — its own impossibility in the age of art's mechanical or technical reproducibility.

While this is not the place for fullscale treatment of the crisis of allegory in Baudelaire (or for Benjamin's ideas about the career of allegory in modern poetics thereafter), a few words are in order. *Allegory* is of course the charged term whose modern reprioritization over *symbol* stems in no small measure from Benjamin's 1928 study of the German play of lamentation, the *Trauerspiel*.[22] For Benjamin, allegory's initial point of departure is that it represents the broken, ruptured truth of attempts at prematurely "symbolic" reconciliation. Hence allegory signifies its own necessarily nonidentical — thus potentially critical and constructionist — character. Suffice to say here that the *Passagen-Werk* section about Shelley, Baudelaire, and allegory is one of the key instances where Benjamin articulates his formal theory (of allegory's proto-critical, constructionist nature) together with an historical instance of a lyric poet whom Benjamin, Brecht, and their circle definitely regard as progressive and committed: whom they regard, indeed, as *den grossen revolutionären Dichter*.[23]

Activated by Brecht and reconstellated by Benjamin, the 1938 matrix of Shelley, Baudelaire, and allegory generates two trajectories that presently concern us: towards the later art of Brecht himself, and towards the philosophical aesthetics of Adorno. Brecht, already having brooded over the poetic kindling, finds it reignited when, in his already strange Los Angeles exile, he belatedly learns (in 1941) of Benjamin's suicide at the Spanish border. The news contributes importantly to the devastating *Hollywoodelegien* and to texts bound chronologically, thematically, and formally to them. It's rarely been noticed that, among these texts, not only "Nachdenkend über die Hölle" is indebted to the figure that that poem calls "mein Bruder Shelley." In fact, the larger groupings of related poems and drafts — which include three texts that explicitly treat Benjamin's suicide — are saturated with themes, directly translated quotations, paraphrases, and images from Shelley: especially from *Peter Bell* and the *Mask*, but from the *Defence of Poetry* and other Shelley texts as well.

Just as significant, in these poems, are Brecht's very complex treatments of tonal register, his stereoscopically introduced and mutually dissolving images, and a syntax of deceptive ease and elegance whose unreeling builds rather than releases tension.[24] All of which, Brecht signals time and again, come in no small part from that romantic source, Brecht's "Bruder Shelley," who had clearly found political militancy inseparable from high lyric impulse and formal aesthetic autonomy, not least in time of difficulty and loss. It is not overshooting the mark to say that Brecht's almost too-terrible decision — to write wartime, Shelleyan elegy that could be taken for bitter satire, and vice versa — is a decision that should count as powerful, and intriguingly *late Modernist* evidence for the acute readings various Anglo-American critics have offered of *Peter Bell the Third*'s historical originality: its relentless insistence on thinking modern lyric and satiric impulse together, and on thinking both in relation to modern poetry's ways of taking history's measure.[25] It seems barely necessary to add that Brecht's efforts reinvent, *via Shelleyan lyric autonomy*, exactly the critical possibility Benjamin had seen as fitfully available in Baudelaire (albeit, in Baudelaire, almost against itself, certainly less definitively than *in Shelley*, and perhaps, Benjamin had thought, for its historical endgame).

Brecht gives the Shelley-infused poems to Hanns Eisler, who works with the *Hollywoodelegien* and related texts of what will become the *Hollywoodliederbuch* and who then, one Los Angeles night in October 1942, sits down at the piano and premieres these impossible *lieder* for an audience consisting of Brecht, Hans Winge, and Herbert Marcuse. Brecht only ups the ante by then testily noting Eisler's distressing tendency, when Eisler "speaks about, [though] not when he composes" the settings, to drop the elegies' significance down a rhetorical or formal-stylistic notch.[26] That's a fantastic micro-dispute to consider, because Eisler, far from undertaking a wholesale genre stripping or programmatic leveling of still-too-high elegiac verse, instead so virtuosically runs Schubertian and Schumannesque *lieder*, French *chanson*, and Schönbergian twelve-tone composition in and out of one another, that it is hard to miss the settings' recognizably high modernist *tour de force* of newly achieved form and voice. It's as if the (protopostmodern) levelling holistically occurs in what Brecht hears as Eisler's irritatingly interpretive-judgmental comments, so that the work itself can then move on to enact its real, critical desideratum: modernist virtuosity in the exploration, coordination, and imaginative synthesis of extremely diverse literary-musical materials and dauntingly various stylistic currents. Brecht acknowledges as much when he rather bluntly insists, against Eisler's alleged murmuring about the poems' mere occasionality or jottedness, on the *Hollywoodelegien*'s compressed monumentality and *gravitas*: "these are full-scale poems" and "in fact the compositions are probably really important as music too."[27]

On the page and in Eisler's settings, the poems exert a profound influence, across at least three continents, on an increasingly late, perhaps still stubbornly persisting critical practice of modernist poetry and, to a lesser degree, modernist music composition. Indeed, with their complicated reception histories, the *Hollywoodelegien* and the poems immediately connected to them testify to the unexpectedly continued, vibrant existence *of* late modernism, well into the era commonly called postmodern (and in which modernism is regularly framed as canonical or reactionary object of critique).[28] The very fact of the elegies' modernist aesthetic and declaredly critical-romantic lineage, which for Brecht seems indissolubly linked to the poems' unblinking view of commitment's unpredictable paths in art and life, would appear substantially to reconfigure recent periodizations and style-characterizations of postmodernism and its much maligned antecedent.

That is, Brecht's late enterprise entails the non-parodic revivification of an ostensibly passé, "lyric-aesthetic" poetics, a revivification Brecht in part accomplishes by returning to the Shelleyan-Baudelairean imperative that lyric critically reimagine itself. Though not exactly hermetic, Brecht's negative-sideways, backward-forward path towards postauratic aura effectively identifies lyric vocation with — or as fuel for — Marx's old "ruthless critique of everything existing," which in *its* turn casts a salutarily cold eye upon lyric's criticopolitical pretensions. Brecht's structuring of this fruitful and constitutive tension between aura and protopolitical critique amounts, astonishingly enough (since it's after all *Brecht* that we're talking about), to the reconjuration of a Left Enlightenment, radically formal aesthetics from elegy ash. Recognition of such a project in his later poetry should begin to unsettle long-standard accounts of how Brecht (or Benjamin, for that matter) alternately models an exchange-value Left cynicism, and a mechanical-reproductionist, exhibition-value "avant-gardist anti-aesthetic" (all of which, in solidarity with radically intended postmodernist art and theory, oppose themselves to a more auratic, romantically derived modernism).[29] (In fact, already in 1940 — in the earlier aftermath of his reencounter with Shelley but before Benjamin's death and the poetry Brecht begins to write thereafter — Brecht repeats a very Shelleyan trajectory by emphasizing the progressive value of *Wordsworth's* most seemingly formalist, apparently sociopolitically inconsequential, lyricism. Moreover, Brecht's reflections on Wordsworth lead him to make a striking, well-nigh Adornian distinction: "Die Kunst *ist* ein autonomer Bezirk, wenn auch unter keinen Umständen ein autarker [Art *is* an autonomous sphere, though by no means an autarchic one].")[30]

Meanwhile, Benjamin's Brecht-indebted reflections on Shelley, Baudelaire and allegory will serve as one of several seeds for Adorno's attempts, after Benjamin's death, critically to preserve and reanimate his friend's work, and to reassess earlier disagreements (including Adorno's and Benjamin's disagreement over the quality of Brecht's Shelley translations themselves).[31] In a gestural shorthand, sometimes explicitly and more often by implication, Adorno writes this Brecht-derived *Shelley-Bild* into and underneath a key series of texts: "Rede über Lyrik und Gesellschaft," "Engagement," "Parataxis," and *Ästhetische Theorie.*[32] Adorno effectively coordinates Brecht's and Benjamin's Shelley with a range of resonance and Baudelairean *correspondance* that includes Benjaminian angelicism, storm images for allegory, and projections of "critical" lyric. Brecht's "Bruder Shelley" thus participates in what may be Adorno's own most enduring legacy, the attempt to uncover and work out a crucial distinction between aesthetic and aestheticization.

Impelled in part by Benjamin's thinking about lyric and allegory, Adorno finds an anti-essentialist, anti-aestheticist constructivism at the heart of Immanuel Kant's aesthetics and the Kantian Critical Philosophy as a whole, which, Adorno suggests, remains surprisingly central to Marxian dialectics and kindred efforts in critical thought. Underlying Adorno's Kantian account is the aesthetic's *quasi*conceptual and thus *quasi*social quality. The aesthetic (with lyric traditionally at its apex), while looking like conceptual-objective, "useful," content-determined thought or activity, quite precisely only *looks like* them, only mimes them at the level of form. Aesthetic thought-experience in some way precedes conceptual-objective, content-and-use-oriented thought; in that sense, the aesthetic *is* formal because, rather than being determined by, it *provides the form for* conceptual thought or cognition. Aesthetic thought-experience remains free (at least, relative to more properly conceptual thought) from the preexistent rules assumed to govern conceptual thought. In the Kantian lexicon, this makes the aesthetic a site of *reflective* rather than *determinate* judgment. The aesthetic, then, serves as mold or frame for the construction *of* conceptual thought, or for "cognition in general," as Kant puts it.

The aesthetic serves also as formal and imaginative engine for new, experimental (because previously non-existent) concepts. With its quasiconceptual and quasisocial character, the aesthetic can provide a prerequisite of critical thought by offering formal means for the development of new (not even necessarily utopian) concepts. In indispensable acts of critically constructionist estrangement, such concepts may bring to light presently obscured aspects of substantive social reality (aspects of society not already determined by society's own conceptual view of itself). The operative notion is that thought determined by society — by society's own concepts of itself (i.e., status quo, reigning concepts of society) — can never give a satisfactory picture of that society. This finally resolves into a fundamental strain of Adorno's aesthetics, to which the Brecht-Benjamin Shelley contributes far more than an undersong, and that can be expressed as follows: Lyric or aesthetic experiment helps construct and make available the intellectual-emotional apparatus for accessing, and to that extent helps make available the social material of, "the new." And "the new" for Adorno is shorthand for the not-yet-grasped features of the mode of production and, in fact, of all that is emergent in the social. This constructivist theory and practice sees that experiment in lyric — lyric or the aesthetic *as* experiment — helps make new areas of the modern fitfully available *to* perception in the first place. Constructivist estrangement by itself — that is, aesthetic constructivism by itself — guarantees neither progressive subjectivity nor commitment to emanipatory politics, nor any final take on what constitutes correct historical analysis of a given phenomenon. But this construction of perceptual or cognitive capability is prerequisite to such subjectivity, critical thought, commitment, and historicization.[33]

There's good evidence that full awareness of the confluence or overlap between them would have driven Brecht and Adorno nuts. But that itself may be good evidence for its reality, and for its value as a place from which to start thinking about the modernisms that may already be succeeding our late postmodernism. Interestingly enough, the last few decades of experiment in poetry and the other arts offer eloquent, nondiscursive testimonies that connect uncannily to the matrices developed by Brecht, Benjamin, and Adorno. There would be a lot to say about developments on this score in contemporary poetry, drama, painting, and music; about the ways that the question of lyric does or doesn't translate into theater and cinema; about the potential meanings — for today's art, criticism, and theory — of any Brechtian-Adornian convergence. But that discussion will have to wait, at least for a while.[34]

Robert Kaufman

NOTES

For their responses to earlier versions of this essay and/or assistance with translations, I am indebted to Russell A. Berman, Adam Casdin, Norma Cole, Lydia Goehr, Geoffrey Galt Harpham, Stephen Hinton, Robert Hullot-Kentor, Tamara Levitz, and Arthur Strum. Any mistakes are the author's own.

[1] On Brecht's process of thinking within his own art about canonicity, see Russell A. Berman, "Brecht: The Poet and the Canon," unpublished paper delivered at the Brecht centenary celebration, Stanford University, July 1998.

[2] Steven E. Jones, *Shelley's Satire: Violence, Exhortation, and Authority* (DeKalb: Northern Illinois University Press, 1994), 103–5. See too Jones's "Shelley's Satire of Succession and Brecht's Anatomy of Regression: 'The Mask of Anarchy' and 'Der anachronistische Zug oder Freiheit und Democracy'" in *Shelley: Poet and Legislator of the World*, ed. Betty T. Bennett and Stuart Curran (Baltimore and London: The Johns Hopkins University Press, 1996), 193–200. As Jones indicates, some earlier English-language critics had also made valuable contributions towards charting the Brecht-Shelley relationship; cf., e.g., S.S. Prawer, *Comparative Literary Studies: An Introduction* (London: Duckworth, 1973), 92–96, and Richard Cronin, *Shelley's Poetic Thoughts* (New York/London: St. Martin's/MacMillan, 1981), 39–42.

See also Bertolt Brecht, "Der anachronistische Zug oder Freiheit und Democracy," in Brecht, *Gesammelte Werke*, ed. Suhrkamp Verlag in cooperation with Elisabeth Hauptmann (Frankfurt/M.: Suhrkamp), 20 vols. (1967), 4 [*Gedichte*], ed. Elisabeth Hauptmann in cooperation with Rosemarie Hill (1967): 943–49; the text is translated as "The Anachronistic Procession or Freedom and Democracy" in Bertolt Brecht, *Poems: 1913–1956*, ed. John Willett and Ralph Manheim, trans. Willett, Manheim, et. al (London and New York: 1987), 409–14. In the later and more comprehensive German edition — the *Bertolt Brecht Werke: Große kommentierte Berliner und Frankfurter Ausgabe*, ed. Werner Hecht, Jan Knopf, Werner Mittenzwei, and Klaus-Detlef Müller, 30 vols. (Berlin and Frankfurt: Aufbau/Suhrkamp, 1989–1998) — the poem appears under the title "Freiheit und Democracy," 15 [*Gedichte* 5], ed. Jan Knopf and Brigitte Bergheim, in cooperation with Annette Ahlborn, Günter Berg, and Michael Duchardt (1993): 183–88. Unless otherwise indicated, all further references to Brecht's German texts are to the *Werke: Große kommentierte* edition and are cited by volume and page. All translations of Brecht, unless making specific reference to Willett's and Manheim's *Poems* or unless otherwise noted, are my own.

[3] See Percy Bysshe Shelley, *The Mask of Anarchy*, in *Shelley's Poetry and Prose*, ed. Donald H. Reiman and Sharon B. Powers (New York: Norton, 1977), 301–10. Unless otherwise indicated, all further references to Shelley's writing are to this edition. Shelley fashioned the ninety-one quatrain stanzas of the *Mask* in popular ballad style; but as commentators have remarked, Shelley also infused the *Mask* with stylistic elements typically found in his high-lyric mode.

[4] *Shelley's Satire*, 183–84, n.24.

[5] See "Das Paris des Second Empire bei Baudelaire" in Walter Benjamin, *Charles Baudelaire: Ein Lyriker im Zeitalter des Hochkapitalismus. Zwei Fragmente.*, ed. and with an Afterword by Rolf Tiedemann (Frankfurt/M.: Suhrkamp, 1969), 63 n.49 [vol. I.2, ed. Rolf Tiedemann and Hermann Schweppenhäuser (1974): 562 n.51, of Benjamin, *Gesammelte Schriften*, prepared with the cooperation of Theodor W. Adorno and Gershom Scholem, ed. Rolf Tiedemann and Hermann Schweppenhäuser (Frankfurt/M.: Suhrkamp, 1972–1999), 7 vols. in 14 individual vols., plus 3 Supplement vols.]. In English, see "The Paris of the Second Empire in Baudelaire" in Benjamin, *Charles Baudelaire: A Lyric Poet in the Era of High Capitalism*, trans. Harry Zohn (London: New Left Books, 1973), 59 n.48. For the Benjamin-Adorno disagreements over "Das Paris des Second Empire bei Baudelaire," see my n.31 below.

[6] Shelley, *Peter Bell the Third*, "Part Third: Hell," 330, l.147; Brecht *Werke* 15 [*Gedichte* 5]: 46, and *Poems*, 367. In the Brecht *Werke*, the poem is known by its first words, "Nachdenkend, wie ich höre," whereas in the older *Gesammelte Werke* (vol. 4 [*Gedichte*]: 830), it is formally titled "Nachdenkend über die Hölle," by which title it is still often discussed in the critical literature, even where the later, *Werke* text, is cited.

[7] Wolfenstein's translation of the *Mask* stanzas is the first text in the "Übersetzungen [Translations]" section of *Das Wort*'s June, 1937 issue (Heft 6, 1937), pp. 63-65. The translated *Mask* excerpt is titled "Sie Sind Wenige — Ihr Seid Viel! [They are Few — You are Many!]"; an introductory note tells *Das Wort* readers that the stanzas come from the last part of Shelley's *Mask*, and that they have been translated by Wolfenstein.

The German title (and text) translates but reverses the *Mask*'s celebrated, twice-repeated line addressing English workers (a line Shelley simultaneously intends as description, incantation, and exhortation/inspiration): "Ye are many — they are few." (In Shelley's text, these words appear at l.155 and again in the poem's final line [l. 372]). Wolfenstein apparently changes Shelley's word order in an attempt to preserve, in German, what he perceives as the essence of the *Mask*'s rhyme-scheme, syntax, and overall rhythm. The reversal may also reflect Wolfenstein's and *Das Wort*'s political judgment about the importance of ending — that is, ending first the bold-faced, all-capitalized, exclamatory title given to the *Mask*-excerpt; then, the repeated phrase within the translated stanzas; finally, the translated text as a whole — with the "many," rather than the ruling class's "few."

[8] Wolfenstein, "Nachwort" to *Dichtungen* (Berlin: Paul Cassirer, 1922), 87–94; reprinted as "Nachwort zu *Dichtungen* von Shelley" in Alfred Wolfenstein, *Werke*, ed. Hermann Haarmann and Günter Holtz (Mainz: Hase & Hoehler, 1982-1993) 5 vols., 4 [*Vermischte Schriften: Ästhetik, Literatur, Politik*, ed. Hermann Haarmann, Karen Tieth, and Olaf Müller (1993)]: 210–15. The *Vermischte Schriften*, along with the poems, short stories, novels, and plays collected in the other volumes of Wolfenstein's *Werke*, reveal Wolfenstein's writ-

ings to have been thoroughly saturated by his readings in, and responses to, Shelley. For a valuable discussion of how Shelley infuses Wolfenstein's attempts to couple, or put into dialogue, an experimental poetics and a committed Left politics, see Klaus Siebenhaar, "Ästhetik und Utopie: Das Shelley-Bild Alfred Wolfensteins: Anmerkungen zum Verhältnis von Dichtung und Gesellschaft im Spätexpressionismus," in *Preis der Vernunft: Literatur und Kunst zwischen Aufklärung, Widerstand und Anpassung. Festschrift für Walter Huder*, ed. Klaus Siebenhaar and Hermann Haarmann (Berlin: Medusa Verlag, 1982), 121–33. See too Peter Fischer, *Alfred Wolfenstein: Der Expressionismus und die verendende Kunst* (Munich: Wilhelm Fink Verlag, 1968), and Russell E. Brown, "Alfred Wolfenstein," in *Expressionismus als Literatur: Gesammelte Studien*, ed. Wolfgang Rothe (Berne and Munich: Francke Verlag, 1969), 264-276.

[9] Walter Haenisch, "Percy Bysshe Shelley," *Das Wort* (January 1938, Heft 1): 96–110.

[10] On Du Bois's passionate Shelleyanism, see the brief published comments of Herbert Aptheker (once Du Bois's younger colleague and close friend, and eventually, editor of the 40-plus volumes of Du Bois's collected writings) in "W.E.B. Du Bois — A Man for Peace" in *Racism, Imperialism & Peace: Selected Essays by Herbert Aptheker* [*Studies in Marxism* 21], ed. Marvin J. Berlowitz and Carol E. Morgan (Minneapolis: MEP Publications, 1987), 204. (Aptheker has indicated, in correspondence and conversation with the present author, that the above-cited commentary on Du Bois and Shelley represents "only the tip of the iceberg" of Du Bois's recurrent recourse to Shelley.) See also Du Bois's stress on the exemplary status of the second-generation English Romantic poets: "... Byron, Shelley, and Keats, lord, gentleman and cockney, all were social revolutionists"; W.E.B. Du Bois, "*The Great Tradition in English Literature,*" *National Guardian* (March 8, 1954) [Du Bois here paraphrases, and adds his distinct emphasis to, a formulation in the book he is reviewing, Annette T. Rubinstein's Marxian-humanist *The Great Tradition in English Literature: From Shakespeare to Shaw* (New York: Citadel Press, 1954)], reprinted in *Complete Published Works of W.E.B. Du Bois*, ed. Herbert Aptheker (White Plains, N.Y.: Kraus-Thomson, 1982-1986), 38 vols., *Newspaper Columns*, 2 vols., 2 (1986): 924–25. On Du Bois's initial attractions to, and ultimately radical interpretations of, German philosophical idealism, see Russell A. Berman's important "Du Bois and Wagner: Race, Nation, and Culture between the United States and Germany," *The German Quarterly* 70.2 (Summer 1997): 123–35.

See too Ella Reeve Bloor's autobiography, *We Are Many*, Introduction by Elizabeth Gurley Flynn (New York: International Publishers, 1940). And see Ossie Davis's and Ruby Dee's "Martin Luther King: The Dream and the Drum," Episode #302 in *Ossie & Ruby...In Other Words* (PBS Video: Emmalyn II Productions; Episode #302 first broadcast January 15, 1986), with its deliberate inclusion and performance of Shelley in tribute to — as the program consistently articulates it — King's militant radicalism.

[11] Until the publication of Brecht's *Arbeitsjournal* (Frankfurt/M.: Suhrkamp, 1973), the best-known evidence was probably the June–August 1938 section of "Gespräche mit Brecht" in Benjamin, *Versuche über Brecht*, ed. and with an Afterword by Rolf Tiedemann (Frankfurt/M.: 1966), 117–35; "Conversations with Brecht" in Benjamin, *Understanding Brecht*, trans. Anna Bostock, Introduction by Stanley Mitchell (London: New Left Books, 1973), 105–21. The Brecht *Werke*'s generous editorial notes add a good deal to the picture; see citations in my n.19 below.

[12] *Aesthetics and Politics*, ed. Rodney Livingstone, Perry Anderson, Francis Mulhern, and Ronald Taylor, trans. Anya Bostock, Stuart Hood, Rodney Livingstone, Francis McDonagh, and Harry Zohn, Afterword by Fredric Jameson (London: New Left Books, 1977); *Die Expressionismusdebatte: Materialien zu einer marxistischen Realismuskonzeption*, ed. Hans-Jürgen Schmitt (Frankfurt/M,: Suhrkamp, 1973).

The editors of *Aesthetics and Politics* and *Die Expressionismusdebatte*, and other commentators, have asserted that Brecht was only a figurehead for, or, at most, nominally involved in editing, *Das Wort*. See, e.g., *Aesthetics and Politics*, 62. Brecht's journals and letters, as well as some of Benjamin's recollections (and Benjamin's own contributions to *Das Wort*) show this to be an inadequate overall analysis. In fact, Brecht's attitudes towards his participation in *Das Wort* ranged from frustration, cynicism, and disgust, to cautious enthusiasm, to energetic determination to shape the journal more towards his liking (including through active solicitation of manuscripts from writers around the world).

See Brecht's correspondence about *Das Wort* in the Brecht *Werke* 28 [*Briefe* 1] (1998): 562 and 569, and 29 [*Briefe* 2] (1998) [both *Briefe* volumes ed. Günter Glaeser, in cooperation with Wolfgang Jeske and Paul-Gerhard Wenzlaff]: 9, 13, 19, 20, 21, 25–26, 36, 38, 64, 77, 81, 83–84, 101, 106–7, 126, and 147–48. (Most of these letters can be found in the English translation of an earlier edition of Brecht's letters, *Brecht Briefe* [Frankfurt/M.: Suhrkamp, 1981]; see *Bertolt Brecht Letters*, trans. Ralph Manheim and ed., with commentary and notes, by John Willett (London: Methuen, 1990), 163, 235, 239, 240, 246, 247, 248, 256, 259, 260, 271, 276, 279, 289, 290, 295, 315, 607, 610, and 611.)

See too, for further evidence of Brecht's ambivalent attitudes towards, and dealings with, *Das Wort*, the Brecht journal entries cited in my n.19 below.

For a measured assessment of the relevant materials and controversies, see David Pike, *German Writers in Soviet Exile, 1933–1945* (Chapel Hill: University of North Carolina Press, 1982), esp. Chapter 8, "The Literary Popular Front, Part I: *Das Wort*."

[13] They are now all available, with ample editorial notes, in the Brecht *Werke* 22.1 and 22.2 [*Schriften* 2.1 and 2.2], ed. Inge Gellert and Werner Hecht in cooperation with Marianne Conrad, Sigmar Gerund and Benno Slupianek (1993).

[14] See the account of Haenisch's fate given by his widow in *Gut angekommen, Moskau: Das Exil der Gabriele Stammberger, 1932–1954. Errinerungen und Dokumente*, written with and ed. Michael Peschke (Berlin: Basis Druck, 1999). Also on Haenisch, see Hans-Albert Walter, *Deutsche Exilliteratur 1933-1950*, (Stuttgart: J.B. Metzler, 1978–1984) 6 vols., 2 [*Europäisches Appeasement und überseeische Asylpraxis*] (1984): 525–26 n. 4, and 4 [*Exilpresse*] (1978; 1984): 422.

[15] *Werke* 22.1:423–34 and 22.2:1035–37nn. "Weite und Vielfalt" was first published, some sixteen years after its composition, in the series *Brecht Versuche*, Heft 13 (Berlin, 1954): 97–107. The essay was also published — before the 1989–1998 *Werke*'s appearance — in Brecht's *Gesammelte Werke* 8 [*Schriften* 2], ed. Werner Hecht (1967): 340–49.

[16] Brecht is of course often described, by others and himself, as the Left's *plumpes-denken* [*crude-thinking, crude-thought, vulgar*] poet, over against Left writers like Wolfenstein who exhibit a penchant for visionary, sometimes arcane or delicate, symbolist esotericism. It therefore seems entirely natural that Brecht chooses to render Shelley's lines far more literally than had Wolfenstein. Yet paradoxically, it is Wolfenstein's translation that yields the familiar Popular Front verse cadence of ringing hammerbeat, along with a rhetorical thematics that quickly thins to weak abstraction. Meanwhile, Brecht's scrupulously literal, generally unrhymed translation somehow manages — no doubt due to Brecht's terrific feel for other poets' language, and, more specifically, his obvious sympathy with the *Mask* — to convey Shelley's startling ways of simultaneously condensing and exfoliating image, phrase, and line. Brecht, that is, powerfully grasps and identifies with Shelley's manner of marrying rhythmic propulsion to textural density, whereby through syntax, cadence, diction, and tone, an intense forward movement and stingingly precise denotation coexist with an imagistic counter-impulse that, with understated elegance, deftly builds back into the poem a cumulatively thickening self-reflection. The inspired and brilliant literalism of Brecht's translation — Brecht's ability to see (and then to render into an impressive construction of energy, concretion, and transparency) the *Mask*'s interanimation of the material and the ideational, of grit and philosophically-oriented intellection — results in stanzas notably more literary and poetic than Wolfenstein's.

For Benjamin's implicit, and Adorno's and Elizabeth Hauptmann's explicit, assessments of Brecht's Shelley translations (as well as Brecht's later, possibly ambivalent attitude towards the translations), see my n.31 below.

[17] *Werke* 22.1:424–25, 430, 432–33 (emphasis in original ["den grossen revolutionären englischen Dichter P.B. *Shelley*"]).

[18] *Werke* 14 [*Gedichte* 4], ed. Jan Knopf and Brigitte Bergheim, in cooperation with Annette Ahlborn, Günter Berg, and Michael Duchardt (1993): 404–5, 662n. Brecht worked on both the *Mask* and *Peter Bell* translations with his close collaborator Margarete Steffin; see *Werke* 14:662–63nn., and 22.2: 1035–36nn.

The *Werke* presents Brecht's *Peter Bell* translation as part of a larger text titled "Hölle [Hell]," *Werke* 14:404–9, 662–63nn. "Hölle" begins with the nine *Peter Bell* stanzas, and then segues directly into the 25 *Mask of Anarchy* stanzas translated — and otherwise appearing only — in "Weite und Vielfalt." The textual history provided in the *Werke*'s notes leads one to deduce that publication of the *Peter Bell* translation occurred only in (and then after) 1972, when the translation appeared in Benjamin's posthumously organized and published *Passagen-Werk*; see my n.19 below.

[19] Brecht's translated *Peter Bell* stanzas appear in Walter Benjamin, *Das Passagen-Werk*, ed. Rolf Tiedemann (1972; Frankfurt/M.: Suhrkamp, 1982), 2 vols., 1:563–64 [also found in Benjamin, *Gesammelte Schriften* vol. 5.1 (1982): 563–64]; in English, see Benjamin, *The Arcades Project*, trans. Howard Eiland and Kevin McLaughlin (Cambridge, Mass., and London, England: Belknapp Press of Harvard University Press, 1999), 449–50.

The sequence of this sharing of ideas and manuscripts, and copying out of translations, can be reconstructed by coordinating Brecht's "Arbeitsjournal" entries for the period in question, along with the June-August 1938 sections of "Gespräche mit Brecht" in Benjamin's *Versuche über Brecht*, 128–35 ["Conversations with Brecht" in *Understanding Brecht*, 114–21], as well as Benjamin's correspondence (particularly with Adorno; see my n.31 below). In addition to the Benjamin texts just cited, see the Brecht *Werke* 26 [*Journale* 1], ed. Marianne Conrad and Werner Hecht, in cooperation with Herta Ramthun (1994): 312–23, esp. 315, 317, and 319; these entries can be found in English in *Bertolt Brecht Journals* [part of the series *Bertolt Brecht: Plays, Poetry and Prose*, ed. John Willett and Ralph Manheim], ed. John Willett, trans. Hugh Rorrison (London: New York, 1993), 6–19, esp. 10, 13, and 14.

[20] Brecht, "[Notizen über Baudelaire]" and "[Zu *Les fleurs du mal*]," *Werke* 22.1 and 22.2 [*Schriften* 2.1 and 2.2]: 451–53 and 1044–45nn. Brecht had left these fragments untitled; "Notizen über Baudelaire" and "Zu *Les fleurs du mal*" are the bracketed titles supplied by the *Werke*'s editors.

[21] Benjamin, *The Arcades Project*, 370 (translation slightly amended; emphasis in original translation ["*grasp*"]); *Das Passagen-Werk*, 1:468 [*Gesammelte Schriften* vol. 5.1:468] (emphasis in original ["*Griff*"]).

[22] Walter Benjamin, *Ursprung des deutschen Trauerspiels* (Frankfurt/M.: Suhrkamp, 1963) [*Gesammelte Schriften* 1.1, ed. Rolf Tiedemann and Hermann Schweppenhäuser (1974): 203–430], *The Origin of German Tragic Drama*, trans. John Osborne, with an Introduction by George Steiner (London: Verso, 1977).

[23] It is almost impossible to resist juxtaposing Benjamin's insistence on Shelley's powerful *grasp* of allegory (and Benjamin's consequent insistence on Shelley's artistic grasp of *reality*) with F.R. Leavis's notorious claim, made only two years earlier, that Shelley had had a "weak grasp upon the actual." Leavis's indictment arises amidst his specific dismissal of *Ode to the West Wind*: the

poem epitomizes what Leavis deems Shelley's unfortunate manner of being so "essentially lyrical" that, as a poet, Shelley can have "little to do with thinking." For Leavis, Shelley's poetry "induces — depends for its success on inducing — a kind of attention that doesn't bring the critical intelligence into play." F.R. Leavis, *Revaluation: Tradition & Development in English Poetry* (1936; London: Chatto & Windus, 1956), 206–8. For two of the most thorough and impressive rebuttals of Leavis's argument, see Earl R. Wasserman, *Shelley: A Critical Reading* (Baltimore: The Johns Hopkins University Press, 1971) and William Keach, *Shelley's Style* (New York and London: Methuen, 1984).

Leavis's judgment, based as it is on Shelley's lyricism (as Leavis sees it, on Shelley's exaggerated, excessively emotion-oriented lyricism) might for that reason seem removed from Benjamin's attention to *Peter Bell the Third*'s biting satire. Yet the surrounding coordinates of Benjamin's discussion — from the Wolfenstein and *Das Wort* preludes, to the Baudelaire and Brecht variations, to the central motif of allegory itself — make clear that back of Benjamin's interest in *Peter Bell* lies exactly this problematic jointure: on one side, an ethereal or seemingly obscure lyric poetics convinced of the need for *via-negativa* coaxing of reality into provisionally apprehendable form; on the other, a righteous truth-telling that aims to call (with equal recourse to clear observation, active intellection, and sociolinguistic precision) a degraded present by its proper name. Productively to motivate the oscillation or shifting combination of the two sides is the whole point of Benjamin's theory of allegory, whose *raison d'être* is, in a phrase, to gain a grasp upon the actual.

[24] Some, but by no means all of these poems (not to mention the drafts printed in the *Werke* notes) have been published in the English *Poems*. See the poems gathered under the titles *Hollywoodelegien* and *Gedichte im Exil*, *Werke* 12 [*Gedichte 2: Sammlungen 1938–1956*], ed. Jan Knopf (1988): 115–25; in *Poems*, see *Hollywood Elegies*, 380–81, and the texts in the section "American Poems 1941–47." See too "An Walter Benjamin, der sich auf der Flucht vor Hitler Entleibte," "Die Verlustliste," "Nachdenkend, wie ich höre" ["Nachdenkend über die Hölle"], and "Zum Freitod des Flüchtlings W.B.," *Werke* 15 [*Gedichte 5*]: 41, 43, 46, 48; in *Poems*, see "On Thinking About Hell" and "On the Suicide of the Refugee W.B.," 367, 363.

See also the *Werke*'s reprinting of the remarkable 1942 typescript draft that Brecht had provisionally titled "Die Hölle" (which is distinct from the *Werke* text combining the *Mask* and *Peter Bell* translations and titled "Hölle," discussed in my n.18 above); this "Die Hölle" typescript is clearly a preliminary stage of the *Hollywoodelegien*. This 1942 "Die Hölle" typescript, moreover, unmistakably arises from the Shelley-matrix, reworking, in fact, the same ideas and even words about "mein Bruder Shelley" (and the figuration of London and Los Angeles as competing versions of Hell) that appear in the 1941 "Nachdenkend über die Hölle." Both "Nachdenkend über die Hölle" and the "Die Hölle" typescript should be traced, of course, back to the Summer 1938 translations, analyses, and discussions of Shelley, particularly to the *Peter Bell* translation. See *Werke* 12:399–400nn. (The 1942 "Die Hölle" typescript may well have emerged from what would have been a previous, manuscript sketch — evidently not possessed by the Brecht Archive, nor elsewhere known — that would have served as the basis for "Nachdenkend über die Hölle," the *Hollywoodelegien*, and related poems.)

For a more brutal sense of what is at stake in these overlapping materials, contexts, and drafts, where — with Shelley so often providing the stated melody or haunting undersong — Brecht undertakes to write alternately despairing and enraged elegy, see Brecht's seven stark, ultimately discarded lines from the first sketch of "Die Verlustliste [The Casualty List]." Those lines include: "Wo ist Benjamin, der Kritiker? / ...Benjamin ist an der spanischen Grenze begraben. / ...Ich fahre entlang den Bomberwerften von Los Angeles [Where is Benjamin, the critic? /...Benjamin is buried at the Spanish border. /...I drive along the bomber-hangars of Los Angeles]." *Werke* 15:338–39nn.

[25] See, most recently, James Chandler's magisterial *England in 1819: The Politics of Literary Culture and the Case of Romantic Historicism* (Chicago: University of Chicago Press, 1998), 483–554; Jeffrey N. Cox's brief but very suggestive comments in *Poetry and Politics in the Cockney School: Keats, Shelley, Hunt and Their Circle* (Cambridge and New York: Cambridge University Press, 1998), 211–16; and again, Steven Jones's *Shelley's Satire*, 49–69, 149–64.

[26] *Bertolt Brecht Journals*, 257–58 (translation amended) ["wenn er von diesen Kompositionen spricht, nicht wenn er komponiert," *Werke* 27 [*Journale* 2], ed. Werner Hecht (1995): 125]. See too the editors' notes, *Werke* 12 [*Gedichte* 2]: 399–403, and the note in *Poems*, 586.

[27] *Bertolt Brecht Journals* 238; *Werke* 27 [*Journale* 2]: 125 ["Dies sind volle Gedichte"; "in der Tat haben die Kompositionen wirkliche Bedeutung wahrscheinlich auch als Musik..."].

Eisler's 1942 comments on the Brecht poems may not have been as judgmental as Brecht had initially believed, nor, in any case, do they appear to have represented Eisler's final opinion on the texts: Eisler subsequently observed that the *Hollywoodelegien* were his favorite works among all Brecht's poetry. See Hans Bunge, *Fragen Sie mehr über Brecht. Hanns Eisler im Gespräch* (Leipzig: 1975), 244, cited in the Brecht *Werke* 12 [*Gedichte* 2]: 402.

[28] The texts have a staggered publication and reception history, dating from Eisler's 1950s recordings of the *Hollywoodliederbuch* [*Hollywood Song-Book*] (which includes the *Hollywoodelegien* and other Brecht poems), and the volumes of Brecht's later poetry, in German and in translation, that appear from the late 1940s onward. With the Brecht volumes in particular, it happens that a significant number of the early 1940s poems from and around the "Shelley-Baudelaire-critical lyric" matrix become readily available in German only in the '50s and '60s, and in some cases are not translated until the '60s and '70s.

[29] Here I use *avant-gardist* and *anti-aesthetic* in the very specific sense drawn out by Peter Bürger's *Theory of the Avant-Garde*, trans. Michael Shaw (Minneapolis: University of Minnesota Press, 1984). For related thoughts about how currents within today's experimental poetry complicate the usual narrative of

postmodernism's superannuation of modernism, see Kaufman, "A Future for Modernism: Barbara Guest's Recent Poetry," *American Poetry Review* 29:4 (July/August 2000): 11–16, and "Everybody Hates Kant: Blakean Formalism and the Symmetries of Laura Moriarty," *Modern Language Quarterly* 61:1 (2000): 131–55.

[30] *Werke* 26 [*Journale* 1, 24 August 1940]: 417–18, 661n; *Bertolt Brecht Journals*, 90–91; (emphasis in the original German and the English translation). Though hardly dispositive on the question of Brecht's support of or opposition to official Comintern and Party policy, it is worth noting that this *Arbeitsjournal* entry about Wordsworth (probably the English poet most often thought to represent, since Shelley's time, apostasic retreat from sociopolitical *engagement* in favor of aestheticist or reactionary formalism) links Brecht's defense of lyric formal experiment per se to anti-fascist sentiment and activity. That is, Brecht specifically relates the "petit bourgeois" character of (and presumed audience for) Wordsworthian poetic "idyll" to the presumably "petit bourgeois" instincts animating people who are courageously resisting Hitler (a number of whom, Brecht takes pains to note, had previously gone to Spain to fight Franco); *Ibid.* The matter of Comintern or Party line arises because Brecht writes at a moment when the Soviet Union and Comintern continued to describe the British struggle against Nazi Germany as an inter-imperialist contest unworthy of solidarity from progressive forces. On the classic Shelleyan treatment of an ostensibly conservative Wordsworthian poetry — a treatment that Brecht here echoes, recontextualizes, and reimagines — see Kaufman, "Legislators of the Post-Everything World: Shelley's *Defence* of Adorno," *English Literary History* 63 (1996): 707–33, esp. 731n.29.

[31] In his 1 February 1939 letter to Benjamin about "The Paris of the Second Empire in Baudelaire," Adorno questions the fidelity to Shelley of the Brecht *Peter Bell* translation that Benjamin's essay quotes; Adorno wonders whether such "directness and bluntness" [Direktheit und Härte]" can really be found in the original. See Theodor W. Adorno, Walter Benjamin, *Briefwechsel 1928-1940*, ed. Henri Lonitz (Frankfurt/M.: Suhrkamp, 1994), 397; Theodor W. Adorno and Walter Benjamin, *The Complete Correspondence, 1928–1940*, ed. Henri Lonitz, trans. Nicholas Walker (Cambridge, Mass.: Harvard University Press, 1999), 304. An editors' note in *Complete Correspondence*, though not indicating that the rest of Brecht's *Peter Bell* translation appears in the *Passagen-Werk*, does provide Shelley's stanza, and comments that "Brecht's translation does follow the English of Shelley's original very closely," 308 n.32.

Interestingly, Adorno's initial doubts concerning the translation's fidelity or quality are later echoed by Brecht's close collaborator and editor Elisabeth Hauptmann, who observes too that Brecht himself had seriously doubted the *Peter Bell* and *Mask* translations' merit; see the Brecht *Werke* 14: 662–63nn. There is no corroborating evidence, from Brecht or others, that Brecht ever actually shared Hauptmann's view or held the one she attributes to him; Brecht's 1954 publication of the *Mask* translation-essay (in the *Brecht Versuche* series) would seem to count as contrary evidence.

Adorno for his part may subsequently have changed his mind — at least somewhat — about the *Peter Bell* translations, which he in all likelihood would have continued to read, preserved as they were in the Benjamin texts that Adorno helped to edit after Benjamin's death. Significantly, the first line of those *Peter Bell* stanzas reappears in one of Adorno's most important discussions of modern poetics, "Parataxis" (1963). As if at once conceding and yet contesting the same old point, Adorno (here constellating Shelley, Baudelaire, and Hölderlin) quite laudatorily gives the first line from those *Peter Bell* stanzas: but he presents the first half of Shelley's line in German, the second half in English! "Wie Hölderlins Wahlverwandtem Shelley die Hölle eine Stadt ist, much like London... [Just as for Hölderlin's kindred spirit Shelley Hell is a city 'much like London...']." See "Parataxis. Zur späten Lyrik Hölderlins," *Noten zur Literatur* 3:174 [*Gesammelte Schriften* 11:462], "Parataxis: On Hölderlin's Late Poetry," *Notes to Literature* 2:122.

For several years, Benjamin had gone back and forth with Adorno (who usually also represented Horkheimer in these colloquies) about Benjamin's Baudelaire texts and related writings. In 1935, Benjamin had submitted a draft of "The Paris of the Second Empire in Baudelaire" to the Institut für Sozialforschung's [Institute of Social Research's] house organ, the *Zeitschrift für Sozialforschung* [*Journal of Social Research*]. At that point, Benjamin was conceiving "The Paris of the Second Empire in Baudelaire" as the second part of a streamlined, three-part version of the *Passagen-Werk* that would be called *Paris, the Capital of the Nineteenth Century*. In Fall 1938, Benjamin submitted a revised version of the essay, which quoted and briefly discussed the translated *Peter Bell* stanza. For the relevant exchanges about these essays, see *Briefwechsel*, 138 ff., 364 ff., and 388 ff.; *Complete Correspondence*, 104 ff., 280 ff., and 298 ff. (Some of these letters are included in *Aesthetics and Politics*'s section on the Adorno-Benjamin debates.)

Though Adorno and Horkheimer had published Benjamin essays about which they had serious reservations — most famously, "The Work of Art in the Age of Mechanical Reproduction" — they did not, even after further Adorno-Benjamin correspondence (in November 1938), publish the revised "Paris of the Second Empire in Baudelaire." In early 1939 they did, however, publish Benjamin's "Über einige Motive bei Baudelaire [On Some Motifs in Baudelaire]," which Benjamin had intended as the "thesis" of *Paris, the Capital of the Nineteenth Century*. "Über einige Motive bei Baudelaire" can be found in Benjamin's *Illuminationen: Ausgewählte Schriften* (Frankfurt/M.: Suhrkamp, 1961), 201–45, in *Charles Baudelaire: Ein Lyriker im Zeitalter des Hochkapitalismus*, 111–64, and *Gesammelte Schriften* 1.2:605–53. In English, see "On Some Motifs in Baudelaire" in *Illuminations: Essays and Reflections* (New York: Schocken, 1969), 155–200, or in *Charles Baudelaire: A Lyric Poet in the Era of High Capitalism*, 107–54.

For a lucid and compressed history of the initial controversies over Benjamin's Baudelaire writings, see Martin Jay, *The Dialectical Imagination: A History of the Frankfurt School and the Institute of Social Research, 192—1950*, 2d. ed. (1973; Berkeley and Los Angeles: University of California Press, 1996), 197–212, esp. 206–11.

[32] See "On Lyric Poetry and Society," "Parataxis: On Hölderlin's Late Poetry," and "Commitment" in *Notes to Literature*; "Rede über Lyrik und Gesellschaft," "Parataxis. Zur späten Lyrik Hölderlins," and "Engagement" in *Noten zur Literatur* [*Gesammelte Schriften 11*]. See too *Aesthetic Theory*, edited, translated, and with a translator's Introduction by Robert Hullot-Kentor (Minneapolis: University of Minnesota Press, 1997); *Ästhetische Theorie*, ed. Gretel Adorno and Rolf Tiedemann (Frankfurt: Suhrkamp, 1970) [*Gesammelte Schriften 7*].

[33] For more sustained discussions of Adornian constructivism in relation to the history of poetics and critical theory, see Kaufman, "Red Kant, or The Persistence of the Third *Critique* in Adorno and Jameson," *Critical Inquiry* 26:4 (Summer 2000): 682–724, and "Negatively Capable Dialectics: Keats, Vendler, Adorno, and the Theory of the Avant-Garde," *Critical Inquiry* 27:2 (Winter 2001): 354–84.

[34] For a preliminary attempt to consider these and adjacent Brecht-Benjamin-Adorno materials in relation to contemporary art and theory, see Kaufman, "Aura, Still," *October* 99 (Winter 2002).

"There is a Tradition that is a Catastrophe."
The Culture of Memory versus "the Cult of Memory"
in Brecht's *Lucullus* texts (1939)

The years in exile motivated Brecht to a confrontation with imper-
manence and the possibilities of tradition. Two opposed models for
a culture of memory — related to Walter Benjamin's theories of history
— appear in Brecht's texts: on the one hand the necessary textual de-
construction of a history that is objective in appearance only, and on
the other hand a mythical tradition which, through images, opens up
new paths of commemoration. Via the interpretation of cultural material that does not serve the glorification of power, memory can be created even for the powerless, the defeated, and the nameless. The texts
about Lucullus, both of which appeared in the difficult year 1939, and
which reveal numerous autobiographical references, are good examples of Brecht's complex and multilayered attempts at a comprehensive
theory of history and culture.

„Es gibt eine Überlieferung, die Katastrophe ist."
Erinnerungskultur versus „Kult der Erinnerung"
in Bertolt Brechts *Lukullus*-Texten (1939)

Bettina Englmann

N ach dem Tod Walter Benjamins notiert Brecht zu dessen letzter
Arbeit *Über den Begriff der Geschichte*:

> Die kleine Abhandlung behandelt die Geschichtsforschung und könn-
> te nach der Lektüre meines *Cäsar* geschrieben sein (mit dem Benjamin, als
> er ihn in Svendborg las, nicht allzu viel anfangen konnte). Benjamin wen-
> det sich gegen die Vorstellungen von der Geschichte als eines Ablaufs,
> vom Fortschritt als einer kraftvollen Unternehmung ausgeruhter Köpfe, von
> der Arbeit als der Quelle der Sittlichkeit, von der Arbeiterschaft als Prote-
> gés der Technik usw. Er verspottet den oft gehörten Satz, man müsse sich
> wundern, daß so was wie der Faschismus „noch in diesem Jahrhundert"
> vorkommen könne (als ob er nicht die Frucht aller Jahrhunderte wäre). —
> Kurz, die kleine Arbeit ist klar und entwirrend (trotz aller Metaphorik und
> Judaismen), und man denkt mit Schrecken daran, wie klein die Anzahl de-
> rer ist, die bereit sind, so was wenigstens mißzuverstehen. (27:12)[1]

Brechts Lob gilt einem Text von 1940, in dem sich Kulturtheorie ver
bindet mit der Kritik an einer positivistischen Historiographie, die an
scheinhafter Objektivität und an der Vorstellung eines kontinuierlichen
Fortschritts der Menschheit festhält.[2] Die Jahre des Exils haben Benjamins geschichtstheoretischen Entwurf geprägt; manifest wird darin nicht
nur die Entwicklung der deutschen Kultur in den Nationalsozialismus,
sondern auch das sich abzeichnende Scheitern des sozialistischen Experiments in der Sowjetunion. Diese aporetischen Erfahrungen motivieren die Ablehnung jeder affirmativen kulturellen Überlieferung;[3] Benjamin widersetzt sich damit dem ästhetischen Kanon, der Vorstellung
historischer Kontinuität und dem konventionalisierten Kulturbegriff
einer elitären Hochkultur, deren Mängel in den Faschismus-Analysen
des Exils zum angeblichen Antagonismus Kultur-Barbarei sichtbar
wurden. Der Bezug auf die Vergangenheit, dem Fundament kultureller
Identität, bedarf der Überprüfung: „In jeder Epoche muß versucht
werden, die Überlieferung von neuem dem Konformismus abzu-
gewinnen, der im Begriff steht, sie zu überwältigen."[4]

Dass Brecht seinen Fragment gebliebenen *Cäsar*-Roman als Vorbild
Benjamins anbietet, zeigt wieder einmal die Ähnlichkeit der Denkmus-

New Essays on Brecht / Neue Versuche über Brecht
Maarten van Dijk et al., eds., *The Brecht Yearbook / Das Brecht-Jahrbuch*
Volume 26 (Toronto, Canada: The International Brecht Society, 2001)

ter beider Autoren zum Ende der 30er Jahre. Mit *Die Geschäfte des Herrn Julius Cäsar* arbeitet Brecht am *Text* der Historie, er dekonstruiert die Verfahren der Geschichtsschreibung und entmythisiert ihre Würdigung der *Großen Männer*. Doch Benjamins kulturtheoretischer Ansatz in *Über den Begriff der Geschichte* ist vielfältiger als Brechts hier literarisierte Historisierung. Er entwirft das Projekt einer *anderen* Überlieferung, die sich als Erinnerungskultur konstituiert, in dialektischer Verbindung mit dem „Kult der Erinnerung,"[5] den auch Brecht im *Cäsar*-Roman denunziert. Das *Passagen-Werk* wird zum Medium dieser anderen Überlieferung, hier vergegenwärtigt sich Vergangenheit nicht im beglaubigten Text historischer Quellen, sondern in Bildern der Erinnerung, in unfreiwilligen Spuren, in lange unbeachteten Relikten.

Jenseits des *Cäsar*-Romans zeigen sich auch in Brechts Werk komplexe Entwürfe potentieller Bezugnahmen auf die Vergangenheit. Neben einer Theorie der Historisierung beschäftigt er sich mit verschiedenen Bereichen im diskursiven Feld des historischen Gedächtnisses: mit dem Verhältnis zwischen Text und Überlieferung, zwischen kanonischer Literatur und dem eigenen Schreiben, mit der Vergänglichkeit von Texten und Menschen, die nicht erinnert werden. Exemplarisch wird das diskursive Feld textuellen Gedenkens zwischen Vergangenheit, Gegenwart und Zukunft in zwei literarischen Texten Brechts, die sich in Genre und sprachlicher Stilisierung unterscheiden, die aber durch ihren zentralen Protagonisten miteinander verbunden sind: in der Erzählung *Die Trophäen des Lukullus*, die Anfang 1939 entsteht, und im Radiostück *Das Verhör des Lukullus*, dessen erste Fassung Brecht mit Margarete Steffin im November 1939 verfasst. Die Texte um Lukullus wirken als Antipoden zum *Cäsar*-Roman, der über die historische Überlieferung durch Texte — Quellen und deutende Geschichtsschreibung — reflektiert. Brechts *Lukullus*-Texte organisieren dagegen die modellhafte Auseinandersetzung zwischen Erinnerungskultur und *Kult der Erinnerung* in bildhaften Erinnerungsfiguren. Diese motivieren eine mythische Literarisierung — im Gegensatz zur narrativen Dekonstruktion im Roman. Die Texte um Lukullus stehen Benjamins *Über den Begriff der Geschichte* damit näher als der *Cäsar*-Roman.

I   MYTHISCHE ERINNERUNG VERSUS HISTORISCHE DEKONSTRUKTION

> Immer doch
> Schrieb der Sieger die Geschichte des Besiegten.
> Dem Erschlagenen entstellt
> Der Schläger die Züge. Aus der Welt
> Geht der Schwächere, und zurückbleibt
> Die Lüge. (6:158)

Die Fälschungen in der Geschichte der Sieger aufzudecken, war das Anliegen des *Cäsar*-Romans. Doch die Einseitigkeit dieses Projekts, das Brecht 1938 begonnen hatte, musste unbefriedigend bleiben für einen

Autor, der seine Texte nicht den *Schlägern* zudachte, sondern den *Erschlagenen*, den Ohnmächtigen und Unterdrückten. Anstatt einer korrigierenden Dekonstruktion der Geschichte der Sieger zeigt *Das Verhör des Lukullus* eine Erinnerungskultur der Besiegten in der Rekonstruktion verdrängter Spuren. Eine Geschichte der Besiegten muss erst entworfen werden, eine Neudeutung der Quellen ist dazu nicht ausreichend, denn die Quellen schweigen. Brecht versucht daher, eine *andere* historische Überlieferung lesbar zu machen, die jenseits des schriftlichen Mediums liegt. Die Figur des Lukullus wird im *Verhör des Lukullus* durch allegorische Erinnerungsfiguren konstituiert, durch den Gedächtnisort des Grabmals, durch den steinernen Fries, dessen stumme Bilder zum Sprechen gebracht werden, durch die Legenden um Lukullus, die sich historischer Faktizität entziehen, und durch den in die Sprache eingegangenen Begriff des Lukullischen, der nicht an den Feldherrn Lukullus erinnert, sondern an einen, der die Freuden des Diesseits genoss. In diesen Erinnerungsfiguren macht der Autor das „imaginative Übergewicht des Bildes über den Text" nutzbar:

> Bilder entwickeln [...] eine ganz andere Übertragungsdynamik als Texte. Sie stehen, um es auf eine einfache Formel zu bringen, der Einprägungskraft des Gedächtnisses näher und der Interpretationkraft des Verstandes ferner. Ihre unmittelbare Wirkungskraft ist schwer zu kanalisieren, die Macht der Bilder sucht sich ihre eigenen Vermittlungswege.[6]

Die Erinnerung in Bildern setzt imaginative Potentiale frei, während der historische Text Gedenken fixiert.[7] Indem er die mediale Spannung zwischen Bild und Text fruchtbar macht, durchbricht Brecht das Genre der historischen Literatur. Analog dazu beschäftigen sich die *Lukullus*-Texte auch kaum mit dem historischen Raum des antiken Roms oder mit der Biographie des historischen Lukullus.[8] Das Bild der Antike, das hier modellhaft erzeugt wird, setzt stattdessen Bedeutung als ein Raum, in dem sich Erinnerungskultur und monumentaler Gedächtniskult konfrontieren. Jan Assmann schreibt in Anlehnung an Pierre Nora: „Erinnerungskultur hat es mit ,Gedächtnis, das Gemeinschaft stiftet,' zu tun. Im Unterschied zur Gedächtniskunst, die eine antike Erfindung [...] darstellt, ist die Erinnerungskultur ein universales Phänomen."[9] Grundlage einer Geschichte der Besiegten ist eine Erinnerungskultur, die sich dem Gedächtnis der Herrschaft widersetzt und deren Denkmäler nicht würdigt. Im fiktionalen Raum zitiert Brecht — in spezifischer Verfremdung — das mythologische Schattenreich der Antike, das über die Toten richtet. Das Gericht wird über das Gedenken an Lukullus urteilen, indem es das Gedächtnis der Dinge, die ihm in den Erinnerungen an sein Leben zugeordnet werden, archäologisch erschließt. Die Aufgabe der Lektüre besteht darin, diesen Prozess der archäologischen Rekonstruktion mitzuvollziehen, der über die Bedingungen der geschichtlichen Überlieferung und über eine Kultur der Erinnerung reflektiert.

Beide *Lukullus*-Texte sind nicht als Arbeit an einer Kultur der Erinnerung rezipiert worden. *Das Verhör des Lukullus* verursachte 1951 in der späteren Fassung als Oper kulturellen Aufruhr in der jungen DDR, da den realsozialistischen Kulturfunktionären nicht nur der pazifistische Grundton des Textes, sondern auch die moderne Musik Paul Dessaus missfiel. Nach der Absetzung des *Verhörs des Lukullus* vom Spielplan der Staatsoper erklärt sich Brecht bereit, die Kritik der Partei an „Formalismus" und „Negativität" zu berücksichtigen.[10] So entsteht die Fassung *Die Verurteilung des Lukullus*, deren Botschaften zu Krieg und Frieden, zu Heldentum und Fortschritt schließlich die politisch erwünschte Eindeutigkeit erreichen. In dieser letzten — von Brecht ungeliebten — Fassung wird die Figur des römischen Feldherrn Lukullus des *Angriffs*krieges schuldig gesprochen; das Gericht des Schattenreichs stößt ihn ins Nichts, in die totale Vergessenheit. Die *Lukullus*-Erzählung blieb zu Lebzeiten Brechts ungedruckt; in weiser Voraussicht notiert der Autor 1948, als er ihre Aufnahme in die *Kalendergeschichten* kurz erwägt: *„Die Trophäe des Lukullus* streiche ich dafür. Sie scheint mir zu kompliziert." (19:710)

Dass die Oper nach dem schließlich erfolgten Placet als späte Abrechnung mit den Nazi-Generälen, als Anspielung auf die Nürnberger Prozesse, aber auch als Protest gegen den Korea-Krieg rezipiert wurde, verwundert daher kaum. Doch auch die Brecht-Forschung ließ das ästhetische Konzept der Mehrdeutigkeit lange unbeachtet, das in den unterschiedlichen Fassungen des Stückes immer weiter getilgt wurde, das sich aber in der ersten Fassung von 1939 noch unverfälscht zeigt. Lukullus wirkt darin als schillernde Figur, das Urteil der Nachwelt über ihn bleibt offen. Obwohl der offene Schluss der ersten Fassung immer bemerkt wurde, findet sich die Überzeugung, dass Lukullus selbstverständlich verurteilt würde, nahezu durchgängig — eine Überzeugung, deren Eindeutigkeit von den späten Fassungen suggeriert wird. Klaus Völker,[11] Jan Knopf,[12] Klaus-Detlef Müller[13] und Hans Mayer[14] sahen im *Verhör des Lukullus* ein zeitgeschichtlich und historisch referentialisiertes Stück, das entweder über seine Quellen — Texte Plutarchs oder Mommsens — zu interpretieren sei oder als parabolisches antifaschistisches Modell. In diesen Deutungen erscheint Lukullus als Stellvertreter einer römischen Elite, die ihre Herrschaft auf imperialistischen Kriegen und der Ausbeutung der breiten Bevölkerung fundiert hat. Er wird demnach verurteilt für seine Schuld am Tod der römischen Soldaten, für die Versklavung Hunderttausender, für die Zerstörung ganzer Länder. Dass sein Koch und ein Bauer, der ihm die Einführung des Kirschbaums dankt, vor dem Totengericht für ihn sprechen, kann ihn anscheinend nicht retten. Lukullus wird so zu einem zweiten Cäsar Brechts gemacht. Müller schreibt: „[...] auch hier handelt es sich um eine Entmythologisierung des Helden."[15] Diese allzu eindeutigen Interpretationen sind durch Ignace Feuerlicht relativiert worden.[16] Feuerlicht weist auf die zahlreichen Signale im Text hin, die dem Lukullus positive Eigenschaften zuschreiben und die seine Verurteilung — und damit das Stück — in ein anderes Licht stellen. Die Figur des Lukullus hat keinerlei Ähnlichkeit mit einem Nazi-Führer. Entgegen Brechts späteren Behauptungen entstand das Stück auch keineswegs als Warnung *vor* Beginn des Krieges. Eine eindeutige politische Aussage, die sich auf die Nazis beziehen müsste, liegt in dieser ersten Fassung nicht vor. Feuerlichts Hinweise wirken als Ausgangspunkt für eine Re-Lektüre der *Lukullus*-Texte, die den zweischneidigen Diskurs um Erinnerungskultur sichtbar macht.

Im Gegensatz zu Brechts oft erprobter ästhetischer Praxis, den Mythos so weit zu historisieren, dass er auf seine geschichtlichen Ursprünge zurückgeführt werden kann,[17] wird hier der umgekehrte Weg beschritten: Brecht erprobt die Auflösung römischer Historie in den mythologischen Raum und bedient sich gezielt mythischer Strukturen, die eine historisierende Lesart untergraben, indem sie das Spannungsverhältnis zwischen Mythos und Historie fruchtbar machen. Jan Assmann schreibt über die komplexen Relationen von Erinnerung, Geschichte und Mythos im kulturellen Gedächtnis:

> Das *kulturelle* Gedächtnis richtet sich auf Fixpunkte in der Vergangenheit. Auch in ihm vermag sich Vergangenheit nicht als solche zu erhalten. Vergangenheit gerinnt hier vielmehr zu symbolischen Figuren, an die sich die Erinnerung heftet. [...] Auch Mythen sind Erinnerungsfiguren: Der Unterschied zwischen Mythos und Geschichte wird hier hinfällig. Für das kulturelle Gedächtnis zählt nicht faktische, sondern nur erinnerte Geschichte. Man könnte auch sagen, daß im kulturellen Gedächtnis faktische Geschichte in erinnerte und damit in Mythos transformiert wird. Mythos ist eine fundierende Geschichte, eine Geschichte, die erzählt wird, um eine Gegenwart vom Ursprung her zu erhellen. [...] Durch Erinnerung wird Geschichte zum Mythos. Dadurch wird sie nicht unwirklich, sondern im Gegenteil erst Wirklichkeit im Sinne einer fortdauernden normativen und formativen Kraft.[18]

Die Verbindung von Mythos und Geschichte sowie die Differenzierung zwischen einem kollektiven kulturellen Gedächtnis und der individuellen, nicht-öffentlich praktizierten Erinnerung erweisen sich im Text Brechts als äußerst fruchtbar. Es wird deutlich, dass die Erinnerungen an Lukullus sich als mythisches Fundament faktizitätsorientierter Geschichte konstituieren, dass seine Person erst durch die Erzählungen derer, die sich erinnern, geschaffen wird.

Ganz anders als im *Cäsar*-Roman arbeitet Brecht hier mit einer Remythisierung der Antike im Text. Die Spannung zwischen Mythos und Historie zeigt sich auch darin, dass ein Teil der Szenen im römischen Diesseits lokalisiert ist. Die Schwelle zwischen Leben und Tod ist nicht absolut, die Sklaven, die keinen Status in der offiziellen Historie Roms beanspruchen können, überschreiten sie.[19] Im historischen Denken der Nachwelt blieben sie leblos, namenlos. Weitere mythische Substrate sind die fahle Stimme, die als Kommentator wirkt, oder die Erweckung der steinernen Gestalten des Frieses, die für und gegen Lukullus zeugen. Auffällig ist auch die gehobene Sprachebene, die mit metaphorischen Bildern und sehr viel mehr Reimen und regelmäßigen Rhythmen arbeitet, als sonst bei Brecht üblich.[20] „[...] die farblose Monumentalität, die liturgische Monotonie dieser Sprachwelt ist erhöht in ein hymnisch verkündendes Sprechen in mythischen Bildern."[21] Nirgends findet sich ein verfremdender Sprachgestus — Parodistisches oder Ironie —, so dass hier erstaunlich klassische Schemata vorliegen, deren Sprache nicht *durchrationalisiert* ist.[22] Mit der Präsenz der allegorischen Bilder verbindet sich, dass Brecht mehr Wert auf deutlich erkennbare Fiktionen legt, insbesondere auf eine mythische, legendäre Überlieferung anstatt auf historische Faktizität.[23] Der bedeutungsvolle Kirschbaum, dessen Einführung Lukullus zugeschrieben wird, repräsentiert eine derartige Legende. Ebenso legendär die Tränen des Lukullus, die dieser bei der Zerstörung der Stadt Amisos vergossen haben soll. Das kollektive Gedächtnis bewahrt diese Erinnerungen und zeigt sich so als Antithese und Variation der Historiographie. Alternative Gedächtniskonzepte können als Kritik traditioneller Historiographie wirken, da sie die Geschichtsschreibung relativieren. Das Gedächtnis wertet anders, eine Erkenntnis, die in der Geschichtswissenschaft seit einigen Jahrzehnten im Konzept der *oral history* umgesetzt wird.[24] *Das Verhör des Lukullus* stellt sich so als ein metahistorisches Stück dar; literarisiert werden Bezüge auf die Vergangenheit zwischen den verschiedenen Zeiten des Autors und des Lesers, zwischen der römischen Antike und ihrer Nachwelt. Brecht thematisiert nicht die Geschichts*schreibung* wie im *Cäsar*-Roman,[25] sondern die Funktion und die Grenzen der Erinnerung und des Vergessens.

Doch darüber hinaus konstituieren die Lukullus-Texte auch eine zukünftige, utopische Zeitschicht. Das Gericht im Schattenreich wird von Brecht nicht nach mythologischem Vorbild durch ehemalige Könige gebildet, sondern — neben einem nicht näher beschriebenen Totenrichter — durch Tote aus sozial unterprivilegierten Schichten: einen Bauern, einen Bäcker, eine Prostituierte, eine Fischverkäuferin und einen Sklaven, der ein Lehrer war. Brecht schreibt über dieses Gericht im Stück: „Unbestechliche, sie, die Ahnen der Nachwelt" (6:98). Das utopische Bild eines Gerichts, das scheinbar die ersehnte sozialistische Gerechtigkeit zukünftiger Zeiten antizipiert, darf nicht darüber hinwegtäuschen, dass die Nachwelt Roms die Verurteilung des Lukullus nicht vollzogen hat, er war und ist keineswegs vergessen. Die evozierte Nachwelt ist eine immer noch utopische Nachwelt. Die Verurteilung des Lukullus hat nicht stattgefunden. Was dennoch bleibt, ist das metaphysische Konzept einer Herstellung von Gerechtigkeit im Jenseits, ein Traumbild. Brecht verfährt nach heilsgeschichtlichem Vorbild; er will

„eine leidvolle Gegenwart der Vergessenheit durch eine verheißungs-
volle Vergangenheit und eine erfüllungversprechende Zukunft einrah-
men. Erinnerung ist deshalb heilskräftig, weil sie eine Brücke zwischen
den bedeutungsvollen Zeiten der Vergangenheit und Zukunft über die
dunkle Gegenwart hinwegspannt."[26] In der dunklen Gegenwart des
Exils agiert auch Brecht als „rückwärts gewandter Prophet."[27]

Benjamin schreibt im *Passagen-Werk*: „Das träumende Kollektiv
kennt keine Geschichte."[28] Dies impliziert, dass sich utopische Träume
der machtlosen Kollektive auf die Zukunft richten müssen; die Vergangenheit der Historiographie bietet nur mächtige Einzelne, *große* Individuen an. Doch Brecht versucht im fiktionalen Modell des *Lukullus* eine
utopische Historie der ohnmächtigen Vielen zu erzeugen. Exemplarisch
wird dies in der Traumszene der *Lukullus*-Erzählung. Der Traum des
Lukullus zeigt das utopische Bild von der gemeinsamen Rettung eines
bedrohten Dammes. Während das Individuum Lukullus zunächst den
militärischen Sieg durch die Vernichtung des Dammes beabsichtigt,
vereinigen sich die anonymen Kollektive der Soldaten beider Seiten,
um die Ernte zu retten. Auch die Rolle des Lukullus ist utopisch: er
reiht sich ein und hilft. Brecht nutzt die Form des (Wunsch-)Traumes,
um die prinzipielle Möglichkeit der Umwälzung von Autoritäten zu
evozieren. So wird die antike Historie zur Zeit des Utopischen und
verbindet sich im fiktionalen Text mit dem Ideal einer Kultur der Erinnerung, die ihre Hoffnungen auf die Zukunft richtet:

> Was der Raum für die Gedächtniskunst, ist die Zeit für die Erinnerungskul-
> tur. Vielleicht darf man noch einen Schritt weitergehen: wie die Gedächt-
> niskunst zum Lernen, so gehört die Erinnerungskultur zum Planen und
> Hoffen, d.h. zur Ausbildung sozialer Sinn- und Zeithorizonte. Erinnerungs-
> kultur beruht weitgehend, wenn auch keineswegs ausschließlich, auf For-
> men des Bezugs auf die Vergangenheit.[29]

II *DIE TROPHÄEN DES LUKULLUS* — VERGÄNGLICHKEIT ODER RUHM

Daß Erinnerungsfiguren Brechts Literarisierung des Lukullus-Stoffes
konstituieren, zeigt zunächst die Erzählung *Die Trophäen des
Lukullus*, die einen gemeinsam verbrachten Nachmittag von Lukullus
und Lukrez beschreibt. Diese Erzählung widerlegt die These, dass sich
Brecht mit Lukullus beschäftigt habe, um mit einem römischen Feldherrn vor dem Krieg der Nazis zu warnen. Es heißt hier auf der ersten
Seite: „Das Gespräch berührte die politischen Ereignisse zunächst mit
keinem Wort. Man erörterte einige philosophische Fragen" (19:425).
Diese Aussage lässt sich als metapoetischer Kommentar Brechts lesen.
Denn in der Tat sind es philosophische Reflexionen über das Gedenken, die hier erörtert werden, ihre Bedeutung für die Politik ist zwar
groß, aber nicht unmittelbar. Daher taugen die *Lukullus*-Texte Brechts
nicht als aktivistischer Aufruf zum antifaschistischen Kampf im Jahre

1939. Doch sie arbeiten an den zentralen Fragen der Erinnerungskultur: Was wollen wir erinnern? Was dürfen wir nicht vergessen? Was soll vergessen werden? In der Erzählung beantwortet die Figur des Lukrez diese Fragen am Ende eindeutig und weist damit die Sehnsucht nach individuellem Ruhm, die Lukullus repräsentiert, zurück.

Lukullus, „ein kleiner, magerer Herr" (19:425), alt geworden, schon lange nicht mehr im römischen Heer, fürchtet um sein Leben und um seinen Ruhm, als sein Nachfolger und Konkurrent Pompeius siegreich aus den asiatischen Feldzügen zurückkehrt. Er wird von der Öffentlichkeit gemieden, da niemand sich durch die Nähe zu ihm kompromittieren möchte. Auch sein Besucher Lukrez ist verletzlich, geschwächt von Krankheit. Das imaginierte Versagen seiner Autorität im Traum lässt Lukullus an seinem historischen Nachruhm zweifeln. Der folgende Dialog beleuchtet die Dialektik von Erinnern und Vergessen im kulturellen Gedächtnis. Lukullus fürchtet, aus den Geschichtsbüchern gestrichen zu werden, falls der Sieger Pompeius den Ruhm der asiatischen Eroberungen, der dem Lukullus in der Öffentlichkeit Roms vielfach zugeschrieben wird, für sich beansprucht. Er fürchtet daher erstmals auch den Tod, der ihm nun die Auslöschung seiner Existenz repräsentiert—, falls ihm das Weiterleben im Nachruhm unmöglich gemacht wird — und bittet Lukrez um Rat. Jedoch: „Der Dichter sagte nichts" (19:431). Auch wenn er schweigt, für ihn spricht sein Lehrgedicht, *De rerum natura*, das die Todesfurcht zurückweist, und aus dem Lukullus nun zitiert. Brecht hat das Gedicht um einige Strophen ergänzt, Strophen, die die menschliche Gewalt beklagen, die alles Leben prägt, und die die Furcht vor dem Tod als Furcht vor dem Diebstahl des Lebens, das auch nur als Besitz geschätzt wird, deutet.

Die Narrativik der Erzählung wird durch den lyrischen Dialog zwischen Lukrez und Brecht geprägt. Brechts lyrische Zuschreibung verweist auf eine intertextuelle Strategie, die in der Inszenierung eines literarischen Gesprächs zwischen einem antiken und einem modernen Autor auch über den ästhetischen Standort des Schriftstellers im Jahr 1939 reflektiert. In der Hermetik des Exils ist die Antike nähergerückt, die einstige Vertrautheit und Nähe zur Literatur der Gegenwart und ihrer unmittelbaren Vorgeschichte ist dagegen geschwunden. Brecht konstituiert so nicht nur ein schriftliches Gedächtnis für seine Sprache und für seine Zeit, darüber hinaus legt er Spuren in andere Zeiten und erinnert an fremd gewordene Literaturen. Es ist bekannt, dass der historische Lukrez für Brecht zu den wichtigsten Autoren gehörte, ein Band seiner Texte begleitet ihn durch das ganze Exil. Lukrez lesen zu können, wird ihm zum Gradmesser persönlichen Wohlbefindens.[30]

Sowohl ästhetische als auch historische Überlieferungspraktiken sollen nach Benjamins und Brechts Konzept einer Kultur der Erinnerung kritischen Überprüfungen unterzogen werden. Die Bezüge zu einer kontinuierlichen deutschen Literaturtradition sind ihnen fragwürdig geworden;[31] die zeitresistente Gültigkeit eines verbindlichen ästhetischen Kanons wird zurückgewiesen.[32]

> So stark wie der destruktive Impuls, so stark ist in der echten Geschichtsschreibung der Impuls der Rettung. Wovor kann aber etwas Gewesenes gerettet werden? Nicht sowohl vor dem Verruf und der Mißachtung, in die es geraten ist als vor einer bestimmten Art seiner Überlieferung. Die Art, in der es als „Erbe" gewürdigt wird, ist unheilvoller als seine Verschollenheit es sein könnte.[33]

Erinnerungskultur konstituiert sich so über ihre Wandelbarkeit, sie will nicht *bewahren* und entwickelt daher subversive Strategien, die sowohl den klassizistischen Kanon deutscher Kulturtradition als auch das *Erbe*-Ideal des sozialistischen Realismus durchbrechen. „Es gibt eine Überlieferung, die Katastrophe ist."[34] Rettung liegt im ästhetischen Kontext oftmals in der Destruktion. Eine statische Überlieferung, durch die Texte „zu musealen Kopien ihrer selbst erstarren,"[35] ist schlimmer als sie zu vergessen.

Der Lukullus der Erzählung fürchtet das Vergessensein, er fürchtet den Tod, doch ebenso fürchtet er militärischen Ruhm, der ihn bei Pompeius gefährdet. Er fragt den Lukrez, „fast flüsternd, nicht ohne Scham: ‚Was denn, meinst du, könnte mein Ruhm sein?'" (19:433). Er will *Ruhm*; nach Nietzsche artikuliert sich darin „die Anwartschaft auf einen Ehrenplatz im Tempel der Historie":[36] Ruhm „ist der Glaube an die Zusammengehörigkeit und Continuität des Grossen aller Zeiten, es ist ein Protest gegen den Wechsel der Geschlechter und die Vergänglichkeit."[37] Doch dieser Ruhm wird Lukullus nicht zugestanden. Lukrez' Blick fällt auf die Trophäe aus Asien — „auf einen Kirschbaum, der, seine weißen Blütenzweige im Wind wiegend, auf einem kleinen Hügel stand" (19:433). Mit seiner Antwort schließt die Erzählung:

> „Vielleicht ist es der?" sagte der Dichter eifrig. „Der Kirschbaum! Freilich, man wird sich wohl kaum da deines Namens erinnern. Aber das tut nichts. Asien wird wieder verlorengehen. Und deine Gerichte wird man bald kaum noch kochen können, denn da wird Armut sein. Aber der Kirschbaum: einige werden es vielleicht doch noch wissen, daß du ihn gebracht hast. Und wenn nicht, wenn alle Trophäen aller Eroberer zu Staub zerfallen sein werden, wird diese schönste deiner Trophäen im Frühjahr als die eines unbekannten Eroberers noch immer im Wind auf den Hügeln flattern, Lukullus!" (19:433)

Wie Lukullus, die Figur eines ehemals Mächtigen auf die Negierung seiner individuellen historischen Bedeutung reagiert, erfährt der Leser nicht. Lukrez spricht diese bedeutungsschweren Sätze, doch man ist geneigt, die Stimme des Autors mitzuhören. Lukullus wird erinnert werden, nicht für die militärischen Taten, die ihm in einer Geschichte der *Großen Männer* zugeschrieben würden, auch nicht für seine Gerichte, die mit ihrem Luxus die Armut der vielen beschämen. Der blühende Kirschbaum im Wind, dieses poetisch fast zu sehr konventionalisierte Symbol des Lebens und der nährenden Natur wird repräsentativ für Lukullus durch die Zeiten hindurch weiterleben, auch wenn sein Name vergessen wird. Die *Lukullus*-Erzählung schlägt eine Erinnerungskultur vor, die sich individuellem Ruhm widersetzt, aber das Gedenken an die Freuden des Lebens gutheißt.

Der Kulturbegriff, den die *Lukullus*-Erzählung konstituiert, hat wenig gemein mit einer *Verteidigung* der im Exil so oft und so pathetisch beschworenen deutschen Kulturtradition.[38] *Die Trophäen des Lukullus* lassen sich als Kritik ebendieser Tradition lesen, da sie den Ruhm zurückweisen und die Vergänglichkeit begrüßen.[39] Benjamin schreibt in *Über den Begriff der Geschichte*:

> Die jeweils Herrschenden sind aber die Erben aller, die je gesiegt haben. [...] Die Beute wird, wie das immer so üblich war, im Triumphzug mitgeführt. Man bezeichnet sie als die Kulturgüter. Sie werden im historischen Materialisten mit einem distanzierten Betrachter zu rechnen haben. Denn was er an Kulturgütern überblickt, das ist ihm samt und sonders von einer Abkunft, die er nicht ohne Grauen bedenken kann. Es dankt sein Dasein nicht nur der Mühe der großen Genien, die es geschaffen haben, sondern auch der namenlosen Fron ihrer Zeitgenossen. Es ist niemals ein Dokument der Kultur, ohne zugleich ein solches der Barbarei zu sein. Und wie es selbst nicht frei ist von Barbarei, so ist es auch der Prozeß der Überlieferung nicht, in der es von dem einen an den andern gefallen ist.[40]

Die Kultur, die sich als Hochkultur definiert, ist zwangsläufig die Beute des Siegers. Brechts *Lukullus*-Erzählung trug ursprünglich den Titel *Die Beute des Lukullus*, was eine Benjaminsche Perspektive der Interpretation eröffnet. Dass sich Brecht nach Cäsar mit einem weiteren römischen Feldherrn beschäftigt, wird dadurch motiviert, dass Lukullus nicht nur ein General ist, sondern auch ein Kulturträger und Kulturbringer. Brecht hätte seine *Lukullus*-Texte nicht über einen Pompeius schreiben können. Lukullus hat mit Krieg den Baum gebracht — zumindest der legendären Überlieferung nach — und er repräsentiert mit seinem Namen in vielen Sprachen die Esskultur, auch wenn ihm Brecht dieses Gedenken scheinbar abspricht. Sein *Name* ist nicht wichtig, denn der Gedächtniskult um Namen nützt niemandem. „Warum / Soll mein Name genannt werden?" wie Brecht — sich selbst beschwörend — in einem Gedicht fragt. (14:321) Dass er dem Ruhm des eigenen Namens dennoch nicht abgeneigt war, artikuliert sich wiederum lyrisch nach der Ankunft in den USA:

> Wohin ich komme, hör ich: spell your name!
> Ach, dieser „name" gehörte zu den großen! (15:48)

Derartige autobiographisch referentialisierte Gedichte Brechts motivieren Verständnis für die Figur des Lukullus. Dessen Angst vor der Auslöschung, die plötzliche Todesfurcht verweisen auf ähnliche Phänomene im Leben Brechts. Insbesondere lyrische Texte seit 1933 — wie *Besuch bei den verbannten Dichtern* (12:35f) oder *Gedichte im Exil* (14:311f) — thematisieren die Angst vor Tod, Vergänglichkeit und Vergessen — Antagonisten der Erinnerung. Im Schreiben wird Erinnerung beschworen. „Was sie sagen, sagen sie aus dem Gedächtnis" (14:312), wie es bei Brecht über Schriftsteller im Exil heißt. Texte müssen ein schriftliches Gedächtnis für die bedrohten, kollektiv verdrängten Erinnerungen konstituieren, was die *Lukullus*-Texte exemplarisch vorführen.

Der einstige Machthaber Lukullus sieht sein Gedenken bedroht durch die Herrschaft des Pompeius; er fürchtet die politisch motivierten Manipulationen der Macht, die das kulturelle Gedächtnis verzerren, vielleicht sogar auslöschen. Dem Autor Brecht gilt im Exil das kulturelle Gedächtnis der Deutschen als bedrohte Erinnerung, da es den Manipulationen der Nazis ausgesetzt ist. Im August 1939 äußert er in einem Interview die Befürchtung, „daß das, was das Ausland an deutscher Kultur nicht rettet, untergehen wird."[41] Die Vergänglichkeit, die als Gegensatz zur kanonischen Fixierung durchaus positiv gewertet wurde, wird Brecht in diesem Kontext bedrohlich. Da sein Werk überliefert werden soll, versucht er, ihm *Dauer* zu verleihen, und entwickelt ästhetische Strategien des Erinnerns, des Überlieferns, was auch seinen Blick auf die Literatur der Vergangenheit schärft.[42] Die Vergänglichkeit von Menschen und Texten wirkt so als vielschichtiger Diskurs in Brechts Exilwerk:

> Werken eine lange Dauer verleihen zu wollen, zunächst nur eine „natürliche" Bestrebung, wird ernsthafter, wenn ein Schreiber Grund zu der pessimistischen Annahme zu haben glaubt, seine Ideen [...] könnten eine sehr lange Zeit brauchen, um sich durchzusetzen. Die Maßnahmen, die man übrigens in dieser Richtung hin trifft, müssen die aktuelle Wirkung eines Werks keineswegs beeinträchtigen. Die nötigen epischen Ausmalungen des für die Zeit des Schreibens „Selbstverständlichen" stellen für diese Zeit nur wertvolle V-Effekte dar. Die begriffliche Autarkie der Werke enthält ein Moment der Kritik: der Schreiber analysiert die Vergänglichkeit der Begriffe und Wahrnehmungen seiner eigenen Zeit. (27:477ff)[43]

Erinnerungskultur dagegen konstituiert sich durch „Lücken / In der Kette der Gewalttaten" (6:110), wie es im *Verhör des Lukullus* heißt. Die Kette der Gewalttaten, das ist die Geschichte der Menschheit — sie muss gesprengt werden. Dieser Gedanke wird auch von Benjamin vertreten: „Die Rettung hält sich an den kleinen Sprung in der kontinuierlichen Katastrophe."[44] In *Die Trophäen des Lukullus* wird der Geschichte der Kriege und Katastrophen eine Erinnerungskultur entgegengestellt, die die Kultivierung des Kirschbaumes in Europa verzeichnen will, nicht jedoch die Heroisierung von Tod und Zerstörung. Benjamin bedient sich der Kategorie einer notwendigen „Erlösung," um die erwünschten Wandlungen im historischen Denken zu bezeichnen.[45]

Solange das Konzept einer kontinuierlich fortschreitenden Kultur nicht aufgebrochen wird, bleibt nur die Existenz in einer unerlösten Geschichte.

Die Erzählung bricht ab, doch Brecht greift Monate später den Lukullus-Stoff wieder auf, an einem anderen Punkt, der den Gedächtnisdiskurs weiterführt und zuspitzt. Der Lukullus der Erzählung ist keine negative Figur, er ist ein kunstliebender, philosophierender Schöngeist. Wer nur die Erzählung kennt, käme gewiss nie auf die Idee, ihren Protagonisten zu verurteilen und ihn ins Nichts zu stürzen. Er hat versucht, die Stadt Amisos zu schützen und weinend ihrer Brandschatzung zugesehen. Auch wenn der Totenrichter Lukullus' Tränen „Über die Vernichtung von Büchern und derlei wenig Nützlichem" (6:112) im Stück kritisiert, man muss bedenken, wie diese Tränen eines Mächtigen im Kontrast zu den realen deutschen Bücherverbrennern wirken. Bedeutungsvoll ist auch, dass die Geschichtsschreibung von einer Zerstörung dieser Stadt durch die *belagerten* Truppen spricht, der Angreifer, Lukullus, ist dafür nicht unmittelbar verantwortlich.[46] Die Figur des Lukullus wird so gezielt mit positiven Aspekten ausgestattet, nur die ironischen Bemerkungen des Lukrez über seinen Reichtum und Luxus relativieren die Tragik des Entmachteten. Das *Radiostück* geht härter mit ihm um. Die Erzählung stellt die Frage, *warum* des Lukullus gedacht werden sollte, während *Das Verhör des Lukullus* dialektisch die Aspekte abwägt, die für ein Erinnern oder für ein Vergessen dieser historischen Figur sprechen. Reflektiert wird dabei nicht nur über das ob, sondern auch über das wie eines Gedenkens, über die vielfältigen Formen der Gedächtniskultur. Eine geschichtliche Verurteilung des Lukullus zu Vergessenheit ist natürlich fiktiv und sagt sehr viel weniger über den historischen Lukullus aus als über die dem Autor gegenwärtige Erinnerungskultur. Brecht experimentiert damit im fiktionalen Raum am Modell einer anderen Erinnerung, einer anderen Geschichte. Damit verändert er zwar nicht die Realität der Gegenwart — beziehungsweise das kulturelle Gedächtnis—, aber er verändert die Perspektiven auf potentielle Alternativen, die die Zukunft bestimmten könnten.[47]

III *DAS VERHÖR DES LUKULLUS* — DENKMÄLER DER HERRSCHAFT UND DAS GEDÄCHTNIS DER BESIEGTEN

*D*as Verhör des Lukullus zeigt und erprobt Medien des Erinnerns. Das Totengedenken ist ein zentraler Bereich der offiziellen Gedächtniskultur.[48] So gedenkt die Stadt Rom ihres großen Sohnes, des Eroberers Lukullus mit einem Trauerzug, sein militärischer Ruhm wird noch einmal laut verkündet. Auch nach der Grablegung wird Lukullus nicht vergessen werden. Sein Triumphbogen, sein Grabmal, und der riesige „Fries mit dem Bild des Triumphes" (6:89) sollen seine Unsterblichkeit im Sinne ewigen Gedenkens garantieren — steinerne Denkmäler, Bilder der Macht, deren Verfallszeit lange währen kann und soll.

Der Kinderchor aus der dritten Szene, „In den Lesebüchern," belehrt uns über den Wunsch der Stadt, „die Namen der großen Feldherrn [...] / Auf die Tafeln der Unsterblichen zu schreiben" (6:92). Der Name des Lukullus im monumentalen Stein wird Roms Herrschaft und Gedächtnis lange stützen.

Das Schattenreich bildet eine Gegenwelt, „der große Lukullus" (6:89) wird seines Namens beraubt, er wird hier bewusst als *Lakalles* angerufen, mit dem Namen, den ihm die Vorstädte gegeben haben, dem „Der Ungebildeten und des Abschaums" (6:97), wie er empört ruft. Seine Frage „Wißt ihr hier meinen Namen nicht?" (6:97) ist nur rhetorisch gemeint, die Antwort lautet, das Schattenreich will *diesen* Namen, der das offizielle Gedenken Roms repräsentiert, gar nicht wissen. Er wird aufgerufen als „Lakalles, der sich Lukullus nennt" (6:97). Das Schattenreich entstellt seinen Namen und entmachtet ihn damit. Die Macht der Benennung, die Definitionsmacht liegt nun beim Totengericht, das ihn noch weiter enteignet, ihm sogar die entstellte Individualität entzieht, und ihn als „der Neue" (6:95) oder als „Schatte" (6:100) anruft. Das Totengericht wird über das Gedenken der *Nachwelt* urteilen, und Lukullus' Voraussetzungen sind schlecht — was Brecht durch das Sprachspiel mit den Namen deutlich macht. Denn hier zählt das offizielle Gedenken Roms, das Gedenken der Herrschenden, nichts; hier entscheiden die, die sich des *Lakalles* erinnern, und das sind die armen Schichten, die nicht von seinem Ruhm profitierten, und die Mütter der Soldaten, die in seinen Kriegen gestorben sind. Sie repräsentieren ein anderes Rom, das Rom der Beherrschten. Das Rom der Sieger gedenkt des Lukullus in steinernen Zeugnissen, das Rom der Verlierer muss erst entscheiden, ob es des *Lakalles* gedenken will oder ob es „den großen Mann" (6:92) strafen wird durch die Auslöschung jeder Erinnerung. Die Entstellung seines Namens ist ein böses Omen, da Erinnerung nur in Zeichen geleistet werden kann, in Namen, Monumenten, Bildern, Allegorien. *Vergessen* bedeutet, diese Zeichen zu vernichten. Die Vernichtung des Lukullus ist sprachlich bereits in seinem Namen vollzogen, seine Individualität wird vergessen sein.

Lukullus, der verhört wird, erkennt seine prekäre Situation nicht, er sieht nicht, dass er im Schattenreich ein Machtloser ist, ein Unbedeutender, dass hier andere Gesetze herrschen. Seine hochfahrende rhetorische Frage „Ist hier keine Ordnung?" (6:95) verfremdet den Blick auf die Ordnungen der differentiellen Welten. Denn im Schattenreich Brechts sind die Gesetze, die die Weltordnung der Lebenden bestimmen, außer Kraft gesetzt. Die Ordnung der Macht ist ungültig, alle Toten sind gleich. Darin zeigt sich weniger eine sozialistische Gleichheitsutopie als die metaphysische Machtlosigkeit des Menschen im Tod. Lukullus wurde nicht durch die Unterdrückten entmachtet, sondern durch sein Sterben.

L'empereur victorieux Lucullus est montré à un moment où ni gloire ni victoire n'ont de signification: c'est le moment où Lucullus est porté au tombeau. La splendeur de la gloire est détruite en premier lieu par la *vanitas*, c'est-à-dire par la vanité de tout ce qui est terrestre [...][49]

Brecht zeigt, dass die Unsterblichkeit im Ruhm der Denkmäler keinen Trost bietet. Lukullus spürt seine Sterblichkeit deutlich. Als Toter blickt er sehnsüchtig zurück auf das Leben, allerdings nicht auf Macht und Größe. Er vermisst nur den Wind und das Essen.[50] Im Tod ist auch Lukullus kein Sieger mehr. Die Denkmäler der Macht tragen nicht zu einer Weiterführung seiner Existenz bei. Stattdessen ist er angewiesen auf die Erinnerungen der Nachwelt, die nun vor dem Gericht erzählt und beurteilt werden. „Tote bzw. das Andenken an sie werden nicht ‚tradiert'. Daß man sich an sie erinnert, ist Sache affektiver Bindung, kultureller Formung und bewußten, den Bruch überwindenden Vergangenheitsbezugs."[51] Brecht kommentiert damit die Kulturkonzepte seiner Zeit, die der Überlieferung des Vergangenen eher mit Ehrfurcht als mit Beurteilungen begegnen.

Lukullus glaubt, dass es für ein Gedenken der Nachwelt genügt, vor dem Totengericht auf seinen militärischen Ruhm zu verweisen, und wünscht sich als Fürsprecher den großen Alexander, der ein „Sachverständiger / Über Taten wie die meinen" (6:98) sei. Doch Alexander ist vergessen — wiederum ein böses Omen für Lukullus, der nur staunen kann, dass „Der Unvergeßliche" (6:98) ausgelöscht wurde. Und so nähert sich das Stück seinem Höhepunkt, dem Zeugnis der steinernen Figuren des Frieses. Nur Lukullus hält den Stein für stumm; für die, die ihn zu befragen wissen, wird er sprechen. Sie lesen die unfreiwillig hinterlassenen Spuren im Stein, die im Gegensatz zur an die Nachwelt adressierten Stilisierung der Macht „Wahrhaftigkeit und Authentizität" zur Rekonstruktion der Vergangenheit versprechen.[52] Die Bilder im Stein sind vieldeutig und bieten dem Gericht so spezifisch andere, eigene Auslegungen. Ihre Berichte werden die Erinnerung der Nachwelt an Lukullus neu konstituieren und somit einen Lakalles schaffen; in mythischem Gestus wird der Text einer Geschichte der Besiegten geschrieben, die den unbekannten machtlosen Schichten ihren Platz einräumt.

Der Text wiederholt sich nun, Lukullus denkt, dass die dargestellte Eroberung fremder Städte für ihn sprechen würde, doch die Gewalttaten, für die er verantwortlich ist — Mord, Vergewaltigung, Versklavung, Zerstörung — ehren ihn nicht, sie erzürnen das Gericht, so dass der Totenrichter spricht. Er fordert Lukullus auf, nicht mehr von seinen schrecklichen Triumphen zu berichten, die ihm hier schaden, und rät ihm, sich auf seine Schwächen zu berufen — um die *Lücke in der Kette der Gewalttaten* zu finden. Der Versuch, im Totenreich weiterhin „Sein eigenes Standbild" (6:95) zu repräsentieren, ist gescheitert. Doch dann wendet sich das Blatt für Lukullus. Denn zwei Dinge sind auf dem Fries dargestellt, die ihn von den Friesen anderer Herrscher unterscheiden, Dinge, die *nur* den Lukullus charakterisieren, die nicht zum Gedächtnis der römischen Herrschaft beitragen. Was nun über Lukullus bekannt wird, zeugt für ihn, für ein Gedenken. Es sind legendäre Erzählungen über Ereignisse, die der Leser aus *Die Trophäen des Lukullus* kennt. Der Koch des Frieses spricht für ihn, die Gerichte des Lukullus machten *seine* Küche berühmt.

> DER LEHRER
> Was soll uns das, daß er gern aß?
>
> DER KOCH
> Aber mich ließ er kochen
> Nach Herzenslust. Ich dank es ihm.
>
> DER BÄCKER
> Ich verstehe ihn, ich, der Bäcker war!
> Wie oft mußte ich Kleie in den Teig rühren
> Der armen Kunden wegen. Dieser da
> Durfte ein Künstler sein.
>
> DER KOCH
> Durch ihn! Ich nenne ihn menschlich drum.
> Im Triumph
> Führte er mich hinter den Königen
> Und erwies meiner Kunst Achtung.
> Und ich weiß auch
> Daß er in Amisus, der Tochterstadt des herrlichen Athen
> Voll bis zum Rand von Kunstschätzen und Büchern, beir Plünde-
> rung
> Seine Soldaten mit Tränen beschwor, nicht Feuer zu legen.
> Naß von Tränen kam er mir zum Nachtmahl.
> Auch das war menschlich, bedenkt das! (6:110f)

Die Bewertungskriterien der Schöffen, die sich hier manifestieren, machen die Urteilsgerechtigkeit der Nachwelt verdächtig — von rechtlich gebundener Objektivität kann nicht die Rede sein.[53] Jeder Schöffe urteilt für sich, nach seinen begrenzten persönlichen Erfahrungen. Der Koch wird durch den Bäcker unterstützt, weil dieser die Lust an der Nahrungszubereitung nachvollziehen kann. Der Lehrer bleibt dagegen völlig verständnislos. Hier wird erst deutlich, wie parteiisch diese Schöffen sind.

Die Erinnerung der Nachwelt ist abhängig vom Urteil eines Gerichts, das sich fragwürdig macht; es wird kein utopischer Ausblick Brechts auf ein sozialistisches Volksgericht sichtbar, das ein „eigenes Recht" und einen „eigenen Blick auf die Geschichte" vorweisen könnte.[54] Nachdem er vom Tod seines Freundes Sergej Tretjakow erfahren hatte, der als angeblicher japanischer Spion zum Tod verurteilt worden war, schreibt Brecht — ebenfalls im Herbst 1939 — ein Gedicht, das ein Scheitern sozialistischer Ideale andeutet: „Ist das Volk unfehlbar?"

> mein lehrer tretjakow
> der grosse, freundliche
> ist erschossen worden. verurteilt durch ein volksgericht.
> als ein spion. sein name ist verdammt.
> seine bücher sind vernichtet. das gespräch über ihn
> ist verdächtig und verstummt.
> gesetzt, er ist unschuldig?[55]

Nur die erste Fassung des Gedichts nennt den Namen Tretjakows in der ersten Zeile, Brecht hat diesen Namen anschließend durchgestrichen. Auch er selbst, dem die Freundlichkeit immer ein erstrebtes Ideal war, fürchtet die *Urteile* der Volksgerichte, auch er fürchtet um seinen *Namen*, um seine *Bücher*, um *Gespräche*, die ausbleiben, wenn die Medien der Erinnerung vernichtet werden. In der Sowjetunion war nach Tretjakows Tod auch sein Werk dem Vergessen überantwortet worden. Tretjakow stand Brecht nicht nur persönlich nahe, auch als Literat und als Kritiker kultureller Öffentlichkeit sah er in ihm einen *Lehrer*, dessen Auslöschung ihm zum Spiegel wird. Das Gericht über Lukullus könnte autobiographische Referenzen zu dem fatalen Volksgericht aufweisen. Doch auch den *Trophäen des Lukullus* geht im Januar 1939 eine bittere Klage Brechts über das Verschwinden zahlreicher Freunde in sowjetischen Gefängnissen voraus.[56] Ebenfalls im Januar erfährt er von der Vernichtung des Prager Satzes der *Svendborger Gedichte* nach der Besetzung der Tschechoslowakei. Die kühle Distanz des Totenrichters hat Brecht selbst nicht aufbringen können. Er reagiert entsetzt auf die materielle Auslöschung seiner Texte; Ruth Berlau berichtet, er habe sie gebeten, seine Gedichte auswendig zu lernen, um ihre Überlieferung so zu sichern. Die Trauer des Lukullus über die verbrannten Bücher in Amisos erlangt vor diesem Kontext neue Bedeutung.

Noch stärker ändert sich das Bild von Lukullus, als nun der Kirschbaum vom Schöffen, der ein Bauer war, entdeckt wird. Denn nun findet Lukullus bzw. Lakalles seine Sprache wieder; und diese beiden sprechen nun als zwei Gleiche über den Baum, den sie lieben. An alle gerichtet, verkündet der Bauer dann die Utopie des Stückes:

> Ihr Freunde, dies von allem, was erobert
> Durch blutigen Krieg verhaßten Angedenkens
> Nenn ich das Beste. Denn dies Stämmchen lebt.
> Ein neues, freundliches gesellt es sich
> Dem Weinstock und dem fleißigen Beerenstrauch
> Und wachsend mit den wachsenden Geschlechtern
> Trägt's Frucht für sie. Und ich beglückwünsch dich
> Der's uns gebracht. Wenn alle Siegesbeute
> Der beiden Asien längst schon vermodert ist
> Wird jedes Jahr aufs neue den Lebenden
> Wohl diese schönste deiner Trophäen noch
> [...] im Wind von den Hügeln flattern. (6:112)

Dieses Bild, das auch die Schlussworte des Lukrez in der Erzählung bestimmt, evoziert die Versöhnung der Klassen, Freundlichkeit unter Gleichen, Kultivierung ohne Gewalt. Doch diese Versöhnung hat keinen Ort im Reich der Lebenden.[57]

Auf die Frage, wie sich die fiktionale Gedächtniskultur zur Figur des Lukullus verhalten soll, ist die Antwort vielschichtig. Das Stück schließt mit der Szene „Spreu und Weizen" (6:112), von einer Trennung, die eine Verurteilung motivieren könnte, ist nicht die Rede. Diese Szene ist übrigens in den späteren Fassungen gestrichen worden, wodurch die anfängliche Mehrdeutigkeit des Stückes zurückgenommen wird.[58] Der Autor Brecht setzt in seinen *Lukullus*-Texten sowohl auf ein konstruktives Erinnern als auch auf ein konstruktives Vergessen. Der Ruhm des Lukullus, der Ruhm eines einzelnen, nützt nur den Herrschenden, die herrschende Geschichtsschreibung, die die Kriege verzeichnet, wird so ebenso zurückgewiesen wie die offizielle Gedächtniskultur, die den *Kult der Erinnerung* organisiert. *Das Verhör des Lukullus* und *Die Trophäen des Lukullus* stellen die Frage nach einer richtigen Vergangenheitsvariante, die in jeder Kultur auftritt. Doch jede erinnernde Fokussierung wird die faktische Vergangenheit zwangsläufig verzerren, verwandeln. Brecht evoziert die Möglichkeit einer Gegengeschichte für unterdrückte Erinnerungen. Im Medium der Schrift kann ein oppositionelles Gedächtnis geschaffen werden, das den Kanon kultureller Überlieferung durchbricht. Das aktive auslöschende Vergessen der *Großen Männer* aus dem Buch der Menschheit ist dabei unabdingbar.

Doch dies bleibt dem fiktionalen Raum vorbehalten; die geschichtstheoretischen Aporien des Exilanten Brecht bleiben — mit den Worten des Lukullus der Erzählung — ohne Lösung, bleiben *unerlöste Geschichte*, deren Gedächtnis sich in den Körper eingeschrieben hat:

> Die Menschheit [...] erinnert sich im allgemeinen länger der Mißhandlungen, die sie erfährt, als der Liebkosungen. Was wird aus den Küssen? Aber die Wunden hinterlassen Narben. (19:430)[59]

ANMERKUNGEN

[1] Brecht-Zitate im Text — mit Bandzahl und Seitenangabe — folgen grundsätzlich der GBA: Bertolt Brecht, *Große kommentierte Berliner und Frankfurter Ausgabe*, hrsg. Werner Hecht, Jan Knopf, Werner Mittenzwei und Klaus-Detlef Müller, 30 Bde., Berlin/Frankfurt/M. 1988 ff.

[2] Walter Benjamin, *Gesammelte Schriften*, hrsg. Rolf Tiedemann und Hermann Schweppenhäuser, 8 Bde., Frankfurt/M., 1972 ff, Bd. 1.2, 691–704.

[3] Vgl. dazu auch Herbert Marcuses kritische Studie *Über den affirmativen Charakter der Kultur* von 1937, über eine deutsche Kultur, die soziale und politische Ungerechtigkeit mit Idealismus verbrämt hat. Herbert Marcuse, „Über den affirmativen Charakter der Kultur," in: H.M., *Kultur und Gesellschaft*, Bd. 1, Frankfurt/M. 1965, 56–101.

[4] Benjamin, GS 1.2:695. Auch Brecht stellt sich im historischen Kontext des Exils gegen eine affirmative Überlieferung kultureller Selbstsicherheit: „Wenn die Barbarei von der Barbarei kommt / Dann kommt die Güte von der Güte und ist unbezwingbar / Und die Schönheit ist schön, und wenn sie bis zum Hals in der Jauche steht" (14:289).

[5] Benjamin, GS 7.1:360.

[6] Vgl. Aleida Assmann, *Erinnerungsräume. Formen und Wandlungen des kulturellen Gedächtnisses*, München 1999, 227.

[7] Vgl. dazu die Wirkung der *imagines agentes*, ebd., 221ff.

[8] Mit Marja-Leena Hakkarainen, die das Konzept der Interfiguralität in Texten Brechts dargestellt hat, lässt sich die Figur des Lukullus als montierte Figur deuten, in der die Texte der Literatur und der Geschichte übereinander projiziert werden. Der reale Lukullus wird aus seinem historischen Kontext herausgelöst und — fiktional gebrochen — in einen neuen Text eingefügt. Dementsprechend unterscheiden sich die Charakterisierungen des Lukullus in der Erzählung und in den unterschiedlichen Fassungen des Stückes beträchtlich. Die historische Individualität des Lukullus spielt bei Brecht überhaupt keine Rolle. Vgl. M.-L. H., *Das Turnier der Texte. Stellenwert und Funktion der Intertextualität im Werk Bertolt Brechts*, Frankfurt/M. u.a. 1994, 229 f.

[9] Jan Assmann, *Das kulturelle Gedächtnis. Schrift, Erinnerung und politische Identität in frühen Hochkulturen*, München 1992, 30.

[10] Die Auseinandersetzung um die Lukullus-Oper in der DDR ist dokumentiert in: Joachim Lucchesi, *Das Verhör in der Oper. Die Debatte um die Aufführung „Das Verhör des Lukullus" von Bertolt Brecht und Paul Dessau*, Berlin 1993, hier 80.

[11] Klaus Völker, *Brecht-Kommentar zum dramatischen Werk*, München 1983, 202 ff.

[12] Jan Knopf, *Brecht-Handbuch*, Bd. 1, Stuttgart 1980, 195–201.

[13] Klaus-Detlef Müller, *Die Funktion der Geschichte im Werk Bertolt Brechts. Studien zum Verhältnis von Marxismus und Ästhetik*, (*Studien zur deutschen Literatur* 7), Tübingen 1972, 142–45.

[14] Hans Mayer, „Brechts Hörspiel *Das Verhör des Lukullus*," in: H.M., *Vereinzelt Niederschläge*, Pfullingen 1973, 218–27.

[15] Müller, *Funktion der Geschichte*, 142.

[16] Ignace Feuerlicht, „Bertolt Brecht's *Das Verhör des Lukullus,"* in: *Monatshefte* 75.4 (1983): 369–83.

[17] Z.B. die *Berichtigungen alter Mythen* (19:340f) oder Brechts *Antigone-Modell*. Allerdings setzt er den Mythos auch ohne Dekonstruktion ein, wie seine Fragmente zu *Mythen für den intimen Gebrauch* zeigen. Vgl. den Band zur Ausstellung „Bertolt Brecht, 1898–1998" der Akademie der Künste Berlin, 25. Januar–29. März 1998: ... *Und mein Werk ist der Abgesang des Jahrtausends." 22 Versuche, eine Arbeit zu beschreiben,* hrsg. Erdmut Wizisla, Berlin 1998, 12 ff.

[18] Jan Assmann, *Das kulturelle Gedächtnis*, 52.

[19] So spricht der Totenrichter: „Sie / Trennt nur so weniges von den Toten. / Von ihnen kann man sagen / Daß sie nur beinahe leben. Der Schritt von der Welt oben / Herab in das Schattenreich / Ist für sie nur ein kleiner" (6:99).

[20] Vgl. Feuerlicht, „Brecht's *Verhör des Lukullus,"* 378 f.

[21] Walter Hilfrich, „Bertolt Brecht: *Das Verhör des Lukullus,"* in: *Die Pädagogische Provinz* 21/1967, 273–88, hier 282.

[22] Vgl. Wilfried Barner, „,Durchrationalisierung' des Mythos? Zu Bertolt Brechts *Antigonemodell 1948,"* in: *Zeitgenossenschaft. Studien zur deutschsprachigen Literatur im 20. Jahrhundert*, hrsg. Paul Michael Lützeler, Frankfurt/M. 1987, 191–210.

[23] Auch Heinrich Mann arbeitet im Exil mit dem Roman von *Henri Quatre* gezielt an legendarer Geschichte.

[24] Vgl. Jan Assmann, *Das kulturelle Gedächtnis*, 51.

[25] Vgl. dazu Harro Müller-Michaels, *Geschichte zwischen Kairos und Katastrophe: historische Romane im 20. Jahrhundert*, Frankfurt/M. 1988, besonders 54–77.

[26] Aleida Assmann, „Zur Metaphorik der Erinnerung," in: A.A./Dietrich Harth (Hrsg.), *Mnemosyne. Formen und Funktionen der kulturellen Erinnerung*, Frankfurt/M. 1991, 13–35, hier 30.

[27] Benjamin, GS 1.3:1250.

[28] Ders., GS 5.1:578.

[29] Jan Assmann, *Das kulturelle Gedächtnis*, 31.

[30] Brecht notiert in Santa Monica: „Das Haus ist sehr schön. In diesem Garten ist der Lukrez wieder lesbar." (27:120). Auch Brechts Fragmente des Lehrgedichts *Das Manifest* (vgl. 15:120–57) „über so etwas wie die Unnatur der bürgerlichen Verhältnisse" (29:348), wie er an Karl Korsch schreibt, beziehen sich ästhetisch auf Lukrez.

[31] „Denn der Begriff der Tradition verschleiert den Bruch, der zum Entstehen von Vergangenheit führt, und rückt dafür den Aspekt der Kontinuität, das Fort-

schreiben und Fortsetzen, in den Vordergrund. [...] dieser Begriff verkürzt das Phänomen um den Aspekt der Rezeption, des Rückgriffs über den Bruch hinweg, ebenso wie um dessen negative Seite: Vergessen und Verdrängen." Jan Assmann, *Das kulturelle Gedächtnis*, 34.

[32] Vgl. Brechts Gedicht *Der Gedanke in den Werken der Klassiker* (14:337f).

[33] Benjamin, GS 1.3:1242.

[34] Ders., GS 5.1:591.

[35] Ders., GS 2.2:641.

[36] Friedrich Nietzsche, „Vom Nutzen und Nachtheil der Historie für das Leben," in: F.N., *Werke. Kritische Gesamtausgabe*, hrsg. Giorgio Colli und Mazzino Montinari, Bd. 3.1, Berlin/New York 1972, 239–330, hier 255.

[37] Ebd., 256.

[38] Exemplarisch wird dieses emphatische Kulturideal in den Essays Heinrich Manns; „Verteidigung der Kultur" titelt ein Aufsatz von 1935, der aus Manns Referat für den „Internationalen Schriftstellerkongreß zur Verteidigung der Kultur" hervorgegangen ist. Vgl. Heinrich Mann, *Verteidigung der Kultur. Antifaschistische Streitschriften und Essays*, Hamburg 1960, 132–37.

[39] Vgl. auch Brechts Gedichte *Die Tuis und das Erbe* (14:283 f) und *Über die geistige und materielle Kultur* (14:285).

[40] Benjamin, GS 1.2:696.

[41] Zitiert in: Werner Hecht, *Brecht Chronik*, Frankfurt/M. 1997, 583.

[42] Vgl. Jochen Vogt, „*Damnatio memoriae* und ‚Werke von langer Dauer'. Zwei ästhetische Grenzwerte in Brechts Exillyrik," in: *Peter Weiss-Jahrbuch* 7 (1998): 97–114.

[43] Vgl. auch Paul Peters, „Schmerz Hekabes. Brecht und die Vergänglichkeit," in: *Weimarer Beiträge* 39.1(1993): 69–84.

[44] Benjamin, GS 1.2:683.

[45] Ders., GS 1.2:693.

[46] Aufgrund derartiger Entstellungen sieht Hakkarainen „karnevalisierte Geschichte in Brechts Lukullus-Versionen." Vgl. Hakkarainen, *Turnier der Texte*, 196 ff.

[47] „Das kollektive Gedächtnis operiert daher in beiden Richtungen: zurück und nach vorne. Das Gedächtnis rekonstruiert nicht nur die Vergangenheit, es organisiert auch die Erfahrung der Gegenwart und Zukunft." Vgl. Jan Assmann, *Das kulturelle Gedächtnis*, 42.

[48] Brechts literarische Beschäftigung mit Grabmälern und Totengedenken hat sich seit den 20er Jahren gewandelt. Vgl. Sigrid Thielking, „‚L'homme statue'?

Brechts Inschriften im Kontext von Denkmalsdiskurs und Erinnerungspolitik," in: *The Brecht Yearbook/Das Brecht Jahrbuch* 24 (1999), 54–67.

[49] Elisabeth Scheele, *„La Guerre de Troie n'aura pas lieu* de Jean Giraudoux et *Procès de Lucullus* (*Das Verhör des Lukullus*) de Bertolt Brecht," in: *Neohelicon* 23 (1996): 223–35, hier 223.

[50] Vgl. ebd., 228.

[51] Jan Assmann, *Das kulturelle Gedächtnis*, 34.

[52] Vgl. Aleida Assmann, *Erinnerungsräume*, 209.

[53] Fredric Jameson schreibt über die verbreiteten Gerichtssituationen bei Brecht: „In diesem Sinne bestätigt Brechts revolutionärer *casus* nicht die Norm oder das Gesetz, sondern stellt es zur Diskussion; und in diesem Sinn fordert Brechts Dramatisierung des Widerspruchs zu einem Urteil auf, das nicht die Wahl zwischen zwei Alternativen ist, sondern ihre Verdrängung im Licht eines neuen, utopischen Urteils [...]" Vgl. F.J., *Lust und Schrecken der unaufhörlichen Verwandlung aller Dinge: Brechts Methode*, übers. Jürgen Pelzer, Berlin 1998, 114.

[54] Vgl. Knopf, *Brecht-Handbuch*, 199.

[55] Vgl. die frühere Fassung des Gedichts in: *„...Und mein Werk ist der Abgesang des Jahrtausends,"* 60 f. Die spätere Fassung in der GBA nennt Tretjakow nicht. (vgl. 14:435f) Tretjakows bereits 1937 erfolgte Hinrichtung blieb lange geheim, erst im Herbst 1939 wurde sein Tod bekannt gegeben. Vgl. Vladimir Kolyazin, „„How Will He Go To His Death?' An Answer to Brecht's Question about the Death of His ‚Teacher,' the ‚Tall and Kindly' Tretiakov," in: *The Brecht Yearbook/Das Brecht Jahrbuch* 22 (1997), 169–79.

[56] Vgl. 26:326 f.

[57] Zur Rolle der Freundlichkeit bei Brecht vgl. Benjamins Kommentar zur *Legende von der Entstehung des Buches Taoteking auf dem Weg des Laotse in die Emigration*: Benjamin, GS 2.2:570 ff.

[58] Diese Absicht zeigt sich in zahlreichen weiteren Änderungen; gestrichen wird die Erwähnung der Tränen vor Amisos, niemand nennt den Lukullus noch menschlich. Stattdessen tritt dieser als deutlich erkennbarer Bösewicht auf, er beschimpft die Zeugen. Der feindliche König wird als Verteidiger gefeiert; das Gericht erhebt sich gar zu seinem Lob. Die Erwähnung des Kirschbaums wird als Bestechungsversuch gewertet. Auch formale Details sind von Bedeutung: dass der Begriff der „Bilder" (6:100) gestrichen wird, geht einher mit der Ersetzung der mythischen Elemente. Die artifiziellen Sprachformen werden dem Umgangssprachlichen weiter angepasst.

[59] Die Traumata und Narben Brechts artikulieren sich in der Lyrik. Vgl. z.B. *Ich, der Überlebende* (12:125) und *In den Zeiten der äußersten Verfolgung* (15:21).

Bertolt Brecht und das Internet

Bertolt Brechts theoretische Überlegungen zum Film in den 30zigerJahren und Hank Barrys Überlegungen zum Internet im Jahr 2000 zeigen, wie neue innovative Technologien die jeweils fest etablierten ethischen, sozialen und juristischen Ideologien einer Gesellschaft herausfordern. Dieses Essay bringt die aktuellen Kontroversen zum Gebrauch des Internet, die sich an dem Fall Napster entzündet haben, in Verbindung mit den Debatten um Brechts „Dreigroschenprozess." Es zeigt, wie Brecht die allzu ökonomischen Konnotationen der Begriffe "Apparat," „Kollektiv" und „Ware" abstreift und ihre dominant sozialen Implikationen herausarbeitet, um ihr innovatives Potential zur Reformierung der Weimarer Film- und Medientheorie offen zu legen. Brechts Neudefinition dieser Begriffe antizipiert Perspektiven die auch die heutigen Debatten um den kreativen und nicht kommerziellbestimmten Gebrauch des Internets lenken und eventuell vorantreiben können.

Bertolt Brecht and the Internet

Dorothee Ostmeier

The advent of new technologies challenges the ethical, social and legal ideologies of society. At the beginning of the 21st century it is the World Wide Web with its infinite possibilities for the exchange of information which has called the commercial conventions of the capitalist society into question. Arguably the most visible challenge to date arose during the last year with the advent of software facilitating exchange of MP3 music files over the Internet without payment to copyright holders. The explosive popularity of the idea led in short order to a lawsuit filed by A&M Records in December 1999 "against Napster, Inc., an Internet start up."[1] The suit, backed by the Recording Industry Association of America (RIAA) and joined by seventeen record companies, demanded that Napster cease operation. The RIAA's lawsuit provoked diverse discussions in court, in the popular press and on the Internet centering on conflicts between the profit-driven interests of the recording industry and the interests of its artists and customers who criticize the industry's criteria and business strategies for the production, distribution and marketing of music. While some object to the exchange of music without payment others focus their criticism on the industry. Popular artists Courtney Love and Prince,[2] for example, sharply disparage the music industry's bolstering of consumerism at the expense of the music lovers' demand for artistic productions. They complain that the marketing and packaging of their work as "disposable entertainment" (Prince 1) undermines its artistic merit, especially when, for example, single songs are taken from their original albums in order to attract buyers to an otherwise "poor selection of forgettable songs" (Prince 2).[3]

These criticisms echo Bertolt Brecht's 1930 fight against the then-fledgling film industry's controlling power when the Nero film company altered plot and substance of *Die Dreigroschenoper* without consulting him. Claiming that the company had ignored parts of the contract with him Brecht, the author, filed a lawsuit against the company on 30 September 1930, shortly after the film production had started on 19 September 1930.

As in the Napster case the conflicts between the interests of the industry and the avantgarde were based on issues of intellectual property, censorship,[4] and the relationship between artists, art and its patrons and audience. Brecht objected to the industry's focus on commercial success and

New Essays on Brecht / Neue Versuche über Brecht
Maarten van Dijk et al., eds., *The Brecht Yearbook / Das Brecht-Jahrbuch*
Volume 26 (Toronto, Canada: The International Brecht Society, 2001)

its demotion of the audience to customers; Napster provided software which freed the customers from their dependence on the industry's music selections. I discuss Napster here as an avantgarde business which — founded by a college student — collected no revenues and charged its clientele no fees[5] before it started to collaborate with the German media giant Bertelsmann October 31, 2000.

This essay relates the controversies about the use of the Internet technology to debates of the late 1920s and early 1930s, especially to discussions centering on Bertolt Brecht's lawsuit against Nero Film Company. Brecht uses his report and commentary about the lawsuit in his essay *Der Dreigroschenprozeß* — written in spring and summer 1931 and published in January 1932 — as a means to reflect on the relation between the commercial and aesthetic aspects of film production. After examining the social activism of the "Prozeß" I will zero in on Brecht's revision of the terms *Apparat*, *Kollektiv* and *Ware* and demonstrate how he associates their economic and social connotations with his aesthetic concerns. He rejects the bourgeois aspects of these terms and explores their innovative potential for reforming film production in the Weimar Republic. The social structures inherent in the use of film technology become the model for the production of anti-bourgeois art. This new definition offers criteria for the re-evaluation of avant-garde film and media theories of his time, and I will investigate how these criteria offer new perspectives on the current debates shaping the Internet.

Brecht studied Marx' *Das Kapital* in 1928, but this as well as the few other texts by Marx and Engels, which had been edited before 1933, did not present systematic ideas about the fundamental structures of proletarian art and film (Gallas 21-22). Thus it fell to the proletarian revolutionary authors — who were organized in the "Bund proletarisch-revolutionärer Schriftsteller"(BPRS)[6] founded in 1928 — to evaluate and reform the established artistic genres and to explore their capacity to revolutionize bourgeois society. Between 1927 and 1932 Brecht extended his reformation of poetic and theatrical forms to include also radio theory and film. *Der Dreigroschenprozeß*[7] is Brecht's first far-reaching text about film which links social issues to film theory before he produced *Kuhle Wampe* between August 1931 and February 1932 together with Ernst Ottwald and Slatan Dudow.

Brecht lost the suit against Nero and chose not to appeal. Soon thereafter he reviewed the proceedings critically in *Der Dreigroschenprozeß*. The text is designed as a montage of legal documents, of newspaper articles, interpersed with Brecht's commentary: He describes first the proceedings of the actual lawsuit, then quotes in chronological order miscellaneous excerpts from newspaper articles which outline the issues raised by the suit, and finally he offers his own commentary reflecting on his experiences with the bourgeois legal system and its depiction in newspapers and journals. The montage of conflicting newspaper excerpts confronts the reader with a conglomeration of varying perspectives.[8] Then

Brecht reveals to the reader that such conflicting statements all stem from the same ideological prejudices:[9]

> Die ideologische Schizophrenie des Kleinbürgers, der die Zeitungen schreibt, zeigt sich in dem Beisammensein verschiedener Vorstellungskreise...Er hat mindestens zwei Vorstellungen zu einer Sache: Die eine bezieht er aus der großen bürgerlichen Idealität, welche das Individuum, die Gerechtigkeit, Freiheit und so weiter gegen die Wirklichkeit durchsetzen wird, die andere aus der Wirklichkeit selber.... (182–83)

Undermining the independence of each newspaper and author, he treats all journalists alike as "Kleinbürger," as representatives of bourgeois thought. The aggressiveness of Brecht's attack becomes apparent when he labels besides Dr. Frankfurter, Nero's lawyer, also Siegfried Kracauer — since 1921 an editor for the "Feuilleton" of the renowned leftist *Frankfurter Zeitung* — members of the petite bourgeois class. Promoting an ivory-tower-aestheticism Dr. Frankfurter discourages collaboration between artists and film industry in order to protect their artistic work from commercialization. Kracauer, in contrast, encourages the industry to employ artists in order to refine film.[10] Both authors insert a typically bourgeois art-film dichotomy: art as an idealistic, film as a realistic project, which involves industrial production and marketing. Brecht claims: "Selbst unsere Freunde von links fanden den Prozeß überflüssig" (183). Since they argue within the parameters of the pre-established ideological system Brecht labels these authors a "Kollektiv" in furthering the proletarization of society:

> Hier ist ein Kollektiv an der Arbeit, das den Einzelteil an der Produktion unkenntlich macht. Wodurch wird es gebildet? Es wird durch den Klassenkampf gebildet. Durch die gemeinsame Arbeit des Proletarisierens und das gemeinsame Schicksal des Proletarisiertwerdens. (182)

Between 1929 and 1933 "collectivation" was central for the policies of the Soviet government which rigorously pursued the transformation of traditional agriculture. "The peasantry were forced to give up their individual farms and join large collective farms (kolkhozy)."[11] While this was considered an innovative economic strategy at the time, Brecht ironically utilizes the term "collective" to describe the bourgeois press' traditional system of argumentation. He refers to its reactionary double standard, the split between idealism ("bürgerliche Idealität") and realism ("Wirklichkeit"), present in Kracauer's and Frankfurter's views which sustain the capitalist economy of the bourgeois system.[12]

Brecht views the representatives of the Weimar judiciary as members of this reactionary collective. Winning or losing the lawsuit was not his main purpose. He filed the suit in order to provoke the legal and journalistic institutions into action and thereby to demonstrate their ideological bias:

> Man konnte ihn nicht von Anfang bis Ende mit dem Bestreben führen, ihn zu
> gewinnen, oder dem Bestreben, ihn zu verlieren — er hätte dann nichts erge-
> ben. Man mußte sich ihm anvertrauen und lediglich darauf bauen, daß er in
> irgendeiner Weise etwas Klarheit über die Art und Weise, wie heute geistige
> Dinge sich materiell umsetzen, schaffen würde.(153)

Subjecting Weimar jurisdiction to his analysis and evaluation, Brecht's
investigation demonstrates the limits of bourgeois concepts of art, film and
commerce which underlie the rulings and do not reconcile artistic with
commercial, intellectual with materialistic interests. Thus the title of the
essay "Prozeß" has three different meanings or at least connotations. First
of all, it refers to the actual lawsuit, secondly to the public thought processes and debates stimulated by the suit, and thirdly to Brecht's critical
examination of the ruling's underlying ideology. His investigation is not
only a theoretical and analytical endeavor — as investigator himself Brecht
plays an active role by challenging the constituents of the social fabric.
Indeed, he actually disputes the legality of Nero's business strategies, the
legal system which promotes them and the journalism which discusses
them. His essay sets an example for cultural criticism in that it does not
only represent only the theoretical endeavor of a single author and is not
only content-oriented. As an "experiment" it presents diverse social processes before analyzing their results. The subtitle of the treatise defines this
"Prozeß" as "soziologisches Experiment." The social reality — and not a
theory — becomes the object of the investigation. For Brecht, cultural
theory is cultural practice: The law suit "schafft Klarheit." He insists:

> es hat nämlich keinerlei Aussicht auf Erfolg, sich eine bestimmte „Kultur"
> auszudenken, zu der man die Realität überreden will. Durch solche Dedukti-
> onen nimmt man sich nur die Möglichkeit, das Funktionieren der Realität zu
> begreifen und so herauszufinden, was an dem schon Vorgehenden revolutio-
> näre und was reaktionäre Tendenzen sind. Das Experiment mobilisiert die
> Widersprüche dieser Art in den Dingen und Vorgängen und hält den Vorgang
> selbst während der Untersuchung in Gang. (208)

Contemplation of culture only abstracts from reality, applies its theories
without being engaged in it. Brecht calls his sociological experiment an
expression of a scientific method which analyzes and reviews generally
unnoticed social processes.[13] Reflecting on the verb "begreifen" he privileges its literal over its abstract connotations. "Das Begreifen...ist ein Griffe
finden" (209). Definitions should make their substance "handlich" (207)
and render a "Zugriff" and "Handhabung des Stoffes" (207). As the conductor of the experiment Brecht is affected by its outcome. At each stage
of the proceedings he has to modify his action. "Begreifen" and "Griffe
finden" implies risk taking. This is especially visible when he first rejects a
settlement fee offered by Nero's lawyer, arguing: "Es handelt sich nicht
um die materielle Seite"(145). Only after the ruling does he accept Nero's
offer to cover the legal fees and to return the filming rights to him. The
acceptance of the money does not undermine his goal to expose Wei-

mar's reactionary legal system at this time.[14]

This avant-garde social activism was inspired by his encounter with the Russian poet, author and theoretician of art, Sergei Tretiakov whom Brecht's poem "Ist das Volk unfehlbar?" calls "Mein Lehrer."[15] Walter Benjamin quotes Tretiakov as one of the most radical anti-bourgeois authors. In "Der Autor als Produzent" (April 1934)(686) he writes:

> Als 1928 in der Epoche der totalen Kollektivierung der Landwirtschaft die Parole: „Schriftsteller in die Kolchose!" ausgegeben wurde, fuhr Tretjakow nach der Kommune „Kommunistischer Leuchtturm" und nahm dort... folgende Arbeiten in Angriff: Einberufung von Massenmeetings; ...Inspektion von Lesesälen, Schaffung von Wandzeitungen und Leitung der Kolchos-Zeitung; Berichterstattung an die Moskauer Zeitungen....[16] (686–87)

Tretiakov transferred his poetic competence to organizing the communal life of the kolkhos. The title "Schriftsteller in die Kolchose!"[17] quotes the official Moscow formula which Tretiakov actually followed when he left Moscow in 1928.[18] In his lecture "Der Schriftsteller und das sozialistische Dorf" presented in Berlin to the "Gesellschaft der Freunde des Neuen Rußland" on January 21, 1931, Tretiakov describes his experiences as "ständiger Mitarbeiter im Rat des Kolchos, Leiter der Bildungsarbeit" by outlining his concept of the "operierenden Schriftsteller" and of "faktographische Literatur." He insists that — in order to change the social reality in the kolkhoz — new genres have to be explored and that the author must be de-professionalized:

> Operative Beziehungen nenne ich die Teilnahme am Leben des Stoffes selbst. Grob gesagt: eine wichtige Sache auszudenken — ist belletristischer Novellismus; eine wichtige Sache zu finden - ist die Reportage; eine wichtige Sache aufzubauen — ist Operativismus....Der Arbeiter am Sozialismus, mit literarischem Können ausgerüstet — das ist der Ausgangspunkt der neuen Literatur. Der berufsmäßige Schriftsteller gliedert sich organisch in die Aufbauarbeit ein und lernt nicht nur die Kunst, das Leben zu konterfeien, sondern auch das Leben zu verändern. („Der Schriftsteller und das sozialistische Dorf," 120–21)

With this turn against such classic realist authors as Tolstoi, Dostoyevski — strongly supported and canonized as "schöne Literatur" by the "Russische Assoziation proletarischer Arbeiter" (RAPP, 1928–1932),[19] Tretiakov does not distinguish between the fictional and biographical subject. Promoting the art of political and/or social intervention, "utilitäre Produktionskunst" (Trommler 592), he initiated the realism of the socialist avant-garde artist who explores social processes by mingling with society and utilizing his art to innovate, provoke or challenge given conditions.[20] Aesthetization or thematization of social conflicts is not sufficient; art has to accentuate its pragmatic edge.

Where Tretiakov cultivates the everyday life in the Russian kolkhoz[21] Brecht revolutionizes German political art. As widely discussed in the scholarship of the last thirty years Brecht not only propagates revolutionary themes but also actively reinvents and rearranges the setting and functions of the bourgeois theater in order to engage the audience through epic devices into the theatrical process or to turn the audience into acting participants in the "Lehrstück."[22] H.L. Gruman reports that "Brecht's 1930 Production of *Die Maßnahme* [...] used the audience as an active 'Control Chorus.'" This collaboration between actors, producer and audience carries on the tradition of the leftist collective theater movement in Weimar Germany (1928-1933) which was inspired by Soviet proletarianism and was further developed by the Piscator-Kollektiv founded in November 1929 after the Piscator Bühne closed.[23] All initiatives shared the common goal to subvert the bourgeois theater's aura of high culture. Brecht transposes this motivation into his actual theatrical experiments, his theater theory and his clearly directed and aggressive attack on the representatives of legal and public institutions in *Dreigroschenprozeß*.[24] The actual Dreigroschenprozeß uses legal means to stir up a public debate before the essay, "Der Dreigroschenprozeß," analyzes the presentation of these discussions of the legal system's strategies and values in journals and newpapers. Here Brecht applies Tretiakov's approach to let the otherwise silent reality speak (Knopf 179) by uncovering the obliviousness of the cultural politics of conservative and leftist intellectuals.

His theoretical writings about theater — "Anmerkungen zur Oper 'Aufstieg und Fall der Stadt Mahagonny'"[25] — and film are linked by his insertion of economic and technological vocabulary in the discussion. Viewing opera, "Schaubühne" and journalism as "Produktionsapparate" Brecht reveals to their artists, writers, journalists that they are not, as they imagine, in control of the apparatus; rather, the economically motivated apparatus is in control of their work. They are unknowingly pushed in the role of suppliers and/or contractors:

> Ihre Produktion gewinnt Lieferantencharakter. Es entsteht ein Wertbegriff, der die Verwertung zur Grundlage hat. Und dies ergibt allgemein den Usus, jedes Kunstwerk auf seine Eignung für den Apparat, niemals aber den Apparat auf seine Eignung für das Kunstwerk hin zu überprüfen. (1005)

Subjecting art to their economic interests, cultural institutions commodify it, censor it, and control its market value. This is a vivid example of the proletarization of artists by capitalist ventures. We will see later that this argument is still used today by popular artists against their producers.

Brecht explores the potentials of the film genre by presenting film as an ideal alternative to the backward opera and by uncovering innovative connotations of the terms "apparatus," "collective" and "commodity." The social apparatus of the opera has a long-standing tradition of separation between composer and institution, since the institution uses the composer's work as a commodity.[26] As Brecht experienced with the sale of his film script this is also true for the cinema: producers buy filmscripts and assume all rights to manipulate them. The sale encompasses the intellectual property of the artist.[27]

Brecht's term "neue Apparate" for film technology stresses his alteration of the concept "Apparat" by distinguishing the inventive capacity of the camera from its reactionary use by the ignorant entertainment industry. Contrasting the "Schöpfungen der Apparate" (159) with those of bourgeois art he subverts their closed ideological concepts of the omniscient and all-pervading author and the psychology of characters. He emphasizes that films, especially silent films, view persons from an external perspective. Characters are controlled by social acts, "menschliche Handlungen" and "gesellschaftliche Prozesse," and not by their individual psyche. Thus the concept of type replaces that of characters.[28] Film technology becomes the paradigm for Brecht's art criticism. Neither epic nor dramatic art is immune from the influence of film. Its construction of reality, of "Künstliches," "Gestelltes" (162), undermines the mimetism of the bourgois novel, drama and film. Twice Brecht attacks Thomas Mann's essay "Über den Film"[29] and its promotion of "lebenswahres und wirklichkeitsechtes szenisch-mimisches Erfindungsdetail" in film (169) and its exclusion of the apparatus from the definition of art and humanity (207). Appropriating Marx' definition of man as toolmaking animal (207)[30], Brecht inscribes mechanistic vocabulary in the definition of man and replaces the individual "Erlebnis" by the "Verdinglichung der menschlichen Beziehungen"(161). "Die eigentliche Realität ist in die Funktionale gerutscht," Brecht argues (161).[31] The terms "Verdinglichung," and "Funktionale" link his views on film and his anti-aesthetic to his social and economic considerations. Freeing the term "apparatus" from being vaguely used as a metaphor for the functions of bourgeois institutions ("Produktionsapparate") and from being loaded with these institutions' ideological history, Brecht examines the social implications of the term: film technology sets social norms by demanding collaboration among its users.

> Tatsächlich sollte der Film nichts machen, was ein Kollektiv nicht machen kann...Was für ein Kollektiv haben wir heute im Film? Das Kollektiv stellt sich zusammen aus dem Financier, den Verkäufern (Publikumsforschern), dem Regisseur, den Technikern und den Schreibern. (172)

Since the production of film is based on the close collaboration of artists and producers Brecht replaces the concepts of the author through the concept of the collective. The representatives of commercial interests are not privileged over the artists. In fact, the produced film should not indicate the contributions by single collaborators. "Wer wünschte da nicht sofort, der Einzelanteil an der Produktion möchte unkenntlich sein?" By not insisting on individualistic or corporate financial interests the members of the film collective collaborate on a common mission to teach and to turn the audience into a collective itself. "Tatsächlich kann ein Kollektiv nur Werke schaffen, welche aus ‚Publikum' Kollektive bilden können."(173). The social requirements of the apparatus determine the strategies of production and therefore their product, the film as well as its effect on the audience.[32]

Brecht distinguishes two concepts of the collective contrasting progressive collectives which are fashioned by the social potentials of innovative technology, in this case film, with the reactionary collectives of journalists, and lawyers which are controlled by pre-given ideological values. Journalism and law sustain the bourgeois social order which the innovative film work overthrows. He discusses actual film techniques only indirectly by reference to photography. He privileges the daguerreotype over the light-sensitive cameras of his time in order to outline his ideas of innovative film techniques. "Bei den alten lichtschwachen Apparaten kamen mehrere Ausdrücke auf die ziemlich lange belichtete Platte; so hatte man auf dem endlichen Bild einen universaleren und lebendigeren Ausdruck, auch etwas von Funktion dabei."(174).

What promoters of light-sensitive cameras view as a disadvantage of daguerreotypes Brecht sees as their advantage: they do not imitate reality but make visible the functions of the apparatus. They become a model for his speculation about the possibilities of most modern cameras: "Vielleicht gibt es eine Art zu photographieren, den neueren Apparaten möglich, die Gesichter zerlegt?"(174). These cameras construct new perceptions of reality and make its hidden and invisible aspects visible. As an example Brecht alludes to photographs of factories:

> Eine Photographie der Kruppwerke oder der AEG ergibt beinah nichts über diese Institute...Die Verdinglichung der menschlichen Beziehungen, also etwa die Fabrik, gibt die letzteren nicht mehr heraus. Es ist also tatsächlich "etwas aufzubauen", etwas "Künstliches", "Gestelltes". Es ist also ebenso tatsächlich Kunst nötig. (161–62)

Socially critical art examines and analyzes the appearance of reality, its "Gesicht," its facade, and exposes its conditions. It deconstructs in order to construct. Brecht applies this logic also to the filming process. "Die Filmtechnik, die nötig war, um aus dem Nichts ein Etwas zu machen, war gezwungen, vorher aus dem Etwas ein nichts zu machen."(176). New technology defamiliarizes the ordinary and opens up new perspectives. Brecht strongly encourages producers to utilize those functions of the cameras which are least likely to produce an imitation of reality.[33]

The production of *Kuhle Wampe* serves as an example for Brecht's actualization of collective collaboration.[34] The film's visual montage of Anni Bönike's hallucinations exemplifies its capacity to construct realities hidden by mimetic realism. The retrospective record of the film taken by W. Gersch and W. Hecht lists twenty-eight shots which associate a wide array of images — sections of the sign of a gynecologist, advertisements for baby formula, cosmetics and other medicine, resignation notes, window displays of coffins, baby shoes etc. — for one and a quarter minutes. The montage literally displaces Anni's head. The script reads: "Kindergesichter kreisen um sie. Ihr Kopf wird allmählich ausgeblendet. Es setzt eine Montage ein."[35] The images from different social contexts indicate Anni's confusion after her boyfriend's disinterest in her pregnancy. While Anni loses control of her perception, the visual reality disintegrates into fragments. They constitute the visionary reality of the tensions, anxieties and hopes which mark Anni's uncertain state between mortality and fertility. These moments of total estrangement indicate also the beginning of her alienation and ensuing emancipation from the patriarchal social order. Thus the montage interrupts the rhythm of the *mise-en-scène,* highlighting the editor's presence and the silent reality hidden behind words and appearance.

Brecht's concept of the apparatus links technological to social advancement, and film production becomes the paradigm for his ideas for restructuring society. Around 1931 he writes:

> Der Kollektivist setzt nicht seinen Gruppenapparat gegen die Masse, sondern in die Masse hinein. Die Menschen wirken aufeinander. Die Masse besteht nur aus Agenten. Der Kollektivist sieht die Menschheit als einen Apparat, der erst teilweise organisiert ist. (Schriften 1.5:21, 518)

The bourgeois dualism between individual and the masses, idealism and reality is missing here and is replaced by the interaction between collectives and their agents. Brecht inverts the relation between "individuum" and "dividuum." The individuum is defined by its external participation in several collectives; it is dividable and thus a dividuum, whereas the collective cultivates more and more individual features.[36] Film art offers a means for this invention of the individuum: collectives produce their artistic work which gives these collectives their individual features.

In *Der Dreigroschenprozeß* Brecht goes a step further than in his learning play *Das Badener Lehrstück vom Einverständnis* (1929) which also links technological to social advancement. Having survived a crash, the aviators face their wrecked plane and invoke Lindbergh's transatlantic flight and fight for their physical survival. This fight turns into a reexamination of their ethical values and only those two aviators who adjust to the demands of a life as a collective, to the erasure of the individual's assertiveness, will be allowed to construct the plane's new motor. Their avaricious colleague — who bases his self-confidence on his individual accomplishments as aviator ignoring his collaborators[37] — is expelled: "denn / Der uns brauchte und / Dessen wir bedurften: das / War er." In this play the supervision of the "Gelernte[r] Chor" precedes technological advancement. It is not the social requirement of the apparatus, in this case the motor of the plane, which demands restructuring of the group of engineers. In *Der Dreigroschenprozeß* a control such as the "Gelernte[r] Chor" and its ideology is missing and replaced by Brecht's explication of the social and technical demands of film technology. Brecht is leaving behind his explicit insistence on ideology.[38] Instead technology becomes an instrument for social progress, for the formation of collectives.

How does Brecht deal with the commercial aspects of film production and with film as commodity? As he experienced with the sale of his manuscript to Nero, film companies automatically assume all rights to manipulate the manuscripts and can ignore any further contracts with the author. Brecht had originally asked to be actively involved in the production of the "Dreigroschenfilm." When he complained that Nero had not solicited his input the company tried to renegotiate this part of the contract. By losing the lawsuit against Nero Brecht found that the appropriation of intellectual property by strong financial and marketing interests is sanctioned by law (180). Manuscripts turn into commodities, and by losing all rights to their work authors are forced to leave their manuscript prey to every possible manipulation and distortion. In 1933 Brecht responds to the question "Was, meinen Sie, macht den Erfolg der ‚Dreigroschenoper' aus?":

> Ich fürchte, all das, worauf es mir nicht ankam: die romantische Handlung, die Liebesgeschichte, das Musikalische. Als die "Dreigroschenoper" Erfolg gehabt hatte, machte man einen Film daraus. Man nahm für den Film all das, was ich in dem Stück verspottet hatte, die Romantik, die Sentimentalität usw., und ließ den Spott weg. Da war der Erfolg noch größer.
> Und worauf wäre es Ihnen angekommen?
> Auf die Gesellschaftskritik. Ich hatte zu zeigen versucht, daß die Ideenwelt und das Gefühlsleben der Straßenbanditen ungemein viel Aehnlichkeit mit der Ideenwelt und dem Gefühlsleben des soliden Bürgers haben." (GBA 26, 299)[39]

This strategy of reversing the author's intentions, ironically contradicts the bourgeois ideals of the artist's intellectual property and personal freedom. The freedom of artistic production is corrupted as soon as the manuscript turns into a commodity for the film industry. Exposing this inconsistency which marks bourgeois culture Brecht demonstrates the logical necessity of redefining the term "Ware." He agrees that film — "auch der künstlerischste" (167) — is a commodity, but instead of complaining about this fact he espouses his redefinition. Offering a shortcut through Marx' detailed analysis of the commodity he criticizes essayists who argue that art frees the film from falling into the status of a commodity:

> Wer das meint, hat keine Ahnung von der ummodelnden Kraft des Warencharakters. Die Tatsache, daß im Kapitalismus die Welt *in der Form der Ausbeutung und der Korruption* in eine Produktion verwandelt wird, ist nicht so wichtig wie eben die Tatsache dieser *Verwandlung.* (167)

The mobility of the commodity supercedes temporary economic systems, in this case the capitalist system. And since the process of commodification is not restricted to things but involves people as well, they lose their priviledged status; the commodity equalizes things and people. The exchange value is seen qualitatively and not in quantitive and materialistic terms. Its social implications are stressed:

Aber nur wer die Augen schließt vor der ungeheuerlichen Gewalt jenes revolutionären Prozesses, der alle Dinge dieser Welt in die Warenzirkulation reißt, ohne jede Ausnahme und ohne jede Verzögerung, kann annehmen, daß Kunstwerke irgendeiner Gattung sich hier ausschließen könnten, denn der tiefere Sinn des Prozesses besteht ja darin, kein Ding ohne Beziehung zum andern zu lassen, sondern alle zu verknüpfen, wie er auch alle Menschen (in Form von Waren) allen Menschen ausliefert, es ist eben der Prozeß der Kommunikation schlechthin. (168)

Brecht stresses the communal and collaborative aspects of the commodity exchange which undermine capitalist exploitation. He abstracts the social aspects of the commodity from its economic reality, suggesting that these social aspects should control the economic reality. Applied to film this reversal of emphasis challenges the profit-driven industry. The industry's financial preoccupation ignores the collaborative implications of its technology which equally subjects actors, bodies, body parts, props, and other objects to its filming and editing devices. Thus the film's production is the perfect means of establishing new alliances between things, people, film producers and audiences. Brecht introduces it as paradigm for a universal process of communication.[40]

The concepts of the commodity and the collective overlap: as commodities people are subjected to each other, and as agents in collectives they actively affect each other. The two terms outline the passive and active attitudes which mark the social collaboration among members of collectives.

Brecht's arguments against the closed structure of the bourgeois apparatus, his concerns about intellectual property and especially his view about the communicative function of film technology anticipate a comment by Napster's CEO, Hank Barry in July 27, 2000 about the communicative functions of the Internet: "Napster shows that the Internet is designed for file sharing."[41] Barry refers to the eighteen months during which Napster users were able to log on to each others' hard drives in order to download music files *gratis*. This new technology allows users to form anonymous collectives which share common interests. They can access and copy popular and rare music and are not restricted by the choices offered by the record industry. This special software empowers the customers to put together their own music selections and to explore music otherwise unpublished. It also "allows artists to communicate directly with their audiences," Courtney Love, the popular singer, argues.[42] The essay "Courtney Love Does the Math" sharply disparages the record industry as ruthless financial and intellectual exploitors of their artists. As in Brecht's case the industry claims ownership of the artistic work, which involves nowadays not only ownership of copyrights but even the artists' name for a Web address.[43] Love concludes: "Recording artists have essentially been giving their music away for free under the old system, so new technology that exposes our music to a larger audience can only be a good thing"

(Love, 4). She encourages artists to leave the boring culture of the status quo by buying into new technology and selling music for less. Then artists might "sell 100 million copies instead of just a million"(Love, 6) and more artists will have a chance to present and distribute their work successfully.

With the emancipation of customers and artists from their dependence on record companies Napster's software enforced a concept of the commodity which Brecht theoreticaly explored in the *Dreigroschenprozeß* as "Prozeß der Kommunikation schlechthin."(168). The commodity is freed from purely economic and arbitrary corporate interests.[44] Scott Rosenberg, *Salon's* managing editor, distinguishes the phenomenon and idea "Napster" from the company and argues that the idea of "peer to peer" software will remain although individual companies might lose court battles.[45] Hank Barry claims in a interview of July 27, 2000 that "there are over 21 million members of the Napster community who think one-to-one file sharing is legal."[46] Alternate projects like Gnutella and Freenet which offer Napster-like MP3 file transfer capability without being linked to one central server will go underground. By creating "a world of total connectivity" (Love, 9) internet technology gains the power to undermine corporate interests. The commodity enters a new phase. Web and Internet technology replaces the mediating and profiteering industry, and the commodity circulates without its intervention and creates collectives of people with the same interests. Courtney Love designs her utopia of a new economy:

> [I will] allow millions of people to get my music for nothing if they want and hopefully they'll be kind enough to leave a tip if they like it...A new company that gives artists true equity in their work can take over the world, kick ass and make a lot of money. We're inspired by how people get paid in the new economy. Many visual artists and software and hardware designers have real ownership of their work." (7/8)

Love knows that the artists' and audience's criteria for the production and reception of the artistic product have to change. Artists have to become independent of being promoted to celebrity status[47] and the audience has to be liberated from being manipulated by advertising: "people who've enjoyed the experience I've provided will be happy to shell out a little more money to cover my costs. Especially if they understand this context, and aren't being shoveled a load of shit about 'uppity' artists" (8/9). Relationships are centered on the shared interest in the artistic work, and not based on the manipulations through promotion techniques.[48]

The Web's power to associate customers and artists with each other is one example how the technology of the 21st century realizes Brecht's utopian vision of overcoming the conventional concept of the commodity. In *Der Dreigroschenprozess* he argues:

> In diesem Sinne ist die Umschmelzung geistiger Werte in Waren (Kunstwerke, Verträge, Prozesse sind Waren) ein fortschrittlicher Prozeß, und man kann ihm nur zustimmen, vorausgesetzt, daß der Fortschritt als Fortschreiten ge-

dacht wird, nicht als Fortgeschrittenheit, daß also auch die Phase der Ware
als durch weiteres Fortschreiten überwindbar angesehen wird. Die kapitalisti-
sche Produktionsweise zertrümmert die bürgerliche Ideologie. (201/204)

Wrecking the commodity status of the commodity is Brecht's and Love's
goal. Love is in the position to take the control in her own hands, to hire a
"Webmistress" (7) and to circulate her own music files. This empowers the
artist to outline his/her criteria for companies of the new economy. Love
advises: "If you're going to start a company that deals with musicians,
please do it because you love music" (13). Resisting being a service to the
industry she switches the roles around: companies provide a service to the
musician and the musician provides a service to the audience. The term
"service" should replace the term product. Thus she privileges the social
function of the commodity over the economic function and she trusts that
business based on social responsibility will outlive profit-oriented commerce.[49]

Her view mirrors Brecht's view although there is one major difference
between both artists: Brecht stresses the educational function of art,
whereas Love is committed to offering an enjoyable experience to her
audience, "Kunstgenuß," an attitude Brecht criticizes.[50] The philosophical
intentions of both might be different, but their view of technology as a
challenge to bourgeois business strategies is the same. In shifting Marx'
focus on class struggles to his focus on the relation between capitalist
business strategies and the social implications of technology, Brecht predicted that capitalism will become its own enemy, that it created technological means which undermine the systems on which it is based.[51]
Brecht's approach to film technology is radicalized by Love's view of the
democratizing functions of the Internet and their potential of creating new
societal interactions.

During the composition of this article in Fall 2000 Napster's service
changed. The New York Times reported November 1, 2000: "Napster...
agreed yesterday to a plan to change course and charge a fee for its service, distributing part of the fee as royalties to record companies."[52] Chal-
lenged by the high costs and the uncertainty of the lawsuit's outcome the
company agreed to accept the financial assistance of Bertelsmann which
in turn received an option to buy a stake in the company. Bertelsmann is
one of the companies which sued Napster for copyright infringement.
Thus the suit served the capitalist enterprise and Napster's business is in
danger of turning again to the status quo: the company compromised the
Napster idea ignoring the innovative social potentials of its own technology. With this reactionary move Napster acceded to industrial interest. It
is not clear if and how the move compromises the company's original
cutting-edge social impact. Will royalty fees again go to the record companies and the artists' needs and rights be ignored?[53] The renewed em-
powerment of the industry boosts its control over the production and
distribution of music files. But file sharing programs without a central

server, as for example Gnutella, Bearshare, LimeWire et al., have gained enormous popularity and will continue to operate, giving users the chance to boycott corporate business. Popular file sharing could slowly subvert the bourgeois order that is the basis for the continuance of the capitalist enterprise. It will at least split social attitudes and social consciousness; Internet file sharing promotes the communicative functions of the commodity as they were envisioned by Brecht and overcomes the commodity's profit margin.

NOTES

[1] "Full text of Judge Patel's Ruling." n.d.: 2.
< http://news.cnet.com/News/Pages/Special/Napster/napster_patel.html >

[2] Courtney Love. "Courtney Love does the math."
< http://www.salon.com/tech/feature/2000/06/14/love/print.html >
    Prince. "4 [sic]The Love Of Music. 2 Very Different Approaches."
< http://www.npgonlineltd.com/ >

[3] At present, October 2000, the controversy has spread and also involves software companies, book publishers, radio and film industries which fear to lose business to software providers who pirate their services and offer them for free. Charles C. Mann reports that he accessed "Pamela Anderson Video," computer software, French television shows, "Yo Yo Ma's latest version of the Bach solo-cello suites," "cheat files for a computer game named 'Obsidian,'" "a plain text copy of *Riding the Bullet*," "and a preliminary version of a DivX software kit for ripping and playing DVDs" ("The Heavenly Jukebox." *The Atlantic Monthly*, September 2000, 58–59). On the other hand, the physicians association support Napster because they are concerned about the lawsuit's restriction of the free flow of information.

[4] In the Napster case issues of censorship were indirectly raised by the industry's choice of the artists it marketed.

[5] "Full text of Judge Patel's Ruling," 4.

[6] The "Bund proletarisch-revolutionärer Schriftsteller"(BPRS) had been founded in October 1928 to address questions about the relationship between modern art forms — inner monologues, epic theater, twelve tone music etc — and class consciousness. Are these art forms expressions of class consciousness or of modern communication- and reproduction techniques and the demands of their new audiences? (Helga Gallas, *Marxistische Literaturtheorie. Kontroversen im Bund proletarisch-revolutionärer Schriftsteller* (Frankfurt/ M.: Roter Stern, 1978), 96, 109 — 10). Helga Gallas points out that Bertolt Brecht, Walter Benjamin and Hanns Eisler as members of the BPRS represent unique positions in their approach to Marxist aesthetic theory. They were ignored or sharply attacked by G. Lukács, the most articulate representative of the BPRS and its journal *Die Linkskurve*, which represented the position of the RAPP (Gallas 96, 109–10). H. Gallas argues that the controversies between the revolutionary authors of the Weimar period, the proletarian as well as bourgeois authors, anticipated the controversies of the *Expressionismus Debatte*, which arose after 1933 between the exiles in the Moscow journal *Das Wort* (18–30).

[7] Bertolt Brecht. "Der Dreigroschenprozeß. Ein soziologisches Experiment." *Gesammelte Werke in 20 Bänden*, ed. Suhrkamp Verlag in Zusammenarbeit mit Elisabeth Hauptmann, 18 (Frankfurt/M.: Suhrkamp, 1967): 139–209. (Page numbers of references to this essay are given parenthetically in the text; references to this edition are cited as GW, Gesammelte Werke).

[8] Brecht quotes from *Neue Zeit des Westens*, *Berliner Tageblatt*, *B.Z. am Mittag*, *Frankfurter Zeitung*, and from film journals *Der Film*, *Der Scheinwerfer*, et al.

[9] Brecht views the tension between the diverse opinions and the similarity of their underlying ideology as most humorous: "Die Pressestimmen sind im großen und ganzen chronologisch geordnet, aber die Anordnung zieht ihren Humor daraus, daß die Auszüge aus verschiedenen Zeitungen so stehen, wie sie auch in einer einzigen hätten stehen können"(182).

[10] In a *Frankfurter Zeitung* article from 18 April 1931 (160), Siegfried Kracauer grants film producers the right to view art as service to the capitalist enterprise: "Sie [die Produzenten] brauchten meinetwegen nichts von Kunst zu verstehen, aber sie müßten imstande sein, ihren Nutzwert einzukalkulieren" (160). As long as art refines the film ("veredeln," 160) the film functions only as a technological device for the dissemination of bourgeois art. The apparatus is not seen as an independent and detached artistic medium. It is raped by art, Brecht says (161). Bourgeois art is so dogmatic and inflexible that it kills the inventive functions (Brecht/Benjamin) of new technology. Satirically Brecht equates the commercial interests of the movie theater owners with those of the "Fueilletonisten" calling them "Physiker and Metaphysiker" of "Publikumsgeschmack."

Brecht often does not identify the authors of the introductory quotes of his sub-chapters, he mostly refers to the journals in general. In regard to the *Frankfurter Zeitung* he only mentions Dr. Frankfurter, the lawyer of Nero, by name. But since the publishers of *Große kommentierte Berliner und Frankfurter Ausgabe* have identified the quote Brecht's criticism of the "Feuilletonisten" seems to be indirectly addressed to Kracauer. Bertolt Brecht. *Schriften I. Große kommentierte Berliner und Frankfurter Ausgabe*. 21, ed. Werner Hecht, Jan Knopf, Werner Mittenzwei, Klaus Dieter Müller (Berlin, Weimar: Aufbau; Frankfurt/M.: Suhrkamp 1992), 783. (Quoted as GBA).

[11] "Collectivization." Britannica.com. 1 December 2000. < http://www.britannica.com >

[12] Brecht dismisses the art-film dichotomy as typically bourgeois and develops an alternative approach: he introduces film as art and modern art as filmic arguing that art in the time of cinematography forfeits all conventional elitist and sublime connotations. Walter Benjamin explores this topic further in 1935 when he scrutinizes the rise of fascism as resulting from the discrepancy between technological advancement and the limits of bourgeois ideology in "Das Kunstwerk im Zeitalter seiner technischen Reproduzierbarkeit."

[13] This social activism can function as an early very practical example for the critical "Haltung" which Brecht demands later from the audience in his theater. In *Kleines Organon für das Theater* he writes: "Welches ist die produktive Haltung gegenüber der Natur und der Gesellschaft, die wir Kinder eines wissenschaftlichen Zeitalters in unserem Theater vergnüglich einnehmen wollen? Die Haltung ist eine kritische" (GW 16, 671).

[14] Ludwig Marcuse accuses Brecht of covering up his financial interests in the lawsuit (see "Kommentar" in GBA 21, 779). My approach does not speculate about Brecht's personal intentions, it analyzes his text *Der Dreigroschenprozeß* as a new innovative genre for his social criticism.

[15] Brecht knew Tretiakov at least by April 1930, but probably by 1929. Fritz Mierau argues that Brecht re-edited Tretiakov's play *Ich will ein Kind haben* in

1929 and that this was the only Sowiet play which interested Brecht. (Fritz Mierau, "Sergej Tret'jakov and Bertolt Brecht. Das Produktionsstück ‚Ich will ein Kind haben' (Russian title). *Zeitschrift für Slawistik* 20.2 (1975): 226–41, and F.M., *Erfindung und Korrektur. Tretjakows Ästhetik der Operativität* (Berlin: Akademie Verlag, 1972), 33, 278 Anm. 52. As author of the socialist revolution Tretiakov was invited for a lecture tour to Germany in December 1930 where he was already well known through performances of his piece *Brülle China* by the Meyerhold Theater in Moscow (Ingrid Belke, "Siegfried Krakauer als Beobachter der jungen Sowjetunion." In *Siegfried Krakauer. Neue Interpretationen* ed. Michael Kessler and Thomas Y. Levin (Tübingen: Stauffenburg 1990), 17–38. Brecht defended the performance in a fragmentary piece in April 1930 (GW 15:204–5) and introduced Tretiakovs presentation "Der neue Typus des Schriftstellers" for the Berliner *Internationale Tribüne* in April 19, 1931 (Belke 30). The friendship between the two authors is evidenced by the exchange of letters and other texts. In 1976 F. Mierau published the letters Tretjakov sent to Brecht between 1933 and 1937. See F. Mierau, *Erfindung und Korrektur*, 258–72. Only three of Brecht's letters to Tretiakov have survived (GBA 28:357, 370, 398–99). In a letter of May 27, 1934 (Mierau 262), Tretiakov mentions the publication of his translations of Brecht's epic dramas, and in the same year he publishes his essay "Bert Brecht" in *Internationales Theater*. (Sergei Tretiakov, "Bert Brecht," in *Die Arbeit des Schriftstellers. Aufsätze, Reportagen, Porträts*, ed. Heiner Boehncke, tr. Karla Hielscher (Reinbek bei Hamburg: Rowohlt, 1972), 146–58. About the similarity between Brecht's and Tretiakov's avantgardistic social realism see Heiner Boehnke "Nachwort," 199–200.

[16] Walter Benjamin, "Der Autor als Produzent." *Gesammelte Schriften* 2.2, ed. Rolf Tiedemann, Hermann Schweppenhäuser (Frankfurt/.M: Suhrkamp, 1980), 686, 687. Benjamin links Tretiakov's to Brecht's agenda utilizing the vocabulary of both authors. Besides Brecht he also refers to the work of Eisler (694), John Heartfield (693), and Aragon (700) and distinguishes these intellectuals of the radical left from more conservative ones, as for example, from Heinrich Mann, Döblin, Tucholsky, etc., who thematize the revolution but do not change the traditional bourgeois genres. Fritz Mierau explains: "Benjamin reagierte damit auf den aktuellen deutschen Streit um die Rolle der Zeitung" and names Rudolf Borchart and Gottfried Benn as other opponents of Benjamin's agenda.(31)

[17] Sergei Tretjakov, "'Schriftsteller in die Kolchose!'" *Die Arbeit des Schriftstellers. Aufsätze Reportagen Porträts*, 103–10.

[18] Belke, 31. Tretiakov's talks and essays about his experiences point out the discrepancy between the official instructions for his mission and the reality of his work. The conflicting instructions see the writer either as informant or as psychologizing realist. They either demand — "Beobachtet vor allen Dingen, wie die Kolchose wirtschaften. Den Zügen des Alltagslebens schenkt keine Beachtung. Das Alltagsleben ist eine zweitrangige, abgeleitete Erscheinung" — or they ask, "Von Wirtschaft habt ihr sowieso keinen Schimmer, Brüder von der Feder...Schreibt von ‚lebendigen Menschen,' ihren Wünschen, Gedanken, Erlebnissen. Gebt ein Bild des Alltags" (Tretiakov, 103).

[19] See Heiner Boehncke, "Nachwort," 193.

[20] Tretjakow, "Woher und Wohin?" Quoted in Heiner Böhncke, "Nachwort," 200.

[21] Walter Benjamin refers besides Sergei Tretiakov to Bertolt Brecht as an author whose work does not only present an ideology but also is actively involved in altering and challenging its institutional structures: "Er [Brecht] hat als erster an den Intellektuellen die weittragende Forderung erhoben: den Produktionsapparat nicht zu beliefern, ohne ihn zugleich, nach Maßgabe des Möglichen, im Sinne des Sozialismus zu verändern" (Walter Benjamin, "Der Autor als Produzent," 691). Benjamin as well as Tretiakov in his short sketch "Bert Brecht" refer to Brecht's theater, especially to *Die Maßnahme*, as example, but never to the *Dreigroschenprozeß*.

[22] In "Anmerkung [zu den Lehrstücken]" (first published in 1957) Brecht writes that the *Lehrstücke* were designed as "Stücke, die für die *Darstellenden* lehrhaft sind. Sie benötigen so kein Publikum" (GW, 17:1035). See also Klaus Dieter Krabiel, *Brecht's Lehrstücke: Entstehung und Entwicklung eines Spieltyps* (Stuttgart and Weimar: Metzler, 1993). Also Reiner Steinweg ed., *Auf Anregung Bertolt Brechts: Lehrstücke mit Schülern, Arbeitern, Theaterleuten* (Frankfurt/M.: Suhrkamp, 1978), and *Das Lehrstück. Brechts Theorie einer politisch-ästhetischen Erziehung.* (Stuttgart: Metzler, 1972).

[23] Harris L. Grumann gives a short introduction to the tradition of the Weimar theater collectives in "The *Piscator-Kollektiv*: Form and Content in the Political Theater." See *Brecht: Performance. Brecht: Aufführung. The Brecht Yearbook* 13, 1984. 21-37, 22. In contradiction to Joel Schechter("Beyond Brecht: New Authors, New Spectators." *The Brecht Yearbook* 11 [1982]), who stresses Brecht's innovative contributions to audience-participation theater Gruman views Brecht merely as an important recorder of the Piscator-Kollektiv's experiments. Gruman 36, Endnote 24. See also the comprehensive and detailed documentation *Theater der Kollektive Proletarisch-revolutionäres Berufstheater in Deutschland 1928-1933 Stücke, Dokumente, Studien,* ed. Ludwig Hoffmann (Berlin: Henschelverlag, 1980). See also D. Ostmeier's short summary of the controversies about how Brecht's learning plays engage actors and audiences: Dorothee Ostmeier, "The Rhetorics of Erasure: Cloud and Moon in Brecht's Poetic and Political Texts of the Twenties and Early Thirties." *German Studies Review* 23 (May 2000): 276.

[24] The theatrical and theoretical re-evaluation of the conventional opera paves the way for the attack on the representatives of legal and public institutions in "Dreigroschenprozeß." Brecht suggests that his opera *Aufstieg und Fall der Stadt Mahagonny* — composed in 1929 after *Die Dreigroschenoper* and before the actual law suit against Nero-Film AG — thematizes and satirizes its own genre, the irrational, culinary and pleasurable aspects emphasized by the musical setting of each opera. *Mahagonny* grotesquely demonstrates how pleasure as the essence of the opera turns into a commodity. "Sie [die kulinarische Oper] war ein Genußmittel, lange bevor sie eine Ware war"(GW 17:1006). *Mahagonny* employs anti-aesthetic means to sabotage the conventional opera's aestheticism.

[25] Brecht published the "Anmerkungen" in the second volume of his journal *Versuche* (1930) before *Der Dreigroschenprozeß* which appeared together with the filmscript *Die Beule* in the subsequent third volume Wolfgang Gersch describes Brecht's radically sharpened attack on the conditions of the bourgeois society in *Die Beule*. See Wolfgang Gersch, *Film bei Brecht* (München: Hanser, 1975), 48-58.

[26] As a counterexample Brecht refers to Richard Wagner's operas as a "Gesamt-kunstwerk" which serve reactionary purposes: they use modern technology to arrange the spectacle of the stage and reduce the ideological content to its pleasurable aspects. Brecht seems not to be familiar with or ignores alternative concepts of the "Gesamtkunstwerk" which promote collaboration of the artists and the arts as, for example, Wassily Kandinsky's approach. Of course, Kandinsky's abstract aestheticism does not address social or political concerns.

[27] Brecht argues that the genre of film should annihilate such a violation:

> Um mit den neuen Apparaten die Wirklichkeit zu fassen, müßte er [der Regisseur] Künstler sein, schlimmstenfalls Wirklichkeitsgenießer, aber keinesfalls Kunstgenießer, also stellt er, was einfacher ist, mit ihnen "Kunst" her, die bekannte, erprobte, die Ware. Er hat den Ruf eines geschmackvollen Arrangeurs, es heißt: er "versteht etwas von Kunst"! als ob man von Kunst etwas verstehen könnte, ohne von der Wirklichkeit etwas zu verstehen! Und hier fungiert als Wirklichkeit gleichzeitig mit dem Stoff der Apparat. Eine solche Situation schaffte den neuen Apparaten nicht die Möglichkeiten, die für sie an sich bestünden. (161)

[28] The first part of *Kuhle Wampe* — independently produced by Brecht, Slatan Dudow and Hanns Eisler between summer and spring 1931/1932 — presents the suicide of an unemployed young man, portraying the economic disaster of the lower classes after the reduction of unemployment benefits for young people by Brüning. The success of this typification became obvious when a censor complained: "Ihr Arbeitsloser ist kein richtiges Individuum, kein Mensch aus Fleisch und Blut...Er ist ganz oberflächlich gezeichnet...aber die Folgen sind politischer Natur und zwingen mich, Einspruch gegen die Zulassung Ihres Filmes zu erheben. Ihr Film hat die Tendenz, den Selbstmord als typisch hinzustellen...als Schicksal einer ganzen Klasse" (Bertold Brecht. "Kleiner Beitrag zum Realismus." Bertolt Brecht, *Kuhle Wampe. Protokoll des Films und Materialien*, ed. W. Gersch, W. Hecht (Frankfurt/M: Suhrkamp 1969), 93–96.

[29] *Schünemann's Monatshefte*, August 1928 (quoted. in GBA 21:787).

[30] See reference in GBA 21:787.

[31] Brecht introduces the general difference between mimetic bourgeois art and anti-realist film art without detailing the technical aspects as, for example, Rudolf Arnheim does in "Film als Kunst" (1932) or without distinguishing his concepts of film from the expressionist fantasies, abstract montages, or experimental films of the 1920s. He also does not outline a list of stereotypical film motifs which represent the daydreams of bourgeois ideology in Kracauer's articles for the *Frankfurter Allgemeine Zeitung* (March 11–19, 1927). See Kracauer's, *Das Ornament der Masse* (Frankfurt/M.: Suhrkamp 1977), 280.

[32] By privileging the collective over the individual, Brecht undermines the definition of the collective in capitalist production which attributes singular and unique works to individuals, and the common and ordinary work to mass production, that is, to say, to proletarian collectives.

[33] In his thorough study, Wolfgang Gersch does not mention this alienating function of the camera. *Film bei Brecht* (München: Hanser 1975).

[34] Film critics in 1932 always refer to *Kuhle Wampe* as a "Gemeinschaftsarbeit" of Bert Brecht, Ernst Ottwald, Hanns Eisler and S. Dudow (Gersch, Hecht 143, 153, 157), and Bernhard von Brentano uses most appropriately the term "Kollektiv" when he writes: "Fast ein Jahr lang arbeitete ein kleines Kollektiv miteinander, um neben der Industrie einen Film zu produzieren. Brecht, Dudow, Ottwald, Eisler unterstützt von den Schauspielern Thiele und Busch und einer Anzahl proletarischer Kultur- und Sportorganizationen." See *Bertolt Brecht. Kuhle Wampe. Protokoll des Films und Materialien*, ed. Wolfgang Gersch, Werner Hecht. (Frankfurt/M.: Suhrkamp, 1969) 162).

[35] Gersch, Hecht 40.

[36] In the end of 1929 he writes in his notebook: "Was sollte über das Individuum auszusagen sein, solang wir vom Individuum aus das Massenhafte suchen. Wir werden einmal vom Massenhaften das Individuum suchen und somit aufbauen" (Bertolt Brecht. GBA 21, *Schriften* 1:359).

[37] This functions as the antithesis to the aviators in the preceding learning play *Der Ozeanflug*" (1928/1929). The eight aviators speak of themselves in the first person singular as "I" and upon their arrival in Paris they praise the "Kameraden in den Ryan Werken von San Diego" who manufactured the motor. "Aber meldet meinen Kameraden in den Ryanwerken von San Diego / Daß ihre Arbeit gut war." Bertolt Brecht. GW 2, *Stücke* 2:584.

[38] About the weakened function of the "Kontrollchor" in *Die Maßnahme* see Dorothee Ostmeier, "The Rhetorics of Erasure: Cloud and Moon in Brecht's Poetic and Political Texts of the Twenties and Early Thirties," 282–83.

[39] The commentary speculates that this text presents a fictional interview designed by Brecht in the second half of 1933 (GBA 26:595; GBA 22.2:883).

[40] Wolfgang Gersch undermines these far-reaching progressive functions of Brecht's definition of the commodity when he claims: "Als Ware aktiv auf Bedürfnisse der Konsumenten reagierend, neue Zwecke schaffend, ist der Film für Brecht Beispiel einer funktionsbestimmten Kunst, wobei ihn in diesem Fall nur die Tatsache der Funktion, nicht aber deren soziale Sinngebung interessiert" Gersch 83.

[41] Cecile Barnes, "Napster CEO fights for life of music" 7/27/2000.
< http://news.cnet.com/news/0-1014-201-2366873-0.html >

[42] "The present system keeps artists from finding an audience because it has too many artificial scarcities: limited radio promotion, limited bin space in stores and a limited number of spots on the record company roster. The digital world has no scarcities" (Love 6).

[43] "But the bill also created an exception that allows a company to take a person's name for a Web address if they create a work for hire" (Love, 3).

[44] Courtney Love lists the arbitrary "factors that made a distributor decide to push a recording through the system" (7).

[45] Scott Rosenberg, "Why the music industry has nothing to celebrate." 27 July 2000.
< http://www.salon.com/tech/col/rose/2000/07/27/napster_shutdown/print.html >

[46] Cecily Barnes. "Napster CEO fights for life of music firm." 27. July 2000.
< http://news.cnet.com/news/0-1014-202-2366873-0.html >

[47] "In a society of over 300 million people, only 30 new artists a year sell a million records. By any measure, that's a huge failure" (6).

[48] "Let us do our real jobs. And those of us addicted to celebrity because we have nothing else to give will fade away. And those of us addicted to celebrity because it was there well find a better, purer way to live..."(7).

[49] An editorial, "King'a Closure," in the *New York Times* on 1 December 2000 suggests that the suspension of Stephen King's online serial novel *The Plant* constitutes a failure of electronic publishing and thus could be seen as counter example to Courtney Love's utopian vision of internet publishing. Stephen King's response does not support this claim. See < http://www.stephenking.com >

[50] "I'm doing good work, I believe that the people who enjoy it are going to want to come directly to me and get my music because it sounds better... I'm providing an honest, real experience" (Love 8).

[51] "Die Wirklichkeit kommt dann an den Punkt, wo das einzige Hindernis für den Fortschritt des Kapitalismus der Kapitalismus ist"(204). Brecht here contrasts impersonal capitalist production with its ideology of personal intellectual property.

[52] Matt Richtel and David D. Kirkpatrick, "Napster to charge fee for Music Rights." 1 Nov. 2000. < http://www.nytimes.com/2000/11/01/technology/01MUSI.html >

[53] While proofreading this article in October 2001 I checked again the news on the Napster Website. In order to comply with legal demands Napster is still working on developing a new technology. The company promises now that "file sharing...will be back" and that it reached a "preliminary agreement with the National Music Publishers' Association (NMPA) which means that songwriters will get paid when their works are shared" (< http://www.napster.com >). This new business direction indicates that the controversial debates about the lawsuit against Napster have forced the NMPA at least to rethink and redesign their atitude towards the artists. it is not clear at this point "whether Napster's millions of users will return to it when it reopens its doors in its new incarnation — as a for-pay service..." and if it will regain its prominence as "the largest widely accessible library of music ever assembled" (Scott Rosenberg, "Revenge of the file sharing."
< http://www.salon.com/tech/col/rose/2001/07/20/napster_diaspora/
    index.htm >

Vom Chaos zur Veränderung: Brechtische Geschichten *Im Dickicht der Städte.*

Seit dem frühesten Anfang seiner Karriere suchte Brecht radikal neue Wege, Geschichte darzustellen, ohne in die Falle einer kohärenten Geschichtsschreibung zu fallen. In *Dickicht der Städte* präsentiert Brecht die theatralische Zerstörung traditioneller Ansichten über Geschichte und Subjektivität, indem er mit traditionellen theatralischen Mimesiselementen experimentiert. Im Stück führen zwei Chicagoer Gangster eine fortdauernde und scheinbar sinnlose Fehde. Während sie sich gegenseitig nachahmen, untergehen sie soziale und rassische Verwandlungen. Brecht verwendet Mimesis, um die Inkohärenz und Kontingenz der natürlichen Geschichte als eine Alternative traditioneller Geschichtsschreibung zu präsentieren. Indem der Zweikampf als grundlos und unerklärlich dargestellt wird, unterminiert das Stück subjektives Handeln und Begriffsvermögen. Deshalb fällt Brechts Geschichtskonzept zwischen Foucault, mit seiner Genealogie der Körper und Systeme der Macht, und Walter Benjamin, der Mimesis — der Drang zur Ähnlichkeit — als die treibende Kraft der Menschheitsgeschichte versteht. *Im Dickicht der Städte* demonstriert die genealogische Nachahmung zweier Männer, die nicht durch vorsätzliches Handeln vorwärtskommen, sondern durch ihren Drang, in Verbindung zu bleiben; ein Drang, der sich in ihren Körpern manifestiert. Die Situierung von Brechts Vorstellung über das unbeabsichtigte Machen der Geschichte innerhalb der philosophischen Konstellation Benjamins und Foucaults zeigt, dass er einen theatralischen Materialismus schon vor seinen Marxstudien entwickelt hat und stellt deshalb Konventionen in Frage, die die durchgehende Vorrangstellung marxistischer Ideologie in seinem Werk behaupten.

From Chaos to Transformation
Brechtian Histories *Im Dickicht der Städte*

Astrid Oesmann

In the middle of his career Bertolt Brecht issued what became a famous theoretical aphorism that numerous critics have linked to his commitment to Marxism. "Verfremden" he claimed "ist historisieren," and with this statement he linked his concept of theatrical estrangement to a broad and self-consciously revolutionary concept of human history. If, however, critics have tied this vision to Brecht's Marxism, they have been careful to show how he imported modernist aesthetic principles into his historical vision, thus developing a political and philosophical perspective that grew out of Marx, but rejected simplistic orthodoxies of any sort.[1] What is sometimes implied in these critical appraisals, but has never been adequately traced or theorized, is the way Brecht's aesthetic modernism shaped his approach to history prior to his turn to Marxism. This essay traces his struggle to stage human history in *Im Dickicht der Städte* and shows the way he developed a "theatrical materialism" that would shape and enrich his later turn to historical materialism.

If we consider Brecht's work in the context of theatrical materialism, it becomes obvious that his relationship to history must have been shaped by modernist skepticism toward any historiography that believes in truthful representations of the past. He presents "den Kampf zweier Männer in der Riesenstadt Chicago" as an historical event that defies categories like historical causation and subjective agency.[2] This paper consists of two parts. The first part argues that *Im Dickicht der Städte* seeks the destruction of traditional historical narrative by making the validity of character and events subject to constant dispute. The second part shows how the no-longer-coherent narrative opens one's eyes to the role instinct plays in understanding social interaction, a process Brecht presents through bodily transformation.

By presenting the fight as causeless and unexplainable the play undermines subjective agency and comprehension. As a result Brecht's concept of history falls somewhere between that of Michel Foucault with his genealogies of bodies and systems of power, and that of Walter Benjamin who sees mimesis — the drive toward similarity — as the most powerful force in human history. Placing Brecht's vision of the

New Essays on Brecht / Neue Versuche über Brecht
Maarten van Dijk et al., eds., *The Brecht Yearbook / Das Brecht-Jahrbuch*
Volume 26 (Toronto, Canada: The International Brecht Society, 2001)

unintentional making of history within this philosophical constellation shows that he developed a theatrical materialism before studying Marx, and thus challenges conventions regarding the primacy of Marxist ideology throughout his work.

THE UNORGANIZED MATERIAL

In his critique of historical representation Brecht writes:

> Die Geschichte der Menschheit ist ein Haufen ungeordneten Materials. Schwer erkennbar ist es, wer immer die Verantwortung trug für seine Zeit. Das Hervortreten der großen Typen, die Kreierung der großen Ideen, die nicht immer in Schlachten und Revolutionen deutlich wurden, müßten zusammengefaßt werden. Jener Typus, der im Jahre 1923 den ersten Kampf aus Kampfeslust führte, jenen ersten uninteressierten Kampf, C. Shlink, ist eine historische Person. (21,180)[3]

Lamenting the disorderly nature of human history does not seem to fit either the "anarchic" Brecht, nor his Marxian successor. We should not read that quotation as a complaint about the state of historiographical narratives, because we know from other sources (including his own theatrical practice) that he was suspicious of imposed order as a disguise of conflict. As the passage continues, it reveals his suspicion of written history's ability to present the forces that "are responsible for its time." The emergence of the "great types" and the "creation of great ideas" are not always recognizable in what is conventionally considered a historical event like a war or revolution. He assumes a disjunction between human actions and ideas, and the way that both influence historical reality and historiography. He rejects any simple causal relationship between "progressive" and "conservative" thought and the direction of social change. Historical insight, then, depends on what he calls "zusammenfassen," the recognition that coherent narratives can only be created when imposed upon a chaos of historical reality. The emphasis on "fassen" (to grasp) underscores the active distortion inherent in seizing events in order to perceive them as history. What he suggests here is a reorganization of the production and perception of history, and he seeks to replace the traditional narrative of character and events with a theatrical presentation that focuses on inconsistencies and contradictions.

With this approach to history Brecht comes remarkably close to Michel Foucault, who, in his essay, "Nietzsche, Genealogy, History,"[4] examines Nietzsche's critique of historicism in light of his own critique of power and knowledge. Foucault describes Nietzsche's concept of "wirkliche Historie" ("effective history") as a history that "introduces discontinuity into our very being — as it divides our emotions, dramatizes our instincts, multiplies our bodies and sets it against itself."[5] With this discontinuity any assurance regarding cause and effect in historical events, identity in historical characters, or meaning in historiography ceases to exist. Moreover, a history that considers itself to be a genealogy of bodies, instincts, and emotions reveals meaningful historiography to be the product of the "passion of scholars." Here Foucault asserts that scholars use academic discourse to disguise "the personal conflicts that slowly" became transformed "into weapons of reason."[6]

In *Im Dickicht der Städte* Brecht takes the opposite trajectory. Reason and the meaningful narratives that it creates are destroyed and what remains is the bare reality of social and physical conflict. Shlink, the "historical person" that he introduces in the play, emerges from the disorganized material of society as an historically significant figure, who is set against himself because of the disinterested pleasure he takes in fighting. Shlink's importance, according to him, lies less in his achievement as a fighter than in his indifference toward winning or losing in comparison to the simple pleasure he takes in the fight. Shlink's fight for pleasure — and his pleasure in fighting — is played out in *Im Dickicht der Städte*. Shlink publicly attacks Garga, an impoverished clerk in a library in Chicago, for no apparent reason. He gets the clerk fired, forces his girlfriend into prostitution, and gains access to Garga's family by hiring his sister as a housemaid. Garga responds to this challenge and the two men take turns bankrupting and criminalizing one another. Each ends up isolated from his original social network — Garga from his family and Shlink from his gang. They finally withdraw completely and spend three weeks hiding out together, having sex and talking before Garga hands Shlink, a Malayan, over to a lynch mob. Shlink forestalls the lynching by committing suicide and Garga retreats to New York.

The play explores the fight between Shlink and Garga as an example of the unorganized material of life which creates various histories: social history is created when Garga's family is destroyed; economic history arises through various business transactions involving Garga and Shlink; cultural history is produced when they experience changes in class and sexual orientation, and even natural history can be perceived through their physical transformation. The lack of organic comprehension that Brecht observes in historiography's desire to divide the aspects of a single set of events appears in the play itself, because it lacks clarity of plot and character. The foreword announces the drama as the unexplainable "Ringkampf zweier Menschen" and directly addresses the audience with the words: "Zerbrechen Sie sich nicht den Kopf über die Motive dieses Kampfes, sondern beteiligen Sie sich an den menschlichen Einsätzen..." (I, 438). Instead of searching for meaning and motivation, the audience is encouraged to participate in the fight — either by taking sides or by betting on the winner. This brings to mind Brecht's address to the audience in another play, *Das Elefan-*

tenkalb, where he explicitly invites people to talk and smoke during the performance and to visit the bar to bet on the winner.

By presenting these plays as boxing matches, Brecht moves the cultural setting of the theater where *Im Dickicht* takes place, to the street.[7] The public life of the streets is especially emphasized in the first of the two versions of the play where "Stimmen von Zeitungsweibern und Zeitungsjungen" shout out headlines that relate to the fable, such as "Verbrechen des Malaiischen Mörders," and "Lynchjustiz der anständigen Bevölkerung" (I, 345). He demonstrates the chaos of social reality by revealing that Shlink is not a murderer, and by rendering unsuccessful the mob's attempt to murder him. But we also know that newspapers are a major source for historiography, and Brecht complicates the question of sources further when he says in the foreword that *Im Dickicht* presents "...lediglich die wichtigsten Sätze, die hier an einem bestimmten Punkt des Globus zu bestimmten Minuten der *Menschheitsgeschichte* fielen" (I, 345). He confronts the concept of transcendent historical importance with the specificity of any individual event's time and place. In the jungle of Chicago Brecht presents the transformation of two people through a variety of economic, cultural, and sexual transactions. Such microcosmic transformations are presented as the key to understanding social change.

For him history is neither a coherent narrative nor a body of knowledge, but an accumulation of events that may or may not be recorded and that may or may not produce meaning for those involved. *Im Dickicht der Städte* does not provide us with meaningful developments or interactions, but with interests, actions and reactions which are subject to constant dispute. In this dispute the sides taken do not remain constant and each contestant appropriates the opponent's arguments in different settings. The struggle can also be read as a fight for representation, not only between Shlink and Garga, or among all characters in the play, but also between the play and the audience, when Brecht suggests that what really happened is a matter of betting (winning or losing). The characters dispute while they are interacting because they find themselves in a chaos of action and meaning, rather than as "representatives" of transcendent historical forces.

Such is the case at the very beginning when Shlink enters "C. Maynes Leihbibliothek in Chicago." Garga, who works there as a librarian, understands this to be a place for books and readers, while Shlink considers it, like any other public place, to be a site where he can pick a fight with anyone he chooses. Garga's conviction that the library is his domain is destroyed when Shlink declares war on him: "Und an diesem Morgen, der nicht wie immer ist, eröffne ich den Kampf gegen Sie. Ich beginne damit, daß ich ihre Plattform erschüttere" (1/441). Shlink stages a performance in the library that throws Garga's life into chaos, culminating with his being fired and losing his girlfriend. Garga had firmly and unreflectively believed in the stability of his professional and private life: that he was the rightful employee of C. Maynes, the responsible lover of Jane Larry, the caring son of his parents; that he lived up to his responsibilities an agent who acts according to his position and that he fulfills his responsibility by handling books, visiting his lover, and earning a living for his family. Shlink upsets this coherent picture by presenting Maynes as a rigid businessman, Jane as an alcoholic who readily rejects her impoverished lover, and, eventually, Garga's parents as greedy exploiters who would accept any breadwinner as their son. The play's opening combines with the turn of events it presents to destabilize the identities of the characters to undermine the possibility of any coherent recording of the historical events presented, or, by extension, of any social process.

The play's critique begins in the economic realm, then moves to the social and finally extends to the cultural when Shlink upends Garga's value system. Shlink begins by attacking Garga's economic position. He offers to buy the librarian's judgment about the quality of different books. In the course of the argument he belittles Garga for his poverty and insists that he should gladly accept money for his literary opinions. Garga refuses: "Ich verkaufe Ihnen die Ansichten von Mister V. Jensen und Mister Arthur Rimbaud, aber ich verkaufe Ihnen nicht meine Ansicht darüber" (I, 439). According to Garga, a book is a materialized thought that can be sold as commodity, while his opinion about the book is a subjective achievement, something that should be excluded from market relations or public dispute. His opinion is part of himself, so selling it would be prostitution (I, 440). In the fight that follows Schlink destroys Garga's belief that intellectual freedom is more important than social and economic bondage. Shlink and his men consider personal opinion a luxury that is beyond Garga's social status as is shown when Skinny asks Garga: "Sind Sie aus einer transatlantischen Millionärsfamilie?" (1/440).

Skinny then introduces the split between moral principles and social life that Brecht traces throughout the play: "Daß Sie Ansichten haben, das kommt, weil Sie nichts vom Leben verstehen (I, 440)." Skinny shows that Garga tries to rise above social struggle by assigning superior value to thought, and in rejecting that effort Skinny hints at the incompatibility of life and thought. The tension between life and thought also provides the perspective from which Shlink and his men mock authorship: "Die Schriftsteller rächen sich am Leben durch ein Buch, das Leben rächt sich dadurch, daß es anders ist." They reject the notion that anyone can comprehend life through the inanimate medium of print or through abstract intellectual inquiry. The revenge that they foresee (revenge never refers to the battle between Shlink and Garga because that is not what motivates them, but to the pleasure of fighting), arises out of this tension produced by an author's attempt to reduce social life in its material complexity — a complexity that includes the corporal existence of the writer as well as of his subjects — to the abstract thought embodied in print. Material life takes revenge on the intellectual life of print by contradicting its narrative presentations of coherent meaning. The cruelty we perceive in nature arises from the intellectual imposition of supposedly rational moral meaning on the amoral process of life. By presenting this conflict to the civilized social body, Brecht shows the city to be a jungle, and he shows that the jungle is home to the contradictions between thought and the "individual's" life and the social body.

Garga builds his identity as a librarian by conceiving of thought as separate from life, as he shows by asserting that material goods are less important than and unrelated to, immaterial goods. Shlink reveals his desire to unite the material and the immaterial worlds by calling his fight with Garga a "metaphysische Aktion": "Sie haben nicht begriffen, was es war. Sie wollten mein Ende, aber ich wollte den Kampf. Nicht das Körperliche, sondern das Geistige war es" (1/493). While Shlink insists that his impulse to fight is spiritual ("das Geistige"), he merges the spirit with the realm of physical action by speaking of understanding as "begreifen" (to grasp) rather than "verstehen" (to understand). Shlink's approach to fighting is informed by Brecht's notion of "das Geistige" as a social interaction that receives and records its experience and the knowledge produced by that experience through and upon the body. Garga ultimately proves unable to learn this lesson.

Brecht thinks "das Geistige" is achieved through physical contact and contrasts it with "understanding" which is an artifact of language. Following their three-year-long fight and before Garga's final retreat to New York, the two men spend three weeks together living off the fruits of their fight and making sense of it. Ultimately, as Garga notes, they fail: "Ich habe Ihnen jetzt drei Wochen zugehört.... Warum sitze ich und verliere meine Zeit? Sind wir nicht drei Wochen hier gelegen?" (1, 492). Shlink, recognizing that they have gained neither sense nor a reliable bond from their three weeks together, asks "Und niemals, George Garga, wird ein Ausgang dieses Kampfes sein, niemals eine Verständigung?" (1, 492). Garga responds, "Die Sprache reicht zur Verständigung nicht aus" (1, 491). Understanding, or the acceptance of its impossibility, reaches an impasse when Garga proves unable to follow Shlink to a less conventional approach. Shlink says:

> Ich habe die Tiere beobachtet. Die Liebe, Wärme aus Körpernähe, ist unsere einzige Gnade in der Finsternis! Aber die Vereinigung der Organe ist die einzige, sie überbrückt nicht die Entzweiung der Sprache. (1, 491)

Schlink's commitment to fighting derives from his observation of animals, and a relationship based on animalistic enmity does not entail understanding.

Like antagonistic animals, Shlink and Garga have tracked one another during their battles. Fighting has kept them close for, as Shlink remarks early in the play, to possess one's hate, as Garga does, is the same as to possess one's love, and in either case one is loath to lose contact. Shlink defines love physically as warmth produced by the closeness of bodies, and he distinguishes it from mere talk, which seeks ineffectually to produce understanding. Shlink has no expectations of the "meaningful" love produced by talk and he accepts language's arbitrariness. The division between the signifier and the signified, rather than mediating between language and life, signifies the difference between them, and it is that very difference that fuels Shlink's initial attack on Garga. The "Entzweiung der Sprache" meets the "unendliche Vereinzelung des Menschen," rendering impossible any connection between people through language and understanding and making even "eine Feindschaft zum unerreichbaren Ziel" (1/491). With spiritual connection rendered impossible, fighting offers a way to initiate contact between bodies, and thus to escape the trap produced by the gap separating life (or social reality) and thought (or writing).

Even in hindsight Shlink's causeless and senseless — literally irrational — enmity resists valid coherent representation, because, as both antagonists come to realize, the arbitrary nature of language renders all meaning fictional. Shlink accepts this and realizes it is impossible to "make sense" of the fight. Garga does apply "sense" by excluding "das Geistige" and opting for survival which he defines as success: "Und das Geistige, das sehen Sie, das ist nichts. Es ist nicht wichtig, der Stärkere zu sein, sondern der Lebendige" (1/493). While Schlink fights to produce a distinct quality of intellectual and physical comprehension, Garga fights only to win in the most conventional sense. When he knows that the lynch mob is coming for Schlink, he takes pride in the prospect of his own survival, and of winning, once and for all, his contest with Shlink. Shlink comprehends life as a perpetual fight with others and he seeks nothing else; Garga, on the other hand, longs for solitude. He declares victory over Shlink to achieve solitude thus ending their relationship. By winning and separating himself from Shlink, Garga abandons the fight. Shlink counts this abandonment as a loss of life.

Garga desires this break in order to pursue a different form of life, and the conflicting goals of Garga and Shlink reflect their differing conceptions of time and history. When Garga opts out of the fight in order to live in solitude, Shlink perceives him to be opting out of history:

> Die Etappen des Lebens sind nicht die der Erinnerung. Ich habe Reis gegessen und mit vielerlei Volk gehandelt. Meine Eingebungen habe ich nicht ausgeschwatzt. Der Schluß ist nicht das Ziel, die letzte Episode nicht wichtiger als irgendeine andere. Schließlich entsprach der Gewinn genau

dem Einsatz. (1, 427)

Shlink cannot understand what it would mean for the fight come to an end and survive only an object of verbal memory. His whole life has taught him to distrust language as much as he trusts physical contact and conflict. Memory — reliable memory — is imbedded in the fight rather than in verbal narrative, so it is social rather than solitary, contested rather than consensual, and in the present rather than in the past. For Shlink, Garga's withdrawal from the fight — his withdrawal into verbal memory — is a withdrawal from life. Shlink "remembers" past battles — and he has engaged in many over the course of his life — only as an integrated part of whatever fight currently animates and produces meaning in his life. Fights do not come to an abrupt end and then get stored safely in a memory bank; they recur and inform one another, producing ever-changing meanings precisely because the chaos of social reality ("unorganisiertes Material") resists stable and unchanging meaning.

Garga rejects Shlink's insight and longs for the solitude in which he can create a meaningful narrative, a goal he articulates retrospectively at the play's end: "Allein sein ist eine gute Sache. Das Chaos ist aufgebraucht. Es war die beste Zeit" (1, 497). He speaks these words while pocketing the money he made selling his sister and Schlink's business. He welcomes the solitude, but he acknowledges that, chaotic as it was, the fight with Shlink was productive — "Es war die beste Zeit." Now, with the fight over, the social conflict that produced history — Brecht's "unorganized material" — grinds to a halt. Progressive memory can no longer be produced through contestation; instead, the once productive fight between Garga and Shlink is consumed, ordered and tamed by memory. When Garga interprets the fight in accordance with his interests, he domesticates it and drains it of its potential for change. This, Brecht's play insists, is the way historical narratives consume social reality.

This involvement, more than any fictional "outcome" that Garga envisions, creates what Foucault calls "effective history":

> An event, consequently, is not a decision, a treaty, a reign, or a battle, but the reversal of a relationship of forces, the usurpation of power, the appropriation of vocabulary turned against those who had once used it, a feeble domination that poisons itself as it grows lax, the entry of a masked other. The forces of history are not controlled by destiny of regulative mechanisms, but respond to haphazard conflicts.[8]

The fight between Shlink and Garga is an "event" in Foucault's concept of genealogy because both men were engaged in a contest that enriched and impoverished them, transformed them, and sacrificed their social networks. The fight alters "a relationship of forces." By presenting the two men's shared struggle as driven by the desire for closeness,

Brecht enables us to witness the perpetual reversal of rules and domination that Foucault sees as historical change. The changes that the struggle between Shlink and Garga produces are partly result of their intention; however, other unintended changes occur that affect the participants of the fight.

INSTINCTS AND TRANSFORMATIONS

> Die Zeiten ohne Instinkte haben das Mißtrauen gegen den Kopf... und es sind die Leute ohne Leiber, die sich etwas erwarten von der Unterbindung des Kopfes. Es gibt eine Phantasie des Körpers und eine Phantasie des Geistes (das heißt, es gibt eher zweierlei Art von Phantasie als die Grenze von Körper und Geist), beide aber sind mehr wert als die dunklen Mischungen in den Venen, die man Gefühle nennt. (21, 239)

Instinct can be defined as the drive to survive, and the means by which a particular species exercises that drive, and it is conventionally considered more the province of animals than humans. Brecht, however, considers instinct and intellect to be mutually dependent human qualities. Though Brecht refuses to consider one without the other, he keeps them separate and distinct. In their conflictual dependence — their dialectical relationship to one another — each serves as a reminder of the other's difference and incompatibility. Brecht uses them together to sharpen the perception of what is physical and what is intellectual. In *Im Dickicht der Städte* he presents the instinctive fight for survival as a means of intellectual comprehension with surprising results. While the fight between Shlink and Garga is without reason, it produces unexpected physical and mental changes. The fight takes place in a racist context — Garga even exploits racism to "win" the fight — and yet both men come to realize and then embody their sameness by transforming into one another.

Shlink instinctively chooses Garga as his opponent and discovers to his delight that he has found a fighter (1/440). Garga survives the initial assault — in spite of his inexperience — by abandoning any attempt to find the reasons behind Shlink's attack, and by employing his instinct for survival. Shlink initiates the fight out of his need for human contact and succeeds in establishing this contact: he invades Garga's work place and his relationships. Through a variety of moves Shlink keeps in touch with Garga without bonding — their contact remains impersonal not only during the three years of their fight but also through the three weeks of their love affair. Throughout the play they address one another as "Sie" rather than "Du." At the end of the play Garga and Shlink meditate on different varieties of contact in which no traces of bonding can be detected. According to Shlink, "Unsere Bekanntschaft war kurz, sie war eine Zeitlang vorwiegend, die Zeit ist schnell verflogen" (I, 490). Acquaintance — pure, simple and persistent acquaintance — is the fruit of contact between Garga and Shlink.

The fight that initiates this acquaintance begins, according to Garga, with a catch:

> Ich weiß nicht, was man mit mir vorhat. Man hat mich harpuniert. Man zog mich an sich. Es scheint Stricke zu geben. Ich werde mich an Sie halten, Herr. (I, 447)

Garga describes his encounter with Shlink as an attempt to make contact rather than simply as an attack. He uses passive terms to describe his connection to his attackers. By accepting his inferiority, Garga enters the fight with the prospect of surviving. He uses "Herr," a public and hierarchical signifier when addressing Shlink and he signals a commitment to staying in contact with his antagonist through the term "sich halten an," which in German entails holding onto something, but also accepting someone as a role model. Committed to staying close to his attacker, watching him, and acting responsively, Garga enters the fight.

By instinctively staying in touch with one another, each man transforms himself. After destroying Garga's economic livelihood, Shlink makes his antagonist more like himself by turning his timber business over to Garga; Garga accepts this gambit and continues to move toward Shlink by immediately donating the business to the Salvation Army. Garga becomes, like his enemy, a former owner of the timber business. Both men experience extreme physical changes over the course of the play. In the first scene Shlink's men "skin" Garga by frightening him out of his clothes; the clothes are returned, but when Garga once again dons his outward "skin," he notices that Shlink's men are dressed just like him. They have entered his skin. Shlink, in turn, assimilates Garga's class status by working in the coal mines, and this alters his body. In this way the antagonism between the men is something other than purely personal. It brings two social spheres into contact. This process continues throughout. When, for example, Garga is imprisoned for business fraud, Shlink replaces him within his family and becomes the breadwinner. Shlink transforms himself from millionaire businessman to coal-mining family member. Garga gains a lucrative business and a life of economic ease, but loses a family. Following this exchange of places, each moves on, but remains in antagonistic contact and continues to take social and economic positions in response to the other. Brecht roots their transformations in a thoroughgoing materialism, though he wrote the play years before turning to Marxism.

Physical and social economies structure not only the fight between Shlink and Garga, but also their love interests. Both men articulate their erotic interests in one another through detached physical and verbal means. For example, neither man's connection to women is rooted in sexual interest; women are simply a medium through which they express homosocial interest in one another. When Shlink says to Garga, "Ich belade Sie mit dem Schicksal Ihrer Schwester. Sie haben ihr die Augen geöffnet, daß sie in alle Ewigkeit ein Objekt ist unter den Männern," (1, 471) he points out that both men are using women to stay in touch with one another. Women are a site for their struggle and a disguise for homoerotic attraction, rather than a cause for fighting, a reward for victory, or an independent force in either man's life.

Their mutual attraction cannot be traced in terms of cause and effect, but it is obvious long before Shlink articulates his love for Garga in the last scene; Garga is, in fact, the one who suggests it earlier in the play. His comment undercuts the primacy critics have conventionally attributed to Shlink's desire, and provides a genealogy for their attraction that extends to the fight itself rather than to individual desire. When Garga arrives at the Chinese hotel inhabited by Shlink's gang, Wurm observes "Die Harpune sitzt fester, als wir glaubten... Jetzt liegt er drinnen in Shlinks Zimmer und leckt seine Wunden" (1, 463–64). Garga originally used this metaphor of penetration to describe Shlink's actions in initiating the fight. Thus while it is Wurm who makes this metaphor explicitly sexual, it echoes Garga's description of his interactions with Shlink:

> Ich nenne ihn meinen höllischen Gemahl in meinen Träumen, Shlink, den Hund. Wir sind von Tisch und Bett geschieden, er hat keine Kammer mehr. Sein Bräutchen raucht Virginias und verdient sich was in die Strümpfe." Das bin ich! (1, 464)

Garga anticipates Shlink's homoerotic longing precisely because he recognizes his own homoerotic interests. This allows him to render Shlink's death as an erotic allegory when he says, "Ich werde einmal seine Witwe sein" (1, 464). By calling himself Shlink's widow, Garga anticipates winning the fight, but he does more. "Witwe" also invokes his status as Shlink's surviving lover after their three-week-long honeymoon. In their longing for one another the men become interchangeable. Garga calls Shlink a dog while behaving like one himself; he calls Shlink his hellish consort in order to affirm his own identity.

The interchangeability of Garga and Shlink is dependent on the symbolic economy of their physical and mental existence. Both men take account of their past and their fight, by comparing each other in genealogical terms. The play remains in the privileged realm of the external, by examining different genealogies of the skin. In Shlink's case, the skin develops through the hardships of social and racial injustice that he, as the older man, has endured over long periods of time, as the growing thickness of his skin shows:

> Die Menschenhaut im natürlichen Zustande ist zu dünn für diese Welt, deshalb sorgt der Mensch dafür, daß sie dicker wird. Die Methode wäre

> unanfechtbar, wenn man das Wachstum stoppen könnte. Ein Stück
> präpariertes Leder zum Beispiel bleibt, aber die Haut wächst, sie wird
> dicker und dicker. (1, 462)

Shlink's skin has grown progressively thicker through numerous humiliations over a long time. This is the sign that Garga has found himself in battle with a professional fighter, and it explains why Shlink and "Skinny" begin the fight by "skinning" the thin-skinned librarian. According to Garga: "Sie haben Prärie gemacht. Ich akzeptiere die Prärie. Sie haben mir die Haut agbezogen aus Liebhaberei. Durch eine neue Haut ersetzen Sie nichts" (1, 448).

Garga survives the fight by adapting to the situations that others create for him: "Ich verstehe nichts, Sir, bin dabei wie ein Neger, bin mit einer weißen Fahne gekommen, jetzt entfalte ich sie zur Attacke" (1, 451). Brecht presents Garga's organic adaptation to new social circumstances with various tropes of changing skin: Garga's loss of his clothes is a "skinning" and leaves him, in his own estimation, a "negro." Losing his work clothes is far more than a superficial and temporary embarrassment; for Garga it is essential and transforming: "Ich hatte meine Kindheit noch vor mir. Die Ölfelder mit dem blauen Raps. Der Iltis in den Schluchten und die leichten Wasserschellen" (1, 490). The natural metaphors Garga uses to describe his loss of childhood underscore the rapid acceleration of evolutionary change that he experiences. According to Shlink, "Richtig, das war alles in ihrem Gesicht. Jetzt ist es hart wie Bernstein, man findet mitunter Tierleichen in ihm, der durchsichtig ist" (1, 490). The changes through which Garga rushed are preserved, however, like fossils in amber (Bernstein). The long duration of evolution has been condensed for Garga into three years and three weeks. The amber face with its preserved fragments of Garga's life also resembles Shlink's "yellow" Malayan skin. Shlink recognizes this transformation. In the course of the play Shlink and Garga turn into one another, a process they can only perceive by observing and tracing one another as their fight requires.

Brecht defines race not in biological but in historical terms — in terms of the life a person lived: history for him materializes in the body. It is the social relation based on instinct that overcomes racial division for the sake of being human. But this awareness is not the result of a "shared humanity," a concept that Brecht destroys in the first scene. Instead, this assurance emerges out of a combination of physical instinct and intellectual recognition of two opposite concepts equally employed in the struggle.

In his "Metaphysisch-Geschichtsphilosophischen Studien" Walter Benjamin writes that Mimesis, by which he means the creation of similarity, is the driving force of human history: "Die Gabe, Ähnlichkeit zu sehn, die wir besitzen, ist nichts als nur ein schwaches Rudiment des ehemals gewaltigen Zwanges, ähnlich zu werden und sich zu verhalten."[9] If we consider the fight between Shlink and Garga from this perspective it becomes obvious that instead of creating meaning and responding to motivation according to the conventions of traditional theater, both men follow a drive to become similar to one another, and the similarity that emerges does so in spite of, or at least without reference to, their intention. Here Brecht moves from a social history as disorganized material to a natural history as it plays out in the fast-paced urbanism of the twentieth century. The city jungle invalidates traditional forms of living, forms that the play presents as empty shells. These forms — the family, romantic partnerships, traditional modes of employment — force those who seek to fulfill them to re-activate the drive for mimesis in order to adapt and form new and unpredictable social units. Attraction and enmity tie together those who succeed in provoking one another. The battle that ensues is a shared collective activity whose effects can be traced through the antagonists' bodies.

Through the attraction and transformation between Garga and Shlink, Brecht presents the history of their fight in terms congruent with Foucault's concept of genealogy. Foucault distinguishes identity as a result of traditional historiography, whereas genealogy traces the descent of the body as "the locus of a dissociated Self (adopting the illusion of substantial unity), and a volume in perpetual disintegration."[10] Garga and Shlink leave their environments and dissolve their own identities in order to maximize their ability to fight. Yet in their moves the men also appropriate the other's identity and environment. Each replaces his former line of descent based on a cultural identity with the line of descent of his opponent. According to Foucault, "Genealogy, as an analysis of descent, is thus situated within the articulation of the body and history."[11] Brecht's articulation of the past through the body bypasses meaningful representations of history, as becomes obvious when neither Garga nor Shlink can make sense of the cause and effect of their fight; instead, they are the carriers of the history their fight produced.

In spite of their transformation, important differences between the two figures remain, and these differences are rooted in Shlink's traumatic past. The genealogy of Shlink's skin varies in interesting ways from that of Garga's. The famous forty-year-long loneliness that Shlink seeks to overcome by fighting Garga is halved by his previous encounters with the lynch mob:

> Das Geschrei kenne ich. Es ist 20 Jahre her, aber ich habe es nicht aus dem Gehirn gebracht. Sie werfen einen Mann wie einen Holzstamm auf den Asphalt, diese Tiere kenne ich. (1, 419)

Shlink distinguishes between different sorts of fighting. He sees lynching as the absence of fighting, and perceives the lynch mob as consisting of those "die nicht bezahlen wollen" (1, 419). The mob refuses a fair fight, rejecting the rules that Shlink and Garga set up for themselves. Fighting for Brecht depends on the mutual acceptance of the fight as a living and a social matter. Shlink's previous experience with a lynch mob traumatized him because it turned him into a victim who could not fight back. By surviving that experience, he learned how to endure.

In the course of his life Shlink brings endurance to perfection. He transforms fear and memory into action and takes masochistic pleasure in doing so. When he applies to the Garga family to take him in as their breadwinner he not only tolerates racist treatment, but pushes matters further with his remark, "Ich habe an allem Geschmack, mein Magen verdaut Kieselsteine" (1, 460). Enduring racist violence becomes an extension of this process when Shlink hesitates to escape the lynch mob that Garga has unleashed for the first time: "Aber es ist noch nicht das richtige Geschrei, das weiße. Dann sind sie da. Dann haben wir noch eine Minute. Horch, jetzt! Jetzt ist es das richtige! Das weiße Geschrei!" (1, 489). Shlink has transformed the fearful and traumatic memory of the lynch mob into a stimulant he can enjoy, because through his fights he has acquired the ability to escape and to fight back. He has endured through struggle.

Transformation plays a key role in endurance. Garga explains Shlink's superiority as a fighter — "Sie kämpfen leicht. Wie sie verdauen" (1, 490), the result of harmony between his way of fighting and his body. This distinction rests on the years that separate him from Shlink, years in which Shlink was victimized by racial violence, an experience he transformed into a fighting technique. Their differences in experience are overcome through further mutual transformation. Garga begins his fight with Shlink as a self-acknowledged inferior, and Shlink changes his persona to that of a humble servant who accepts the stereotype of racial inferiority by referring to his "gelbe Haut" (1, 460). Shlink transforms himself to match Garga, a transformation that allows the fight to continue for longer than first appeared likely. Shlink finds advantage in accepting the disadvantages of self-abnegation. He works within the racist structure he has knows all his life, changing himself in accord with it in order to seek his own death in battle with a "carefully chosen" white man. Garga, as that white man, can and does activate a lynch mob. By engaging with a racist power structure Schlink can exercise his strength as a fighter and his endurance in a way that permits him simultaneously to fight and to submit to his chosen death.

Garga comes to fear Shlink learned so much that he cannot be beaten. According to Garga, Shlink has a "zu dicke Haut. Er biegt alles um, was man hineinstößt" (1, 416). This renders Shlink invulnerable, because it allows him to transform attacks into counterattacks. But despite his apparent invulnerability the memory of lynching manifests itself in Shlink's skin — his most external feature. As in *Trommeln in der Nacht,* Brecht presents the past not through a narrative, but as an imprint on the body, as a genealogy that combines physical and social history. As Garga puts it: "Jetzt geht es also durch Ihre Haut? Die Geschichte mit den Spießen" (1, 419). The harpoon that Shlink aimed at Garga penetrated his body and propelled him into a new public sphere. Shlink is perforated by history and memory, a perforation that provides Garga with the information he needs for the final triumph when he hands Shlink over to the mob.

But Shlink's fighting techniques cannot accept Garga's attempt to organize the chaos of the fight in terms of winning and losing. In fact, both men get from the fight what they want — Shlink does, after all, want death. Here lies the split between the two men: Garga fights to live but Shlink to die, as he elaborates to Garga: "Ein Weißer, gemietet, mich hinunterzuschaffen, mir etwas Ekel oder Moder in das Maul zu stopfen, daß ich den Geschmack des Todes auf die Zunge kriege" (1, 493). After engaging Garga in love and metaphysics, Shlink engages him in his death. Thought and love are conventionally perceived as non-material and personal entities; death is considered inevitable and biological, and beyond the realm of subjective or social interference. Shlink is old and determined to transform the biological act of dying into a social event. He succeeds in this goal, and the fight enables him to distill as much life out of his death as he can.

The fight as "uninteressierter Kampf" lacks meaning, but as the "Geschichte mit den Spießen" (1, 419) it signifies historical change. Harpoons link disinterested people through penetrated skin, and the battle that results from that link transforms them visibly and in traceable ways into one another. Brecht's later notes regarding transformation in history may well have their origins in his *Dickicht* plays, as under-scored by his theoretical assertion that history should be seen primarily as genealogy:

> Es soll nicht bestritten werden, daß Bürger sich wie Adelige benehmen können zu einer Zeit, wo sich Adelige schon nicht mehr wie Adelige benehmen oder wie Bauern, die sich niemals so benähmen wie Bauern, wenn sie nicht Felder bearbeiteten, der bürgerliche Mensch löst adeligen, der proletarische den bürgerlichen nicht nur ab, sondern er enthält ihn auch. (21, 522)

Class struggle when viewed as genealogy becomes more complicated than a story of political commitment within a progressive narrative of historical development. When history as genealogy produces contain-ment, the assurances of cause and effect, of right or wrong, are subject to constant change. If the succession of struggle produces containment, an elevated position of moral integrity becomes an illusion. From this perspective, class struggle includes cultural and physical seduction as well as economic and political conflict. Parties to such struggle can only achieve "victory" by accepting their antagonists and adapting to the world they initially seek to change. The process of "enthalten" might be misunderstood for what is conventionally called assimilation, but one should keep in mind that Brecht's concept of becoming similar is based on permanent conflict and is thus not unidirectional. It is mutual or multi-directional. The importance of the habitual mimesis in *Im Dickicht der Städte* is that dominance constantly shifts between the two opponents.

If we consider containment the result of habitual mimesis, we may subsume "enthalten" into Brecht's vast concept of "Haltung" and thus add a historical component to this concept. As one of the key terms of Brechtian theater, "Haltung" contains such diverse aspects as social attitude and physical posture. According to Brecht, "Haltung" as an essentially theatrical concept is the physical signification of thought; it thus needs an audience to decipher it. In *Im Dickicht der Städte* Garga and Shlink come to "contain" one another as a result of their conflictual engagement, but each man develops a different attitude, as is obvious in their final evaluation of the outcome of their fight:

> GARGA ... Wenn Sie längst Kalk über sich haben, durch die natürliche Ausscheidung des Veralteten, werde ich wählen, was mich unterhält.
> SHLINK Was nehmen Sie für eine Haltung ein? Ich bitte Sie, Ihre Pfeife aus dem Mund zu nehmen. Wenn Sie sagen wollen, daß sie impotent geworden sind, dann tun Sie das mit einer anderen Stimme. (1, 293)

The German "unterhalten," as used by Garga, entails such different concepts as subsistence and entertainment. He opts out of the fight in favor of a life free from conflict, but also passive, solitary, and asocial. He separates himself from Shlink in two ways: first he declares Shlink expelled from the fight; then he moves from the social commitment of fighting to the atomizing act of choosing. Garga envisions a state of luxury where he will be able to choose his subsistence and entertainment without making any personal investment, just as, in the beginning of the play, he insisted that opinions could be held "freely." Shlink, on the other hand, is an advocate of "Haltung" in the materialist sense, when he seeks to extend the fight into the realm of intellectual cognition. Such is the case when in the end he seeks to combine fight, philosophical reflection, and sex into one conflictual interaction. Accordingly, Schlink responds to Garga's longing for entertainment with contempt. He perceives Garga's desire for solitude as passivity and sexual impotence. Shlink sees this "choice" as a rejection of social and sexual opponents/partners. Sex, like thought, depends on social contact and conflict, and, like fight and philosophical reflection, it must be performed in an appropriate manner.

Im Dickicht der Städte presents the various elements of Brecht's concept of "Haltung." In the beginning he uses it for human contact in terms of "sich halten an" when Garga holds on to Shlink in order to learn how to survive the fight. Garga acts instinctively by enduring Schlink's attack, and he gains the attitude and the posture of a fighter by accepting Schlink as a role model who is a master in endurance. By cleaving to one another over time the two men transform into one another in terms of "enthalten" as historical containment. Finally, the fight can be understood as the demonstration that thought as mimetic activity hinges on social conflict and physical endurance when Brecht writes, "Denken findet nur im Kampf statt" (21, 427).

Cognition for Brecht does not take place inside the subject, but emerges as the result of successful social labor. He advocates a "Philosophie der Straße" that shares much with Shlink's conception of a fighting life: "Wenn die Leute das Wort ,philosophieren' verwenden, tun sie es meist im Sinne von ,aushalten von etwas.'" The German "aushalten" includes the English verbs to endure, to bear, to suffer, to sustain, and to stand up to. "Haltung" is a physical, social, intellectual and historical position and thought gains content through physical struggle. As Brecht outlines in his Keuner stories, thought "hat keinen Inhalt." This becomes clear when Keuner responds to the lecturing philosopher: "Ich sehe dein Ziel nicht, ich sehe deine Haltung" (18, 13). While bodies are containers of historical conflicts, thought remains devoid of content. However, thought when acted out and released into a social context, can be observed by others and become subject to dispute. The exchange of thought then does not rely on understanding, but on physical and social imitation which results from social conflicts and rapid cultural changes characteristic of the 20th century. *Im Dickicht der Städte* demonstrates the genealogical re-creation of two men who progress not through intentional acts, but through their drive to stay in touch, a drive that manifests itself in their bodies. In this play Brecht located historical change and intellectual comprehension strictly in the social and the physical, and in the process he developed a distinct theatrical materialism years before he turned to the historical materialism of Marx. It is through this "pre-Marxian" and distinctively theatrical materialism that Brecht continues to challenge and enrich Marxism.

NOTES

[1] Brecht links his concept of epic theater inseparably to history. This historical perspective also ties him to Marx, though, as Hans Mayer has convincingly shown, more in terms of historical materialism than in terms of revolutionary teleology. See Hans Mayer, "Brecht und die Tradition," in *Brecht* (Frankfurt/M.: Suhrkamp, 1996), 309–22. But, as Reinhold Grimm has argued, Brecht's historical materialist perspective on the past was complicated by an epistemological skepticism reminiscent of Nietzsche. See Reinhold Grimm, *Brecht und Nietzsche oder die Geständnisse eines Dichters: Fünf Essays und ein Bruchstück* (Frankfurt/M.: Suhrkamp, 1979), 55–77. Frederic Jameson triangulates Brecht between modernity, actuality, and historicity. Jameson argues that Brecht's concept of historicity result from his understanding of progress as productivity. See Frederic Jameson, *Brecht and Method* (London, New York: Verso, 1998), 177.

[2] On Brecht's destruction of subjective agency see Astrid Oesmann, "The Theatrical Destruction of Subjectivity and History: Brecht's *Trommeln in der Nacht*, in *The German Quarterly* 70:2 (Spring 1997): 136–50. Rainer Nägele points out that Brecht's early plays *Im Dickicht der Städte* and *Mann ist Mann* "reject the basis of traditional drama: motivation." See Rainer Nägele "Brecht's Theater of Cruelty" in *Reading after Freud: Essays on Goethe, Hölderlin, Habermas, Nietzsche, Celan, and Freud* (New York: Columbia UP, 1987), 132. Hans-Thies Lehmann and Helmut Lethen place Brecht in a continuum along with Marx, Nietzsche, and Freud, by pointing out that each of them seeks to undermine any idealist notion of the subject and thus the basis coherent historical representation. Elizabeth Wright offers postmodern readings of *Im Dickicht der Städte* where she focuses on sadism and masochism. See Elizabeth Wright, *Postmodern Brecht: A Re-Presentation* (New York: Routledge, 1989).

[3] All citations follow the *Große kommentierte Berliner Frankfurter Ausgabe* (GBA) (volume/number) (Berlin, Frankfurt/M: Aufbau/Suhrkamp, 1988–1999) ed. Werner Hecht, Jan Knopf, Werner Mittenzwei, and Klaus-Detlef Müller.

[4] Michel Foucault, "Nietzsche, Genealogy, History," in *Language, Countermemory, Practice*: Selected Essays and Interviews by Michel Foucault, ed. Donald F. Bouchard (Ithaca, New York: Cornell University Press, 1977), 139–64).

[5] Foucault, 154.

[6] Foucault, 142.

[7] Wolf-Dietrich Junghans has shown how Brecht's interest in boxing matches is intertwined with his concept of the public sphere in that the fight enables people to gain experience when participation and observation are not separated. Wolf-Dietrich Junghans, "Öffentlichkeiten: Boxen, Theater und Politik," *drive b:, Theater der Zeit/The Brecht Yearbook* 23 (1998): 56–59.

[8] Foucault, 154.

[9] Walter Benjamin, "Lehre vom Ähnlichen," Walter Benjamin, *Gesammelte Schriften* 2.1, ed. Rolf Tiedemann, Herrman Schweppenhäuser (Frankfurt/M.: Suhrkamp, 1980): 210.

[10] Foucault, 148.

[11] Foucault, 148.

Brechts (Nicht-) Philosophisches Theater

Dieser Aufsatz vergleicht die klassische Formulierung der Verwunderung (to thaumazein) als das Prinzip der Philosophie und des Theaters bei Platon und Aristoteles mit der marxistischen Kritik seiner Tradition, insbesondere mit der althusserischen Perspektive auf die neue Ausübung der Philosophie und auf das materialistische „philosophische" Theater. Vorgeschlagen wird die Situierung von Brechts Theater in den Kontext, den Althusser als ein (nicht-) philosophisches, marxistisches Eindringen der Praxis in die Geschichte der westlichen Philosophie bezeichnet. Wenn für Aristoteles die Tragödie eine „Nachahmung oder Darstellung von Handlung" ist, ist für Brecht das Schauspiel hauptsächlich die Handlung der Darstellung, ein Schauspiel „möglicher Darstellungen," oder mit anderen Worten, eine Praxis, die beabsichtigt, die Gesellschaft anhand eines Schauspiels der Verwunderung zu beeinflussen. Solch ein Schauspiel ruft das Gefühl der „Intellektuellen Freiheit und hoher Mobilität" hervor, das auf die praktische, politische Umformung der Welt ausgerichtet ist.

Brecht's (Non-)Philosophical Theater

Max Statkiewicz

Brecht n'a cessé, toute sa vie, de mettre en rapport direct le théâtre et la philosophie.

> Louis Althusser, "Sur Brecht et Marx"[1]

Das Theater wurde eine Angelegenheit für Philosophen, allerdings solcher Philosophen, die die Welt nicht nur zu erklären, sondern auch zu ändern wünschten.

> Bertold Brecht, "Vergnügungstheater oder Lehrtheater?"[2]

B recht' s theater is often called "philosophical." Since in Western thought there is an old tradition of "philosophical theater" associated with Aristotle and because Brecht has always insisted on the non-Aristotelian character of his theater, it is necessary to examine his alternative, "non-Aristotelian," sense of the philosophical. I will attempt such an examination by comparing the classical formulations of the principle of philosophy in Plato and Aristotle with the Marxist critique of the classical tradition, and in particular with the Althusserian interpretation of Marx's theory of the new practice of philosophy. I will propose to situate Brecht's theater in the context of what Althusser considers to be a (non)phil-osophical irruption of praxis in the history of Western philosophy.

Very early in his career Brecht associated the idea of the epic theater with philosophy. In 1929, in his article "Last Stage: Oedipus," for example, he says that "the future of the theater is philosophical" and it is, of course, in the epic theater that he sees the realization of that future; he relates it to the German philosophical past and in particular to Marxist philosophy.[3] Almost a quarter century later, in the "Epic theater" (Notes on *Katzgraben* from 1953), Brecht still calls his theater "philosophical," this time in a "naïve" sense, that is, simply involved in the "actions and opinions of people" (*Verhalten und Meinen der Leute*).[4] Brecht's friend, admirer, and interpreter, Walter Benjamin, is more explicit in his defense of Brecht' s philosophical aesthetic of the theater in his unpublished essay "What is Epic Theater?" (first version): "One may regard epic theater as more dramatic than the dialogue (it is not always): but epic theater need not, for that reason, be any less philosophical."[5] Benjamin refers in this context not only to Plato's philosophical method and his favorite literary

New Essays on Brecht / Neue Versuche über Brecht
Maarten van Dijk et al., eds., *The Brecht Yearbook / Das Brecht-Jahrbuch*
Volume 26 (Toronto, Canada: The International Brecht Society, 2001)

genre but also to his typical "undramatic" character, the sage. Later in the text, he explicitly calls this kind of theater "Socratic," and Stanley Mitchell, in his introduction to the English edition of Benjamin's essays on Brecht, goes so far as to talk about a "truly Platonic drama" in the epic theater (*UB* XV). Are these epithets legitimately used to explicate the meaning of the philosophical and yet "non-Aristotelian" character of Brecht's aesthetic?

Let us begin by considering the "beginning" and "principle" (*arkhē*) of philosophy as it is generally conceived in the tradition of Western thought. "The beginning of philosophy is wonder, amazement (*thaumazein*)," says, for example, Socrates in Plato's dialogue *Theaetetus* (155d): "there is no other *arkhē* of philosophy than this." For once, Aristotle does not dissent from "*amicus Plato*" when he states in his *Metaphysics* (982b): "It is through wonder (*dia to thaumazein*) that men now begin and originally began philosophizing." Philosophical amazement is caused, to use Socrates' language in Plato's dialogue *Parmenides* (128e-130a), by the contradiction (*aporia*) in the "visible things," such as "stones, sticks, and the like," which seem at once like and unlike, singular and multiple, static and in motion. This pertains also to human beings, who appear at the same time tall and short (*Phaedo*), beautiful and ugly (*Hippias*), just and unjust (*Republic* I). Philosophy — the philosophy of the Intelligible Forms — should dissolve the aporia by showing that all visible things participate in different Forms, such as unity and plurality, motion and rest, justice and injustice, etc., and that the latter are not contradictory. The world of Forms, of mathematical objects, of divine justice is to "save" the world of phenomena. For example, the amazement before Zeno's famous paradoxes disappears once the Forms are separated from the sensuous things; the latter are only apparently contradictory, says Socrates in Plato's *Parmenides*, through the participation in contrary Forms:

> [I]f anyone showed that the like itself becomes unlike, or the unlike like, that would be a wonder; but if he shows that things which partake of both become both like and unlike, that seems to me not at all strange, not even if he shows that all things are one by participation in unity and that the same are also many by participation in plurality; but if he shows that unity itself is also many and the many one, then I shall be amazed. The same applies to all other things. (Plato, *Parmenides*, 129b-c)

And the same pattern of explanation applies to most other Western philosophical "cosmodycies," to most other justifications of our world through the separation and introduction of another, ideal one. Once this is done, amazement disappears. What is wonderful (*ti thaumaston?*), Socrates keeps asking, if the things in our world are contradictory? If one could show that they are contradictory in the ideal world, this would be really amazing, but it would be the end, not the beginning of philosophy (*Parmenides*, 135a-c).

For Aristotle, who cannot afford the luxury of the ideal realm, the solution of aporia, which philosophy and sciences should provide, must be found in this world. A causal explanation should "save phenomena" by rendering them rational, and thus suppressing amazement. Once astronomy explained the reasons of the phenomenon of the eclipse, for example, it no longer provoked amazement; one would rather wonder if things were to happen otherwise. And if they really did, the amazement would lead to the revision of the rational explanation. The telos of philosophy and of the sciences, for Aristotle as for Plato, is a coherent, noncontradictory picture of the world. If it remains amazing, it is in the Kantian sense of *Verwunderung* shading into *Bewunderung* or admiration before the "wonderful" order of the "starry sky" and of the "moral law in the human heart." It is in this sense — the sense of puzzlement (*aporia*), mixed with and eventually transformed into admiration — that Aristotle brings together the amazement of the lover of myths (*philomuthos*) and of the lover of wisdom or knowledge (*philosophos*) in the *Metaphysics* (982b19).

If all Western philosophers seem to agree with Plato and with Aristotle that the beginning of philosophy is wonder before an aporia, a contradiction, a paradox, most of them tend to focus on philosophy's *end* as the solution of aporias, overcoming of contradictions, and suppression of wonder. The initial bewilderment and uneasiness before the object of inquiry is not supposed to persist in the advanced philosophical state, the state of *sophia* (wisdom or knowledge); it is to be replaced by the ease of understanding and familiarity with its object. The state of wonder before the world "out of joint" is to be transformed into an admiration before the "new wonderful world," a comprehensive world of natural or divine laws. Such a world is often an ideal realm set against the chaotic and unjust world of everyday experience.

Aristotle's understanding of the principle of amazement (*to thaumaston*) in his influential *Poetics* comes close to his general epistemological view. When analyzing the end (*telos*) of tragedy, which is to arouse pity and fear in order to achieve catharsis of these and similar emotions, Aristotle insists on the suppression of bewilderment and amazement. This statement comes just after his proclaiming tragedy more philosophical (*philosophōteron*) than history (*Poetics*, 1452a4, 1451b5). As in natural sciences, the end of tragic plot is admiration in the face of the triumph of the rational and just order of the universe.[6]

Brecht seems to agree with the founders of the classical tradition in philosophy and the theater when in *A Short Organon for the Theater*, he proclaims entertainment (*Unterhaltung*) the principle of his "philosophical" theater, and then locates the beginning of theatrical/philosophical pleasure in wonder. In order to be pleasurable, the epic theater must first of all "surprise its public" (*sein Publikum wundern machen*).[7] Moreover, Brecht seems to have in mind the Aristotelian kind of progress from initial amazement to rational scientific explanation when he talks of "the great Galileo," who observed with wonder (*verwundert*) the pendulum motion of a swinging chandelier. He was amazed "as if he had not expected it and could not understand its occurring, and this enabled him to come on the rules by which it was governed" (*ShO* 44). Would not the same characterization apply to the principle of amazement in Brecht's epic theater, which "must surprise its public" and which should lead to the wisdom that comes from the solution of problems (*die Weisheit, welche von der Lösung der Probleme kommt*) (*ShO* 24)? The purpose of Brecht's philosophical theater would thus be to uncover the rules of social life, to reveal the rational world beyond the contradictions, and eventually to suppress the initial amazement. If we add that Brecht seems to share with the author of the *Poetics* the view on the importance of plot (*muthos, Fabel*) in achieving amazement, we might conclude that the author of the non-Aristotelian drama is amazingly close to Aristotle.

In fact, such a rapprochement between the two authors of "*Organons*" would be overly simplified. Aristotle's *muthos* and Brecht's *Fabel* are not identical: the latter is always a "limited episode" (*begrenztes Geschehnis*) caught up in the complex play. The amazement of the epic theater should never change into an admiration before the beautiful order (*kosmos*) of the world but should rather bring into focus ever new contradictions, and thus remains what Althusser might call a "continual beginning." What radically distinguishes Brecht's theory of the theater from Aristotle's is this notion of a continual amazement stemming from the theatrical praxis, that is, the action of representation and its displacement. One might say briefly that if for Aristotle tragedy is "an imitation or representation of an action" (*mimēsis praxeōs*) (*Poetics*, 1449b24), for Brecht, the play is mainly an action of representation, a play of "workable representations" (*die praktikablen Abbildungen*) that is a praxis directed toward influencing society wholly and entirely as play (*ganz und gar als ein Spiel*) (*ShO* 24). Thus, the apparently limited technique of "a playlet within the play" (*ein Stückchen im Stück*) (*ShO* 67) is to become in a larger sense the general pattern of the epic theater.

The philosophical character of the epic theater does not conflict — as it is commonly assumed in Western Aristotelian tradition — with its being practical at the same time. Brecht's principle of *Verwunderung* refers neither to the purely theoretical puzzlement before the enigma nor to the satisfaction of its solution, neither to the intellectual bewilderment before the threat of chaos nor to the reassurance brought by the return of order. Amazement is "practical" all through; it has its origin in the observation of "people's behaviour and opinions" (*Verhalten und Meinen*) (16:815), it makes them "as strange as possible, thus as objective as possible" (*möglichst fremd, also möglichst objektiv*) (*GW* 15:220), and eventually it aims at their transformation. It is this focusing on the action of transforming behaviour and opinions that earns the epic theater the label "poetical" in the etymological sense of the word (from *poiein* — to make). Indeed, a productive attitude (*produktive Haltung*) (*ShO* 21) is the necessary counterpart of Brechtian amazement. Brecht's theater aims to generate a "po-etical," that is, productive and transformational attitude in the spectator ([*der Zuschauer*] *ist nicht mehr Konsument, sondern er muß produzieren*) (*GW* 15:222), and indirectly towards nature and society. To be sure, it is understanding and not cathartic *Einfühlung* (empathy) that should result from the epic play — not, however, a purely rational understanding de-void of feeling but a thoughtful passion for the transformation of the world, a "great passion for producing" (*große Leidenschaft des Produzie-rens*) (*ShO* 21):

> We need a type of theater which not only releases the feelings, insights and impulses possible within the particular historical field of human relations in which the action takes place, but employs and encourages those thoughts and feelings which help transform the field itself. (*ShO* 35)

Not a contemplative philosopher but an architect of irrigation dams, a fruit farmer, and a builder of vehicles are the models for the spectators of this theater. The epic theater should help them to develop a critical atti-tude (*kritische Haltung*) towards the existing social order with its illusion of coherence and necessity, and eventually to turn them into the "over-turners of society" (*Gesellschaftsumwälzer*) (*ShO* 22).

The critical attitude begins with the (hypo)critical acting of the Brechtian actor. Rather than playing a part, s/he should "display" a charac-ter (and her/his role in the social structure of the play), and thus frustrate any temptation of empathy (*Einfühlung*) on the side of the spectators. The latter should see "through" the characters, the conditions (*Zustände*), and relations (*Verhältnisse*) responsible for their prosperity or their plight. Pas-sion when directed against institutions of oppression is not free from sym-pathy (*Mitleid*).[8] It does not operate, however, through an identification with the traditional individual hero but rather in solidarity with the op-pressed (*mit dem Unterdrückten*), and it is mixed with anger (*Zorn*) (*ShO* 24). The latter — in itself a destructive emotion, hardly compatible with the principle of pleasure — functions as a powerful source of energy, as the beginning of what Brecht elsewhere calls a "revolutionizing effect" (*revolutionierende Wirkung*) (*GW* 15:212). In a dialogue with the play-wright Friedrich Wolf, Brecht passionately dismisses the slogan "Reason this side, Emotion that" and the opposition epic/dramatic — both some-times attributed to him — as simplistic. The epic theater

> by no means renounces emotion, least of all the sense of justice, the urge to freedom, and righteous anger; it is so far from renouncing these that it does not even assume their presence, but tries to arouse or to reinforce them. The "attitude of criticism" which it tries to awaken in its audience cannot be pas-sionate enough for it. (*BTh* 227)

These are, then, the end results of Brecht's *Verfremdung* as the counterpart of the philosophical amazement: the sympathy with the oppressed, the anger caused by the display of social conditions and the critical attitude towards system that guarantees these conditions, and finally the passion for its productive transformation. In accord with the eleventh thesis on Feuerbach, they allow the spectator to amplify the philosophical principle of amazement and to carry it over from the sphere of the pure theoretical contemplation to the sphere of practical and poetical/productive "acting."

The rapprochement between Marx's intervention in the history of philosophy and Brecht's intervention in the history of the theater is not arbitrary. The eleventh thesis on Feuerbach, condemning philosophy for its lack of concern for praxis — the active role in the transformation of the world — also played a crucial role in challenging the traditional relationship between philosophy and the theater — and precisely because of Brecht's intervention. Among other texts referring to the eleventh thesis, Brecht recognized the inspiration of his revolutionary theater in his notes to Erwin Strittmatter's play *Katzgraben*, by repeating almost *verbatim* the thesis: "The principle that I wanted to apply in theater is that one should not be satisfied with the interpretation of the world (*die Welt zu interpretieren*), one should change it (*verändern*)."[9] Thus, drawing a parallel between the "interpretive" attitude in philosophy and in the theater, Brecht displaces the terms of the traditional opposition between philosophy and the theater: not simply philosophy versus theater but rather the contemplative/philosophical mode of gazing at the world versus the practical/poetic — here theatrical — mode. And Brecht unequivocally sides with the theatrical practice against philosophy and the philosophical theater in the Aristotelian sense.

Let us rephrase our initial question: Is there a contradiction between Brecht's philosophical aspirations on the one hand and his implicit rebuff of the philosophical theater as merely interpreting the world, on the other? The Gramscian notion of a new "philosophy of praxis" has been applied in answering this question.[10] Its danger, according to Louis Althusser, is to posit a new principle — *praxis* — that tends to function in the same way as other supreme philosophical principles: Idea, Totality, Being, Transcendental Subject, Origin, Meaning, etc., and thus leads to another philosophy of Truth.[11] It is important, in Althusser's view of the relationship between philosophy and *praxis*, to maintain the position of the latter as independent from the former — as its other:

> *Praxis* is not a substitute for Truth of an indestructible philosophy: it is on the contrary what destroys philosophy; it is this other, which, in its entire history (under the form of errant cause or of class struggle), philosophy has never been able to subdue. (*Sph* 153)

"Philosophy of praxis," combining the two terms of the historical contradiction, would be a non-dialectical notion in danger of obliterating the actuality of the political and artistic struggle, comparable to the notion of philosophical tragedy in the Aristotelian and neoclassical tradition.[12] If

Brecht occupies an important place in the history of Western philosophy, it is not as a philosopher in the traditional sense of the word but, paradoxically — but the same paradox has been shown by Althusser to be that of Marx's and Lenin's impact on the history of philosophy[13] — as a "non-philosopher."

"*Les professeurs de philosophie ont tort,*" says Althusser, in "Sur Brecht et Marx" (*Épp* II 544f.). They are wrong, philosophy professors, in not taking advantage of the particular insight, the unique perspective which Brecht's theater is able to provide. To be sure, Brecht did not write a philosophical book, did not produce a coherent philosophical system; his discourse, even in his theoretical writings, is not strictly speaking philosophical, produced "as philosophy" ("*le produit de la philosophie comme philosophie*") (*Sph* 173). Still, philosophy professors are wrong to overlook these writings, and especially wrong not to pay attention to Brecht's theatrical practice — a paradigmatic case of resistance to the totalistic disposition of Western philosophy. The latter has been usually employed, according to Althusser, in the task of deferring all social practices to the regime of the dominant ideology.

The status of philosophy was discussed by Althusser and his collaborators[14] in the Fall of 1967 and the Spring of 1968, as part of the preparations for the publication of a collective work with the provisional title *Éléments de matérialisme dialectique*. A direct conversation followed by an exchange of letters was contemporary with the preparation of Althusser's conference paper "On Brecht and Marx" and the essay "Lenin and Philosophy."[15] The participants in the discussion concluded by crediting philosophy with a potentially revolutionary function of *rupture* as distinguished from the *coupure* of scientific practice (both usually translated into English as "break"). The latter break (*coupure*) should be understood as an opening of a field of inquiry beyond the realm of a particular ideology, i.e. beyond the circle of (mis)recognition. Such an opening leads necessarily to questioning a given ideology; it threatens its very basis: its obviousness. Philosophy is able to record (*enregistrer*) — and it usually does — a radical epistemological break as a *rupture* of the ideological continuity, a rupture between the theoretical and the ideological. The relationship of *rupture* to *coupure* is essential as it indicates the relationship of philosophy to a particular — ideally scientific — practice in Althusser's and his collaborators' view.[16] An epistemological break (*coupure*) usually precedes a philosophical break (*rupture*) and makes it necessary. In a later text, Althusser presents a case of a reverse relationship though: a philosophical rupture or revolution rendering possible an epistemological break. The case is well known: Marx's revolution in philosophy which, in disengaging itself from the bourgeois and petty-bourgeois ideology, allowed the inauguration of a materialist science of history, and eventually an actual, "material" revolution.[17] Philosophy has this revolutionary potential because it always records the tension between the material praxis and ideology even if it only in exceptional cases proclaims a radical break in the form of revolution.[18]

But can philosophy, a discipline devoted to the production of a world view, limit itself to recording the epistemological break (and the break in the ideological continuity) and leave the definite interpretation of this event open? The basic opposition of Marx's eleventh thesis on Feuerbach — mere interpretation versus transformation — would suggest such a possibility. In fact, it is not likely that a "pure" philosophical interpretation of the world would be possible at all. Brecht himself, who took the eleventh thesis on Feuerbach as his credo, doubted it. He did not understand it as a strict opposition between transformation and interpretation. The latter is rarely "pure," suggests Brecht's *Me-ti*. Most interpretations are in fact the justifications (*Rechtfertigungen*) of the existing world order and worldview.[19] Far from promoting a new *Weltanschauung* and *Weltordnung* they usually play the politically conservative role. They are not neutral interpretations but rather apologias for the status quo, just like the realist theater, which under its pretension to objectivity sacrifices in fact to "the god of the things such as they are" (*der Gott der Dinge, wie sie sind*) (*GW* 15:218). Another text is even more explicit in the direction of questioning the common understanding of the eleventh thesis: every interpretation has to face the possibility of transformation of the world in the form of the alternative: to encourage or to oppose it. In fact, thinking itself is always already practical: "Conditions and things, which are not to be changed by thinking (which do not depend on us) cannot be thought" (*GW* 20:155). Thought is here understood as directly and necessarily performative, as productive of real changes in conditions (*Zustände*) and things (*Dinge*). A pure philosophical contemplation is impossible. To assume the existence of such pure *theōria* is already tantamount to an act of endorsing the status quo, and it manifests either naiveté or bad faith.

Neither theater nor philosophy can just "contemplate," "watch" (*theas-thai, theōrein*) an economic, political or aesthetic development of society without taking a position in the struggle that underlies it, especially in a situation of crisis. In order to preserve the purity of speculation, such a *Weltanschauung* would have to find an impossible place beyond the world, a place modeled on the auditorium of the neoclassical and bourgeois theater.[20] According to Althusser, an outlook that would ignore the interpreter's position in the economic, social, and political conjuncture, that would disregard its own political position, is inconceivable in the situation of break (*coupure*), which always initiates a particular philosophical interpretation. Any claim to such purity of contemplation is a sham — a "denial" (*Verneinung, dénégation*) in Freud's terminology. "In fact, no philosophy is satisfied with the interpretation of the world," says Althusser, and "all philosophies are politically active, but most of them spend their energy in denying their political commitment" (*Épp* II, 547).[21] The latter consists in producing a coherent interpretation of the world that justifies it as the best possible world or at least a necessary one. Althusser calls such *Weltanschauung* a "philosophy of the 'interpretation' of the world" and "philosophy of *dénégation*" (*LPh* 66). Marx's intervention in the history of philosophy consisted precisely in dispelling the illusion of philosophy's autonomy. The thesis on Feuerbach is not so much an inversion of the classical opposition between contemplative philosophy and praxis as a questioning of the traditional tripartite division of human "activity" into *theōria*, *praxis*, and *poiēsis*.[22] In spite of the efforts of governments to keep philosophers in the lofty sphere of pure contemplation, in spite of the will of philosophers themselves, eager to obtain their tenure there, they must descend to the cave, or rather they should never let themselves be dragged out of it in the first place. Philosophizing, whether philosophers admit it or not, constitutes a political act. In the latter case it is an act of denial, contributing to the production of a dominant ideology; in the former it could be a conscious ideological act, a "theoretical praxis," a "class struggle on the level of theory."[23]

Brecht denounces the same kind of pretension to interpretive neutrality in realist theater when he points to the discovery of the "partiality of objectivity" (*die Parteilichkeit der Objektivität*) as the result of contemporary German — mainly Piscator's and his own — experiences in the theater (*GW* 15:225). It was the very structure of Western "philosophical" theater that guaranteed the theoretical, "speculative" objectivity of the spectacle. In this theater, the separation between imitation and its object (reality, *ta erga*, in Aristotle's words) played a role comparable to the separation between the world of Forms and the world of the things that participate in them, in Plato's metaphysics;[24] both accounted for the limited reality of the derived, actual world and for its imperfection. The verisimilitude of representation (*to eikos*, *verisimilitudo*, *vraisemblance*), at once true and not true, was guaranteed by the resemblance with the true model and the distinction from it. Aristotle's mimesis, e.g., simultaneously links and separates the two worlds. The events on the stage are necessary and plausible. The characters resemble us so as to provoke a dreamy *Einfühlung* or empathy (Brecht, *ShO* 26), but not a real identification (in the sense of Plato's mimesis). Although the theater world resembles our world, there is no danger of confusing the two (e.g., Aristotle, *Poetics*, 1448b9–12). A certain familiarity with the events on the stage does not preclude the transcendent, mytho-logical authority they exercise on the audience and hence the sense of their plausibility and necessity. Aristotle never tires of repeating that the events of the plot should follow from one another "probably or necessarily" (*kata to eikos ē to anankaion*) (*Poetics*, 1451a12–13, 1451a38, 1451b91452a24, and especially 1454a33-36). This phrase, which brings together natural necessity and rhetorical and theatrical verisimilitude, has a precise ideological function of rendering the existing social order as natural as nature itself.

The famous "necessity and verisimilitude" of the sequence of events are in fact the correlate of the ideological familiarization, of the "stamp of familiarity" (Stempel des Vertrauten) (ShO 43) that Brecht says marks the audience even before entering the theater. Every story (muthos), every retelling of the story reinforces this sense of mytho-logical order. As the principle of ideology, the story, the myth, the plot (muthos, Fabel) is no less important for Brecht than it is for Aristotle. And Brecht's emphatic agreement with the latter concerns also the necessity and probability of the central ideological plot. Except that this is only "half of the story." The other half — or rather another story — consists in the displacement of the episodes of the first so that they transcend the inert plot, appear unaccept-able and unnecessary in the ordinary ideological framework and thus in need of replacement in a new framework. It is the spectator that is made a producer of this new framework, that is, new plot: "[Der Zuschauer] ist nicht mehr Konsument, sondern er muß produzieren" (the spectator is no longer a consumer; s/he has to produce) (Brecht, GW 15:222).

In order to achieve the estrangement of the dominant plot another plot has to be woven "in the wings," as it were. In the Threepenny Opera, for instance, the impromptu arrival of the royal messenger as presented by Peachum would be only the mark of a bad plot — just as the flight of Medea mars Euripides's tragedy in Aristotle's opinion — were it not for Peachum's own "plot" to disturb the royal wedding, a plot further dis-placed by some readers of Brecht such as, for example, the producers of G. W. Pabst's film from 1931, into their own plot, namely Peachum's failure to contain the army of beggars on their way towards the center of power. As it is, Macheath's "unbelievable" peripeties become a foil to the difficult but plausible reversal caused by the army of the paupers involved in Peachum's enterprise and in his plot. However, the new revolutionary framework derives its plausibility from the dialectical relationship to the new alliance between Macheath and Peachum, destined to save the old order by channeling and turning to their advantage the new-discovered popular energy.

It is this open interpretation of each single action, each single episode through its possible involvement in different plots, (con)texts, in different ideological frameworks which constitutes the necessary counterpart of the intellectual mobility of the audience — a conditio sine qua non of their political mobility. Such an opening towards "practical action" — which would be a "poetic fault" in terms of the classical unity of action and of poetic justice — radically distinguishes Brecht's notion of emplotment from Aristotle's muthos. It also justifies the constant tendency, accentuated towards the end of Brecht's writing career and of his life, to call the kind of theater he promoted "dialectical."[25]

The relative strength of the concurrent frameworks is indeed essential for achieving a dialectical tension of a play, a tension that should reflect the reality. Brecht has never forfeited the claim made in the famous debate with Lukács that his notion of the theater and of art was truly realist. In *A Short Organon for the Theater*, for example, he states that the theater "has to become geared to reality if it is to be in a position to turn out effective representations of reality" (*ShO* 23), and he often points to the contradictory character (*Widersprüchlichkeit*) of reality as the principle of its changeability (cf. *ShO* 52). Moreover, Brecht explicitly refers to dialectical materialism as a method of "unearthing society's laws of motion" (*ShO* 45).[26] In the posthumously published revising notes to *A Short Organon*, Brecht reaffirms the realist claim of the theater ("The fact remains that the theater has to represent the world and that its representations must not mislead") (*GW* 16:707; *BTh* 279) and again associates this claim with the dialectical exigency. After quoting Lenin on the necessity of dialectics and in particular of the law of the unity of opposites for the explanation of the development of reality, he writes: "If Lenin's view is right, then [the representations of the world] cannot work out satisfactorily without knowledge of dialectics — and without making dialectics known" (*GW* 16:707; *BTh* 279). Dialectics, an ontological and epistemological theory, a principle of the development of reality and of knowledge, signifies also an autonomous method,[27] hence Jameson's "reduction" of Brecht's aesthetic theory to "method," modeled on Lukács's comparable "reduction" of Marxism to "method."[28]

However, such a method should be understood most broadly. In order to resist the reduction of dialectics to an exclusively aesthetic method, philosophically and politically independent, an effort must be made to keep it consciously within the framework of existing ideology, that is, the accepted "opinions of people." As Althusser points out, the materialist theater begins when the audience shares the same story or plot with the actors and characters: "*Nous partageons bien la même histoire — et c'est là que tout commence.*"[29] Brecht clearly affirms the necessity of such ideological situating in the last paragraph of his addendum to *A Short Organon*, when he lays aside the subjective and individualist forms of art: they have asocial effects (*asoziale Wirkungen*) as the counterpart of their ideological independence; they are out of touch with the (social) reality because they are out of touch with its ideology, with its social mythology. The epic or better dialectical theater should make dialectics known through "dialecticizing" (*Dialektisierung*) of this mythology in the form of the ideological plot (*muthos*). It was Manfred Wekwerth, one of Brecht's last interlocutors, who reported the term *dialektisieren* used by Brecht, a useful complement of the earlier and more common verb *episieren*.[30] Indeed, Brecht considered narrating a story in the epic theater and dialecticizing the events to be one and the same action. He said explicitly to Wekwerth in August 1956 that "[d]*as Erzählen einer Fabel auf der Bühne sei letztens Endes auch ein ‚Dialektisieren' der Vorgänge.*"[31] Thus the epic theater will have been dialectical from the very beginning.

It is significant that Brecht insists at the same time on the dialectical and dramatic character of his theater.[32] In the addendum to *A Short Organon* he admits that some statements of the latter might have given the impression that the concept of the epic was "too inflexibly opposed to the concept of the dramatic" (*GW* 16:701; *BTh* 276). The dialectical telling of a story on the stage combines the Brechtian notions of narrative, of character, and of drama. A narrator in the epic theater is an actor as well, and vice versa. A story should always be attached to a particular character as its representative and advocate, and thus submitted to a cross-examination in a juridical manner.[33] The trial structure is indeed a common feature of Brecht's theater. Even if Brechtian "heroes," like Mother Courage or Galileo, seem to accept their fate, the spectators are not supposed to do so; rather, they are supposed to act as a jury, that is, listen to the arguments and make up their mind. Instead of *representing* characters, as in the traditional theater, Brechtian actors *present* their cases, hence the technique of speaking in the third person and in the past tense (*GW* 15:344).[34] The traditional Platonic and Aristotelian distinction between diegesis (or narration) and mimesis and the Schillerian distinction between rhapsode and mime are transcended in the dramatic trial of the dialectical theater. An actor is a mime *and* a rhapsode, although not a rhapsode of the Ion type described by Plato (a rhapsode drowning the audience with tears and creating the famous magnetic chain of empathy). Nor should s/he be a totally uninvolved type of narrator/rhapsode mentioned by Schiller in his correspondence with Goethe.[35] Rather, a Brechtian actor should combine the two functions of impersonation and narration: "*In lebendiger Darstellung erzählt er die Geschichte seiner Figur*" (*ShO* 50).[36] An actor (*hupokritēs*) becomes thus a judge (*kritēs*) of her/his own character, and s/he transfers this power of judgment onto the spectator. If one can speak of identification in Brechtian theater, it would not be an empathy with a particular character on the stage but an identification with an actor as a "praxis-oriented" *judge* and *critic*.

The dialectics of the dramatic and of the epic marks the limits of the "autonomization" considered by Jameson the core of Brecht's method. Episodes, scenes, and actions cannot always be made autonomous, that is, arbitrarily transformed into *gestus*; plot cannot be "stretched out and sliced up like a sausage" (Jameson, *Brecht and Method* 51f.). On the contrary, the articulations between the episodes of the plot must be clearly registered: "the individual episodes have to be knotted together or linked (*verknüpft*) in such a way that the knots (*Knoten*) are easily noticed" (*ShO* 66). Knots are the bastions of an ideological *muthos* and cannot be outflanked but have to be confronted head-on. The transformability of the plot must be achieved *in spite of* its real strength, not because of its supposed weakness. The play *Roundheads and Peakheads*, for example, gives emphasis to this "in spite of" when it precedes the final reappearance of the revolutionary sign of the sickle by the toast of the viceroy to what *is*

(*"Trinkt, Freunde, trinkt! Auf daß da bleibt, was ist!"* — Drink, friends, drink! So that what is may continue!). The song of the landowners that follows the toast immediately questions "what is" politically and ideologically by exaggerating their forced, artificial "reality":

> Perhaps all men will praise and not defy.
> Perhaps the nights will trespass on the days.
> Perhaps the moon will cease to change its phase.
> Perhaps the rain will fall from earth to sky.[37]

Political transformation requires the recognition of both the strength and the artificiality (and hence fragility) of the "unnatural" ideological apparatus designed to preserve the *status quo* through the exact reproduction of the existing social structure. In order to achieve this recognition, the events on the stage of the epic theater must display a kind of "unnaturalness" (*etwas Unnatürliches*) and hence become open to action (*handelbar werden*) (*ShO* 40), that is to say, open to practical transformation.

An excellent means of rendering the events changeable consists in presenting the story (*historia, histoire*) as if it were historical (*historisch*), that is to say, as if it were already gone by, developed, transformed (*ShO* 37). Indeed, the best evidence of the transformability of the conditions is that they have already been transformed. Thus, Brecht recommends not only to stage the old plays as old plays — that is, without modernizing them, without making them appear modern, "humanly relevant," familiar — but also to stage the modern plays in the same historical mode:

> [I]f we stage plays dealing with our own time as though they were historical, then perhaps the circumstances under which [the spectator] himself acts will strike him as equally odd (*besonders*); and this is where the critical attitude begins. (*ShO* 37)

The sense of "particularity" results from the alienation of the present entering into a dialectical tension with other historical forces and disturbing the continuous, linear progression of the plot. The way Brecht historicizes drama in epic theater undermines in a sense the viability of "simple" epic theater. This leads to a more complex dialectical theater in which the *telos* of epic theater is retained and at the same time put into question. In this way, dialectical theater becomes the true beginning of the critique (*der Beginn der Kritik*). The abolition of bourgeois property laws, presented in the prologue to the *Caucasian Chalk Circle* and then reenacted by the judge Azdak in the play itself, is an excellent example of this procedure. It clearly refuses the solace of the Aristotelian *telos* of tragedy, i.e., catharsis, which stipulates rationality as the basic characteristic of the tragic world.[38] For Brecht, it is irrelevant whether the *ideal* world is good and rational or not; what is important is that the "conditions" of *this* world are insufficient (*unzulänglich*) and that they lead to injustice: "*Doch die Verhältnisse, sie sind nicht so*" (But the conditions are not such [as to allow for "human kindness"), sings Peachum in *Threepenny Opera*. Yet Brecht's world is not the Beckettian "endgame" world without meaning and without hope. The conditions might well be insufficient but they are changeable (*veränderbar*), and if there is a didactic dimension to the epic theater, it consists precisely in this display of the changeability of the material conditions of social life.

The opposition between narrative and mimetic mode and between epic and dramatic genre, introduced by Socrates in Plato's *Republic* and taken over by Aristotle in the *Poetics*, has become a commonplace of Western theory of literature. Brechtian theater undermines this opposition. Its being "epic" does not make it "non-dramatic." On the contrary, it presents a dramatized challenge of the most "epic" element of the theater, namely plot, as well as a mythologization of characters "dramatic" *par excellence*. Narrative plays a double role in Brecht's theater. As plot (*Fabel*), it is the principal *object* of estrangement. Through the actors' "recounting (*erzäh-len*) of their characters," narrative becomes a *means* of estranging their identity and of criticizing their conditions. Whereas for Aristotle plot is the *arkhē* in the full sense of the word, the beginning and the principle of tragedy, for Brecht, it is only a beginning. The genuine principle of epic/dialectical theater is *Verfremdung*, which provokes the sensation of "intellectual freedom and high mobility" directed toward the practical, political transformation of the world. More than any other aspect of Brecht's theater, this dialectical displacement of the plot marks its departure from the Aristotelian tradition of the Western theater and moves drama in the direction of praxis.

Brecht's eventual opting for the term "dialectical theater" reflects this displacement.[39] The resistance to the classical theater consists above all in the resistance to the principle of plot coherence, and it is paradoxically this resistance that renders the epic/dialectical theater philosophical in the sense of presenting an initial aporia. Since, however, Brecht's aporia always interrupts an ideological continuity, one has to accept, with Althusser, the continuous character of *Verfremdung*, which corresponds to the "eternal" character of ideology.[40] It is this notion of "continual wonder" that also accounts for the displacement effected by Brecht in the tradition of the philosophical theater. For Brecht, it is less a question of making theater philosophical or philosophy theatrical, than of thinking and performing the relationship between the two — the old debate between philosophy and theater — as the best way of affirming the continued actuality of the ideological struggle. If, in a sense, the epic/dialectical (non-) philosophical theater is more philosophical than philosophy, it is because it keeps wonder alive — a wonder supplemented by a political solidarity with the oppressed, by an anger against the ideology of the status quo, and by a passion for the transformation of the world.

NOTES

This essay is dedicated to the memory of Michael Sprinker, teacher and friend.

[1] "Brecht never tired, throughout his life, of directly relating theater to philosophy"; where not specified translations are mine.

[2] "The theater became an affair for philosophers, but only for such philosophers as wished not just to explain the world but also to change it" (Willett's translation).

[3] Bertolt Brecht, "Letzte Etappe: *Ödipus,*" in *Schriften zum Theater* 1, in *Gesammelte Werke* 15 (Frankfurt/M.: Suhrkamp Verlag, 1963): 184; English translation by John Willett, *Brecht on Theater* (New York: Hill and Wang, 1964), 24 [henceforth cited as *GW* and *BTh*, respectively]; cf. the program note for the 1928 Heidelberg production of the *Im Dickicht der Städte*: "This is a world and a kind of drama where the philosopher can find his way about better than the psychologist" (*GW* 16:67; *BTh* 24).

[4] "My theater (and it can hardly be held against me) is in a naïve sense a philosophical one." Brecht, *GW* 16:815; *BTh* 248; the relationship between the epic theater and philosophy is a constant theme in Brecht's writings: see, for example, "*Der Philosoph im Theater,*" in *GW* 15:252 ff.

[5] Walter Benjamin, *Understanding Brecht*, trans. Anna Bostock (London: New Left Books, 1973), 6 [henceforth *UB*].

[6] See, e.g., Jonathan Lear, "Katharsis," in Amélie Oksenberg Rorty, *Essays on Aristotle's Poetics* (Princeton, NJ: Princeton University Press, 1992), 315–40.

[7] *A Short Organon for the Theater* [henceforth cited as *ShO* plus paragraph] in (*GW* 16:682; *BTh* 192).

[8] On the combination of passion and critical distance in Brechtian tradition, see Eric Bentley, *The Brecht Commentaries* (New York: Grove Press, 1987), 56ff.; cf. Herbert Blau, *To All Appearances: Ideology and Performance* (New York Routledge, 1992), 143f.

[9] "[Es kommt] *nicht nur darauf an [...] die Welt zu interpretieren, sondern sie zu verändern.*" Brecht, „*Katzgraben*-Notate" (1953) in *GW* 16:815; cf. Karl Marx, "Thesen über Feuerbach" in Karl Marx, Friedrich Engels, *Werke* vol.3 (1932; Berlin: Dietz Verlag, 1969), 7: „*Die Philosophen haben die Welt nur verschieden interpretiert, es kömmt drauf an, sie zu verändern*"; another text of Brecht (an unpublished essay *Das epische Theater* from 1936) refers also to the eleventh thesis: "The theater became a matter for philosophers — for those who wished not only to explain (*erklären*) the world, but also to change (*ändern*) it." — *GW* 15:266; cf. also *ShO* 35.

[10] See, for example, Wolfgang Fritz Haug, *Philosophieren mit Brecht und Gramsci* (Berlin, Hamburg: Argument Verlag, 1996), especially chapter 2.

[11] See Louis Althusser, *Sur la philosophie* (Paris: Éditions Gallimard, 1994), [henceforth *Sph*] 144, 148ff.

[12] For Althusser's position see "Sur Brecht et Marx," in Louis Althusser, *Écrits philosophiques et politiques* vol. 2, ed. François Matheron (Paris: Stock/IMEC, 1995): 546 (hereafter quoted as *Épp* 2); and *Sph* 153, with an important change in the assessment of Gramsci's position in this matter.

[13] See, e.g., Althusser, "Lenin and Philosophy," in *Lenin and Philosophy and Other Essays* [henceforth *LPh*], trans. Ben Brewster (New York: Monthly Review Press, 1971), 31 *et passim*, and "La transformation de la philosophie" in *Sph* 162ff., especially 173–78.

[14] Pierre Macherey, Étienne Balibar, Alain Badiou, François Regnault, and Jean Savéant.

[15] Some of the documents concerning this event, mainly Althusser's reflexions, have been recently published; see "*Notes sur la philosophie* (1967–1968)" in *Épp* 2:299—48.

[16] The notion of *rupture épistémologique* (with an ideological discourse preceding the science) has been elaborated by François Regnault in an (unpublished) *Cours de philosophie pour scientifiques (1l)*; see *Épp* 2:344.

[17] See "Reply to John Lewis" in Louis Althusser, *Essays in Self-Criticism*, trans. Grahame Lock (London: New Left Books, 1976), 68 ff.

[18] Western philosophy itself has been constituted as such a break between the theoretical field of Plato's *epistēmē* and the field of *doxa* of the (democratic and Sophistic) ideologies (Pierre Macherey's example in *Épp* 2:310f.).

[19] „Ma-te fragte: Wird die Welt nicht schon dadurch verändert, dass sie erklärt wird? Me-Ti antwortete: Nein. Die meisten Erklärungen stellen Rechtfertigungen dar." (Ma-te asked: Is not the world already changed by its explanation? Me-ti answered: No; most explanations constitute justifications.) *GW* 12:549.

[20] Empathy in the traditional Aristotelian aesthetics is not socially determined.

[21] In "Lenin and Philosophy," Althusser registers the "theoretical denial (*dénégation théorique*) of [philosophy's] own practice, and enormous theoretical efforts to register this denial in consistent discourses (*dans des discours cohérents*). Althusser, *Lenin et la philosophie* (Paris: Maspero, 1969), 53, *LPh* 64.

[22] See also Étienne Balibar, *La philosophie de Marx* (Paris: La Decouverte, 1993), 15ff., especially 40–41, *The Philosophy of Marx*, trans. Chris Turner (London: Verso, 1995), 13ff., especially 40–41.

[23] See, e.g., Althusser, *For Marx*, trans. Ben Brewster (London: Verso, 1969), 165ff., and the interview with Maria Antonietta Macciocchi in *LPh* 18.

[24] Remarkably, Socrates identifies participation with imitation in Plato's *Phaedo*.

[25] See, e.g., Brecht's essay "[Notizen über] Die dialektische Dramatik" from 1931 in *GW* 15:211–25; on the development of Brecht's dialectic method, see especially Peter Brooker, *Bertolt Brecht: Dialectics, Poetry, Politics* (London: Croom Helm, 1988).

[26] On Brecht's debt to dialectical materialism, see in particular Brooker, *Bertolt Brecht: Dialectics, Poetry, Politics*, 27–29.

[27] It is this latter sense that Brecht seems to have in mind when associating dialectics with his theater. Indeed, the whole paragraph in the addenda to *A Short Organon* begins with the statement that "it is a matter of indifference whether the theater's main object is to provide the knowledge of the world."

[28] Fredric Jameson, *Brecht and Method* (London, Verso, 1998), 24ff.

[29] "We share the same story — and it is there that everything begins." Althusser, "Le 'Piccolo Teatro': Bertolazzi et Brecht" in *For Marx*, 150.

[30] Manfred Wekwerth, *Sinn und Form* (Berlin: Henschelverlag Kunst und Gesellschaft, 1957), Nos. 1–3.

[31] "Narrating a story on the stage will have been actually a 'dialecticizing' of the events as well."Manfred Wekwerth, *Schriften* (Berlin: Henschelverlag Kunst und Gesellschaft, 1973), 72; cf. *BTh* 282.

[32] See Brooker, *Bertolt Brecht: Dialectics, Poetry, Politics*, 33ff.

[33] See, e.g., Brecht, *GW* 15:345; cf. Mordecai Gorelik, *New Theaters for Old* (New York: Citadel Press, 1940), and Darko Suvin, *To Brecht and Beyond: Soundings in Modern Dramaturgy* (Sussex: The Harvester Press, 1984), 121.

[34] Cf. Timothy J. Wiles, *The Theater Event: Modern Theories of Performance* (Chicago: The University of Chicago Press, 1980), 72.

[35] See Schiller's letter to Goethe from 26 December 1797, quoted by Brecht in *A Short Organon* (50) and in the Foreword to his *Antigone* (*BTh* 210); cf. Martin Esslin, *Brecht: A Choice of Evils* (London: Methuen, 1959), 113f.

[36] "He narrates the story of his character by vivid portrayal" *BTh* 194.

[37] Bertolt Brecht, *Roundheads and Peakheads*, trans. N. Goold-Verschoyle in *Jungle of Cities and other Plays* (New York: Grove Press, 1966), 279–80.

[38] In the words of a recent reader of Aristotle's *Poetics*, the function of catharsis is to provide the consolation "that even when the breakdown of the primordial bonds occurs, it does not occur in a world which is in itself ultimately chaotic and meaningless." Lear, "Katharsis," in Oksenberg Rorty, *Essays on Aristotle's Poetics*, 334–35.

[39] A displacement that in fact occurred at the very beginning of his career: see Brecht's notes to the *Threepenny Opera* from 1931, and Willett's note on p. 46 in *BTh*.

[40] This practice of Verfremdung shows precisely "this other out of which one can not only unhinge philosophy but also begin to see [one might say *theasthai*] clearly in it." Althusser, *Sph* 153; cf. Balibar, *La Philosophie de Marx* 19ff., *The philosophy of Marx* 17ff.

Brechts Quellen für *Furcht und Elend des III. Reiches*: Heinrich Mann, persönliche Freunde, Zeitungsberichte

Bis zu diesem Zeitpunkt sind die Quellen, auf denen Brecht *Furcht und Elend* basierte, nie klar identifiziert worden. Dieser Aufsatz untersucht zwei von ihm mit großer Bestimmtheit benutzte Quellen und eine dritte, von der er Szenen des Alltags im Dritten Reiches herbeizog. Die erste Quelle, eine Serie von Minidramen, die Ende 1933 als ein Teil von Heinrich Manns Werk *Der Hass* erschienen, verschaffte ihm Situationen (z. B. in einem Konzentrationslager) und Themen (z. B. ein Rechtsanwalt, der zwischen den Anforderungen der Gerechtigkeit und den Drohungen der S. A. verstrickt ist), die in seinem Stück als spezifische Zustände und Konflikte wieder auftauchen. Eine zweite Quelle bezog sich auf „Die jüdische Frau." Die Darstellung ihres Dilemmas widerspiegelt genau, was mit Sadie Leviton, einer Freundin von Helene Weigel, geschah, die Brechts Freund aus Kindeszeiten, Otto Müllereisert — ein Arzt in Berlin—, heiratete, aber dann dazu gezwungen wurde, sich von ihm zu scheiden, weil sie Jüdin war. Die dritte Quelle besteht aus Zeitungsausschnitten über Geschehnisse in Nazideutschland, von denen Brecht nicht nur die spezifische Handlung in Szene 21 (Der alte Kämpfer) herbeizog, sondern auch den exakten Wortlaut des Schildes, das an dem toten Metzger, der in seiner Darstellung Selbstmord verübt hatte, umgehängt war. Diese Quellen weisen auf die Notwendigkeit hin, andere Materialien aufzuspüren, die als spezifische Inspiration für jede der Szenen im Stück dienten.

Brecht's Sources for *Furcht und Elend des III. Reiches*: Heinrich Mann, Personal Friends, Newspaper Accounts

James K. Lyon

Though scholars in recent decades have uncovered most of the sources Bertolt Brecht drew on to create his full-length dramatic works, one puzzle remains. To this point no one has clearly identified the material he used to write the series of scenes he published under the title *Furcht und Elend des III. Reiches*. The limited information about these sources is so general as to be almost meaningless.

In his *Brecht Handbuch* of 1980, for example, Jan Knopf notes only that "ab 1935 beginnt Brecht nach Augenzeugenberichten und Zeitungsnotizen kleine charakteristische Szenen auszuarbeiten,"[1] which eventuated in this play. And volume 4 of the *Grosse kommentierte Berliner und Frankfurter Ausgabe* published in 1988 adds only slightly more information. It states that:

> Ab 1934/34 stellt sich Brecht, unterstützt von Margarete Steffin, aus Pressemeldungen und Augenzeugenberichten Material über Alltagsereignisse in Hitler-Deutschland zusammen. In der Folgezeit entstehen einige Gedichte zu dieser Thematik. Die Materialsammlung und die Gedichte geben erste Anregungen für die Szenenfolge *Furcht und Elend des III. Reiches*.[2]

Regarding a writer who throughout his lifetime borrowed openly and took few pains to hide his sources, this paucity of information represents a marked contrast to the abundance of material known about the origins of his other plays. What follows is a first attempt to fill this lacuna by identifying some probable and known sources.

Among Heinrich Mann's extensive writings, few are less familiar to non-specialists than a book-length work published in late 1933 by Querido Verlag, Amsterdam under the title *Der Hass. Deutsche Zeitgeschichte*. Though this obscure work almost certainly served as one of Brecht's major sources, its connection to *Furcht und Elend*, which he wrote several years later, and which was first published in 1938, has escaped general attention. In this collection of twelve anti-Nazi essays, the individual titles reflect the bitterness of Mann's polemic against the hatred that he believed was the moving force behind Nazi ideology. The opening treatise under the superscript "Vor der Katastrophe" bears the title "Das Bekenntnis zum Übernationalen." The second grouping

New Essays on Brecht / Neue Versuche über Brecht
Maarten van Dijk et al., eds., *The Brecht Yearbook / Das Brecht-Jahrbuch*
Volume 26 (Toronto, Canada: The International Brecht Society, 2001)

under the general heading "Nachher" presents eleven more essays with the titles: "Auch eine Revolution;" "Der Hass;" "Der grosse Mann;" "Im Reich der Verkrachten;" "Goering zittert und schwitzt;" "Ihr ordinärer Antisemitismus;" "Wohin es führt;" "Die enttäuschten Verräter;" "Die sittliche Erziehung;" "Der sichere Krieg;" and "Die erniedrigte Intelligenz." More immediately relevant for *Furcht und Elend* is an appendix ("Anhang") entitled "Szenen aus dem Nazileben." It contains six dramatic scenes written by Mann that deal with daily life in Nazi Germany. Their titles are: 1. "Auf der Strasse;" 2. "Im Konzentrationslager;" 3. "Die Vermissten;" 4. "Man muss sich zu helfen wissen;" 5. "Hitler bei Hindenburgh;" and 6. "Der Zeuge." It appears almost certain that these short dramatic portrayals gave Brecht the idea for his own play and, besides serving as a general model, provided him with situations and themes for specific scenes in *Furcht und Elend*.

There is no question that at the very least, the playwright knew of Mann's book and its general contents. Soon after it appeared in late 1933, Brecht, who was living in a Paris hotel at the time, met with Walter Benjamin, Siegfried Kracauer, André Germain, Klaus Mann, and Hermann Kesten on November 12, 1933 in the restaurant "Deux Magots." According to Klaus Mann's journal entry of that date, they heard Kesten read aloud a review he had written of Mann's recently published work.[3] Brecht also might have learned more about it from other sources he was reading at the time. Within the next three months, reviews of Mann's *Der Hass* by Lion Feuchtwanger, Heinrich Fischer, and Ernst Ottwalt appeared in *Das neue Tagebuch, Die neue Weltbühne, and Neue deutsche Blätter* respectively,[4] journals Brecht is known to have read regularly while in Danish exile.[5] From this it is clear that *Der Hass* was well known and no doubt discussed among exiled German artists and intellectuals. While there is no absolute proof that Brecht read it, I would argue that his voracious reading habits, coupled with his interest in all types of anti-Fascist literary expressions being written by friends and colleagues in exile, as well as his presence at Kesten's reading of his review of the work, suggest the strong possibility that he did in fact read it. Since it was common practice among financially strapped exiles to borrow and lend books to each other that one of their number had recently published, it is no stretch of the imagination to assume that at the very least he obtained a copy of it from one of his friends.[6]

The most compelling argument for Brecht's familiarity with it derives from similarities and correspondences between Mann's six scenes and his own *Furcht und Elend des III. Reiches*. Here circumstantial evidence seems too strong to be coincidental. Beyond Mann's title for his scenes "Szenen aus dem Nazileben," which describes precisely what Brecht was trying to represent in *Furcht und Elend*, other resemblances are conspicuous. Both works, for example, portray inmates in a concentration camp — Mann in the scene entitled "Im Konzentrations- lager," which consists of three separate sub-scenes, and Brecht in the scenes "Dienst am Volke" (scene 4), "Die Internationale"(scene 14), and "Moorsoldaten" (Anhang), each of which is also located in a con- centration camp. In the latter scene, Brecht reproduces a situation which, in its dramatic conflict, is identical to one of Mann's scenes. In each, inmates who had been enemies in their pre-internment days refuse to unite against their Nazi oppressors. Instead, they carry old hostilities into the concentration camp. In each the scene ends when the bickering between the former foes results in punishment by the SS man guarding them.

The second of two further sub-scenes from Mann's "Im Konzentra- tionslager" shows a banker who is confronted by a former employee, now his guard and tormenter in the concentration camp, who was dismissed from his bank for incompetence. The guard announces his revenge by informing the banker that he will not leave the camp alive. The third sub-scene contains a dialogue similar in its essential elements to that reproduced in Brecht's scene "Zwei Bäcker" (scene 19). In Mann's dramatization, one women asks the other why she is in the camp. The second, who operated a house of prostitution before 1933 and is designated as a "Sadistin," replies that after being picked up on suspicion of her occupation, the SA took her to a police station and inadvertently led her down a wrong corridor, where she saw photos of horribly mutilated people. She then states that she is interned not be- cause she saw them, but because despite the sadistic practices to which her occupation exposed her, she almost fainted when she saw these unspeakable photos. In short, her knowledge of and inability to tolerate Nazi brutality made her a security risk, and they interned her.

In Brecht's "Zwei Bäcker" (scene 19), two inmates (in a Third Reich prison rather than a concentration camp) repeat the same question that one woman asked the other in Mann's dialogue, viz. why the other person is there. In an irony as bitter as that in the final episode of Mann's concentration camp scene, each answers that it was for failure to conform to the expectations of the new state. Their responses de- scribe a crime as absurd as that of the sadistic madam who could not bear the sight of mutilation — the one baker had mixed potatoes and bran into his bread dough when it was forbidden, the other had not mixed it in after the State began requiring it of bakers.

Another structural and thematic similarity emerges from Mann's scene called "Der Zeuge." Like the scene "Rechtsfindung"(scene 5) in Brecht's *Furcht und Elend*, it involves a judge caught in the impossible dilemma of administering justice in the Third Reich. An accused young Communist testifies before this judge about the shooting death of a policeman and an SA man in a pub where a group of Communists were seated. He describes how the policeman blocked the doorway against Brownshirts who were trying to enter. Denying the charges that the Communists inside the pub killed the two, the young man notes that the policeman was shot in the heart from the front — clearly by the SA men who were trying to get past him — and that the SA man —an extremely unpopular figure among his colleagues — was shot in the back – clearly by his own Brownshirts — as he tried to enter. The judge, terrified by the Stormtroopers singing the Horst Wessel song outside his chambers, tries to persuade the young man to testify that the Communists in the pub caused the two deaths and implies that he will received a mild sentence. But his plea "Ich möchte Sie retten. Helfen Sie mir!" fails to change the young man's version of what happened, and the judge's assessor — obviously a fanatic Nazi — says that it is now too late for the witness and the judge, since the latter's attempt to help save the young man makes him, too, an enemy of the state.

Though the other four of Mann's six scenes do not resemble or duplicate situations in Brecht's Furcht und Elend as closely as these do, at least one in Mann's series anticipates and coincides in part with a theme Brecht treats in "Die jüdische Frau" (scene 8). In a reception set in the palace of Hermann Goering, president of the Reichstag, part of the scene "Man muß sich zu helfen wissen" includes a conversation between Pfitzner, president of the Prussian Academy of Arts, and one of its members, Belling. Pfitzner insists that the latter resign from the Academy, since Belling is married to a Jewess ("Durch meine Ehe bin ich verjudet," Belling laments). In the conversation, one learns that Pfitzner himself became the conductor of the Städtische Oper as the replacement for a Marxist Jew who had been forced out. Four years after Mann wrote this scene dramatizing the effects of being married to a Jewish wife, Brecht's "Die jüdische Frau" brilliantly captures the dilemma of a Jewish woman married to an Aryan man from the perspective of the woman whose husband was beginning to feel the detrimental effects of their marriage in his professional life.

One other scene among Mann's mini-dramatizations of life in the Third Reich —"Hitler bei Hindenburg" — adds a small piece of circumstantial evidence to the claim that Brecht knew and borrowed from this obscure work. As the title suggests, Mann's scene — written shortly after the actual historical event in 1933 — dramatizes the meeting between Hindenburg and the newly-elected Chancellor of Germany. In several points it anticipates a scene in Brecht's Arturo Ui, a work he conceived in 1934 but did not complete as a drama until 1941. In it the title character — a thinly veiled version of Hitler —meets with Dogsborough — a transparent caricature of Hindenburg. In both Brecht's and Mann's dramatic renderings, Hindenburg's and Dogsborough's son Oskar is present; in both versions the father and son express contempt for Hitler's boorishness and alarm at his brutal use of force to gain his ends; and in both, Hitler and Ui force the father and son to lend the feeble old man's good name to his cause by threatening to expose the father's involvement in a huge financial scandal.

Though the evidence here, too, is circumstantial, and though there are significant differences in Mann's other one-acters — for example, he satirizes and caricatures Nazi big-wigs and makes them appear grotesque, while Brecht, at least in *Furcht und Elend,* never portrays them — the sum of similarities, duplications of situations, and thematic overlaps make a strong case for the appended dramatizations of "Szenen aus dem Nazileben" in Heinrich Mann's *Der Hass* as being one of the sources from which Brecht borrowed general ideas and specific motifs and situations for his play *Furcht und Elend.*

Another apparent source for this play surfaced late in 1999 with the publication of Klaus Völker's book *"Ich verreise auf einige Zeit". Sadie Leviton. Schauspielerin, Emigrantin, Freundin von Helene Weigel und Bertolt Brecht.*[7] Though it is known that Brecht consciously sought out information about daily life in the Third Reich from friends and acquaintances who visited him in Denmark, until the appearance of Völker's book nothing was known about the specific source for his piece "Die jüdische Frau" (scene 8). Völker makes a compelling case that Sadie Leviton, a Jewish friend of Helene Weigel's from the 1920s, was Brecht's model for this scene. Indeed, events from her life in Berlin after the Nazis came to power duplicate some basic features of his brief but powerful dramatic portrayal of a marriage that is undermined by official anti-Semitism.

The unidentified Jewish wife in Brecht's play is married to a physician. In real life Sadie Leviton in 1932 had married one of Brecht's closest friends from his youth in Augsburg, Otto Müllereisert, who by this time was a physician in Berlin. After Hitler's ascent to power and the introduction of state-sponsored anti-Semitism, it would have been strange indeed if Brecht had not known of or grasped the conflict that this marriage of an Aryan friend to a Jewish woman in the Third Reich engendered, and it is easy to imagine that he and Helene Weigel spoke with Sadie or her husband about it. Like Brecht's Jewish wife, they, too, had friends with whom they played bridge each week, and they, too, found these friends growing increasingly distant without articulating the reasons for their coolness. In Brecht's dramatization, the Jewish wife realizes that by staying married to her husband, she is also jeopardizing his medical career, which in turn motivates her to flee. But she also lies to herself, her friends, and her husband by saying she will not be gone for long ("ich verreise auf einige Zeit," GBA 4:385–86), a lie her husband echoes by acknowledging that it will be only for a few weeks ("schliesslich sind es nur ein paar Wochen," GBA 4:390).

In her own life, Sadie Leviton concluded soon after the Nazis came to power that staying married to her husband would embarrass him and ultimately spell the end of his medical career. To avoid this, she divorced him in November, 1933, though Müllereisert did not want the divorce and asked her to remain. She then went into exile — first to Denmark, where she stayed with the Brecht's, then to Argentina. Like Brecht's Jewish wife, Leviton tells her husband and her mother that she is not leaving permanently. While the playwright added details he doubtless heard from others or created from his own imagination, it now appears, according to the information provided by Völker, that the substance of this scene, like others in *Furcht und Elend*, was drawn directly, though inevitably modified, from real-life events in the lives of these friends. One can only speculate on what she discussed with the Brechts in Denmark, but it is probably safe to assume that from her the playwright had an abundant source of first-hand information for his creation of the "Jewish wife" scene in this play.

As a third source for *Furcht und Elend*, Brecht drew on general and specific information from newspapers that reached him in Danish exile. A voracious newspaper reader, he saved literally hundreds of articles about daily life in the Third Reich. From the vast number preserved in at least ten different folders in the Brecht-Archives,[8] it is evident that he had access to an unusually high number of newspapers or newspaper articles —some of them from a clipping service — published both inside Germany and in other countries. From within the Third Reich he saved articles from the *Völkischer Beobachter; Der Stürmer; Berliner 12-Uhr Blatt; Berliner Tageblatt; BZ am Mittag; Berliner Börsen-Zeitung; Berliner Volkszeitung; Hamburger Fremdenblatt; Der Heidelberger Student; National Zeitung; Deutsche Zentral-Zeitung;* and the *Frankfurter Zeitung.* Further, he collected articles from various German-language newspapers published outside the country. They included the *Neue Zürcher Zeitung; Neues Wiener Tageblatt; Der Bund* (Switzerland); *Der Blitz* (Vienna); *Wiener Montagblatt;* and the exile newspapers *Deutsche Freiheit* published in Paris and the *Deutsche Zentral-Zeitung* published on Moscow, all of which reported extensively on life within Nazi Germany. Additionally, he kept numerous articles from American, British, French, and Danish-language newspapers, among them the *London Times* and the Danish newspaper *Politiken.* Notations confirm that some of the American, English, and French articles came from a clipping service. Others no doubt originated with friends and acquaintances inside and outside Germany. Taken together, they reveal the playwright's keen interest in what was happening in his homeland.

The array of topics in these articles ranges from major political happenings at a state level to mundane incidents from daily life. One entire folder (BBA 302) contains clippings from English, French, and German-language newspapers on the trial of the alleged perpetrator of the Reichstag fire. Several articles report on the murder of Horst Wessel and the trials of his two assailants. A single article describes the assas-

sination of Ernst Röhm and the Night of the Long Knives. In additional
ones he found information on subversive actions by the common people in Germany, such as a note posted on a bulletin board in a Berlin-
Wilmersdorf artists' colony that the police quickly removed because of
its treasonable content. It read: "Tausche wenig gebrauchte Fahne für
ein Viertelpfund Butter." An Associated Press article that caught his
attention cites the *Verbandsorgan der deutschen Polizisten* and its recently announced list of "crimes against the state" in Nazi Germany,
which included derogatory jokes about the government; failure to raise
the right arm in the "Hitlergruss" when the Horst Wessel Lied was
sung; spreading false rumors; positive descriptions of life in the Sowjet
Union; negative remarks about Nazi leaders; and attempted suicide. As
justification for criminalizing this final subversive act, it noted that
attempted suicide "wastes the human material of the nation" ("weil sie
[Selbstmordversuche] das Menschenmaterial der Nation vergeuden").

Anti-Semitism reported in the daily press also caught Brecht's attention, as reflected in various articles he saved, including one entitled
"Der ewige Jude," which published photos of six "hebräische Unter-
menschen," or an account of a "Volksfest" in Wels from another paper
which took it as an occasion to reproduce an anti-Semitic poster. A
further article from the "Jüdische Presseagentur" of December 28,1935,
reports on the first "racial purity" trial of an Aryan in Berlin who had
had sexual relations with a Jewish woman. Until then, it states, the
Nuremberg Laws had been directed only against Jewish men who con-
sorted with Aryan women.

In a significant number of articles, Brecht read of the mass arrests,
internment in concentrations camps, torture, and death of innocent
victims — usually workers — and of those who openly resisted. An
undated one, apparently from 1933 or 1934, names well-known figures
who had been sent to the Oranienburg concentration camp. Yet another describes the mass arrest of workers in Saxony and Thuringia, all
of whom were sent to the concentration camp Schloss Osterstein. And
an undated article from the Moscow-based German-language newspaper *Deutsche Zentral-Zeitung* — probably May, 1935 —describes in
lurid detail under the heading "Massenverhaftungen und Morde in
Nazi-Deutschland" how working class resisters were arrested and tor-
tured to death by the Gestapo.

While none of the articles described to this point appears to have
provided specific material for *Furcht und Elend,* one clipping does
contain dramatic elements that might have served as the model for one
of the central motifs in his scenes from daily life in the Third Reich —
the dissatisfaction with and oppositional attitude of large segments of
the population toward the Nazi regime, a concept Brecht thematized
repeatedly in *Furcht und Elend.* One unidentified newspaper clipping
in his collection contains a fictitious monologue written by Ernst

Ottwalt entitled "Friseur Zenker halt Monolog." In it, an obviously prosperous owner of a barber shop unburdens himself to a Herr Hegemeister, whose hair he is cutting. In the same breath that he expresses support for Hitler, he complains that high taxes are ruining his business and raises questions that in Nazi Germany were disloyal at best, and treasonable at worst. Though couched in ambivalence, his comments make it clear that Hitler's policies do not support the small business man. Precisely this kind of equivocal speech in support of the government over a layer of underlying dissatisfaction is typical of the discourse used by various figures in *Furcht und Elend* one thinks of the father in the scene "Der Spitzel" (scene 9), or the two scientists in "Die Physiker" (scene 7) And in this small clipping, Brecht also read about an abbreviated form of the "Hitlergruss" — perhaps for the first time — that recurs in his own play *Schweyk im Zweiten Weltkrieg* — the contraction "Heitler' for "Heil Hitler."

A second newspaper article that Brecht read and saved appears to be a stronger candidate for the source of a specific scene in *Furcht und Elend* than any of those mentioned so far. Taken from the Berlin newspaper *12 Uhr Blatt* of February 7, 1933, it might have come to his attention while he was still in Germany (he did not flee until three weeks after it appeared). Reporting on shootings in Berlin-Charlottenburg at 1:30 am. of the same morning, the account describes how a group of six S.A. men — "an ihren Parteiuniformen erkenntlich" — were standing on a street corner. Suddenly one who was wearing a military overcoat left to follow two young men who were headed for a local pub on the Galvanistrasse known to be frequented by Communists. Just before reaching the pub, the Brownshirt pulled out a revolver and, without warning, shot one of them in the stomach. The young man's companion tried to stop the gunman, who then fired five more times at him, but only grazed his head. At this point the S.A man fled in a taxi.

Though it differs in a number of details, it is possible nevertheless that this real-life account well might have given Brecht the idea for the opening scene in *Furcht und Elend* entitled "Volksgemeinschaft." It, too, takes place immediately after Hitler's election as Reich Chancellor, and it, too, happens at night in Berlin where two drunken SS men are staggering down a street and reveling in their new-found power. It, too, portrays one of the Nazis as being armed with a revolver and as shooting indiscriminately against those he supposes to be Communists. Though there is no absolute proof that this newspaper report was the basis for Brecht's scene, which is more tightly constructed and dramatically focused than the version given in the press, his dramatization nevertheless reproduces a real-life situation in Nazi Germany that he found reported at least this once in a newspaper that had not yet come under state control. From this one can adduce that here and elsewhere he probably did not invent the basic situations in *Furcht und Elend*.

They sound authentic because, for the most part, they appear to have had been based on actual events.

The relationship between the two aforementioned articles and scenes in *Furcht und Elend* is based on conjectures about general similarities. But a third article found among his collected newspaper clippings offers indisputable proof that Brecht knew and used it as the basis for the scene entitled " Der alte Kampfer" (scene 21) in *Furcht und Elend*. In this case he constructs his dramatization around and borrows literal wording from two episodes he read in a newspaper story found in the Brecht Archives in folder 470/10.

In this scene, which takes place early in the morning on the sidewalk in front of a butcher shop and a dairy products shop, one woman explains to another that again there is no butter to be had, but she is deterred from further criticism of the government by the presence of a rabid young Nazi. The dairy products shop owner appears and, referring to the butcher shop next door, relates how the butcher's son was picked up the night before (presumably by the police or the Gestapo) because his father recently created a public furor when he refused to hang cardboard maché reproductions of meat in his shop window as the government demanded of him. The butcher, himself an "alter Kampfer" who had been in the party since 1929, was incensed that he was being asked to deceive his customers about the meat shortage. He would rather leave his display window empty. Fortunately he was out of town the previous night, or he, too, would have been picked up. The butcher's wife joins the other women in front of the shops and pretends not to know that her son has been picked up. But when a light goes on, they turn to look at the butcher shop and see that something is in fact hanging in the display window. It is the butcher who has hanged himself and now wears a sign saying, "ICH HABE HITLER GEWÄHLT."

In an unidentified newspaper report that repeated stories gathered from German-language newspapers, Brecht read two accounts that provided the unmistakable raw material for this scene. The common elements in both are men who hang themselves (one a butcher) in their shop windows and make a demonstrative statement against the government with signs that specifically name Hitler as the cause of their suicide. The two accounts, which are compiled in a single article, read:

> Der Prager „Gegenangriff" berichtet: "Vor einigen Tagen machten einige Bewohner von Altona, die zeitlich morgens die Strasse betraten, eine grausige Entdeckung. Im Schaufenster eines Fleischerladens hing die Leiche des Besitzers. Der kleine Gewerbetreibende glaubte, die unerträgliche Lage, in die er durch die Fleischnot geraten war, nur durch Selbstmord beenden zu können. Aber in seiner grenzenlosen Verzweiflung benutzte er diesen Selbstmord zu einer grausigen Demonstration: Die Leiche war mit einem deutlich lesbaren Zettel versehen auf dem die Worte geschrieben standen: **Fleisch für Hitler.**"

Das erschütterndste an diesem Vorkommnis ist die Tatsache, daß dieser einzigartige Vorfall eine Wiederholung fand. Ein anderer Kleinhändler in Barnbeck erhangte sich bald darauf, ebenfalls im Schaufenster seines Ladens. Er brachte an seinem Körper eine Inschrift an, die womöglich noch aufpeitschender ist als die andere. Er schrieb einfach: **Ich habe Hitler gewählt.**

Brecht's dramatic scene conflates these two episodes into a powerful single event. In his version the man who hangs himself is the butcher mentioned in the first episode. Brecht also appropriates the man's motive for suicide from the first episode — despair at lack of meat to sell in his butcher shop. From the second episode, which describes the victim only as a small business man who hanged himself in his shop window (no specific occupation is given), his dramatization cites verbatim the bold-faced words that appear on the inscription which he attached to his clothes: "**ich habe Hitler gewählt.**" While the final words of the sign on the butcher's body ("Fleisch für Hitler") might have been more appropriate for the occupation of a butcher, Brecht gives added power to the second phrase by making the butcher in his scene an "old fighter' ("alter Kämpfer'), a veteran member of the Nazi party since 1929. Since neither of the two episodes reported in his source mentions anything about the victims' political affiliation, it appears that the dramatist took this creative liberty to underscore the deep disillusionment with Hitler's policies that he believed was widespread among all classes and political persuasions in Nazi Germany, and that he believed would eventually lead to the overthrow of the regime.

In addition to works described above, Brecht undoubtedly drew on additional material in writing *Furcht und Elend* that has yet to be identified. Some of it might have originated in oral reports from friends or acquaintances whom he met during his Danish exile or his travels in Europe and America between 1933-38, in which case there would be no written record. But given his practice of generous borrowing from or basing his other dramas on written material, it seems logical to assume that in addition to Heinrich Mann's *Der Hass*, biographical data from Sadie Leviton's life, and the many newspaper articles he read, there are other sources yet to be discovered before the material basis for *Furcht und Elend* has been clearly and fully established.

NOTES

[1] Jan Knopf, *Brecht Handbuch. Theater. Eine Ästhetik der Widersprüche* (Stuttgart: Metzler, 1980), 144.

[2] Bertolt Brecht, *Grosse kommentierte Berliner und Frankfurter Ausgabe. Stücke 4* (Berlin: Aufbau and Frankfurt/M: Suhrkamp, 1988), 523. Hereafter abbreviated as GBA, followed by the volume and page number.

[3] Klaus Mann, diary entry of 12 November 1933, *Tagebücher 1931–1933.* Ed. Joachim Heimannsberg, et al. (Munich:edition spangenberg, 1989), 321.

[4] Lion Feuchtwanger, *Das neue Tagebuch* 22 (Paris, Amsterdam, 1933): 526–27. Heinrich Fischer, "Der Hass," *Die neue Weltbühne* 47 (Prague, 1933): 1478–81. Ernst Ottwalt, *"Das gute Beispiel." Heinrich Mann "Der Hass. Deutsche Zeitgeschichte."* Lion Feuchtwanger, *Die Geschwister Oppenheimer. Roman* (Querido Verlag, Amsterdam), in *Neue deutsche Blätter* 1 (Prag, Wien, Zurich, Paris, Amsterdam [1933–34]): 373–79.

[5] Brecht's library held by the Bertolt Brecht Archives includes one copy of *Neue Deutsche Blätter* from August, 1935 and several issues of *Die neue Weltbühne* between 1937–39.

[6] Though no copy of Mann's *Der Hass* exists in Brecht's posthumous library, this does not constitute an argument against his knowing it. Dozens of books he is known to have read did not make it through his exile years.

[7] Berlin: Transit, 1999.

[8] Articles are found in Bertolt Brecht Archive, files no. 302; 387; 390; 391; 470; 474; 560; 1151; 1211; and 1387.

"Brecht is Being Spat on Here," or
"*Kim*: Could Not Be Identified."
The Scandalous Commentary on Brecht's Letters

Using the *Große kommentierte Berliner und Frankfurter Ausgabe* of Brecht's works, the author analyzes the commentary on the letters that Brecht wrote in exile between 1933 and 1948. Producing symptomatic examples, he shows that the commentaries are frequently inexact, misleading, or wrong, and that in other cases annotations are missing completely. Serious mistakes from the 1981 East Berlin edition of Brecht's letters were simply repeated, and commentaries from other editions of the letters were copied without fact-checking or even citation of sources. Many of Brecht's allusions are not recognized as such and therefore not decoded. Even with respect to personalities of world politics, names and facts are occasionally mistaken. Historical events are sometimes dated incorrectly and interpreted in a bizarre way. Such inadequacies could easily have been avoided by using authoritative secondary literature and by consulting reference works.

Hier wird Brecht gespuckt oder „*Kim*: konnte nicht ermittelt werden." Die skandalöse Kommentierung von Brechts Briefen

Hans-Albert Walter

Die im vergangenen Jahr abgeschlossene *Große kommentierte Berliner und Frankfurter Ausgabe* von Brechts Werken ist wohl für absehbare Zeit das sozusagen „letzte Wort" der Brecht-Edition. Das bestimmt auch das Maß der Erwartungen, mit denen man insbesondere da an ihre Kommentare herantritt, wo sie neue Quellen begleiten und erschließen sollen; also beispielsweise in den drei Brief-bänden, die 1998 an die Stelle der einbändigen Ausgabe von 1981 traten. Diese alte Edition enthielt rund 900 Briefe und war von Günter Glaeser verantwortet worden, einem Mitarbeiter des Berliner Brecht-Archivs. Die neue Ausgabe bringt fast 2400 Briefe und wurde wiederum von Glaeser betreut, diesmal unter Mitarbeit von Wolfgang Jeske und Paul-Gerhard Wenzlaff.

Wie sind sie mit ihrer komplexen Materie umgegangen? Wie mit einem Briefschreiber, der, man weiß es, dem schriftlichen Austausch den mündlichen entschieden vorzog, und dessen Briefen man das auch anmerkt? Tatsächlich sind Brechts Briefe meist ein (oft nur mäßig stilisierter) Gesprächsersatz. Nicht für die Nachwelt bestimmt, sondern einzig für den Empfänger, behandeln sie Dinge von gemeinsamem Interesse, so dass Brecht ohne lange Vorrede gleich zu dem kommen konnte, worüber der Adressat genauso Bescheid wusste, wie er selbst. Dies lakonische medias in res macht für Außenstehende vieles kryptisch.

Wie etwa sollen sie verstehen, was Brecht im Sommer 1935 aus dem dänischen Svendborg an seinen nach London emigrierten „marxis-tischen Lehrer" Karl Korsch schrieb? „Abends glauben wir immer Tritte zu hören, das müssen Sie sein. Aber Sie sind es nicht. Auch uns erweist sich Old Merry England als unsicherer Verbündeter!" Dazu muss man wissen, dass Korsch aus England ausgewiesen werden sollte, weil ihn

New Essays on Brecht / Neue Versuche über Brecht
Maarten van Dijk et al., eds., *The Brecht Yearbook / Das Brecht-Jahrbuch*
Volume 26 (Toronto, Canada: The International Brecht Society, 2001)

jemand als Naziagenten denunziert hatte. Brecht hatte ihn eingeladen und wartete ungeduldig auf den, für den sich England als „unsicherer Verbündeter" erwiesen hatte. Das war England inzwischen aber nicht bloß für Korsch. Kurz zuvor hatte es ein Flottenabkommen mit dem Dritten Reich geschlossen und so der bis dahin illegalen deutschen Aufrüstung den Segen gegeben — zur großen Ernüchterung von Brecht. Weshalb der Korsch gewissermaßen zu trösten suchte: *„Auch uns erweist sich Old Merry England als unsicherer Verbündeter."*

Womöglich noch geheimnisvoller wirkt die beiläufige Frage, die Brecht im Mai 1937 seinem Freunde Lion Feuchtwanger stellte: „Übrigens: wieso loben Sie den Schönherr?" Der Naturalist Karl Schönherr war nach 1900 mit erdverbundenen Dramen und Erzählungen aus dem Tiroler Bauernleben bekannt geworden, doch warum hätte Feuchtwanger diesen fast Vergessenen noch 1937 loben sollen? Er hatte nicht einmal über ihn geschrieben. Sehr wohl aber hatte er jüngst ein erdverbundenes Bauerndrama von Julius Hay gerühmt, das Schauspiel *Haben*. Der im Moskauer Exil lebende Naturalist Hay gehörte zur Clique um Georg Lukács, die dem „Avantgardisten" Brecht zu schaden suchte, wo sie nur konnte. Mit dem Hymnus auf Hay hatte Feuchtwanger seinen Freund Brecht somit peinlich bloßgestellt. Überdies wollte er die Rezension im *Wort* veröffentlichen, der Zeitschrift, die er, Brecht und Willi Bredel gemeinsam herausgaben. Brecht hätte das mit einem Veto verhindern können, doch darauf hat er — aus vermutlich wohlerwogenen Gründen — verzichtet. Er begnügte sich mit einem Nasenstüber, einer provozierenden Frage, die der naive Feuchtwanger nach einigem Grübeln vielleicht sogar verstanden hat: „Übrigens: wieso loben Sie den Schönherr?"

Soll der Leser etwas von ihnen haben, dann müssen Brechts Briefe sehr sorgfältig kommentiert werden. Doch daran hapert es. Ein gut Teil der Werkverweise erinnert an die Bibelexegese. Wie dort Matthäus aus Jesaia gedeutet wird und Jesaia Matthäus legitimiert, so wird Brecht zumeist aus Brecht erklärt, nur dass es sich hier nicht um Heilsbotschaften handelt, sondern um Literatur. Dies werkimmanente Gestrüpp mag Brechtologen faszinieren, kaum aber den an Brecht wirklich interessierten Leser. Sucht der nun gar Rat in anderen Dingen, so sieht er sich nicht selten im Stich gelassen. Sofern die Kommentare nicht ganz fehlen, sind sie vielfach ungenau, irreführend und voller Fehler. Anscheinend hat das niemand bemerkt, obwohl die Briefe allgemach seit gut drei Jahren auf dem Markt sind. Die zünftige Literaturkritik kümmert sich um Editorisches ja kaum. So blieben die Herausgeber von Brechts Briefen bislang ebenso ungescholten, wie seinerzeit Inge Jens für ihre grandiose Betreuung von Thomas Manns Tagebüchern weithin unbedankt geblieben ist.

Schon die in Ost-Berlin entstandenen Kommentare der Vorläufer-Edition von 1981 wiesen mancherlei orts- und zeitspezifische Defizite auf. So war als Erscheinungsort der *Süddeutschen Zeitung* Stuttgart angegeben — die Westpresse war Günter Glaeser anscheinend nicht zugänglich. Das war gewiss nur grotesk. Anderswo wurde es ernster. In einem Brief an Egon Erwin Kisch hatte sich Brecht 1939 sehr kritisch über Alfred Kerr geäußert, der seit den Tagen der *Dreigroschenoper* sein Intimfeind war. Kisch war zuvor öffentlich für den Mitemigranten Kerr eingetreten, und um darzulegen, weshalb er das für falsch hielt, nahm Brecht mögliche Gegenargumente vorweg: „Aber ihm [Kerr] geschieht jetzt doch auch Unrecht? Ja, aber welches? Daß die ihn diesmal (zugegeben unter nichtigen Vorwänden) nicht mitmachen lassen!" „Letztes Mal" nämlich, 1914, hatte Kerr den deutschen Krieg verherrlicht und sich militaristischer gebärdet als mancher General. Brecht unterstellte also, dass Kerr auch bei Hitler mitmachen würde, von den Nazis aber daran gehindert werde, „unter nichtigen Vorwän-den," seiner jüdischen Herkunft wegen. Das ist starker Tobak, doch die Behauptung ist nicht etwa deshalb unkommentiert geblieben. Vielmehr wurde Kerr geschont, weil er im Londoner Exil eng mit Kommunisten zusammengearbeitet hatte und zeitweise sogar Präsident einer kulturel-len „Front"-Organisation, des Freien Deutschen Kulturbundes, gewesen war.

Ein weiteres Beispiel betrifft den Schriftsteller Bernard von Brenta-no. Anfang der dreißiger Jahre hatte Brentano der KPD mindestens nahe gestanden, im schweizerischen Exil sich aber allmählich von ihr abgewendet. Brecht hielt zu dem nun als „Renegaten" Verfemten gleichwohl noch lange Kontakt. Er schätzte den Autor Brentano, und im März 1937 dankte er ihm für sein letztes Buch:

> Den neuen Roman habe ich mit allergrößtem Interesse gelesen, wie alles, was Sie schreiben. Er ist so leicht und elegant geschrieben, wie man bei uns sonst nicht eben oft schreibt, und wenn ich mit etwas unzufrieden bin, dann damit, daß er zu kurz ist. Eine Nebenbemerkung: das Buch liest sich wie eine Konkretisierung des Kafkaschen „Prozeß."

Den Titel hat Brecht nicht genannt — warum hätte er es auch tun sol-len? Der Kafka-Vergleich zeigte ohnehin, dass nur der Roman *Prozeß ohne Richter* gemeint sein konnte. Dieses mit kaum 200 Seiten wirk-lich kurze Buch ist eine beziehungsreiche Verfremdung von Schaupro-zessen in Diktaturen — Prozessen, charakteristisch nicht für Hitlers Berlin, sondern für Stalins Moskau. Soweit gut. Günter Glaeser jedoch hatte — statt *Prozeß ohne Richter* — *Theodor Chindler* für Brentanos „neuen Roman" gehalten, eine umfangreiche Familiengeschichte, die bereits ein ganzes Jahr vorlag. Glaeser hatte somit keines der beiden Bücher gelesen, und das verwundert wenig. In der DDR stand der „Renegat" Brentano im Giftschrank, und selbst parteitreueste Wissen-schaftler brauchten jedes Mal Sondergenehmigungen, wenn sie derlei Bücher lesen wollten.

Tempi passati. Die DDR gibt es nicht mehr, und ihre Giftschränke sind dortigen Lesern ebenso frei zugänglich wie die Westpresse. Indes erscheint in der neuen Briefausgabe die *Süddeutsche Zeitung* noch immer in Stuttgart, die Anspielung auf Kerrs Hurrapatriotismus von anno 1914 ist noch immer nicht entschlüsselt, und noch immer auch hat Brecht *Theodor Chindler* gelobt, statt den *Prozeß ohne Richter*, der ihm ideologisch so wenig gefallen konnte. Die Kommentare von 1981 sind nämlich zum gut Teil in die Neuausgabe übernommen worden, unbesehen, ungeprüft, bedenken- und gedankenlos.

Anderseits hatte die alte Ausgabe auch Vorzüge. Als Philologe verstand Glaeser sein Handwerk. Bei schon publizierten Briefen hat er stets den Druckort genannt, so, wie es sich gehört, und die Kommentare hat er im Imperfekt gegeben, wissend, dass sie von längst vergangenen Dingen handeln. Auch hat er ein Personen- und Institutionen-Register angelegt, das man nur vorzüglich nennen kann.

Die Neuausgabe dagegen verzichtet auf die Annotation von Erstdrucken, ignoriert sogar den Briefband von 1981, und überdies verweigert sie dem Leser eine Konkordanzliste. Das ist deshalb besonders misslich, weil — gegenüber 1981 — viele Briefe umdatiert worden sind, da um Wochen, dort um Monate, so dass sich in einen Irrgarten versetzt wähnt, wer etwas vergleichen möchte.

Die Tempora bilden ein weiteres Ärgernis. Statt beim Imperfekt zu bleiben, huldigt man nun in einer unseligen Liebe dem historischen Präsens: als ereigne sich alles in dem Moment, da der Leser die Seiten umblättert. Bislang war das historische Präsens eine Domäne des Kitschs, der Sensations- und der Regenbogenpresse. Es ist eine Neuheit, aber keine gute, dass es mit seiner trüben Action-Brühe nun auch Werkkommentare überschwemmt.

Im Register schließlich sind Institutionen nicht mehr aufgeführt, ferner fehlen die biographischen Notizen, die Glaeser bei entlegeneren Namen mit Recht für nötig gehalten hatte. Das hat Folgen für die Kommentierung. 1937 etwa erwähnte Brecht im Kontext einer Pariser Aufführung der *Dreigroschenoper* eine Frau Tallon, und im Register der alten Ausgabe hatte Glaeser angemerkt: „Tallon, Ninon, leitete das Pariser Théâtre Pigalle; für André Mauprey hatte sie eine französische Rohübersetzung der ‚Dreigroschenoper' angefertigt." In der Neuausgabe taucht sie natürlich ebenfalls auf, doch im Kommentar liest man, was uns noch beschäftigen wird, weil es uns so überaus häufig begegnet: „Frau Tallon: konnte nicht ermittelt werden."

Eine weitere Neuerung ist das klammheimliche Abschreiben, die nicht belegte Übernahme von Anmerkungen aus Büchern anderer Leute. 1991 hatte der amerikanische Germanist Harold von Hofe Feuchtwangers kleinere Briefwechsel herausgegeben, darunter den mit

Brecht. Dabei hatte er es auch mit der mysteriösen Schönherr-Stelle zu tun bekommen und sie so kommentiert: „Möglicherweise bezieht sich Brechts Frage auf einen Aufsatz [Feuchtwangers] über Karl Schönherrs Drama *Glaube und Heimat* in der *Schaubühne* vom 23. März 1911. [...] Zeitnahes ließ sich bibliographisch nicht ermitteln." Derlei vergisst man nicht so leicht, und so durfte ich noch einmal lachen, als ich es bei den Brecht-Editoren wiederfand. Den letzten Satz haben sie paraphrasiert, das andere haben sie, wie auch mehrfach sonst, bei von Hofe wörtlich abgekupfert. Es fehlt nicht einmal das Zitat aus Feuchtwangers Schönherr-Kritik, das ich eben weggelassen habe. Eines fehlt aber in allen diesen Fällen. Die Quellenangabe.

Bei manchen Erklärungen fühlt man sich an östliche Tabus und Sprachregelungen von einst erinnert. Wenn vom *Braunbuch über Reichstagsbrand und Hitlerterror* die Rede ist, sucht man vergebens nach Willi Münzenberg, der nicht nur die *Braunbücher* initiierte, sondern auch die gesamte kommunistische Reichstagsbrandkampagne. Weil er sich 1938 von der KPD getrennt hatte, wurde Münzenberg in der DDR totgeschwiegen. Erst in den achtziger Jahren verlor das Tabu an Kraft. Die Kommentatoren jedoch — befolgen sie es noch immer? Oder wissen sie über Münzenbergs Rolle beim *Braunbuch* bloß nicht Bescheid?

Solche Fragen stellen sich auch, wenn man über André Gides Reisebericht *Zurück aus Sowjetrußland* erfährt: „Dieses Buch enthält heftige Ausfälle gegen die Sowjetunion." Kein wahres Wort. Das Buch dokumentiert Gides große Enttäuschung über die Sowjetunion, es ist ganz präzise in der Wiedergabe der ernüchternden Erlebnisse, aber auch ganz ohne Polemik. Es war nicht Gide, der „heftige Ausfälle" gegen die Sowjetunion, es waren Stalinisten aus aller Herren Länder, die sie gegen sein Buch gerichtet hatten. Bewegen sich die Herausgeber also in den Fußstapfen von Gides Verleumdern, oder haben sie seinen Reisebericht nicht gelesen?

Genauso dunkel bleibt für mich, weshalb zu massiven politischen Irrtümern von Brecht jedes klärende Wort fehlt. Nach der von den Siegern bei der Konferenz in Jalta beschlossenen Annexion Ostpreußens phantasierte er: „Der ostelbische Landarbeiter aber wird vermutlich von den siegreichen Polen Land bekommen. *Sie* werden ihn dort ansiedeln, nach tausend Jahren bloßer ‚Anwesenheit'." Das haben weder die „siegreichen Polen" vorgehabt noch gar die Sowjetunion, und das Potsdamer Abkommen schuf darüber mit Artikel XIII unmissverständlich Klarheit: statt der Ansiedelung des deutschen Landproletariats auf eigenem Grund verfügte er seine Vertreibung. Über das Potsdamer Abkommen hat Brecht einen euphorischen Brief geschrieben, zu Artikel XIII allerdings hat er sich ausgeschwiegen. Beide Male schweigen aber auch die Editoren, sei es, weil sie Brechts politische Blöße bedeckt halten wollten, sei es, weil sie von Jalta nichts wussten und auch nichts von Potsdam.

Bei den meisten Nicht- oder Falschinformationen scheiden ideologische Motive freilich aus. Sie müssen andere Ursachen haben. Im Herbst 1933 bat Brecht seinen nach Zürich emigrierten Freund Brentano, er möge jemanden namens Hartung „mal fragen, ob er für die ‚Maß für Maß'-Bearbeitung Interesse hat. Dann würde ich sie ihm schicken." Anmerkung zu Hartung: „Der frühere Intendant des Hessischen Landestheaters Darmstadt Gustav Hartung." Was soll man damit anfangen? Die sachdienliche Information hätte ungefähr lauten können: Der aus Deutschland emigrierte frühere Intendant...war jetzt Regisseur am Zürcher Schauspielhaus, der für exilierte Dramatiker wichtigsten deutschsprachigen Auslandsbühne.

Wurde der Leser hier mit einem Scheinhinweis abgespeist, so bekommt er noch viel öfter Auskünfte, die nicht bloß irreführend sind, sondern eindeutig falsch. An Willi Bredel, seinen Mitherausgeber beim Wort, schrieb Brecht im Sommer 1938: „Lieber Bredel, vielen Dank für Ihren Brief. Das ist schön, daß Sie wieder in Reichweite sind!" Kommentar: „Bredel kommt im Juni 1938 aus Spanien nach Moskau zurück." Aus dem Spanischen Bürgerkrieg ja, doch nach Moskau mitnichten. Nach Paris vielmehr, weil in Moskau der Terror regierte, das Große Morden, und Bredel — begreiflicherweise — das unkalkulierbare Risiko des Genickschusses scheute, nachdem er sich am Ebro vor den Kugeln gerettet hatte, die immerhin von vorn gekommen waren.

Wieland Herzfelde wiederum übersiedelte, den Anmerkungen zufolge, mit seinem Malik-Verlag gleich zweimal nach London, 1934 und 1939, und da den Editoren nicht einmal dies auffiel, wissen sie auch nicht, was sich 1934 resp. 1939 tatsächlich ereignet hatte. Oder nehme man den Zürcher Verleger Emil Oprecht. Im Kommentar taufen ihn die Editoren in Ernst Oprecht um, was nicht hindert, dass er im Register mit seinem richtigen Vornamen erscheint. Unter „Emil Oprecht" rubriziert das Register indes auch Emils Bruder Hans, der nicht Verleger war, sondern Vorsitzender der Schweizer Sozialdemokraten. Kurz, Brecht hat neben dem Verleger Oprecht auch den Politiker gleichen Nachnamens gekannt und genannt, das Register seiner Briefe aber kennt und nennt ihn nicht.

Mit Namensduplizitäten haben die Herausgeber öfters Probleme. So halten sie den Schriftsteller Friedrich Hagen für einen wichtigen Mann im New Yorker Council for a Democratic Germany. Künstlerpech! Zur fraglichen Zeit, im März 1944, lebte Friedrich Hagen illegal in Frankreich und kämpfte mit der Résistance gegen die Wehrmacht. Im New Yorker Council hingegen agierte und agitierte der Politiker Karl Borromäus Frank — und zwar unter seinem allbekannten Decknamen Paul Hagen. Weiter. Brecht polemisierte gegen die im Zweiten Weltkrieg weltweit verbreitete These von der deutschen Kollektivschuld — und gegen ihre bekanntesten Verfechter, „die Ludwigs, Vansittarts, Ehrenburgs." Obwohl Brecht auch hier der kommentierungser-schwerend niederträchtigen Gewohnheit folgte, Vornamen wegzulas-sen, sind die Herausgeber mit Vansittart und Ehrenburg zurechtge-kommen. Mit dem Dritten war es aber anscheinend nicht so einfach. Statt auf Emil Ludwig, den seinerzeit weltberühmten Serienproduzen-ten von Biographien „großer Männer" (das Repertoire reichte von Christus bis Stalin), statt auf diesen Bestsellerfabrikanten sind sie — nun, sie sind wahr und wahrhaftig auf den Dichter Otto Ludwig verfal-len; nur dass der ein Zeitgenosse von Heine war und seit 1865 tot.

Warum soll aber für die Ludwigs nicht recht sein, was den Editoren für die Roosevelts billig dünkt? Eine Briefbemerkung zum Tode des Präsidenten Franklin Delano Roosevelt wird so erläutert: „Theodore Roosevelt stirbt am 12. April 1945." Nein, möchte man einwenden, am 6. Januar 1919! Da sie aber die Roosevelt-Präsidenten schon nicht auseinanderhalten können, würden die Herren die Ironie wohl nicht verstehen. Im Register haben sie Roosevelt ja auch stets unter „Theodo-re" gebucht. Gemeint war allemal Franklin Delano — den es für diese Briefbände einfach nicht gab. Was verschlägt es da noch, dass der Eintritt der USA in den Zweiten Weltkrieg vorverlegt wird, vom 8. Dezember auf den 8. Oktober 1941? Die Editorentrinität schreibt die Weltgeschichte um.

Und wie im Großen so im Kleinen. Den Namen eines prominen-ten kommunistischen Journalisten halten sie für ein Pseudonym und dichten ihm einen bürgerlichen Namen an, der das Pseudonym eines sozialdemokratischen Journalisten war. Aus einer sozialdemokratischen Zeitung machen sie eine „konservative," aus einem überparteilich ge-tarnten, sowjetfinanzierten Pariser Verlag eine Außenredaktion von Brechts Zeitschrift *Das Wort*. Und nun gar Namen, mit denen sie nichts anfangen können. Die ignorieren sie einfach. Das trifft den Vorsitzen-den der dänischen KP und die Gründerin der sozialdemokratischen deutschen Arbeiterwohlfahrt, es trifft einen wenig bekannten schwedi-schen Lyriker und einen achtbaren deutschen Prosaschriftsteller mit DDR-Werkausgabe, einen emigrierten Komponisten, mit dem Brecht in Hollywood Schach spielte, und einen Literaturagenten, der außer für Brecht für Feuchtwanger tätig war, für Werfel und Thomas Mann.

Es trifft eben, wen es trifft, und nur über eines wird man in diesen Kommentaren wirklich glänzend informiert — über den Horizont der Herausgeber. Ob der aber jemanden interessiert, außer Freunden, Be-kannten und Verwandten? Im Kommentar zu den zwischen 1933 und 1948 geschriebenen Brecht-Briefen — und nur die habe ich unter die Lupe genommen — bin ich über einhundertsechzigmal auf Lücken gestoßen, auf Verzeichnungen, Klitterungen oder Fehler. Genannt habe ich hier nur einige Fälle, exemplarische, die sich knapp darstellen lie-ßen. Komplexere Beispiele musste ich beiseitelassen. Mitunter hätten eines oder zwei allein so viel Raum gekostet, wie mir insgesamt zur

Verfügung steht.

Natürlich kann niemand überall Bescheid wissen, ein Narr, wer das erwartete und verlangte. Aber dass Herausgeber sich informieren und nachschlagen, das kann man erwarten und verlangen, und dass Glaeser, Jeske und Wenzlaff es offenkundig unterließen: das ist das eigentlich Niederschmetternde an dieser tristen Geschichte. Den moskaufinanzierten Pariser Tarnverlag etwa, die Editions du 10. Mai, hat David Pike porträtiert. Sein Buch zum sowjetischen Schriftstellerexil liegt seit 1981 vor, und wie die Brecht-Briefe ist es bei Suhrkamp erschienen. Über Gustav Hartungs Zürcher Exil hat Werner Mittenzwei, einer der Hauptherausgeber der „großen, kommentierten" Brecht-Ausgabe, mehrfach geschrieben, das erste Mal, soweit mir bekannt ist, schon 1978. Genauso hätte sich in der engsten Umgebung der Briefeditoren leicht herausfinden lassen, wann und warum Brechts wichtigster Exilverleger den juristischen Sitz seines Unternehmens von Prag nach London verlegte, und wann er selber von Prag nach London floh, ohne jedoch seinen Verlag mitnehmen zu können. Wieland Herzfelde hat selber darüber berichtet, 1967, in einer Publikation der Berliner Akademie der Künste, zu der das Brecht-Archiv meines Wissens seit je gehört.

Ob Tagebücher, Briefbände oder Autobiographien, ob wissenschaftliche Arbeiten oder Lexika: die Liste der *nicht* konsultierten Literatur ist ansehnlich, und sogar der Große Meyer figuriert auf ihr. Die Editoren-Trinität hat aber nicht nur nicht nachgeschlagen. Ich fürchte, sie hat gar nicht bemerkt, dass sie es hätte tun müssen, geschweige dass sie gewusst hätte, wo sie es hätte tun können.

Nun lassen schon der groteske Schönherr-Lapsus und die nicht kommentierte England-Stelle in dem Brief an Korsch ahnen, dass sich ihre Inkompetenz nicht auf das „Umfeld" von Brecht beschränkt. Sie wissen nicht bloß in seiner Zeit und Welt nicht Bescheid, nein, auch bei ihm selber kennen sie sich nicht aus. Denn bei den Beispielen, mit denen ich schließe, ist man im Zentrum von Brechts Esse. Man weiß, wie hoch Brecht Karl Kraus geschätzt hat. Der Dreiundzwanzigjährige schon hat ihn gelesen, und in den Kämpfen mit Kerr wurde die Beziehung noch enger. Es war denn auch nicht zufällig Kraus, auf den Brecht sich berief, als er mit einem Verleger stritt, der verschandelnd in eine Übersetzung eingegriffen hatte: „Handelt es sich [...] um einen Abscheu vor Fremdwörtern, so kann ich nur sagen, daß ich den nicht teile. Karl Kraus hat über dies Thema meiner Meinung nach Klassisches formuliert." Auf Anhieb wusste ich nicht, was Brecht meinte. Indes steht Kraus im Regal, und in dem Band *Die Sprache* bin ich fündig geworden. Gleich der erste Text im Buche ist es — „Hier wird Deutsch gespuckt" —, und ebenso kommt der nächste Aufsatz — „An die Anschrift der Sprachreiniger" — in Frage. Meine Suche hat keine zwei Minuten gedauert. Die Editoren aber: „Karl Kraus... Klassisches: konnte nicht ermittelt werden."

Prägender noch als Kraus ist Rudyard Kipling für Brecht gewesen, im Werk stößt man wieder und wieder auf seine Spuren. Brechts Indien und Brechts Tommies in *Mann ist Mann* sind undenkbar ohne Kiplings Indien und Kiplings Tommies, manche Brecht-Gedichte wirken wie Kipling-Imitate, und noch für *Mutter Courage* hat sich der Mann mit den laxen Eigentumsbegriffen bei Kipling ähnlich „bedient" wie, ein Jahrzehnt zuvor, für die *Dreigroschenoper* bei Villon. Kiplings Roman *Kim*, sein größter und schönster, scheint im Hause Brecht sogar sprichwörtlich gewesen zu sein. Jedenfalls hat der Stückeschreiber lakonisch auf ihn verwiesen, als er Margarete Steffin über New York berichtete und über sein dortiges Geschick als nichtemanzipierter Mann: „Bei der Wäsche hat [mir] Lou Eisler geholfen und sich dadurch (siehe Kim!) Verdienst erworben." Die von Brecht unterwiesene Proletarierin Steffin verstand. Die brechtgelahrten Herausgeber der an sie gerichteten Briefe Brechts verkünden lauthals ihre Ignoranz: „Kim: konnte nicht ermittelt werden."

Worauf sie ihn flugs — Erde zu Erde, Staub zu Staub — ins Personenregister expedierten, die nicht existierende Romangestalt zum nicht gemeinten amerikanischen Präsidenten. Nein, mit ihren Kommentaren hat sie kein Verdienst erworben, diese Herausgeber-Dreieinfältigkeit. Statt Brecht zu erklären, hat sie mit ihm angestellt, was Karl Kraus so formuliert haben könnte: Hier wird Brecht gespuckt.

Letter from Barbara Brecht-Schall

Lieber Herr Silberman,

ich habe erst jetzt mit Bewußtsein das Interview mit Manfred Wek-
werth im „Brecht-Jahrbuch" gelesen, das er eigentlich, so glaube ich,
Ihnen gegeben hat. Nun muß ich doch schreiben, um etliche grobe
Fehler zu korrigieren.

    Helli hatte nicht „Atherosklerose" (es heißt doch wohl richtig „Ar-
teriosklerose"), sie hat sich sehr gut an Dinge erinnert. Wie die Autop-
sie später belegte, hatte sie Arthritis, das hat nichts mit dem Gedächtnis
zu tun. Wenn Helli ihn aus Schweden zu sich bestellte, so wird sie ihre
Gründe gehabt haben, und sicher wichtige und dienstliche. Zur Kündi-
gung seinerseits kam es, weil er unbedingt die Leitung des Hauses
übernehmen wollte und Hehl keine Lust hatte, sie ihm zu geben, was
ja wohl verständlich war. Daß er nicht Brecht spielen wollte, ist lächerlich. *Die Kipper* von Volker Braun, da hat Helli sich ungeheuer be-
müht, das Stück in den oberen Gremien durchzusetzen. Der Wekwerth
hatte, und hier greife ich auf den nächsten Punkt vor, sich damals mit
Helli Gründgens' Inszenierung der *Heiligen Johanna der Schlachthöfe*
ansehen könnnen. Darin spielte Hanne Hiob, deren Karriere im Westen erstklassig verlief, die Hauptrolle. Wekwerth wollte dann natürlich
die „Johanna" auch am Berliner Ensemble machen, am liebsten mit der
Hiob, um zu zeigen, daß er sehr viel besser als Gründgens sei. Gegen
die Warnungen der Weigel und auch gegen die Bedenken der Hiob,
der bewußt war, daß ihre Karriere großen Schaden nehmen könnte,
wenn sie im Osten spielt, hat er durchgesetzt, daß die Hiob engagiert
wurde. Danach gab es verschiedene politische Probleme, so daß diese
Inszenierung fast 1½ Jahre verschoben wurde. In der Zwischenzeit hat
Wekwerth seine jetzige Frau Renate Richter kennengelernt und wollte
unbedingt, daß sie jetzt die Johanna spielt. Von ihm kam diesbezüglich
der hervorragende Satz: „Ich mag dieses Familien-Theater nicht, ich
will, daß meine Freundin die Rolle spielt." Die Weigel hat ihm ganz
klar gesagt, daß sie keine Schauspielerin 2 Jahre auf eine Rolle warten
lassen kann und sie dann einer anderen gibt. Erst recht könne sie das
Brechts Tochter nicht antun. Dann kam Wekwerth mit der glorreichen
Idee, er wolle statt dessen die *Johanna von Döbeln* spielen. Helli sagte
ihm, daß er erst dann die Parodie spielen könne, wenn das Original
gespielt worden ist. So, wie es damals mit der *Courage* war, wo die
Flinz ein Riesenerfolg wurde, weil die Leute den Bezug sehr wohl
verstanden. Also mußte er zuerst die *Heilige Johanna der Schlachthöfe*
machen mit der Hiob, und nachher durfte er natürlich die *Johanna von
Döbeln* machen mit seiner Freundin. Die *Johanna von Döbeln* war
übrigens einer der größten Flops, die wir je hatten.

Im übrigen hat die Helli überhaupt nicht für mich gekämpft. Der Brecht hat mir zur Bedingung gemacht, wenn ich Schauspielerin werde, daß ich erst in einem anderen Theater einen Erfolg haben müßte. Diese Bedingung habe ich erfüllt in *Polterabend*, Regie Curt Bois, im Deutschen Theater. Daraufhin hat Brecht eine Rolle für mich gesucht und fand *Held der westlichen Welt*, in einer hervorrangenden Ubersetzung von Peter Hacks. Er wollte gern, daß Benno Besson es inszeniert (Brecht hielt nicht viel von Wekwerth). Das war mir gar nicht so lieb, denn ich war nicht so begeistert von Besson wie Brecht, auch aus persönlichen Gründen. Als Benno dann sagte, er mache es mit der Lutz, war ich sehr froh dem Brecht vorzuschlagen, daß Wekwerth/Palitzsch, die erst nur eine kleine Inszenierung gemacht hatten (*Hirse für die Achte*) damit vielleicht einen Anfang erhalten könnten. Das wurde auch gemacht, und es war eine sehr schöne Inszenierung. Wekwerth vergißt leider sehr gern, daß er durch mich seine erste Chance bekommen hat.

Seine Behauptungen über das Testament, über das so viele Gerüchte umgehen, stimmen ebenfalls nicht. Der Brecht hat, unverständlich für ihn als alten Krimi-Leser, ein Testament gemacht, maschinengeschrieben und keine Zeugen. Die Hehl hat sehr wohl versucht es durchzusetzen, es gelang ihr aber nicht. Sie hat trotzdem, so es in ihrer Macht stand, Brechts Wünsche erfüllt. Die Hauptmann erbte natürlich keine Teile an der *Dreigroschenoper*, sondern ihr Anteil war ja schon in den Verträgen mit Suhrkamp festgelegt. Die Berlau hat natürlich gar nichts geerbt. Nach seinem Tod hat Helli das Haus in Dänemark, das Brecht der Berlau zugedacht hatte, abbezahlt. Die Tatsache, daß sie es in kürzester Zeit „versoffen" hat, nach Berlin kam und der Helhi auf der Tasche lag, ist nebensächhich. Käthe Rühicke hat nichts an der *Mutter* geerbt. Isot Kilians Kinder sollten Teile aus den „Songs"-Tantiemen in der DDR bekommen. Als Nachlaßverwalterin wurde die Weigel eingesetzt. Als Brecht im Sterben lag, sagte er zur Helli (und ich war selbst dabei, im Gegensatz zu Herrn Wekwerth): „Mach' das weiter, so lange es das Berliner Ensemble ist. Du kannst das, Weigel". Daß eine Beratung der sich erwähnt Hoffenden stattfand, klingt schauderhaft, wie eine Versammlung von Aasgeiern, hat aber mit dem Testament nichts zu tun. Die Weigel hat das Testament nicht angefochten, wie gesagt, sondern das Gegenteil war der Fall.

Zu dem nächsten Satz kann ich nur fragen, woher er wissen will, was Brecht gesagt hat, er war ja nicht dabei. Auch seine Beschreibung, wie er alles neu geschrieben hat und viel besser, würde ich mit einer Riesenladung Salz nehmen. Es ist auch eine Tatsache, daß die Weigel nicht nur dachte, daß er ihren Intendanten-Stuhl wollte, er hat das auch ganz klar formuliert. Und er kündigte, weil er dachte, mit dieser Erpressung könne er die Künstlerische Leitung und überhaupt die Leitung des ganzen Hauses übernehmen. Dabei wäre folgendes zu berücksichtigen: In den späten Sechziger Jahren wurde die Partei plötzlich ganz engstirnig und verlangte, daß alle Leiter Partei-Mitglieder sein sollten, was ja die Weigel nicht war. Der Hager ritt besonders darauf herum und stellte sich sehr hinter Wekwerth.

Die Sache mit dem Brief ist lächerlich. Helli ging ins Krankenhaus am 1. Mai. Daraufhin wurde erst einmal klar, wie krank sie wirklich war, denn ich hatte es all die Monate für mich behalten. Anscheinend hat Vera Tenschert dann den Tenschert in London angerufen und gesagt, daß die Weigel jetzt im Krankenhaus sei. Daraufhin hat Wekwerth schnell einen Brief formuliert, in dem er sich einschleimen wollte. Helli verstarb am 6. Mai. Der Brief landete keineswegs im Weigel-Archiv sondern ca. Mitte Mai im Büro der Bertolt-Brecht-Erben, wo er noch immer liegt. Also kann er ihn nicht im Weigel-Archiv gefunden haben.

Es stimmt, daß ich mir verbeten habe, daß er zur Trauerfeier kommt. Verhalten in den letzten Jahren der Weigel gegenüber sah ich keinen hat trotzdem eine 5- bis 10minütige Rede gehalten, in der 57 Mal (ich kreuzte es an) das Wort „ich" vorkam.

Das sind ungefähr grob die Fehler in dem Artikel. Ich wollte sie wirklich nicht unwidersprochen lassen und zulassen, daß Herr Wekwerth sich da als Held und Märtyrer aufputzt.

Übrigens hat er tatsächlich eine neue Fassung der „Leitungstätigkeit" geschrieben, in der jeder vorkam, von der Putzfrau bis zum Bühnenarbeiter. Es fehlten nur alle Schauspieler und die Weigel. Diese Fassung kursierte im Ensemble und wurde die „Apfelböck-Version" genannt, nach dem Gedicht von Brecht: „Erschlug den Vater und die Mutter sein und blieb im Hause übrig, er allein". Merkwürdigerweise verschwand diese Aufstückelung nach Weigels Tod völlig aus allen Akten. Sie wird nur ab und zu erwähnt als eine „weise Schrift", ohne daß sie einmal jemand zu sehen bekommen hätte.

Mit besten Grüßen

Ihre
Barbara Brecht-Schall

27.07.2000

Book Reviews

D. Stephan Bock. *Coining Poetry. Brechts „Der gute Mensch von Sezuan".* *Zur dramatischen Dichtung eines neuen Jahrhunderts.* Frankfurt am Main: Suhrkamp, 1998. 516 Seiten.

Zum Brecht-Centennium stellte der Suhrkamp Verlag unter anderem ein Buch von 516 Seiten über *Der gute Mensch von Sezuan* vor, dessen ungewöhnlicher Titel, *Coining Poetry,* doppelt neugierig macht. Allerdings dachte ich gleich an Gide: hoffentlich kein *Faux-monnayeur.* Die Aufregung im Lektorat verrät der Klappentext: „Eine kleine Sensation: ein Klassiker Bertolt Brechts liest sich auf neue Weise!" Dieser metaphorisch köstliche Text nennt auch gleich den Grund dafür: Brecht „erzeugt poetisches Scheidewasser." Womit man sich jedoch leicht die Finger verbrennen kann!

Die These des Autors ließe sich *in nuce* so beschreiben: bis zur Erscheinung seines Buches hat noch niemand die durch dieses Stück markierte literarische Wasserscheide geokulturell ausgemessen. Daher der enorme Aufwand an gesammeltem Material. Die anthropologische Aufregung, geht es doch um die Entdeckung beinahe der ganzen Kultur Ostasiens im Stück, wird von einem Konvertiteneifer begleitet und energisiert. Wie konnte die wirkliche Bedeutung des Ostasiatischen für Brecht bloß so lange übersehen werden, zumal die Zukunft **„einer internationalisierten dramatischen Dichtung wie eines internationalisierten Theaters"** (387, *sic*) auf dem Spiel steht?

Das Buch enthält weder Register noch Bibliographie. In einer zwölfseitigen, kleingedruckten Anmerkung mitten im Text listet der Autor ihm wichtig erscheinende Bücher auf (204–215; diese oft kuriose Liste — *Talks in Tokyo, A Guide to English Conversation for Japanese Students* — soll jeder Schulklasse die notwendigen Kenntnisse bieten, die ihr „keine ‚Brecht-Sinologie' zu vermitteln vermag," 208). Da die Bücher der Gerügten offenbar nicht konsultiert wurden, und folglich nicht aufgeführt werden, kann man die unverständliche Kurzsichtigkeit jener Vorgänger nur ihrer „Überheblichkeit" zuschreiben. Im ganzen langen Text wird lediglich aus einem einzigen einschlägigen, auch nicht bibliographierten *Artikel,* „nach **langem** Widerstreben und dann nur aus einer Laune heraus nachblätternd," ein paar uneinsichtige Sätze zitiert, auf die ich zurückkomme. Die darin enthaltenen, verständnislosen Bewertungen verrieten, sage und schreibe, rassistisches Vorurteil (205).

Richtet man sich nach den hier aufgestellten Wegweisern, betritt man ein merkwürdiges Gelände, das zuerst wie Neufundland erscheint. Nach den gängigen Brechttouren freut sich wohl jeder auf die in Aussicht gestellten Entdeckungen. Die ungewöhnliche Reisebeschreibung verblüfft angesichts der ausgewählten Sehenswürdigkeiten. Aber in einem fremden Land ist guter Rat teuer und bei neuen Geschichten hört man zunächst gerne zu. Allerdings führen die recht ausgefallenen, pausenlos angewendeten rhetorischen und orthographischen Überraschungen allmählich zu einer immer wachsenden Verwunderung. Was zuerst sprachlich amüsant vorkommen mag, womöglich kritisch wachrüttelt, und daher akzeptabel erscheint — etwa, zu einer noch nie entdeckten Thematik passt auch ein innovativer Stil—, verläuft jedoch als neuer Duktus immer manieristischer.

Die sprachlichen Mätzchen — z.B. „die Hinterfotzigkeiten des tschajnataunesischen Örtchens" (167) — verlieren dann nach einer Weile ihren anfänglichen Charme. Sie gestalten sich immer mehr zu einer Art Privatsprache, die nur durch eine konzentrierte Lektüre des ganzen Texts überhaupt zu entziffern ist, wiewohl es beim Lesen weiterhin offen bleibt, ob sich die Mühe dieses langen Wegs überhaupt lohnt. Deswegen hier gleich eine für diesen Text absolut typische Kostprobe:

> „Augenspinner, Kommafalter, Weiße C? Erste Lexikale offenbart, TE setzt Schmetterlingswolken COURAGEirt teutsch, vollendet Bertolt ‚Einstein der neuen bühnenform' konshenial[hochte]. TE schreibt endgültig in den IrrWitz & erzeugt dabei das nicht faßbare Wunder — Smetterlingschaos im Gleitflug." (361, *sic*; man beachte unter anderem den leicht übersehbaren, hier aber wirkungsmächtig gedachten Fettdruck in der Endsilbe der hochgesetzten Buchstaben: „hoch**te**.")

Was hier mitgeteilt wird, bleibe vorerst das Geheimnis des Autors. Eines steht fest: Zahllose, nur in diesem Text konstruierte Assoziationsketten müssen ständig präsent sein, sonst scheitert die Lektüre. Folglich kommt die Interpretation eines derart verschlüsselten, ja geradezu hermetisch erscheinenden Textes praktisch seiner Re-lektüre gleich. Entweder hat er eine entsprechend originelle rhetorische Meisterleistung vorgelegt oder ein autistisches Desaster zustandegebracht. Darüber entscheiden vor allem die gewonnenen „Erkenntnisse."

Zuerst fällt der Widerspruch zwischen einer jedenfalls sehr mit sich selber beschäftigten Rede und dem Anspruch auf kulturübergreifende und -vergleichende Perspektiven auf. Offenbar kann dieses seltsame Territorium nicht anders beschrieben werden. Denn hinter den Sprachspielchen steckt eine „Methode," so seltsam sie erscheinen mag. Obwohl ein narzisstischer Zug überdeutlich wird, sind sie daher keine *rein* selbstgefälligen Spielereien. Der Text enthält auch ziemlich versteckte, thematisch geschweige denn theoretisch nicht besonders hervorgehobene, im allgemeinen Wortschwall und im interkulturellen Beziehungswirrwarr daher leicht zu übersehende Hinweise, dass nämlich hier nicht nur mit einer *Methode*, sondern auch anhand eines bestimmten *Modells* gedacht und geschrieben wird. Dem Verlag zufolge habe sein Autor „eine unvergleichliche LesArt" vorgelegt. Dem ist unbedingt zuzustimmen. Da schon von „Klassikern" die Rede war, denke ich aus mehreren Gründen eher an: „Das Unbeschreibliche, / Hier ist's getan!" Machen wir trotzdem den Versuch, dieses Unbeschreibliche zu entziffern und auf seinen intellektuellen Gehalt hin zu prüfen. Man kann es auch anders sagen: Wie soll dieses Modell theorisiert werden?

Nicht jeder wird sich ein Urteil über diese „unvergleichliche LesArt" erlauben, da die bis in die allerletzten Verästelungen hinein vorgestellte, aufgrund des anvisierten Stückes auch irgendwie naheliegende „chinesische Textur" zu unbekannt, womöglich zu wesensfremd und allemal nicht genügend überprüfbar erscheint. Viele werden das Buch deswegen gar nicht erst lesen, oder nach einem kurzen Durchblättern vermutlich beiseitelegen. Wir erfahren z.B., dass Brechts „Chima" mit dem japanischen Wort für Insel — „shima" — zusammenhängt (368). Was dem Brecht nicht alles eingefallen ist! Über eventuelle Konsequenzen für ein besseres Verständnis der Texte wird hier allerdings nichts mitgeteilt. Es ist nun einmal so.

Der Autor macht es solchen Lesern, d.h., fast der ganzen Leserschaft, auch nicht leichter. Denn dieses Neuland kann nur als Labyrinth begangen werden. Dadurch zwingt er jeden, der sich hinein begibt und nicht unverrichteter Dinge einfach kehrtmacht, dem angelegten narrativen Pfad bis zum Ende zu folgen, in der Hoffnung der lange Weg wird doch zu den immer wieder angedeuteten neuen Kenntnissen führen. Genau wie im ursprünglichen Labyrinth nähert sich dieser Weg immer wieder dem „Zentrum" seiner Wahrheit, um dann gleich den nächsten Schlenker zu machen, der vorerst in eine ganz neue Richtung führt. Er muss so schreiben, die intellektuelle Methode verschweigen, die Gestalt seines Entwurfs verschleiern, sein Modell verstecken, mit den vorgegaukelten Erkenntnissen zurückhalten, die Hauptfrage immer wieder anrühren und die Antwort darauf verweigern, ja fast bis zum Schluss hinauszögern, weil sonst niemand nach den ersten drei Seiten seines Texts weiter lesen würde, wenn er dort erklärt hätte, was ihm vorschwebte und wie er es zu begründen hoffte. Er vermeidet tunlichst jedes Abstrahieren. Er will höher hinaus: ins Poetische. Denn das war auch Brechts Anliegen.

Müsste diese Methode begründet werden, statt lediglich in ihrer unnachahmlichen Ausführlichkeit vorgeführt, wäre es bald um jenen Höhenflug geschehen. Es käme recht bald zu einem Absturz. Da sie jedoch nur vorausgesetzt werden muss, bewegt sich der ganze Text im nie versagenden Aufwind der eigenen Rhetorik. In diesem schwerelosen Medium sind die tollsten Drehungen, die kühnsten interpretorischen Purzelbäume möglich. Die entferntesten Assoziationen können aus solcher Höhe sofort erspäht werden. Nichts muss in diesem durch rhetorische Ekstase und mit einer Konjunktiv-Philologie sich aufbauschenden Textes anhand irgendwelcher bodenständigen Kriterien geprüft werden. Der Phantasie sind keine Grenzen gesetzt. Träume gehen in Erfüllung, und „so darf geträumt werden" (496).

Und wie lautet etwa die praktisch bis zum Ende aufgehobene zentrale Frage? Im Grunde: Warum heißt das Stück *Der gute Mensch von Sezuan*?

Wie bitte? Also: Warum schreibt Brecht ausgerechnet „Sezuan" und nicht etwa „Szechuan" oder eine andere der im Westen gebräuchlicheren Transkriptionen des Namens jener chinesischen Provinz? Dazu muss „der Einstein der neuen Bühnenform," wie Brecht hier ständig genannt wird, einen Grund gehabt haben, zumal das Stück nicht nur eine geheime, bewusste und feinmaschige Kodierung chinesischer Kultur, sondern darüber hinaus die Form der dramatischen Dichtung des neuen Jahrhunderts darstellt. Das kann also kein Zufall sein.

Lassen wir die rhetorischen Mittel fürs erste aus dem Spiel. Der Autor meint eine vergleichende Untersuchung vorgelegt zu haben, die kulturelle Verhältnisse beschreibt, wie sie noch nie gesehen, verstanden und geschildert wurden. Da niemand auch nur annähernd die Breite und Tiefe der chinesischen Bezüge in Brechts Stück erkannt hat, ist sein Ziel, sie aufs genaueste zu beschreiben. In den 516 Seiten steht jedoch kein einziger zusammenfassender Satz über die Fabel des Stücks, besser gesagt: über die Fabel, wie man sie als Gegenstand einer kritischen Auseinandersetzung bislang ausgelegt und kommentiert hat. Der Autor geht ganz anders vor. Neben zahllosen Hinweisen auf erdachte, buchstäblich weithergeholte Beziehungen zwischen dem Stück und der klassischen Kultur, z.B. der *Reise nach dem Westen*, aber auch einmal der kulturellen Gegenwart, Liu Sola (512), gilt seine Aufmerksamkeit hauptsächlich den im Stück verwendeten „chinesischen" Namen. Aus ihnen entwickelt er nach und nach eine ausführliche Hermeneutik. Diese Methode ist in Wirklichkeit eine Art Onomantik, die in anderen Zeitaltern als eine Wahrsagekunst aus Namen verstanden wurde.

Denn die Namen sind allesamt Bedeutungsträger, die geheime Quelle jener sträflich vernachlässigten, unser Verständnis des Stücks nunmehr grundsätzlich erweiternden, ja umwerfenden Interpretation. Sie enthalten eine geheime „Botschaft" (286). Behauptete doch Tynjanov: „Im Kunstwerk gibt es keine nichtssagenden Namen" (169). Und „Brecht und seine Autorinnen," eine zweite ständig rekurrierende Formel, haben es gewusst. Hat man dies endlich mit allen dazugehörigen Konsequenzen erfasst, steht das Stück in einem ganz neuen Licht da. Und vieles andere auch!

Also werden sämtliche Namen, die im Stück vorkommen oder beim Umschreiben wieder herausgenommen wurden, semantisch ausgepresst. Diese überraschenden Ergebnisse sollen das seltsame, enthusiasmiertpedantische Vorhaben rechtfertigen. Wegen einer vorausgesetzten Eigentümlichkeit der chinesischen Sprache ermöglichen jene Signifikanten eine angeblich beinahe uferlose Mehrdeutigkeit, wodurch eine bislang unvermutete semantische Anspielung immer im richtigen Augenblick der Interpretation plötzlich herausspringt. Darüber hinaus stammen diese dadurch freigesetzten Signifikate auch und gleichzeitig aus mehreren Sprachen.

Das Chinesische allein reicht also bei weitem nicht aus, will man die ganze Spannweite der intendierten und simultan vielsagenden Bedeutungen erfassen. Das Japanische gibt auch viel her, wie selbstverständlich das

Englische und das Anglo-Amerikanische, vorausgesetzt freilich, dass die über jene Sprachen gewonnenen Signifikate sich mit einem jeweiligen, in *deutscher* Orthographie wiedergegebenen chinesischen Morphem lose verbinden lassen, etwa mit SHEN oder TE. Kommen einem eventuell Zweifel über die rapide zunehmenden und wirklich sehr gezielt angewendeten Sprachkenntnisse Brechts, wird mehrmals an das „Sprachgenie" (450) Steffin erinnert, der solche Leistungen ohne weiteres zuzutrauen wären. Auch wird großes Vertrauen in Elisabeth Hauptmann gesetzt: „Undenkbar bei dieser Akribie und Gewissenhaftigkeit (und: Liebe), dass Elisabeth Hauptmann nicht gewußt haben soll, wie etwas ‚japanisiert' werden mußte" (217, auch 368).

Diese Methode erinnert mich aus mehr als einem Grund an zwei Stellen in *Gulliver's Travels*. Womit neben der onomantischen Methode das Thema des hier verwendeten Modells schon angeschnitten wird. Im dritten Teil seiner Reisebeschreibung fragt Gulliver die Einwohner der vor der Küste „Japons" fliegenden Insel Laputa über die Bedeutung des Namens ihrer Heimat aus:

> The word, which I interpret the *Flying* or *Floating Island*, is in the original *Laputa*; whereof I could never learn the true etymology. *Lap* in the old obsolete language signifieth *high*, and *untuh* a *governor*; from which they say by corruption was derived *Laputa* from *Lapuntuh*. But I do not approve of this derivation, which seems to be a little strained. I ventured to offer to the learned among them, a conjecture of my own, that *Laputa* was *quasi Lap outed*; *lap* signifying properly the dancing of the sun beams in the sea; and *outed* a wing, which however I shall not obtrude, but submit to the judicious reader. (Kapitel II)

Gesucht wird selbstredend eine „wahre Etymologie" und Gulliver wartet mit poetisch wirksameren Vorschlägen auf. Der Versuch, diese Sprache durch Auslegung des metaphorischen Gehalts zusammengesetzter Wörter besser zu verstehen, wird dann um einiges erschwert, als er die Große Akademie von Lagado besichtigt:

> [The first professor] then led me to the frame about the sides whereof all his pupils stood in ranks. It was twenty foot square, placed in the middle of the room. The superficies was composed of several bits of wood, about the bigness of a dye, but some larger than others. They were all linked together by slender wires. These bits of wood were covered on every square with paper pasted on them; and, on these papers were written all the words of their language in their several moods, tenses, and declensions, but without any order. The professor then desired me to observe, for he was going to set his engine at work. The pupils at his command took each of them hold of an iron handle, whereof there were forty fixed round the edges of the frame; and giving them a sudden turn, the whole disposition of the words was entirely changed. He then commanded six and thirty of the lads to read the several lines softly as they appeared upon the frame; and where they found three of four words together that might make part of a sentence, they dictated to the four remaining boys who were scribes. This work was repeated three or four times, and

> at every turn the engine was so contrived, that the words shifted into new places, as the square bits of wood moved upside down. (Kapitel V)

Dieser merkwürdige Vorgang, offenbar einem nicht auf Anhieb einsehbaren poetischen und hermeneutischen Zweck gewidmet, ist nicht frei erfunden. Damit satirisiert Swift die mechanischen Vorrichtungen der Kabbala-Interpreten der jüngsten Barockzeit, die aus verstellbaren Buchstaben und Wörtern Dichtung und Einsicht in die Wahrheit maschinell herzustellen hofften. Georg Philipp Harsdörffers *Fünffacher Denkring der teutschen Sprache* war eine drehbare poetologische Mechanik, die alle vorhandenen Silben verschieden zusammensetzen ließ. Athanasius Kircher ersann eine Metaphernmaschine, durch die Bilder übereinander gestellt und dann gedanklich miteinander kombiniert werden konnten. Quirinus Kuhlmann erfand eine Sprachmaschine, die als „allgemein durchgehendes Sprachwechselrad" alle Sprachen kombinatorisch miteinander verbinden lassen sollte. Es waren handgreifliche, quasi mit Bedienungsanleitung versehene dreidimensionale Modelle, die nach dem Prinzip der Buchstabenversetzung der Kabbala aufgebaut waren. „Wenn der Nam zu keiner Erfindung dienen wil / so kan man die Buchstaben versetzen und eine andere Meinung heraus bringen" (Harsdörffer, *Poetischer Trichter*). Swift mokierte sich darüber.

Mit der wiederentdeckten Kabbala wollte die Romantik einen platten Rationalismus bekämpfen. Schlegel schwebte vor, daraus ein Modell für die neue Ästhetik zu entwickeln. Hamann verwendet andauernd kabbalistische Strategien. Seine „Sprache weist performativ vor, was sie thematisiert. Die allusive Schreibart der Kabbala ist selbst im Modus der Allusion vorgetragen."[1] Eine neuerliche Beschreibung der rhetorischen Folgen passt zu *Coining Poetry* wie die Faust aufs Auge:

> Hamanns Stil ist wirklich furchtbar: verschlungen, dunkel, voller Anspielungen, Abschweifungen und unerfindlicher Bezugnahmen, voller privater Witze, Wortspiele in Wortspielen, Anagramme und Kryptogramme, voller Geheimnamen für Personen der Vergangenheit und Gegenwart, für Begriffe und unsagbare Visionen der Wahrheit. Wo das Fleisch der Worte den Geist nicht zu offenbaren vermag, da versucht er, der zurecht vergessenen kabbalistischen Ausdrucksweise der Mystagogen der Vergangenheit nachzueifern — in Formulierungen, von denen nicht zu sagen ist, wo die Imitation endet und die Parodie beginnt.[2]

Bei Hamann wie bei Bock haben wir es mit kabbalistischer Sprachmagie zu tun. Durch Vertauschung der „zweiundzwanzig hebräischen Buchstaben und der Gottesnamen" wie auch „durch Kontemplation ihrer linguistischen Elemente" soll „eine in göttlichen Buchstaben und Namen geschriebene Textur" entziffert werden.[3] Die Gottesnamen sind letztlich Umsetzungen des immer großgeschriebenen Tetragramms IHVH. Oftmals „dauerentflammt" und „in Fieber gesetzt...bis in den Exzeß" (194), schreibt auch Bock die bei Brecht vorkommenden Namen immer in Makulatur oder, wie wir sahen, im Fettdruck zur Hervorhebung ihrer mehrdeutigen Bedeutsamkeit: SHEN und TE, SHUI und TA. Das ist also kein Zufall.

Wohl deswegen finden sich Anspielungen auf die Kabbala (181, in Bezug auf Borges, wohlgemerkt Bocks stilistischer Gegenpol); und auf jede herstellbare Verbindung zwischen jüdischer und chinesischer Kultur (305, Richard Wilhelm suchte nach solchen Bezügen; 328, die Vermutung, im Fettdruck, „daß hebräisches und chinesisches Frauenideal im wesentlichen identisch seien"), wie auch zwischen hebräischen Buchstaben und chinesischen Ideogrammen (430). Statt die Buchstaben bzw. das Wort zu versetzen — aber das macht er auch—, tauscht Bock die chinesischen Zeichen, die irgendwie mit dem in deutscher Schreibart gleich scheinenden Laut annähernd verbunden werden können. Dadurch ergießt sich über die 516 Seiten ein onomantischer Strom der Bezüge, der in jede beliebige Richtung geleitet werden kann.

Jeder stellt sich einmal die Frage, ob nicht die Namen in *Der gute Mensch von Sezuan* eventuell zum Verständnis des Stücks beitragen. Als ich vor etlichen Jahren Brechts Beziehungen zu China zu untersuchen begann, fiel auch mir auf, dass *Shen Te* und *Shui Ta* etwas „bedeuten" bzw. zum Sprechen gebracht werden konnten. Die Figurennamen wurden im Zuge des Schreibens auch umgeändert, hießen sie doch in einem früheren Stadium *Li Gung* und *Lao Go*. Dies wiederum bestärkte die Vermutung, dass etwas dahinter steckte. In *Li Gung* und *Lao Go* sah ich zwar chinesisch klingende Namen aber im Gegensatz zu den späteren keinen auf die Figuren beziehbaren Sinn. Die weiteren Figurennamen waren gleichfalls ohne erkennbaren Bezug. Da auch andere, für ungeschulte europäische Ohren irgendwie chinesisch klingende, aber im Chinesischen unmögliche Namensformen — Wung, Shung — verwendet wurden und zumal neben Sezuan zwei andere Namen, offensichtlich gleichfalls Provinzen oder Gebiete, womöglich auch Städte, die es nicht gibt — *Schun* und *Kwan* — im Vorspiel erwähnt werden, schloss ich auch wegen der Unerheblichkeit und der grundsätzlichen Unwahrscheinlichkeit eines solchen Unterfangens aus, dass diese Namen geheime Bedeutungsträger sein konnten.

Genau dies behauptet nun Bock. Da meine Meinung mir jetzt jenen Rassismusvorwurf einträgt, war ich natürlich neugierig, wie Bock neben *Sezuan* auch noch aus den Gebietsbezeichnungen *Schun* und *Kwan* Bedeutsames herausholen würde. Das wird im Handumdrehen auf eine Weise gemacht, die bislang niemandem eingefallen ist. Wir erfahren, dass *Schun* einen mythischen Kaiser bezeichnet, während mit *Kwan* selbstverständlich die volkstümliche buddhistische Göttin der Barmherzigkeit gemeint sein muss. In Wirklichkeit heißt diese Figur *Kwanyin* (Pinyin: Guanyin). *Kwan* alleine sagt gar nichts oder eben auch alles, und nach dieser Methode verfährt er im ganzen langen Buch: „Schun und Kwan holen vielmehr die Personage chinesischer ‚goldener Legende' ins Gedächtnis, ohne die selbst eine ‚halb europäisierte' Parabel nicht auskommt: die mythischen Kaiser und Herrscher" (281). Die Stellung des Namens im Stück spielt keine Rolle mehr, auch z.B., dass Shen Te und Shui Ta eine Person sind. Hier geht es höher hinaus, assoziiert doch SHEN TE sprachmagisch nunmehr „Kwan."

Diese Provinznamen werden zu drei Figurennamen *Fo, Su, Tscheng,* die Herr Buddha, Witwe Rein und Herr Stadt hergeben sollen, und dann zu den drei Göttern in Beziehung gesetzt. Dies löst eine das Buch durchlaufende Kette von zahlenmystischen Spekulationen aus, die manchmal auf das Druckbild einwirken und zum Arsenal der Kabbalistik gehören. Infolgedessen sei es auch unmöglich — solche Formulierungen werden ständig verwendet, da nichts hier „belegt" werden muss noch wird, denn Belegen gehört zu den niederen, spaßverderbenden Künsten—, dass rein zufällig von *drei* Provinzen geredet wird, denn in der gleichzeitig im Stück einkodierten chinesischen Geschichte war *Sezuan* bzw. der historische Vorgänger, aber was tut's, eins der drei Reiche, die z.B. im klassischen Werk *Die Geschichte der Drei Reiche* vorkommen. Dieser seitenweise sich ausbreitenden Assoziationskette zufolge, ist *Sezuan* folglich, „Drittes Reich poetischer Zunge" (303). Womit der Bezug zur Zeitgeschichte wieder einmal hergestellt wird. Diese Exkursion in die klassische chinesische Kultur bringt auch insofern einen unverhofften Bonus, als die (völlig anderen) Namen der auf dem Gebiet des jetzigen Sezuans befindlichen Provinz und deren Hauptstadt damals identisch waren, womit für unseren Autor erklärt wird, warum „Brecht und seine Autorinnen" zuerst den Namen der Provinz mit der Hauptstadt verwechselten und die „Hauptstadt Sezuan" schrieben.

Da *Shen Te* durch das überreichte Geld von den Göttern gewissermaßen „erfunden" und am Ende dann verlassen wird, schlug ich als Bedeutung „göttliche Wirksamkeit" vor, denn die Wörter können so ausgelegt werden.[4] Bock zitiert ohne Namensnennung einen kurzen früheren Artikel von mir, um anzumahnen, dass „göttliche Wirkkraft" weit besser wäre, denn bei ihm gerät *Shen Te* zu einer Heiligenfigur, eben zu jenem Leitbild für das neue Jahrhundert. Die unterschiedliche Auslegung dieses Namens weist tatsächlich auf eine Kluft zwischen den Interpretationen.

Aber wie steht es mit dem fallengelassenen Namen *Li Gung*? Um es kurz zu machen, bezieht Bock das Wort *Li,* verwendet man seine onomantische Methode der Gleichsetzung der europäischen Lautschreibung mit allen auch nur entfernt damit kombinierbaren chinesischen Zeichen jener lautarmen Sprache, aus Hunderten von möglichen Auslegungen hier auf eine Bedeutung in der klassischen chinesischen Kultur: auf das konfuzianische Ritual. *Gung* kann nach dieser Methode beinahe endlos interpretiert werden, berücksichtigt man alle damit verbindbaren Zeichen in allen auf Chinesisch jedoch anders klingenden Tonhöhen. Aus dieser Fülle wählt er „öffentlich" aus, um festzustellen, dass *Li Gung* daher „RituelleRitualisierte Öffentlichkeit" (*sic*) oder **„Sittliche Öffentlichkeit (für**

alle!)" (454f., *sic*) bedeutet. Wozu das gut sein soll? Jeder wird dabei gleich einsehen, dass hier der Junge Genosse aus *Die Maßnahme* gemeint sein muss. Infolgedessen signalisiert der Namenswechsel von *Li Gung* auf *Shen Te*, denn hier wird auch eine heimliche Autobiographie konstruiert, eine Abkehr von der Politik und eine Hinwendung zu der erträumten, neuen und vor allem *poetischen* Welt. Diese Welt muss auch universal sein. Deswegen werden die schier endlosen chinesischen Bezüge bewusst eingebunden, geht es doch um die Zukunft der Menschheit, die ohne eine chinesische Beteiligung undenkbar wäre.

Dieses methodische Vorgehen in seiner detaillierten Komplexität gebührend zu schildern, käme, wie schon angedeutet, einer nochmaligen Lektüre des Buches gleich. Ich erwähne deswegen nur noch vier Beispiele.

1. Es gibt eine Figur mit Namen *Feng*. Nicht jeder wird sich daran erinnern, denn sie redet nicht. Gemeint ist der kleine Sohn des Schreiners *Lin To*. Über diesen Namen ergießt sich jedoch ein Platzregen von Anspielungen und Assoziationen. Das fängt mit dem klassischen *Buch der Lieder*, dem *Shijing*, an und hört mit den ständig herangezogenen Wörterbüchern auf, zu denen auch *Japanisch für Globetrotter* (315) und *Chinesisch in 24 Stunden* (365) gehören. Eins der vielen Schriftzeichen, *Feng*, bezeichnet einen Teil jener Liedersammlung. In der traditionellen konfuzianisch-moralischen Auslegung jenes Werks enthielten diese sogenannten Volkslieder eine verklausulierte Kritik uneinsichtiger Herrscher. Brecht müsse die Assoziation einer sozialen Kritik behalten haben, weil das Wort von Waley erwähnt und in den Anmerkungen zu den chinesischen Gedichten zitiert wird. Nun wird „die Kühnheit des Brechtschen Historisierens" (443) erst richtig erkennbar: „Der kleine FENG zeigt sich damit nicht nur als personifizierte ‚Kritik an den Herrschenden', sein Name tut auch noch kund, wie diese Kritik zu verstehen ist: als Volkslied" (444). Damit ist aber die Bedeutsamkeit dieser stummen aber beredten Figur bzw. ihres Namens noch lange nicht ausgeschöpft. Denn forscht man mit dem Vergrößerungsglas in den einschlägigen Wörterbüchern nach, findet man bei Matthews unter den vielen Fengs eben diese obskure Bedeutung: „a district in Szechwan said to be near the entrance to the infernal regions." Die „Härte und Wucht," mit der Brecht den Namen setzt, zeige sich nun folgendermaßen: „Kaum beachtet und doch kindlich geradeaus hat der kleine FENG die Szene dorthin gelenkt, wo sie der inneren Mathematik nach hinlangen mußte: an die Schwelle zum 8., zum Fabrik-Bild" (493). Diese Fabrik ist selbstredend die Hölle.

2. Der Autor erklärt folgendermaßen die Bedeutung von SHUI TA: „Wer ist es?" Auf Chinesisch müsste man dafür sagen: „Ta shi shui?" Verstellen gehört aber zur Methode. Spielt man mit SHUI TA weiter herum, ergibt sich neben einem „englischen" „Showy ‚Thank you'" (177) „anagrammatisch" (265) eine Antwort auf diese Frage, „Wer ist es?" denn *huida* bedeu-

tet „Antwort." Die „Wörter" HUI STA lassen sich auch durch eine Buchstabenversetzung daraus konstruieren und damit hat man über UI (Arturo) und STAlin, die zwei Hauptschergen des 20. Jahrhunderts, gleich beim Namen genannt. Da auf Russisch und Polnisch die Silbe „hui" (aber ein „h" auf Russisch?) eine sofort erkennbare anzügliche Bedeutung hergibt, wird jeder einsehen, was hier gemeint ist: „HitlerSchwanzficktStalin" (175).

3. Anhand dieser unerschöpflichen Lust zu anagrammieren (266), zu visionieren (359) und unentwegt zu assoziieren, entsteht ein ekstatisches mehrsprachiges Wörterbuch von Auslegungen für SHEN TE. Mir vergeht die Lust, sie alle aufzuzählen. Eine erwähne ich bloß: *shanty*, wohnt sie doch in einem Armenviertel. Was der Kabbala *Adam Qadmon* war, ist für Bock Brechts SHEN TE: die göttliche Verbürgerung der Zukunft. Brechts Ziel sei gewesen: „im tiefsten Exil eine neue Schöpfungsmythe zu setzen" (419). Daher habe sein Text „kosmische wie überzeitliche Tragweite" erlangt (430).

4. Warum schrieb Brecht nun *Sezuan* und nicht etwa Szechwan? Dazu kam es über einen Leo Greiner, der offenbar irgendwo irgendwann mal „Si-Tsüan" schrieb. Da Brecht bzw. dem Einstein der neuen Bühnenform und seinen Autorinnen alle denkbaren Assoziationen mehrsprachig ständig präsent waren, kann das nur eines bedeuten: eingeschrieben sei sprachmagisch und wegen der ähnlichen Vokalisierung sowohl ein Wort für Drama, *qü*, und ein anderes für eine bekannte lyrische Form, *ci*, das auch als *tzu* und in vielen anderen europäischen Versionen auftaucht. Damit gestalte sich das Stück sowohl dramatisch wie auch lyrisch zum langanhaltenden Echo chinesischer Kultur. Deswegen heißt es dann *Der gute Mensch von Sezuan*. Aber nicht *nur* deswegen. Denn Wilhelms Übersetzung von Zhuangzi (Dschuang Dsi): *Das Wahre Buch vom Südlichen Blütenland* spiele auch eine Rolle. Mit dem südlichen Blütenland ist selbstredend Sichuan (Sezuan) gemeint, wohin der von Brecht geschätzte Li Bai ins Exil ging usw. Infolgedessen solle man sich Brechts Titel als Hommage an diesen Text denken, denn durch Überkreuzung verbinden sich wahr und gut, Buch und Mensch.

Wie sieht die anfänglich exzerpierte Kostprobe nun aus? Der ganze Text ist ja sprachmagisch angelegt. Der Autor arbeitet mit Fettdruck und Makulatur, um durch das Druckbild Wirkungen zu suggerieren, die logisch, philologisch und kulturell unsinnig sind. Heißt es doch anderswo: „TE verabschiedet|e SchriftZüge, die Brecht und mit ihm seine Autorinnen an die Grenze zum Irrsinn gebracht hatten" (364, *sic*). TE, als „Tugend," gleichlautend mit DE, als „Wirkung erzielen," und viele andere Assoziationen schreiben sich sprachmagisch ins Deutsche und dadurch ohnehin auf einer anderen Ebene quasi unbewußt in die Werke Brechts hinein: „TE setzt Schmetterlingswolken COURAGEirt t**e**utsch."

Dann enthält das kongeniale „konshenial" die magische Ausstrahlung des Zauberwortes SHEN, weil alle Morpheme, sprachübergreifend, eine universale Verbindlichkeit herstellen. Die magische Ausstrahlung der tugendhaften TE wird dem deutsch-tschajnataunesischen Wort „konshenial" noch im Superskript angehängt, seine Wirkung somit erheblich, ja potentiell ins Unermessliche steigernd[hochte]. „Smetterlingschaos" ist eine Anspielung auf die dänische Aussprache von Ruth Berlau. Was nun „Weiße C" usw. bedeutet, habe ich ehrlich vergessen. Um es herauszubekommen, müsste ich das ganze Buch noch einmal lesen. Lieber nicht. Ezra Pound hat die chinesischen Zeichen auseinander genommen und in ihre bildhaft-metaphorische Bestandteile zerlegt. Daraus entstand manchmal eine geniale Lyrik. Bock geht ganz anders vor. Er assoziiert mehrsprachig denkbare, durch Lautvertauschung potentiell ins Unermessliche reichende Auslegungen, aus deren Kombinationen er sein schrulliges Wortgebäude zusammenstellt.

Dem Autor gebe ich darin recht, dass Brechts schönes Stück im Theater oft verhunzt wird. In Augsburg sah ich einmal eine Inszenierung, die alle lyrischen Stellen, also die Stimme des sozialen Unbewussten, einfach gestrichen hat. Da wurde noch immer verdrängt. Aber neben den schlimmsten habe ich von diesem Stück auch zwei der besten Brecht-Aufführungen gesehen: eine in Berlin, die andere in Beijing. Es waren nicht zufällig Studentenaufführungen und beide stellten solche Verdrängungen ins Zentrum des Geschehens. In Beijing sagte mir eine chinesische Bekannte, sie habe nicht verstanden, dass Brecht China so gut kannte. Aber Brecht „kannte" China nicht — er wollte partout Folklore vermeiden — und schon gar nicht, wie Bock sich das vorstellt, obwohl die ostasiatische Kultur sein Werk und sein Denken teilweise entscheidend beeinflusst hat. Dafür waren ihm menschliche Verhaltensweisen nur allzu bekannt und die waren in China genauso anzutreffen wie anderswo auch. Das Archivmaterial zeigt die Anstrengungen, die der Stoff gekostet hat. Deswegen habe ich betont, dass das Stück nicht *chinesisch* sein wollte, sondern einfach menschlich glaubhaft, auch weil es damals und wohl immer noch als märchenhaft (Reich-Ranicki) abgetan wurde. Erstaunlich ist es übrigens, dass Bock bis auf zwei Zitate, andere aus der chinesischen Kultur, auch die in Erwägung gezogenen aber im Stück dann nicht verwendeten, offenbar nicht kennt.

Dieses Buch erträumt sich eine andere Rezeption des Stücks und möchte „chinesischdeutsch" berichten „Vom guten Menschen singend aus Theaterland" (464). Wenn hier in der Tat das Unbeschreibliche getan ist, dann führt auch die ewig-weibliche göttliche Wirkkraft der mildtätigen, universalierten SHEN TE *buchstäblich* ins nächste Jahrhundert hinan. Meines Erachtens hat dieses Buch mit „Brecht" und mit „China" wenig zu tun und noch weniger mit „Brecht und China." Dafür ist es einschließlich des zur onomantischen Methode dazugehörigen prophetischen Begehrens in seiner phantasiegetriebenenen Erweiterung des dahinter liegenden sprachmagischen Modells eine schlechterdings unübertreffliche kabbalistische Chinoiserie.

Antony Tatlow
University of Dublin

ANMERKUNGEN

[1] Andreas B. Kilcher, *Die Sprachtheorie der Kabbala als ästhetisches Paradigma. Die Konstruktion einer ästhetischen Kabbala seit der Frühen Neuzeit* (Stuttgart: Metzler, 1998), 267.

[2] Isaiah Berlin, *Der Magus des Nordens. J. G. Hamann und der Ursprung des modernen Irrationalismus* (Berlin 1995), 43.

[3] Kilcher, *Die Sprachtheorie der Kabbala*, 33.

[4] Wer sich dafür interessiert, kann nachlesen in: Antony Tatlow, *The Mask of Evil* (Bern: Peter Lang, 1976), 267ff.

Vladimir Koljazin, Hrsg. *Brecht i chudoschestvennaja kultura XX veka. Materialy nautschnoj konferencii. Archivnye dokumenty. Publikacii. Chronika.* [Brecht und die künstlerische Kultur des 20. Jahrhunderts. Materialien einer wissenschaftlichen Konferenz der Russischen Brecht-Gesellschaft zum 100. Geburtstag Bertolt Brechts (12.–13. März 1998).] Moskau 1999. 288 Seiten.

Vorliegender Band dokumentiert mit den Beiträgen einer wissenschaftlichen Konferenz, den bibliographischen Nachweisen zu Publikationen der Mitglieder der Russischen Brecht-Gesellschaft, den Interviews mit dem Theaterregisseur Jurij Ljubimow und dem Komponisten Lew Solin sowie den abgedruckten Archivalien den aktuellen Stand des Umgangs mit Person und Werk Brechts in der postsowjetischen Wissenschaft, Kunst und Öffentlichkeit. Da es in folgendem vor allem um die hier veröffentlichten Archiv-Dokumente (44 Seiten von insgesamt 288 Seiten) gehen soll, zum Ganzen nur so viel: hier zeigt sich eine neue Generation von Brecht-Forschern, die sich streitbar in die internationale Brechtforschung einbringt, den Theatermann und Theoretiker als Einheit zu betrachten sucht und durch Bereitstellung sowjetischer Quellen zu Brecht und seinen Zeitgenossen die in den letzten 10 Jahren stattgefundene Debatte um Brechts Verhältnis zu den totalitären Systemen des 20. Jahrhunderts zu historisieren hilft. Gleichzeitig ist aber nicht zu übersehen, daß die miserable finanzielle Ausstattung der Forschung im heutigen

Rußland auch Folgen für die wissenschaftliche Qualität mit sich bringt. Sachanmerkungen sind recht fehlerhaft und geben oft nicht den außerrussischen Forschungsstand wieder. Darüberhinaus sind etliche Archivdokumente mit Ellipsen wiedergegeben, was ihren Wert für die Forschung reduziert.

Es ist Koljazins Verdienst, der bereits mit dem Band *Laßt mich frei!* (Moskau 1997) wichtige KGB-Dokumente zugänglich gemacht hat,[1] diesmal aus dem Russischen Staatlichen Archiv für Literatur und Kunst (RGALI) 30 Dokumente in russischer Übersetzung zu veröffentlichen, die aus dem im Fond 631 (Sowjetischer Schriftstellerverband) aufbewahrten Redaktionsnachlaß der Zeitschriften *Das Wort* und der *Internationalen Literatur* (russische Ausgabe) stammen. Die Auswahl erfolgte unter dem Aspekt der Rolle und Mitarbeit von Brecht sowie seiner (Nicht-) Veröffentlichung in diesen Zeitschriften. Unter der Überschrift „Aus dem Briefwechsel der Zeitschrift *Das Wort* 1936-1938" lesen wir Briefe von Maria Osten, Margarete Steffin und Fritz Erpenbeck. Überschrieben „Aus dem Briefwechsel der Zeitschrift *Das Wort* im Zusammenhang von Brechts Tätigkeit als Redakteur" findet man Briefe von Alfred Kurella, Lion Feuchtwanger, Willi Bredel und Fritz Erpenbeck.

Es folgen zwei von der Zeitschrift *Internationale Literatur* in Auftrag gegebenen „Gutachten" von Mai bzw. Juni 1941, die ein ablehnendes Urteil über *Der gute Mensch von Sezuan* (Ms. 81 Seiten) sowie die Erzählungen „Der Mantel des Ketzers," „Der Augsburger Kreidekreis" und „Das Experiment" abgeben. Während das Drama im Unterschied zu seinen früheren klaren Stücken als „Mysterium" oder als philosophischer Scherz über den Zusammenhang von kraftlosen Göttern und Menschen, das eventuell für das Puppenspiel geeignet sei, zum Druck abgelehnt wird, bekommt die Prosa wegen ihrer „Zeitlosigkeit" und „allegorisch-symbolistischen" Fabeln eine Rüge. Die Bemühung Brechts um russische Veröffentlichungen stand im Kontext seiner geplanten Transit-Durchreise und der Hoffnung auf Honorar. So brachte Becher in der deutschen Ausgabe der *Internationalen Literatur* im Juniheft 1941 den „Augsburger Kreidekreis" und im Juliheft einige Antikriegs-Gedichte aus den „Finnischen Epigrammen," die dem „Gutachter," der sie als „sehr schwach" bewertete, ebenfalls vorgelegen hatten.

Koljazin wertet die von ihm veröffentlichten Briefe zu Recht als wichtige Dokumente zur Rekonstruktion des redaktionellen Alltags der Zeitschrift *Das Wort*, als „Einblicke in die Moskauer literarische Küche," in der — so könnte man weiter fabulieren — zu viele Köche zeitweilig den antifaschistischen „Brei" zu verderben drohten. Koljazin merkt an, daß die Original-Briefe Brechts fehlen, sich aber diverse Kopien erhalten haben. Es ist für mich unverständlich, warum er diese bis auf einen jedoch nicht abdruckt, zumal auch nur einige wenige davon in der neuen Brecht-Ausgabe enthalten sind. Er fragt, wer diese Briefe entnommen haben könnte und wo sie zu suchen wären. Sicher in den Beständen des KGB, aber auch in den Unterlagen der Auslands-Kommission, bei Apletin als dem Nachfolger von Sergej Tretjakow und Michail Kolzow. Aber bevor sich jemand an diese Aufgabe macht, sollten wir uns an das halten, was jetzt schon einsehbar ist. Zumal zweifelsfrei ist, daß die Brecht-Kopien echt sind.

Gerade für den umstrittenen Komplex Brecht und der Stalinismus bieten seine in Moskau lagernden kommentierenden und intervenieren-den Briefe an Erpenbeck und Kurella aufschlußreiche Einblicke in Brechts strategisches und taktisches Verhalten.

Um nur zwei Beispiele aus eigener Moskauer Lektüre zu geben: nachdem sich die Krise zwischen Brecht und Erpenbeck wegen der Be-handlung Hanns Eislers sowie der Verzögerung des Abdrucks der Memoi-ren von Martin Andersen Nexö zugespitzt hatte, schrieb Brecht am 25. November 1938 an Erpenbeck:

> Wie denken Sie sich eigentlich unsere zusammenarbeit? Was ist mit der demokratischen grundlage unserer redaktionsarbeit? ich bestehe darauf, daß diese abmachung durchgeführt wird und der abdruck in der januar-nummer beginnt. ich bin nicht gewohnt, als strohmann auf titelblättern geführt zu werden, wenn sie eine alleinige herrschaft durchführen wollen, müssen die herausgeber m.m.n. daraus die konsequenzen ziehen. wie immer wieder betont, bin ich auch empört über die art, wie unserem freund eisler bei uns das wort entzogen wird. in dem großen und schweren kampf gegen den faschismus stehend, müssen wir unsere freunde ehrlich und menschlich behandeln.

Anfang Januar 1939 teilte Brecht seine Bestürzung darüber mit, daß Eislers „Entgegnung" nun statt im *Wort* in der *Weltbühne* erschienen ist.

> ich habe immer wieder darauf gedrungen, daß sie bei uns erscheint, da ja auch der angriff bei uns erschien. zumindestens von bredel weiß ich positiv, daß er ebenfalls für den abdruck war. ich muß also der redaktion hier sabotage zur last legen [. . .] da ich nun seit wochen keinerlei antwort mehr auf meine anfragen und nicht einmal bestätigungen für den eingang von manuskripten, die ich abschickte, bekomme, in den mir zugeschickten materialien für neue hefte meine forderungen aber einfach unberücksichtigt finde, muß ich Euch bitten, mir die adresse der stelle im verlag mitzuteilen, der Ihr verantwortlich seid. mit kameradschaftlichem gruß brecht.

Die in diesem Band abgedruckten 30 Briefe (der Moskauer Bestand zum *Wort* enthält mehrere hundert Briefe) beziehen sich auf die oben angedeu-teten Probleme Brechts, seine Intentionen in der Zeitschrift durchzuset-zen. Sie stammen bis auf zwei aus dem Jahre 1938 und dokumentieren vor allem Fritz Erpenbecks Bemühungen, sich bei Bredel und Feuchtwan-ger Hilfe gegen Brecht zu holen. Erpenbecks mit „Die Redaktion" ge-zeichneter Beitrag zum „Abschluß unserer Expressionismus-Diskussion" (Heft 6/1938) mußte durch Brechts entschiedenen Einspruch um jene Passagen gekürzt werden, in denen die Realismus-Auffassung von Lukács sanktioniert werden sollte. Brechts Post-scriptum in dieser Sache lautete am 2. Mai 1938: „Wir müßten übrigens, in diplomatischer Form, Lukács nahelegen, in seinen Arbeiten für das WORT unbedingt dieses ständige Zensurenerteilen, überhaupt diese autoritäre Allüre des Marxismus-pächters, zu unterlassen, ein solcher Ton, wie er ihn gegen Eisler, einen großen revolutionären Musiker, anschlägt, schickt sich nicht im WORT" (192).

Die Briefe zeigen die unterschiedlichen literarischen Auswahlkriterien der Herausgeber sowie der Redakteure Erpenbeck, Kurella, Maria Osten, das peinliche Unverständnis etwa, das Erpenbeck gegenüber Walter Benjamin als „wissenschaftlich tuendem Schaumschläger" artikulierte. Zwei Briefe stammen aus der Anfangszeit der Zeitschriftengründung: Maria Osten fragt bei Lydia Scheinina, in Moskau in der Redaktion tätig, im Juli 1936, warum die erste Nummer noch immer nicht erschienen ist. Sie teilt mit, daß Brecht ganz und gar gegen die Veröffentlichung von Ernst Ott-walts Kritik an Ignazio Silone sei und kündigt bei eventuellem Erscheinen einen Skandal an. Vom Londoner Plenum der Internationalen Schriftstel-lervereinigung, an dem sie für die Redaktion teilnahm, zeigt sie sich am 24. Juni 1936 an Scheinina „enttäuscht," weil die Empfänge wichtiger als die Arbeit gewesen sei. Maria Ostens Bedeutung für *Das Wort* bedarf erst noch einer ausführlichen Darstellung, die ihre antifaschistische engagierte Arbeit sowie ihr organisatorisches Geschick gleichermaßen zeigen würde. Ihre Funktion als „vielseitiger literarischer Kurier" (161) zwischen den Exilländern war es dann auch, die zur konstruierten NKWD-Anklage wegen Spionagetätigkeit gegen die UdSSR im Dienste der deutschen und französischen Aufklärung beitrug, in deren Folge sie am 8. August 1942 in Saratow erschossen wurde.

Nicht zuletzt können wir die postalischen Schwierigkeiten nach-vollziehen, die zwischen Moskau, Kopenhagen, Paris und Sanary sur Mer einem pünktlichen Erscheinen der Monatszeitschrift im Wege standen, die von 1936 bis 1939 für die Entwicklung der antifaschistischen Literatur als Publikationsort wie als Diskussionsforum wichtig gewesen war. Die hier abgedruckten Briefe machen die Notwendigkeit deutlich, den Gesamtbe-stand der Redaktion durch eine sorgfältig kommentierte Ausgabe öffent-lich zugänglich zu machen. Hierzu bedarf es in Zeiten knappen Geldes sicher einer klugen internationalen Kooperation, die jedoch für die politi-sche Kultur des 20. Jahrhunderts singuläre Zeugnisse bereit stellen würde.

Simone Barck
Zentrum für zeithistorische Forschung, Potsdam

ANMERKUNG

[1] "Vernite mne svobodu!" Memorialnuy sbornik dokumentov iz archivov byvschevo KGB. Dejateli literatury i isskusstva Rossii i Germanii — Schertvy

stalinskovo terrora ["Laßt mich frei!" Erinnerungsband von Dokumenten aus den Archiven des früheren KGB. Literaten und Künstler Rußlands und Deutschlands – Opfer des stalinistischen Terrors]. Moskau: Medium, 1997. Enthält Verfolgungs-, Prozeß- und Rehabilitierungsunterlagen zu 20 Personen, darunter zu Carola Neher, Alexander Granach, Hans Hauska, Asja Lacis, Helmut Damerius, Herwarth Walden, Maria Osten, Berhard Reich.

Susanne Winnacker, guest editor, "German Brecht, European Readings," Special section of *TDR — The Drama Review* 164 (Winter 1999). 184 pages.

American readings of Bertolt Brecht's oeuvre tend to focus on the humanist plays. *Galileo, Mother Courage and Her Children,* and *The Good Person of Szechwan* dominate critical analysis and classroom exposure of Brecht. *The Drama Review's* Winter 1999 Special Section on Brecht, however, provides a more European focus on texts like the *Lehrstücke* or learning plays, the *Fatzer* fragments, and the *Mahagonny* songs. Titled "German Brecht, European Readings," the extended section is in some ways a project meant to free Brecht studies of what editor Susanne Winnacker calls the "obstinate desire to pacify Brecht by owning him and fitting him into a social reality" (9). Instead, the fifteen articles assembled by Winnacker shift emphasis back onto the texts, which she argues become "buried underneath" critical fashions, "changing paradigms, political, ideological, and psychological lines" that render author and texts "for a time invisible" (8-9). Hence, issues of language and translation here supersede negotiations of biographical material and issues of Brecht's "moral duplicity" and "personal opportunism," though telling details of Brecht's life are regularly woven into analysis. Discussions of performances and literary artifacts alike approach Brecht as a text-maker first and theater artist second.

Perhaps the most accessible articles for American readers are Carol Martin's "Brecht, Feminism and Chinese Theatre" and Gerd Gemünden's "Brecht in Hollywood: *Hangmen Also Die* and the Anti-Nazi Film." Martin's essay attempts to "rethink Colonial assumptions in the opposite direction," contextualizing and historicizing Brecht's praise of Mei Lanfang with background on traditional Chinese performance and current feminist and materialist theory. Gemünden explores how the construction of memory, national loyalty, and cultural identity in Hollywood anti-Nazi films by exiled artists vary from more mainstream films. As such, both participate in a kind of cultural analysis of film conventions or gender in history familiar to American scholars. Perhaps the most challenging and obscure contribution is Friedrich Dieckmann's "Brecht's Modernity: Notes on an Obscure Author," which draws on French psychoanalytic theory, wrestling with Brecht's modes "self-sublation" and "self-preservation" in both his texts and his life (13).

As Winnacker points out, the collection represents the engagement of a younger generation of scholars with new theoretical approaches and the fruits of research made possible by the opening of the East German archives after the fall of the Berlin Wall in 1989. The new Brecht edition, jointly published by Suhrkamp Verlag and Aufbau Verlag, also shapes these new "exemplary" approaches to Brecht (10). Inspired by new research, new translations, and recent productions, the substance of the articles breaks down into three categories: those concerned with theorizing translation and documentation, those negotiating Brecht's legacy in performance, and those dedicated to the linguistic analysis of his texts. Only one article, Hans-Thies Lehman's "BRECHTBLOCK," is not printed in English. The rest offer their provocations in English, calling for a new energy to be devoted to translating and documenting Brecht's entire body of work, searching for ways to adequately address the blend of "theory and practice, text and performance, language and body" found therein (Primavesi 54).

Two of the most outstanding articles in the collection traverse the textuality and performativity of Brecht's corpus through the theoretical investigation of Brecht's "documents" and of his views on translation. Judith Wilke's article "The Making of a Document: An Approach to Brecht's *Fatzer* Fragment" wonderfully ponders Brecht's manipulation of the "increasing popularity of documentary drama and literature in the 1920s." Wilke views the fragments of *The Downfall of the Egoist Johann Fatzer* as part of a counter rhetoric about documents Brecht launched while working at Piscator's theater. By calling his failed play the "Fatzer-dokument," Wilke asserts that Brecht plays with conventional meanings like "certificate," "record," or "piece of evidence, exposing them to a certain ambiguity between true and false, real and fictitious." Crucially, Wilke points out, Brecht is developing an idea of the document in theater as an "artifact that would become 'authentic' only by provoking conflicting interpretations" (122-123). This idea of the document as "real" but also an "enormous lie" prompts Wilke's affirmation of Brecht's theater as a "collective experience" and "cognitive process" based on the interdependence of production and reception, acting and watching, reading and examination, document and commentary. Though Brecht struggles "with the fact that an author cannot restrict the interpretations of his works," his innovation was to envisage a theater where the spectators would also be able to take part in the "making of documents" (126-127).

Wilke's analysis finds a brilliant match in Patrick Primavesi's article "The Performance of Translation: Benjamin and Brecht on the Loss of Small Details." Reading Brecht and Benjamin on the "Task of Translators," Primavesi builds toward a definition of what might be called "gestic translation." Invoking Benjamin's dictum that poetic language "demands" to be altered or transformed and Brecht's line-by-line translation/enactment of *Galileo* with Charles Laughton, Primavesi investigates how translation is like performance. With Brecht, Primavesi rejects a model of translation that most values resemblance: "while being translated into another language, poems usually get damaged most strongly through the effort of translating too much. Perhaps one should be content with the translation of the poet's thoughts and his attitude"(57). Attitude, or *Haltung*, is also, of course, the key of theatrical *gestus* as Brecht defines it. Primavesi instead finds in the Brecht-Benjamin dialectic a theory of translation that deconstructs traditional theories about how translation reflects "the communications of intentions and messages" (54). "Brecht used the gap between language and the process of translation as material for theatrical thoughts," he declares (57). Primavesi's message is that productive translations are "theatrical thoughts," something translators and directors of Brecht should always bear in mind.

Translation and documentation form the subject of Erdmut Wizisla's contribution "Editorial Principles in the Berlin and Frankfurt Edition of Bertolt Brecht's Work" as well, but Wizisla's methodology partakes of the philological. Wizisla traces three models of selection for the versions of Brecht's texts used in editions of the collected works: "*aus frühester Hand*" (the principle of earliest version), the "text corpus" principle, and the "authorization" principle. Offering examples of how all three principles were upheld and broken, and doubting the possibility of an edition to take the place of "authentic literary remains," Wizisla concludes with a citation of Brechtian insouciance: "principles stay alive by being violated" (38).

The issue of "authentic literary remains" ghosts all the articles that concern themselves, as Wizisla does, with negotiating Brecht's legacy. The memory of performances, or the vision of performances as they should be, join "authentic literary remains" as the chorus to which productions of Brecht's plays must always respond. Two of the articles that treat specific performances explicitly read the productions at hand in light of a type of cultural and literary reception/reaction around the legacy of Brecht. But the two articles that are more specifically production histories also become perforce commentaries on the cultural position of Brecht. Judith Rudakoff's interview with Yugoslavian director Alexander Lukac, "Theatre Offensives from Belgrade to Toronto," compares two productions of *Baal* from 1982 and 1998. Andrzej Wirth's "The Lehrstück as Performance" likewise records productions or readings of *The Measures Taken* or the *Fatzer* fragments directed by Wirth in 1973, 1976, 1977, 1979, 1987, and 1994. The two men cannot help but comment on the changing efficacy of Brecht's work in relationship to North American and European audiences. Wirth's astonishing, prolonged involvement with the *Lehrstücke* in production particularly lends detail to his insight about the changing "utopian project" of the learning play. He sees the *Lehrstück* as a meeting of two radical concepts: "the theatre as metatheatre and society as changeable" (113). His observation that the proletarian ("an anachronistic concept") message of the plays has withered in no way undercuts his belief that the *Lehrstücke* are a place for "artistic sensibility and elementary camaraderie" to be transmitted to young people (120).

Wirth and Lukac ask the most basic question about Brecht's legacy: can his plays still provoke society? The cultural analysis in Stefan Mahlke's "Brecht +/- Müller: German-German Brecht Images Before and After 1989" and Günther Heeg's "Einar Wie Eva: Towards an Economy of the Feminine in Schleef's *Puntila*" presents more complicated questions about how directors and critics imagine Brecht through production. Mahlke's fascinating account of Heiner Müller and Ginka Tsholakowa's 1982 *Macbeth* turns on anachronistic criticism the production received from Brecht scholar and critic Ernst Schumacher that attempted to ally itself "*with* Brecht *against* Müller" (40). Spurred by this reaction, Mahlke uncovers the competing critical formulations of Brecht, from post-war "dialectical three-step" criticism through to Müller's still potent formulation of the "uncompensated Brecht" (41; 47) seen in Einar Schleef's 1996 *Puntila*, which Mahlke praises as a paradigmatic example of "how to make critical use of Brecht." Heeg extends this in his article, discovering in *Puntila* a depersonalized oratorio that "releases character and fabel" and delves into the "fear center" of the play. Heeg veers into murky psychological territory as he untangles the action of male alliances exorcising the feminine that becomes images of descent from the cross and burial, consent and labor, coffin and grave (93). Nevertheless, his reading, like Mahlke's, advances the paradoxical Brecht in performance, the Brecht of actions that are "not...but" and the Brecht who makes contradictions dance.

Paradox reigns in the three very fine articles that proceed by close reading of Brecht's poetry and songs as well. In her study of the *gestus* of Brecht's poems, Helen Varapoulou is the least concerned with paradox. Yet, her article, "Brecht's *Gestus*: Brecht and C.P. Cavafy. And Heiner Müller," raises the revealing point that the anti-Aristotelian Brecht responds to C.P. Cavafy's poem "Trojans" in his poem "Reading a Late Greek Poet" by transforming an "elegy-oriented, reflexive poem into a scene" (62). Brecht's poem employs a *gestus* of the past and an address to the "*sembable*" or "*frère*" that slyly renders modern commentary on its invocation of Troy's fall, but Varapoulou finds more links between Cavafy and Müller, who she feels, unlike Brecht, works by allegory and not by analytic history.

Hans-Thies Lehmann and Nikolaus Müller-Schöll get to the heart of the paradoxes that propel most of the Brecht scholarship in this special section in powerful parallel studies of the *Mahagonny* songs. Lehmann's "Newness and Pleasure: *Mahagonny* Songs" attacks the paradox embodied in the city Mahagonny: that capitalism produces pleasure as well as alienation. His detailed readings of the songs in both the *Hauspostille*

(*Manual of Piety*) and *The Rise and Fall of the City of Mahagonny* reveal a pattern of images of waste, excess, spending, pleasure, and newness. The songs posit an equation where newness and pleasure equal freedom, but freedom equals death, thereby Mahagonny, which has been a paradise of consumption becomes a hell. Müller-Schöll's "...just an invented word" probes the metaphysical dimension of this *Mahagonny* world. When Brecht concludes the *Mahagonny* songs with "Mahagonny — that is just an invented word," he is, Müller-Schöll argues, avoiding a "twofold danger: the represented shall not be confounded with reality ... as if it were nothing but its imitation (*imitatio*); at the same time it shall not only be regarded by itself — as an autonomous absolute work of art" (27). What emerges is the hoped-for paradox of estrangement — that a "parable" or "invented world" makes the discussion of reality possible.

Movement between pleasure and alienation, between the invented world and the real world, characterizes the most fertile engagements of the entire selection of articles, including Lehmann and Müller-Schöll's textual rigor, Mahlke's masterful cultural history, Primavesi and Wilke's assessment of boundaries in translation and documentation, and Martin's clear reminder to feminist scholars to approach Brecht with his paradoxes in mind. "German Brecht, European Readings" will do nothing if not provoke pursuit of these paths.

Sara Freeman
University of Wisconsin, Madison

Margarete Steffin. *Briefe an berühmte Männer: Walter Benjamin, Bertolt Brecht, Arnold Zweig.* Hrsg. und Vorwort von Stefan Hauck. Hamburg: Europäische Verlagsanstalt, 1999. 358 Seiten.

„ich muss doch bald einen millionär totschlagen, es bleibt mir gar nichts anderes übrig. odense (Sie wissen, es liegt 1 1/2 stunden von hier) soll viele millionäre haben, und schließlich kostet die rückfahrkarte nur 4 kronen 80, am sonntag sogar weniger, das sind für eine million nicht zu hohe unkosten" (262). So schreibt Margarete Steffin Ende 1937 aus Svendborg an Walter Benjamin — enthalten in dem beachtenswerten und größtenteils sorgfältig edierten Band von Stefan Hauck, dessen Titel allerdings ein peinlicher Missgriff ist — als habe hier Verlagskalkül geboten, die Autorin der Briefe hinter dem späteren Ruhm ihrer Briefpartner verschwinden zu lassen. Insgesamt ist wenig Fröhliches in den hier erstmals vollständig herausgegebenen Briefen zu lesen. Schließlich erlebte die aus einfachsten Verhältnissen stammende Kommunistin, Theaterpraktikerin (schreibend, spielend, inszenierend), Mitarbeiterin und Geliebte Brechts Jahre des Elends — finanziell und emotional — im Exil, bis sie 1941 im Alter von nur 33 Jahren in Moskau an der Tuberkulose, wegen der sie sich seit Jahren immer wieder vergeblich Kuren unterzogen hatte, starb. In einem Brief an Brecht vom März 1936 findet sich eine der wenigen Passagen, in denen Steffin das Herzzerreißende ihrer Lage offen zur Sprache bringt:

> und wenn ich auch verstehe, dass Du „zu hause" sein willst einige zeit, so stösst mir natürlich mächtig auf, dass ich kein 'zu hause' habe. nirgends. ich muss immer für mich und meine koffer um einen platz bitten, und kann mir nicht mal bücher kaufen, weil wo soll ich sie hinstellen? dann natürlich sehe ich immer ganz klar, es geht doch nicht. wenn Du dann auch so selten schreibst, was auch die gründe sind, so wird es in einem masse schlimm, wie ich es nicht sagen kann (194).

Und doch blitzt, auch unter schwierigsten Bedingungen, immer wieder jener trockene Humor auf, von dem man wünscht, das Leben hätte ihr viel mehr positiven Anlass dazu gegeben; beispielsweise, wenn sie Benjamin mitteilt: „meine werke sind noch unveröffentlicht, zum grössten teil auch noch nicht geschrieben" (203). Und in einem Brief an Zweig heißt es: „schicken Sie unbedingt fotos, alle würden sich sehr darüber freuen. von brecht Ihnen eines zu schicken, hat keinen zweck, er sieht genau so aus wie damals" (234).

Steffins Briefe sind eher von biographischem als literarischem Interesse — meist kunstlos, oft unter Zeitdruck geschrieben, liegt ihr Wert vor allem in den Einsichten, die sie uns ermöglichen in die deutschsprachige Exillandschaft, in das Netz von Kommunikation und Beziehungen zwischen den Emigranten, und ebenso in die Alltagserfahrungen, die die Exilerfahrung prägen. Sie sind ergänzend (gelegentlich auch widersprechend und relativierend, z.B. im Vergleich mit Ruth Berlaus Erinnerungen aus der gleichen Zeit in dem von Hans Bunge 1985 herausgegebenen Band *Brechts Lai-Tu*) zu lesen zusammen mit Brechts Tagebüchern und Briefen, mit Benjamins Briefen und mit anderen Exilschilderungen. Eine Reihe von Überschneidungen mit dem 1991 von Inge Gellert herausgegebenen Band *Konfutse versteht nichts von Frauen* sind unvermeidlich: Zum einen finden sich von Gellert veröffentlichte Gedichte und autobiographische Texte Steffins hier als Teil ihrer Briefe an Brecht wieder; zum anderen hatte bereits Gellert eine Auswahl aus Steffins Briefen zugänglich gemacht.

Warum gerade diese Briefe und keine anderen gewählt wurden, teilt der Herausgeber nicht mit. Ging es darum, dem Etikett „berühmte Männer" zu genügen? Die überwiegende Anzahl der Briefe geht an Brecht, der auch in den Briefen an Benjamin und den wenigen an Zweig gerichteten häufig vorkommt — oft mit ausgerichteten Aufträgen, Fragen und Grüßen, und häufig explizit charakterisiert als Nichtschreiber, an dessen Statt eben Steffin die Korrespondenz führt. Nicht nur das, immer wieder berichtet

Steffin halb amüsiert, halb empört, dass Brecht Briefe — auch an sie gerichtete — einfach einbehält oder nicht mehr herausrückt.

Die Briefe geben einen anschaulichen Einblick in die Vielfalt von Steffins Tätigkeiten und Aufgaben — sie kommentiert und ediert Texte, versucht in Paris eine Agentur für deutsche Exilautoren zu etablieren, kümmert sich um Veröffentlichungsmöglichkeiten, übersetzt selber aus mehreren Sprachen und stellt selbst während Sanatoriumsaufenthalten Theaterprojekte auf die Beine. Die Briefe demonstrieren Alltagsschwierigkeiten des Exils — viel Energie geht immer wieder in Versuche, Honorare einzufordern, dem Verbleib von Büchern (z.B. verliehener und später dringend benötigter Bände) nachzuforschen, den Transport notwendiger Materialien an neue Exilorte zu organisieren, und überhaupt Bücher zu bekommen. Am 20. Juli 1937 klagt Steffin in einem Brief an Benjamin: „ich kann keinen kriminalroman mehr auch nur von weitem sehen, und alle andern bücher, dir mir erreichbar waren, hab ich längst zweimal gelesen" (247). Welche Rolle — neben Klagen über Kälte und abgewetzte Farbbänder — Geldsorgen spielen, geht vor allem aus den zahlreichen detaillierten Kostenaufstellungen hervor, mit denen beispielsweise Steffin Benjamin das skandinavische Exil schmackhaft zu machen versucht, oder der peniblen Weise, in der sie mit Benjamin die Tabaklieferungen — Kaufpreis und Porto — abrechnet, mit denen sie ihn immer wieder versorgt und deren häufiges Verlorengehen zu einem Leitmotiv ihrer Korrespondenz wird.

Lohnend ist der Band nicht zuletzt durch Haucks solides und informatives Vorwort und wegen der recht ausführlichen Annotierung, die ergänzt wird durch 22 Seiten Chronologie und ein nützliches und detailliertes 15seitiges „Biographisches Glossar." Nur gelegentlich hätte man sich zu einzelnen Punkten, wie auch auffälligen zeitlichen Lücken in der Korrespondenz, Auskünfte über das Gebotene hinaus gewünscht, und ein letzter Redaktionsdurchgang hätte die Zuweisung einzelner Annotationen noch verbessern können, die gelegentlich nicht die erste, sondern eine spätere Nennung erläutern. Redundant ist die verschiedentlich quasi wörtliche Übernahme der Einträge aus dem „Biographischen Glossar" in Anmerkungen — hier hätte es auch ein Verweis getan. Doch diese kleinen Kritikpunkte sollen den Verdienst des Herausgebers nicht schmälern, der uns mit diesem Band zwar nicht weltbewegende neue Einsichten vermittelt, aber doch ein facettenreiches und detailgesättigtes Bild von Steffins Persönlichkeit, Arbeit und Rolle im Exilnetzwerk um Brecht.

Sabine Gross
University of Wisconsin, Madison

Jürgen Schmid. *Brecht und Haindl. Berthold Friedrich Brechts "Chronik der G. Haindl'schen Papierfabrik Augsburg" von 1899.* Augsburg: Wißner-Verlag, 1999. 280 Seiten.

Jürgen Hillesheim. *Augsburger Brecht-Lexikon. Personen — Institutionen — Schauplätze.* Würzburg: Königshausen & Neumann, 2000. 207 Seiten.

Wolfgang Bömelburg, *Hobellied für Bertolt Brecht. Ein Theatertischler erzählt.* Berlin: Eulenspiegel, 1997. 128 Seiten.

Despite generic differences these three samples of recent Brechtiana share an emphasis on biography and locale. The first two focus on Augsburg, one reproducing the *Haindl Chronicle* by Brecht's father and describing its origin, nature, and related issues; the other a reference work (subject catalog) pertaining to Brecht in Augsburg. The third offers recollections by a long-time member of the Berliner Ensemble, presenting us with the challenges of stage construction spiced by human and all-too-human episodes.

Schmid's volume is a model of thorough documentation. The meticulously annotated edition of the 1899 *Chronicle of Haindl's Paper Factory* (here published for the first time, on prime quality paper, in the year of the 150th anniversary of the successful firm in which Brecht's father rose to directorship) is followed by succinct commentaries on the chronicle's binding (Ursula Kohler), its paper and script (Klaus Wengenmayr), its artistic design (Petra Riesterer), and a comparison with another "family history" in Mann's *Buddenbrooks* (Michael Friedrichs). The subsequent part on the chronicle's historical context sketches the rise of the genre in Germany (a sort of *Festschrift* celebrating a company's achievements) and evaluates Berthold Friedrich Brecht's loyalist perspectives ("between entrepreneur and worker"). While this section dwells conscientiously on the firm's development and also includes its social contributions to the workers, it neglects contemporary problems such as industrial pollution, the workers' socio-political conditions in the late nineteenth century, or the role of women in the work force. Other issues reflected in the chronicle (developments in paper production, Augsburg's industrial growth, sources of information, salary lists of employees) are commented in the context of available research. The biographical part on members of the Brecht family focuses on Brecht's father (Ralf Witzler), the role of the Haindl firm in Eugen Brecht's own literary development (Helmut Gier), and the playwright's brother Walter Brecht, professor of paper technology (Jürgen Schmid). Brecht's father, a "liberal" conservative, emerges as an impressive, success-oriented business man with remarkable tolerance, generosity, even fatherly pride towards his provocative poet-son, who, in turn, did his part in not letting frictions turn into full-fledged father-son conflicts. The discrepancies young Brecht experienced during his simultaneous exposure to the wealthy industrial establishment and the life of the workers are highlighted in detail as a lasting influence on his life and work. The Haindl firm also played an important role in the development of Eugen's brother Walter. But despite similar upbringings, fundamental differences existed between the personalities and careers of the two distinguished brothers, who over the years maintained a loose family contact. The book's title, *Brecht and Haindl*, thus expresses more than one interconnection. The various relationships between the Brechts and the firm come to life in an engaging blend of well-presented information, ample illustrations, and other pertinent documentation from the Haindl archives, not to speak of the abundant footnotes. The treatment is exhaustive and the reading rewarding, but there remains a tantalizing question implicit throughout the book. If the father's writing is addressed in such detail, and the strong impact of the Haindl firm on the poet elaborated with such emphasis: did the son know the father's chronicle of the firm? This question may seem irrelevant, yet the epigraph to Schmid's whole volume is Brecht's well-known "Ode" (for his father's 50th birthday), whereas the father used well-known Goethe mottos in his chronicle (for the Haindl firm's 50th birthday). All these headings pointedly invoke the joint theme of what the younger generation owes to the older — coincidence or intertextuality within all the contextuality?

Hillesheim's volume, too, is well-researched and plentiful, listing in alphabetical order over 150 relatively brief entries relating to "Brecht in Augsburg." The collection draws on numerous new findings in recent years and includes not only persons, places, and matters of importance to Brecht's formative early period, but also his birth city's efforts on behalf of its famous son. After initial controversies, these efforts had their ups and downs, their merits and pitfalls, of which Hillesheim is well aware. At any rate, the term "Augsburger" is expansive and lists (in the "person" category) fellow citizens of Brecht as well as recent Augsburg Brecht scholars. Even non-Augsburgers become important Augsburgian acquaintances of Brecht (from Aretino to Villon, Bach to Wagner, Büchner to Nietzsche, Grabbe to Shakespeare, and so forth). One might miss some influential names in this extensive array (Homer? Luther?), but as Hillesheim points out in his thoughtful introduction, limits had to be drawn, selections had to be made. Augsburg localities, then and now, are commented (from Barfüßerkirche, Gablers Taverne, Steinerner Mann to Bert-Brecht-Straße, Bert-Brecht-Shop, etc). Overlapping with the "places" category are "institutions" (e.g., schools, daily newspapers, Stadttheater, Plärrer, Bertolt-Brecht-Forschungs- und Gedenkstätte). Among other topics we find, e.g., Dreigroschenheft, Die Ernte, Räterepublik, Reservelazarett, Tagebuch Nr. 10, Weltkrieg. The various entries offer much factual information, specifying the ties to Brecht and his early projects, and also point to relevant sources. Furthermore, a network of cross-references connecting the entries allows us to read this book profitably in various directions, despite some redundancies. Interpretations of individual Brecht texts were beyond the book's scope, but its author managed to unfold, in easily accessible form, a comprehensive picture of "Brecht in Augsburg," suggesting the emergence of certain traits that would become characteristic of the man and his work. Starting at the earliest stage, this is a useful handbook up to a point, however, it seems unlikely that its format would prove suitable for later stations of Brecht's complex life and work.

Bömelburg, occasionally using Brecht proverbs in his own way, aims to shed light on those who are not seen in the dark. He offers a concise account of his own professional life, of which forty-five years were spent with the Berliner Ensemble. His illustrated memoirs, though episodic, amount to a kind of theater history as perceived by a stage technician who was part of all performances of the Ensemble at home and abroad. Having been fired by an irascible Brecht and reemployed by a level-headed Helene Weigel on his first assignment, Bömelburg becomes a valued colleague helping with inventive solutions to numerous technical problems. A perceptive observer with an eye for oddities, he not only gives us enlightening details of his tasks and everyday surroundings, but also amusing anecdotes of unexpected situations and peculiar happenings in close quarters as well as on the road. Bömelburg's "Hobellied" (joiner's song) is dedicated to Bertolt Brecht, but is a tribute to Helene Weigel no less, and a lively testimony to the exciting work with a great theater company.

Herbert Knust
University of Illinois, Urbana-Champaign

Therese Hörnigk und Alexander Stephan, Hrsg. *Rot = Braun? Brecht Dialog 2000. Nationalismus und Stalinismus bei Brecht und Zeitgenossen*. Berlin: Theater der Zeit, 2000. 258 Seiten.

Dieser Band fasst 13 Vorträge zusammen, die bei den Brecht-Tagen 2000 vom 6. bis 11. Februar 2000 im Literaturforum im Brecht-Haus Berlin gehalten wurden. Sie sind drei großen Themenkreisen zugeordnet, die jeweils auch Diskussionsbeiträge einschließen. Der Titel ist zu Recht mit einem Fragezeichen versehen, denn er will provokativ sein und nicht die schon tot geglaubte Totalitarismus-Debatte aus den Zeiten des kalten Krieges wieder aufwärmen, die in manchen Darstellungen nach dem Fall der Mauer wieder fröhliche Urständ feiert.

Im ersten Teil ("Bertolt Brecht und die Zuschreibung des Totalitären") sollen die Grundlagen für die weitere Diskussion gelegt werden, was nur teilweise gelingt. Gerhard Scheid versucht, Hannah Arendts Totalitarismuskonzept nachzuzeichnen, bleibt aber zu sehr im Abstrakten stecken. Konrad Jarausch dagegen bietet einen klaren und konzisen historischen Abriss über die Versuchung der Intellektuellen durch Kommunismus / Sozialismus und Faschismus, wobei er sich oft auf Viktor Klemperers Tagebücher stützen kann. Manfred Lauermanns Beitrag über Horkheimer und den Totalitarismus lässt leider eine klare Linie vermissen und verliert sich in langen Zitaten und schier endlosen Anmerkungen. Entsprechend unergiebig bleibt auch die nachfolgende Diskussion.

Nachdem der Leser sich durch den ersten, theoretischen Teil hindurch gearbeitet hat, wird der Band jedoch in den folgenden Teilen — mit ganz wenigen Ausnahmen — wirklich spannend und anregend. Im zweiten Teil sind unter dem recht lockereren und nicht immer zutreffenden Titel „Brecht und die Faschismustheorien" fünf Beiträge zusammengefasst, die sich zwar mit Brechts Faschismustheorien befassen aber auch mit Brechts Haltung zur jüdischen Frage und Brecht als „antistalinistischer" Stalinist. In einer kurzen aber bedeutsamen Miszelle beleuchtet Silvia Schlenstedt den kuriosen Wunsch Brechts im Jahre 1945, „daß das Jiddische Staatstheater von Mikhoels aus Moskau in Berlin mit meinen 'Rundköpfen und Spitzköpfen', diesem Stück gegen Rassismus, gastiert" (85). Das ist in der Tat ein recht befremdlicher Wunsch, denn Brecht hat sich nie mit der jüdischen Frage auseinandergesetzt, wie Manfred Voigts in seinem Beitrag ausführt. Bekanntlich ist die Rassenfrage im genannten Stück für Brecht nur Vortäuschung, um die Klassengegensätze zu übertünchen; sie verschwindet „im marxistisch orientierten Sozialismus" (Voigts, 112). Von dieser Haltung ist Brecht nie abgerückt, und auch Schlenstedt vermag diesen seltsamen Wunsch Brechts nicht zu erklären, es sei denn, er war an einem doppelten Verfremdungseffekt interessiert. Schlenstedt wirft somit mit ihrem kurzen Beitrag ein bezeichnendes Schlaglicht auf Schwachstellen in der Brecht-Biographie, zumal Brecht auch nie wissen wollte, dass Stalin Solomon Mikhoels später ermorden ließ. Wie Detlev Schöttker ausführt, hat Brecht nie eine zusammenhängende Faschismustheorie entwickelt; für ihn war im echt marxistischen Sinne Faschismus nur als Kapitalismus zu bekämpfen (davon zeugen ja nicht zuletzt auch *Die Rundköpfe und die Spitzköpfe*). Das wird auch in Brechts Hitlerparodie *Der aufhaltsame Aufstieg des Arturo Ui* deutlich, die für Jost Hermand ein Drama aus der „Geschichte der skrupellosen Marktwirtschaft" (124) darstellt. Es verwundert daher, dass sich Brecht gerade mit diesem Stück einen Erfolg in den USA versprach. Wie Hermand nachweist, war dagegen die einzige andere wirksame Hitlerparodie, Charlie Chaplins Film *Der große Diktator*, der Brecht bis auf die Kapitalismuskritik in seiner Analyse des Faschismus in vieler Hinsicht folgte, wesentlich erfolgreicher.

Die ambivalente Haltung Brechts zum Stalinismus wird in mehreren Beiträgen diskutiert, von Klaus Völker (im 2. Teil) sowie von David Pike und Gerd Rienäcker (im 3. Teil „Bertolt Brecht im Spannungsfeld zwischen Avantgarde und Staatskunst"). Für Völker zeigt gerade *Die Maß-*

nahme, „wie wenig Brecht Stalinist war" (134). Leider bleibt er den Beweis schuldig, denn viele Kritiker sahen gerade *Die Maßnahme* als Brechts stalinistischstes Werk. Auch für Rienäcker war Brecht kein Stalinist, während Pike da wesentlich skeptischer ist und von seiner Position, die er vor rund 15 Jahren in seinem Buch *Brecht und Lukács* (1986) vertrat, kaum abrückt. Wie brisant und problematisch das Thema immer noch ist, zeigt Pikes äußerst behutsames Vorgehen (sozusagen in der Höhle des Löwen, im Brecht-Haus) und Rienäckers versteckte Kritik an Pike. Es gibt in der Tat zahlreiche Stellen in Brechts Werk, in denen Brecht selbst den stalinschen Terror zu unterstützen scheint; Kritik an Stalin findet sich zumeist nur in privaten Äußerungen. Rienäcker plädiert jedoch nicht zu Unrecht dafür, die finsteren Zeiten zu berücksichtigen, in denen Brecht lebte, und von denen sich die „moralingesäuerten Urteile" (214) einiger Kritiker aus dem sicheren Westen keine Vorstellung machen. Michael Rohrwasser fragt in seinem Beitrag, warum Brecht kein Renegat wurde wie viele andere Marxisten und kommt zu dem Schluss, dass Brecht seine Apologien für Stalin als „Schutzmaßnahme für die eigene Produktivität" (228) brauchte. Zu erwähnen sind noch der informative Aufsatz Jürgen Scheberas zur Übernahme von kommunistischen Arbeiterliedern durch die Nazis und Rainer Grübels Versuch, Brecht in die Opferdiskurse der europäischen Kulturgeschichte im allgemeinen und der russischen Literatur der 20er und 30er Jahre im besonderen einzuordnen. Nach Grübel kannte Brecht die russischen Opferromane, doch die interessante Frage, ob sie Einfluss auf Brecht / Eislers *Die Maßnahme* hatten, bleibt offen.

Der Band schließt mit vielen Fragen, die zwar im Text mehrmals angesprochen und diskutiert aber nie endgültig beantwortet werden. Doch das ist vermutlich auch gar nicht (oder noch nicht) möglich. Da kann man nur mit Brecht schließen: „so viele Fragen und so wenig Antworten," oder im Anschluss an Brechts *Guten Menschen*, der „Vorhang zu und alle Fragen offen." Doch der Leser steht nicht „enttäuscht" und „betroffen" vor dem Ergebnis, denn es obliegt ihm, sich Gedanken zu machen und zu eigenen (und vorläufigen Schlüssen) zu kommen. Den Herausgebern ist zu danken, dass sie auch die Diskussionsbeiträge eingebaut haben. Nur wünschte man zu erfahren, wer sich hinter „Publikum" verbirgt, handelt es sich doch anscheinend um ausgewiesene Brecht-Kenner. Überhaupt sind die Diskussionsbeiträge zuweilen interessanter als manche Vorträge, tragen sie doch zur Erhellung einiger wichtiger Fragen bei. Das trifft vor allem auf die Diskussion nach dem 2. Teil zu.

Was bleibt am Ende der Lektüre? Brecht war nicht der einzige deutsche Linksintellektuelle, der von den Verbrechen Hitlers und Stalins wusste — wenn auch nicht so umfassend wie wir heute — ohne sich je ausführlich damit auseinander zusetzen. Eine Judenfrage existierte für ihn nicht und Stalins Verbrechen werden zum Teil sogar gerechtfertigt. Das ist für uns Nachgeborene schwer zu verdauen, und man kann sich fragen, ob das eine vertretbare moralische Position war. Doch sind wir deswegen berechtigt, den ersten Stein auf ihn zu werfen? Und noch eins wird nach der Lektüre deutlich: trotz zahlreicher Parallelen ist rot nicht gleich braun, auch wenn der Monumentalstil der abgebildeten Illustrationen aus stalinistischer und nationalsozialistischer Zeit darauf hinzudeuten scheint.

Karl-Heinz Schoeps
University of Illinois, Urbana-Champaign

Werner Hecht. *Helene Weigel: Eine große Frau des 20. Jahrhunderts.* Frankfurt am Main: Suhrkamp, 2000. 343 Seiten.

Den Büchern zum einhundertsten Geburtstag von Brecht, Weigel oder Eisler verdanken wir neben bislang unbekannten historischen Materialien auch manchen neuen Blickwinkel. Was Helene Weigel betrifft, so haben die neuen Publikationen viel deutlicher als in früheren Jahren das Bild einer von Brecht verschiedenen und von ihm unabhängigen Person entworfen. Mittlerweile können wir sie uns in ihrer eigenartigen Beharrlichkeit vorstellen, ohne sie dabei zu einer Funktion Brechts zu machen.

Daran hat auch das Buch *Helene Weigel: Eine große Frau des 20. Jahrhunderts* von Werner Hecht seinen Anteil. Hecht hat viele Jahre als Dramaturg am Berliner Ensemble gearbeitet, gut zehn Jahre davon unter Helene Weigels Leitung. Dabei lernte er sie nicht nur als Schauspielerin und als Intendantin kennen, sondern arbeitete auch als Herausgeber von Brecht-Texten mit ihr zusammen. Als unübertroffener Sammler von Fakten und Daten legt er ein vielseitiges Buch vor, das in fünf Abschnitte gegliedert ist. Die ersten beiden sind persönlicher Art. Sie umfassen den Abdruck eines langen Gesprächs zwischen Hecht und Weigel von 1969 und Hechts Erinnerungen an die Weigel aus der Zeit der gemeinsamen Arbeit zwischen 1959 und 1971. Die letzten drei Abschnitte des Buches sind im Unterschied dazu sachlicher Natur. Hier finden sich eine ausführliche Darstellung aller Rollen, die die Weigel zeit ihres Lebens gespielt hat, eine umfangreiche Zitatensammlung aus zeitgenössischen Rezensionen über ihr Spiel und zum Schluss des Buches eine kurze Chronik ihres Lebens — etwa in der Art, wie wir sie von Hechts *Brecht-Chronik* (1998) kennen, nur summarischer und wesentlich kürzer. Ergänzt und unterbrochen werden diese drei Überblicksdarstellungen durch einer Fülle von Fotos, Kopien von Briefen und Dokumenten sowie durch diverse Texte über die Weigel von Karen Michaelis, Bertolt Brecht, Anna Seghers, Herbert Ihering, Bernhard Dort und Jürgen Rühle. Manches überschneidet und doppelt sich in jenen beiden Abschnitten, die sich der schauspielerischen

Laufbahn der Weigel und den zeitgenössischen Kritiken widmen, einige der alten Texte über sie sind bereits vielfach gedruckt und bekannt. Dessen ungeachtet hat Hecht hier einen lange schon nötigen Überblick über Biographie und Rollenverzeichnis der Weigel zusammengetragen, der zum Nachschlagen einlädt und dem nur eines fehlt — ein Register.

Wichtiger als diese sachlichen Informationen waren dem Autor jedoch die persönlichen Begegnungen mit der Weigel und seine Erinnerungen; ihnen ist die erste Hälfte des Buches vorbehalten. Erinnerungen handeln vor allem von denen, die sie erzählen, und darauf kommt es Hecht auch an. In den Episoden, die er über die Weigel erzählt, spart er nicht mit Informationen zur eigenen Person. So erfahren wir nicht nur, wie sich die Weigel als Intendantin burschikos über die Politbürokratie in der DDR hinwegsetzen konnte, sondern auch, dass sich der junge Hecht während seines Studiums in Leipzig nicht SED-konform verhielt (74). Wir erfahren nicht nur Interna über die Krise des Berliner Ensembles am Ende der sechziger Jahre und über damalige Reformvorschläge der Weigel, sondern auch, dass Hecht während dieser Krisenzeit ihr engster Vertrauter war. In seinem Besitz befindet sich jener — nun im Buch abgedruckte — Notizzettel, auf dem die Weigel ihre Vorstellung von einer veränderten Leitungsstruktur des Berliner Ensembles kurz vor ihrem Tod entwarf. Dieser Entwurf, so lesen wir, sah Hecht als zukünftigen Chefdramaturgen und außerdem neben Ruth Berghaus, Wolfgang Pintzka und Peter Kupke als zukünftigen Regisseur des Theaters vor (118f.). Gleichzeitig erfahren wir, wen Hecht für den Bösewicht in der damaligen Krise hält: Manfred Wekwerth, Regisseur und späterer Intendant des Hauses, erscheint bei Hecht als verlängerter Arm der SED, der die Weigel damals verriet und zum Königsmörder wurde (113ff.). Liest man zufällig parallel zu Hechts Buch die Memoiren von Wekwerth oder das Interview mit Pintzka, das im *Brecht-Jahrbuch* 25 (2000) publiziert ist, so wird deutlich, wie verschieden ihre Blicke auf die Vergangenheit ausfallen. Ebenso deutlich zeichnet sich ab, dass der Kampf der ehemaligen Mitarbeiter des Berliner Ensembles um ihre Plätze in der Geschichte des Theaters begonnen hat und jeder an seiner Selbststilisierung arbeitet.

Die Geschichten, die hier über die Weigel zum Besten gegeben werden, sind jenen Lesern und Leserinnen, die sich schon mit ihr beschäftigt haben, zumeist bekannt, irgendwo und irgendwie sind sie alle schon einmal erzählt worden. Im Unterschied dazu konnte man den vollständigen Wortlaut jenes Gesprächs, das Hecht 1969 mit der Weigel führte, und das er zu Beginn seines Buches zum ersten Mal abdruckt, noch nirgendwo lesen. Und trotzdem erscheint es nicht neu. Es ist eine irrige Annahme, dass Gespräche, geführt in einer früheren und völlig anderen Zeit, heute noch kommentarlos für sich selber sprechen könnten und wie seinerzeit Brisanz und Bedeutung hätten. Ohne Kontext, ohne Verweis auf das damals Relevante in den Fragen und Antworten, führt das Gespräch nur vor, dass Hecht und Weigel über Vieles miteinander gesprochen haben. Das

Bild von der Weigel, das Hecht mit diesem Gespräch und mit seinen Erinnerungen hervorkehrt, ist nur ein Grund für die Publikation. Der andere ist Hechts eigene Geschichte. Insofern ist das Buch nicht nur vielseitig sondern auch zwiespältig.

Petra Stuber
Universität Leipzig

Adolf Dresen. *Wieviel Freiheit braucht die Kunst? Reden, Briefe, Verse, Spiele.* Hrsg. von Maik Hamburger. Mit einem Essay von Friedrich Dieckmann. Berlin: Theater der Zeit. 2000. 396 Seiten.

Zum 65. Geburtstag des Regisseurs Adolf Dresen brachte die Zeitschrift *Theater der Zeit* im Frühjahr 2000 in der „Recherchen"-Reihe einen Band mit Dokumenten und autobiographischen Notizen Dresens aus drei Jahrzehnten Theaterarbeit heraus. Auf knapp vierhundert Seiten wird der ungewöhnliche Lebensweg des Verfassers durch beide deutschen Staaten und darin ein wesentliches Stück zeitgenössischer Theatergeschichte dokumentiert. Dresens Arbeit hat im Laufe seines Lebens eine Reihe von Texten begleitet, die er teils zur Selbstverständigung, teils zur Verständigung mit Freunden und Kollegen, teils für öffentliche Anlässe über Fragen der Kunst und Gesellschaft schrieb. Ein Teil davon wurde durch den Dramaturgen Maik Hamburger zu einer Chronologie sieben verschiedener Lebensetappen zusammengestellt. Die Texte — Konzeptionspapiere, Tagebuchnotizen, Gedichte, Briefe, Reden, Essays — sind trotz unterschiedlicher Entstehungszeit und mitunter zu gänzlich anderen Anlässen aus der Rückschau geschrieben und den jeweiligen Begebnissen zugeordnet. Eine abgeklärte Draufsicht entsteht trotzdem nicht, vielmehr werden die Geschehnisse durch die verschiedenen Blickwinkel außerordentlich plastisch. Wo nötig, gibt es knappe Anmerkungen und Hintergrundinformationen des Herausgebers. Lebensdaten und Inszenierungsverzeichnis liefert der Anhang.

Dresen, Jahrgang 1935, machte erste Theatererfahrungen an der Studentenbühne der Universität Leipzig. Man erfährt, dass Dresen eher dem Segelfliegen als dem Studium zugeneigt war und eher zufällig an die Theaterarbeit geriet. Im germanistischen Seminar bei Hans Mayer lernte er die deutschen Klassiker und bei Ernst Bloch die dialektische Schule von Hegel und Marx kennen. Hans Mayer war es, der Dresens voller politischer Anspielungen steckende Studentenbühnenaufführung des *Frieden* von Aristophanes zur Generalprobe sah und den Beteiligten dringend zur Absetzung riet. Die Theatermacher ließen widerwillig die Premiere „aus techni-

schen Gründen" ausfallen. Mayer hatte sie damit vor dem Zuchthaus bewahrt. Kommilitonen von Dresen hatten nur einige Jahre später weniger
Glück.

Dresens weiterer Weg ging in die Provinz. In Greifswald fiel er mit
einem der ersten „Theaterskandale" der DDR auf. Er inszenierte im
Shakespeare-Jahr 1964 auftragsgemäß einen *Hamlet*. Sein Konzept, *Hamlet* als Stück über das Versagen von Vernunft aufzuführen, lag definitiv
nicht auf der Linie der DDR-Kulturpolitik. Aufführungsverbot der beim
Publikum höchst erfolgreichen Inszenierung nach wenigen Vorstellungen
war die Folge. Konzept und Begebnisse sind im ersten Teil des Buches
dokumentiert. Ebenso Dresens anschließende Zeit als Bohrarbeiter auf
einem Erdölfeld in Mecklenburg. Seine Tagebuchaufzeichnungen beschreiben den Arbeitsalltag als eine Realität jenseits aller heldischen Ar-
beitsweltklischees, eine Realität, aus deren Distanz die kulturpolitischen
Querelen um *Hamlet* im nahen Greifswald andere Relationen annehmen.
In der Produktion hat Dresen einige Male gearbeitet; teils freiwillig, teils
als Strafversetzung. Die kritisch reflektierenden Texte und Beschreibungen, die dabei entstanden, waren in er DDR weder zu veröffentlichen
noch aufführbar.

Als die prägendste Zeit für Dresen erscheint die Arbeit am Deutschen
Theater in den Jahren 1964 bis zu seinem Weggang aus der DDR 1977,
eine außerordentlich bewegte Zeit und eine der produktivsten der Thea-
terkultur im Lande. Nach dem Scheitern der neuen ökonomischen Politik
leitete die zweite Bitterfelder Konferenz 1964 und das 11. Plenum des
Zentralkomitees der SED ein Jahr später eine dirigistische Wirtschafts- und
Kulturpolitik ein, in der jede künstlerische Äußerung durch ein enggefass-
tes ideologisches Schema gezwungen werden sollte. Diese Entwicklung
wurde 1971 teilweise korrigiert. Schon 1968 plädierte der Literaturwissen-
schaftler Wolfgang Heise auf dem internationalen Brecht-Dialog „Politik
auf dem Theater" für ein „Theater als Laboratorium der sozialen Phantasie." Doch die ideologischen Abwehrreaktionen gegen die sogenannte
euro-kommunistische Abkehr der westeuropäischen Linken von der
KPDSU verschärften sich. Die Ausbürgerung des Sängers Wolf Biermann
1976 markierte eine ideologische Eiszeit. In den Spannungsverhältnissen
dieser Zeit entwickelten sich in der DDR produktive und experimentier-
freudige Teams von Theatermachern mit Regisseuren wie Adolf Dresen,
Benno Besson, Ruth Berghaus, Einar Schleef, B.K. Tragelehn, den Drama-
tikern Heiner Müller, Peter Hacks, Volker Braun, dem Bühnenbildner
Horst Sagert. Die Arbeit dieser Theatermacher war immer an den Rändern
des politisch Geduldeten angesiedelt und rang um eine ständige gesellschaftliche und „handwerkliche" Neudefinition der Bandbreite von Kunst.
Dies machte den großen Erfolg, das Einverständnis beim heimischen Publikum und auch die wachsende internationale Beachtung dieser Teile des
DDR-Theaters aus.

Vom damaligen Intendanten Wolfgang Heinz gegen den Protest des Kulturministeriums engagiert, begann Dresen am DT mit Einaktern des Iren O'Casey. Er brachte einen neuen Ton auf die Berliner Staatsbühne, einen Gleichklang von Poesie, Chaos und plebejischem Humor. Aus dieser Zeit stammen mehrere Texte zur Arbeit des Schauspielers und zum Handwerk des Theaterspielens, mit denen sich Dresen auch an öffentlich geführten Diskussionen im Haus beteiligte. „Ein Regisseur darf nicht zuviel erklären, auch dann nicht, wenn es richtig ist, was er sagt — man erklärt einem Tausendfüßler auch besser nicht, mit welchem Bein er zuerst losgeht" ("Die Kunst des Scheiterns oder die Tücke der Tücke des Objekts").

Dresens nächste und wahrscheinlich wichtigste und folgenreichste Arbeit überhaupt wurde der *Faust* (1968). Die Proben begannen während des Einmarsches der Truppen des Warschauer Paktes in Prag, zu dem der Theaterverband eine billigende Erklärung abgegeben hatte. Es entstand eine Inszenierung, die den Text äußerst sorgfältig analysiert hatte, überraschende Konstellationen entdeckte und ihre Herkunft aus spannungsreicher Gegenwart nicht hinter Klassizität verbarg. Zur Premiere verließ die Politprominenz in der Schlussszene demonstrativ ihre Plätze. Die über 60 Änderungsanweisungen, die dem Theater anderntags übermittelt wurden, wurden vom Ensemble teils befolgt, teils sabotiert, im wesentlichen aber erfüllt, um ein Verbot zu vermeiden. Ein neuer neuralgischer Punkt war getroffen: eine Klassikeraufführung war zum Politikum geworden, der Text eines sakrosankten und scheinbar vereinnahmten Autors hatte überraschende Sprengkraft erhalten und das Verbot ausgerechnet der ersten *Faust*-Inszenierung in der DDR-Hauptstadt stand im Raum. Um einen Eklat künftig zu verhindern, wurde die offizielle Bevormundung und die geheimdienstliche Kontrolle der Arbeit Dresens und des DT entschieden verschärft. Aus gleichem Jahr stammt folgendes Gedicht:

Der Pessimist
Sylvester 68 entzünden sich folgende Leute
auf den Treppen des Staatsratsgebäudes:
1. Dresen
2. Bredemeyer (eventuell)
3. Goldmann (eventuell)
4. Hamburger (eventuell)
Das heißt, Hamburger lehnt es ab, weil es angeblich keinen Zweck hat.
Er ist Pessimist durch und durch.

Dresen gab die Vorbereitungen für *Faust 2* auf, die Arbeiten scheiterten wenig später und der Intendant Wolfgang Heinz trat zurück. Aus dieser Zeit sind auch einige Texte überliefert, die Dresen mit Mitarbeitern aus der *Faust*-Mannschaft im Rahmen einer Recherche für eine Operette über den bevorstehenden Abriss alter Häuser in der Berliner Innenstadt zusammentrug.

In den siebziger Jahren liest man in Dresens Dokumenten die zunehmende Distanz, die er dem real existierenden DDR-Sozialismus gegenüber entwickelte. Über die Auseinandersetzung, wie kulturelles Erbe zu behandeln sei, kommt er zur Frage der ungelösten deutschen nationalen Identität. In diese Zeit fällt auch seine fundamentale Kritik an der Marxschen Revolutionstheorie, in der er die bei Marx postulierten Identität von sozialer und technischer Revolution als Befreiungsakt hin zur Gesellschaft der frei assoziierenden Individuen in Frage stellt. Dresen setzt dagegen die These, gesellschaftliche Entwicklung in ihrer evolutionsimmanenten Dialektik von Kooperation und Konkurrenz zu sehen ist. Den auszugsweise zitierten Aussagen Dresens ist ein ausführlicher Kommentar am Ende des Buches beigefügt. Er stammt von Friedrich Dieckmann, einer der wenigen, unter denen das Manuskript kursierte und damals Dramaturg am Berliner Ensemble war. In seinem Essay „Die Pyramide und die Sphinx" analysiert er rückschauend die Gesamtheit der Dresenschen Argumentationslinien bis hin zu dessen vernichtendem Schluss, dass es eine Kritik des Stalinismus vom Marxismus aus nicht geben könne, da „Stalinismus nicht Deformation sondern Konsequenz des Marxismus" bedeute. Die neue Gesellschaft aber sei „...ein Zwitter, von Kapitalismus wie Sozialismus gleichermaßen getrennt durch den Wunsch der Herrschenden, ihre Macht aufrechtzuerhalten...." Dresen glaubt an keine Alternativen jenseits der Grenze. Ist im Osten „Einheit ohne Einzelnheit, Freiheit nur hin zum Allgemeinen," so sieht er im Westen, wo er 1974 das erste Mal inszenieren durfte, „Einzelnheit ohne Einheit, Freiheit nicht in, sondern von der Gesellschaft." Die Distanz wird zur Ortlosigkeit.

Heimat
Am Lenindenkmal Friedrichshain
Da steht ein großes Haus
Unten ziehn die Leute ein
Und oben springen sie raus.

1974

Maik Hamburger merkt dazu an: „Von D. am Leninplatz aufs Pflaster geschrieben, war der Vers lange Zeit zu lesen, bevor der Regen ihn wegwusch."

1975 bittet Dresen in einem Brief an seine Parteigruppe, ihn aus der SED-Mitgliedschaft zu entlassen. Der Ausschluss wurde ein Jahr später vollzogen. Seine letzten großen Inszenierungen galten Kleist: ein Doppelprojekt *Prinz Friedrich von Homburg / Der Zerbrochne Krug* und *Michael Kohlhaas*. Im preußischen Kontext arbeitete er das Thema Freiheit und Notwendigkeit, Räson und Regelbruch auf. Der bekannte Satz, wonach Freiheit Einsicht in die Notwendigkeit bedeute, wurde dahingehend erweitert, dass die Notwendigkeit dann auch ein Einsehen in die Freiheit haben müsse. Das Drama vom rechtschaffenen Pferdehändler Kohlhaas, der das Recht, seinen Staat beim Wort zu nehmen bis zum Amok wahrnimmt, fiel in die Zeit der Biermann-Ausbürgerung und schien mit jedem Satz die DDR-Wirklichkeit zu beschreiben. 1977 wird Dresen eine Inszenierung am Theater Basel gestattet. Er kehrt nicht in die DDR zurück, wird aber nicht ausgebürgert. Sein Wegbleiben wird Jahre später mit einer dauerhaften Ausreisegenehmigung legitimiert. Im Januar 2000, fünfundzwanzig Jahre nach seiner Marx-Kritik, hofft Dresen in einer Anmerkung zum Abdruck im Buch, dass sich aus dieser Kritik eine neue Theorie entwickelt, die die Kritik und die Veränderung der gesellschaftlichen Verhältnisse einschließend, sich wieder auf Marx berufen könnte: „Es wird keine Linke geben, die Marx links liegenläßt."

Die folgenden beiden Kapitel beschreiben Stationen seiner langen Ankunft im Westen, Erfolge und Niederlagen. Vier Jahre ist er am Wiener Burgtheater, anschließend drei Jahre Leiter des Schauspiels Frankfurt. Am Ende jeder Etappe steht ein ehrlicher und freundschaftlicher Brief an den Intendanten, in dem er Bilanz zieht und Gründe seines Weggehens beschreibt. Es gibt Vergleiche der westlichen und der östlichen Theaterarbeit, westlicher und östlicher politischer Attitüden: sichtbar wird die Unbehaustheit, die einer wie Dresen in beiden Deutschlands empfindet. Die Leitung des Frankfurter Schauspiels übernimmt er mit einer Vorlaufzeit von wenigen Monaten und ohne bestehende personelle Bedingungen ändern zu können. Das Mitbestimmungsrecht — eine Ikone des politischen Aufbruchs nach 68 — aussetzend, braucht er sich um Feinde keine Sorgen mehr zu machen. Das Ensemble verliert zwar den gegen ihn angestrengten Prozess, aber Dresen lernt die Macht des Feuilletons kennen.

Er flieht aus der Schauspielarbeit in die Oper. In einem Brief an Hans Mayer konstatiert er, dass er damit seinen eigentlichen Beruf, vielleicht besser seine Berufung — als Ensembleentwickler, als zutiefst politisch denkender Regisseur, der mit gesprochenem Text kollektiv arbeitend sich in gesellschaftliche Prozesse einmischt — an den Nagel gehängt hat. Er eröffnet sich jedoch die Chance, außerhalb des deutschen Sprachraums inszenieren zu können. London, Brüssel und Paris werden wiederholt Stationen seiner Arbeit, noch 1988 auch wieder die DDR mit *Onegin* an der Komischen Oper. Trotz der fokussierenden Macht der Musik, die die Intensität der Arbeitsprozesse stärker abschirmt als im Schauspiel möglich, konstatiert er, dass auch in der Oper „Destruktion als letzte Form der Originalität, der Skandal zum Markenartikel...wird" ("Opernboom und Selbstzerstörung," 1986).

Im Schlusskapitel entwickelt Dresen noch einmal sein Leitmotiv: das Verhältnis von Freiheit und Kunst als Dialektik von Regelbruch und notwendiger Regelsetzung, von Aufbruch und Scheitern im Spannungsfeld von künstlerischem Handwerk und Genie. Er warnt vor dem Siegeszug der Unverbindlichkeit, der „Sinnverschmutzung," angesichts derer Kunst ihre

Negationskraft verliert. An Überschreitungsvorgängen stellt er deren Janusköpfigkeit — sozialer Fortschritt oder Auflösung des sozialen Körpers — heraus. Auf die historische Verantwortung eines jeden einzelnen verweisend — und damit ist er wieder beim *Faust* — sieht er gerade darin Grund für unbändigen Optimismus: In welche Richtung sich die Geschichte entwickelt, hängt vom Menschen selbst ab.

    Wieviel Freiheit braucht die Kunst vereint über vier Jahrzehnte authentische Innenansicht des Theaters in beiden deutschen Staaten und scharfsinnige Analyse der Wirkungsbedingungen von Kunst in der Gesellschaft. Die Vielgestaltigkeit der Texte und ihre sorgfältige Zusammenstellung machen das Buch zu einer mit Genuss lesbaren und sehr informativen Lektüre, die eine Vielzahl von Anregungen zum Nach- und Weiterdenken enthält.

Thomas Engel
Internationales Theater Institut, Berlin

Carola Stern. *Männer lieben anders: Helene Weigel und Bertolt Brecht.* Berlin: Rowohlt Berlin Verlag, 2000. 223 Seiten.

Finally, a post-unification book about a successful and relatively happy woman, a woman who, so the author often reminds us, was a committed socialist to boot. Carola Stern's presentation of the life and legendary stature of Helene Weigel is refreshingly straight-forward and simple: she was an unusually talented and courageous woman who realized early on that men, especially ambitious men such as her husband Bert Brecht, "love in a different way." (All translations are my own, H.F.) To support this claim, the impressive catalogue of Brecht's extra-marital affairs from Neher and Hauptmann to Reichel and Kilian is once again enlisted. Weigel, Stern suggests, lived in a marital and working partnership with a brilliant but emotionally deficient, sexually unfaithful man, relying on her inner strength and wit to make the most of her lot in life, whereupon she blossomed and thrived.

    Neither a biography nor a fact-filled chronicle, the book is conceived in the dramatic vein. The plot of this prose melodrama in three acts is predictably linear: two feisty independent souls are caught up in the "bohemian" life (31) of Weimar, endure the hardships of exile, and forge a successful working partnership in the GDR. Weigel, we are told, rose to just about every occasion, whereas Brecht is characterized early on as a "polygamist" (22) who failed to meet his ideals in his personal life: "The poet who wanted to help create the new man was himself unable to be a new man. He didn't even try. Why should he have tried? Life up till now had been good to him" (57). This moral indictment is thereupon tempered on the basis of the life experiences of the exiled Brecht, described by Stern as seasoned by one humiliation after another, and his years in the GDR, where belated maturity enabled him to share more of his life work with Weigel, albeit ever remaining the man who would "love in a different way." Stern's drama ends at the gravesite in the famous Berlin Dorotheen cemetery where, she reminds us, Weigel was rightfully buried alongside her husband, not at Brecht's feet as she had requested. Thus ended a full, extraordinarily productive, and for Stern, exemplary life.

There is much to irritate the reader for whom this book is not the first introduction to its subject matter. As already noted, Brecht and Weigel are portrayed for the most part as participating in an extended family melo-drama, not as the architects of epic theater. In fact there are few references to theater. For its part, history is quaintly summarized, as in this rendering: "Certainly, in 1920s Berlin, especially in bohemian circles, much is per-mitted and accepted as a matter of course. Everyone sleeps with everyone else. Fidelity is an old-fashioned notion. Being a virgin at sixteen is con-sidered an insult" (31). No less curious is the summary tone of serial pat phrases. Elisabeth Hauptmann is presented as an "intelligent, chic young woman" whose "movements are charming" and whose "beautiful brown hair has a silken shine" (21). Margarete Steffin is a "delicate, lively, indeed life-hungry, but also a bit dreamy, tubercular young woman" (53). This "hushed, inconspicuous, rather shy little creature" (85) pales all the more next to her soon-to-be rival, the infamous Ruth Berlau, introduced by Stern as dressing "fashionably," wearing "expensive furs and fine jewelry," driv-ing "an exclusive car," while being at the same time a "dedicated and active member of the Danish CP," in other words, "attractive, assertive, at times arrogant, a vivacious young woman eager for adventure" (85). And so forth. But for all her verbiage it is Stern's preference for the all-consuming present tense that most confounds this reviewer, as if time and history had stood still in the enduring moment of the Brecht-Weigel love story, lending universal relevance, and no little sentimentality, to their trials and travails.

Is this book a weighty contribution to Brecht and Weigel scholarship? No, it is not. Is it timely and important? By all means. Written for a wide readership by a well-established liberal journalist with a particularly strong following among women, Carola Stern's book is much more than mere melodrama. If Stern eschews scholarly convention (most obviously, quota-tions and other references are not supported by footnotes), she has un-doubtedly done her homework. While she does not engage in critical dialogue, a careful reading of her book makes evident that she is thor-oughly acquainted with her subject matter as well as the wide-ranging primary and secondary sources listed in the bibliography at the back of the book. The quotations and detailed descriptions of conversations and events are well-chosen, and as far as I can tell, accurate. The text also demonstrates that the author relied on a series of personal interviews as well as research conducted in archives in Germany and the United States.

Particularly significant to me was the evidence brought by Stern of the extent to which Weigel was the continuous object of Stasi surveillance in the fifteen years between Brecht's death and her own. Paradoxically, some of this surveillance was carried out by Brecht's and Weigel's most trusted younger colleagues at the Berliner Ensemble, who because of their personal ties to dissenters and reformers were particularly vulnerable to Stasi pressure and blackmail. Stern's main example is the unfortunate Isot Kilian, former wife of the imprisoned reformer Wolfgang Harich, to whom she remained close and whom she felt obliged to protect from further reprisals taken against him, reprisals with which the secret police threatened her into complying, at least nominally, with its demands for information about Weigel and the inner workings of the BE. The disarray within the BE in the sixties was thus infinitely more complex in nature than what we have previously been led to believe by critics who all too simply attribute its problems to Weigel's supposedly outdated concept of epic theater, her hen-pecking style of management, her alleged political dogmatism and rigidity vis-à-vis the next generation. Stern portrays the elder Weigel as a political pragmatist who did her best to protect her flock while knowing all the while that at the helm of the BE she herself remained unprotected in the posture of a wise, humble, generous soul. Reading Stern's assessment of Weigel, we are inclined to believe it.

Stern's book provides an interesting contrast to John Fuegi's misguided *Brecht & Co.* (Grove, 1994; now resuscitated in German translation). Whereas Fuegi, in undisguised oedipal/pre-oedipal fashion, depicts Weigel as a modern-day harpy who fed off Brecht and his disciples while collaborating with the GDR state, Carola Stern portrays a woman who bravely confronted hardship and injustice throughout her life: her first struggles to become an actress, the difficulties as a wife and mother in exile, the impact of the Holocaust which claimed her father and relatives, her years in the United States without work as an actress and under FBI surveillance, and later efforts to maintain the integrity of the Berliner Ensemble amidst continuous threats and interference coming from the SED and GDR security police network. While Fuegi's book, which boasts its own curious style, is fraught with malicious posturing, unfounded character assassination, and hundreds of factual errors (see the list compiled by Willett, Lyon, Mews, and Nørregard in *The Brecht Yearbook* 20, 1995), the more modest account authored by the journalist Carola Stern is thoroughly researched, intelligently argued, and has no mean-spirited agenda — no, not even toward men who "love in a different way." In spite of its melodrama, it impresses me as an altogether honest book. Its only bias may be an enlightened point of view. Or as Brecht, and Weigel, might have said: it is useful.

Helen Fehervary
The Ohio State University

Sabine Kebir. *Abstieg in den Ruhm. Helene Weigel. Eine Biographie.*
Berlin: Aufbau, 2000. 425 Seiten.

I n the first full-length biography of Helene Weigel by someone outside
the circle of those who knew her personally, Sabine Kebir provides her
readers with the same even-handedness, thoroughness, breadth and
depth of knowledge, and new information on her subject that marked her
earlier books on the women in Brecht's life. Besides her commanding
overview of the extensive published works on Weigel, she draws on an
impressive array of unpublished sources from archives in Germany and
Sweden, including many writings by Weigel herself; interviews with
Weigel and with others who knew her; and extensive government and
personal documents from the former GDR relevant to her subject, including Weigel's Stasi file. While her 981 endnotes spread over more than 60
pages seem daunting at first, they document her work convincingly and,
as nearly as I can determine, responsibly. To make them more "user-
friendly," she includes in the notes biographical sketches of dozens of
persons who played a role in Weigel's life, a catalog that enhances the
readability of her main text by reducing biographical excursions about
lesser players while supplying information in the endnotes for anyone
who wants it. This practice ought to be a standard feature in all biogra-
phies.

Building on the well-known general outline of Weigel's life, Kebir
adds countless details, nuances, and new information that makes almost
every phase of her career more intelligible. Besides describing the origins
of various life-long friendships that began in her early years at Eugenia
Schwarzwald's progressive school for girls, e.g., with Karin Michaelis,
Kebir illuminates how this schooling also determined the broad-gauge
feminist thinking that enabled her to play so skillfully the various roles she
assumed at different points in her life as an actress, political activist,
mother, homemaker, and administrator, not to mention as the wife of a
great writer and difficult husband. Her insightful, convincing portrayal of
Weigel in the 1920s as essentially a character actress with a wild, turbu-
lent, and noisy manner ("Die lärmendste Schauspielerin Berlins") and an
attention-grabbing voice establishes the basis for one of the main theses in
her book. According to Kebir, over the years Weigel gradually discovered
that quiet, even silent playing could be more effective than the loud, exu-
berant manner of her youth. The year 1932 and her performance in *Die
Mutter*, for which she rehearsed by working closely with Brecht, not only
convinced him of her greatness as an actress, it became pivotal in her
development toward a new style of acting that she reflected through "ein
erlernter asiatischer Habitus" (9) — a balanced, unemotional style that did
not eschew, but increased emotion by controlling it through understated
language, stylized movement, and non-histrionic action. Kebir provides

evidence that throughout her exile years, Weigel worked on cultivating this new "epic" style that Brecht found so appealing. She studied and saw examples of acting, primarily but not exclusively Chinese, discussed them with Brecht, and practiced them in private. The acting lessons she gave in Sweden and the USA helped her to refine these views and her own skills. All the trademark features of her later acting — her mode of speech, her posture, and her various gaits (Kebir cites the sexy "Millionen-Dollar Gang" she learned from Mae West and used as the governor's wife in *Der kaukasischer Kreidekreis*) — were not spontaneous or natural, but assiduously cultivated habits she learned and refined during her fifteen years of exile.

As a second major undertaking, Kebir attempts to unravel the enigma of what held Weigel and Brecht together despite his notorious womanizing and her conditioning as a sovereign, emancipated woman who planned to leave him in 1932 and actually did separate from him for six months in Berlin in 1953, only to take him back. One of the ironies implicit in her account is that if Hitler had not come to power and forced them to stay together in exile, she might never have gained fame for a style of epic acting that could only have been realized in his theater, and he might never have written plays with the powerful roles for mothers and women that were created specifically for her and clearly determined his career as a playwright. Eschewing psychoanalytical explanations, Kebir sees a complex "symbiosis" at work (61, 92) that defies formulation in terms of conventional love, though she offers evidence that they continued to have sexual relations till the end. She points instead to economic considerations. In the first years Brecht was economically dependent on her, whereas in exile the roles were reversed. There was also their shared ideology and the chance to promulgate it through the theater. Brecht obviously admired her commitment to Communism, while she admired him as an ideologically committed writer and appreciated the opportunities his reputation and writings gave her to convey a Marxist message. This ideological conviction also allowed her to see Brecht's feminine collaborators as political comrades rather than as competitors (114). Further, the symbiosis existed through mutual respect and need for what the other contributed to the theory and practice of theater. Kebir calls her "die lebendige Inkarnation [von Brechts] Arbeit" (183) and "das Medium seiner Kunst" (276) and theorizes that without her he would have had far greater difficulties revolutionizing the theater. In addition, they shared a general attitude toward the world that Kebir formulates in the word "Aktivität" (55), by which she means a view of the equality of all humans and solidarity with any type of action that supported that position.

Kebir claims, however, that in contrast to many leftists who believe that changing socio-economic conditions was enough, Weigel translated her political convictions into concrete actions on behalf of others. In fact, she developed what Kebir calls "ein geradezu obsessives Helfersyndrom...bei dessen Ausleben sie ungeheuere Energie und Phantasie an den Tag legte" (55). This obsession with helping the weak explains, at least in part, her role in the symbiotic relationship toward Brecht and the distress of his exile. It extended to many of Brecht's women, including Margarete Steffin in Denmark, who, Kebir claims, became Weigel's "adopted child" (174), and later to Ruth Berlau, whom she supported during the latter's final years of life. One might say of her that, like Kattrin in *Mutter Courage*, she too "leidet an Mitleid." Her selfless efforts on behalf of others continued till the end of her life through countless small acts of kindness, through political intervention for acquaintances, friends, and members of the Berliner Ensemble, and through direct and extensive involvement in correcting problems of the production of basic consumer goods in the GDR, such as children's shoes, detergents, cosmetics, etc. And to some degree this compassion was what drove her into the ultimate conflict that caused Manfred Wekwerth to leave the Berliner Ensemble after she insisted — unnecessarily, one could argue — that Hanne Hiob, Brecht's daughter by his first marriage, play the title role in *Die heilige Johanna der Schlachthöfe.*

Though Weigel's stoicism was severely tested during her marriage to Brecht, Kebir does not attempt to glorify her subject's well-documented toughness. In fact, she provides insights into her human side with passages from Weigel's letters or statements to friends that occasionally reveal frustration, depression, and even anger. Nor does she fail to mention those who, at various points in her life, saw her as brusque, unfeeling, and insensitive. What emerges, however, is the picture of a tough-mind, resilient, highly gifted, often self-effacing woman with strong desires, controlled passions, and an even stronger commitment to caring for others. In short, she presents a Weigel whose human skills were as highly developed as her artistry in the theater, foremost among which was a keen sense of humor and the ability to laugh at herself and the world.

Kebir's biography is by no means a feminist reading, for she demonstrates that Weigel was much more than that and cannot be easily co-opted by contemporary feminists. But the author's viewpoint as a woman clearly informs the text as she skillfully addresses issues or raises questions that a man might not treat in the same way, if at all, e.g., why Weigel did not leave Brecht, or how she related to Hauptmann, Steffin, and Berlau. In addition, Kebir's academic training in political science manifests itself repeatedly. She supplies useful and balanced information about and analyses of political matters that affected Weigel and Brecht, especially but not exclusively during their years in the GDR. Occasionally one senses on the author's part a certain yearning for the grand but failed experiment in socialism that she saw in that country, and her claims for Brecht as a promoter of "Basisdemokratie" are questionable enough that one wonders if they belong here. Some might fault her for including too much about Brecht in a biography devoted to Weigel, though the balance seems to be about right as she attempts to contextualize a life that was inextricably bound up with his.

This reviewer found the most engaging new details in this well-written, highly readable narrative to be about Weigel's/Brecht's long-running struggles to maintain the Berliner Ensemble as an island of theatrical experimentation and to publish his works over the opposition of cultural and political authorities in the GDR. In them, almost every side of her enormous gifts and complexity as a person emerge — her courage, her uncompromising principles, her tactical skills in battling bureaucrats, her kindness toward almost everyone she knew, her involvement in urging the government to improve the quality of basic consumer goods, her commitment to a state that labeled her "politically unreliable" (325), her role as a mother to members of the Berliner Ensemble, her undiminished skill as an actress, and her unflinching stamina in the face of declining health.

Despite a few factual errors and far too many typos for a book of this high quality, Kebir's representation of Weigel, while sympathetic, is not an exercise in hagiography. Its primary feature is what characterizes any good biography. From a balanced, engaging, well-researched presentation emerges a complex and admirable woman whose flaws, gifts, and personal charm simultaneously engage readers and leave them wishing that they had known her personally, in part to have experienced greatness on an ordinary level, in part to try and grasp the essence of this or any fascinating person that ultimately goes beyond what even the most skilled biographer can convey.

James K. Lyon
Brigham Young University

Stefan Mahlke, Hrsg. *„Wir sind zu berühmt, um überall hinzugehen".
Helene Weigel: Briefwechsel 1935-1971.* Berlin: Theater der Zeit und Literaturforum im Brecht-Haus, 2000. 255 Seiten

"Ich habe viel zu lange nicht geschrieben." Mit dieser Entschuldigungsfloskel beginnen viele Briefe von Helene Weigel, die an anderer Stelle aber auch von sich sagt: „Ich bin ein Briefschwein, und ich gedenke es zu bleiben." Helene Weigel hat viel korrespondiert. Dabei wirken ihre Briefe vor allem wie Geschäftspost. Private Dinge werden meist als Einstieg benutzt, um ganz praktische und taktische Anfragen und Mitteilungen machen zu können. Deshalb ist es nur konsequent, dass im zum 100. Geburtstag der Weigel herausgekommenen Briefwechsel-Band auch zahlreiche Notate und Dossiers, Anweisungen und Verweise für

Ensemblemitglieder sowie Anfragen an Ministerien abgedruckt sind.

23 Ordner umfasst Helene Weigels Korrespondenz im Archiv des Berliner Ensembles, aus dem Herausgeber Stefan Mahlke seine (durch Briefe aus dem Helene-Weigel-Archiv ergänzte) Auswahl traf. Gegen das in der Öffentlichkeit angeblich vorherrschende Bild der Weigel als Mutter Courage auf der Bühne und im Familienleben des Exils soll laut Vorwort mit dieser Auswahl einer anderen Weigel „die Bühne bereitet werden," nämlich der „arbeitenden Intendantin." Das führt leider zu einem diffusen Auswahlprinzip: statt zu versuchen, mit ausgewählten Briefen einzelne Vorgänge transparent zu machen, wird auf die Darstellung von Weite und Vielfalt der Aktivitäten der Schauspielerin und Intendantin Helene Weigel gesetzt. Also geht es in den Briefen um Proben und Spielpläne, um Spielweisen und Gastspiele, um Schminke und Seife, um Ministerbriefe und Kostüme, um einen Vorschuss für Heiner Müller und das Honorar von Benno Besson, um Artikel über Brecht im Ausland und Kontakte mit westdeutschen Theaterkünstlern. Heraus kommt ein Lesebuch, das für den Leser ohne Vorinformationen überhaupt nicht und für den Fachmann nur mit ständiger zusätzlicher Recherche nutzbar ist.

Neben einem äußerst knapp gehaltenem Personenverzeichnis gibt es keinen Anmerkungsapparat, was bei zahlreichen Briefen, die in der Regel ohne die entsprechenden Antwortbriefe abgedruckt sind, dazu führt, dass der Leser zwar eine bestimmte Haltung und Atmosphäre mitbekommt, aber letztlich gar nicht weiß, worum es konkret geht. Wer z.B verstehen will, warum Helene Weigel sich 1966 „auf dem kurzen Wege," nämlich über Blacky Bork, die Leiterin des Künstlerischen Betriebsbüros des Berliner Ensembles, bei deren Mann Kurt Bork über einen Artikel in *Theater der Zeit* scheinbar informiert (in Wirklichkeit aber beschwert), der muss in anderen Quellen recherchieren. Nur dann erfährt er, dass Kurt Bork stellvertretender Kulturminister war und dass der von der Weigel als „schwachsinnig und fehlerhaft" bezeichnete Artikel von einem Hallenser Schauspieler stammt, der mit der Forderung nach „unbedingter theoretischer Klarheit und Einmütigkeit der Genossen in allen ideologischen Fragen" nach dem 11. Plenum gegen die Stücke *Marski*, *Der Bau* und *Paul Bauch* wettert, indem er deren Autoren Lange, Müller und Braun (mit denen das BE zu arbeiten versuchte), eine verbildete Sicht auf „unsere sozialistische Wirklichkeit" vorwirft. So unkommentiert, wie diese Ausgabe ihre oft ungeschickt wirkende Auswahl ausbreitet und viele Themen gleichzeitig nur anreißt, stellt sie ein editorisches und inhaltliches Ärgernis dar.

Die Briefe von und an Helene Weigel (Briefe von Brecht sind nicht aufgenommen) sind in sieben Kapiteln chronologisch angeordnet. Im 1. Kapitel werden die verschiedenen Stationen des Exils beleuchtet. Es geht in Briefen an Familienmitglieder und an Piscator und Benjamin vor allem um Arbeitssuche, um Weigels Auftritt in *Furcht und Elend*, um Care-Pakete nach Deutschland und um den Alltag des Exils. Das (zu) umfängliche 2. Kapitel breitet den Briefwechsel mit der befreundeten Schauspielerin Therese Giehse aus. Deutlich wird die praktische Fürsorge der Weigel, mit der sie sich bei ihrem langjährigen Versuch, die Giehse als Gast ans BE zu holen, um Geld und Visum, Wohnung und Verträge, Honorare und Rollen kümmert. Im 3. Kapitel geht es um die Zeit zwischen 1950–1956, in der das BE als Gast beim Deutschen Theater unterkriechen musste. Es ist eine Zeit der ständigen organisatorischen Konflikte, der Reibereien mit Wolfgang Langhoff um Spieltermine und das Verhalten der Bühnenarbeiter. Mit flexibler Strategie, immer konsequent in der Sache, vermag sich die Weigel durchzusetzen. Bei Konflikten wendet sie sich gleich an den Kulturminister Alexander Abusch. Diese Taktik der Weigel, sich beim kleinsten Anlass sofort an die höchste politische Stelle zu wenden, wird als Grundhaltung in allen Kapiteln des Buches deutlich. Mit taktischer List variiert sie dabei bereits in der Anrede die Haltung, sie wechselt zwischen kollegialer Anfrage und Anmerkung auf gleichberechtigter Leitungsebene, und sie zeigt mit dem Gestus „ich bin für Rat und Hilfe dankbar" immer eine scheinbare Kooperationsbereitschaft.

Die letzten vier Kapitel — „Jahre nach Brecht" (1956-61), „Mühen um den Standard" (1961-66), „Krise des BE" (1966-69) und „Die letzten Jahre" (1969–1971) — geben eine Fülle von Anmerkungen zum nachbrechtischen Alltag am BE, der vom Kampf um die Brecht-Deutungshoheit und von einer unangenehmen Streitatmosphäre geprägt scheint, wobei jeder zur Begründung der eigenen Position mit Brechtzitaten hantiert. Die endgültige Lossagung von Manfred Wekwerth geschieht laut Helene Weigel, „weil Wekwerth nicht mehr den Weg Brechts" ging. Und im ausgiebig dargestellten Konflikt um Uta Birnbaums *Mann ist Mann*-Inszenierung 1966/67, bei der Helene Weigel (wie sie es zu allen Inszenierungen, auch zu Repertoirevorstellungen tat) seitenlang kritische Anmerkungen zu Inszenierungsdetails lieferte, wehrt sich Frau Birnbaum gegen ein Perfektionsstreben natürlich mit einem Brechtzitat über die Vorzüge der Unfertigkeit.

In keinem Augenblick gibt Helene Weigel die Deutungshoheit über Brechts Werk auf. Sie gestattet sogar niemandem eigenständiges Nachdenken über Brecht. Sie lässt sich ständig Dossiers anfertigen, d.h., Gutachten über andere Theater, über Kritiker, über Bücher und Texte zu Brecht. Arnolt Bronnen wird aufgefordert, seine Biografie in Bezug auf Brecht nach ihren Wünschen zu ändern, und auf einen Artikel von Klaus Völker im *Kursbuch*, der sich im Archiv Material zu seiner Brecht-Biografie angesehen hat, reagiert sie mit einem bösen Brief an den *Kursbuch*-Verleger Unseld („Sensationshascherei" und „trübe Art, sich Quellen zu verschaffen"). Auf John Willets Wunsch, sich zu seiner Brecht-Biografie zu äußern, antwortet sie mit einem vernichtenden Brief und meint, ihn über das englische Theater belehren zu können. Und ein Beschwerdebrief an Kulturminister Becher endet mit dem Satz: „Sollte Langhoff die Ansicht Brechts über Brecht nicht teilen, könnte er vielleicht belehrt werden."

Helene Weigel erweist sich in ihren Anmerkungen zu Aufführungen vor allem als patente Theaterpraktikerin, die Kluges über Dauerwellen und Stimmlagen, über Schminken und Spielweisen anzumerken weiß. Wenn sie grundsätzlich und dramaturgisch wird, überzeugt das weniger, so, wenn sie Müllers *Philoktet* zwar für großartig, aber nicht für ein Theaterstück hält. Das Verhältnis zum Westen wird in vielen Anmerkungen thematisiert, wobei man manches gern genauer wüsste. Da gibt es eine Anfrage von Gudrun Ensslin um einen Antikriegstext; da geht es um Verhandlungen mit Wolfgang Neuss; da wird von Plänen zu einem Gründgens-Gastspiel berichtet und vom Versuch, den westdeutschen Schauspieler Hans-Christian Blech zu engagieren. Die Staatlichen Schauspielbühnen Berlins bekommen ihren Plan, O. E. Hasse den Brechtschen Galilei spielen zu lassen, recht rüde um die Ohren geschlagen, und das Verhältnis zur Schaubühne am Halleschen Ufer ist gleichermaßen von Konkurrenzneid wie von einer Skepsis über „linksradikale anarchistische Tendenzen" bestimmt (Notat von Joachim Tenschert für Helene Weigel). Bedauerlich ist, dass so viele Themen nur vage angerissen werden. Insgesamt gibt der Helene-Weigel-Briefwechsel-Band mehr Fragen auf, als dass er Antworten liefert.

Jutta Phillips-Krug
Berlin

Books Received

Carmen-Maja Antoni und Johanna Schall. *Bertolt Brecht gesungen von Antoni & Schall* (Klavier Karl-Heinz Nehring). CD with Brecht-Weill-Eisler songs. Düsseldorf: Patmos, 1999.

Ernst Josef Aufricht, *Und der Haifisch, der hat Zähne: Die Aufzeichnungen eines Theaterdirektors*. Nachwort von Klaus Völker. Berlin: Alexander, 1998. [Reprint der Originalausgabe *Erzähle, damit du dein Recht erweist*, 1966].

Bertolt Brecht. *Brecht on Film and Radio*. Edited, translated, and with introduction and line commentaries by Marc Silberman. London: Methuen, 2000.

Bertolt Brecht. *Registerband*. Bearbeitet von Günter Berg, Karin Flörchinger und Wolfgang Jeske. Große Berliner und Frankfurter Ausgabe. Berlin und Frankfurt am Main: Aufbau und Suhrkamp, 2000.

Barbara Brecht-Schall, *BBS 70: Barbara Brecht-Schall im Gespräch* [mit Werner Hecht, Joachim Lang, James K. Lyon, Ingeborg Pietzsch, Giuseppe de Siati 1978-2000]. Frankfurt am Main: Suhrkamp, 2000.

Adolf Dresen. *Wieviel Freiheit braucht die Kunst? Reden, Briefe, Verse, Spiele 1964 bis 1999*. Hrsg. von Maik Hamburger. Berlin: Theater der Zeit, 2000.

Werner Hecht. *Helene Weigel: Eine große Frau des 20. Jahrhunderts*. Frankfurt am Main: Suhrkamp, 2000.

Jürgen Hillesheim. *Augsburger Brecht-Lexikon: Personen – Institutionen – Schauplätze*. Würzburg: Königshausen & Neumann, 2000.

Theresa Hörnigk and Alexander Stephan, Hrsg. *Rot = Braun? Brecht Dialog 2000. Nationalismus und Stalinismus bei Brecht and Zeitgenossen*. Berlin: Theater der Zeit, 2000.

Sabine Kebir. *Abstieg in den Ruhm: Helene Weigel. Eine Biographie*. Berlin: Aufbau, 2000.

Helmut Koopmann, Hrsg. *Brechts Lyrik – neue Deutungen*. Würzburg: Königshausen & Neumann, 1999.

Vladimir Koljazin, Hrsg. *Brecht i chudoschestvennaja kultura XX veka. Materialy nautschnoj konferencii. Archivnye dokumenty. Publikacii. Chronika*. [Brecht und die künstlerische Kultur des 20. Jahrhunderts. Materialien einer wissenschaftlichen Konferenz der Russischen Brecht-

Gesellschaft zum 100. Geburtstag Bertolt Brechts (12.-13. März 1998)] Moskau 1999.

Stefan Mahlke, Hrsg. *"Wir sind zu berühmt, um überall hinzugehen":* *Helene Weigel, Briefwechsel, 1935-1971.* Berlin: Theater der Zeit, 2000.

Heiner Müller, *Die Stücke I.* Hrsg. von Frank Hörnigk. Frankfurt am Main: Suhrkamp, 2000.

Michael Opitz und Erdmut Wizisla, Hrsg. *Benjamins Begriffe.* 2 Bände. Frankfurt am Main: Suhrkamp, 2000.

Albrecht Riethmüller, Hrsg. *Brecht und seine Komponisten.* Laaber: Laaber-Verlag, 2000.

Nina Sandow (Gesang) und Jens Stoll (Klavier). *Brecht, Majakowski, Hans Albers* [CD with live recording from a performance at the Berliner Ensemble on January 15, 1999]. Freibank Musikverlag.

Carola Stern. *Männer lieben anders: Helene Weigel und Bertolt Brecht.* Berlin: Rowohlt Berlin, 2000.

Christof Šubik. *Philosophieren als Theater: Zur Philosophie Bertolt Brechts.* Wien: Passagenverlag, n.d. [1999].

Jürgen Schmid. *Brecht und Haindl: Berthold Friedrich Brechts "Chronik der G. Haindl'schen Papierfabrik Augsburg" von 1899.* Augsburg: Wißner, 1999

Ronald Speirs, ed. *Brecht's Poetry of Political Exile.* Cambridge and New York: Cambridge University Press, 2000.

Stiftung Archiv der Akademie der Künste, Hrsg., *Chausseestrasse 125: Die Wohnungen von Bertolt Brecht und Helene Weigel in Berlin Mitte.* Fotografiert von Sybille Bergemann. Berlin: Stiftung Archiv der Akademie der Künste, 2000.

Stiftung Archiv der Akademie der Künste, Hrsg., *"Unerbittlich das Richtige zeigend": Helene Weigel (1900-1971).* Katalog einer Ausstellung vom 21. April bis 19. Mai 2000 in der Dresdner Bank (Pariser Platz, Berlin). Berlin: Stiftung Archiv Akademie der Künste, 2000.

Susanne Winnacker, guest editor. "German Brecht, European Readings." Special section of *TDR* 164 (Winter 1999).